Atonement and the Logic of Resurrection in Hebrews 9:27–28

"This work is one of the most unusual on Hebrews I have ever read. In this massively researched book, William Henry takes us on a detailed investigative excursion into what for many will be virgin territory. Interacting with Hebrews 9:27–28, Henry advocates for the position that Jesus leads believers into heaven after death and judgment. This entrance constitutes final salvation and has spatial/temporal connotations. Whether you agree with Henry or not, this is a fascinating journey that will surely open up new vistas on this wonderful book of Hebrews."

—DAVID L. ALLEN, distinguished professor of practical theology, Mid-America Baptist Theological Seminary

"This book is the culmination of the author's lifelong, passionate search for biblical and theological answers, first as a medical doctor and then as a seminary student, regarding Christ's present role in heaven and the timing of believers' entry into heaven after death. Anchoring the discussion with Hebrews 9:27–28 as the keystone, the author argues that Jesus leads believers to heaven shortly after death. This perspective will likely provoke many questions and challenges from biblical scholars. Nonetheless, the book offers numerous thought-provoking ideas and merits careful reading."

—S. AARON SON, professor of biblical studies, Dallas Baptist University

"William Henry's work challenges traditionally held views concerning the interpretation of Hebrews 9:27–28, which he sees as a key text for the larger context of his work. He maintains that Jesus intercedes a short while after death at judgment to bring into heaven those who believe in his offering for sin. Scholars may not agree with Henry's conclusions, but they will have to consider his meticulous research."

—TERRY L. WILDER, professor of New Testament and Greek, Campbellsville University

Atonement and the Logic of Resurrection in Hebrews 9:27–28

Jesus's Ministry to Lead Believers for Salvation into Heaven a Very Little While after Individual Death and Judgment

WILLIAM W. HENRY JR.

WIPF & STOCK · Eugene, Oregon

ATONEMENT AND THE LOGIC OF RESURRECTION IN HEBREWS 9:27–28
Jesus's Ministry to Lead Believers for Salvation into Heaven a Very Little While after Individual Death and Judgment

Copyright © 2024 William W. Henry Jr. All rights reserved. Except for brief quotations in critical publications or reviews, no part of this book may be reproduced in any manner without prior written permission from the publisher. Write: Permissions, Wipf and Stock Publishers, 199 W. 8th Ave., Suite 3, Eugene, OR 97401.

Wipf & Stock
An Imprint of Wipf and Stock Publishers
199 W. 8th Ave., Suite 3
Eugene, OR 97401

www.wipfandstock.com

PAPERBACK ISBN: 979-8-3852-1886-8
HARDCOVER ISBN: 979-8-3852-1887-5
EBOOK ISBN: 979-8-3852-1888-2

09/04/24

To

my wife, Tammy,

and my children,
Charity, Jordan, William, and Stephen,

and my family, friends, and enemies,

for their love, support, and testing, as
I have sought to increase faith understanding
about the growing city of believers in the heavens.

Hebrews 11:13–16

Contents

List of Illustrations and Tables | ix

Permissions | xi

Preface | xiii

Acknowledgments | xxi

Abbreviations | xxiii

1. Get Ready . . . Get Set: Introduction to Hebrews 9:27–28 Macro Conclusion/Summary about Entrance into Heaven | 1

2. Go! First Steps: The Word(s) to Place(s) in Hebrews 9:27–28 | 18

3. Steady Stride on the Right Course: Consistent Conversation, by Those Listening, about the Word of Christ into the Eternal/Perpetual-*Place*(s) | 90

4. Consistent Splint Times: The Place(s) of the Pastor's Discourse Unit Conclusions about Death, Judgment, Intercession, and Salvation | 186

5. Finish Well: Prompt Completion of God's People in God's Place in the Pastor's Main Conclusion of Hebrews 9:27–28 | 396

Excursus A: Other Runners' Corresponding Place(s) of Other NT Gospel Sequences: A Nodal Example and Area for Further Research | 405

Excursus B: Avoiding Missteps—An Example of a Detour toward Other Place(s) from Heaven: Martin Luther's Misstep after Five Hundred Years | 419

CONTENTS

Appendix 1 | 441
Appendix 2 | 455
Appendix 3 | 474
Bibliography | 475
Author Index | 509
Subject Index | 511
Scripture Index | 547

List of Illustrations and Tables

LIST OF FIGURES

1. A Minister of the Holy Places | 441
2. Confidence to Enter the Holy Places | 442
3. Judgment of Unbelievers at Death | 443
4. Senses of the Heaven(s) | 444
5. Definition of Typology in Hebrews | 27
6. First-Century Interpretation Methods | 445
7. Source Filter for Word Meanings | 42
8. The Pastor's Historical Thematic and Verbal Links | 51
9. Sifter to Filter the Pastor's Words | 52
10. Dying Sequence and Rising Sequence of Salvation | 447
11. Discourse Mapping Terminology | 448
12. Discourse Structural Mapping of Hebrews | 449
13. Section 1 (Heb 1:1—4:13) Discourse Unit Structural Mapping | 450
14. Section 2 (Heb 5:1—10:18) Discourse Unit Structural Mapping | 451
15. Section 3 (Heb 10:35—13:21) Discourse Unit Structural Mapping | 452
16. Discourse Chiastic Structure of Hebrews | 454

LIST OF ILLUSTRATIONS AND TABLES

LIST OF TABLES

1. Words in Hebrews Linked with God | 457
2. Words in Hebrews Linked with Creation | 460
3. Words in Hebrews Linked with People | 464
4. Words in Hebrews Linked with Other Spiritual Beings | 469
5. Summary Words of Hebrews 9:27–28 | 469
6. Modern English Words Unknown by the Pastor | 20
7. The Pastor's Words with Different Background Meaning | 21
8. LXX δεύτερος with Object of Proposition ἐκ | 77
9. Spatial Syntax Cohesion in Hebrews | 470
10. Ministry Comparison in Unit F (Heb 8:1—10:18) | 474
11. Ps 109:2–3 LXX Semantic Correspondence with Hebrews 8:1–2 | 291
12. Early Greek Manuscript and Latin Translator Accuracy of the Greek New Testament Plurals of ουρανος | 426
13. Pre-Luther Greek Collated Textual Accuracy by Erasmus of the Greek New Testament Plurals of ουρανος | 428
14. Pre-Luther German and English Translator Accuracy of the Greek New Testament Plurals of ουρανος | 429
15. Luther German and Post-Luther English Translator Accuracy of the Greek New Testament Plurals of ουρανος | 433

Permissions

Scripture quotations marked (AKJV) from The Authorized (King James) Version. Rights in the Authorized Version in the United Kingdom are vested in the Crown. Reproduced by permission of the Crown's patentee, Cambridge University Press.

Scripture quotations marked (NASB, NASB95) are from the New American Standard Bible. Copyright The Lockman Foundation 1960, 1962, 1963, 1968, 1971, 1971, 1973, 1975, 1977, 1995. Used by permission.

Scripture quotations marked (ESV) are from The Holy Bible, English Standard Version. Copyright © 2016 by Crossway Bibles, a publishing ministry of Good News Publishers. All rights reserved.

Scripture quotations marked (RSV) are from The Revised Standard Version. Copyright 1946 by Division of Christian Education of the National Council of Churches of Christ in the U.S.A., and are used by permission. All rights reserved.

Scripture quotations marked (NSRV) are from the New Revised Standard Bible, Copyright © 1989 by Division of Christian Education of the National Council of Churches of Christ in the U.S.A., and are used by permission. All rights reserved.

Scripture quotations marked (NIV) are from from the Holy Bible, New International Version®, NIV®. Copyright © 1973, 1978, 1984, 2011 by Biblica, Inc.™ Used by permission of Zondervan. All rights reserved worldwide. www.zondervan.com The "NIV" and "New International Version" are trademarks registered in the United States Patent and Trademark Office by Biblica, Inc.™

Scripture quotations marked (NLT) are from the Holy Bible, New Living Translation. Copyright © 1996, 2004, 2015 by Tyndale House Foundation. Used by permission Tyndale House Publishers. All rights reserved.

Scripture quotations marked (NET) are from the NET Bible®. Copyright © 1996, 2019 used by permission from Biblical Studies Press, L.L.C. All rights reserved.

Scripture quotations marked (HCSB) are from the Holman Christian Standard Bible. Copyright © 2002, 2003, 2009 by Holman Publishers. Used by permission.

PERMISSIONS

Holman Christian Standard Bible® are federally registered trademarks of Holman Bible Publishers.

Scripture quotations marked (LEB) are from the Lexham English Bible. Copyright 2012 Logos Bible Software. Lexham is a registered trademark of Logos Bible Software.

Scripture quotations marked (NABRE) are from the New American Bible: revised edition. Copyright © 2010, 1991, 1986, 1970 Confraternity of Christian Doctrine, Washington, DC, and are used by permission of the copyright owner. All rights reserved. No part of the New American Bible may be reproduced in any form without permission in writing from the copyright owner.

Translation of New Testament Bible passages from Nestle-Aland Greek New Testament, 28th Edition (NA28). Copyright 2012 by Deutsche Bibelgeselschaft. Used by permission. All rights reserved.

Translation of Old Testament Bible passages and Scripture quotations from Septuagint with Logos Morphology (LXX). Copyright 1935, 1979 by Deutsche Bibelgeselschaft. Used by permission. All rights reserved.

Scripture quotations marked (CSB) are from the Christian Standard Bible®, Copyright © 2020 by Holman Bible Publishers. Used by permission. Christian Standard Bible® and CSB® are federally registered trademarks of Holman Bible Publishers.

Scripture quotations marked (NCV) are from The Holy Bible: New Century Version®, copyright © 2005 by Thomas Nelson, Inc. Used by permission.

Scripture quotations marked (NKJV) are from the New King James Version. Copyright 1979, 1980, 1982 by Thomas Nelson, Inc. Used by permission. All rights reserved.

Scripture quotations marked (TNIV) are from the Holy Bible, Today's New International Version™ TNIV.® Copyright © 2001, 2005 by International Bible Society®. All rights reserved worldwide.

Scripture quotations marked (ISV) are from the Holy Bible: International Standard Version®. Copyright © 2000 by The ISV Foundation, 2200 N. Grand Avenue, Santa Ana, 92705-7016. Used by permission of Davidson Press, Inc. All rights reserved internationally.

Translation of Old Testament and Scripture quotations from Biblia Hebraica Stuttgartensia (BHS). Electronic ed., edited by K. Elliger, W. Rudolph, and Gérard E. Weil, © 1967, 1977, 5th corrected edition, prepared by A. Schenker 1997. Deutsche Bibelgesellschaft: Stuttgart, 2003. Used by permission.

Translation of Old Testament and Scripture quotations from *Biblia Hebraica Stuttgartensia* (BHS). Electronic ed., edited by K. Elliger, W. Rudolph, and Gérard E. Weil, © 1967, 1977, 5th corrected edition, prepared by A. Schenker 1997. Deutsche Bibelgesellschaft: Stuttgart, 2003. Used by permission.

Preface

The fascination of the places described in the biblical narrative of Hebrews inspires for many an interest in biblical cosmology/cosmogeny. Due to images beyond earthly geography, this project focuses narrowly upon the commonly held notion of a perpetual heavenly place for eternal life at death when promptly seeing Jesus and other brethren in completed salvation (Heb 11:13–16; cf. Matt 27:52–53; 1 Cor 15:12–58; 2 Cor 4–5; Phil 1:21–24; 3:17–21).[1] This global faith claim arouses interest in the sense of the language portraying the optimistic destiny in the unseen heavens for deceased believers by the gospel, so-called, with atonement in cleansing of sin through the ability of Jesus, as the Christ, to prepare and provide the way (Heb 9:27–28; cf. John 14:1–6).

In the sermon of Hebrews that had been circulated as a letter among the churches and later canonized into the NT, the Pastor entreats

---

1. E.g., in the Spring of 2018 Billy Graham passed away at age ninety-nine. As president of the Southern Baptist Convention, Steve Gaines, in the *Baptist Press*, said, "Billy Graham is with Jesus. He has seen and talked with our beloved Savior." Frank S. Page, president of the SBC Executive Committee reflected, "Heaven is a richer place today." Baptist Press Staff, "Billy Graham," para. 3, 5. Franklin Graham, in a press release from the Billy Graham Evangelistic Association, lovingly wrote, "My father's journey of faith on earth has ended. He has been reunited with my mother and has stepped into eternal joy of Heaven in the presence of his Savior, in whom he placed his hope." Franklin Graham, email message to author, Feb 21, 2018. His grandson Will Graham tweeted, "Even though my grandfather has physically died, he is very much alive in heaven. And you will see him there one day if you have asked Jesus to forgive you of your sins and made him Lord of your life." Graham, "Even though my grandfather." Even Billy Graham in his last column for the *Gaston Gazette* wrote, "By the time you read this, I will be in heaven." Graham, "By the Time." Graham testified just before his one hundredth birthday and death that the features of Jesus coming with his angels and trumpets apply to each individual believer at death. Graham, *Extraordinary Journey*.

his listeners, "Let us run with steadfastness the race set before us!" (Heb 12:1).[2] In a corresponding fulfillment with the journeys of millions of others listening to his metaphoric life challenge, in June 1982, I started to run this race in beginning the project set before you during preparation for a Wednesday night Bible study on the tabernacle in an isolated rural pastoral study at Hickory Ridge, Arkansas. As I taught a series that month on the symbolism of the individual tabernacle sections using Paul Kiene's beautiful color tabernacle pictures and slides, an unquenchable calling to a heavenly goal to be with Jesus commenced.[3] Over forty-years later, I am now at the current race-marker sprinting through the final details of this book, still on a course not quite complete yet, till I hear Jesus's call to come into heaven.[4]

In the quietness of my pastoral study, during reflection on the text of Heb 8:5, the phrase "copy and shadow of heavenly things" (AKJV) exploded in meaning as I mapped the tabernacle sections of holiness to their corresponding heavenly places. Once drawn out, questions arose about the connections of the movement of the high priest ministry of Jesus, as the Christ mentioned by the Pastor in the Letter to the Hebrews, through the whole of the tabernacle of all creation "not made with hands" (Heb 9:11, 23).[5] The working out of Heb 8:5 in relation to the heavenly

---

2. I use the *Nestle-Aland Greek New Testament*, 28th edition for Greek NT text. Other Hebrew, Greek, Latin, and Aramaic texts supply the source. All English translations are mine unless otherwise noted.

3. Kiene, *Tabernacle of God*.

4. I understand this exercise as only one point along the total journey of God's purpose in a race during life. Yet in my case, the experience represents a metaphoric ultra-marathon by covering about two-thirds of my life experience. Most PhD candidates write while they are young under the strict guidance of a supervisor or committee. Years later, many produce a *magnum opus* concerning their major insights. My journey experience involved writing a dissertation late in life. This book is a slight revision of that project. As I believe it was for the Pastor, my race completion finalizes at the goal of meeting Jesus either coming from heaven to lead me into heaven at death or, if still living in the flesh, at his second coming to earth for future ministry in joining those who have died now with him. This preface serves to assist the runner/reader to understand my previous steps with respect to my personal perception of God's calling over a lifetime. As a fellow listener for God's speech, this composition contributes but one of many strides in faith seeking understanding of what I hear. The personal accounting neither claims perfect truth nor supports absolute correctness but explains the late life, perceived, heavenly calling to this project.

5. Strong, *Tabernacle of Israel*. Strong warns about focus on individual parts with omission of the meaning of the whole. Since reading his warnings, I attempt to avoid the many possible micro applications and to pursue the macro meaning of the whole in relation to the gospel.

PREFACE

things led to a crude stick-figure outline for mimeograph distribution about Jesus's high priestly intercessory movement in the current plural heavens and earth.[6] This outline, as the heavens and earth field upon which the battle against sin and death was being victoriously remedied by God through Jesus, as the Christ, was employed in childlike faith for years of biblical teaching. God said it; it must be true.

Along years of running toward Jesus in a faith that embraced biblical discovery through the lens of plural heavens, the providential "training" (παιδεία) of the Lord next led to the addition of the practice of medicine. This holistic bi-vocational ministry led to an understanding about the chaotic functioning decay of the present visible creation from the smallest cells to the macrosystems that enable the energy for independent life from God's presence and light. The exposed realism about creation and humanity both shocked this naive young Pastor and reinforced the biblical description concerning the current crumbling condition and obsoleteness due to a lack of holiness concerning both created beings and people in the dark cosmos apart from the eternal/perpetual creation of God's light and dwelling.

Unable to provide permanent physical repair of the sin related disorders and the separateness of the earthly system that greatly contrasted with the biblical descriptions concerning the peace of the invisible, perpetual, promised creation now in God's presence, a thematic change came in a two-week preaching revival in 2000. A heavenly focus emerged that centered on Heb 11:13–16. The outline of the play-by-play activities of

---

6. The many sources and ideas demonstrating the concept of current plural heavens in what I call version 1.0 are not original. Scant sources were available in 1982 in the isolated farm town of four hundred souls. God led to a pastorate in the isolated rural delta several hours away from seminary. There was no internet in those days. The distance providentially impeded advanced religious education. I had completed only a couple of years by intermittent commutes either full or part-time. My initial basic religious education came from very conservative revised dispensationalists in the shadow of W. A. Criswell. Along with the book by Kiene on the tabernacle, which I purchased from the seminary bookstore, was my recommended *Scofield Reference Bible*. As instructed, I never read it from the bottom up. Scofield commented about plural heavens but I could not get his view to make sense and fit the pattern of Jesus' ministry. Cf. Scofield, *Scofield Bible Reference Bible*, 1113. Also, no longer extant in my files was a mimeograph outline copy of the plural heavens from some unknown source. It had the traditional view of Jesus going down to Hades and saints moved to the holy of holies of heaven from Hades to paradise as the beginning of the process of his fleshly resurrection. As will be discussed in later writing, I no longer hear from God's speech the traditional view of believers in Hades after death or as lesser incomplete souls in the holy of holies as the later defined Latin transliteration "Sanctuary."

God between the plural invisible heavens and the temporary decay of visible creation were applied diachronically (over time) in a biblical theology from the beginning of Genesis until the foretold final reconstruction of Revelation. The messages mapped God's solution of Jesus as Christ for man's sin and the problematic obsolete creation upon the outline of the heavens.[7] This spawned a 2001 publication of an unpolished biblical theology in a book entitled *Heaven Past Present Future: The Fulfillment of the Times* that plotted biblical events in the plural heavens and earth.[8]

Once published for free distribution on the Internet in 2002, the initial details that charted activities across the plural heavens outline had many incorrect theological presuppositions that were slowly corrected by the influence of kind discussion from many people from around the globe.[9] By 2006, seven chapters had expanded to twenty-one, with seven each respectively for heaven past, heaven present, and heaven future. By 2008, color graphics of the plural heavens replaced the outline and

---

7. While not the main subject of this project, this diachronic theology now expands temporally for immeasurable time *before* Gen 1:1. My theological view moves beyond my early teaching by Missionary Baptist professors in Little Rock, Arkansas, concerning the dispensational concepts of L. D. Foreman and the revised dispensational views of the "gap theory" in W. A. Criswell's study Bible. Cf. Foreman, *Bible in Eight Ages*; Criswell, *Criswell Study Bible*. I would now argue that while Criswell's and Foreman's concept of perpetual time of creation before the dark chaos described in Genesis is true, the text of Gen 1:1–2 does not support a gap. The Genesis creation at the beginning is made from the previous perpetual creation of unmeasurable time before Genesis. My current organization of the creation, with eternal-places of plural heavens above, mandates a *precosmic* introduction of sin by other heavenly created beings before the historically accurate Genesis account. Precosmic sin necessitates the present construction of dwelling levels of holiness for sinful volitional creations in separated realms of heavens that were cast down from the eternal-place creation of measureless perpetual time (cf. Heb 1:10–12, 11:3; Ps 90:1–4). More biblical theology on this faith-view, perhaps held by the Pastor, is presented in chapter 3 regarding the plural eternal/perpetual-*places* of Hebrews. In later research, I hope to discuss the missteps by later dispensationalists in collapsing dualism to an earth-centric hope more in-line with other commonly held earth-centric views.

8. Henry, *Heaven Past Present Future*. After multiple publishing house rejections due to lack scholarly credentials and name recognition, this was a personal printing of about three thousand copies. Due to many errant, theological presuppositions, at times I would like to recall them. Yet, the missteps serve as reminders of a race with training that is not finished and that hears continual instruction of the Lord. There is still much to learn. I remain awed daily over all that God continues to reveal and awaits discovery from his word till my arrival at the throne of Jesus in heaven. I look forward to knowing for sure, all the while knowing God's promises are much better than I could ever imagine.

9. A pin map tracked comments from all continents and many countries. I remain thankful for their discussion contributions and encouragement along the way.

PREFACE

stick figures, and emphasis changed to simply "The Heavens" in 2009. In teaching about Jesus in the heavens, many adjustments led to multiple chart versions distributed in churches and on several international mission trips.[10]

In early 2010 while working in a basement publishing studio on a book revision and video segments, the desire for conversation correctness concerning the believer's relationship to the truth of the heavens heavily influenced a yearning for a return to seminary. Early ministry pastoral demands and pre-Internet distance obstacles providentially hindered completion of a bachelor's degree from 1975 to 1985. God emphatically closed those seminary education doors three times before opening the opportunity for secular education that ended in a medical degree and the practice of medicine added to ministry. Years later, through the advice of the author's friendship of associational missionary Ronnie Toon, God led to enrollment in classes at Southwestern Baptist Theological Seminary. The wonderful professors at Southwestern, first by Dr. Tim Deahl at the Little Rock extension campus, provided the proper biblical hermeneutic for the study of the plural heavens as related to believers in Jesus as Christ.

My pre-dissertation research mapped the narrative of Jesus's heavenly journey as exemplar upon the typological outline of the earthly tabernacle parallels with plural heavens (Heb 8:1–6). Jesus's ministry models open heavenly access to the holy places of the living God, and symbolically links eternal life with postmortem promises in heavenly places. However, prolonged fruitless attempts to completely harmonize the background and language of long held traditions urged search for better tools to interpret the biblical claims.[11]

While learning the craft and skills for better biblical interpretation, I felt both shock and surprise over the lack of scholarly unity in opinions

10. The current color version in vertical synthesis of gospel movement is version 8.1. The current color horizontal and vertical synthesis is version 10.0. At times I wish I had could get previous versions back due to significant changes along the race. Each served as a part of a lifelong learning experience about the heavens. It is unfortunate the color versions are not allowed but I will publish them later.

11. E.g., Rogers, *Place Called Heaven*, 6. Rogers answers the question of when we arrive, stating, "The next thing we need to know is that the saved go to heaven immediately upon death." However, Rogers also taught a flesh body resurrection at the earthly second coming in complementary separate events. Cf. Matt 11:25; John 3:10; 12:34; 14:1–12; 21:23. The cosmic restricted views of Israel and the early disciples logically led to incorrect theological conclusions. In later footnote discussion, I address these in light detail. They are still popular and provide a large reservoir for future research.

about the unseen heavens mentioned in Scripture. It seemed the more religiously educated, that biblical descriptions of faith become less real and more figurative as one interprets texts and concepts that involve biblical descriptions about the invisible heavens. Only a handful of recent scholars have ever attempted a synthesis of a literal, coherent, topographical structure for God's creation beyond what is visible. Major scholars thus push back against any possible consistent and coherent pattern based on the tabernacle outline for plural heavens. Their conclusions are based both on a long tradition of previously admitted failures by influential scholars and long-established, traditional, lexical views that primarily promote an earth-centric ideology against a present, literal, heavenly entrance by believers to Jesus at death.[12]

Undaunted from nearly thirty-years of biblical topographical studies involving the unseen heavens, nearly every paper that I submitted in seminary developed some spatial aspect about deceased believers in relation to the present heavens and earth creation. With each paper and seminary course, the surrounding details within the overarching cartographic outline changed but the tabernacle outline of plural heavens remained stable. The desire to explore the current tension and disconnect concerning accessible plural heavens through the tools of a scholarly approach based on Hebrews led in 2011 to Dr. David Allen at Southwestern, who had written the New American Commentary on *Hebrews*.[13] Dr. Allen graciously accepted guidance of a masters level thesis by an appeal based on his understanding of one who had taken a path less traveled through his experience in publication of *Lukan Authorship of Hebrews*.[14] He graciously accepted guidance of a masters thesis on related tabernacle mapping topics.[15] His later PhD seminar on atonement, in relation to attendance of the ETS section from 2013 to 2018 on the place and timing of atonement in Hebrews, sparked even greater interest.

During prospectus development, Dr. Terry Wilder, as PhD supervisor, nudged for a narrow text with prospects for a thesis question to further explore assertions about the spatial-temporal background previously

---

12. Established theological presuppositions and methodology that must change based on a unified cartography of Scripture present as the main obstacles. It is easier to deny creational cartographic unity than change long held confessional traditions and methods that negate a dualistic view.

13. Allen, *Hebrews*.

14. Allen, *Lukan Authorship of Hebrews*.

15. Henry, "Cosmology of the Heaven(s)."

studied in multiple research and seminar papers concerning the place and timing issues of atonement and salvation. Surprisingly, the chosen text of Heb 9:27–28, when investigated by the tools of lexical semantics, biblical theology, and discourse analysis, appears to summarize the Pastor's previous exposition on the matters of question in the recent atonement debate.[16] No dissertation level inquiry has been done on this text, due to an assumed concrete warrant of tradition for parenesis about the earthly second coming. This project presents exploration of the Pastor's macro conclusion/summary of Heb 9:27–28 in search for correspondence with the view of prompt eternal life in heaven after death.

While professors at SWBTS have reminded several times that they did yet not fully agree (most admit to a faith for going to heaven to see Jesus when they die), they graciously listened in their busy schedules and made important points of problematic areas on multiple occasions. Their wise probing insights to my initial mapping and movement schemes revealed necessary modifications for proper correspondence with the textual propositions surrounding Jesus's experience beyond death in rising to God. E.g., Jesus now no longer in his gospel travel goes to Hades at his death but as an eternal bodily spirit enters the heavenly holy of holies in completion of the events of a biblical death, which requires a onetime approach and presentation at judgment before God that is modeled by both the OT daily sacrifices and the Day of Atonement.

Also, after the pattern of the movement of Jesus's entrance into the holy of holies beyond the unseen heavenly veil, the deceased saints are now bodily complete with him in heaven instead of either the traditional view advocating location in a lesser holy realm of the unseen heavens or living as an inferior disembodied soul awaiting a future entrance into the holy of holies during the gathering of all believers for the second coming. Further, a believer's first probable opportunity for literally seeing Jesus as their Savior is greater at the moment of death than while still living in the flesh, where during the second coming to earth the living in the flesh are gathered to himself and the living dead who are already with him.[17] These

---

16. In my original dissertation, the nomenclature of Hurst and Buck is used, where *Auctor ad Hebraeos* refers to the author of Hebrews. This application offers the advantage that Hebrews views primarily through a lens as both a literary and an oral work by one author. See Hurst, *Epistle to the Hebrews*, 4. For simplicity in this publication, I use the term "the Pastor" to refer to the author of Hebrews.

17. The popular continually future eschatological lens embraced over the last one hundred years either overlooks or explains away the nearly two thousand years of a present reality in heaven for those who have died with faith in Jesus. Those billions

are just some of the many changes to inner detail of mapping within the stable outline of plural heavens during studies at Southwestern.

In many ways, the Pastor's race analogy in Heb 12:1–13 corresponds to the living activity of a study of this type. I use a similar race analogy to keep readers oriented in the topical surroundings and purpose of each chapter. In a study of this scope, it is easy to get lost in the minutia, of which I have provided much to consider that relates to the thesis.[18]

There is much still to learn in and by cartographic studies of the heavens. In this book project, if there is any truth or wisdom to encourage fellow believers during the discouragement of this world—it is only from the Holy Spirit who gives understanding.[19] If there is any error, it is solely my own inaccuracy for not listening more carefully to God's speaking of his word. As always, readers are encouraged to test the spirits to see if the conversation herein is of God or of the world (1 John 4:1–6; Matt 24:5).[20]

---

of believers, who have died before Jesus' return, saw the appearance of Jesus as their intercessor at judgment to begin rising to God in spirit. They abide just a brief time in heaven before the transformation of their spiritual bodies for his promised second coming ministry to the temporary earth. This lacuna of the present promise fulfilment for the dead inspires the thesis of this work that is stated in chapter 1 and drives the subsequent extensive exploration of the message of Hebrews in the chapters that follow.

18. The footnotes and chapters are numerous and lengthy due to many contacts with scholars and the interpretative issues related to the exploration of the thesis that concerns whether believers literally enter heaven to be with Jesus at death by his intercession at their judgment according to Heb 9:27–28. The boundaries of this study do not outline a cove, bay, or inlet that is easily charted in a quick survey but an ocean in magnitude due to the nature of the question about what is beyond in relation to peoples' common experience of death. A proper dissertation requires a complete scholarly and literary in-depth engagement with the greater conversation surrounding the spatial movement of both Jesus and his believers at death, rather than a smaller focus on one issue in the overarching conversation. The product is a life-long labor over forty years that will require interested readers some time to digest. It is written for scholars, students, and non-academic seekers, who desire a comprehensive analysis about what is beyond death from a pure biblical view of God's speaking revelation in promises to those who believe in Jesus.

19. Truth as accurate perception of the unseen realities of God's promises, now not seen, cannot be fully understood except by revelation of the Holy Spirit (1 Cor 2:9–10).

20. Not everything taught builds correctly on the foundation of Christ, even among those who claim Jesus is the Christ (Matt 7:21–23; 22:41–45). In compiling this work by faith in seeking understanding, all spiritual teaching should be tested before adoption by others.

Acknowledgments

I offer special thanks and gratitude to my family for listening to numerous conversations dominated by a focus on the eternal/perpetual-place heavens—at times they are ready to let me go there before my finished race. Also, along the way in a race that spans over fifty-years of ministry, God sent (1) many friends who listened and ran part of the way with encouragement and support,[1] (2) grace-filled hospitals and patients who allowed incessant sharing about the kingdom of the heavens and faith in Jesus as the way to the so much better conditions of God's dwelling,[2] (3) patient assemblies of believers small and large who heard much commentary on the cartography of the gospel of Jesus as the Christ in the heavens,[3] (4) professors who heard persistent conversation and read long, detailed research and seminar papers,[4] and (5)

---

1. These include Buddy Ritter, Thurman Cossey, Danny Bradley, Rusty Roebuck, Gary Self, David Avery, Brad Sullivan, Bob Cooper, Allen Waldrup, Larry White, Ronnie Toon, Lewis Hershey, Rich Byers, Gene Tulberg, Eddie Cox, Jim Sproles, and Stacy Reed.

2. This includes, in Arkansas, Ashley County Medical Center, St. Bernard's Regional Medical Center, Northeast Arkansas Baptist Medical Center, and Izard County Medical Center in Calico Rock. In Texas, Faith Community Hospital in Jacksboro and USMD Surgical Center in Fort Worth. Special thanks to Southern Emergency Services, Concord Medical Group, Correct Care Emergency Services, and TeamHealth for schedule accommodation.

3. This includes, in Arkansas, Hickory Ridge Missionary Baptist, Hickory Ridge; Gethsemane Missionary Baptist, Walnut Ridge; Butterfield Missionary Baptist, Malvern; Temple Baptist Church, Jonesboro; Oak Grove Missionary Baptist, Jonesboro; First Baptist of Crossett; Mount Olive, Crossett; and First Baptist Church of Batesville.

4. This includes professors Tim Deahl, Hal Dixon, Jonathan Watson, John Howell, Jason Duesing, Robert Caldwell, S. Aaron Son, David L. Allen (thesis supervisor), John Taylor (first-year PhD supervisor/NT major), Craig Blaising (BT minor), Mark Taylor, Ryan Stokes, Paul Hoskins, and Terry Wilder (supervisor).

the students and scholars at SWBTS, ETS, IBR, and SBL, who were approachable to discussion about a subject foreign to their ears due to the formal closure by many of the biblical text concerning Jesus's ministry within the plural heavens.

For contributions in dissertation assistance in critique and editing, I extend extra appreciation to Vickie Lowery, Charles Martin Jr., and Bill Johnson. These kind people helped me express the concepts about the heavens in my heart. Special thanks to my dissertation Supervisor Dr. Terry Wilder, second reader Dr. Jim Wicker, and third reader Dr. John M. McKay Jr. for their stamina during review. Most of all I am especially grateful to my wife, Tammy, for her patience living with a lifelong attempt to know more about God's promised heavenly country of Heb 11:13–15 during often tenuous tracking of the treatise of Hebrews through the proposed macro summary lens of Heb 9:27–28.

A word of special gratitude goes to the editorial staff of Wipf and Stock for offering publication and seeing that the project comes to completion. All remaining mistakes and missteps of imperfection are mine. May the reader be patient and see the message more than any inferior prose, lengthy verbose sections, deviations from scholarly form, or inconsistencies in governing methodology. As one of two million books published this year alone, I don't expect to make the best sellers lists. Tammy often reminds me that our motivation for my writing to this point came by thinking about the one person who we might meet in heaven due to their reading this lifelong effort. We, and perhaps "one more" who we shall meet later, may thank those at Wipf and Stock for making this conversation about Jesus's often forgotten present ministry in the unseen heavens available, when after death and judgment following our great Shepherd of the sheep into the eternal/perpetual realms in reunion together (Heb 9:27–28).

William W. (Bill) Henry Jr.
Batesville, Arkansas, USA

Abbreviations

SCRIPTURE ABBREVIATIONS

Hebrew Bible / Old Testament

Gen	Judg	Neh	Song	Hos	Nah
Exod	Ruth	Esth	Isa	Joel	Hab
Lev	1–2 Sam	Job	Jer	Amos	Zeph
Num	1–2 Kgs	Ps (pl. Pss)	Lam	Obad	Hag
Deut	1–2 Chr	Prov	Ezek	Jon	Zech
Josh	Ezra	Eccl (or Qoh)	Dan	Mic	Mal

New Testament

Matt	Acts	Eph	1–2 Tim	Heb	1–2–3 John
Mark	Rom	Phil	Titus	Jas	Jude
Luke	1–2 Cor	Col	Phlm	1–2 Pet	Rev
John	Gal	1–2 Thess			

Apocryphal / Deuterocanonical Books

Tob	Wis	1–3 Esd	Sg Three	Bel	3–4 Macc
Jdt	Sir	Ep Jer	Sus	1–2 Macc	Pr Man
Add Esth	Bar				

DEAD SEA SCROLLS

1QS Rule of the Community (Manual of Discipline)
4Q400

OTHER ABBREVIATIONS

ABD	*The Anchor Bible Dictionary.* 6 vols. Edited by David Noel Freedman. New York: Doubleday, 1992.
ABR	*Australian Biblical Review*
AKJV	Authorized King James Version
ANE	Ancient Near East
ANRW	*Aufstieg und Niedergang der Römischen Welt*
AUSS	*Andrews University Seminary Studies*
BBR	*Bulletin for Biblical Research*
BCE	Before the Common Era
BDAG	Walter Bauer, Frederick W. Danker, William F. Arndt, and F. Wilber Gingrich. *Greek-English Lexicon of the New Testament and Other Early Christian Literature.* Chicago: University of Chicago Press, 2000.
BDF	Friedrich Blass and Albert Debrunner. *A Greek Grammar of the New Testament and Other Early Christian Literature.* Translated and revised by Robert W. Funk Chicago: University of Chicago Press, 1961.
BHS	*Biblia Hebraica Stuttgartensia: SESB Version.* Stuttgart: German Bible Society, 2003. Electronic ed.

Bib	*Biblica*
BNTS	Daniel B. Wallace. *The Basics of New Testament Syntax: An Intermediate Greek Grammar*. Grand Rapids: Zondervan, 2000.
BSac	*Bibliotheca Sacra*
BT	*The Bible Translator*
BTB	*Biblical Theology Bulletin*
BTLNTG	Hermann Cremer. *Biblico-Theological Lexicon of New Testament Greek*. Edinburgh: T&T Clark, 1883.
BTS	Biblical Tools and Studies
BZ	*Biblische Zeitschrift*
CBQ	*The Catholic Biblical Quarterly*
CE	Common Era
CHAL	William Lee Holladay and Ludwig Köhler. *A Concise Hebrew and Aramaic Lexicon of the Old Testament*. Leiden: Brill, 2000.
CNTTS	*The Center for New Testament Textual Studies: NT Critical Apparatus*. Edited by Bill Warren. New Orleans, LA: New Orleans Baptist Theological Seminary, 2010.
COED	*Concise Oxford English Dictionary*. Edited by Catherine Soanes and Angus Stevenson. Oxford: Oxford University Press, 2004.
CTJ	*Calvin Theological Journal*
CurBR	*Currents in Biblical Research*
DI	Level 1 Discourse Introduction (appendix 1, fig. 11)
DJG	*Dictionary of Jesus and the Gospels*. 2nd ed. Edited by Joel B. Green, Heannine K. Brown, and Nicholas Perrin. Downers Grove, IL: InterVarsity, 2013.
DLNT	*Dictionary of the Later New Testament and Its Developments*. Edited by R. P. Martin and P. H. Davids. Downers Grove, IL: InterVarsity Press, 1997.

ABBREVIATIONS

DNTB	*Dictionary of New Testament Background:* Edited by Craig A. Evans and Stanley E. Porter. Downers Grove, IL: InterVarsity, 2000.
DOTP	*Dictionary of the Old Testament Prophets: A Compendium of Contemporary Biblical Scholarship.* Edited by Mark J. Boda and J. Gordon McConville. Downers Grove, IL: InterVarsity, 2012.
DPL	*Dictionary of Paul and His Letters.* Edited by Gerald F. Hawthorne and Ralph P. Martin. Downers Grove, IL: InterVarsity Press, 1993.
DSS	Dead Sea Scrolls
DTIB	*Dictionary for Theological Interpretation of the Bible.* Edited by Kevin J. Vanhoozer, Craig G. Bartholomew, Daniel J. Treier, and N. T. Wright. Grand Rapids: Baker Academic, 2005.
DUC	Level 2 Discourse Unit Conclusions/Summaries (pl. UC) (appendix 1, fig. 11)
DVNT	J. M. Harden. *Dictionary of the Vulgate New Testament.* London: Macmillan, 1921.
EDEJ	*The Eerdmans Dictionary of Early Judaism.* Edited by John J. Collins and Daniel C. Harlow. Grand Rapids: Eerdmans, 2010.
EDNT	*Exegetical Dictionary of the New Testament.* 3 vols. Edited by Horst Robert Balz and Gerhard Schneider. Grand Rapids: Eerdmans, 1990–.
ETS	Evangelical Theological Society
EvQ	*Evangelical Quarterly*
FGT	Functional groupings of text
GELS	T. A. Muraoka. *Greek-English Lexicon of the Septuagint: Chiefly of the Pentateuch and the Twelve Prophets.* Leuven, Belgium: Peeters, 2002.
GGBB	Daniel B. Wallace. Greek *Grammar Beyond the Basics: Exegetical Syntax of the New Testament.* Grand Rapids: Zondervan, 1996.

GHAIS	T. A. Muraoka. *A Greek ≈ Hebrew/Aramaic Two-Way Index to the Septuagint*. Leuven, Belgium: Peeters, 2010.
GNTG	Friedrich Blass. *Grammar of New Testament Greek*. Translated by Henry St. John Thackeray. London: Macmillan, 1911.
GTJ	*Grace Theological Journal*
HAL	*The Hebrew and Aramaic Lexicon of the Old Testament*. Edited by Ludwig Koehler, M. E. J. Richardson, and Johann Jakob Stamm. Leiden: Brill, 1994–2000.
HeBAI	*Hebrew Bible and Ancient Israel*
HolGNTAp	Michael W. Holmes. *Apparatus for the Greek New Testament: SBL Edition*. Bellingham, WA: Logos, 2010.
HTR	*Harvard Theological Review*
HTS	*Harvard Theological Studies*
IDB	*The Interpreter's Dictionary of the Bible*. 4 vols. Edited by George A. Buttrick. New York: Abingdon, 1962.
Int	*Interpretation*
IVPBBCNT	Craig S. Keener. *The IVP Bible Background Commentary: New Testament*. Downers Grove, IL: InterVarsity, 1993.
JBL	*Journal of Biblical Literature*
JE	*The Jewish Encyclopedia: A Descriptive Record of the History, Religion, Literature, and Customs of the Jewish People from the Earliest Times to the Present Day*. 12 vols. Edited by Isidore Singer. New York: Funk & Wagnalls, 1901–1906.
JETS	*Journal of the Evangelical Theological Society*
JR	*Journal of Religion*
JSNT	*Journal for the Study of the New Testament*
JSOT	*Journal for the Study of the Old Testament*
JTI	*Journal of Theological Interpretation*
JTS	*Journal of Theological Studies*
L&N	Johannes P. Louw and Eugene Albert Nida, eds. *Greek-English Lexicon of the New Testament: Based on Semantic Domains*. 2nd ed. New York: United Bible Societies, 1989.

LCL	The Loeb Classical Library
LSJ	Henry George Liddell, Robert Scott, Henry Stuart Jones, and Roderick McKenzie. *A Greek-English Lexicon*. 9th ed. Oxford: Clarendon, 1996.
LXX	Alfred Rahlfs. *Septuaginta: With Morphology*. Stuttgart: Deutsche Bibelgesellschaft, 1979. Electronic ed.
McNTS	McMaster New Testament Studies
MCS	Macro Conclusion/Summary of Hebrews 9:27–28
MHT	James Hope Moulton and Wilbert Francis Howard. *A Grammar of New Testament Greek: Accidence and Word-Formation*. 4 Vols. Edinburgh: T. & T. Clark, 1963–2006.
MM	James Hope Moulton and George Milligan. *The Vocabulary of the Greek Testament: Illustrated from the Papri and Other Non-Literary Sources*. London: Hodder & Stoughton, 1930.
MT	Masoretic Text
MTS	Münchener theologische Studien
NA28	*Nestle-Aland Novum Testamentum Graece*. Edited by Barbara and Kurt Aland, Johannes Karavidopoulos, Carlo M. Martini, and Bruce M. Metzger. 28th ed. Westphalia: Deutsche Bibelgesellschaft, 2012.
NA28App	Eberhard Nestle and Erwin Nestle. *Nestle-Aland: NTG Apparatus Criticus*. Edited by Barbara Aland, Kurt Aland, Johannes Karavidopoulos, Carlo M. Martini, and Bruce M. Metzger, 28th rev. ed. Stuttgart: Deutsche Bibelgesellschaft, 2012.
NDBT	*New Dictionary of Biblical Theology*. Edited by T. Desmond Alexander and Brian S. Rosner. Downers Grove, IL: InterVarsity Press, 2000.
Neot	*Neotestamentica*
NICNT	The New International Commentary on the New Testament
NIDNT	*New International Dictionary of New Testament Theology*. Edited by Lothar Coenen, Erich Beyreuther, and Hans Bietenhard. Grand Rapids: Zondervan, 1986.
NovT	*Novum Testamentum*

NRSVApo	*The New Oxford Annotated Apocrypha*. 3rd edition. Edited by Michael D. Coogan, Marc Brettler, Carol Newsom, and Pheme Perkins. Oxford: Oxford University Press, 2007.
NT	New Testament
NTS	*New Testament Studies*
OT	Old Testament
OTGP	Ken Penner and Michael S. Heiser. *Old Testament Greek Pseudepigrapha with Morphology*. Bellingham, WA: Lexham, 2008.
OTP	*The Old Testament Pseudepigrapha*. 2 vols. Edited by James H. Charlesworth. New York: Yale University Press, 1983.
PAGM	Peder Borgen, Kåre Fuglseth, and Roald Skarsten. *The Works of Philo: Greek Text with Morphology*. Bellingham, WA: Logos, 2005.
PAE	Philo. *Philo*. Translated by F. H. Colson, G. H. Whitaker, and J. W. Earp. Vols. 1–10. LCL. Cambridge, MA: Harvard University Press, 1929–1962.
PRSt	*Perspectives in Religious Studies*
Pt	Point
RCT	*Revista catalana de teología*
ResQ	*Restoration Quarterly*
S	Level 1 Discourse Section (appendix 1, fig. 11)
SBL	Society of Biblical Literature
SBJT	*Southern Baptist Journal of Theology*
SbPt	Level 4 Discourse Unit FGT Support Subpoint (appendix 1, fig. 11)
SJT	*Scottish Journal of Theology*
SR	Studies in Religion
ST	Second Temple
StC	*Studia catholica*
STL	Second Temple Literature
STr	Level 1 Discourse Section Transition(s) (fig. 11)

ABBREVIATIONS

SwJT	*Southwestern Journal of Theology*
SUBBTO	*Studia Universitatis Babeș-Bolyai Theologia Orthodoxa*
TD	*Theology Digest*
TDNT	*Theological Dictionary of the New Testament.* 10 vols. Edited by Gerhard Kittel and Gerhard Friedrich. Translated by Geoffrey W. Bromiley. Grand Rapids: Eerdmans, 1964–2006.
TJ	*Trinity Journal*
TLZ	*Theologische Literaturzeitung*
TynBul	*Tyndale Bulletin*
UC	Level 3 Discourse Unit FGT Conclusion/Summary (sg.) (appendix 1, fig. 11)
UI	Level 3 Discourse Unit FGT Introduction (appendix 1, fig. 11)
UPt	Level 3 Discourse Unit Point (appendix 1, fig. 11)
VC	*Vigiliae Christianae*
VUL	*Biblia Sacra Iuxta Vulgatam Versionem.* 3rd ed. Stuttgart: Deutsche Bibelgesellschaft, 1969.
VULAp	Robertus Weber and R. Gryson. *Biblia Sacra Iuxta Vulgatam Versionem. Apparatus Criticus.* 5th Revised Edition. Stuttgart: Deutsche Bibelgesellschaft, 1969.
WBC	Word Biblical Commentary
WFJ	Flavius Josephus. "The Jewish War: Books 1–7; Greek Text." Edited by Jeffrey Henderson, T. E. Page, W. H. D. Rouse, and E. Capps. Loeb Classical Library. Cambridge, MA: Harvard University Press, 1927–1928.
WTJ	*The Westminster Theological Journal*
ZAC	*Zeitschrift für Antikes Christentum*
ZNT	*Zeitschrift für Neues Testament*
ZNW	*Zeitschrift für die neutestamentliche Wissenschaft und die Kunde der älteren Kirche*
ZTK	*Zeitschrift Für Theologie und Kirche*

1

Get Ready . . . Get Set
Introduction to Hebrews 9:27–28
Macro Conclusion/Summary
about Entrance into Heaven

INTRODUCTION

This chapter sketches the "Get Ready! . . . Get Set!" preparations for exploration of a prompt, postmortem, heavenly entrance through the fulfillment of the promised covenant ministries of Christ outlined by Heb 9:27–28. Surprisingly, modern reader conceptions for a present ministry of Christ for a *place* of destiny and continuance of life *immediately* at death never emerge. The global faith perception by many for swift heavenly entrance by both Christ and people, when mapping the Pastor's corresponding spatial-temporal guides, suggest possible tension with the lengthy postponements and alternative endpoints for salvation often presumed upon authorial intensions. For multiple millennia both directions before and after the first century CE, the *where* and *when* of salvation questions have generated intense debate. However, the delayed and detoured sense heard for salvation fulfillment is today rarely questioned. Usually, the text hearing in the academy interprets as a warrant for only the earthly second coming with added philosophical proposals for logical discourse about fleshly resurrection.[1]

For evaluation of this observation and the elements of the old debate, first, this chapter offers more questions that suggest tension concerning the place and time now consistently assumed in the Heb 9:27–28 narrative. Then a thesis statement ensues for evaluation of a possible route hardly embraced in the academy regarding the destiny and time of arrival for people with faith in the ministry of Christ in relation to this first-century CE afterlife summary. Next, samples of conversation are briefly introduced that raise concerns surrounding a believers lengthy eternal life interruption and projected finish locale of popular supported positions. A methodology for charting an ancient and neglected teaching follows about the prompt heavenly shepherd ministry by Jesus as Christ. For study foundation, readers are then encouraged to train their thoughts by familiarization with the Pastor's words provided in categories of the appendix 1 tables to facilitate accurate assessment. Finally, a conclusion summarizes preparations before beginning chapter 2, in search for word correspondence with an often-unconsidered journey regarding the completion of salvation a very little while after death as described in Heb 9:27–28.

PLACE AND TIME QUESTIONS ABOUT THE PASTOR'S MACRO CONCLUSION/SUMMARY

"*Where* are we going *when* we die?" The response of most believers in Jesus, as the Christ, and his gospel, condenses to a simple answer: I am going to Jesus in heaven.[2] An optional translation of Heb 9:27–28 encompasses this thought in more complexity. The Pastor's context could

---

1. For this project, philosophy defines as the use of any rational or logically constructed, extracanonical term or concept beyond the textual meaning of the original biblical authors. In this practice, when by this method derived precepts are constructed and substituted back upon the original text, the textual interpretive exercise consists of philosophy, rather than biblical theology in accurate reflection of the meaning of God's literal speech through the original authors. Concerning academic commentary on Hebrews, many specialized terms and concepts are anachronistic, constructed straw men built in traditions for antithetical argument or supportive for ideology that either cannot be found in the available historical and biblical writings of the time, or consider only one of two or more competing available views (Col 2:8).

2. Cf. Paul's spatial-temporal endpoint as "the result to depart and to be with Christ" (Phil 1:22–24).

conclude his expositional summary with sense that after the appointed time of death, Christ, who as an offering for sins, and who similarly endured the same experiences of death and judgment, for salvation after death at judgment of people waiting for him, will appear "from a second *place/position* [throne in heaven] without sin" (ἐκ δευτέρου χωρὶς ἁμαρτίας Heb 9:28).[3]

This contextual, idiomatic, spatial-temporal reading, rather than the more common temporally restricted reading of Heb 9:27–28, hears in God's speech a strong connection with immediate *heavenly* entrance by the *present* ministry of the fulfilled purpose of Christ according to the Pastor's thematic text of Ps 109:1, 4 (LXX; 110:1, 4 MT). The validly requires exploration of the context of Hebrews. In this setting, the Pastor advances hope as present living with Jesus after fleshly death that instantly begins bodily with rising to God as an eternal/perpetual-*place* spirit (cf. Heb 6:18–20; 10:5).

TENSIONS ABOUT THE PASTOR'S MACRO CONCLUSION/SUMMARY

The academy commentary since this first-century CE statement *overwhelmingly* delays and reroutes this expected completion after death to an earthly locale. Even with other texts supporting believers *living* with Jesus in heaven after death, the inquiring mind quickly startles to a puzzling realization. The faith acceptance of the answer of *going promptly to Jesus in heaven* based upon any biblical text tracks inversely proportional to religious knowledge about traditional options.[4] Theology and philosophy easily obscure the expectation *to Jesus in heaven* by the

---

3. This possible translation does not exclude the common NT options concerning Jesus's future appearing to again minister on earth (Acts 1:11). From the position of his throne in the heavens, as a minister of the holy-*places* (Heb 8:1–2), Jesus may "come" (ἔρχομαι/παρουσία), "appear" (ὁράω/φανερόω), and "bring" (φέρω/ἄγω) people who call upon him to himself (Heb 7:25). Jesus saves people both during approach to God at individual death (Heb 1:3c; 10:35–39; 13:20; cf. John 14:1–6; 1 Thess 5:6–11; 1 Cor 4:5; 2 Cor 5:10; Col 3:1–4; 1 John 2:28; 3:1–3) and brings the fleshly dead who are now alive in heaven with him to meet in the air all those remaining alive in the flesh at his return for a second earthly ministry (Matt 24:29–31; Acts 1:11; 1 Thess 4:13–18; 2 Thess 2:1).

4. Since before writings of the NT, rational conceptions have plagued possible messianic ministry understanding (cf. Matt 11:25; Mark 8:33; Luke 19:11; 24:21; John 3:10; 12:34; Jas 2:5).

present ministry of Christ with myriads of questions, clarifications, thematic interests, schemes, and unknowns.

The sound of other viewpoints, however, creates distortion from hearing God's speech in the text's condensed claims. Jon Laansma, when surveying the explosion of interest in Hebrews in the modern era, remarks, "In many respects, the book remains a 'riddle,' though not for attempts to unlock it."[5] Any agreement of modern hearing on the thematic message of Hebrews remains elusive due to assumptions arising both before and since the first-century CE summary statement.

The barrier of a modern culture and a different language, distanced from the first-century CE author and recipients, stands foreboding as the most ominous obstacle. This situation creates perplexing hermeneutical and methodological challenges. Errors of "parallelomania" muddle the time and place of salvation.[6] Hebrews 9:27–28 explores upon a different spatial-temporal background that is like attempting sense of a narrative about playing American football on a European soccer field. Primarily, academic interpretations mainly consist of parallel conclusions derived from long held conceptions about the heavens and earth, which the adherents assimilate into proof texts supportive of orthodox traditions.[7]

Since the circulation of Hebrews, much of the Pastor's play-by-play of both Jesus's ministry "to atone" (Heb 2:17–18) for sin and his subsequent ministry in high-priestly intercession (Heb 7:25–26), omit the actual participation of people into heaven simply due to spatial-temporal conceptions retained from long before the first-century CE that are often codified into prescribed traditions. A situation develops where the optional *background* of biblical *aiōn-field* (apocalyptic) revelation concerning people collapses into the limited orthodoxy and expectation of a visible *cosmic-field* fulfillment.[8]

---

5. Laansma, "Hebrews," 8.

6. Sandmel, "Parallelomania," 1–13.

7. Bauer, *Orthodoxy*. Bauer correctly finds the terms "heresy" and "orthodoxy" as inappropriate and anachronistic. He also observes "heresy" sometimes antedates "orthodoxy." In the first century CE, the term carried strong weight for a different school of thought—e.g., unique teaching of a Pharisee, scribe, Sadducee, or Jesus. For late second-century CE development of a pejorative force to exclusion of others, see Le Boulluec, *Notion of Heresy*. It is important to ask, does the second- to third-century CE state church view that prevailed in forceful exclusion of others, properly portray God's speech in his word about his people?

8. The term *cosmic-field* maps visible, material, spatial-temporal reality, and *aiōn-field* includes unseen, material, substance-reality of any *heavenly* movement in space and time narrative. The *cosmic-field* is a subset of the material, spatial-temporal reality

For example, the anti-evolution apologetic of the recent era added to developments of the Enlightenment, now strongly shapes the assessment of all of God's historical activities as only within a cosmic-*field* with features of both short duration and earth limited experience. With this background setting, current inquiry of God's speech often hears the afterlife of people in the biblical text with ears accustomed to a cosmic-limited humanity. The resultant textual dissonance and disorientation of compressing *aiōn-field* language pressures readers toward a myriad of new, continually evolving, cosmic-*field* restricted, salvation solutions. Martin Luther examples common steps toward this muted heavenly theme that modulates away from an eternal/perpetual-*place*, heavenly hope (Heb 11:13–16; 12:22–24), toward a *dark-creation* Eden restoration.[9] Collectively, these dampen hearing a first-century CE optional understanding of atonement and the present hope after death of joining Jesus in the eternal/perpetual substance-reality of the unseen kingdom.

In first-century CE understanding, the lexeme κόσμος (cosmos, world, universe) encompasses all recent observable creation, often with a focus on people.[10] It is unfortunate this term also operates as a referent for the unseen heavens in skirting over the different word choices of the Pastor. The Greek lexemes αἰών (*aiōn*) and οἰκουμένη (*oikoumenē*) expand broader creation conceptions than his use of κόσμος (*kosmos*). The term αἰών includes the κόσμος, and also, more comprehensively the eternal creation of unobservable material beyond God himself.

The referent οἰκουμένη encompasses God's order and rule in dominion over invisible substance creation.[11] Within the αἰών and current

---

of the Pastor's *aiōn-field* background apocalyptic language.

9. The term *dark-creation* serves as a biblical geographic descriptor (Heb 12:18; cf. John 1:5; 12:35, 46; Acts 26:18; Col 1:13). Both earthly Eden and the prophetic earthly conditions promised in other canonical texts, which are like Eden (cf. Isa 51:3; Ezek 36:35), function as an antitype of the true type of unseen heavenly realities (cf. Ezek 28:13). Martin Luther held to heavenly access after death but his translation of the Greek plurals of "heaven" (οὐρανός) as singular help scholars of modern translations maintain earthly kingdom paradigms taught formerly by educated church elders since the fourth century CE. See excursus B and Henry, "Cosmology of the Heaven(s)," 28–62.

10. Cf. BDAG, "κόσμος," 561–63. Bauer remarks, "The other philosoph. usage, in which κ. denotes the heaven in contrast to the earth, is prob. without mng. for our lit." Cf. Adams, "Graeco-Roman," 5. Adams writes, "Cosmology seeks to explain the origin, structure, and destiny of the physical universe." Cf. Wright, *Cosmology in Antiquity*, 3–8; Kahn, *Anaximander*.

11. A lack of modern conceptions about the unobservable eternal/perpetual creation results in no current single English gloss to delineate the functional weight of

οἰκουμένη, everything created consists of stuff in the first-century CE known as "substance-reality" (ὑπόστασις Heb 11:1), in an interim observable and unobservable duality (cf. Heb 11:3).[12] All created visible and invisible substance-reality moves through space, experiences time, and at the present remains at a coordinate location of relationship to God's holiness. Everything collectively exists as God's "house" (οἶκος Heb 3:4; 10:21) and "tent, tabernacle" (σκηνή Heb 8:1) within provisional boundaries of the plural heavens and the visible earth (figs. 1–3). The visible and some invisible regions exist either temporary or decaying apart from God's immediate presence (cf. Heb 1:10–12; 12:18–19, 25–27). The invisible creation endures eternally for measureless time (cf. Heb 1:2; 9:11; 12:27; 13:14; cf. 2 Cor 4:18).

This brief spatial-temporal background context for God's speech in Hebrews and perhaps any other biblical narrative serves as the control to govern narrative events of referents in verbal activity.[13] For proper

---

their contextual meanings. Cf. Allen, "Forgotten Ages," 144–51. The lexemes αἰών and οἰκουμένη are errantly translated "world, universe" in a sensed equivalence to the visible creation "world."

12. Whitlark, "Cosmology," 118, 121. Whitlark contends, "According to Hebrews, God has structured his creation with two key realms: a mortal and an immortal one. Both realms simultaneously exist, though, as we will see, they are temporally related concerning the Christian community's experience of them. . . . Again, there are two simultaneous 'created realms'—the present mortal realm where God's faithful people eagerly wait to enter into God's immortal resting place."

See further, Martin, *Corinthian Body*, 1–37. Martin asserts the conclusions from modern Cartesian philosophy that dominate scholarly categories and dichotomies today were only a minor option in first-century CE thinking. René Descartes rejected the ancient definition of the study of nature as the sum of all things. He constructed the category of nature to include only those parts of the universe that could be observed "scientifically." This of necessity resulted in a new category of the "supernatural" and "nonmaterial" in contrast to the "physical" or "material" scientifically sensed world. The redefinition provided him freedom to scientifically study the observable world without regulation by the state church. In this newly invented "physical" or "material" world, this supernatural category could not be analyzed as reality by rational means. Adapting this new dualism as compatible opposites, common-sense theological development led to modern scholarly assertions that this supernatural spiritual reality is either timeless or psychological in only a matter of the mind. Instead, first-century CE thinking primarily held to a "hierarchy of essence." Martin calls the unseen "stuff" for lack of a good English term. This unseen and invisible substance creation is identified in the NT by the term "spiritual" (πνευματικός) and can only be known by revelation, since it is inaccessible by rational scientific study. Biblical revelation never portrays this reality of *spiritual substance* as timeless, psychological, or absolutely inaccessible by the substance of the visible cosmos.

13. Laansma, "Cosmology," 125, 127. Laansma correctly recognizes "cosmology is certainly *there* behind and within the Letter's theology and argument" (italics Laansma). He further states, "Cosmology may not be the main theme in this homily

interpretation, one must accurately determine the narrative *background field*, the features of *referents* involved, and *verbal movements* as understood by the listeners of the original message—without adaptation to either other preconceptions or later anachronistic deductions.[14] Distortion of the original sense heard exponentially increases by use of another space-time background field.[15] The interpretative result by a cosmic-*field* constriction for people either ignores or spiritualizes gospel activity in the invisible creation described by the Pastor.[16] Any temporal description of spatial movement must remain in the background reality utilized by the speaker of Hebrews without orphaned typological antitypes or metaphoric reduction of heavenly types for modern hearing foreign to the original intent.

THESIS ABOUT THE PLACE(S) OF THE PASTOR'S MACRO CONCLUSION/SUMMARY

The key question concerns the place and timing of the atonement for believers and their subsequent salvation experience in Christ as expressed in the *macro conclusion/summary* (MCS) of God's speech in Heb 9:27–28. When and where do believers need and receive literal intercession

---

but it cannot be construed as extraneous to the book's actual interests and so it must be considered as an aspect of its *theology*" (italics Laansma).

14. Wenell, "Kingdom," 135–50. Wenell recognizes a current imbalance between space-based and time-based kingdom of God scholarly studies since the groundbreaking early twentieth-century influence of Weiss and Schweitzer combined with Dalman's definition of the kingdom of God as "kingly rule." She rightly critiques the "prioritizing of context" in spatial studies to the neglect of the message of actual text. Her critique applies easily to scholarly studies in Hebrews, which often neglect the spatial-temporal background language as it appears in the text. Rather, scholars speculate preconceived theoretical differences of space-time concepts, with Jewish as a temporal emphasis and Hellenistic as spatial emphasis. The actual text cannot carry the weight from sources outside the text of the modern proposed division between Jewish and Hellenistic concepts.

15. Cotterell and Turner, *Linguistics*, 96. Cotterell and Turner, concerning author/listener/reader presupposition pools, warn, "If we do not share the presupposition pool of the intended hearer/reader we are prone to misunderstand; perhaps even totally."

16. E.g., *COED*, s.v. "spiritual." In this era, the term "spiritual" senses as "relating to or affecting the human spirit as opposed to material or physical things." In modern context, to *spiritualize* refers to negation of the possession of the features of natural, material substance, thereby considering something with spiritual attributes as supernatural in a presumed, *non-material*, eternal, unseen creation. In the first-century CE context of the Pastor, the modern, contrasting, material-spiritual categories most often now utilized are not so neatly separated where the material cannot enter the spiritual realm. The spiritual realm also consists of material reality of substance.

from judgment for sin after death, by the priestly ministry of Jesus as the Christ, who has completed atonement for sins? An answer should be governed by the background *aiōn* (αἰών) and *oikoumenē* (οἰκουμένη) of the reality envisioned by the Pastor.

The academy is far from monolithic concerning the when and where of Jesus's atonement.[17] Recent conversation about Hebrews among evangelicals attempts to unite atonement and salvation, as part of a lengthy atonement *process* yet complete, that hinges not *only* on the completion of the suffering of the cross but includes perpetual atonement and the logic of Jesus's fleshly resurrection to heaven—with no one yet saved, or ever in heaven.[18]

This project investigates if Jesus's enthronement and exaltation describe a separate promised covenant feature from Jesus's suffering "to atone" (ἱλάσκομαι Heb 2:17; appendix 1, fig. 1, no. 4), regarding a twofold, new covenant ministry of Christ expressed in Hebrews. Further, the inquiry asks if events of exaltation and enthronement occur during Jesus's human death experience *promptly after* the proceedings of heavenly justification, *immediately* at his rising *of* the dead from the cross (appendix 1, fig. 1, no. 2), and *before* his unmentioned and assumed fleshly "rise" (ἐγείρω) *from* the dead three days later in his visible proof of "resurrection" (ἀνάστασις, appendix 1, fig. 1, no. 5; Heb 6:2; 11:35; cf. John 2:18–22).

In relation to the Pastor's earthly tabernacle "outline" (ὑπόδειγμα Heb 8:5, fig. 2), the analysis asks if God expects the teaching of the listeners to "imitate" the same sequence events of Jesus at death (appendix 1, fig. 2, no. 1). It inquires, for the Pastor in Hebrews, if spirits of the dead promptly approach to the throne for judgment (appendix 1, fig. 2, no. 2), where Christ "will appear for salvation from a second *place/position* without sins to those who are eagerly awaiting him" (Heb 9:28) to intercede a very little while after death at judgment (appendix 1, fig. 2, no. 3). Additionally, it asks if Jesus's shepherd intercession (Heb 13:20) allows believers "entrance" to the Father into the holy of holies (appendix

---

17. Jamieson, "When and Where," 347–49.

18. E.g., Moffit, "Further Reflections." In defense of the implications of his work upon the atonement meaning of the cross, Moffit clearly states he views the flesh resurrection of Jesus and later flesh ascension to the Father as part of the *process* of atonement. In his view, atonement would include the sacrifice of the cross but expands to ascension after fleshly resurrection and even, as still unfinished, embraces Jesus's present ministry of intercession.

1, fig. 2, nos. 4–5) with other "brethren" (Heb 2:10–13) before the later corporate resurrections "to complete" those still living (Heb 11:39–40).

The research examines if both Jesus's crucifixion and fleshly resurrection occur as polar endpoints of a sequence of death and rising movements due to accomplishment of atonement for sin before God in heaven promptly at Jesus's death (appendix 1, fig. 10). If true, then does achievement of atonement initiate a process of heavenly events *after* Jesus's human sacrificial offering on the cross that occur *before* his fleshly resurrection, that promptly continue in his subsequent heavenly journey of approach as the forerunner and exemplar for entrance into the way which leads to the Father in heaven (Heb 1:3–9; 6:19–20; 12:2; see appendix 1, fig. 1)? This possible scenario appears in conversation among scholars.[19] Yet, there has been no investigation to test the propositions of the speculated sequence of events, especially since Heb 9:27–28 mainly serves as a warrant for salvation and resuscitation of the flesh at the second coming.

Based upon the lacuna for research testing these conjectures, this project explores for evidence that supports if the Pastor's message, as summarized in the unit conclusion (UC) of Heb 9:27–28, (1) emphasizes Jesus's two-fold, new covenant ministry concerning his completed offering of atonement on the cross and logic of his continual, postresurrection, priestly intercession *in heaven* "to save" (Heb 5:7; 7:25). Also, if (2) for those who have believed in faith (Heb 11:6), that Christ appears for salvation during a prompt similar approach to God after death (Heb 4:16; 7:25–26; 10:22; 12:22–24; fig. 2). Further, if (3) this promised intercession for salvation occurs in a corresponding resurrection experience with Jesus as the Christ (Heb 6:19–20), in the way of the holy-*places* (Heb 9:8), after fleshly death, and before the later proof for his rising to God of fleshly resurrection (Heb 11:39–40; cf. John 2:18–22). This project appraises the thesis that Jesus now intercedes a very little while after death at judgment to bring into heaven those who believe in his offering for sin, in the same way God promptly raised him in salvation from the dead into heaven, recaps Heb 9:27–28, as the true heart conversation of the Pastor's entire exposition, exhortation, and rhetoric.

---

19. Jeremias, "Zwischen Karfreitag," 194–201; Backhaus, *Der Hebräerbrief*, 87. Cf. Eisele, *Ein Unerschütterliches Reich*, 84–85; Zimmerman, *Das Bekenntnis der Hoffnung*, 201; Karrer, *Der Brief an die Hebräer*, 2:170–71; Rowland and Morray-Jones, *Mystery of God*, 169–73.

With the lens of the proposed thesis, the Pastor addresses the recipients need for endurance in a proper teaching "conversation" (ῥῆμα Heb 1:3b) concerning their confession of eternal/perpetual-*place* hope by Jesus's atonement and heavenly salvation soon after death at judgment.[20] It is unfortunate modern glosses utilize the English "word" for both ῥῆμα and λόγος, leading to an *illegitimate totality transfer* fallacy.[21] With some overlap, the term λόγος usually refers the revelation speech-action from God, whereas ῥῆμα refers to external conversation about words, speech, or teachings concerning the actual source λόγος. The Pastor's exhortation for proper conversation about Jesus, as the Christ, governs all confession about the Word (speech-action) of God (Heb 4:12–13).

BACKGROUND TO THE PLACE(S) OF THE PASTOR'S MACRO CONCLUSION/SUMMARY

Contextual Background

Once neglected, the sermon of Hebrews by an unknown author in the early decades of the newly-formed Christian churches now claims an explosion of academic attention. After enduring challenges, its place in the canon for now remains secure. Hebrews occupies a unique place on the margins of transition from the OT to the NT.[22] The Pastor's extensive use

---

20. The Pastor chooses the verbal noun "conversation" (ῥῆμα) as his term for proclamation of messianic salvation. Cf. BDAG, "ῥῆμα," 905. Bauer remarks, "Gener. the sing. brings together all the divine teachings as a unified whole, w. some such mng. as *gospel*, or *confession*." The Pastor does not use the verbal noun of the word "gospel" (ευαγγελιον) to describe God's salvation work in Christ. He does use the verbal activity "to proclaim good news" (εὐαγγελίζω Heb 4:2, 6) concerning both past and present gospel reception. The theme "conversation" (ῥῆμα) has a close connection to other NT writers use of the term "gospel" (εὐαγγέλιον Rom 1:16). Salvation is promised when a person believes after hearing the "conversation" about God's ability as Christ, in the personal intercession of Jesus to bring people to himself by entrance into heaven at judgment after death (cf. Rom 10:17; Eph 1:13). This "conversation" theme introduces in the chapter 4 DI (Heb 1:1–4) as the first of three adjectival participles sequencing the ministry of the Son. The Pastor states, "While bringing all things by the conversation of his ability" (φέρων τε τὰ πάντα τῷ ῥήματι τῆς δυνάμεως αὐτοῦ Heb 1:3b; cf. Rom 1:16). Most modern English translations use the word "power" for δύναμις (*dynamis*), which loses the specific activity of the gospel in exchange for a general descriptive characteristic about God in relation to his creation. The Pastor encourages and warns his listeners concerning a need for proper *conversation* of God's speech and exegetes the OT as God's speech in detail.

21. Cf. Barr, *Semantics of Biblical Language*, 218.

22. The background for this exploration Hebrews views as sermon of early date 66–70 CE likely from Rome after early victories in the Jewish War (66–70 CE), to Jewish Christians

of the LXX supports a likely provenance of a Judeo-Hellenistic synagogue by an author with probable rabbinic training and rhetorical literary skill.

Hebrews is the only extant record of a complete, orated, congregational message from the NT period.[23] It is internally labeled as "word of exhortation" (Heb 13:22; cf. Acts 13:15). The *Sitz im Leben* is likely a well-crafted homily designed for a synagogue gathering, with a cohesive letter-ending for circulation (Heb 13:22–25).[24] The sermon genre matches common first-century CE expositional-exhortative midrash of two OT texts (cf. Acts 13:14–31, 42, 44; Luke 4:16; 18:4).[25]

Rather than primarily evangelistic in concern for listeners personal salvation, the sermon provides assistance for some "brethren," "holy brethren," "sons," and "his people," to *again* resist persecution and pressures to teach inaccuracy concerning Christ (Heb 10:32–35; 12:3–4).[26] The Pastor encourages his audience to hear and imitate what God "spoke" (ἐλάλησεν Heb 1:1–2), for a proper "conversation" (ῥῆμα Heb 1:3b; 6:5), as "teachers" (διδάσκαλοι Heb 5:12) with "maturity, completeness" (τελειότης Heb 6:1) "of the word/message of Christ" (τοῦ Χριστοῦ λόγον Heb 6:1). This thematic purpose of Hebrews supports a monotheistic secondary christological didactic.[27] The Pastor primarily counsels believers in proper hearing and teaching maturity of their "confession"

---

in a synagogue. The recipients were pressured by growth of Jewish nationalism and further messianic expectation to fall away from Christian confession, congregational assembly, and teaching, in return to former Jewish cultural norms. Cf. Allen, *Hebrews*, 23–93.

23. Walker, "Place for Hebrews?," 376–88.

24. For recent structural considerations of Hebrews, see Coetsee, "Die sprekende God," 41–80.

25. Gelardini, "Hebrews," 25–26. Contra, Heinemann, "Triennial Lectionary Cycle," 41–48.

26. Allen, *Hebrews*, 61–70. The Pastor calls his listeners "brethren" (ἀδελφοί) nine times, "holy brethren" (ἀδελφοὶ ἅγιοι), and "his people" (τὸν λαὸν αὐτοῦ) once. The previous experience of persecution when coming to Christ and returning to their previous foundation strongly supports believers who after a season of peace face new challenges in the practice of their faith. This carries great weight against the likelihood of a second less grounded or apathetic generation as supposed by some interpretations of Heb 2:3. Contra, Marshall, "Soteriology in Hebrews," 253–72.

27. Notably, the Pastor places more emphasis on the actions of the Son's "ability" (τῆς δυνάμεως Heb 1:3; 7:16) as a person during his similar experience of human death (2:9–18), than his (Jesus's) identity as "being the radiance of his [God's] glory and representation of his substance-reality" (ὢν ἀπαύγασμα τῆς δόξης καὶ χαρακτὴρ τῆς ὑποστάσεως αὐτοῦ Heb 1:3). His thematic exegesis supports issues not on the latter, with his listeners over *who Jesus is as the Christ*—but the former, about *what Jesus humanly was able to do* as God in fleshly death as the Christ that was incongruent with what his listeners were tempted to repetitively do and teach.

Atonement and the Logic of Resurrection in Hebrews 9:27–28

(Heb 3:1; 4:14; 10:23), in an *effective* salvific christological Word (speech-action) (λόγος Heb 2:1–4).²⁸ This God-centered revelation begins in the discourse introduction (DI) (Heb 1:1–4) with the subject-predicate "God . . . spoke" (ὁ θεὸς . . . ἐλάλησεν Heb 1:1–2).²⁹ On this foundation, the homily orates God's speech—what God did and continues to do by the Son, as the Christ fulfillment in Jesus, that the listeners should hear and teach with maturity in their "conversation."³⁰

Recent Background Discussion

In recent years past, David Moffitt's book *Atonement and the Logic of Resurrection in the Epistle to the Hebrews* has triggered a flurry of discussion.³¹ As part, the Invited Section on the Epistle to the Hebrews of the Evangelical Theological Society meetings in 2018 completed six years of papers focused on atonement in Hebrews.³² Mainly, concerning Moffitt's proposals, the presentations in the early years incited vigorous debate over when and where Jesus made his offering of atonement based upon Hebrews.³³ The argument stimulated a taxonomy of recent scholarship by Robert Jamieson on the issue.³⁴

Academy dialogue often openly negates possible spatial-temporal background features behind the Pastor's views and assumes "clear"

---

28. In his introduction, Ceslaus Spicq, concerning the contents of the Hebrews epistle, comments, "A la différence de celle Saint Paul, la théologie de l'Épître aux Hébreux est théocentrique et non christocentrique." Spicq, *L'Epitre aux Hébreux: I*, 41; Cf. Ellingworth, *Epistle to the Hebrews*, 66. Ellingworth comments, "If Christology is the centre of the epistle's teaching, that Christology is rooted in teaching about God."

29. Allen, *Hebrews*, 95. Allen comments, "The structural weight of the entire 72 words in Greek rests upon a single finite verb *elalēsen* and its subject *ho theos*: 'God . . . has spoken.' The author's use of rhetorical techniques such as alliteration, meter, rhythm, phonetic and semantic parallelism, syntactical/semantic repetition, and chiasm are all evidenced in this sentence."

30. Coetsee, "Die sprekende God," 122–23. Coetsee discovered, that 73 percent of the time, the author used something spoken in the past, to apply either urgently to the present or as a reality in the perfect. This urgent present in authority of God speaking allowed the author to command his listeners that God was still speaking today, and they needed to listen and properly teach what God says.

31. Moffitt, *Atonement*.

32. Laansma et al., *So Great Salvation*.

33. Marshall, "Yes, But." The death of Howard Marshall perhaps prevented publication into *So Great Salvation* of the discussion push-back to David Moffitt in the first 2013 session. Cf. Kibbe, "Is It Finished?," 25–61; Schenck, "Through His Own Blood."

34. Jamieson, "When and Where," 338–68.

dichotomies perhaps foreign to him. For example, Victor (Sung Yul) Rhee writes concerning eschatology, "Thus it is *clear* that eschatology set forth by the author of Hebrews is not based on Philo's spatial idea of the invisible world, but on the Jewish understanding of the temporal idea. . . . Thus far, the discussion has been centered around whether the eschatology of Hebrews is spatially or temporally oriented. The evidence indicated that the temporal idea is more convincing."[35] This background spatial-temporal position erects an impossible false dichotomy between the temporal and spatial language in Hebrews.[36] The Pastor includes detailed spatial-temporal background information of his present era and spoke his message under the assumption his readers would already understand it (see fig. 4).

The author-reader interaction with narrative operates much like how the modern listener of a play-by-play football game would understand the organization of the field as one's mind follows the movements and activities of the players.[37] In similar mental mapping, original readers could follow the movements of Jesus in a play-by-play manner on their perceived background field of God's salvific efforts. The author and readers really believed these described, unseen places existed (Heb 11:13–16). Craig Keener recognizes, "Unlike Plato, the writer of Hebrews does not see the heavenly reality only as an ideal world to be apprehended by the mind: Jesus really went there."[38]

Modern solutions plausibly miss the Pastor's first-century CE understanding by negation of any promised, present, and heavenly entrance for people. In the early last century, in dissatisfaction with the realistic achievement of their earth-centered views, the academy moved from a present earthly fulfillment involving a thick social gospel. The new options view salvation promises as inaugurated, internally realized, and

---

35. Rhee, *Faith in Hebrews*, 50–51, (italics mine).

36. Käsemann, *Das wandernde Gottesvolk*. Käsemann interprets spatial orientation in both a present and future eschatological lens. Also, he does not feel the present is emphasized as much as the future. However, a major foundational weakness in his position is the impossibility for perception of time without relative movement of created objects through space. Timelessness in God's creation cannot exist if there is life.

37. Gould and White, *Mental Maps*, 1986.

38. Keener, "Hebrews 8:1–5." Cf. Guthrie, *The Structure of Hebrews*, 121–124. Guthrie, concerning the structure of Hebrews, concludes the arguments are spatial. He writes, "In Hebrews an emphasis on spatial orientation to either heaven or earth resides primarily in the expositional material." He points out that this spatial theology is textually driven from the author's exegesis of spatial points of reference in Ps 110:1 and Ps 8.

future at the end of the age. However, the retained closed transcendent heaven for people on the same limited cosmic-*field* still rationally leaves no present place for continuous eternal living for the dead in a prompt resurrection or allowance for the Pastor's present ministry of Christ, as shepherd, leading believers into the unseen accessible reality of heaven.

Several "clear" dichotomies of modern scholarship need revisiting for better understanding of the process of rising to God after death heard in first-century CE background descriptions. For example, concerning the evidence suggesting the cosmic limitation of people after death, John Collins warns against the simple adversarial dichotomy of the Greek belief in immortality of the soul and Jewish belief in the flesh resurrection.[39] Neither argued assertions are sustainable by the evidence at hand. The possibility that the Pastor describes complete, immediate living, in afterlife activity of believers apart fleshly resurrection, is ripe for further investigation by the removal of errant antithetical warrants no longer supporting the traditional superstructure of cosmic-*field* restriction.

METHODOLOGY FOR EVALUATION OF THE PASTOR'S MACRO CONCLUSION/SUMMARY

The thesis herein explores the feasibility of a "paradigm shift" entailing a change in the background field behind the message in Hebrews.[40] It tests an *aiōn-field* background for the narrative concerning the atonement and logic of Jesus's resurrection in Heb 9:27–28 as promptly after his death with experience upward into the way of the holy-*places* three days before fleshly resurrection (appendix 1, fig. 1). It also evaluates the probability for Jesus's postmortem transformation in spirit-resurrection to priestly intercession *in heaven* promptly after fleshly death for a common immediate resurrection for those who believe in faith in a near parallel experience (appendix 1, fig. 2).

In methodological overview, the appraisal progresses with this chapter as introduction, three subsequent chapters in consideration of the thesis, and a conclusion. It applies the tools of lexical semantics, Koine Greek grammatical-historical exegesis, biblical theology, discourse analysis, narrative analysis, and rhetorical analysis. These tools pale in comparison to the Pastor's understanding of "the Holy Spirit's

---

39. Collins, "Afterlife in Apocalyptic Literature," 129.
40. Kuhn, *Structure of Scientific Revolutions*.

presently revealing these things" (Heb 9:8; cf. 1 Cor 2:9–16) available to all believers. Priority centers on *God's speech* as the primary evidence above that of the secondary tools and secondary sources. Also, for completeness, historical major shifts in NT studies possibly influencing other views in an alternative cosmic-*field* away from the Pastor's *aiōn-field* will be addressed.

The arrangement for exploring evidence for the proposed thesis will first encourage frequent reflection upon the Pastor's lexical choices found in appendix 2. Properly understanding his contextual meaning begins by becoming acquainted with his lexical choices more than those who write/speak later, with other words about his words.

The table lists are not prescriptive for the Pastor's meaning.[41] Meaning (semantics) always resides at the syntactical level of the sentences, literary devices, discourse rhetorical units, and thematic, cohesive interconnections of the collective work. The initial exercise, therefore, is not to determine meaning, which is a task which must follow later. Thus, this chapter seeks a familiarity with the cohesive word pool so that variant background options and proposals quickly raise suspicions for proof texting.

Chapter 2 first lays foundation steps for successful identification of the discourse lexemes employed by the Pastor. Lexical analysis of the words of Heb 9:27–28 samples probable to possible sources for evidence of meaning corresponding to the proposed thesis. A modified sampling method assists to filter his large word pool noted in the tables 1–4 due to the impossible magnitude of diachronic word studies for every word from all possible sources in a study of this size.

Collectively, the meaning of the lexical units assembles into a proposed *biblical theology* of the Pastor through a theocentric lens.[42] Chapter 3 analyzes the background *aiōn-field* for cohesive mental mapping of the thesis in the Pastor's discourse and rhetoric. Rather than modern

---

41. Young, *Intermediate New Testament Greek*, vii. Young observes, "Many grammars assume that what a particular structure meant before the Koine Greek period dictates what it means when used by NT writers. The historical school therefore tends to be prescriptive, a notion shunned by modern linguists. The descriptive school, on the other hand, recognizes that usage in context determines meaning, not prior usage."

42. Köstenberger and Patterson, *Invitation to Biblical Interpretation*, 697–99. Biblical theology aims to understand a passage of Scripture in its own historical setting. Further, Scripture is studied "*on its own terms*, that is, pay special attention, not merely to the concepts addressed in Scripture, but to the very words, vocabulary, and terminology used by the biblical writers themselves" (italics Köstenberger, 698).

systematic categories and issues of later debates pressed upon his text, the assembled biblical theology attempts to tease out the Pastor's own categories with *his* terms. Admittedly, this is a challenging task due to the impossibility of eliminating one's own presuppositions, the powerful pressure of later traditions, the overwhelming scholarly superstructure built upon alternative views in specialist technical language, the acknowledged cultural temporal distance, and the Greek to English gloss language obstacles. However, the method has a higher probably discerning the Pastor's theology and philosophy to answer the propositions posed concerning Heb 9:27–28 than the more common method of pressing modern categories from later issues and unrelated technical terms. Thus, the assembled biblical theology seeks to place the sermon in the Pastor's own contextual philosophical and theological paradigm.

Chapter 4 builds upon previous lexical semantics and biblical theology with discourse analysis and exegesis.[43] It adds rhetorical, narrative, and story analysis along with first-century CE interpretation methods from the Pastor's use of the OT. It evaluates the validity of the overall function of the lexical parts within the whole sermon on a first-century CE apocalyptic background. Specifically, it assesses if Heb 9:27–28 functions as a MCS, a proposed discourse function by Teun van Dijk, whose methods are utilized in discourse analysis by Linda Neeley.[44] Theoretically, in Greek rhetorical discourse, embedded unit conclusions together should form a MCS. If an accurate proposition, then the derived semantic meaning of the embedded discourse conclusions should integrate into a MCS congruent with Heb 9:27–28. Once formed, this MCS compares with the thematic assertions set forth in the thesis. Exegesis of these units answers the question whether the proposed theme of Heb 9:27–28 fits the other discourse unit conclusion (DUC) themes.

In later footnote discussion the resultant compiled MCS compares with points of contact with other language of NT writings concerning possible spiritual living after death. Future research can include additional points of contact with other contemporary canonical and non-canonical writings. These NT works are mined for both continuity and discontinuity with the derived context for the Pastor's referents, verbal actions, of spirit existence in relation to requirements to enter the places

---

43. For introductory principles, see Black, *Linguistics for Students*, 170–72; Dooley and Levinsohn, *Analyzing Discourse*.

44. Van Dijk, *Some Aspects of Text Grammars*, 6, 10–11. Cf. Neeley, *Discourse Analysis*, 28.

of God's holiness. The question addressed focuses on whether other primary writers maintain that believers not only see Jesus, as the Christ, at his coming to earth, but also at his coming in intercession for those approaching by transformation to a complete, bodily spirit by God at death.

The result of chapters 2 through 4 compares with arguments against the thesis throughout this work. Brief survey provides possible historical, theological, and philosophical changes and alternatives that project away from the proposed thesis both before, during, and after the first-century CE written recorded sermon.

Chapter 5 summarizes the findings, lists the compiled evidence for the thesis, provides experiential observations learned during the dissertation investigation, and proposes areas for future research. It concludes with an invitation to believe for approach to Jesus by faith, for entrance of the way of the holy-*places* to God, and for freedom at eternal/perpetual-*place* judgment to eternal/perpetual-*place* life.

Finally, two excursuses introduce areas of needed further investigation. Excursus A provides a nodal investigation of the flesh-spirit juxtaposition in relation to the meaning of resurrection for believers in other NT texts concerning the theme of the gospel. Excursus B examines a path of missteps away from heavenly completion at death by Martin Luther and his subsequent influence on the accuracy of modern Bible translations.

CONCLUSION

This chapter introduces questions about a link between the summary of God's speech found in Heb 9:27–28 and the simple faith for living approach and entrance promptly after death to Jesus in his unseen heavenly kingdom that may be heard in Hebrews. Is it possible the faith of the general body of believers, who believe they are going to Jesus when they die, have it right? The evidence of the possibility of the answers to this question in the affirmative explores in chapters 2–4. After the reader reviews the words spoken by the Pastor in appendix 2, the next step in the investigation should proceed with chapter 2.

2

Go! First Steps

The Word(s) to Place(s) in Hebrews 9:27–28

INTRODUCTION

The Pastor exhorts his audience, "Let us run with perseverance" (Heb 12:1). Analogous to running, this chapter starts the "Go!" It covers foundational steps for determining the meaning of the Pastor's word choices within his intended understanding.

This segment listens to the first-century CE summation of God's speech in Heb 9:27–28 with tools of linguistic analysis. The first step establishes familiarity with the Pastor's chosen words more than commentary about those words. Steps following briefly review the thesis question, translation difficulties, and related traditions against translating Heb 9:28 with *ek deuterou* (ἐκ δευτέρου) as an idiom with both spatial and temporal weight, rather than the usual temporal only rendering. A summary of common first-century CE hermeneutics follows. How the Pastor *intended* and how the *audience received* the words greatly enhance understanding. The next step introduces challenges of first-century CE Jewish apocalyptic (*aiōn-field*) language. Interpreter outlook toward this background field for revelation has weight for predeterminations about the Pastor's word meaning. Also, the next step reviews the sense of the traditional translation.

Continuing toward an efficient stride, next, a methodology which stratifies both available first-century CE sources and later related resources from "most probable" to "least possible" is applied. This evaluation technique enables evidence stratification and necessary filtering of available options for word meaning (fig. 9). The method provides a foundation for a sampling of the Pastor's available sources and historical evidence for thematic and verbal correspondence with his word pool. Determination of the overall theme and common verbal associations of his available sources enables selection of his most probable intended meanings. Finally, a chapter conclusion summarizes the findings in preparation for a smooth and steady stride in chapter 3 toward the contextual background for the meaning of the Pastor's words in Heb 9:27–28.

STEP 1: BASIC LEXICAL SEMANTICS

Basic principles of lexical semantics provide a starting point for the optional place(s) explored.[1] Not unlike running techniques, certain communication rules regulate the essentials for successful understanding. After determination of genre and background, the interpretative movement must focus on identification of the most probable "referent" and "sense" intended for word choices. A *referent* is what in a context is being spoken about, and the *sense* is what is being said about the referent.[2] The sense of the Pastor's referents in speech consists not only in the public meaning of definition, etymology, sound, or feeling, but must consider the Pastor's own meaning in tone and context. The Pastor's meaning is not automatically homogeneous with others.[3]

---

1. Principles of lexical semantics assist to determine authorial meaning. This tool should not be held as the only ultimate *key* to proper interpretation of meaning. The method of first identifying word meanings, as a reduction and simplification of the overall complexity of God's provision of communication, provides only some of the necessary components for the overall context that determines authorial meaning of speech; e.g., Tuen van Dijk recognizes that the mental activity of a listener/reader assembled context does not contain a recitation of *each individual word* with associated meanings. Rather, it always *summarizes* speech meaning as much greater than the sum of the individual meanings of the words. Van Dijk calls this mental construction the "SUMMARY" (caps van Dijk) as the "macro-structure" of the meaning of a text. Van Dijk, *Some Aspects of Text Grammars*, 6, 10–11.

2. Caird, *Language and Imagery*, 39.

3. Caird reminds, "The danger here is that we should think of culture in fixed and exclusive terms." Caird, *Language and Imagery*, 53.

Table 6—Modern English Words Unknown by the Pastor

Modern English Words Unknown by the Pastor		
trinity	Philonic	supernatural
dualism	Platonic	transcendent
monistic	mysticism	dichotomy
nonmaterial	Sanctuary	trichotomy
hell	rapture	church
universe	cosmology	dispensation
afterlife	disembodied spirit	anthropology
intermediate-state	apocalypticism	pseudepigrapha
apocalyptic (adj.)	Gnosticism	session
apocalypse (genre)	biblical theology	heavenly tabernacle

Understanding the Pastor's meaning requires learning *his* language in *his* culture. Interpretative steps must filter available lexical data for the most suitable glosses for the Pastor's intended understanding. Tables 6 and 7 list both post-sermon words unknown by the Pastor and the Pastor's words with different modern meaning. Awareness of these anachronistic hazards guards against misinterpretation. Regarding differences in word meanings, David Black recognizes, "However, few words retain their original meanings throughout their history and migration from one language to another."[4]

The tables provide words often freighted with other meanings. Caution should be observed in translation with meaning foreign, limited, expanded, or oblique to the Pastor. It is best to maintain concept and summary terminology as close as possible to his words and meanings as determined by his *aiōn-field*, first-century CE usage. Table 7 lists drift in word meanings since the sermon that can alter interpretative perceptions.

---

4. Black, *Linguistics for Students*, 122.

Table 7—The Pastor's Lexemes with Different Background Meaning

Greek	Pastor's Aiōn-field Meaning	Limited Cosmic-field Meaning
οὐρανός (ouranos) (space)	substance heaven(s) (singular or plural)	material cosmos with non-material heaven
ἡμέρα (hēmera) (time)	day(s) (both earthly and eternal/perpetual-*place* time)	day(s) (earthly time only; heaven usually timeless eternal present)
διαθήκη (diathēkē)	covenant(s) (present and future fulfillment at death)	covenant(s) (only one future eschatological fulfillment)
ναός (naos) (not in Hebrews)	temple (type—all creation of invisible substance heavens)	temple (local creation in transcendent–timeless heaven)
σκηνή (skēnē)	tabernacle/tent (type—all or part[s] of creation)	tabernacle/tent (local creation only in heaven)
ὑπόστασις (hypostasis)	reality and substance of the heavens and earth	forensic perceived assurance, confidence on earth
πνεῦμα (pneuma)	spirit (substance-reality)	spirit (nonmaterial])
κατάπαυσις (katapausis)	rest (after death with Jesus)	rest (peaceful fleshly life)
λαλέω (laleō)	God's speaking/revealing acts	audible speech of God
ῥῆμα (rhema)	conversation (about λόγος)	Word (scripture or revelation)
λόγος (logos)	God's Revelation in/by Christ	Word (scripture or revelation)
δύναμις (dynamis)	ability (specific gospel acts from death to resurrection)	power (general trait of God's sovereign omnipotence)
προσέρχομαι (proserchomai)	approach (life-worship + after death approach to Jesus)	worship (type elevation as reality only in fleshly life)
εἰσέρχομαι (eiserchomai)	enter (at death after judgment led by the Shepherd Jesus)	worship (type elevation as only reality in fleshly life)
ἐσχάτου τῶν ἡμερῶν τούτων (eschatou tōn hēmerōn toutōn)	during these last days (present and future)	at these last days (mainly future only)
αἰών (aiōn)	eternal/perpetual-*place*(s); All/part(s) of eternal & temporary creation	world/universe (visible) or age, eternity, everlasting (time)

οἰκουμένη (oikoumenē)	ordered dominion over αἰών from eternity past	God's rule over only rational visible creation of Genesis
υἱός (huios)	Son (human/God)	Son (God/human)
ἐκκλησία (ekklēsia)	assembly (earthly antitype + believers in heaven as type)	church (local, on earth only)
ἀποθνήσκω (apothnēskō)	death (flesh + eternal unseen relationship away living God)	death (flesh only)
κρίσις (krisis)	judgment (at fleshly death)	judgment (future only)
ἀποκάλυψις (apokalypsis)	revelation (all figurative as a reality of seen and unseen truth)	revelation (figurative only, limited reality to cosmic truth)
κόσμος (kosmos)	earth and celestial host	all creation beyond God
πνεύματος ἁγίου (pneumatos hagiou)	holy *place* spirit (person)	Holy Spirit (God)
πνεύματος αἰωνίου (pneumatos aiōniou)	eternal/perpetual-*place* spirit (person)	Holy Spirit (God)
πατρὶ τῶν πνευμάτων (patri tōn pneumatōn)	the Father of spirits (people)	only fleshly life now and future (no place for fleshly dead)
πνεύμασιν δικαίων τετελειωμένων (pneumasin dikaiōn teteleiōmenōn)	to spirits of righteous having been completed (in heaven)	only fleshly life now and future (no place for fleshly dead)
τοῦ πνεύματος τοῦ ἁγίου (tou pneumatos tou hagiou)	the Holy Spirit (God)	the Holy Spirit (God)

STEP 2: PROPOSED WORD MEANINGS AVOIDING SOLUTION MISSTEPS

The proposed thesis for exploration rests on evidence with contextual weight for addition of *place/position* sense to the idiomatic force of ordinal idiom *ek deuterou chōris hamartias* (ἐκ δευτέρου χωρὶς ἁμαρτίας Heb 9:28) that corresponds to Jesus's position in the *aiōn-field* background governing the message. The option translates that Christ will appear for salvation "from a second *place/position* without sins," which concerns the holy space location of his enthronement for his present ministry of the new covenant.[5]

5. In this optional proposal, the nom. sg. Hagia (Ἅγια Heb 9:2) designates the "holy

In this option, the gen. adjectival construction "out of a second... without sin" links with the same previous adjectival construction *"second tent"* (δευτέραν Heb 9:7) about the "tent, which is called holy of holies" (Heb 9:3)—"from, out of" Christ will appear (Heb 9:28). As an ordinal idiom serving in a unit summary of previous exposition, it has both adjectival and adverbial space and time properties determined by context.

Proper testing should explore whether the listeners and later first- to third-century CE readers likely heard, based on the Greek ordinal adjectival/adverbial construction under the weight of the previous spatial exposition, an idiomatic meaning of "from a second *place/position* without sin."[6] If true, this statement evokes the Pastor's thick conceptions of Jesus's continual *second ministry* as Christ as an active, heavenly, priestly mediator from the right hand of God after completion of atonement (cf. Heb 1:3, 13; 8:1; 10:12; 12:2). Jesus appears quickly to individually meet approaching believers after fleshly death for salvation in continuance of their possession of eternal/perpetual life.

By this construction as his main UC, the Pastor summarizes four synchronized tracks of his exposition in sections 1–2 (Heb 1:1—10:18): (1) testimonial faith in hope after *death* for a heavenly inheritance, (2) God's *judgment* of Jesus's offering at his substitutionary human death, (3) Jesus's current heavenly ministry of *intercession*, and (4) *salvation* into a present, new, covenant relationship for believers resulting in forgiveness of sin during approach to God in heaven after death. These parenetic pathways come together in Heb 9:27–28, which functions as the main MCS.

Evidence for this proposal faces obstacles. First, it builds on a minority theological position, both historically and among modern scholars, of life promptly after fleshly death.[7] The possibility that even Jesus experienced

---

place" and combined form Hagia Hagiōn ('Άγια Άγίων Heb 9:3) refers to the "holy of holies." The native koine Greek gen. pl. ἁγίων (*hagiōn* Heb 8:2; 9:3; 9:8; 10:19) and acc. fem. sg. *hagia* (ἅγια Heb 9:12, 24, 25) in the tabernacle context then consistently serve as a referent for the collective recently achieved heavenly (holy-*places*) by Jesus's entrance (appendix 2, table 9). For discussion, see Barnard, *Mysticism of Hebrews*, 92–93.

6. Nida and Charles, *Theory and Practice of Translation*, 163. Nida and Taber in their chapter, "Testing the Translation" state, "There should not be anything in the translation itself which is stylistically awkward, structurally burdensome, linguistically unnatural, and semantically misleading or incomprehensible, unless, of course, the message in the source language has these characteristics (the task of the translator is to produce the closest natural equivalent, not to edit or to rewrite)."

7. E.g., Jesus corrected the theology of the Sadducees in Mark 12:18–27, by revealing that Moses taught by the Scriptures, that God is the God of the "living" Abraham,

continued living in approach to God "according to the ability of an endless life" (Heb 7:16), and "through a spirit of an eternal/perpetual-*place* himself" (Heb 9:14) after fleshly death and before fleshly resurrection, cuts across the theological structure of traditional cosmic-*field* limited views.[8] A continuous state of death requires assimilation of all Jesus's postmortem heavenly activity into ascension after fleshly resurrection (Mark 16:19; Luke 24:51; Acts 1:2, 9, 11, 22). This includes for adherents Jesus's atonement of sin, movement in "the way of the holy-*places*" (Heb 9:8), his similar rising *of* (all) the dead *people*, judgment and vindication by God, rising *from* the dead, approach, passing through the heavens, entrance, offering, and bringing/leading into/through the heavenly places.[9]

Biblical narrative about Jesus's approach in spirit, vindication in judgment, entrance into the holy of holies, enthronement as God's Son, worship by angels, and the first human in spirit birth (Heb 1:3c–14)

Isaac, and Jacob—even after their fleshly death. For Jesus, the present tense "I am the God of your fathers" (Ἐγώ εἰμι ὁ θεὸς τοῦ πατρός σου Exod 3:6 LXX) evidences a continuous *living* relationship with God for these patriarchs, even after death. Also, Jesus promises, "The one who hears my word [τὸν λόγον μου (Jesus's speech-action as the Christ)] and believes him who sent him, continually has eternal/perpetual-*place* life [ἔχει ζωὴν αἰώνιον] and does not come into judgment, but has moved from death into life [μεταβέβηκεν ἐκ τοῦ θανάτου εἰς τὴν ζωήν]" (John 5:24). The recurrent phrase "eternal/perpetual-*place* life" (ζωὴν αἰώνιον) has both temporal and spatial weight as life in the unseen eternal/perpetual-*places*. The pres. tense in Jesus's hermeneutic carries force for continuous possession of a life that is fulfilled by uninterrupted extension of life for entrance into the eternal/perpetual-*place* creation. The perf. tense suggests completion of everything necessary for the present effect of further movement from death to life (cf. John 5:25–32). Further, Paul's language of comfort for grieving Thessalonian believers over their recent dead in comparison to most others, speaks of present conscious alertness in a domain of light for the believing dead, in comparison to a destiny in suffering of drunken darkness for unbelievers (1 Thess 5:1–11).

8. A major issue hinges on translation of δύναμις (*dynamis*) when linked with ζωῆς ἀκαταλύτου ("endless life," Heb 7:16). The word δύναμις carries weight of a potential ability to function in a certain sequence of actions. BDAG, "δύναμις," 262–63. The modern English "power" carries more general, nonspecific, possibilities of activities. Jesus continued living, specifically during the three-day period after death of the flesh until his resurrection, must carry more than a general potential of a possibility. The entire theology of the gospel hope and promise crumbles without this basic fact of Jesus's "endless life" (Heb 7:16) at his judgment by God, even temporarily after the situation of fleshly death in inactivity by crucifixion of the flesh body. The sense of δύναμις that tracks through Hebrews is addressed in the chapter 4 "Discourse Introduction (1:1–4)."

9. Nelson, "He Offered Himself," 255. Nelson assumes, "Hebrews thus unites Christ's resurrection and exaltation/ascension into a single concept (13:20)." Cf. Schreiner, *Ascension of* Christ, 106–8; Moffitt, "It Is Not Finished," 157–75; Moore, "Sacrifice, Session, and Intercession," 521–41; Moffitt, "Jesus as Interceding High Priest," 542–52.

logically follows flesh resurrection in various methodological rejection under the philosophical term *dualism* (table 6) for a finished and complete spirit life outside of flesh.[10] For adherents, nothing humanly happens after death until after Jesus's resurrection and return—which since for Jesus's correspondence with all human death (Heb 2:9–18) extrapolates to believers with no conscious living after death until a fleshly resurrection.[11]

The second obstacle locates in the late fourth century CE, three hundred years after the Pastor's sermon. Since that time, Heb 9:28 rarely interprets with present spatial force for those waiting.[12] However, the evidence of tradition weakens when critically analyzed. Mainly, this limited option for only the earthly second coming fulfillment appears quite late, as distant from the sermon in time, language, and culture. Use of the tradition argument to counter or affirm a spatial translation follows the fallacy of the argument from silence. Also, interpretation by allegorical symbolism later overshadows the Pastor's authorial-intended method for interpretation of God's revelation.[13]

---

10. Baugh, "Whose Spirit?"; Lohfink, *Die Himmelfahrt Jesu*, 50; Wright, *Surprised by Hope*; Wright, *New Testament*, 97; Mackie, "Son of God in Hebrews," 114–29; Mackie, "Exordium of Hebrews," 437–53; Laansma, "Hidden Stories in Hebrews," 9–18; Laansma, "Heaven in the General Epistles," 111–18; Schenck, *Cosmology and Eschatology in Hebrews*.

11. E.g., Ellis, *Christ and the Future*, 120–28; Ellis, *Pauline Theology*, 16–17n45.

12. Heen and Krey, *Hebrews*, 147. The earliest commentary on record by Ephrem the Syrian on Heb 9:28 in the late fourth century CE states, "'He will appear a second time,' not in order to die for the sins, for which he has already died once, but in order to appear in a new world, where there will be no sins on the part of those who in hope expect salvation through him." The statement demonstrates that by Ephrem the Syrian's time, any vertical hope of heavenly fulfilment in the context had changed emphasis more toward a temporal hope of an earthly "new world" fulfillment as only an ethical with earthly change.

13. Goppelt states, "Allegorical interpretation, therefore, is not concerned with the truthfulness or factuality of the things described." Goppelt, *Typos*, 12. As a possible biblical hermeneutical method, allegorical interpretation overshadowed all other authorial intended revelation-interpretation methods by those religiously educated, until the sixteenth-century Reformation with the return to a desire for a literal interpretation of Scripture. Baird, *History of New Testament Research*, 1: xvii. Allegory primarily links referents to explain truth by correspondences of word-context patterns in symbolic language that does not carry weight of a representation of literal reality. NT writers found use for allegorical interpretation in their texts; e.g., Paul uses "allegorically speaking" (ἀλληγορέω) in Gal 4:21–26.

STEP 3: THE PASTOR'S INTENDED INTERPRETATION METHODS

The once overshadowing method of allegory in biblical interpretation was joined with the previous second-century CE transition away from hearing the eternal heavenly language of canonical texts in the concrete reality intended by first-century CE authors. Once revelation concerning the eternal "substance-reality" (ὑπόστασις) of faith (Heb 11:1; 12:2) viewed as allegory, with no realistic corresponding connections, textual interpreters ignored the authorial-intended methods of interpretation.[14] The Pastor primarily embraces realistic links in methods of either direct prophecy, analogy, or typology.[15] His quotation of OT texts consists mainly of a variant of the rabbinic midrashic method.[16]

Initially, scholars recognized first-century CE typological interpretation with realistic links.[17] In this line, typology defines in this project

---

14. Ferguson, *Backgrounds of Early Christianity*, 544. Analysis for the *middot* or formal interpretative rules credited to Hillel are beyond the scope of this work. For the Pastor's use of the second rule of *gezera shawa* ("verbal analogy"), see deSilva, *Perseverance in Gratitude*, 34–35. For critique, consider, Alexander, "Rabbinic Judaism," 246. Alexander reports there is no evidence that this interpretational technique was unique to Judaism. He suggests, based on work of other scholars on the *middot* issue, that, "From their very nature the rules in question may be 'natural' to human discourse or argument, or typical in general of early rhetoric."

15. E.g., by *direct prophecy*, the Pastor conveys prophetic truth about living referents in the past, present, and future (Heb 11). By use of *typology*, the Pastor reminds his listeners how Moses was told the priests of the tabernacle "serve to outline and shadow of the heavenlies *ministry*" (τῶν ἐπουρανίων Heb 8:5). Moses also was told, "You will make everything according to the 'type' [τύπον], the one being made known to you on the mountain." The Pastor proceeds to explain the correspondence between the movements in the holy-*places* of the earthly priesthood "antitype of the true *places*" (ἀντίτυπα τῶν ἀληθινῶν Heb 9:24). He further details Jesus's past movements (1) in the heavenly realities, (2) since resurrection in a present ministry in the "path of the holy-*places*" (Heb 9:8–9), and (3) in future appearing from the holy of holies (Heb 9:28), which the earthly antitype literally represents, for a heavenly fulfillment in a greater way. Modern descriptions of typology invert the first-century CE terminology of Hebrews, Peter, and Philo.

16. Steyn, *Quest*, 406–7. Steyn recognizes that the Pastor in his OT quotations places these mostly in pairs like the rabbinic midrashic method with commentary or midrashim usually attached to the longer of the two quotations. Regarding the Pastor's OT quotations, these often combine with typological interpretative functions to provide parenesis for Jesus's activities in the process of atonement; e.g., much of the evidence for Jesus's enthronement in Heb 1 comes from multiple consecutive OT quotations in direct prophecy, analogy, or typology.

17. Frei, *Eclipse of Biblical Narrative*. Frei discusses the collapse of traditional typology and narrative of the biblical text with the result of a loss of its reality for recent scholars. Cf. Goppelt, *Typos*, 7. Goppelt states, "The typological use of the OT in the NT

as an author-chosen method for revelation of truth, used heavily in *aiōn-field* background (apocalyptic) language, using *antitypes* (visible cosmic-*field* examples, outlines, copies, and patterns) concerning people, places, events, or institutions, that are linked in greater correspondence to other referents, as either future cosmic-*field* antitypes/types, or, *types* of *aiōn-field* heavenly reality fulfillment in places by people, in events and institutions (figure 5—Definition of Typology in Hebrews).[18] Any visible typological event on earth has corresponding truth that God intends in revelation of unseen heavenly matters.

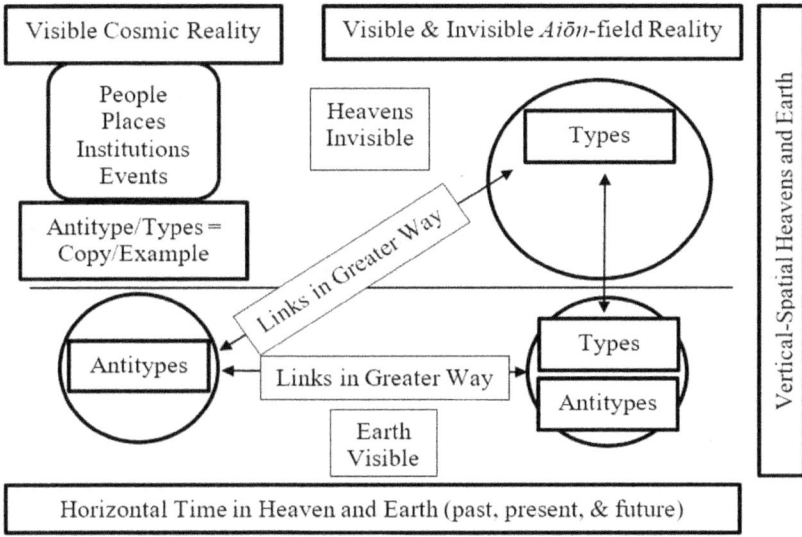

Figure 5—Definition of Typology in Hebrews

---

has always provided an example of a more profound interpretation of the OT and has motivated the search for a meaning that goes beyond the literal grammatical-historical explanation." He recognizes, "For typological interpretation, however, the reality of the things described is indispensable. The typical meaning is not really a different or higher meaning, but a different or higher use of the same meaning that is comprehended in type and antitype." Goppelt, *Typos*, 12. Fishbane concludes, "Typologies of within the Hebrew Bible are broader than the mere 'historical.'" Fishbane, *Biblical Interpretation in Ancient Israel*, 351n94.

18. Antitypes always limit to the cosmic-*field* of historical observable reality and link with types both in the visible cosmic-*field* and/or the unseen *aiōn-field* reality that the antitypes are meant by their link to describe in greater correspondence. These antitypes or types may fulfill either historically past, present, or future and/or vertically in both the seen and unseen spatial realities as determined by context. Also, antitypes never replace antitypes. New antitypes link with change in truth of heavenly reality.

Diverse conclusions arise from tenuous attempts to harmonize this recovered hermeneutic with long held cosmic-*field* constrained traditions without an *aiōn-field* substance-reality for people.[19] Typological realism, especially any spatial-vertical verbal movement about Jesus in the heavens promptly after death, often suffers, without debate, toward only symbolic meaning.[20] Also, popular interests in horizontal future eschatology only scantly consider realistic, vertical heavenly existence for people.[21]

For proper understanding of the Pastor, this imbalance needs correction by additional realistic weight of his original spatial intentions in vertical movement of the Christ, especially as linked in his typology. Appendix 1, figures 6a and 6b offer a balanced approach for first-century CE hermeneutics in a simplified flowchart. This synthesizes more from inductive observation of the biblical authors than from the later conclusions derived from the discussion of the debate over first-century CE hermeneutics.[22]

Six observations can be deduced about first-century CE interpretation. First, each method carries a distinct application for truth about a referent(s) or OT text(s) to guide the understanding.[23] Second,

---

19. Cf. Fairbairn, *Typology of Scripture*; Stek, "Biblical Typology Yesterday and Today," 133–62; Moo, *Old Testament in the Gospel*, 56–58; Ellis, *Prophecy and Hermeneutic*, 165–69; Young, "Typology," 29–48; Davidson, "Eschatological Hermeneutic of Biblical Typology," 5–12; Hoskins, *That Scripture Might Be Fulfilled*, 17–36; Hoskins, *Jesus as the Fulfillment*, 27–31; Baker, "Typology and the Christian Use," 313–30; Ribbens, "Typology in Types," 81–96.

20. E.g., Jamieson lists scholars who view the vertical, heavenly, typological language of the place and timing of Jesus's atonement language in heaven as only symbolic. Jamieson, "When and Where," 342–46.

21. Davidson, "Eschatological Hermeneutic of Biblical Typology," 5–48; Davidson, *Typology in Scripture*, 99–100; 363–88.

22. This application of revelation-interpretation can only support a modest claim that would be recognized by a first-century CE audience. Understandably, the *English* lexemes, syntax, and semantics are modern. Yet, the act of interpretation concerning revelation of truth in the first century CE could comfortably and logically follow, without objection, these guiding observations set forth. Cf. Lampe and Woollcombe, *Essays in Typology*, 29–30.

23. The differences between each non-OT text interpretative method are determined by three factors in the context, (1) whether there is more than one referent linked by the truth expressed, (2) how the author links the truth correspondences between two or more referents under consideration as either literal reality or only nonrealistic symbolic figures of speech, or (3) whether the truth expression represents referent(s) in greater correspondence than the grammatical-historical context; e.g., the expression of truth of any narrative form (discourse, poetry, proverb, hymn, parable,

interpretational methods are determined by authorial intention—not later function as options for the reader/listener, to use for gain of alternative insights into *the author's* text.[24] Third, these interpretation methods must function seamlessly with natural language without later culturally conditioned accommodation in meanings away from their normative significance.[25] Fourth, these interpretation methods convey truth concerning people, places, objects, or institutions, without inherent temporal or spatial weight in the method itself.[26] Fifth, in the author's revelation choice of typology, the antitype-type correspondence in a text does not

---

psalm, or apocalyptic) about a single referent signals direct prophecy in a statement of truth. For two or more linked referents in comparative correspondence: (1) if no reality, then the method is allegory, (2) if only similar patterns of verbal movement and/or referent characteristics, then it is an analogy, and (3) if greater vertical and/or horizontal links, then it is typology. These categories anchor the interpretation of objects under consideration regardless of other contextual elements added.

OT quotations typically determine in a similar fashion by three factors in the context: (1) if the meaning of the text is paraphrased, (2) if two texts are linked to provide greater meaning, (3) and if the text is considered a fulfillment of a past hidden event or experience. The affirmative determines the methods of targumic, midrashic, and pesher, respectively. The negative means the text is interpretatively intended as a non-OT quotation textual method.

24. Goppelt, *Typos,* 9. Hermeneutical methods do not have a layered function with some weight found in every possible method that a reader/listener can compile in a greater and overall meaning.

25. Goppelt, *Typos,* 8. An audience interpretational method should mean to the reader/listener no more than that which the author designed in normative application of lexical semantics of his context. There should be no hidden meanings to an author's text unless purposely cryptically designed when conveyed, and only then, when a text in some way signals as cryptic by the author.

26. Literary rhetorical devices and both spatial and/or temporal elements for audience orientation may or may not be added to the surrounding context by the author. These may express truth about referents in humanly understood terms in two directions, either about (1) the temporary visible and/or invisible, eternal, vertical realities, or (2) the earthly historical and/or heavenly, horizontal time movements. No revelation-interpretive method carries time or spatial weight. The context determines both the time elements of past (historical), present (eschatological), and/or future (eschatological) truth or any vertical elements of earthly or heavenly, spatial truth—nothing inherent in the author's chosen method. For verbal expression of truth about their chosen referents, after choice of literary form, biblical authors then choose a revelation-interpretation method. Next follows their added contextual information for orientation in choices of (1) either horizontal language elements (no time, all-time, past, past to present, present, present to future, or future) and/or vertical language elements (none, all creation, things under the earth, on the earth, and in the heavens), and/or (2) literary rhetorical devices "such as alliteration, assonance, *inclusio*, and a host of others." See Allen, *Hebrews,* 29n31 for sources listing those used by the Pastor. The contextual vertical and horizontal aspects do not function as opposites but can variably combine as desired by the author.

later replace or apply to another antitype-type link in succession, unless the connection is restated.[27] Sixth, typological links between an antitype and type as ministerial parenesis serve to testify about gospel truth of salvation promises, not as a means to obtain the salvation promises of entrance to God at judgment.[28] These guiding observations that consistently

---

27. The historical activity links between antitype/type in typological referents carry weight in a ministerial function to reveal truth either in the temporary or eternal creation. Referent antitypes *fulfill* spoken truth in their appropriate context of place and time—but their revelatory links never *replace* one antitype with another in succession unless the link is restated anew. Revelatory-linked truth between referents is always truth and does not change, since spoken by God, who cannot lie (cf. Heb 6:18); e.g., the Sinai covenant reveals truth about the relationship between the eternal/perpetual-*place* God in heaven and the people of the temporary creation. The Pastor states about the earthly Sinai covenant, "But, one becoming obsolete and growing old near for destruction" (Heb 8:13). In the temporary, changing cosmos responding to God's salvation plan to bring his people to himself in the eternal/perpetual-*places* of heaven, the heavenly typological content of Sinai covenant was fulfilled in Jesus as the Christ (cf. Matt 5:17). This completion also introduced his beginning fulfillment of the promises of the new covenant. The truth of the first covenant served for the duration of time and space appointed in its purpose. Its function ends with the new, but its spoken truth between the referents involved continues true for its appointed time and space. Truth does not replace truth, and truth does not transfer to another referent unless restated in a new revelatory link with a new referent. Therefore, linked revelation of truth concerning referents by direct prophecy, allegory, analogy, or typology is not succeeded by the connections with other referents. For further discussion on successionism, see Ounsworth, *Joshua Typology*, 176–84. Ounsworth introduces this thought line in negating proposed ideas of supersessionism of the temple by the Pastor after its destruction. Cf. other essays on the topic of temple supersessionism in Bauckham et al., *Epistle to the Hebrews*, 151–225.

28. In the temporary earthly ministry of truth revelation, a referent "antitype" (ἀντίτυπα Heb 9:24; cf. 1 Pet 3:21) links as (1) "examples, outlines, copies" (ὑποδείγματι Heb 4:11; 8:5; 9:23), (2) "types, examples" (τύποι Heb 8:5; cf. 1 Cor 10:6), and (3) "typological [adv.]" (τυπικῶς 1 Cor 10:11). A concise list of linked earthly antitypes includes revelation by the tabernacle/temple, Israel, the Sabbath observance, the land promise, ceremonial law, local church, water baptism, Lord's Supper, the Lord's day of first day of the week, Christ's millennium rule on earth, etc. Antitypes function as examples within the temporary creation of unsensed eternal truth and never to replace the true referent "types" (cf. Heb 8:5) they represent in greater correspondence in the eternal/perpetual-*place* creation. When their revelatory use in ministry completes, they may become obsolete, and other referents may reflect the circumstantial parenetic changes in space and time, but these are not referent-truth replacements in successionism. Also, these antitypes in ministry may fulfill eternal typological realities either negatively or positively; e.g., when Moses (antitype) strikes the rock (Num 20:11), the positive, desired typological ministry in example of speaking to God for his eternal provision of promised salvation crumbles. Thereby, in proper negative fulfillment, Moses in ministry (antitype) is not allowed in the promised land (antitype). His ministerial failure does not negate his salvation in heaven by faith (Heb 11:23–28 [cf. "sixth" observation above]). Moreover, the Joshua (antitype) in his ministry for leading Israel into the land of promise (antitype)

shape first-century CE author-audience interpretation of truth should guide modern evaluation of the Pastor's message.

STEP 4: FIRST-CENTURY CE APOCALYPTIC (AIŌN-FIELD) WORD STOCK

First-century CE literature, that both was possibly available to the Pastor and containing revelations of the heavens in language of substance-reality, often carried the genre label "apocalypse" by the second century CE.[29] Modern analysis, upon rediscovery of these works in the mid-nineteenth century, initially viewed the typological frame of apocalypse narrative from a different, well-entrenched, cosmic-*field* limited background.[30]

---

should not be interpreted that he replaces Moses either in salvation or ministry, but that both served truth as a referent antitype of Christ corresponding to Jesus (type) leading people to God in heaven (type). Furthermore, this rule of referent-truth correspondences in ministry would hold true for verbal activity of examples regarding God's "people" referents; e.g., the *antitype* example of the fleshly people of the temporary local church in ministry on earth neither replaces the referent eternal *type* concerning the people of spiritual Israel now assembling at death in heaven (cf. Rom 9:8) nor the now-assembling church of the firstborn in heaven at death (Heb 12:22–24).

29. Smith, "On the History of ΑΠΟΚΑΛΥΠΤΩ," 9–20. BDAG, "ἀποκάλυψις," 112. Cf. Aune, "Apocalyptic and New Testament Interpretation," 237–59. Aune traces the modern academic reclaiming of the genre of Jewish apocalypse in understanding from the third century BCE. During the first century CE it was the "prime mover" in Christian views (242). His synthesis reveals a defining characteristic in the belief of two ages with both temporal and spatial aspects (245). In literature of this category, some emphasize open heavens for human interaction. Rowland observes, "Apocalyptic has a vertical dimension which is just as important as any predictions made about the future." Rowland, *Open Heaven*, 2. Vines argues one of the genre's most peculiar features concerns the relationship of time and space. Vines, "Apocalyptic Chronotope," 112–14. Cf. Sturm, "Defining the Word 'Apocalyptic,'" 17–48; Ziegler, *Militant Grace*; Collins, "Introduction: Towards the Morphology," 1–20; Collins, "Genre Apocalypse Reconsidered," 21–40; Collins, *Apocalyptic Imagination*, 352. As part of his summary, Collins states, "Jewish apocalypses were not produced by a single 'apocalyptic movement' but constituted a genre that could be utilized by different groups in various situations. . . . It also involved a conceptual framework which assumed that life was bounded by the heavenly world of the angels and by the prospect of eschatological judgment. . . . The problems to which these revelations are addressed vary in kind. . . . The constant factor is that the problem is put in perspective by the otherworldly revelation of a transcendent world and eschatological judgment."

30. Barnard, *Mysticism of Hebrews*, 172–75; Koch, *Rediscovery of Apocalyptic*. Koch traces the positive scholarly development in rebirth of apocalyptic and the negative responses of established dogmatic tradition proponents. Cf. Käsemann, "Beginning of Christian Theology," 82–107. Käsemann, as a student of Rudolf Bultmann, declared, "Apocalyptic was the mother of all Christian theology" (102). Such a view surprised

For the first one hundred years, until the 1970s, scholarship negativized such literature as esoteric and away from mainstream Orthodox Judaism, which seemed more supportive of their own long held assumptions.[31] From the orthodox perspective, John Collins defines the modern *apocalypse* genre, stating, "'Apocalypse' is a genre of revelatory literature with a narrative framework, in which a revelation is mediated by an otherworldly being to a human recipient, disclosing a transcendent reality which is both temporal, insofar as it envisages eschatological salvation, and spatial insofar as it involves another supernatural world."[32] By adding "transcendent," "supernatural," and "otherworldly" noted in table 6, John Collins brings in foreign sixteenth-century philosophical presuppositions in a

---

scholarship by declaring apocalyptic as mainstream in opposition to the dominant view which saw apocalyptic bordering on heresy; e.g., Bietenhard, *Die himmlische Welt im Urchristentum*. Bietenhard claims the cosmological speculations in the NT are peripheral and form no essential part of the gospel. *Contra* Käsemann, "Zum Thema Der Urchristlichen Apokalyptik," 257–84. In his lengthy article he attempts to answer scholarly criticism over why he had claimed apocalyptic was the mother of all Christian theology (284). He argues that to ignore the apocalyptic context obstructs access to the hope of early understanding of the Easter kerygma, which was not just about resurrection from the dead (263). Cf. Pannenberg, *Basic Questions*, 15–80. As an unknown scholar at the time, a year before Käsemann, Pannenberg reintroduced the horizontal presuppositions spanning the whole of Christian theology of the apocalyptic background field. The spatial apocalyptic presuppositions are still currently in limited acceptance with little investigation or debate.

31. The assumptions, which built on the anachronistic foundations of late second-century CE Judaism dominated by Sadducean schools of thought, by pressures previously noted above had changed substantially in both philosophy and theology. The probable Sadducean influence is further addressed in chapter 3.

32. *Pace* Collins, "Introduction: Towards the Morphology," 9. Also Collins, "Genre Apocalypse Reconsidered," 28. Collins recognizes many of the elements of apocalyptic writings, "bear structural weight, as they shape an implied view of the *world*. These were elements singled out in the definition, by reference to the manner of the revelation and to the *transcendent* reality, both spatial and temporal. The content of the genre implies a distinctive worldview" (italics mine). Collins agrees with Vines on the "temporal and spatial unboundedness of apocalypse" which "affords a divine perspective on human activity." Vines, "Apocalyptic Chronotope," 113. However, the idea of the divine heavenly spatial and temporal elements as "transcendent" injects the questionable weight of modern philosophical categories foreign to the first century CE. After evaluation of the details of apocalyptic literature, Jean Carmignac simplified his definition of the genre as "genre littéraire qui décrit des révélations célestes à travers des symboles." Carmignac, "Description du phénomène de l'Apocalyptique," 165. Carmignac does not prove this simplified definition, but it more naturally fits the language of the first-century CE literature better than pressing it comparatively through a developed sixteenth-century philosophy or later eschatology.

cosmic *field* that points perpendicular to the *aiōn-field* used by the Pastor and others using "apocalyptic language" style of revelation.[33]

This definition was emended later by Adela Collins considering suggestions of David Hellholm and David Aune, to read that, "apocalypse ... intended to interpret *present*, earthly circumstances in light of the *supernatural* world of the *future*, and to influence both the understanding and the behavior of the audience by means of divine authority."[34] John Collins later claims, "All the apocalypses, however, involve a transcendent eschatology that looks for retribution beyond the bounds of history. In some cases (*3 Baruch, Apocalypse of Zephaniah*) this takes the form of the judgment of individuals after death, without reference to the end of history."[35] By pressing all first-century CE debates about apocalyptic revelation of heavenly (*aiōn-field*) matters "future" into twentieth-century eschatology and into philosophical, nonhistorical, "transcendent" reality in modern views of heaven, both the revised definition by Adela Yarbro Collins and the summary of John Collins still ignore the *realized*, vertical-horizontal, *aiōn-field* motifs related to a *present* hope in complete, continuous, prompt living in death, which were conveyed in some writings of the first century CE.

33. Collins utilizes the term "apocalyptic" as adjectival. Collins, *Apocalyptic Imagination*, 1–52. He attempts to define the nomenclature of the discussion with the literary genre as "apocalypse" (3–14), the use of "apocalyptic" limited as an adjective (2), and "apocalypticism" (15–17), as reflective of varied social movements in reaction to problems addressed contextually in the literature. The term "apocalypse" refers to a group of literature collectively with vast differences but having some common particular traits and distinctive elements (3–14). The term "apocalyptic" as an adjective refers to usage of some of these traits and elements in description (2). Collins debunks correctly the "apocalyptic myth" which suggests "a worldview or a theology which is only vaguely defined but which has often been treated as an entity independent of specific texts" (2). As asserted above, the background-view or theology of first-century CE authors is not inherent in the genre or interpretational method and must be determined by the context. Also, Collins does concede, in other modern terms, another crucial point, that a constant trait within the apocalypse genre is a top-down revelation from the unseen heavenly reality, which he labels as "transcendent." This top-down emphasis is distributed differently than the various works with bottom-up earthy understanding, which Collins labels "history." (7, 352).

34. Adela Yarbro Collins, "Introduction," 7.

35. Collins, *The Apocalyptic Imagination*, 15. Collins recognizes the objection of Rowland, "that there is not *distinctive* apocalyptic eschatology" (italics Collins). He further states, "The genre is not constituted by one or more distinctive themes, but by a distinctive combination of elements, all of which are also found elsewhere." These observations support the previous assertion that the horizontal elements in interpretation arise from the context and not the literary narrative frame or author-audience interpretation method. Cf. Rowland, *Open Heaven*, 29–37, 71.

Rowland attempts to distinguish apocalyptic from eschatology by reserving to the latter the future hope of Judaism and Christianity. He claims apocalyptic literature was an attempt to understand more how things are *now* rather than predict the future.[36] The spatial and time elements of first-century CE apocalyptic language in typology, direct prophecy, or analogy were established by the context; neither the genre frame nor the author-audience interpretative method that was used to convey space and time. Similarly, Adela Collins takes the position in later work that spatial and time elements must function together when included in the text of an author. She bases this claim on the observation that *both* spatial and temporal elements, in differing degrees of emphasis depending on the contextual background, are most always present in literature employing apocalyptic language.[37]

The book of Revelation serves as an example of a pure apocalypse. Other NT books such as the Gospels, Hebrews, Ephesians, Colossians, and 1 and 2 Peter commonly employ apocalyptic language and concepts.[38] Second-century CE Christian churches, commonly still fluid with Judaism in the diaspora due to their common heritage, preserved the apocalyptic literature of ST Judaism.[39] In the second century CE and later, many apocalypse type works appear which address various problems from diverse theological, noncanonical points of view.[40] However, two major pressures from both without and within the slowly diversifying Jewish and Christian cultures against heavenly theological matters changed the attitudes and usage among leadership.

---

36. Rowland, *Open Heaven*, 1–2.

37. Yarbro Collins in reaction to tendencies of scholarly polarization toward either mysticism or eschatology, later combines her definition with John Collins as support for her position "that the classic apocalypses combine the two concerns [eschatological and mystical dimension], so that contact with knowledge of the heavenly world provides an understanding of history and supports a particular way of life." Yarbro Collins, *Cosmology and Eschatology*, 7. Adela Collins applies the assertions of Hirsch by interpretation of the apocalypses in two moments of "meaning" and "significance" as determined by and in fidelity with the intent of the author in context. Hirsch, *Aims of Interpretation*, 79–81. Adela Collins, based upon Hirsch, correctly claims that proper interpretation must include fidelity to both spatial and temporal elements in authorial context before modern interpretative application to the present.

38. Collins, *Apocalyptic Imagination*, 321–51.

39. Harlow, "Early Judaism and Early Christianity," 258.

40. Yarbro Collins, "Early Christian Apocalypses," 60–121; Fallon, "Gnostic Apocalypses," 122–58; Rowland, *Open Heaven*, 349–441; Evans, *Ancient Texts*, 256–67; Himmelfarb, *Apocalypse: A Brief History*; Nickelsburg, *Jewish Literature between the Bible*; Berthelot, "Early Jewish Literature," 181–200.

First, under the pressure of Jewish, messianic hope, the first-century CE revelation of this literature for many readers was already interpreted with an endpoint as having only a heavy, cosmic-*field* constrained fulfillment (cf. Luke 19:11; Acts 1:6).[41] This explanatory view escalated tension in the ministry of Jesus, even resulting in his crucifixion (cf. Matt 2:2; 27:11, 29, 37; Luke 19:38; John 20:9). The same continued misuse and misapplication by Jewish Zealots and sympathizers also generated extreme social, political, and religious tensions with their Roman Empire relationships.[42] Resulting Jewish violence against Roman imperial rule ensued, with the destruction of their temple in the Jewish Wars from 66–70 CE.

In the second century CE, further uprising in the Diaspora Revolt of 115–117 CE resulted in decimation or destruction of the Jewish settlements in Egypt, Libya, and several other places. Later in recovery from another uprising in the devastating Bar Kokhba Revolt of 132–135 CE, surviving Rabbinic Judaism of the diaspora, as mainly Saducean in philosophical thought, heavily suppressed apocalyptic genre writings, opting mainly for the OT canon with emphasis on the law in one's *earthly* relationship with God (fig. 4).[43] Modern negativism toward apocalyptic concepts arose from this later position of Judaism that is antithetical to other views in Jewish STL of the first century CE.

Amid the Jewish movement that later became Christians, who both held in faith a spatial "heavenly" hope and observed the escalation of conflict in the death of millions, the leadership in later state-supported churches turned to the safer hermeneutic of allegory (*Hist. eccl.* 7.14.1–3; *Cels.* 4.87; *Princ.* 2.11.2–3).[44] By the fourth century CE, this method universally applied to the prophetic earthly kingdom and millennial texts, regardless of authorial intent, to ease tensions toward peaceful interpretative solutions.[45]

---

41. Collins, "Jewish Apocalypses," 30–36.

42. Portier-Young, "Jewish Apocalyptic Literature," 145–46; Wessinger, "Apocalypse and Violence," 423–24; Mendel, *Vision and Violence*, 30–45.

43. Gruenwald, *Apocalyptic and Merkavah Mysticism*; Scholem, *Jewish Gnosticism*; Scholem, *Major Trends in Jewish Mysticism*, 41–79. Cf. Alexander, "Mysticism," 704–32; Alexander, *Mystical Texts*; Alexander, "3 (Hebrew Apocalypse of) Enoch," 1:223–54. Cf. Eskola, *Messiah and the Throne*. More on this historical observation follows in chapter 3.

44. Fredriksen, "Apocalypse and Redemption," 154–55.

45. Fredriksen, "Apocalypse and Redemption," 155–68.

Second, later Christians, in response to the pressure of heresy within by leaders who considered themselves Christians, applied allegorical redefinition to the earthly-heavenly, antitype-type correspondences of spatial typological revelation. The first major heresy reaction surfaced from Christian incorporation of early Jewish gnostic elements containing privileged knowledge of heavenly matters.[46] A criticism against apocalyptic language arose by the late second century CE in the reaction of Irenaeus and others against the heresy.[47] Also, a second heresy arose in the new prophecy of Montanism with claims for an imminent expectation of the descent of the new Jerusalem that instilled still more reaction.[48] Early

---

46. Scholem, *Jewish Gnosticism*, 34; Wilson, *Gnostic Problem*, 64–96, 116–48. Wilson is probably correct, that the gnostic error was not in the common parallels of the apocalyptic language from Judaism added with Hellenistic philosophy and mythology, but instead, the ideas and concepts in the context of how the common apocalyptic language of each was used; e.g., in the mid-third century CE, it is not the *aiōn-field* "diagram" or realities of human access to heaven after death that Origen refutes against Celsus (*Cels.* 6.24–39), but the incorrect concepts in its teaching containing gnostic heresy. Cf. Williams, *Rethinking "Gnosticism."* Williams points out that many of the conclusions of generalized statements contained within the modern scholarly category of Gnosticism do not bear out in historical documents. In agreement with his argument, use the term of the "gnostic" demarcates the heretical ideas themselves, rather than the modern broad conclusions against all apocalyptic language, or its vertical dualism. After his discussion of recent studies in review of the distinguishing features of Gnosticism and apocalypticism, Burns comments, "Consequently, the traditional basis for associating 'Gnosticism' and 'apocalypticism' has been dissolved." Burns, "Apocalypses Among Gnostics and Manichaeans," 358.

47. Irenaeus reputes strongly the gnostic *privileged* knowledge of heavenly revelation and entrance of selected souls thereby into the heaven of God's domain before death and their denial of fleshly resurrection after death (cf. *Haer.* 5.31.9; 5.31.1). His defense negativized the apocalyptic language of the revelation of the heavenly matters in the gospel due to gnostic association. This unfortunate side-effect for early Christian teachers such as Irenaeus and others eventually placed an imbalanced emphasis of the center of eternal/perpetual-*place* hope, away from the time of death in approach/entrance into heaven which Irenaeus held (cf. *Haer.* 5.31). In his defense against heresy, Irenaeus allegorically interprets "flesh and blood" (1 Cor 15:50) as "fleshly works" (*Haer.* 5.13.3), rather than as a later resurrection with fleshly transformation to spiritual bodies (cf. 1 Cor 15:35–50; 1 John 3:2). Thereby, he heavily weights the promises of a future hope as only a flesh resurrection on earth. This involves a flesh "regeneration" to incorruption, which the believer initially receives by observance of another, allegorical, antitype elevation of drinking and eating Jesus's "flesh" in the Eucharist (cf. *Haer.* 5.2.2). Further evaluation of these and other patristic responses provide a topic for further research. The influence of Irenaeus and his mentor Justin regarding pejorative redefinition of *hairesis* ("heresy") in the late second century CE against the long-held view for prompt transformation from flesh to spirit bodies follows in chapter 3.

48. E.g., Metzger, in analysis of the effects of Montanism in the mid-second century CE, writes, "The influence of Montanism in this regard was twofold: the production of new 'sacred' scriptures, and the development within the Great Church of a mistrust of

Christian apologists, like good surgeons, removed with wide margins the cancer of perceived heresy (cf. Rev 2:2–3). The later nineteenth-century approach of the *religionsgeschichtliche* school demonstrates a widespread problem in Christian churches since the second century CE. Objections to perceived heresy viewed as non-Orthodox frequently reduces to flattened, general definitions, which often result in repudiation of all common parallel elements, rather than the erroneous concept itself.

These second-century CE tensions propelled church leaders in the direction of a preferred allegorical hermeneutic that gave rise to two major theological changes. The first change moved errantly toward a closed spatial reality. In consequence, the orphaned biblical earthly antitypes, that previously corresponded to heavenly types, were then escalated in replacement of the new vacuum for the types in the heavenly reality they portrayed.[49] The second change escalated biblical, prophetic, revelatory history of future earthly antitypes as *final termini*, having no links with heavenly types.[50] These symbolic antitypes became the salvific final

---

apocalyptic literature, including even the Johannine Apocalypse. Some Catholics also rejected the Epistle to the Hebrews because of the use that Montanists made of [Heb] vi.1–6." Metzger, *Canon of the New Testament*, 102. Metzger described the backlash of the anti-Montanist reaction that brought the Apocalypse of John under a cloud of suspicion because of its usefulness in supporting the "new prophecy" (104). Some influential leaders in the Eastern churches even removed it from their canon (105).

49. E.g., the church, which errantly became ideologically the authoritative kingdom only on earth, emerged with little consideration of the heavenly corresponding type it represents (see fig. 4). Before this flattening, the earthly assemblies represented Jesus's building of his church, whereby deceased believers currently are assembling in heaven with him when at the gate of Hades in death (cf. Matt 16:18; Heb 12:23). Also, due to flattening, the observances of baptism and Eucharist became legally sacramental. Observers attained merely a legal incorruption on earth before God to wait postmortem as *inferior quality spirits* for a possible later merited fleshly resurrection through the authority of the earthly church and intercession by other saints with its sacraments, indulgences, and relics. Before modification, these contained an antitype-type symbolic correspondence where believers, as complete (Heb 12:23), would follow Jesus's typological gospel pattern after death in the way of the holy-*places* in heavenly events before return with Jesus for the living believers before the earthly day of the Lord judgments.

50. E.g., Jesus's millennial, messianic kingdom rule and Israel's Edenic-like, land fulfillment (cf. Acts 1:6; 3:21) are elevated to final endpoints of God's desired goals, rather than being symbolic of later heavenly fulfilment of all things "toward himself" (εἰς αὐτόν Col 1:20 [spatial acc.]; cf. Eph 1:10). This elevation of earthly Eden rationally results in the concept of a general judgment, which to adherents occurs when Jesus returns to earth to be with his church. Cf. Schnabel, "Viability of Premillennialism," 785–95.

endpoint of God's purposes rather than later fulfillment in their corresponding heavenly types in the eternal creation (cf. Rev 21–22).[51]

By the second to third century CE, extant writings of Christian leaders which embrace a limited cosmic-*field* for people, flatten NT biblical direct prophecy and typological teaching about access and entrance into the eternal creation at death in such texts as Heb 9:27–28. The later patristic emphasis, which so heavily emphasized acknowledgment of an orthodoxy toward the future resurrection of the fleshly body, influenced interpreters to determine the promised transformation as an eternal fleshly life. These changes limit salvation to a merited incorruptibility by sin and death, without any of the revealed eternal creation transitions to a "heavenly body" or "spiritual body" (cf. 1 Cor 15:40, 47–49; 1 John 3:2; Phil 3:20–21).[52]

STEP 5: TRADITIONAL TRANSLATION OF HEBREWS 9:28

This tradition, originating three hundred year after the Pastor's writing, continues without critique, advocating in relation to the Pastor's emphasis of the temporal adverb "once" (ἅπαξ), only the horizontal temporal preference for a translation of a "second *time*."[53] Few critically consider the obvious difficulty with the syntactical contortion, "will appear a second

---

51. E.g., the issue of orphaned antitype escalation or degradation in typological interpretation forms the basis for most theological debate among the Christian faith and in Hebrews. Interpreters either intensify the antitype as the end or means of Christian hope, with no or little eternal heavenly expectation, or they reduce the antitype so flat in earthly fulfillment that it either ignores or blurs the symbolism to the heavenly corresponding type.

52. E.g., in the fourth century CE, Augustine in his *City of God* insists on the corporeality of this spiritual body (*Civ.* 22.21). A survey of second- and third-century CE extant patristic literature, both in defense against heresies and in theological parenesis, reveals little consideration for promises of the resurrection and bodily transformation of the flesh, away from obsolete vestigial functions in a decaying dark-creation (cf. Rom 8:11; 1 Cor 15:35–50; 1 John 2:2) to characteristics necessary for eternal living in the dwelling presence of God (Rev 21:3; Matt 5:8). By the fourth century CE, these bishops, like Israel before them, anticipate a hope toward the cucumbers, onions, and lentils of Egypt, than the milk and honey of the promised land (cf. John 3:17, see fig. 4). The Pastor finds the same tendencies in his audience that he attempts to correct in his parenesis (Heb 3–4). Cf. Engberg-Pedersen, *Cosmology and Self*.

53. Zimmerman, *Das Bekenntnis der Hoffnung*, 201. Zimmerman recognizes the second coming option as from tradition of the early church rather than later redaction. Exploration in this project centers not on the tradition of the second coming theme itself, but whether this tradition should have become the only traditional option for the parenesis of the Pastor and other NT authors.

time without *reference* to sin" (NASB).[54] Mainly, the translation results in a contextual shift to other unstated, biblical, overarching themes.[55] It also discounts the natural, ordered, syntactical use and semantic meaning of the Pastor's words, his excellent Greek prose, the parallel contextual themes of the embedded DUC, and the possible function of Heb 9:27–28 as a MCS of other surrounding thematic content.

Translation should hinge on whether interpretation provides "functional equivalence" with the Pastor's contextual meaning. Carson considers "functional equivalence" replacing "dynamic equivalence," as a corresponding term for the same translation theory.[56] Eugene Nida states, "Dynamic equivalence is therefore to be defined in terms of the degree to which the receptors of the message in the receptor language respond to it in substantially the same manner as the receptors in the source language. This response can never be identical, for the cultural and historical settings are too different, but there should be a high degree of equivalence of response, or the translation will have failed to accomplish its purpose."[57]

This raises a question, if this traditional "prestigious" sense of "second *time*" would have been immediately recognized, then applied by listeners and early readers, who knew already about multiple other earthly appearances of Jesus after death and flesh resurrection (cf. 1 Cor 15:5–8). When the typological and apocalyptic (*aiōn-field*) thematic frame that controls the optional sense of ἐκ δευτέρου ("from a second . . .") is orphaned outside the heaven-earth and type-antitype authorial intended associations, an array of errant interpretative proposals abound for this

---

54. E.g., Daniel Wallace does not list this syntactical option for ἐκ with the genitive. The temporal aspect lists with weight of separation as "temporal: *from, from [this point] . . . on*." *GGBB*, 371. This option creates great theological tension with the Pastor's claim of judgment after his appearing, if from the point of his appearing, there is no reference to sin.

55. Carson, "The Limits of Functional Equivalence in Bible Translation," 88. The alternative sense of Heb 9:28 considered avoids any question of orthodoxy, since both options are attested in Scripture. Carson comments on a comparable situation, "But it is *not* a matter of theological orthodoxy, since understanding the text one way does not mean that the translator (or the commentator) is *denying* the complementary truth but is merely asserting that the complementary truth is not in view here" (italics Carson).

56. Carson, "The Limits of Functional Equivalence in Bible Translation," 65.

57. Nida, *The Theory and Practice of Translation*, 24. Fundamental priorities are listed as: "(1) contextual consistency has priority over verbal consistency (or word-for-word concordance), (2) dynamic equivalence has priority over formal correspondence, (3) the aural (heard) form of language has priority over the written form, (4) forms that are used by and acceptable to the audience for which a translation is intended have priority *over the forms that may be traditionally more prestigious*" (14; italics this author).

and other issues in Hebrews.[58] Ideas expand exponentially by antitype escalation into morphed earthly replacements and successionism due to the void created from their neglected, corresponding, heavenly types.

STEP 6: SIFTER FOR THE PASTOR'S FIRST-CENTURY CE WORD MEANINGS

Both the amount of available first-century CE literature, and later commentary providing interpretation surrounding Hebrews, collectively comprise another obstacle to proper interpretation of possible spatial meaning.[59] A concise study, which should include lexical analysis, requires a method to screen the evidence. After a quick review of the word tables in the appendix 2, readers probably already acknowledge tension; the Pastor is quite a Greek wordsmith by alternating multiple cognates and idiomatic thematic phrases to avoid repetition.

This vast sea of information connected with postmortem themes in Hebrews logistically overwhelms any *thematic* investigation. Narrow historical and theological topics or section studies, by nature, filter themselves. A quest concerning the words of Heb 9:27–28 as a contextual MCS requires mastering a vast ocean. If not sifted, the word meaning assembly of the tables easily burgeons into a colossal lexicon with optional glosses and catalog of opinions.

Consequently, a sampling method of the words is applied to sift the available information that follows two lines of stratification. The first line forms vertically by comparison of his words, cognates, and related thematic phrases to possible sources of influence upon the Pastor by order of importance from highest to lowest. The second line forms horizontally, based upon their principal functions. His words are evaluated

---

58. E.g., Thompson, "Outside the Camp," 58–60. Cf. Mason, "Call to Renunciation of Judaism or Encouragement to Christian Commitment?," 400–402. Thompson recognizes the Pastor's earthly-heavenly link, rather than orphaned earthly solutions toward either rejection of Judaism or matters concerning community purity threats from eating unclean foods.

59. Laansma, "Hebrews," 1–3. Laansma finds confidence in the increased "cultivation of historical work related to Hebrews, for it plays an essential part in the global ecosystem of meaning" (3). He comments, "We may confidently predict, in fact, that the gates to a richer harvest of the historical fruits will be opened precisely through a full integration of the theological and historical. In a global ecosystem, all the habitats and all the species are mutually sustaining" (3n7). This project attempts a MCS of the "full integration" which Laansma predicts.

for meaning based on correspondence with his source authority, repetitions, discourse unit summary deployments, and his chosen historical narrative. These two lines function together forming a grid to sample the Pastor's terms in Heb 9:27–28 for possible spatial weight in probable first-century CE sources. The results from the samplings filter out the most probable sense of the words. The grid results can be compared to the word translations and interpretations of commentaries, monographs, and articles for relevance in message cohesion.[60]

Vertical Filter Grid Line

The first grid line involves vertical stratification of the Pastor's words against other available first-century CE information, from most probable to least possible. It filters on the premise that even though sources may share a common language and themes of the first-century CE Hellenistic-Jewish culture surrounding the Pastor, some sources have a higher probability for influence upon his meaning and audience understanding than others. A few sources have definite utilization with evidential direct influence. Other sources only distantly relate with possible indirect influence, either by correspondence of lexical root or form, Greek language and culture, or a common thematic topic, OT scripture usage, era, or locale. The possible sources that should be considered would include: (1) Hebrew OT recension(s) similar to the MT, (2) Greek recension(s) of OG/LXX with apocryphal writings, (3) other NT literature, (4) other circulating copies of the library of the DSS, (5) Greek works of Philo, (6) Greek Jewish pseudepigrapha, especially those with apocalyptic language, (7) Jewish talmudic literature, (8) and Hellenistic Greco-Roman and surrounding cultural literature.[61] Figure 7 illustrates the vertical line filter.

60. Hilber, *Old Testament Cosmology*, 5–15; Streett, "New Approaches," 14–17.

61. The Pastor had to communicate in language understood by an audience steeped in the literature available to the Hellenistic-Jewish culture. His verbiage should have verbal and thematic correspondence with the available literary works of the time. This necessity supports the inclusion of other categories for evaluation beyond the OT. However, it must be noted, that a possible knowledge or use in a level of correspondence with another literary work does not imply any sense of a personal or cultural recognition of revelation authority. The Pastor probably only considered the OT and LXX as authoritative Scripture, as God speaking in revelation concerning the messianic hope of salvation in Jesus as Christ. In the first-century CE, the Letter of Aristeas reflects a Jewish legend reaching back to the second-century BCE, that views both the LXX and Hebrew OT of equal authoritative value. Notwithstanding, the "authority" of the LXX resides in its use by the writers of the New Testament, not inherently.

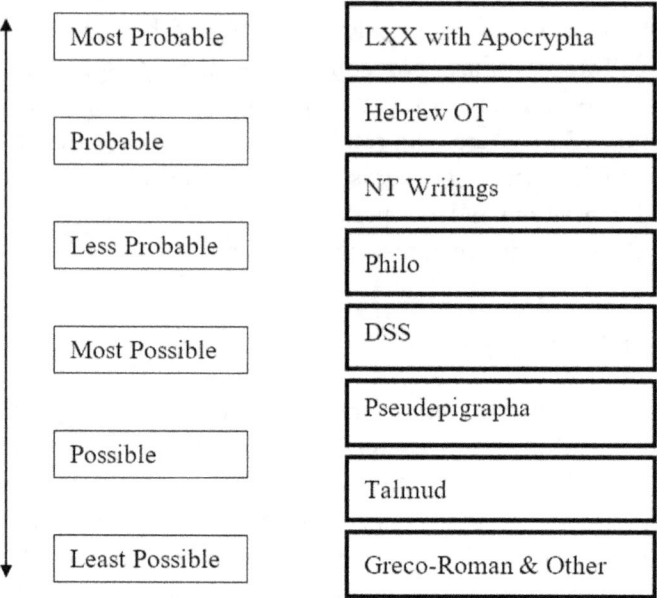

Figure 7—Source Filter for Word Meanings

Koine Greek served as the common language of the Greco-Roman Empire at the time of the Pastor's sermon, which models immaculately written Koine Greek prose. Koine Greek served as the lingua franca in multiple recensions as the Greek OT text by the first century CE. This was due to few Jews of the diaspora knowing Hebrew and Aramaic as the primary language of Palestinian Jews.[62] The Hebrew OT was first translated into Greek in the mid-second century BCE with semantic fields of words weighted from Aramaic influence.[63] This Greek LXX includes the Apocrypha of STL compositions.[64]

The LXX with the Apocrypha serves as the most probable direct source of influence for the Pastor's word meaning.[65] Several observations

---

62. Jobes and Silva, *Invitation to the Septuagint*, 20; deSilva, *Letter to the Hebrews*, 10.

63. Jobes and Silva, *Invitation to the Septuagint*; Loiseau, *L'influence de l'araméen*. Loiseau observes in his research, that the LXX semantic word fields reveal translators of the Hebrew OT had a strong Aramaic influence.

64. DeSilva, *Introducing the Apocrypha*; Harrington, *Invitation to the Apocrypha*; Harrison, *Introduction to the Old Testament*.

65. Harrington, "Old Testament Apocrypha," 200–202. Apocryphal works, containing possible later redaction, must be evaluated on their historical merits since there

support this contention. The Pastor's content utilizes the LXX with thirty-eight Scripture quotations, excluding many allusions and echoes.[66] He does not directly quote the apocryphal books. Also, his selected connections of narrative taken from the LXX witness provide his evidence for his claims at two major points. First, he presents his chosen LXX textual and verbal links with a christological lens as focused upon the Christ activity of Jesus. Second, he highlights the ministry experiences both of Jesus and others related to Christ as a typological faith by describing their referent antitype examples in the *aiōn-field* background expressed in the LXX. Further, the Pastor freely engages without necessary explanation, both Greek rhetorical devices and Jewish OT hermeneutics.[67] The most probable source for the Pastor's word meanings should be derived from thematic and verbal correspondences of the words in his chosen narrative with the authoritative Scripture of the LXX.[68] Therefore, the contextual usage of his corresponding words in the Greek language, with the specialized terms surrounding both faith and ministry in the LXX with the available Apocrypha, carries the highest probable weight.

A second probable source for the Pastor's word meanings derives from an unknown *Vorlage* of the Hebrew OT text, that differs from the Masoretic text as known today.[69] There appears weight of some direct

---

is no direct evidence of verbal or thematic influence by quotation in the sermon. These works may have probable indirect influence; e.g., Heb 1:3 may verbally link "reflection" (ἀπαύγασμα) with Wis 7:26 and descriptions of the wisdom of God in similar passages (cf. Col 1:15–20; John 1:1–18). Also, Hebrews may find either indirect influence or common cultural thought with Wisdom of Ben Sira in the theme of "rest" in concordance involving the theme of death. From the perspective of finding comfort and rest in grief over a dead one in Sir 38:3, he states, "He will refresh/rest from work among the dead. Please Rest! In your remembrance and Be Comforted! On account of him when going out of his spirit" (Sir 38:3 LXX; cf. Rev 14:13). Harrington, *Invitation to the Apocrypha*, 86–87.

66. Steyn, *Quest*, 2, 378–412. Steyn states, "Apart from the fact that the author utilized a number of quotations from already existing early Jewish and early Christian traditions, there are definite indications, on the one hand, of an alternative *Vorlage* than that as represented in the eclectic editions of the LXX and NT today. But the unknown author of Hebrews himself, on the other hand, is also creatively involved in some stylistic and theological changes to his quotations" (412). Cf. Guthrie, "Hebrews," 919–93.

67. Martin and Whitlark, *Inventing Hebrews*, 6–19. Cf. Garuti, *Alle Origini Dell'omiletica Cristiana*, 7–31; deSilva, *Perseverance in Gratitude*, 35–70.

68. Lindars, *Theology of the Letter*, 124–25; Steyn, *Quest*, 4; Kistemaker and Hendriksen, *Exposition of Hebrews*, 107.

69. Jobes and Silva, *Invitation to the Septuagint*, 20; deSilva, *Perseverance in Gratitude*, 32–33; Guthrie, "Hebrews," 922.

influence, since some of his OT quotations, allusions, and echoes mirror the Hebrew OT textual tradition.[70]

The circulating NT writings provide a third probable influence. These would include the early Aramaic and Greek written traditions compiled cooperatively by the main four apostolic-led missions historically detailed in the NT writings.[71] These documents, for over thirty years before the Pastor's sermon, circulated among the apostolic missions until later replaced, due to destruction by intense persecution and ordinary depreciation, by the surviving four gospels and other circulated letters. The written Petrine and Pauline mission history of Acts, and later letters of Paul, John, and Peter find less probable influence since created about or later than the same period. However, even though the sermon contains no recognized direct NT quotations, the Pastor does make common use of OT messianic textual traditions with other NT writers, Philo, and the DSS.[72] Further, due to his heart connection with fellow "brethren" and "faith" in interpreting the OT through the lens of Jesus as Christ, the Pastor would identify and probably read circulating material of similar messianic hope.

A fourth less probable influence is that of Philo, a first-century CE Hellenistic Jew from Alexandria.[73] The Pastor's language highly corre-

---

70. Allen, *Hebrews*, 161–63.

71. Ellis, *Making of the New Testament Documents*.

72. Steyn, *Quest*, 379, 382–83, 404, 410. In his conclusion concerning the Pastor, Steyn states, "He [the Pastor] was familiar with the Scriptural reference tradition of early Judaism and that of early Christianity—with an 85% overlap between the quotations used by himself and those in the DSS, Philo and the NT."

73. Williamson, *Jews in the Hellenistic World*, 1–27. Williamson comments that Philo presents as a Jewish contemporary of the first-century CE early Christian movement in Judea. Contemporary with the ministry of Jesus, John the Baptist, and early Paul, Philo appears as a Jewish leader and elder, probably in his late fifties and living in Alexandria. Philo, later writing in his sixties or seventies, probably represents both a normative, devout, monotheistic Jew, and loyal citizen of the Roman Empire. He was geographically distanced by the diaspora from the events of Jesus's life and ministry and never mentions him. Williamson paints the life and faith of Philo through a twentieth-century lens with modern terms of "transcendent," "supernatural," and "immaterial." For example "transcendent" translates the Greek "better" (κρείττων *Opif.* 8) as a comparative form of "good" (ἀγαθός) to Philo's view of God and the eternal creation. Also, "immaterial" translates Greek "bodiless" (ἀσώματα *Praem.* 30). However, when Williamson's later philosophic terms are extracted away, Philo, from his own voluminous literature, remains a first-century CE messianic Jew with repentance of sin (14) and faith (*Abr.* 268) in the mercy of God (*Praem.* 117). Further, he demonstrates an eschatological hope (14) and believes he will see God (*QE* 2.51) in a restoration of Israel (164–68) in changed bodily form and earthly conditions with the nations governed

sponds both verbally and thematically with the Jewish-Hellenistic culture of the diaspora in Egypt.[74] However, there is no evidence of direct dependence on Philo.[75] Still, the language of Hebrews easily supports a probable normative literary source, at least in Alexandrian provenance, and possible cutting across the entire Jewish culture.[76] This observation

---

under the law of Moses (*Praem.* 169–72, *Mos.* 2.17) by the Logos creator (*Alleg. Interp.* 3.96). He asserts the converts to Judaism who accept its moral law and its philosophical ideas and ideals–a place in heaven (*Praem.* 152).

In all his writings, Philo never mentions Jesus or Messiah but through his concept of the *logos* (λόγος), similar to both the Pastor and the apostle John, probably represents an OT salvific Jewish faith similar to the OT faith of Abraham and pre-Damascus road Saul of Tarsus. Yet, Philo expresses his faith with some of the language of Platonic philosophy of a Hellenized world due to his desired audience, much like the Pastor. Cf. Thompson, *Strangers on the Earth*. The Pastor's use of the language Hellenistic philosophy very likely serviced the necessity to curtail ongoing persecution and possible martyrdom if an ordered worship of Emperor Caligula enforced against his Jewish rejection. Thereby, the language of both Philo and the Pastor probably derive from a normative, first-century CE apocalyptic symbolism with language of a future messianic hope expressed in common cultural Platonic terms. The difference is that the Pastor, like other similar Jews looking forward in faith as Philo, finds faith in Jesus as the beginning of the fulfillment of the promises of the revealed OT Logos/Christ. Cf. Schenck, *Brief Guide to Philo*, 73–76. Schenck avers that Philo was viewed favorably by Christians until the seventeenth century.

Modern background field changes of Christianity, in antitype escalation, resulted in antisemitism and negativization of the proper OT faith of Philo and other messianic Jews; e.g., for Paul, consider, Fredriksen, "Paul, the Perfectly Righteous Pharisee," 112–35. Fredriksen argues that Paul claims that he achieved righteousness under the law faultlessly against the common *adversus Judaeos*, which developed later in organized Christianity. Paul of the NT is probably a faith-based messianic Jew, who believed in Christ for salvation in heaven as the law revealed, even before his Damascus road experience, where he pointedly understood Jesus is his Christ of the law (Phil 3).

74. Williamson, *Philo*, 410; Barrett, "Eschatology of the Epistle," 169–70; Schenck, "Philo" 184–208; Ellingworth, *Epistle to the Hebrews*, 28.

75. Williamson, *Philo*, 576–80.

76. Source influences upon the Pastor have oscillated from Philonic dependence in Spicq's commentary in 1952, to deconstruction by Ronald Williamson in 1970, then affinities with first-century CE apocalyptic traditions. Cf. Schenck, "Philo," 184–86, 201–2. Also Schenck avers, "Indeed, it is interesting that even though Williamson himself accepted that the author had come under Alexandrian influence, he was so preoccupied with the desire to distance Hebrews from Philo that he often went to the opposite extreme. Thirty years later, with a better understanding of both Hebrews and Philo, it seems possible to reach a more balanced conclusion" (186).

This common Jewish cultural language often finds rejection because of tension between the philosophical ideas presented and their diversity from the now dominant background views. Cf. Williamson, *Jews in the Hellenistic World*, 103. Williamson observes, "It is always, however, difficult for a modern mind to grasp wholly what it is that an ancient writer—especially one who is avidly devoted to both scriptural Judaism and Greek philosophy—had in mind, and one suspects more than once that what looks like

finds some weight due their common (1) selection of OT quotations,[77] (2) background apocalyptic *aiōn-field* with Philo, NT writers, and the DSS,[78] (3) features of Middle Platonism,[79] and (4) use of typological interpretation as Philo under the pretext of all things hidden as allegory.[80]

---

an inconsistency, or a contradiction, does so because of the intellectual and religious viewpoint of the (usually non-Jewish) reader of his works." Schenck concludes, "While we cannot prove that the author of Hebrews was dependent on Philo, we can plausibly assert that all three writers were passing on common Alexandrian traditions at these points" (Schenck, "Philo," 201). Therefore, Schenck correctly observes that the more balanced assumption points "with confidence to a common milieu" (202).

77. Steyn, *Quest*, 382–83. Steyn recognizes this represents more than a coincidence, that he picked such a large amount of same OT quotations. However, a common language or quotation source does not provide comprehensive evidence for completely similar views.

78. Barrett, "Eschatology of the Epistle," 169. Barrett claims, "It has been urged in this essay that certain features of Hebrews which have often been held to have been derived from Alexandrian Platonism were in fact derived from apocalyptic symbolism. This is in itself an important conclusion, but it is not the whole truth. The author of Hebrews, whose Greek style is so different from that of most of the N.T., may well have read Plato and other philosophers, and must have known that his images and terminology were akin to theirs. He had seized upon the idealist element in apocalyptic, and he developed it in terms that Plato—or, better, Philo—could have understood."

79. Schenck, "Philo," 199–204. Schenck elaborates that both Philo and the Pastor possess a three-tiered view of reality consisting of (1) God beyond all creation, (2) an eternal intermediary realm which served both as a copy/image/shadow of God and provided patterns for the sense-perceptible world, and (3) the temporary sense perceptible world which consisted of copies/images/shadows of the intermediary realm. Thereby, the λόγος ("Word" [speech-action]), similar to the wisdom imagery of the Wisdom of Solomon, is viewed as a representation of the mind/thought of God in directives to his dualistic creation. Also, the tabernacle carries a Platonic interpretation as the copy and shadow of the heavenly tabernacle. Schenck, concerning this, avers, "I personally believe that we have in Hebrews 8:5 another instance where the author is thinking far more exegetically than ontologically" (203). However, Schenck admits, "Since Christ's entrance into the heavenly sanctuary corresponds to his exaltation to the right hand of God, it is tempting to see the heavenly tabernacle in Hebrews after the model of the universe as God's temple, a view that appears occasionally in Philo's writings" (204). Schenck footnotes this background-view in an apocalyptic lens with Platonic language and a dualistic view of creation beyond God, then held by both Philo and Josephus, showing that the view was widely held. He lists from Philo, *Somn.* 1.215; *Spec. Laws* 1.66; *Mos.* 2.88; *QE* 2.91 and Josephus, *Ant.* 3.123; 3:180–87 (204n104). I would also personally note that the term "heavenly [sing.] tent/tabernacle" does not appear in Hebrews or other STL. Further consider on another topic, Schenck, "Philo," 192. Schenck recognizes that, similar to Philo and Plato, the Pastor may have a realistic body-soul dichotomy of corporeal/incorporeal substance different from the more modern Cartesian dualism of material/immaterial. STL cannot support the antithetical straw man claims of the modern "heavenly tabernacle," material/immaterial camp.

80. Philo self-labeled as "allegory" his own interpretational method of searching for underlying meaning of an OT text (*Ios.* 28; *Prob.* 83). In *On Dreams* his prayer states,

Some Jews in Palestine resisted apocalyptic and platonic language due to focus on the local temple ministry. For example, the Hasmonaean priesthood in power escalated the intended antitype of the tabernacle as the final type of God's revelation, as demonstrated in their response against Stephen's statement thirty years before circulation of Hebrews (Acts 7).

Across the reaches of the diaspora, other circulating copies of the literary works contained in the DSS at Qumran provide a fifth most possible influence on the Pastor.[81] The Jewish citizens there resided as more

---

"O Sacred Guide, be our prompter and preside over our steps and never tire of anointing our eyes, until conducting us to the hidden light of hallowed words thou display to us the fast-locked lovelinesses invisible to the uninitiate" (*Somn* 1.164 PAE). Philo also used the Greek term τύπος (*typos*) metaphorically as (1) an impressed image (*Leg.* 1.61), (2) typologically with an Egyptian god as a type of Jethro, the father-in-law of Moses (*Ebr.* 36), and (3) typologically of the instruction to Moses on the Mount about that "invisible without substance with unseen form" as a "type of pattern" stamped on the mind of Moses (*Mos.* 2.76). He used the term ἀντίτυπος (*antitypos*) once typologically and metaphorically, concerning resistance by some to wax "impressions" (ἀντίτυπος) from instruction of the invisible divine things being rejected on the soul, even as Laban is compared to Jacob (*Her.* 181). Philo's typological use of τύπος for the invisible and unseen substance of divine creation, and ἀντίτυπος for visible patterns or impressions, corresponds with the typology of the Pastor.

The realistic greater correspondences of referents used by Philo match first-century CE typological interpretation—even when used in conjunction with his overarching, nonliteral, allegorical applications. Like allegory, Philo recognized typological interpretation in acknowledgment that the eternal creation can only be understood in the mind since the eternal cannot be seen rationally or empirically. Paul as a converted faith-based, messianic Jew, makes this same argument in 1 Cor 2:6–16. Spiritual understanding must be spiritually discerned, i.e., only in the mind till final arrival to reality. Philo's typology is often mistakenly cast as allegory, thereby missing the positive comparison with the Pastor. Cf. Trotter, *Jerusalem Temple in Diaspora*, 195–200. In discussion of Philo's allegorical method, Trotter recognizes the tension with Philo's "reality," but in traditional bias against both Philo's dominant exegetical method and typological representation of the temple as *all* creation, rejects the comparison.

Contra Sowers, *Hermeneutics of Philo and Hebrews*, 91. Sowers concludes, "It should not be surprising that typological exegesis is totally absent from Philo's writing, and the word *tupos* (τύπος) does not appear as a technical exegetical term there as it does in the N.T. and Apostolic Fathers." Based upon Philo's usage in the above references, Sowers may have pushed too far his typology criteria. Cf. Williamson, *Philo*, 519–38. Williamson follows Sowers in a complete contrast between Philo's allegorical method and the typology of the Pastor. Schenck offers a more balanced approach. Schenck, "Philo," 194–95. He writes, "One significant area in which Williamson's treatment of Hebrews and Philo was seriously deficient was his discussion of their respective exegetical techniques. While it is true that Philo favored allegory and Hebrews' exegesis was more typological, those of Williamson's generation had latent biases that overemphasized the implications of this difference." Schenck goes on to demonstrate Philo's use of both literal and allegorical approaches.

81. VanderKam and Flint, *Meaning*; Tigchelaar, "Dead Sea Scrolls," 163–180;

a part of the diverse first-century CE Hellenistic-Jewish milieu than as an isolated esoteric Jewish sect.[82] The scrolls display a multilingual people versed in Hebrew, Aramaic, and Greek. Further, they collected literature which presented both a strong messianic hope in apocalyptic language and a dualistic creation having both spatial and temporal verbal and thematic correspondences.[83] Still, beyond common OT quotations, fifty years of research cannot find one direct link to Hebrews.[84] Even though geographically distant, the contents of the Qumran library may not have been much different from the other reaches of the Jewish diaspora such as Egypt.

A sixth possible influential source comes from Jewish intertestamental pseudepigraphic writings, especially those with apocalyptic language.[85] The Pastor uses similar language which makes him at least aware of the common frame of these writings.

A seventh possible source is that of a Palestinian influence upon the Pastor's Jewish educational background popular in rabbinic schools, which would provide some knowledge of the talmudic commentary literature.[86] These collections, compiled several centuries before him in

---

Attridge, "How the Scrolls Impacted Scholarship," 203–30.

82. Attridge, "How the Scrolls Impacted Scholarship," 207. Attridge summarizes, "The contemporary scholarly consensus holds that the scrolls in a significant way illuminate aspects of the general Jewish milieu out of which Christianity, including the Greek-speaking variety evidenced in Hebrews, emerged, but that there is no direct literary dependence between this bit of Christian rhetoric and the scrolls. Most scholars would also agree that there are analogies between the community of the scrolls and the early Christian movement, occasioned by the common sectarian situation and eschatological orientation. The consensus is largely correct, although the publication of scrolls in the last decade has added important details to the picture."

83. Hurst, *Epistle to the Hebrews*, 43–66; Cf. Attridge, "How the Scrolls Impacted Scholarship," 208–30.

84. Hurst, *Epistle to the Hebrews*, 230.

85. Adler, "Pseudepigrapha in the Early Church," 211–28; Bauckham et al., *Old Testament Pseudepigrapha*; Gurtner, *Introducing the Pseudepigrapha*.

86. Fraade, "Targum, Targumim," 1278–81. Talmudic commentaries in Aramaic likely functioned to accompany the authority of Scripture in the social context of the synagogue to both preserve and teach the fixed Hebrew OT text. Evidence suggest many of these groups were multilingual into late antiquity, especially in rabbinic circles, but also served those who no longer understood the then dead language of Hebrew. After reading in Hebrew, an Aramaic oral rendering in a rabbinic venue followed each verse of the Torah, or up to three verses of the Prophets, called a targum. The continued rabbinic practice of targum led to the learned oral teaching of the Mishnah. The writing of the oral teaching of the Mishnah into dialectical commentary formed the talmudic commentary literature. Cf. Alexander, "Jewish Aramaic Translation," 217–53;

Babylon and Persia, contained running summaries, in Aramaic commentary, of the fixed Hebrew OT text. Scholars working on *Vorlage* of the Hebrew OT quotations do not mention direct influence of Aramaic semantic field correspondences in Hebrews but note the Pastor's exegetical method as close to midrash.[87] This Jewish literature only carries an indirect influence from educational exposure.

The final, least probable influence is Hellenistic Greco-Roman and other distant cultural literature, philosophy, mythology, and life. The Pastor does use Greco-Roman Hellenized philosophical terms to relate to his audience.[88] Some of his analogies reveal syncretism with secular areas of Greco-Roman life such as medicine, athletic games, nautical terms, legal specifications of testaments, and the vocations of a temple priest and shepherd. There is no evidence of a line of influence from Greek-Roman mythology such as "the redeemed redeemer," astral associations with the Greek-Roman gods, an anti-imperial polity in reaction to god claims of the Roman Caesars, concerns of audience participation in the Roman temple worship by eating meat offered to idols, or celebration of Hellenistic festivals. His ethical and religious parenesis follow common Jewish lines and issues with little regard for the more permissive polytheistic Greek-Roman and surrounding Mediterranean society. While his common apocalyptic language of heavenly living after death also thematically corresponds beyond Hellenism with other cultures such as Persia and Egypt, the Pastor's maintains a Jewish theological and philosophical *aiōn-field* view that is normative as apocalyptic. Other surrounding first-century CE cultures have the least possible influence upon his word pool.

The persecution that the Pastor mentions more than likely came either from fellow Jews that stirred a Roman reaction toward preservation of peace or the leadership of imperial Rome.[89] Since probably written from Rome at the beginning of the Jewish War, the Pastor may anticipate Roman persecution and possible death more than the restoration

---

Alexander, "Rabbinic Judaism," 237–46. Cf. Levine, *Ancient Synagogue*, 147–51.

87. Loiseau, *L'influence de l'araméen*, 249. Cf. Steyn, *Quest*, 406–7. Steyn recognizes correspondence to midrash in the Pastor's placement of commentary, or midrashim, particularly to the second quotation of each given pair of presented quotations; Allen, *Lukan Authorship of Hebrews*, 341–42. Allen comments on the statement of Eusebius in his *Ecclesiastical History* in *Hist. eccl.* 6.14 that Clement of Alexandria claimed Hebrews was written by Paul in Hebrew or Aramaic. He contends, "Few, if any, modern scholars would argue for a Greek translation of a Hebrew or Aramaic original."

88. Thompson, *Beginnings of Christian Philosophy*.

89. Allen, *Hebrews*, 621–22.

Atonement and the Logic of Resurrection in Hebrews 9:27-28

promises of the prophets in the renewed early war nationalism.[90] This may explain his omission of his and other's personal information and his encouragement to maintain their assembling in worship, especially in the face of the possible "day" (Heb 10:25) that they would meet the Lord in death by such persecution in martyrdom.[91]

Other unlikely influences arise from issues surrounding either temple destruction or delay of the parousia.[92] The Pastor applies the tabernacle ministry as temporary antitypes of the true eternal type in the heavens, similar to Stephen, and that in the true temple of all creation. If the proposal concerning Heb 9:28 finds any validity, then the promises of the second coming are not the major focus of the Pastor's concern, but only part of the theme he conveys.

Horizontal Filter Grid Line

The second grid line involves a historical survey of the Pastor's thematic and verbal correspondences. Within the total word pool, the Pastor's referent and verbal links of chosen authoritative, repetitive, conclusive, and historical narrative lexemes intuitively suggest his theme, which would be remembered by his audience.[93] Figure 8 illustrates the horizontal filter.

---

90. Ellingworth, *Epistle to the Hebrews*, 33, 547. Ellingworth, concerning the term "suffering" (θλῖψις), notes, "With θλῖψις, Is. 37:3. Frequent in the LXX in connection with declarations of war (1 Sa. [1 Kgdms.] 17:10, 25f., 36, 45; 2 Sa. [2 Kgdms.] 21:21; 1 Chr 20:7; Sir. 47:4" (brackets in the original). *Contra* deSilva, *Letter to the Hebrews*, 52–53.

91. Casey, "Christian Assembly in Hebrews," 323–35.

92. Werner, *Formation of Christian Doctrine*. Werner conjectures a crisis in the early church due to speculation over a delay of parousia that was taken up by scholars after the second World War. For critique of this conjecture, see Koch, *Rediscovery of Apocalyptic*, 71–72. In apocalyptic messianic interpretation of Jesus as Messiah in the early church, there is no eschatological delay—Jesus comes in the last day either at death or his coming again to earth. The ideology of delay likely did not dominate again until later prevalence for rational theological solutions for the material kingdom transferred from heaven to earth.

93. Van Dijk, *Some Aspects of Text Grammars*, 6, 10–11; van Dijk, "Recalling and Summarizing Complex Discourse," 49–118; van Dijk, *Text and Context*, 157. Van Dijk recognizes in the process of communication of a textual discourse, the audience does not remember all the individual words but forms a macro summary from the author's macrostructure of the discourse. This literary crafted macrostructure is required for any text to be classified as a discourse. Building on van Dijk's observations, this filtering method attempts reduplication of an innate audience summarization. A macro summary can form by sampling the Pastor's word pool for LXX translations of the Hebrew OT, repeated words, discourse unit conclusions, and historical narrative connections

His thematic MCS forms by blending words and their cognates in their function as referents, verbal nouns, and verbal activity.

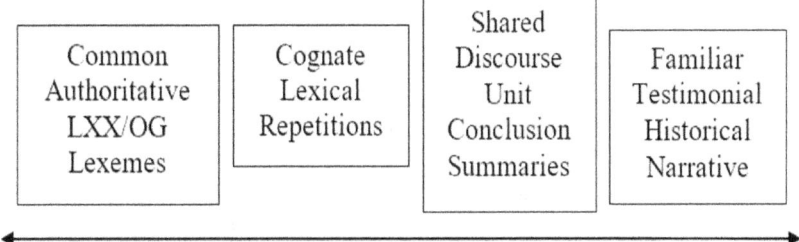

Figure 8—The Pastor's Historical Thematic and Verbal Links

The LXX is the source for the Pastor's authoritative words. Most LXX quotations are introduced with some lexical form of God speaking. The blending of words, cognates, related phrases, and themes of his LXX quotations should provide weight toward his MCS. His lexical repetitions adds other summary weight.[94] These resonate with natural receptive importance, especially when unnaturally negativized with repeated "once" (ἅπαξ Heb 6:4; 9:7, 26–28; 10:2; 12:26–27 and ἐφάπαξ Heb 7:27; 9:12; 10:10).

Also, the word summaries of his DUC provide the Pastor's own sifted summaries. An audience listening to discourse mentally assembles these together to affirm the MCS which the Pastor rhetorically provides. Finally, his historical evidence of familiar testimonial narrative adds more weight to the overall summary desired to be understood by his audience. If crafted appropriately, when this rhetorical evidence blends, an audience then cognitively ascertains and affirms the Heb 9:27–28 thematic MCS. Knowledge of the Pastor's word pool assists in eliminating unlikely influence by improbable available first-century CE sources, historically later presuppositions, or foreign words for commentary with weighted philosophical/theological terms with meanings for audiences later than the first century CE. Figure 9 illustrates the sifting function of both vertical and horizontal lines. These two lines form a sifter for interpretational glosses proposed either from historical correspondences or from later writers since the sermon. Those word meaning options

---

that make up the discourse macrostructure in Hebrews.

94. Moore, *Repetition in Hebrews*.

closest to the Pastor's theme in Heb 9:27–28 have a higher probability for interpretational accuracy than those following other unrelated themes.

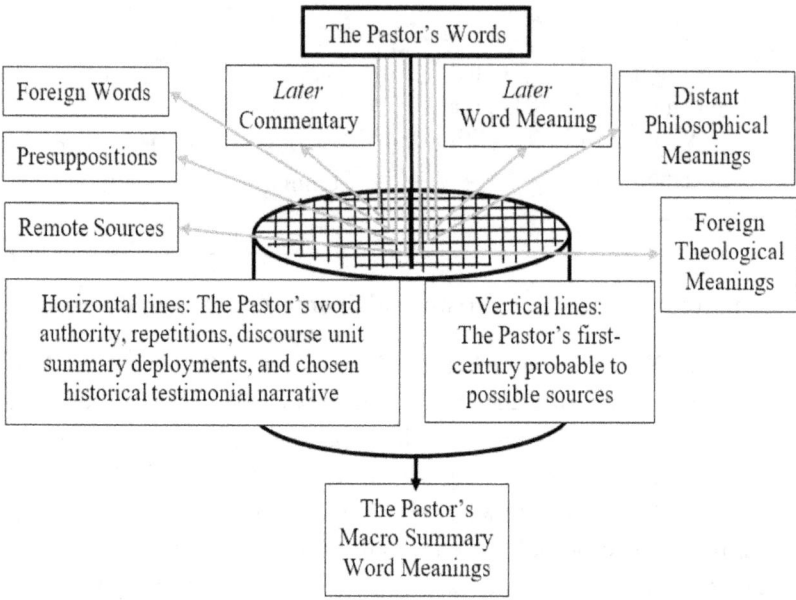

Figure 9—Sifter for STL and Anachronistic Influence on the Pastor's Words in Hebrews

STEP 7: SIFTING SOURCES WITH THE PASTOR'S WORDS IN HEBREWS 9:27–28

Evaluation of the proposed spatial translation necessitates the step of sifting the words and phrases of Heb 9:27–28. The search domain limits to the Pastor's most probable to most possible sources unless findings in possible sources merit mention by significant topical correspondence. The process samples available data for correspondences in vertical and horizontal *aiōn-field* categories. This includes either topological information or spatial-temporal activity related to his available vertical and horizontal substance-reality for words presented as evidence for his rhetorical claims.

"And in Accordance with This" (καὶ καθ')

The connective-preposition combination καὶ καθ' followed by an acc. case object in Greek discourse often syntactically functions as a device that can either connect corresponding ideas or introduce a summarizing conclusion to previous statements.[95] The Pastor uses the device twice. His first use in UPt3 of unit D at Heb 7:20 introduces a new subject of "oath" (ὀρκωμοσίας).[96] The point compares correspondences between the priesthood of Jesus with the Levitical priesthood.[97] His second use in his unit F UC at Heb 9:27 signals correspondence of the MCS to both his immediate unit and the overall discourse. His narrative asserts homogeneity in death by Jesus with all people.

"Just As . . . So" (ὅσον . . . οὕτως)

For the acc. object of his conjunction-preposition καὶ καθ', the Pastor adds a correlative conjunction.[98] This device serves to join two clauses in some related degree.[99] The placement of clauses as the object of καὶ καθ' indicate that these devices function together to frame his explanations of the correspondences within his previous parenesis.

The "just as . . . so" (ὅσον . . . οὕτως) form appears in the LXX to establish the degree of a relationship between two assertions. With the Pastor's two applications, the first, which emerges in Heb 7:20, functions in his historical parenesis concerning Melchizedek. The second, in Heb 9:27–28, frames his parenetic summary of the correspondence between the postmortem events of Christ and believers. This correlative conjunction does not appear in any of his LXX quotations or other DUC. Still,

---

95. BDAG, "κατά," 512. Bauer finds the usage in the acc. commonly as "marker of norm of similarity or homogeneity, *according to, in accordance with, in conformity with, according to*." He, in this category, mentions a common contextual use as "the norm according to which a judgment is rendered, or rewards or punishments are given."

96. Neeley, *Discourse Analysis*, 87–88.

97. Allen, *Hebrews*, 426–27.

98. Cf. MM, "ὅσος," 461. Moulton observes, "Καθ' ὅσον, 'in proportion as,' is found in Hebrews 3:3; Hebrews 7:20; Hebrews 9:27."

99. BDAG, "ὅσος," 729. Bauer signifies this use as "pert. to degree of correlative extent." Cf. L&N, "78.52 ὅσος η, ον; τοσοῦτος, αὕτη, οὗτον," 1:692. L&N observes in the connection, "a degree of correlative extent—'to the degree that, to the same degree, as much as.'"

his use after καὶ καθ' would provide weight for the provided comparative statements as his MCS for his overall point.

"It Is Reserved" (ἀπόκειται)

The verb ἀπόκειται appears four times in the LXX (Gen 49:10; 2 Macc 12:45; 4 Macc 8:11; Job 38:23).[100] Jacob's use of the term in Gen 49:10 has weight for an expectation of messianic mediation for his son Judah. This messianic figure is presently reserved at his side until a time of rest, which occurs after his enemies are subdued and all the peoples should obey him.[101] Jacob's prophecy seems to include uninterrupted mediation for his son Judah by a future messianic coming to him.[102] The need for mediation in possible protection harmonizes with the Pastor's use of ἀπόκειται in Heb 9:27–28 in the subtopics of judgment after death.

---

100. BDAG, "ἀπόκειμαι," 113. Bauer's glosses from historical context find reference to put away for safekeeping in a time of need, a reserve for reward or recompense, or something reserved in result of an unavoidable circumstance. The main idea seems something exists that is reserved. The time or nature of what is reserved determines by context. Cf. L&N "ἀπόκειμαι," 2:29. Louw-Nida glosses "put away," "exist," and "be necessary" perhaps adding the weight of the context to the word, and thereby, moving away from something laid up or reserved. Cf. MM, "ἀπόκειμαι," 63–64. After review of primary contextual uses and secondary literature, Moulton and Milligan state, "The word is common in the sense 'to be stored.'" For correspondence with Heb 9:27, they mention a late Alexandria reference quoted from Kaibel, *Epigrammata Graeca ex Lapidibus Conlecta*, 416. It states, "As having known that for all mortals it is reserved to die" (ὡς εἰδὼς ὅτι πᾶσι βροτοῖς τὸ θανεῖν ἀπόκειται).

101. The LXX translates, "And the ruler will not depart from Judah, even the one himself leading the way from his side, until the one himself reserving should come to him, and he is the expectation of the nations" (Gen 49:10 LXX). The pres. mid./pass. ptc. ἀποκείμενα provides possible weight for Judah having a current reservation or laying up for the appropriate time by a ruler currently leading at his side. The pres. mid./pass. ptc. ἡγούμενος infers a present continual leading. Cf. L&N, "ἡγέομαι," 1.464–65. Louw-Nida recognizes ἡγέομαι in a semantic field with προΐσταμαια, κατευθύνω, φέρω, and ἄγω. The latter two find expression five times in Hebrews and one time respectively as descriptive of Jesus's shepherd motif for mediation of believers raising up to God at death.

102. The prophecy of Jacob, by singling out personal messianic mediation for his son Judah, may serve typologically in greater escalation as an antitype of a messianic coming from the tribe of Judah (Heb 7:14; cf. Num 24:17; Isa 11:1; Mic 5:2; Matt 2:6; Rev 5:5). The most likely place and time that Judah would personally need mediation by a ruler would involve the divine judgment of his eternal destiny at his death (Heb 10:26–39, cf. Luke 16:19–31). This eternal destiny decision predetermines as a judgment of condemnation until belief in God's personal provision for mediation (Heb 4:3; 11:6; cf. John 5:24–32).

The second- to first-century BCE author of 2 Macc. 12:45 uses ἀποκείμενον in probable reference to a reserved postmortem "grateful reward" for those who "fall asleep" or die with godliness.[103] Judas Maccabeus had holy and pious thoughts of such reward after death. For Judas Maccabeus, such worship practice of atonement for the dead would only be valid if the dead were still alive due to their godliness. This implies a judgment event linked with prompt resurrection to God's presence. In reference to the sin of some fallen brethren, Judas made an atonement for those who had died so that they might be delivered from their sins at judgment for reward "which is presently being reserved."[104]

The first-century CE author of 4 Macc. 8:11 recounts the second-century BCE event of Antiochus Epiphanes's torture of Eleazer, his seven brothers, and their mother, who would not break God's law when ordered to eat pig meat.[105] Antiochus threatens the seven brothers after torturing to death Eleazer stating that only the rack "is being reserved" (ἀπειθήσασιν) for them "to die" (ἀποθανεῖν) if they do not eat. This

---

103. GE, "χἄριστήριος." The term "grateful reward" (χαριστήριος) refers to a reserved reward as a return offering of thanks from God for godly service. The terms "sleep" (κοιμάω and καθεύδω) are commonly recognized, in Jewish literature, as a euphemistic reference to the event of dying with entrance into the created spiritual realm with resurrection. Cf. 4 Macc. 7:18–19; 16:25; Jub 23:31; 1 En. 92:3; 100:5; Dan 12:2. The lexeme κοιμάω (koimaō) generally refers to the event of fleshly death whereas καθεύδω (katheudō) to the state of complete decay of the flesh in death. Cf. Jackson, *Investigation of Koimaomai*. *Contra* Bailey, "Sleep," 161–67. Bailey surmises the state of the deceased best follows the formula *"in* Christ—*with* Christ," with "in Christ" in the present, and "with Christ," in the future and knowing nothing after death until later flesh resurrection. No evidence is presented that negates the possibility that the idiom *"with* Christ" begins at death or that "sleep" serves as a biblical term for the bodily spirit of the dead people *with* Christ before the resurrection of the earthly living. This observation from silence is weak.

No work has been done for evaluation of "sleep" or *"with* Christ" in relation to the presence of an *aiōn-field* context in sources for these terms linked with apocalyptic language. Chapters 3 and 4 will briefly explore OT and NT context for the *aiōn-field* background. Jackson, Cullmann, and Michel are correct to avoid modern philosophical baggage of the term "the intermediate-state." The Pastor uses neither term, opting for ἀποθνῄσκω ("to die" Heb 7:8; 9:27; 10:28; 11:4, 13, 21, 37) for the event of dying and νεκρός ("dead" Heb 6:2; 9:17; 11:19, 35; 13:20) to identify his subject as one dead.

104. The syntactical use of the adjectival pres. mid./pass. ptc. ἀποκείμενον, signifies a present reward. Nothing in the text implies a distantly future judgment. The gesture functioned not toward their salvation, but typologically, both for demonstrating the atonement covering of sin in salvation (2 Macc. 12:42) and for rewards of the godly postmortem in a judgment at a prompt resurrection (2 Macc. 12:44–45).

105. Evans, *Ancient Texts*, 55; NRSVApo, "4 Maccabees," 362. Wilson dates the work 20–54 CE with a range of the late first-century BCE to first-century CE. Also, as an appendix addition to the Greek LXX, the work was probably available to the Pastor.

combination may echo, in Heb 9:27, the themes of persecution of faith found in Hebrews, as a reversal of the claims of Antiochus Epiphanies in the face of threats of martyrdom. Expectation of life rewards continues beyond reserved death at expected judgment that can be atoned.

After asking Job and his companions a series of questions exposing the limitation of man's knowledge, God derisively states in Job 38:23 LXX, "But you came into the treasures of the snow. But you have seen the treasures of the hail. But it is reserved to you for a time of enemies, in a day strife and dispute." God reveals metaphorically that these men had some treasury knowledge of the snow and hail. He then continues with more questions pointing out their knowledge within a human view meets with chaos and death that ἀπόκειται ("is reserved") for them. The word associates with God's reserved judgment as revealed in the chaotic visible cosmos.

NT authors also used ἀπόκειται (Luke 19:20; Col 1:5; 2 Tim 4:8; Heb 9:27). Jesus refers to it in a parable with a nobleman's judgment of his servants. A servant had been "reserving" his mina by sewing it in a facecloth. Since the word carries weight of judgment from the LXX and MT above, the servant's own words appropriately reserve the judgment he receives when he was brought into account.

Paul writes Col 1:5 to believers about their hope "reserved" (ἀποκειμένην) "in the heavens" (ἐν τοῖς οὐρανοῖς), which they heard in the word of truth of the gospel. In the gospel sequence, the processes of salvation take place over plural heavens of both the temporary and the eternal unseen kingdom (fig. 2). For the believer at judgment is reserved a journey of hope (Heb 6:18–20). Paul also states in testimony shortly before his death, "There is reserved [ἀπόκειται] for me a last thing, that of a crown of righteousness, which the Lord, who is a righteous Judge, will reward me in that day, but not only to me, but also to all who have loved his appearing" (2 Tim 4:8). Paul's thoughts here center on death—the time of his departure as being poured out as a drink offering (2 Tim 4:6). With the completion of his ministry (2 Tim 4:7), his next move consisted of the judgment of the Lord and the expectation of his "appearing" (ἐπιφάνειαν). Paul testified "there is reserved" (ἀπόκειταί) a last thing for him of a crown of righteousness on that day.[106] In the context of his life

---

106. *GGBB*, 140. Paul places himself personally as a dat. of indirect object of the pass. "there is reserved" (ἀπόκειταί) showing he receives the subject of the verb. The subject antecedent of ἀπόκειταί identifies in the dependent clause to follow as "the Lord, who is a righteous Judge." Paul anticipated the personal intercessory judgment of

and teaching, "that day" of the Lord's judgment would refer to the day of his death—the time of his departure and being poured out as a drink offering before God (2 Tim 4:6; cf. Phil 1:23).[107]

The Pastor only speaks ἀπόκειμαι once and avoids it in descriptions of death in his historical testimonials but his choice for introducing his summary conclusion is significant. In the first century CE, in other parallel writings, as laid out by surrounding context, ἀπόκειμαι dominantly sets for an audience the background *aiōn-field* of a reserved judgment linked with one's death.

"For People" (τοῖς ἀνθρώποις)

The word "man, people" (ἄνθρωπος) is ubiquitous in the Pastor's world.[108] The Pastor quotes from two OT texts of the LXX that use ἄνθρωπος from Ps 8:5 LXX (8:4 MT) in Heb 2:6 to introduce, in the form of parallel Hebrew poetry, the contrast of "man" and "the Son of Man," whom he interprets as Jesus.[109] Psalm 117:6 LXX (118:6 MT), in Heb 13:6, uses a rhetorical question to remind of man's limitations when enduring persecutory harm, in respect to God's plans after this life. Also, the Pastor's use of ἄνθρωπος ten times increases the weight of the substantive as a choice for his MCS. The Pastor declares of his examples, "All these died corresponding to faith" (Heb 11:3). This familiar narrative of the faith experience of people that pleased God as they looked for entrance into the heaven after death also supports the subtopic of ἄνθρωπος (cf. Heb 11:13–16).

The stability of meaning across the large numbers of the Pastor's sources, the use in two OT LXX quotations of Ps 8:5 LXX (8:4 MT) and Ps 117:6 LXX (118:6 MT), his parenesis including multiple cognate subcategories, message repetitions, and his personal illustrations of familiar

---

the Lord as a righteous Judge in reward of a crown of righteousness.

107. Paul uses both the verb "to depart" (ἀναλῦσαι Phil 1:23) and the noun "departure" (ἀνάλυσις 2 Tim 1:6) in reference to his own personal death. Combining these similar ideas, Paul anticipated, at the departure of his earthly death, an appearing of the Lord to be with Christ (cf. 2 Cor 5:6–8).

108. GELS, "ἄνθρωπος," 37–38. Muraoka glosses LXX usage as either "man (with no particular reference to maleness), *human being*" or "w. special reference to male" (italics Muraoka), as in Gen 2:24. The terms "man," "men," or "mankind" herein carry no weight of male limitation unless specified. This writer attempts to follow a first-century CE worldview of the Pastor as close as possible. However, an attempt for cultural accommodation of modern gender issues foreign is applied to the text by use of "people."

109. Johnson, *Hebrews: A Commentary*, 90.

narrative about faith in death all support ἄνθρωπος as a fitting choice for a summary conclusion of his correspondence between man with Christ in the comparative statements of the MCS (see appendix 3).

"Once" (ἅπαξ)

Audience contextual understanding beyond the ordinal function of the adverb ἅπαξ is determined from the temporal and spatial scope of the other referents in the MCS. In Hebrews the Pastor quotes Hag 2:6, commenting on the importance of ἅπαξ in the phrase "still once" ("Ἔτι ἅπαξ Heb 12:26, 27). He uses a cognate form "once for all" (ἐφάπαξ) three times, once in the UC of Heb 7:25-28.[110] Also, after concluding the parenesis of his rhetoric in Heb 9:26 with use of ἅπαξ, he places it twice more for emphasis in both of his corresponding summary statements in comparison of the death of man and death of Christ in Heb 9:27-28. These two statements both have ἅπαξ, and pair the adverbial terms with the adjectival object of preposition "second" (δεύτερος Heb 9:7; 9:27-28; cf. Jude 5). The first occurs in Heb 9:7 where "but into the second *tent*" (εἰς δὲ τὴν δευτέραν) contextually refers to high priest movement into the holy of holies.

These observations support the Pastor's word choice of ἅπαξ as a key understanding of the concluding corresponding statements of his MCS. Also, it is essential to note the term, in all probable and possible influences upon the Pastor, carries only numerical or ordinal weight in narrative. Any implied temporal end, duration, repetition, or spatial activity must come from the surrounding context.

"To Die" (ἀποθανεῖν)

The verbal "to die" (ἀποθνῄσκω) appears often in the Pastor's environment as an event common to humanity.[111] In the LXX it overwhelmingly indicates man's physical death in correspondence to the concept of

---

110. BDAG, "ἐφάπαξ," 417–18. For meaning in Hebrews, Bauer remarks, "Taking place once and to the exclusion of any further occurrence, once for all, once and never again."

111. The referent ἀποθανεῖν semantically functions as the subject of the sentence as the antecedent of the pronoun "it" in the main verb (appendix 3). Also, ἀποθανεῖν functions as the subject of the two corresponding statements in a MCS of his discourse narrative that tracks from the introduction.

Hades.[112] The LXX translators chose ἀποθνῄσκω for five different Hebrew words related to physical death in the MT with links to concepts of Sheol.[113] It carries a meaning distinct from ideas of continued living or from the state of "death" (θάνατος), a term often used to translate postmortem terms.[114] The NT authors crafted sentences with ἀποθνῄσκω 111 times, with the infinitive ἀποθανεῖν 16 times, mainly for physical death, with one textual use as figurative extension (cf. Luke 16:22; Rev 3:2).[115]

112. GELS, "ἀποθνῄσκω," 53–54. Muraoka glosses the lexeme "to come to an end of one's physical existence." E.g., "But from the tree of which to know good and evil, do not eat from it, since that day you should eat from it, yourselves will die to death" (Gen 2:17 LXX). This delineation is not as clear in the Hebrew of the MT, which has the literal phrase מות תמות (Gen 2:17 BHS), can translate "to die you will die" or for emphasis, "you will surely die." HAL, "מות," 562–63. In Gen 2:17 the LXX translators used θάνατος as a noun in dat. masc. sing. form θανάτῳ, as a gloss, syntactically of a dat. of direct object, for the Hebrew infinitive verb form "to die" (מות). The LXX translators chose the Greek "Hades" (ᾅδης) for the Hebrew "Sheol" (שאול). GELS, "ᾅδης," 8. Muraoka glosses the term "Hades, the underworld as the abode of the dead." The term has correspondence with the verbal idea of physical death as both the location of the flesh and a postmortem moment before rising in resurrection; e.g., "Moreover, my flesh will dwell in hope, because you will not abandon my soul in Hades" (Ps 15:9–10 LXX [16:9–10 MT]).

113. GHAIS, "ἀποθνῄσκω," 14. Cf. Johnston, Shades of Sheol, 69–85. Johnston recognizes the term as a personal description in narrative context as people "die" or experience "death." As a personal expression, "go down to Sheol" corresponds with "to die" in physical death, with visible understanding of the place of the body. The NIV translates it as "grave." Johnston observes that Sheol also can refer to postmortem activity in the underworld by the wicked and the righteous dead. In a wholistic flesh view, he limits people as an inseparable category, so that, a person cannot be considered in two places at once, as separable from fleshly living. This presupposition causes the OT Sheol descriptions to seem contradictory. The OT describes (1) the righteous in death as in Sheol (Gen 37:35, 42:38, 44:29, 31; Job 14:13; Ps 88:3; Isa 38:10), (2) the wicked speaking in the realm of the dead (Isa 14:9–10; Ezek 32:21), and (3) that only the righteous after entrance to the grave, then move on to the presence of the Lord in heaven in the way of life (Ps 16:8–11). So, how can one be both in Sheol, where one cannot escape, and at the same time, dwell in heaven? The logical conclusion in wholistic flesh only paradigms is that the terms must be figurative, with no conscious living until flesh resurrection, i.e., people no longer exist after death, but only in the mind and plan of God, as "in Christ." However, the Pastor's normative of apocalyptic Jewish dualism allows for the mortal body to remain in the grave, whereas the soul/spirit body of the righteous rises to enter the presence of God to heaven in the way of life to await a collective completion with others (cf. Eccl 12:5–7).

114. The Greek θάνατος (thanatos) usually served as a gloss of Hebrew words in context for the postmortem state after physical death. GHAIS, "θάνατος," 55. Like LXX translators, NT writers in an apocalyptic view maintain this contrast (cf. Rev 9:6). Cf. Williamson, Death and the Afterlife.

115. E.g., "Now, he happened to die, the poor man, to be taken away by angels into the bosom of Abraham. Now also, the rich person died, and he was buried" (Luke

The Pastor chooses a form of ἀποθανεῖν seven times (Heb 7:8; 9:27; 10:28; 11:4, 13, 21, 37). It serves as his main thematic verb in his D1ʹ UC concerning the "elders" (πρεσβύτεροι Heb 11:2) in Heb 11:13. The Pastor claims, "All these died in correspondence with faith," referring to their faith as their "testimony of approval" (ἐμαρτυρήθησαν Heb 11:2) before God, after they had died. It is a fitting term for his MCS, since the theme of physical death overshadows his examples and illustrations of his testimonial narrative.

"But After This" (μετὰ δὲ τοῦτο)

The phrase does not appear in the LXX. In Hebrews, the Pastor crafts the successive ordinal indicator on three occasions (Heb 4:8; 9:3; 9:27). The first, as part of his historical narrative, "concerning another he would not have spoken after this day" (Heb 4:8), has temporal weight to signal another day after the day of the original author of the OT text. In Heb 9:3, he says, "But after the second veil a tent which is the one being called the holy of holies." The spatial emphasis has probable weight to successive temporal events in the same discourse unit for the Heb 9:27 phrase "but a judgment after this" (μετὰ δὲ τοῦτο κρίσις). The context supports the probability that the first ordinal event and second are successive but closely connected events.

"A Judgment" (κρίσις)

As a verbal noun, the term "judgment" (κρίσις) and the verbal form "to judge" (κρίνω) carries thematic significance in the LXX.[116] In the Pentateuch, κρίσις labels God's judgments in the Law which determine land blessings.[117] In the prayer of Hannah, there is recognition that the Lord

---

16:22).

116. BDAG, "κρίσις," 569; L&N, "κρίσις," 1:363; BDAG, "κρίνω," 567–68; L&N, "κρίνω," 1:358; GELS, "κρίσις," 331. Muraoka glosses the LXX lexeme usage as (1) "acting as judge," (2) "sentence," (3) "a decision taken," (4) "an act of righteousness," (5) "moral, ethical integrity," or (6) "a court proceeding." Cf. GELS, "κρίνω," 331. Here, Muraoka lists (1) "to act as a judge over," (2) "to take up a legal case for," (3) "to determine or pronounce as a verdict," (4) "to decide," (5) "to contest a legal case."

117. E.g., "If you should hear the commandment of the Lord your God, which I commanded to you today, to love the Lord your God, to walk in all his ways, to keep his decrees, and his judgments, and you will live and you will become great, and the Lord your God will bless in all the land" (Deut 30:16 LXX).

"went up" (ἀνέβη) "into heavens" (εἰς οὐρανοὺς) where "he will judge" (κρινεῖ) the earth, and lift high the horn of his "anointed one, Christ" (χριστός).[118] In the prophets, it links with "to bring, to lead" (αἴρω) and "to rise, to bring" (ἄγω) word groups, with "into death" (εἰς θάνατον) of the suffering servant motif of Isaiah.[119] A devoted reader, with an apocalyptic (*aiōn-field*) lens on the LXX in the early NT era, would likely sense concerning people both a prompt individual judgment between earth and heaven after death and a later corporate judgment in final execution of the pronounced penalty.

The LXX translators chose forms of κρίσις and κρίνω for multiple Hebrew and Aramaic words in the MT which pointed to different details of judgment.[120] The LXX κρίσις serves as a general term for all senses of the entire course of judgment as determined by context, either in part or whole, involving charges/defense, testing in trial, decisions, sentencing, and finally, deliverance or execution of a guilty verdict.

In the NT, κρίσις occurs forty-seven times. It follows the same sense as the LXX for the processes of judgment-related senses with an apocalyptic (*aiōn-field*) emphasis.[121] The importance of the term is supported from

118. E.g., "The Lord went up into the heavens and he will thunder, he will judge the highest places of the earth, and he will give strength to our kings, and he will lift high the horn of his Christ" (1 Kgdms 2:10 LXX).

119. E.g., "In which his judgment will humiliate one being raised, who will describe his generation? Because his life will be raised from the earth, because of the transgressions of my people he was brought into death" (Isa 53:8 LXX).

120. GHAIS, "κρίσις," 71.

121. The NT contextually follows the LXX and MT by use of κρίσις in the sense of (1) the word of the one making judgment (John 8:16), (2) the judgment of a claim (John 3:19; 12:31; Rev 18:10), (3) the decision of vengeance in judgment (Matt 23:33; Jude 15), (4) an interpretation in judgment (John 7:24), (5) the decision of rightness in judgment (John 5:30), (6) the dispute of a judgment (Jude 9), and (7) the Lord's judgment after death between the righteous and the wicked (Matt 3:29; John 5:24, 29; 2 Pet 2:9).

It is doubtful that the NT increase in commentary concerning God's eternal judgment represents a shift in thinking. It is more likely a shift in genre. The bulk of the early OT contains historical revelation from man's bottom-up perspective, with only occasional mention of matters from God's heavenly view. As often suggested, the scant *eternal creation* references should not be taken to mean that authors did not think of eternal/perpetual-*place* postmortem matters but only this life. Pace Johnston, *Shades of Sheol*, 16. However, ossuary and burial practices suggest otherwise, that the OT to NT emphasis is not contradictory. Also, the frequent OT historical connections of death, which contain statement concepts of activity in Sheol, negate ideas of Jewish head-in-the-sand living with their minds only upon the present temporary creation. The tabernacle service itself served as an outline of the both the temporary and eternal creation, with hope in the mercy and provision of God. Rather, the ST increase in eternal

the LXX in the evidence that the Pastor chooses several scriptures which prominently feature God's judgment (Isa 26:11; Deut 32:35–36). In his discussion of the unchangeableness of God, Philo recognizes the saving mercy of God after running the course of life, during the postmortem individual phase of judgment of the sin of man (*Deus* 74–76).[122] Also, the Pastor speaks the specific term κρίσις twice (Heb 9:27; 10:27) and cognates seven times (Heb 4:12; 6:2; 9:27; 10:27; 10:30; 12:23). Further, the Jewish Law contains parenesis of earthly judgment, which served as a "shadow" of the activity of the eternal/perpetual-*places* (Heb 10:1). He considers this antitype-type connection of "of an eternal/perpetual-*place* judgment" (κρίματος αἰωνίου Heb 6:2) as a beginning teaching.[123] In the Pastor's purview, the eternal/perpetual-*place* judgment represents a process of events where individuals who are suspected of charges in a dispute against them are presented before a judge (Heb 4:12–13) to receive a verdict after "testing" (πειράζω Heb 2:18) of a trial.[124] If a verdict of guilty occurs, then the

---

matters reflects changes in genre, with more postmortem reflection in the Psalms and Prophets, in a top-down eternal creation (*aiōn-field*) view. The NT expands the detail of this apocalyptic view of the idea of eternal/perpetual-*place* judgment after rising of dead people (Heb 6:2) and salvation by faith in the intercessory gospel ability of Jesus, as the Christ (Heb 7:25; 9:28).

122. E.g., Philo asserts that all are unworthy of God's mercy and that all stumble during the course of life from birth to death. Philo speaks of God's individual judgment that takes place concerning the course of the entire life, probably after "death's burial" in the "deep mud" (βύθια *Deus* 76 PAGM). Philo does not connect this judgment with any later resurrection but postmortem; e.g., he writes, "So that the people should exist, if more of persons should go into the deep mud, he tempers mercy, by which toward kindness and unworthy benefits, and not only he pities the ones having been condemned, but even condemns the ones having pity" (ἵν᾽ οὖν ὑπάρχῃ τὸ γένος, κἂν πολλὰ τῶν εἰδικῶν βύθια χωρῇ, τὸν ἔλεον ἀνακίρνησιν, ᾧ πρὸς εὐεργεσίας καὶ τῶν ἀναξίων χρῆται, καὶ οὐ μόνον δικάσας ἐλεεῖ, ἀλλὰ καὶ ἐλεήσας δικάζει *Deus* 76 PAGM). Philo deploys κρίσις in the sense of (1) the word of the one making judgment (*Drunkenness* 170, *Heir* 311), (2) the judgment of a claim (*Flight* 118), (3) the decision of vengeance in judgment (*Flight* 196), (4) an interpretation in judgment (*Creation* 109, *Dreams* 1.28), (5) the decision of rightness in judgment (*Heir* 162), (6) the dispute of a judgment (*Dreams* 2.24), (7) and the Lord's judgment after death between the righteous and the wicked (*Flight* 118, 196).

123. This beginning teaching of eternal/perpetual-*place* judgment of mankind presents for the Pastor as a continual process of judgment containing past, present, and future eschatological events from the eternal perspective of "today" (Heb 1:5; 3:7, 13, 15; 4:7; 5:5; 13:8; cf. Acts 17:31).

124. The DUC (Heb 2:17–18) of unit B (Heb 2:1–18) states, "For in which, he has suffered as one being put to the test, he is able to help the ones being tested." In the Pastor's apocalyptic lens, the discourse unit develops Jesus's "testing" (πειράζω) beyond the suffering of life and the cross to include the process of judgment at death. His evidence includes God's judgment of the Son spoken in unit A Upt1–2 (Heb 1:5–12) and the

individual remains outside heaven until a later time when the appropriate sentence is executed. If found righteous in innocence, then the one charged is saved or delivered (Heb 7:25; cf. Ps 119:123).[125]

Son's experience of post-judgment glory and honor in events after his own judgment as a person in unit B UPt1–3 (Heb 2:5–16, esp. 9, 14).

There is no evidence concerning either Jesus or the righteous dead enduring further testing of a future judgment after spiritual bodily transformation in rising to Jesus in heaven. Also, the cross cannot be seen as the only testing that Jesus endured, since another event of judgment for all men must occur after fleshly death (Heb 9:27). Jesus's judgment in the sequence events of death logically must both continue at fleshly death and precede fleshly resurrection from the dead with a verdict of righteous. If there is no verdict of righteousness for a person at judgment after death, there would not be a life continuing to resurrection but a further sequence of events toward a second resurrection of the great judgment and second death (cf. Rev 20:5–6). The Pastor rhetorically employs the testing of Israel (Heb 3:12–4:13) as an antitype of the heavenly type of eternal/perpetual-*place* judgment that occurs before entering with Jesus into heaven. One finds the antitype sequence of deliverance from Egypt, testing in the wilderness, and entrance by faith into the land. The heavenly type fulfills by deliverance from the dark-temporary world of slavery (Heb 2:14–15), testing in approach (Heb 4:11–13), and entrance by faith into the rest of heaven (Heb 4:14–16; 6:18–20).

125. For the Pastor, during Jesus's sequence as a person (Heb 2:9, 14), after fleshly death, he is arguably tested at judgment, found innocent of sin, and exalted above the heavens (Heb 7:26; appendix 1, fig. 1; cf. 1 Tim 3:16b; 1 Pet 2:23). People found guilty of sin endure darkness and gloom outside of the blessings of heaven (Heb 10:26–31; 12:18–21; appendix 1, fig. 3). This infers a "descent" of the fleshly body to the grave (cf. Luke 18:14) and the spirit body remaining in "Hades" (ᾅδης) with failure to rise from the dead (cf. Luke 16:31) in exaltation to heaven, only if after judgment, found guilty (cf. Matt 11:23). In the apocalyptic view, "Hades," the "abyss," and the "cosmos, universe," which includes the earth, represent all temporary creation outside of the domain of the eternal/perpetual-*place* heavens (cf. Gen 1:2 LXX; Rom 10:6–7; Eph 4:9). Jesus's decent into Hades or the cosmos as God in the flesh occurs in his conception and incarnation (Heb 10:5; cf. Matt 3:16; 28:2; Mark 1:10; Luke 3:22; John 1:32–33, 51; 3:13; 6:33, 38, 41–42, 50–51, 58; Rom 10:6–7; Eph 4:8–10). At death, Jesus's body, in the likeness of all men (Heb 2:9–11), descends into a grave (cf. Matt 12:40; 16:21). His spirit bodily ascends from the realm of the dead in Hades outside the gates to heaven (cf. Matt 16:18) toward the reclaimed lesser holy realm of heaven by veil removal before approach to God after judgment (Heb 4:11–13; 9:27–28) in the way of the holy-*places* (Heb 9:8). Since vindicated (cf. 1 Tim 3:16b; Rom 3:4), he enters as the first born-again person into the eternal, now greater and more perfect heaven of God's presence (cf. Heb 1:6; Col 1:18; Rev 1:5; John 3:13; Acts 2:34; Rom 10:6–7; Heb 9:14; cf. chapter 4 unit F UPt2 Heb 9:1–14). Jesus takes with him those previously found innocent by faith (cf. Matt 27:52–53; Luke 23:43; Rom 8:29; Heb 2:11–13; 3:1; 12:23). After fleshly resurrection on the third day, he ascends in flesh into heaven (cf. John 6:62; 20:17; Eph 4:8). The idea of descent outside of the eternal heavens to a place of the dead of Hades (hell), where others, who have been sentenced in judgment temporarily abide, does not harmonize with first-century CE apocalyptic views. *Pace* Emerson, *He Descended to the Dead*; Alfeyev, *Christ the Conqueror of Hell*.

The Pastor appropriately chooses κρίσις to signify typologically a judgment in the eternal creation after death, in facing the presence of sin before God (Heb 6:2; 10:26–31; cf. Rev 11:18). He routinely, according to first-century CE practice, chooses either the verb κρίνω, or verbal nouns κρίσις and κρίμα for the senses of continual individual judgment in life (Heb 13:4), individual postmortem judgment (Heb 10:26–39), and a final corporate judgment of all things "that can be shaken" for removal from God's kingdom presence (Heb 12:25–29). The text of the latter two senses both function as part of the UC of their respective units. The term κρίσις is fitting for his MCS in Heb 9:27–28 for the past (cf. John 16:11), present (cf. John 12:33; Rom 12:2), and future intercession of Christ (cf. John 12:25).

"So Also" (οὕτως καὶ)

The Pastor adds the second part of the correlative conjunction *houtōs* with *kai* (οὕτως with καὶ), of the idiom καθ' ὅσον ... οὕτως mentioned above, to compare the two corresponding statements of his MCS.[126] The καὶ with the adverb οὕτως provides force of adverbial function with inferred meaning of comparison as "in the same way" or "likewise."[127]

The Pastor uses the phrase three times. In Heb 5:3, he states in reference to the offerings the high priest makes for the people, he must "in the same way" (οὕτως καὶ) make them for himself. In Heb 5:5, he speaks the

---

126. BDF, §453, 236. *Pace* Robertson, *Grammar*, 966–67. Robertson comments "This is a classic idiom and occurs only in Hebrews, except once in Mark." On the relative comparative construction, Robertson states of Heb 9:27 that there is no comparative. He writes, "This is probably causal in idea, as is true of καθ' ὅσον in 9:27, where there is no comparative, though we have the correlative οὕτως καὶ." Robertson recognizes the comparative function of the idiom but negates it in Heb 9:27 without stating his reasoning. This literary construction allows the probability that the two relative clauses of Heb 9:27–28 semantically, with the relative pronoun idiom construction, function comparatively, to develop the second adverbial clause as the reason or basis of salvation. The subjects of death and judgment for people in the first clause as a protasis compares to the death and judgment of Jesus's personal death and judgment in his offering for the sins of many people as an apodosis (appendix 3).This provides from the basis for salvation from death and judgment, that he will be appearing to those waiting for him. The question of where and when this truth occurs must come from the surrounding context.

127. BDAG, "καὶ," 495–96. Bauer recognizes in this adverbial construction an additive relation in the contrast, stating, "In sentences denoting a contrast καί appears in var. ways, somet. in both members of the comparison, and oft. pleonastically, to our way of thinking." Louw and Nida translate it most often in six examples as "in the same way."

phrase found in Heb 9:28, "so also Christ" (Οὕτως καὶ ὁ Χριστὸς), as the subject of a second comparative statement with Aaron. The phrase functions to join the two main statements of his MCS of the unit discourse to demonstrate parallel correspondence in the ordinal events.

"Christ"

The substantive "anointed one" (Χριστὸς) appears forty-six times in the LXX.[128] The term at the establishment of the cultic priesthood of Israel refers to "the anointed priest" (ὁ ἱερεὺς ὁ χριστὸς LXX Lev 4:3, 5, 16; 6:15 [6:22 MT]; 21:10, 12) in his consecrated, ministerial activity of the sin offering, guilt offering, and grain offering.[129]

Hannah prophetically speaks, in a messianic foreshadowing, that the Lord "will give strength to our kings and lift high the horn of his anointed [χριστοῦ]" (1 Kgdms 2:10 LXX [1 Sam 2:10 MT]).[130] Further, later in contrast to the priestly unfaithfulness of the sons of Eli in violation of God's offering instructions, Yahweh says, "I will raise up [ἀναστήσω] for myself a faithful priest" (1 Kgdms 2:35 LXX [1 Sam 2:35 MT]), who

---

128. GELS, "Χριστὸς," 600. Muraoka glosses the LXX lexeme usage as "1. *smeared*: s [subject] oil used to consecrate a priest," and "2. subst., *one on whom the act of χρίω has been performed*: Priest, b. 'messiah': God's, . . . Amos 4.13; . . . Hb 3.13" (italics Muraoka).

129. This "anointed priest" offered up burnt offerings for atonement and God's forgiveness of committed unintentional sins that had become known by a person or the priest himself, the people of the congregation, a leader, or the people of the land. They also followed similar procedures in the guilt offering and the grain offering. In execution of the sin offerings, the anointed priest would "lay his hand on the bull and slay the bull before the Lord" (Lev 4:4) as a symbolic transfer of sins to the sacrificial animal. The priest then dipped his finger in the blood and sprinkled it seven times before "the veil of the holy place" (τὸ καταπέτασμα τὸ ἅγιον Lev 4:6). He then applied some blood on the horns of the altar of incense "before the Lord, which is in the tent of testimony" (ἐναντίον κυρίου, ὅ ἐστιν ἐν τῇ σκηνῇ τοῦ μαρτυρίου Lev 4:7). The rest of the bull's blood was poured out at the base of the altar of burnt offering, which is at the doorway of the tent of testimony (Lev 4:7). Specific fat and organs were then offered up on the altar of burnt offering with the ashes (Lev 6:11). The rest was taken "outside the camp" (ἔξω τῆς παρεμβολῆς) where it was burned. The priest would eat selected portions of the sacrifices in the first area of the holy place (Lev 6:15, 26, 29). The priestly path of movement in relation to the tabernacle areas in the activity of these offerings were continually repeated for the entire congregation, a leader, or the people of the land, with slight variations, where the elders would lay their hands on a bull (Lev 4:13–21), or the leader and people of the land would offer a male goat without defect (Lev 4:22–35).

130. The use of Χριστὸς for the priests continued throughout the history of Israel (cf. 2 Macc 1:10).

will always walk himself through the tabernacle ministry.¹³¹ God's judgment reveals the importance of both the obedience in the quality of the offerings, and the movement activities in the respective places of the tabernacle ministry.

By late in Samuel's life, Χριστὸς begins to embrace an application to kings serving before God and ruling over the people (1 Kgdms 12:5–6 LXX [1 Sam 12:5–6 MT]; cf. LXX 1 Kgdms 24:7, 11; 26:11, 16, 23; 2 Kgdms 1:14, 16; 2:5; 19:21; 23:1 [2 Chr 22:7 MT] 1 Sam 24:7, 11; 26:11, 16, 23; 2 Sam 1:14, 16; 2:5 [omitted MT], 19:21; 23:1; 2 Chr 22:7).¹³² Later the Chronicler applies the term to the nation of Israel (1 Chr 16:22 LXX/MT). The lexeme Χριστὸς appears ten times in the LXX Psalms and five times in the Prophets about the antitypes of David, kings of Israel and other nations, early patriarchs, the people Israel, and prophetic events of messianic fulfillment (Cf. LXX Pss 2:2; 17:51 [18:50 MT]; 19:7 [20:6 MT]; 27:8 [28:8 MT]; 83:10 [84:9 MT]; 88:39 [89:38 MT]; 88:52 [89:51 MT]; 131:10 [132:10 MT]; 131:17 [132:17 MT]; Isa 45:1; Lam 4:20; Dan 9:26; Amos 4:13 [MT different]; Hab 13:3).

The LXX translators chose Χριστὸς for two Hebrew words in the MT which point toward individuals chosen for special purposes of God, with a strong messianic typological force of both priest and king fulfillment.¹³³

---

131. The LXX states concerning the faithful priest, "Who will do all things that are in my heart and in my soul, and I will construct for him a faithful house, and he always will pass himself through before me my anointed priest" (ὃς πάντα τὰ ἐν τῇ καρδίᾳ μου καὶ τὰ ἐν τῇ ψυχῇ μου ποιήσει, καὶ οἰκοδομήσω αὐτῷ οἶκον πιστόν, καὶ διελεύσεται ἐνώπιον χριστοῦ μου πάσας τὰς ἡμέρας 2 Macc 7:35 LXX). The LXX translators choose a fut. tense "will go through" (διελεύσεται) for the Hithpa'ēl form of וְהִתְהַלֵּךְ, which from the lemma הלך with meaning based on context "to walk about for himself" that signifies intensive reflexive action, possibly repetitive. Gesenius, *Gesenius' Hebrew Grammar*, 149. Based on the contextual contrast with Eli's sons, this *walk* references the *path* or *way* the anointed priest travels before Yahweh in intercessory offerings for sins in the tabernacle. The priest who Yahweh raises up will always be faithful in this intercessory walk before him. The statement, as a likely reference to Samuel (1 Sam 12:5–6), foreshadows typologically the path through the heavens of the ministry of Christ in the tabernacle of all creation (cf. Heb 8:1–6). The priestly language of the text of 1 Sam 2:35 from the Greek LXX interweaves throughout the message of the Pastor (cf. Heb 2:17; 3:1–7, 14; 4:14; 5:5; 6:1; 9:8, 11, 14; 10:21, 23; 11:11).

132. However, this observation does not suggest the anointed ruler or king conceptualization came later. The Pastor speaks of Melchizedek, to whom Abraham gave tithes, as both a ruler and prince of Salem (Heb 7:1–2). This suggests imbalance in neglect of the sacrificial Christ. Also, cultic sacrifices had been a main observance of humanity since the beginning, as suggested by the offerings of Cain, Abel, and Noah (cf. Heb 6:1–2; 11:4).

133. *GHAIS*, "χριστός," 128. Muraoka lists: (1) נָגִיד (2), מָשִׁיחַ "chief, prince" (Dan

At the dawn of the NT, the Μεσσίας ("Messiah" [Aramaic]) foreshadowing dominated the hope of Israel (John 1:41; 3:28), Samaritans (John 4:25, 29), and eastern nations (Matt 2:1–2) mainly toward the sense of the earthly "anointed king" fulfillment (Matt 2:2; 22:42; Luke 3:15; 17:20; 19:11).[134] It would seem only a minority of Jews considered within the Levitical tabernacle typology, the "anointed priest" as "in the heavens" (ἐν τοῖς οὐρανοῖς) in an apocalyptic (*aiōn-field*) view beyond the earth (Heb 8:1–2; 9:11, 24; cf. Luke 2:25–32).[135] Some Jews, like the Sadducees, even denied the apocalyptic dualistic concepts of the eternal creation and the possibility of continued living in an eternal unseen kingdom after death (Mark 12:18–27; Acts 23:7–8).[136]

9:26). Cf. *HAL*, "645 ",מָשִׁיחַ; *HAL*, "נָגִיד," 667–68. Koehler glosses the lexeme from OT context for leaders appointed by God, which include princes, kings, officers, court officials, and the high priest.

134. John shares the lexeme Μεσσίας as a Greek transliteration of the Aramaic מְשִׁיחָא for the Hebrew מָשִׁיחַ as the Χριστὸς in first-century CE conversation concerning the anointed priest/king. See BDAG, "Μεσσίας," 635.

135. E.g., Jesus's main emphasis on his ministry centered on his role as fulfillment of the anointed priest (Matt 11:2–6; John 14:1–7). Ironically, he both was judged before Pilate over the secondary theme of anointed king (Matt 27:11–14; Luke 23:2; cf. Mark 15:32) and judged by the chief priest over his claim of his coming ministry as the anointed priest (Matt 26:59–68). This popular, imbalanced emphasis, mainly by leaders, about messianic king/priest understanding may explain Jesus's command for his disciples to not share their understanding of him as Χριστὸς (Matt 16:20; cf. Luke 4:41). In the balanced lens linked with a heavenly ministry at individual death and judgment, Caiaphas, the high priest, in his judgment of Jesus, pictures a reversal, where "from now on" (ἀπ' ἄρτι) Jesus would be the one judging Caiaphas on approach to God after death (Matt 26:64; cf. Matt 7:21–23; Mark 14:61–62). Also, concerning Jesus's fulfillment of king and kingdom, the eternal temple not made with hands references his ministry in the temple of the plural heavens of all creation, which he receives by rising from the dead as the anointed priest, after his sacrificial death (Rom 10:4–7). In Jesus's present ministry as the anointed priest, he comes at death with his angels to meet those who taste death (cf. Matt 16:12–28; Heb 9:28). He now builds a kingdom of his assembled believers that is not of this world (John 18:36). Chapter 4 unit F explores observations based upon antitype-type principles, that the destruction of the temple of Jesus's body in relation to the earthy temple does not *replace* the temple typology but *fulfills* both the daily and annual Day of Atonement sacrifices. Also, the Pastor follows this same rhetoric, whereby the sacrificial activities of the earthly covenant are no longer necessary due to incorrect typological teaching (Heb 8:13; cf. 2 Cor 3:14). Since Jesus has fulfilled the new covenant, as the necessary eternal/perpetual-*place* offering, and continues priest/king service in providing a better covenant relationship, the new covenant allows confidence for entrance into heaven at eternal/perpetual-*place* judgment after death for those who come by faith (Heb 7:23–25; Rom 6:8; 14:9).

136. The Sadducean rational conclusion mainly toward a moral, social, kingdom emphasis on earth, with no apocalyptic, *aiōn-field*, background reality creatively existent beyond this visible world, has continued as a messianic cosmic-*field* option since

Writing to interpret OT texts, NT authors deploy Χριστὸς 529 times.[137] These reinforce proper messianic OT concepts (Luke 24:26; John 1:25; Acts 3:18; 17:3; 26:23) and rhetorically explain differences in the contemporary imbalance and errant perceptions of both revelatory antitypes and their unseen eternal reality in type fulfillment (cf. Luke 23:35; John 7:26–27, 31; 12:34; 1 Cor 1:23).

When Χριστὸς stands alone 275 times in statements of the NT, the syncretic emphasis from freighted title designations dissipates toward a focus upon the OT foreshadowing of the anointed priest and king. In these statements, the priestly offering and intercession emphasis overshadows NT parenesis under the mantra of "the gospel" (Rom 15:19–20; 1 Cor 1:17). This fulfills in the self-offering events of Jesus's death and rising to God (Luke 24:26, 46; Rom 5:8) and then continues to those who believe—with access to Christ in the eternal kingdom at individual death (Phil 1:21–23; 1 Cor 15:22–23; 2 Cor 5:8).

Also, when Χριστὸς stands alone in the NT, the contextual sense of expectant king for the antitype of the earthly kingdom occurs infrequently. Most examples occur after the Pastor's message (cf. 1 Thess 4:16; Rev 1:5; 11:15; 12:10; 20:4, 6). This adds overwhelming weight that an audience, after considering the rhetoric and exposition of the NT, would understand Χριστὸς alone as a reference to the anointed, priestly ministry in the heavens in both his own past self-offering for sins of the people

---

before the writings and the gospel events of the NT. Further research is needed for the influence of this ancient view upon modern background *aiōn-field* vs. *cosmic-field* views (cf. Matt 23:13; 24:5; John 9:39; Acts 23:8; 1 Cor 3:19). Later Sadducean influence is addressed in chapter 3.

137. In the NT, Χριστὸς pairs with "Jesus" 226 times, "Lord" 90 times, "heaven(s)" 11 times, "Savior" 11 times, "God" 120 times, "Son" 34 times, and "Son of Man" 1 time. While functioning often with some force as titles, these designations are loaded with the freight from the OT which is often highlighted in their surrounding context; e.g., in Dan 7:13–14 the term "son of man" carries messianic kingly freight without mentioning Χριστὸς. Daniel was told that "the son of man" would travel up into heaven for presentation to the Ancient of Days. This presentation by others (angels) in heaven occurs before receiving the kingdom. Thereby, Jewish leaders by adding Ps 2 and other texts considered the "anointed king" as "the Son of God" (Matt 26:63; cf. Luke 4:41). Jesus integrates the "Son of Man" prophecy of suffering in death with the "anointed priest/king" in being "lifted up" representing both the death of the cross and fulfillment of Dan 7:13 in presentation to God in heaven, which could not be understood by those only viewing the "anointed king" sense (cf. John 12:34). Also, he builds his kingdom in heaven upon the confession that he is "the Christ, the Son of the living God" (John 16:16; cf. 11:27). Mark's gospel account runs under the title "the gospel of Jesus Christ, the Son of God" and details the suffering of the Savior (Mark 1:1) to counter expectations only for an "anointed king" upon the earth.

and his present continuing intercession at approach to God in their own reserved death and judgment.

The Pastor speaks Χριστὸς twelve times and the verb χρίω (chriō) one time. The verb introduces the concept of God's anointing in a LXX quotation of Ps 44:7–8 (45:6–7 MT) concerning God's judgment and enthronement of the antitype of the earthly king who becomes an oil of exultation to his people.[138] The Pastor also uses Χριστὸς in Heb 5:5 with links to Ps 2:7 LXX/OT and Ps 109:4 LXX (110:4 MT) to support that Jesus was God's chosen king-priest who did not choose himself.[139]

He also uses the noun Χριστὸς in both his MCS and his final UC of Heb 13:20–21. He integrates the two senses of Χριστὸς in type as both "anointed king" and "anointed priest."[140] Further, he implies the Χριστὸς

---

138. The latter portion of the verse states, "For this reason, God, your God, anointed you an oil of exultation beyond your companions" (Ps 44:8 LXX). The implication of the acc. case ἔλαιον ("oil") receiving the action of God's anointing, implies the king becomes God's oil in a metaphoric sense to bring exultation to the people in an eternal kingdom that loves righteousness and hates lawlessness. Chapter 4 unit A UPt1–2 (Heb 1:5–12) explores setting of the discourse in Heb 1:3–14 that provides details of the Pastor's MCS concerning the death, judgment, salvation, and enthronement of Jesus by God before his resurrection and ascension for eternal participation as Priest/King. Thereby, Jesus, as God's Son at the right hand of the throne, becomes an oil of exultation (Heb 1:9) to those who believe on him for purification of sins in their own death and judgment.

139. The Pastor interprets both senses of eternal king and priest as both prophetically and simultaneously beginning fulfillment within the events of death to resurrection (see appendix 1, fig. 1).

140. The Pastor, in his main argument and parenesis, deploys "Christ" alone nine times until his concluding summary remarks in Heb 10:10, where he speaks, "By which a will, we are people having been made holy through the offering of the body of Jesus Christ once for all." Two other deployments of "Jesus Christ" are Heb 13:8 and 13:21. This linking integrates the flesh offering of the Son of God and the ministry of the anointed king/priest. Regarding his singular usage in Heb 3:6, the Pastor initially integrates "Christ" and "Son" in the house of all created things of which Moses was a faithful antitype in the tabernacle service (cf. Heb 8:5). In Heb 3:14 he tells his audience they had become fellow partakers in Christ "if we should hold fast the beginning of the substance-reality until the completion." By faith believers follow the reality of Christ through death and judgment into the final eternal kingdom. In Heb 6:1–2, concerning foundation matters in teaching and maturity, the Pastor lists "the word of the beginning of Christ" as a reference to the traditional teachings of "Christ" from before the time of Moses to "the beginning." He asserts that the foundational teaching in the sacrificial system from Abel to Melchizedek to Aaron (see initial discussion this section above for Aaron and Levitical priesthood) contained repentance from dead works, faith toward God, ceremonial washings in purity laws, laying on of hands in transference of sins, and the rising up of the dead in eternal/perpetual-*place* judgment at death. Heb 9:11, 14, and 24 detail the elementary typology of the anointed Priest/King in death to resurrection.

concept even motivates the faith of Moses in his decision regarding his relationship to Pharaoh (Heb 11:26). These observations concerning Χριστὸς reveal that the choice in the MCS serves the Pastor as much more than a title. It invokes a foundation of antitype sacrificial teaching from the beginning concerning God's offering for sin, with promises of Christ appearing at eternal/perpetual-*place* judgment.

"Once" (ἅπαξ)

For syntactic analysis of ἅπαξ, see the same section above. In the first statement, ἅπαξ, as an ordinal adverb, modifies "to die" (ἀπόκειται) but in the second corresponding statement, ἅπαξ modifies the adjectival ptc. "who being offered" (προσενεχθεὶς) which modifies Χριστὸς (see appendix 3).

The use of "once" with the correlative conjunction "just as . . . so" in connecting the two statements in correspondence has significance for Χριστὸς in the activity to follow. As shown in the next section, Jesus fulfills the reservation of death and judgment, and functions in priestly activity of being both the offering and priest in intercession for sins.

"Who Being Offered" (προσενεχθεὶς)

The Pastor's choice "to bring" (προσφέρω) appears 161 times in the LXX and the cognate verbal noun "offering" (προσφορά).[141] Verbally, these lexemes usually refer, generally, to the offering of gifts or an appeal to another.[142] In the sacrificial tradition of the LXX, the προσφέρω deploys

---

141. GELS, "προσφέρω," 492. Cf. L&N, "προσεγγίζω," 1.191.

142. E.g., in the first LXX translator choice, the Lord says to Cain concerning his rejection of his offering, "If you should offer rightly, but not apportion rightly, do you not sin? Be quiet! Its recourse is toward you, and you will master of it" (Gen 4:7 LXX). For the LXX translators, it appears the antecedent of the gen. "it" (αὐτοῦ) was perceived as the sinful offering that was not correctly offered to show the proper symbolism of eternal matters in worship. The MT implies the need for the correct symbolism of a sacrifice "raising up" to God and translates, "Do you not desire raising up? And if you do not do right, sin in regard to the entrance of the offering lies down toward you. And you will rule in it [sin]" (Gen 4:7). The Pastor also implies that the rejection of Cain's sacrificial offering was because it did not properly symbolize a testimony of faith in the ministry of the anointed Χριστὸς (Heb 11:4). In Heb 6:1–2, the Pastor lists six foundation teachings of the priestly sacrificial offerings involving "the beginning word [speech-action] of the Christ" (Heb 6:1). He asserts that proper foundational teaching from the beginning of the sacrificial system embraces these six things, which would include Abel and Cain, Melchizedek, and Aaron. These are (1) "repentance of dead

69 times in Leviticus and 31 times in Numbers alone, with 30 times associated with the technical language of the ministry of the "anointed priest" who presents and offers the required sacrifices up to the Lord for the atonement of sins.[143] The verbal noun προσφορά does not appear in the Law and only appears once in the Psalms (Ps 39:7 LXX [40:7 MT]).[144]

The NT authors choose "bring, present, offer" (προσφέρω) forty-one times and "offering, gift" (προσφορά) nine times. Excluding Hebrews, προσφέρω only refers to the technical activity of the anointed priest two times, where usage still retains the same priestly sense in word meaning as in the LXX and MT.[145] The verbal noun προσφορά, outside of Hebrews in each deployment by Paul, embraces either the sacrificial system of the law or the symbolism of Christ in it (Acts 21:26; 24:17; Rom 15:16; Eph 5:2).

The Pastor speaks προσφέρω twenty times in the same first-century CE general sense of the required movements of the anointed high priests in ministry both in the "continual, daily," (תמיד Heb 8:3–4; 10:11) and the annual "Day of Atonement" (יום כפרים Heb 9:7, 25; 10:1).[146] He also chooses the verbal noun προσφορά five times, all immediately after his discourse MCS of unit F UC of Heb 9:27–28. All placements of προσφορά in the post MCS support of discourse unit F Pt4–Pt6 (Heb10:1–18)

---

works," (2) "faith upon God," (3) "teaching of ceremonial washings," (4) "laying on of hands," (5) "raising up of the dead," and (6) "eternal/perpetual-*place* judgment." The Pastor claims Jesus has fulfilled the earthly, sacrificial typology with its two covenants by the higher priesthood of Melchizedek (Heb 7:1–28), a continuance of the sacrifices of the priests in the days of Isaac (cf. Gen 47:22), and even Abel's sacrificial testimony of his faith in the beginning (cf. Heb 12:24).

143. E.g., "This is the offering of Aaron and his sons, they will bring to the Lord in the day in which you should anoint them" (Lev 6:13 LXX [6:20 MT]).

144. This textual choice in the Psalm by the LXX translators did not miss the attention of the Pastor, who quotes the text as part of his rhetoric.

145. E.g., Jesus told the leper after his healing, "but *please* go! *Please* show yourself! to the priest and *please* offer! concerning your purification, that instructed by Moses, for a testimony to them" (Mark 1:44; cf. Acts 21:26). Only Hebrews elaborates on the symbolic details of the sacrificial offerings of the "anointed priest," but other NT authors assume the same common first-century CE understanding by their audience. For discussion of the background of priestly offerings for the ritual impurity of leprosy, see Thiessen, *Jesus*, 43–68.

146. The scope of the antitype offerings emphasized by the Pastor goes beyond the Day of Atonement to embrace all details of earthly covenant typology back to the beginning of the teaching of Χριστός (Heb 6:1–2). For recent interpretative issues surrounding the Day of Atonement, see Heike and Tobias, *Day of Atonement*. Chapter 4 units D–F discourse analysis explores the antitype spatial-temporal relationships of the daily and annual offerings with the types portrayed in the heavens.

frame in a sacrificial contextual language. In this argument, the Pastor summarizes the "offering" of the "Christ" that God restored at judgment is a "body" (σῶμα Heb 10:5), rather than antitypes about his ministerial self-offering that only picture the type of Christ's heavenly body rise to ministry (cf. Heb 10:5, 8, 10, 14, 18).[147]

The Pastor emphasizes this priestly typological interpretation of προσφέρω and προσφορά in two LXX texts. The first is Ps 39:6–7 LXX (40:6–7 MT) in Heb 10:5–9. After the negativizing of earthly sacrifices, he interprets as messianic the transition of verses Ps 39:6–7 LXX. He views these as the personal statements of one coming physically into the cosmos to do God's will, which in turn foreshadowed God's desire for both his offering and priestly mediation later fulfilled by the body of Jesus.[148]

The second of the Pastor's authoritative links in Heb 10:12 connects the priestly movement of προσφέρω with Ps 109:1 LXX (110:1 MT). He claims, in contrast to the repeated ministry of the antitypes, "but this one, who having offered one sacrifice for sins for all time, sat down at the right hand of God."[149]

The lexeme προσφέρω ("to offer") only appears in the unit F UC of the main discourse unit MCS. However, the activity subtopic does introduce the main discourse unit in Heb 5:1 and continues fifteen times throughout the priestly parenesis in the second main section STr2 (Heb 5:1–10:18). In the third main section S3 (Heb 10:26–13:21), it appears two times in his testimonials of Heb 11 and again in Heb 12 about God's

---

147. The Pastor introduces this final discourse unit of the second main section with the typological language contrast of "shadow" (σκιά) and "image" (εἰκόνα Heb 10:1). He continues to signal a typological lens between the earthly sacrificial ministry symbolizing the two-fold ministry by the anointed priest and the true reality therein portrayed about the two heavenly covenants of promise and fulfillment by Jesus as the Christ.

148. Chapter 4 unit F Upt5 (Heb 10:5–14) explores possible OT interpretation by the Pastor that the use of the Greek lexeme "ear" (ὠτίον Ps 39:6 LXX) and Hebrew "ear" (אזנים Ps 40:6 BHS) functions figuratively in synecdoche as part of a whole human person with a "body" (σῶμα Heb 10:5), who after his fleshly offering in death receives from God a spiritual body to become an interceding eternal/perpetual-*place* priest continually coming into the "cosmos" (κόσμος) for approaching believers.

149. Chapter 3 explores the semantics of the attributive ptc. προσενεχθεὶς forming a dependent clause which modifies "this one" (οὗτος). Some manuscripts have "he" (αυτος) for an adverbial participle phrase, "but *he* having offered one sacrifice for sins for all time, sat down at the right hand of God." Neither syntactical choice changes meaning of the semantic function. Chapter 4 explores the discourse analysis concerning Jesus's atonement offering as complete when he sits down for priestly intercession a moment after death.

offering of himself as a Father in training believers as sons in the ministry of Jesus.[150]

The Pastor utilizes προσφέρω in two faith testimonials. The first testimonial is that of Abel in Gen 4:7, whose correct offering in worship testified to his faith. The second faith testimonial appears in Heb 11:17–19, stating, "By faith Abraham has offered Isaac, when being tested, and was offering his only Son, the one [Abraham] receiving the promise, to whom it was said that, 'in Isaac a seed will be called,' having himself considered that even God is able to raise up from the dead people, by which he [Abraham] received him [Isaac] back in a parable."[151] For the Pastor, Abraham considered that God was able to raise up *from* the dead *people* [cf. resurrection *of* the dead, Heb 6:2, i.e., all dead people], one offered as the promised "seed" (σπέρμα) of the covenant (Gen 22:18; cf. Heb 2:16).[152]

---

150. E.g., "You endure with respect to training, God offers himself to you as a son, for what son does a father not train?" (Heb 12:7). It is best to keep the priestly offering sense of the lexeme προσφέρω consistent with the rest of the Pastor's message. With "God" as the nominative subject, then προσφέρεται can portray either the pres. pass. "God is offering to you as a son," or mid. "God offers himself to you as a son." In context, the middle voice carries better the weight of God's now speaking through his Son at the right hand of God, who presently trains sons in a better priesthood of the new covenant (Heb 12:1–17).

151. Chapter 4 unit D2′ SbPt2a (Heb 11:17–19) explores this activity of προσφέρω, where both Abraham and Isaac in Gen 22 testify as an antitype of the type of the anointed Christ, without Isaac having to die. God provides a substitute ram, which reveals the provision of the Christ, and which bestows continued living to Isaac (Gen 22:8–4). The Pastor interprets Isaac's continued living by substitutionary atonement and their belief in rising *from* the dead one offered, as a "parable" (παραβολή Heb 11:19). For cognate meanings for parable, see BDAG, "παραβολή," 759. The Pastor interprets Gen 22 as both typology with Christ and a narrative parable, with importance to illustrate heavenly truth.

152. Abraham understood the messianic typology through the testimony of the sacrificial offering ministry of the anointed priest, that was available from the beginning. According to the Pastor in Heb 6:1–2, part of the beginning teaching of the sacrificial system of the word of the beginning of Christ was "rising up *of* the dead people" (ἀναστάσεως νεκρῶν Heb 6:2). It is probable that Abraham's faith involved more than just Isaac's raising up in flesh from the dead but included both the raising up *of* all dead to God (including Isaac) for judgment and the hope of the one raising up *from* the dead concerning the promised "seed" who would fulfill the sacrificial/priestly Christ typified in the sacrifices before the law and Aaron's anointed priesthood (Gal 3:16, 19, 29; Acts 3:35). Abraham's faith in the sacrifice of Christ, that his own sins would be atoned by one able to rise up *from* the dead, enabled him to perceive the promised "seed" upon Isaac and the same sequence of raising up to God in completion of heavenly living with a spirit body form (Heb 6:15; cf. 7:26; see appendix 1, fig. 2). Chapters 3 and 4 explore if this rising sequence, as determined pre-cosmic in heaven, and revealed by God from

This supports a conclusion for the Pastor's choice of προσφέρω as appropriate for a MCS. The technical term functions as an attributive ptc. modifying Christ, to compare the offering of Christ as equivalent to the first statement's assertion of death and subsequent judgment. The implication of the two statements in the correlative conjunction is that Christ, also in his offering to God, endured the same death and personal judgment to follow reserved for all people. The Pastor's next syntactical unit, by choice of an adverbial inf. of purpose shares the reason Christ endured the same fate of death and judgment.

"For the Purpose to Bear Many Sins" (εἰς τὸ πολλῶν ἀνενεγκεῖν)

The Pastor's choice "bring, carry, bear, offer" (ἀναφέρω) appears 155 times in the LXX. Most usage links it with technical ministry language to sacrificial offerings.[153] The term can refer either to the one bringing the offering for himself or to an anointed priest who, in intercession for collective "sin," brings an offering for all the people.[154] As part of the ritual in the ancient sacrificial observances, from the beginning of the inhabited world inherited by Israel, one would lay hands upon the offering in a symbolic transfer of sins for atonement (Gen 22:6; Exod 29:25; Lev 1:4, 10; 4:4–5, 15, 24, 33; 8:14, 18; 9:22; 16:21; cf. Heb 6:1–2). In the sacrificial usage of ἀναφέρω in the LXX, ἀναφέρω broadly embraces the bringing of varied kinds of offerings to the Lord. The meaning force often

---

the beginning of man's sin, initiates a very little while after death at judgment, and before return to earth for ministry with Jesus. It is this concept that enabled Jesus to speak about the place of "Abraham's bosom" (Luke 16:22).

153. Over half of these contextually link with the acc., either "whole burnt offerings" or "presentation of whole burnt offerings." For distinction, see LSJ, "ὁλοκάρπωμα," "ὁλοκάρπωσις," 1217. In Ezek 43:24 the LXX translators use for Ezekiel's offering instructions both general terms προσφέρω (previous section) and ἀναφέρω. The LXX translators leaned towards ἀναφέρω for the bringing of the whole burnt offerings and προσφέρω for offering activities involving approach to the presence of the Lord. Around fifty uses ἀναφέρω also link with an acc. θυσία ("sacrifice") as a broad term for various kinds of sacrifices specified in recorded OT instructions (cf. 1 Kgdms 6:15 LXX [1 Sam 6:15 MT]). With either term, the implication, figuratively for the one offering, is that the smoke of the offering approaches or ascends up to God to atone for sin and make one pleasing to God (cf. Gen 8:20–21; Num 18:17; Judg 20:38). For an example contextually linking these cultic technical terms, David says after his confession of sins and change of heart, "Then you will be pleased with a sacrifice of righteousness, then they will offer up upon the altar your young bulls" (Ps 50:21 LXX [51:21 MT]). David recognized God is pleased when the offeror and offering are right before him.

154. GELS, "ἁμαρτία," 22.

contextually included the imagery of symbolically bearing the sins of the one making the offering for atonement of God's judgment upon sin (cf. Deut 1:17).[155]

The Greek NT deploys ἀναφέρω just ten times, with broad sacrificial meaning, as in the LXX.[156] For example, outside of Hebrews the word carries the imagery of Abraham bringing up Isaac for sacrifice (cf. Jas 2:21). Yet, it is interesting that both Matthew and Mark choose it from many other cognate options to describe Jesus taking his chosen disciples up on the mountain for his transfiguration before them (cf. Matt 17:1; Mark 9:2).[157] Similarly, Luke links the term to descriptions of Jesus being brought up into heaven at his ascension (Luke 24:51).[158] Also, Peter links the sacrificial term with the eternal spiritual realm in the context of following Jesus in suffering and possible martyrdom (1 Pet 2:5) in following the movement of his pattern in being brought up to God in death (1 Pet 2:24; cf. 1 Pet 3:18, [προσάγω as cognate of προσφέρω in previous section]). In the NT, ἀναφέρω operates as a specialized term for linking earthly people in transfiguration, ascension, or spiritual living in temporal-spatial movement in similar ways, following Jesus's example in being brought up to God in the eternal heaven.[159]

The Pastor crafts ἀναφέρω three times and ἁμαρτία twenty-five times. The problem of "sin" (ἁμαρτία) of the people and its priestly

---

155. Moses instructed appointed judges in Israel "to bring" (ἀναφέρω) matters of difficult judgment to him for the "judgment" (κρίσις) of God. By continuing the priestly and offering observances in place from the beginning of people, Israel in their Law greatly expanded the typology of the atonement of God's judgment of sin.

156. BDAG, "ἀναφέρω," 75; L&N, "ἀναφέρω," 1.533.

157. There are thirty-five cognates of the Greek root φέρω found 256 times in the Greek NT. The mountain imagery has apocalyptic connections (Heb 12:18–22; cf. Ezek 40:2; Rev 21:10; and 2 Bar. 76.3; 1 En. 25.3; 77.4–5, 87). The mountain symbolized God's eternal separated and restricted domain of heaven before the later typology of the tabernacle or temple. Cf. Morales, *Cult and Cosmos*; Morales, *Tabernacle Pre-Figured*; Tănase, "From 'Veil' (κάλυμμα) Theology," 119–82, esp. 122n9. Tănase asserts, "The Tabernacle was meant to be a living extension of Mount Sinai. During the theophany, the mount was separated into three distinct zones of increasing degrees of holiness and restriction of access."

158. E.g., Luke's broader application to Jesus's later bodily ascension indicates later interpretative meaning with emphasis upon the movement between earth and heaven that Jesus bodily opened for mankind in the gospel sequence from death to resurrection.

159. In the NT, only the Pastor links "sin" (ἁμαρτία) and specifically "to bear" (ἀναφέρω) as messianic sacrificial technical terms (cf. Heb 7:27; 9:28). Others use near cognates for other details.

Atonement and the Logic of Resurrection in Hebrews 9:27–28

sacrificial purification and atonement before God thematically occupies his expressed thoughts (Heb 1:3; 2:17; 4:15; 5:1, 3; 7:27; 8:12; 9:26, 28; 10:1–18; 13:11). The term captures a place in his introduction and several DUC including the MCS. To all this, adding the example of Moses's faith in his choice of Christ above the pleasures of sin of Egypt in Heb 11:25–26 demonstrates its importance as a choice for his MCS.

The Pastor speaks eleven cognates of the root φέρω forty-seven times, which includes introductory subtopic usage in the DI (Heb 1:1–4) and three out of six exposition DUC in this sermon, to express the imagery of both Christ's and the believers movement at death between the temporary earth and God in heaven.[160] Functioning as an adverbial infinitive of purpose, the pres. inf. ἀναφέρειν (Heb 7:27) registers the present sacrificial offerings of the earthly priests.[161] For contrast, the aorist inf. ἀνενεγκεῖν (Heb 9:28) refers to Jesus's finished onetime offering of himself up to God. In both deployments as sacrificial technical terms, ἀναφέρω twice links in sacrificial language imagery the offering of a symbolic substitutionary sacrifice being brought up to God for judgment of "sins" (ἁμαρτίας) "for many *people*," (εἰς τὸ πολλῶν Heb 7:27; 9:28; cf. 9:26). The Pastor's allusion in these to Isa 53:11–12 connects prophetically with the suffering servant motif popular in the NT for supporting both the offering and anointed priestly work of Christ.[162] When added to other expressions of spatial movement of "transfer" (μετατίθημι), "approach" (προσέρχομαι), "enter" (εἰσέρχομαι), "entrance" (εἴσοδος), and "the way of the holy-*places*" (τὴν τῶν ἁγίων ὁδὸν Heb 9:8), the evidential weight of descriptive continued living movement in the spiritual reality after death increases.

---

160. The theme of "bringing" in cognates of the root φέρω begins in Heb 1:3–4 of the DI. The Pastor deploys cognates of φέρω in the discourse unit conclusions of Heb 7:25–28; 9:27–28; and 10:15–18. Chapter 4 explores the function of cognates of φέρω in the discourse unit conclusions. An interesting research topic to consider is whether Jesus bears sinners or sins in his movement to heaven. Both senses have good probability in that first he brings on himself the "sins" (ἁμαρτίας) of the people once for all in substitutionary atonement, so that at fleshly death of people he brings the "sinners" (ἁμαρτωλούς) who believe on him, to God, since their sins are atoned by their faith in God's ability.

161. *GGBB*, 590–91. Wallace states the infinitive of purpose is used to indicate the purpose or goal of the action of the controlling verb to answer the question why. It looks ahead to the anticipated and intended result and explains the why Christ allowed himself "being offered" (προσενεχθεὶς) sacrificially? So that in death, he might bring himself to God in substitution for the sins of the people.

162. Guthrie, "Hebrews," 919–93.

Table 8—LXX δεύτερος with Object of Proposition ἐκ

2 Kgdms 14:29	ἐκ δευτέρου	Absalom sent out a second time
3 Kgdms 19:7	ἐκ δευτέρου	angel returned a second time
1 Chr 29:22	ἐκ δευτέρου	Solomon made king a second time
Tob 1:22	ἐκ δευτέρου	set him down from the second position
1 Macc 9:1	ἐκ δευτέρου	Demetrius a second time to send
Jon 3:1	ἐκ δευτέρου	word of the Lord came a second time
Hag 2:20	ἐκ δευτέρου	word of the Lord came a second time
Zech 4:12	ἐκ δευτέρου	Zechariah answered a second time
Isa 61:7	ἐκ δευτέρας	Israel will inherit the land a second time
Jer 1:13	ἐκ δευτέρου	word of the Lord came a second time
Dan 2:7	ἐκ δευτέρου	Daniel answered a second time

"From a Second Place without Sin" (ἐκ δευτέρου χωρὶς ἁμαρτίας)

The ordinal adjective δεύτερος appears 217 times in the LXX with 11 occurrences as an object with the preposition ἐκ.[163] As the object of proposition ἐκ, it operates as second in order of an ordinal event, modifying the subject in repeated verbal activity upon an object or a continued state.[164] The gen. phrase ἐκ δευτέρου linked with ἅπαξ functions as an idiom in shortened form for the understanding—out from the first event then a second event.[165] The space and time of the subject, repeated ordinal

---

163. *GELS*, "δεύτερος," 111. Muraoka glosses the LXX lexeme usage as "a. *second in order*," "b. *the other* of a pair," and "c. adv. δεύτερον 'for a second time.'" E.g., during Abraham's offering of Isaac, the LXX states, "And an angel of the Lord called to Abraham a second time from heaven" (Gen 22:15 LXX/MT).

164. BDAG, "δεύτερος," 220–21; L&N, "δεύτερος," 1.606; *EDNT*, "δεύτερος," 1.291–92.

165. Cf. Porter, *Idioms*, 154–56. Porter illustrates the preposition ἐκ has the restricted sense of "out of" as opposed to its partial synonym ἀπό with basic sense of "out from." *Pace* Moule, *Idiom Book*, 71–74. The preposition ἐκ maintains relationship with the object that modifies the subject it governs. In ordinal or cardinal enumerated events, the subject can only be "second" or beyond if there exists a relationship to the first event of a subject. Porter notes the locative has the basic sense of "movement out of," from which the temporal and instrumental senses are metaphoric extensions. He states of the temporal use, "One of the specific applications of physical or spatial movement is temporal. The preposition ἐκ may be used of a restricted time from which someone or something has moved." In the instrumental use, ἐκ overlaps with the locative to indicate origin or source as the cause or agent which something comes out.

activity, and any object acted upon determines by the context.¹⁶⁶ Also, it carries both adjectival and adverbial weight by indicating a second ordinal event in space and time both for the subject (adjectival) and the main verb (adverbial).¹⁶⁷ As noted, in Tob 1:22 (table 8), the second ordinal event can be repeated and durative for each time the named parties sat down, as a statement of an exercised position.¹⁶⁸

In the NT, "second" (δεύτερος) appears forty-three times, with five of these in Hebrews.¹⁶⁹ Several NT uses craft the phrase ἐκ δευτέρου to identify a successive corresponding ordinal event in a different space and time. In the NT, any space and time emphasis of the successive second

---

166. BNTS, 44. The gen. is usually related to a noun while the acc. is usually related to a verb.

167. Robertson, *Grammar*, 549–50. Robertson states concerning Greek idioms, "But the Greek uses the adjective often where the English has the adverb. That is, the Greek prefers the personal connection of the adjective with the subject to the adverbial connection with the verb." He further states concerning prepositional phrases, "These adjuncts have the substantial force of adverbs."

168. LSJ, "δεύτερος," 382. Lidell lists the sense of second in order or rank. The literary ability and functionality as both adjectival and adverbial force carries great weight in the exploration of the thesis herein. As the phrase ἐκ δευτέρου χωρὶς ἁμαρτίας serves the Pastor in Heb 9:28 adverbially, then the second ordinal event is the appearing of Christ discussed in the next section. As adjectival, then the phrase modifies Christ with meaning discussed in the previous section (see appendix 3). In an adjectival ordinal event, Christ "from a second place without sin" appears in his second ordinal ministry in a repeated and durative *position* of the anointed high priest as intercessor in the eternal/perpetual-*places* (Heb 9:24; cf. 7:25). His first ordinal event as Christ was manifesting from heaven as the offering of sacrifice for sin (Heb 9:26). The first and second ordinal events of Christ as offering, and intercessor [presentation and participation] theologically align with the overall theme of the Pastor's argument. Furthermore, when the phrase is taken adverbially in modification of appearing a second time, then the second ordinal event is Christ's appearing a second time *positionally* in the repeated and durative activity of the anointed priest. It is not impossible that this would include a sub focus on the onetime event of the second coming to earth. Chapter 3 background theology and chapter 4 discourse analysis of syntactical relationships explores for a second coming theme of the anointed king on earth in the Pastor's MCS, the other DUC, or his parenesis. It also further investigates the presence the two-fold work of *Christ* in salvation as both offering and anointed priest for the sins of the people to bring them to a place without sin in the holy of holies of heaven, as the contextual comparison.

169. BDAG, "δεύτερος," 220–21. Bauer makes an interesting point of the contrast in Jude 5, commenting, "τὸ δ. ἀπώλεσεν *the second time he destroyed* Jd 5 (NRSV renders 'afterward', but this is not to be construed as a difft. mng. for Jude's use of δ.: in Jude's pregnant statement the point lies in a contrast between two special moments of display of divine power, one in salvation, and the second in destruction)." With the Exodus motif event of Israel as an antitype, Jude's emphasis as possibly on the importance of faith in salvation for entrance into the type of the eternal/perpetual-*place* kingdom needs further investigation.

ordinal event, if any inequality at all, determines by the context surrounding the idiom and not the idiom itself. The adverbial unit "without sin" (χωρὶς ἁμαρτίας) only occurs in Hebrews (cf. Heb 4:15; 9:28).

For the Pastor's syntax in Heb 9:28, the idiomatic usage of ἐκ δευτέρου both adjectivally modifies Χριστὸς and adverbially governs the verbal activity of "will appear" (ὀφθήσεται, see appendix 3). It can translate as either "a second *time*," "from a second *place*," or "from a second *position*," since the idiom simply specifies a successive second ordinal event in space and time. Any time (when), location (where), or position (subject) specificity for the second ordinal event must come from the surrounding context and related correspondence to the first ordinal event and not reader presuppositions.[170]

The Pastor choses the ordinal δεύτερος five times. In Heb 8:7 the choice identifies the second *ministry*.[171] This second *ministry* does not identify only a onetime event at a particular place but a durative recurring position of Christ available in ministry by God. Next, in Heb 9:3 the ordinal δεύτερος identifies the place behind the veil called the holy of holies.[172] In his third use before Heb 9:28, the Pastor deploys the ordinal for the second place/position in ministry of the high priest once a year.[173]

---

170. Translators usually render ἐκ δευτέρου as "a second time." However, for many, this indicates a presupposition that the second ordinal event is the second coming "once" to earth. Further exploration herein investigates the possibility that the corresponding summary statements of Heb 9:27–28 compare the death of people with the death of Christ. The living people waiting in the MCS context optionally could point to people *after* death and judgment and not those who have yet to die, who anticipate the described summary event of the previous exposition. The MCS point could sum that Christ appears as mediator during the judgment reserved for people *after* death (Heb 6:18–20; 7:25; 10:19–20), and not the unrelated corresponding truth that Christ comes in the distant future *for those living* to complete that salvation process (cf. Heb 11:39–40). The research considers that since the second coming to earth is never explicitly mentioned, perhaps Heb 10:25, 37 has more contextual weight for parenesis referring to Jesus continual coming at death for believers.

171. The Pastor states, "For if the first *covenant ministry* there was blameless, a place should not be sought for a second *covenant ministry*" (Heb 8:7). The Pastor's linking of "place" (τόπος) with "covenant" (διαθήκης) in context implies a durative force that applies an available position of relationship to multiple people, recurring over time to those who come to God in faith.

172. The Pastor comments in his parenesis on the tabernacle, "But after the second curtain a tabernacle, the one being called the holy of holies" (Heb 9:3). He speaks of a second dwelling place hidden beyond sight that typologically represents the highest heaven of God's dwelling. There God is pleased to receive an offering of Christ himself once for sin (Heb 9:26).

173. "But into the second place once a year the high priest alone, he enters not without blood, for himself and the sins committed in ignorance of the people" (Heb

Therefore, when the Pastor, in modification of the subject of Christ, speaks ἐκ δευτέρου in Heb 9:28, the audience could more likely sense understanding "from a second *place/position*" in the recurrent ministry of his new second covenant ministry from heaven. Even the Pastor's summation in Heb 10:9 can follow the same use of the ordinal about the second covenant stating, "He takes away the first to establish the second." The ordinal δεύτερος does not appear in any LXX quotation or any of the Pastor's historical narrative except that of the ministry of Christ.

The adverbial modifier "without sin" governs what it follows. In the only other use in the NT, the Pastor crafts the phrase in the summation of Heb 4:15 stating, "For we have not a high priest who is not continually able to sympathize with our weaknesses, but with all things in correspondence to likeness without sin." The statement claims Jesus Christ, as high priest in ministry, experiences without sin every weakness in all things and man's likeness. This strongly corresponds to Heb 9:28. The *subject* of Christ, in his second ordinal position *activity*, "will appear from a second place without sin" of the holy of holies at the right hand of the throne of God as high priest. The *objects* of this activity are people eagerly awaiting salvation at their individual judgment a very little while after death (Heb 10:37). The adverbial χωρὶς ἁμαρτίας does not apply to those eagerly awaiting salvation as discussed in the previous section. Salvation does not imply that those waiting are without sin but that their judged sin was atoned by Jesus, so that, they as holy people might enter the place of heaven without sin (holy of holies) brought by the priest without sin appearing from heaven (cf. John 5:24).[174]

9:7). In the Pastor's typology, Christ in the second place of the holy of holies is given a second position as anointed priest to continually minister for the sins of the people. He links the second position (Christ as intercessor of anointed priest) with the second place (holy of holies) in the second relationship (new covenant). These connections imply a possible correspondence in the first position (Christ as offering) with the first place (holy place) in the first covenant (sacrificial atonement).

174. The NASB awkward translation, "without *reference to* sin," may miss the point of judgment after death. It infers that there is no address about personal sin after death when Jesus appears. This idea is foreign to the previous teaching of the Pastor and other NT writers (cf. Heb 4:12; 6:2; 10:26–31; 12:23; 13:4; Matt 12:36; John 3:18; 5:22–30; 12:48; 16:8; Acts 17:31; 24:25; Rom 2:3, 5, 16; 14:10; 1 Cor 4:5; 11:29, 31–32; 2 Cor 5:10; 2 Thess 1:5; 2:12; 1 Tim 5:24; 2 Tim 4:1, 8; 1 Pet 4:5).

"Will Appear" (ὀφθήσεται)

LXX translators implement the fut. pass. verb "to become visible, make appearance, present oneself" (ὀφθήσεται) 22 times.[175] Forms of its lemma ὁράω ("see, observe, look at") are used 1754 times. The pass. of ὁράω (*horaō*) does not link directly with "Christ" as subject, but it does link with "LORD" as subject in the pass. voice 16 times.[176] In Leviticus, the LXX translators chose the fut. pass. ὀφθήσεται to describe Moses's promise that the "LORD" will appear to them after Aaron's "approach" (προσέρχομαι) to the "altar" as anointed priest, to make offerings for the atonement of the sins of the people (Lev 9:4, 6; cf. Gen 22:14; 3 Kgdms 9:2 [1 Kings 9:2 MT]).[177]

In the NT, the fut. pass. ὀφθήσεται occurs only in Hebrews and the pass. voice only occurs twenty-two times.[178] In these, the pass. form of ὁράω refers multiple times to the appearances of Jesus to his disciples after his resurrection and sitting in enthronement (cf. Luke 24:34; Acts 13:31; 1 Cor 15:5–8; 1 John 1:1, 3). These records fulfill his promise in John 16:22 to appear to them. Jesus also appears to angels at his vindication

---

175. GELS, "ὁράω," 411–412.

176. The Pastor integrates mainly the messianic LXX terms "Son" and "Lord" with "Christ," and "Jesus" in his message (see appendix 2, table 1 "Words in Hebrews Linked with God"). He begins with "Son" (Heb 1:2), enfolds "Lord" by a quotation from the LXX (Heb 1:10), and follows with "Jesus" fulfillment (2:9). He then adds "Christ" as "Son" (Heb 3:6) in the positive comparison of both the house of Moses and Jesus. The messianic term "Christ" when introduced implies the context of both his self-offering and ministry of his anointed priesthood. Such integration may provide the foundation in the MCS that "Christ . . . will appear." Jesus himself may make the same claim in John 8:56–58 as the Lord in the OT historical context appearing to Abraham (cf. Gen 12:7). If found plausible, such observations could provide substantial weight against an isolated temporal ordinal limitation for the lexeme ὁράω, since, in the LXX, the Lord appears in the narrative multiple times (cf. 3 Kgdms 9:2 LXX [1 Kgs 9:2 MT]).

177. The early chapters of Leviticus contain much of the Pastor's thematic cultic language. Philip, *Leviticus in Hebrews*. See Philip's appendix 4 for the multitude of quotations, allusions, and echoes taken from Leviticus. Cf. Gen 22:14 LXX/OT where Abraham named the place where the Lord provided the ram in substitute for the offering of Isaac (cf. Acts 7:2). The text reads, "And Abraham called the name of the place there, 'the LORD saw,' so that they should say, 'In the mountain the LORD appeared'" (Gen 22:14 LXX). The aorist pass. ὤφθη by the LXX translators shows interpretation of the Hebrew niphal imperfect יֵרָאֶ֑ה as reflexive for the literal "was himself seen" or "appeared himself" meaning. See Seow, *Grammar for Biblical Hebrew*, 288. Cf. 3 Kgdms 9:2 LXX (1 Kgs 9:2 MT), where the LORD appeared to Solomon a second time in a personal appearance.

178. E.g., "Saying that the Lord truly was risen, and he appeared to Simon" (Luke 24:34).

in his judgment (cf. 1 Tim 3:16).[179] Later, Jesus also appears to Saul of Tarsus on the road to Damascus (Acts 9:17; 26:16). NT writers do not limit the appearance of Jesus to *one* second space/time ordinal event after his resurrection or his ascension (cf. 1Cor 15:5–6).

In Hebrews, the Pastor only chooses the pass. of ὁράω one time, in Heb 9:28 regarding his MCS. The syntax of future tense limits the appearance event to a forthcoming appearance after the events described in the two clauses, the first corresponding statement and the dependent clause of the second statement (see appendix 3, "Heb 9:27–28 Sentence Diagram"). Functioning as the main verb of the second corresponding statement, with subject of Christ, the weight of any ordinal, positional, spatial, or temporal properties of the idiom "from a second . . . " (ἐκ δευτέρου) must derive from context.

The Pastor also chooses the lexeme in his LXX quotation of Exod 25:40 in Heb 8:5, concerning God's warning to Moses before building the tabernacle, stating, "For he says, Watch! You will achieve all things in correspondence with the type shown to you in the mountain" (Heb 8:5).[180] The Pastor's insertion of "all things, everything" (πάντα) possibly pushes his interpretation of the tabernacle typology to include more than just a static Christology. He construes that the spatial-temporal (*aiōn-field*) movements and actions of the priests in the first and second holy areas (Heb 9:1–2) of the tabernacle provides a background as antitypes for the christological typology. The addition of πάντα (panta) corresponds to his preceding assertion, where he states, "who serve to outline and to shadow *ministry* of the heavenlies" (Heb 8:5).[181] The Pastor does not flatten the tabernacle ministry and everything ongoing in priestly service of the offerings to only a static sacrifice.

In other historical testimonial narrative, the Pastor chooses cognates of ὁράω to describe faith which centered on heavenly expectation

---

179. Angels often appeared for ministry (cf. Luke 1:11, 22:43; Acts 7:30). People concretely appear after death (and) without fleshly resurrection such as Moses and Elijah (cf. Matt 17:3, Mark 9:4). The hymn of 1 Tim 3:16b has a high probably of referring to Jesus appearing after death "in a spirit of an eternal/perpetual-*place*" before angels in heaven in his common experience with mankind of death and judgment before God and before his fleshly resurrection (cf. Heb 1:5–12; 2:11, 14; 5:7; 9:27; cf. 1 Pet 2:23).

180. The LXX reads, "Watch! You will achieve ['all' not present] in accordance with the type which has been shown to you in the mountain" (Exod 25:9 LXX).

181. This connection explains the Pastor's deployment of many verbs of movement with his christological parenesis and faith that the Lord by making people holy will be literally seen (cf. Heb 12:14).

in death.[182] Enoch by faith was taken up to heaven "with the result to not see" (μὴ ἰδεῖν Heb 11:5) death.[183] Abraham by faith "was expecting/was looking" (ἐξεδέχετο Heb 11:10) for a heavenly city in death. Moses "was looking/was paying attention" (ἀπέβλεπεν Heb 11:26) to promised blessings available in heaven after death through faith in Christ. About Moses, the Pastor further states, "For he endured as one who is continually seeing the invisible *one*" (Heb 11:27). Concerning all the Pastor's faith testimonies, "they died" (ἀπέθανον Heb 11:13; cf. Heb 9:27) without the promises in Christ, having confessed they are exiles and strangers on earth. Further about them, he states, "But ones having seen and ones themselves having welcomed from a distance" (Heb 11:13) the heavenly promises after death. As exampled in these witnesses, he exhorts his audience to run, saying, "While fixing eyes upon Jesus, the author and consummator of faith" (Heb 12:2).

---

182. See discussion Allen, *Hebrews*, 568. Allen makes excellent observations about Eisenbaum and Gordon, esp. 568n367, and associated text. Eisenbaum, *Jewish Heroes of Christian History*, 177–88. Eisenbaum's thesis contends that the Pastor's method of presentation of the list of the Jewish heroes of faith attempts to denationalize them from the land. Thereby, she describes them as distinctly Christian. Allen lists four characteristics of these Jewish heroes as elaborated by Eisenbaum. Allen writes, "First, most experience death or have a near death experience. Second, they all have the ability to see beyond their own day by their faith. Not only did they accomplish remarkable things by faith, but because of their faith they developed the capacity to look beyond their own lifetime. Third, they all experience some alteration of their status. Fourth, they all experience some form of marginalization (Allen, *Hebrews*, 568). Cf. Gordon, "Better Promises," 434–49. Gordon finds that death functions as a sub-theme in Heb 11, whereby, faith overcomes death to better promises than those on earth. Chapter 4 unit D1´ and D2´ explore the Pastor's presentation of historical testimonials, who as the Jewish heroes following the path of Christ distanced themselves from earthly matters and looked beyond the land promise to fulfillment at death in the eternal/perpetual-*place* of the heavens (cf. Heb 11:1–2, 4–5, 9–10, 12, 13–16, 19, 21–22, 26–27, 28–31, 33–35, 35–37; 12:2, 9). For rhetoric in Hebrews focused beyond death, see, Thompson, *Strangers on the Earth*.

183. Enoch's death in Genesis has sparked several thousand years of Jewish and Hellenistic speculation with five collated pseudepigraphic books now known as 1 Enoch. The Pastor, in commentary on Enoch, exegetes the Genesis text without reference to the pseudepigraphic writings available, of which he may have been aware. For the Pastor's treatment of Gen 5:22–24, see, Allen, *Hebrews*, 547–48.

"To the Ones Eagerly Awaiting Him" (τοῖς αὐτὸν ἀπεκδεχομένοις)

The verb ἀπεκδέχομαι (*apekdechomai*) is not found in the LXX.[184] However, it does appear in the NT eight times where each use has a common connection with descriptive language to the events of Christ's personal intercession at judgment. For example, Paul uses this term three times (Rom 8:19, 23, 25) in his parenesis of the discourse unit of Rom 8:1–39. There, he expounds on a corresponding MCS theme of Heb 9:27–28 concerning God's judgment at death of the flesh, with a resulting blessing of continued life at peace with God for those who with their spirit have received the Spirit of Christ (Rom 8:9, 14–16). Like the Pastor, Paul writes that Christ Jesus, who resides at the right hand of God, "intercedes," (ἐντυγχάνει Rom 8:27, 34; cf. Heb 7:25) for those "waiting completion" (ἀπεκδέχομαι Rom 8:19, 23; cf. Heb 9:28). After telling his readers the indicative reality, that "you are about to die" (μέλλετε ἀποθνῄσκειν Rom 8:13; cf. Heb 9:27), at the eternal/perpetual-*place* of judgment, they receive "no condemnation" (κατάκριμα Rom 8:1; cf. Heb 9:27). Paul further adds the spatial aspect of the creation after their death. He declares though they live "in accordance with the flesh" (κατὰ σάρκα Rom 8:13), they enter judgment in spirit into a creation longing for their arrival (Rom 8:19) and not presently seen (Rom 8:24–25). By the dwelling of Christ's Spirit, they embark on a path in the purpose of God in Christ Jesus for reception in the glory of God (Rom 8:23).

In NT usage, it appears at least for Paul, Peter, and the Pastor, that ἀπεκδέχομαι carries a nuanced perfective meaning of awaiting completion

---

184. The root δέχομαι deploys in the LXX sixty-two times. Cf. *GELS*, "δέχομαι," 111. Muraoka glosses δέχομαι as (1) "to receive approvingly or willingly" (cf. Gen 4.11), (2) "to come to terms with, reconcile oneself with," (cf. Gen 50:17), and (3) "+ dat. of beneficiary," (cf. Lev 22:25). The LXX translators chose the cognate ἐκδέχομαι nine times. *GELS*, "ἐκδέχομαι," 159. Muraoka glosses ἐκδέχομαι as (1) "to receive (guest)," "welcome" (Mic 2:12), (2) "to be in store for" (Hos 8:7), (3) "to take in charge" (Gen 43:9).

The addition of the preformative *apo-* (ἀπό) in the first-century CE Greek often inferred a perfective meaning. See MHT, 2:298; MM, "ἀπεκδέχομαι," 56. Moulton describes ἀπεκδέχομαι as a rare word even in profane literature. Due to the rarity and the diverse BCE meanings, later meaning after the first century CE took on theological moorings. James Swetnam speculates that modern lexical senses of "eagerly awaiting" derive from the later Latin Vulgate translation of ἀπεκδέχομαι as *exspectantibus* ("to look for, await, expect") with later escalation to "eagerly await." Swetnam, "On Romans 8,23," 106. Swetnam delineates from early twentieth-century lexicons two main senses of the lexeme determined by context either as temporal "to await" or cognitive "to infer, understand, interpret." The cognitive soteriological sense during waiting for Jesus at judgment has possibly dropped out of later lexicons.

in the eternal/perpetual-*place* at individual death for salvation by Christ's intervention at judgment before God, with situational spatial inferences of events in the spiritual realms of heaven (cf. 1 Cor 1:7–8; Gal 5:5; Phil 3:20; 1 Pet 3:18–22).[185]

The Pastor selects the term ἀπεκδέχομαι only once in this MCS. Since there is no direct evidence of previous use, conclusions cannot be pressed too far. The ἀπο- prefix, as common addition by NT writers in apocalyptic language to "awaiting" (ἐκδέχομαι) is fitting due to its perfective force. It also may suggest a cognitive awareness for the believer both while living and during the probable very short waiting period at judgment for prompt completion of salvation.[186] The dat. phrase "to him" (τοῖς αὐτὸν) places Christ as both appearing before alert believers and the receiving beneficiary, who willingly and approvingly receives them in into the eternal/perpetual-*places* of heaven (Heb 4:14–16; cf. John 14:3).

"For Salvation" (εἰς σωτηρίαν)

The terms "salvation, deliverance, peace, safety" (σωτηρία), "deliverer, savior" (σωτήρ) as verbal nouns, and the verbal "to save, deliver, escape/depart safely" (σῴζω) carry thematic significance in the LXX.[187] In the LXX, σωτηρία (*sōtēria*) combines with κύριος (*kyrios*) over thirty-five times (cf. Gen 49:18 LXX/MT) and "judgment" once (cf. Isa 59:11 LXX/MT) in correspondence with the Pastor's message of deliverance from

---

185. Both Paul, Peter, and the Pastor probably ministered together at Rome in the sixties CE which may account for the common vorlage in use of ἀπεκδέχομαι. Peter even deploys the term concerning God's patience in the days of Noah before the flood, which functions as an antitype, like baptism, to typify the hope of salvation after death by being led by Christ to God.

186. The Pastor describes the believer's movement of "approach" (προσέρχομαι) to the throne of grace in cognitive terms of "confidence, boldness" (παρρησία Heb 4:16) and "to believe" (πιστεύω Heb 11:6). His views of a cognitive experience in judgment drive his parenesis on maintaining a good "conscience" (συνείδησις) during approach (Heb 9:9, 14; 10:2, 22; 13:18). The ideas of either non-existence or sleeping through/until judgment after death pending a flesh resurrection create tension with the Pastor's cognitive concerns for one's conscience during approach, since judgment precedes the appearance of Jesus for salvation and subsequent later spiritual bodily return (Heb 9:27–28). Also, he even speaks of Enoch as "being changed, transferred" (μετετέθη) without seeing death and not being found since God took him, which strongly implies continued, cognitive, animated living (not dead) when changing places to God's presence in heaven (Heb 11:4–6). Even Philo speaks of the dead rising up to heaven (*Alleg. Interp.* 2.58 PAGM).

187. GELS, "σωτηρία," 545–46.

God's judgment.[188] The first usage by LXX translators occurred in Gen 19:17, 20, and 22 in connection to God's judgment upon the sin of Sodom and Gomorrah.[189] The intertwining of salvation from the judgment of sin continues throughout the LXX and MT (cf. LXX Pss 75:10 [76:9 MT]; 53:3 [54:1 MT]; 71:4 [72:4 MT]; Isa 19:20 [19:20 MT]).

For NT authors, it was no accident that God who came in the flesh to bring "salvation" from consequences of sin was given the Greek name "Jesus." They also designated this Savior by the Aramaic מְשִׁיחָא ("Messiah") for the Hebrew מָשִׁיחַ ("Messiah"), which translated in Greek as Χριστός.[190] NT authors deploy σωτηρία forty-six times, with seven of these in Hebrews for connection of Jesus as both Christ and Savior.[191] The term carries weight from the Hellenistic sense of deliverance from acute dangers for the loss of physical life (cf. Matt 14:30; 27:49; Mark 15:20; Luke 23:39; John 12:27; Acts 27:20, 31, 34). However, they also contextually share God's desire for the salvation of people from his judgment of wrath upon sin, beyond the loss of the fleshly life in death, and entrance into his glory—by faith in the substitutionary offering of Jesus, as Christ

---

188. E.g., Jacob prophetically speaks of Dan, "I await the salvation of the Lord" (Gen 49:18 LXX). Also, the language of the Pastor heavily corresponds to the LXX translation of 2 Chr 6, where Solomon in prayer dedicates the temple to the "LORD" (14). He reminds the people that the God of Israel does not dwell in the "house" which he built (2 Chr 6:18; cf. Heb 3:1–6; 10:19–22). He asks God to hear their prayers from his dwelling place in "heaven" (2 Chr 6:21; cf. Heb 8:1–5). Also, he requests God to act and "to judge" the people when "one should sin" (2 Chr 6:23; cf. Heb 9:27–28). He further asks that God's "priests" be clothed with "salvation" (σωτηρίαν) and not to turn away the face "of your Christ" (τοῦ χριστοῦ σου 2 Chr 6:41–42). In this brief survey, one finds similar language of the antitypical ministry described by the Pastor about the anointed priests in portrayal of the ministry of the Lord Jesus Christ in the house not made with hands (Heb 9:11). Similar antitype revelation in other LXX texts consists of return to the land upon repentance and for salvation and deliverance from enemies (cf. 2 Esd 9:8 LXX [Ezra 9:8 MT]; 2 Mac 11:6 LXX). The LXX Psalms contain many statements concerning the salvation of the Lord (cf. LXX Ps 3:9 [3:8 MT]; 11:6 [12:5 MT]; 37:23 [38:22 MT]; 87:2 [88:1 MT]; 117:14–15 [118:14–14 MT]; 139:8 [140:7 MT]; 149:4 [149:4 MT]). The prophetic writings translated in the LXX follow the same theme of salvation in the Lord like the Pastor (cf. LXX/MT Isa 12:2; 38:20; 45:17; 49:8; Jer 3:23; 38:22).

189. Such visible judgment on earth typifies God's unseen eternal/perpetual-*place* judgment upon sin. The deliverance of Lot while vexed with sin reveals God's protection in judgment for those who are his by faith, even though overcome by sinful actions (cf. Heb 10:39; cf. 1 Cor 3:15). Isaiah also depicts God's salvation power, in that, he hears when there is confession of wickedness (Isa 59 LXX/MT).

190. Cf. Luke 1:31; 2:10–11, 21; John 1:41; 3:28; 4:25, 29 for interrelation of the terms Ἰησοῦς, σωτήρ, χριστός, and κύριος.

191. BDAG, "σωτηρία," 985–86.

(cf. Luke 1:76–79; 16:22; Rom 5:9; 13:11; Phil 1:28; 1 Thess 5:9; 2 Thess 2:10; 2 Cor 7:10).[192]

The Pastor chooses the verb "to save" (σῴζειν Heb 5:7; 7:25) twice. Both contexts relate "to approach" (προσέρχομαι) God for judgment after death.[193] In correspondence with the LXX and OT, Jesus is delivered by God from the path of death at his judgment as any other man (see appendix 1, fig. 3). This second ordinal event occurs after death and before his rising to God on a subsequent path of resurrection *of* the dead (appendix 1, fig. 1, no. 2).[194] In death, God raises Jesus up *from* the dead into his presence due to his previous petitions and prayers in the days of his flesh that were made with crying and tears to the one who was able to save him from death (Heb 5:7, appendix 1, fig. 1, no. 3).[195] Jesus, with faith in

---

192. Foerster, "σῴζω and σωτηρία," 989–998. Foerster concludes, "Apart from religious usage σῴζω and σωτηρία occur in the NT only in relation to an acute danger to physical life. The meaning 'preservation' or 'maintaining' of the natural constitution of a person or thing is not found." For the Pastor and other NT writers, salvation involved transformation from the visible world and entrance into the glory of the eternal creation of heaven with God (cf. Heb 10:19–20; 11:4–6).

193. The Pastor chooses the pres. inf. of σῴζω twice to describe the basis both of Jesus's prayer for deliverance from death before God and his present intercessory ministry. The pres. tense inherently possesses weight of ongoing or progressive action. This does not negate the NT language, which considers as "saved" those who accept Jesus as Savior from sin, as in Eph 2:8. The verb σεσῳσμένοι, as a pf. pass. ptc. with syntactic intensive force of a past event with present results, translates simply "being saved." For those coming to Christ in Acts 2:47, the verb σῳζομένους as a substantive pres. pass. ptc. translates "the ones continually being saved," implying a restriction of the term for those who had a personal reception of Christ to a present state of salvation. Believers are both indwelled and sealed by the Holy Spirit as God's guarantee of his offered intercession for salvation (cf. Rom 8:16; 1 John 4:13; Eph 1:13–14; 4:30). This present salvific state/result has future promises of an eternal inheritance at a literal salvation experience before God at judgment from God's wrath upon sin by the mediation of Jesus (Heb 7:25; cf. Matt 7:21–23; Rom 5:9–10; 1 Thess 1:5). The Pastor's message thematically centers on this neglected foundational teaching of every believer at death being experientially saved at κρίματος αἰωνίου ("an eternal/perpetual-*place* judgment," Heb 6:2), before proceeding through other events toward eventual ministry with Jesus by collection of the living and dead in a spiritual bodily return at a second coming to earth (Heb 11:39–40, cf. 1 Thess 4:13–18).

194. Jesus's fleshly suffering for sin completes in the cross. His ministry of atonement continues in spirit by suffering his own death with the rising *of* the dead in judgment before God (Heb 2:9) and subsequent aid to others during the same judgment experience (Heb 2:14–18; 7:25; 9:27–28; cf. 1 Cor 15:21–22; see appendix 1, fig. 1).

195. Bertolet, "Hebrews 5:7," 1–10. Bertolet argues convincingly, the cries of Jesus, that the Pastor points, refer to the Davidic Psalter who "trusts God his Father into and through his death ordeal. This righteous servant's trust is rewarded by an exaltation" (9).

God's ability, both requests and receives life in rising *from* the dead into salvation of God's presence due to his reverential fear.

The Pastor also deploys forms of the verbal noun σωτηρία seven times, with two of these in DUC. The first UC use occurs in Heb 1:13–14, where he shares that the ministry of angels is service on behalf of those about to inherit salvation.[196] Then, in the MCS UC of Heb 9:27–28, the word encapsulates the purpose of God in the Christ as "the source of eternal/perpetual-*place* salvation" (Heb 5:9). The Pastor considers this salvation at judgment as a movement from the temporary creation to permanent existence in time and space of the unseen, perpetual, substance-reality of creation.

He uses this eternal hope for encouragement and warning to his audience (Heb 6:19–20). They will not escape penalty for transgressions and obedience in God's judgment if they neglect to pay attention to what they had heard and drift away in their ministries from propter teaching about the so great a salvation (Heb 2:3). His language of exhortation for them concerns "the better things that are even accompanying salvation" (Heb 6:9). They, by either neglect of their salvation (Heb 2:1–3) or possibly teaching an incorrect gospel with no ability to bring listeners to repentance (Heb 5:11—6:8), do not add to their salvation the available promises of their eternal inheritance (Heb 6:12; 12:17; cf. Matt 19:29; 1 Cor 3:8–15; 1 Pet 3:9).

Finally, in his historical narrative he also explains the testimonial event of Noah building the ark for the coming flood as an action by faith which was "for salvation of his house" (Heb 11:7). This ministry of Noah functioned as an antitype of God's judgment "through which he condemned the world" (Heb 11:7). Like baptism, God historically demonstrates typologically in the flood, that the outcome of those who are judged for sin, who have faith in Christ, is salvation (cf. 1 Pet 3:21–22). Noah's whole burnt offering symbolized one rising to God (Gen 8:20–22). The choice of "salvation" as the final word for emphasis in the MCS fits well his vision of the purpose of God in Christ expressed in his surrounding vocabulary. The semantic relationship to other lexemes in the Pastor's message finds expression in the next chapter.

---

196. The Pastor does not mention the worship of angels. His purpose for angels as ministering spirits centers on the contrast of the efficacy of their ministry with that of Christ. Jesus's ministry is better, in that he, as God and man, can inherit the more excellent name of "Son" at his judgment at completion of atonement for sin (cf. Heb 1:4; 5:7; cf. 1 Cor 15:20–23). His dominion would include the ability for entering the presence of God as a man.

CONCLUSION

This chapter explores the most efficient beginning steps for success in understanding the background (*aiōn-field*) places of the Pastor's words in Heb 9:27–28 as a possible MCS. The first step introduces the basics of lexical semantics concerning word studies. These principles include determination of accurate translation and recognition of modern anachronistic terms that carry freight in totality transfer toward modern concepts foreign to the Pastor's original intent. Step 2 focuses on the proposed interpretative goal and introduces obstacles against acceptance success. Step 3 considers available first century CE intended interpretation methods for his audience. Step 4 introduces the apocalyptic (*aiōn-field*) word stock necessary for understanding the communication about heavenly matters of the first century CE. Step 5 critiques the traditional translation for Heb 9:28. Step 6 proposes a sifter for the evidence concerning the message of Hebrews, from most probable to least possible having influence on the Pastor's word meaning for his audience understanding (fig. 9). Finally, Step 7 surveys and sifts the probable to most possible available evidence for the sense option for words in Hebrews.

After a good start, a well-trained runner next establishes a proper stride toward his goal. Chapter 3 analyzes the Pastor's broader conversation and background (*aiōn-field*) of biblical theology that governs the semantics of his words to evaluate further possible congruence with the proposed thesis.

3

Steady Stride on the Right Course
Consistent Conversation, by those Listening, about the Word of Christ into the Eternal/Perpetual-*Place*(s)

INTRODUCTION

The Pastor challenges his listeners, "Let us run . . . a race" (Heb 12:1). Both a runner's initial steps and his later stride involve strategic differences depending on the chosen course. For excellence, a runner must perform both actions with appropriate precision, which involves different techniques and skills adapted for the course conditions. Likewise, accurate hearing of Hebrews requires knowing the background course conditions and adjusting the perceived conversation of the words for coherent correspondence.[1]

---

1. Tångberg, "Linguistics and Theology," 304. Tångberg comments, "Instead of overinterpreting interesting but isolated linguistic facts, biblical theology must concentrate on carefully interpreting the sentence and still larger discourse units that are able to convey theological information." Cf. Black, *Linguistics for Students*, 138. Black writes, "The distinctiveness of the Bible is therefore not to be found at the lexical or morphological level, but at the syntactic level. Hence, the entire text must be considered before the meanings of its component words and sentences can be determined. This means that the same sequence of words can have a different meaning in a different context." Cf. Silva, *Biblical Words and Their Meaning*, 138–41. Silva rightly asserts that meaning resides from the smallest element of syntax to all that has gone on

The previous chapter suggests that the initial steps for exploration for a MCS UC function of Heb 9:27–28 should commence with word study filtering for the sense of the Pastor's *own* words (fig. 9).² This chapter looks for the background (*aiōn-field* course) that governs the Pastor's word sense to clearly map the motion and reality he perceives.³ Such a compilation should closely resemble the biblical theology underlying the ῥῆμα ("conversation," Heb 1:3b) that he desires for audience teaching.⁴

The thesis consideration investigates whether the idiom ἐκ δευτέρου should contain, from the context, a weight of place(s) based on the Pastor's spatial narrative concerning Jesus's ministry as high priest to his people.⁵ Would a first-century CE audience consider Heb 9:27–28 summarizing a *local present position* of Jesus's *current* intercessional ministry as a high priest after completed atonement of sins (Ps 110)? Especially, would the listeners think of Jesus possibly coming bodily from the holy of holies to the cosmos at a believer's fleshly death (cf. Heb 10:5)? Would this concept of Jesus coming at death merge in cohesion with both his MCS and his other context?⁶

---

before, including the knowledge shared by the speaker and audience up to that point.

2. Austin, *How to Do Things*. Cf. Searle, *Speech Acts*. Austin and Searle demonstrate that meaning of discourse could not be determined by only the dictionary sense of words. They improved communication theory by adding the intent of the author to the understanding of discourse. Cf. Briggs, "Speech-Act Theory," 763–66.

3. Cotterell and Turner, *Linguistics*, 122–23. They state, "In sum, Barr was saying . . . the whole enterprise of trying to establish theology on the basis of *word studies* was fundamentally mistaken. The theology of the Testaments lies in the propositions asserted in the sentences, paragraphs, and whole discourses of its writings, not in the individual words" (italics Cotterell and Turner).

4. Lincoln, "Hebrews and Biblical Theology," 313–38. Cf. Klink and Lockett, *Understanding Biblical Theology*; Barr, *Concept of Biblical Theology*, 4. Barr correctly assumes, "The term 'biblical theology' has clarity only when it is understood to mean theology as it existed or was thought or believed within the time, languages and cultures of the Bible itself." He states, "What we are looking for is a 'theology' that existed back there and then." And, further, "Or, to put it in another way, the more we insist that the Bible is 'theological' in character, the more that same affirmation leads us to look for the theology that motivated it and lived within it in ancient times."

5. Nida et al., *Style*, 74–75. Nida addresses the "special problems of figurative meanings" with translating idioms. He defines idioms as "combinations of two or more words which have meaning which cannot be derived from the meaning of the component parts." He further states, "A failure to recognize idioms can lead to unfortunate misunderstanding." His examples excellently demonstrate the figurative aspects over the literal wording for proper understanding.

6. Beekman and Callow, *Translating the Word of God*, 24. Beekman and Callow present the problem of "idiomatic translation" with examples of past translators such as Jerome and Luther. Their point is well taken that one must consider the "receptor

Atonement and the Logic of Resurrection in Hebrews 9:27–28

To continue testing the MCS hypothesis for Heb 9:27–28, surveys in this chapter analyze the MCS in relation to basic questions underlying his narrative. Who is God? How does God communicate? How does God normally relate to creation near himself? What are God's boundaries and limitations for creation remaining in his presence? How does God meet the needs of sin to bring separated people to himself? Do other beings help him? Where and when does he judge and resolve current issues with people and other created beings regarding sin?

In pursuit of answers, the key referents underlying this proposed MCS are analyzed in relation to the Pastor's conversation/biblical theology through the lens of his main subject, God. This includes how God relates to the present plural heavens and the earth, the holy-places of his tabernacle, sinful people, the eternal/perpetual-*place* judgment, the sacrificial atonement and priestly intercession of the Son, and his other eternal beings. Last, a conclusion summarizes the findings in preparation for chapter 4, which checks his smooth and steady strides against his contextual split times at each UC of his rhetoric, both toward and following the course DUC for the proposed contextual meaning of the place(s) implied by the Pastor's words in Heb 9:27–28.

GOD

In his possible MCS, the Pastor chooses Χριστὸς (Christos) to recap his emphasis about his main subject of "God" and God's link with "people" in their common experience of "living" through both "death" and "judgment." In his construction, the "Christ" serves as the subject of an apodosis in the second of two correlative statements (appendix 3). The correlative conjunction "just as . . . so also," signals Christ's participation in both the protasis and apodosis assertions. Χριστὸς spans the interrelated experiences of both the Pastor's main subjects of God and people in the anticipated event of salvation during the experience of fleshly death and judgment.

---

language" when deciding between a literal or idiomatic translation for conveying the sense of a text. The observation of J. L. Austin is also fitting in this situation. He states, "Along these lines it has by now been shown piecemeal, or at least made to look likely, that many traditional philosophical perplexities have arisen through a mistake—the mistake of taking as straightforward statements of fact utterances which are *either* (in interesting non-grammatical ways) nonsensical *or else* intended as something quite different." Austin, *How to Do Things*, 3 (italics Austin).

GOD SPEAKS

In the DI (Heb 1:1–4), the Pastor immediately cues his listeners to hear God speaking. His opening unmodified ὁ θεός (*ho theos*) serves in a probable mixed audience as a "generic expression" for a supreme being/benefactor in relation to the affairs of everything existing.[7] He later crafts a definition to this theocentric theme that runs throughout the whole letter.[8] Also, at times, both Jesus and the Holy Spirit speak, supporting the three persons of God.[9] Table 1, "Words in Hebrews Linked with God," shows that θεός is voiced sixty-three times in Hebrews, contrasted to "Jesus" fourteen times, "Son/son" twenty-one times, "Christ" twelve times, "Lord" sixteen times, and "Holy Spirit" three times.

In table 1, Χριστός has correspondence with all referents that the Pastor chooses, to provide a spotlight for God's speech. God, who has progressively spoken in the past to reveal his purposes "in many parts and in many ways" (Heb 1:1), "spoke to us in a Son" (Heb 1:2; cf. Heb 2:1–4). He also speaks in the *present* (Heb 9:8–9) and will continue to speak in the *future* as "the Word of God" (ὁ λόγος τοῦ θεοῦ) to people in judgment after death (Heb 4:11–13; 9:28; 10:29–30, 37–38).[10]

---

7. Martin, "Household of God." Cf. deSilva, *Perseverance in Gratitude*, xii, 2–6, 59–64; deSilva, "Exchanging Favor for Wrath," 91–116. Cf. Attridge, "God in Hebrews," 199, 202–3. Attridge states, "The God to whom the Son leads and directs the members of his covenant community is not an abstract or remote entity, but a person related to and intimately involved with humankind."

8. Allen, *Hebrews*, 626–27. Allen asserts that God speaking tracks from the beginning invocation of the exordium to his concluding benediction of Heb 13:20–21. Cf. Lane, *Hebrews 1–8*, cxxvii; Attridge, "God in Hebrews," 95–110; Johnson, *Hebrews: A Commentary*, 31–32; Wider, *Theozentrik und Bekenntnis*; Smillie, "Living and Active."; Lewicki, *Weist nicht ab den Sprechenden!*; Schenck, "God has Spoken," 321–36; Griffiths, *Hebrews and Divine Speech*; Coetsee, "Die sprekende God."; Pierce, *Divine Discourse*.

9. The Holy Spirit speaks in Heb 3:7, 15; 10:15. Jesus speaks in 2:11–13; 10:5, 8–9. Cf. Jobes, "Putting Words in His Mouth," 40–50.

10. Smillie, "Living and Active." Smillie makes a direct affirmation about the word of God in Heb 4:12–13. He also notes that the Pastor considers his own sermon to be the word of God and expects listeners will, through the text, hear God's voice. The Pastor considers both the OT speaking the NT message and the NT interpreting the OT christologically to be the word of God. Cf. Coetsee, "Die sprekende God," 121–23. Coetsee also asserts the formulas confirm that the OT, for the author, is inspired and comes from God's mouth, with several texts having God as the primary speaker (Heb 2:6, 4:4, 7). He further claims that, for the author, the authority of the text lies with the actual speaker and not the text itself. Further, the author deliberately uses texts that are direct speech in thirty-seven out of thirty-eight OT quotations to emphasize God's direct speech through it. Cf. Coetsee, "Unfolding of God's Revelation," 1–8. Coetsee

God speaks to hearers in both the Pastor's hermeneutic of the LXX OT in promised features of the Son and his historical knowledge of the life of Jesus. The Pastor does not listen to the LXX OT and history from the perception that it *points* either to God or even Jesus. Rather, he hears the OT LXX speaking directly from the ministry of Christ as spoken promise-fulfillment in Jesus's atonement and his current perpetual ministry. This ministry now entails continual intercessory travel in the way of the holy-*places* (cf. Heb 1:3; 7:23–24; 9:8–9; 10:37).

With some overlap, the Pastor usually chooses λόγος (*logos*) for revelation by speech-action from the source (Jesus, Christ, God, etc.), whereas ῥῆμα (*rhema*) refers to external conversation about words, speech, or teachings concerning the actual source λόγος. The Pastor frames this theme of *God speaking* with an introductory formula for his LXX OT-quoted texts that are all communicative verbs.[11] Smillie observes that the Pastor, like Philo, introduces the OT text with "say, speak" (λαλέω).[12] The forms of λαλέω appear forty-three times. These deploy most often as a cue to listen to the λόγος as spoken action of the Son, as God (cf. Heb 1:1).[13] Smillie further finds this as a consistent hermeneutical pattern with the perspective that what the Pastor says about the OT text is the direct personal speech/word of God.[14]

Both the Pastor and hearers accept the LXX OT text as authoritative speech from God.[15] However, it is not as if the OT written record has special powers of its own apart from God.[16] Neither does the Pastor embrace misunderstanding, cultivated in the *Religionsgeschichtliche Schule*, that the biblical text was nothing more than unreliable history about conceptions of God in an equality with other comparative religions.[17]

The DI (Heb 1:1–4), establishes the background places within the theology of God, who speaks as creator. In a dependent clause modifying

---

concludes that the Pastor had the conviction that God's revelation unfolded from his so-called "Old Testament" revelation to his "New Testament" revelation in his Son.

11. In all, nine verbs are used by the Pastor to introduce his LXX quotations which all come from the semantic domain of communication. Coetsee, "Die sprekende God," 121–22; L&N, "33 Communication," 1: 388–445. For a listing, see appendix 2, table 1, "Words in Hebrews Linked with God."

12. Smillie, "Living and Active," 51.

13. Smillie, "Living and Active," 95.

14. Smillie, "Living and Active," 97. Cf. Beek, "Hebrews," 13–28.

15. Peterson, "God and Scripture in Hebrews," 118–38.

16. E.g., Hegermann, "Das Wort Gottes," 83–98.

17. Ladd, *Theology of the New Testament*, 13–33.

"the Son," he exclaims "who he appointed an inheritance of all things, through whom also he made the eternal/perpetual-*places*" (Heb 1:2). In this project, αἰών (*aiōn*) translates as "eternal/perpetual-*places*" to convey the Pastor's sense of place and perpetual time reality recently achieved by the Son.[18] He applies "to create, make, do, achieve" (ποιεω) eighteen times to frame a recent change to the state of unseen creation by the Son.[19]

---

18. It is used twelve times in noun form and six times as an adjective. The LXX OT usage of αἰών links its NT use with the OT Hebrew term עוֹלָם. Cf. *HAL*, "עוֹלָם," 798–99. The general term αἰών for his audience governs his message in such a way that, concerning the creation changes achieved by the Son, each of his discussed specific places have varied meaning in overlapping boundaries of space and time as defined by surrounding context. For movement of either the living God or any of his described creation, the Pastor entertains no preconceived notions of the philosophical ideas of timelessness, non-substance-reality, or hints of his heavenly typological language as only imaginary symbols for earthly limited realities. Time for the Pastor always deploys as a natural measure of the living, verbal movement of both the visible and invisible substance-reality in a relationship with the places of created space.

The Greek αἰών is difficult to translate in modern languages that lack referents which include both nuances of meaning of eternal or perpetual time and space. Cf. Allen, "Forgotten Ages," 144–51. The terms "universe" (HCSB, NIV), "world(s)" (NASB, ESV, NET, KJV, NRSV, RSV, NKJV) fall short of the full weight of the meaning in the context of Hebrews by pointing readers only to modern concepts of spatial ideology. The NASB provides the referenced gloss "lit. ages." E.g., Bauer, "αἰών," 32–33, "αἰώνιος," 33. Bauer provides different temporal-focused senses without mention of the necessity of the relative, understood, contextual movement of substance(s) in space that are necessary for the measure of temporal features in narrative even to exist. Cf. Sasse, "Αἰών, Αἰώνιος," 1:197–209. Sasse recognized that Platonic ideas of timelessness were isolated to the Greek world, whereas most other glosses involve some duration of time. In reference to eternity as an adjectival modifier of God, Sasse writes, "But how are we to understand the eternity ascribed to God in the term αἰών? In the older writings of the OT there is a quite simple concept of eternity. The being of God reaches back into times past computation. God has always been. Hence, he is the God of old, as we are really to construe the אֵל עוֹלָם of (θεὸς αἰώνιος Gn. 21:33 LXX). Again, he always will be. In contrast to men, who are subject to death (Gn. 6:3), He is the living God (e.g., Dt. 5:23; 32:40). This primitive idea of eternity changes at a later date. In Deutero-Isaiah אֱלֹהֵי עוֹלָם really means θεὸς αἰώνιος (Is. 40:28), עוֹלָם no longer signifying merely the remote past, but unending time or eternity" (201). Modern lexicographers and translators ignore concepts of existing places before those of Gen 1:1 (not gap theory but perpetual time before Gen 1:1), in a constricted cosmic-*field* background, and short duration for God's creative experience. In line with this narrowed assumption, glosses of αἰών lean heavily toward a temporal bias until forced to recognize the innate spatial weight of the term by a context where a purely temporal focus is nonsensical.

19. L&N, "ποιέω," 1:149–50. Louw and Nida comment, "Any meaning involving 'to cause to be' implies some change in state, and therefore one could classify these meanings under Subdomain B *Change of State*. However, the focus seems to be primarily upon the changed state rather than upon the process of moving from one state to another. The fact that a change of state has taken place seems to be semantically incidental." The Pastor's chosen focus on Jesus's movement in Unit F UPt2 (Heb 9:1–14) does

His narrative about these abilities of the Son take place in a reality with observational features of space-time, rather than philosophical Cartesian ideas of transcendent immaterial timelessness.[20] He embraces the Jewish tradition of the living God, who alone creates or changes the state of ontological reality, in contrast to the gods of other religions that only attempt to explain observations about the visible creation. He also supports a tradition that God has appointed the person of the Son as the owner-agent of an "inheritance," in which God lives in a dwelling relationship to all created things.[21]

---

not support the claim that other derived truth is semantically incidental. Jesus achieved by atonement a change in the unseen eternal places. Also, the Pastor shares the common "conversation" in Heb 11:3 that the visible realm of the eternal/perpetual-*places* was made from things not seen. The Pastor implies a common first-century CE teaching that the eternal/perpetual-*places*, from which the Son created the current changed state of the visible creation, existed before the present visible creation of Genesis and people. Also, his ministry makes necessary changes in creation for people to enter the presence of the living God.

20. Jones, *Time and Cosmos*. Cf. Wright, *Cosmology in Antiquity*, 126–44. Wright reviews how ancient observational understanding of the cosmos, as the home of the everlasting gods, develops into concepts of eternity. Aristotle, out of fears that his house would be destroyed as the atomist claimed, connected his personal desires for the cosmos with Greek term "eternal/perpetual-*places*" (αἰών), as a reaction to the teaching of the atomist that the world would eventually disintegrate (130). His elevated straw man argument for the eternal duration of the cosmos, that for Aristotle did not include the Jewish invisible heaven, contrasted with the more abstract idea of "time" (χρόνος) which referenced earthly past, present, and future events that seemed to lack the eternal stability of the continuance of the observed cosmos in line with the atomist claims. Already, Parmenides contemplated that, "immortality and eternity implied the denial of both starting and finishing in a continual present, for a beginning of being required non-being before it and an end non-being after" (126). Plato, in looking for a solution to the problems raised by Parmenides, suggested an αἰών that has neither past nor future, which was later taken to be a foreshadowing of the concept of the atemporal eternity of the Christian God (131). Greek cosmic metaphysics in connection with αἰών, often leads to a misunderstanding for αἰών as timeless or atemporal. However, emphasis seems to be more on duration or endlessness, without beginning or end in relative comparison to earthly human experience. While the generations of people tend to come and go, the cosmos and its gods appear to endure.

Also, timelessness, as often claimed from Plato, is an unconvincing philosophical idea. Plato's speculation concerns time for the Eternal Being creator *before* the beginning of *any* creation that has any movement in relation to God, i.e., when God was alone (*Tim.* 37D–38A). As such, this contemplation does not apply to descriptions of time in biblical literature conveying a measurable spatial-temporal movement by God's created substances, i.e., angels, Jesus, or believers in the invisible heaven of God's near dwelling living relationships. Cf. Grudem, *Systematic Theology*, 173. Wayne Grudem is probably right to assume that God's creation always has time.

21. Backhaus, *Der sprechende Gott*, 77–100, 302.

GOD SPEAKS AS LIVING

God has eternal, self-revealed, superior qualities in activities beyond and before the current visible places of this creation (Heb 1:8; 5:6; 6:20; 11:3; cf. Pss 90:1–4; 110:4). For both his living eternal beings and mortal people to interact and dwell with God in a relationship, God must have some quality of living nearness. Else, his created living creatures would have no real substantive relationship of any close relatedness.[22]

For the Pastor, the words spoken are "from the living God" (Heb 3:12; 9:14; 10:31; 12:22; cf. 4:12; 5:9). Smillie recognizes, "Of thirty-two instances in Hebrews of 'Word' λεγω in the present tense, twenty-three are references to Scripture, or someone recorded in Scripture, 'speaking.'"[23] The living God *now* personally speaks in a connection with both the eternal creatures, such as angels, and the people, who he recently created through his Word. This speech-act involves a continued *living* movement of both God and his *living* listeners, who should hear some sense of what is spoken by the creative God and engage in conversation about the salvation of that speech (Heb 2:1–4).

Both God and his living relationships are described in relation to both visible and invisible created places that are active and real. Neither God, nor any of his eternal substance creation of places, merely form an idea, type, dramatization, figure of speech, or allegory to just depict some disconnected, transcendent, spiritual concept of God's relatedness. The Pastor, speaking about the Son, says, "Who being the brilliance of glory and reproduction of his substance-reality [τῆς ὑποστάσεως]" (Heb 1:3).

The term "substance-reality" appears three times (Heb 1:3; 3:14; 11:1; cf. 2 Cor 9:4; 11:17).[24] In the first use that modifies God, it implies that his essence of his nature as an entity is that of an actual living being

---

22. Grudem, *Systematic Theology*, 166–67. The assertion that God is living in a personal relationship with his creation does not allow for *process theology* claims that God changes as the creation is changing and therefore is not immutable. Movement and motion in interaction are not at issue. The attribute of immutability refers to an eternality and stability of character and nature without loss by death, decay, aging, or experiences. In Hebrews, God, as both Jesus and the Holy Spirit, "speak" in a living relationship with people. Jesus, as the Son and Lord, now lives in the substance of flesh at the right hand of the throne in a ministry of intercession for man (Heb 2:9–18). Also, the "living God" (Heb 3:12; cf. 4:12; 7:25; 10:31; 12:22) implies a substance existence in a living relationship with the "Holy Spirit" (Heb 3:7, 15; 10:15) and the "Father" (Heb 1:5; 12:9).

23. Smillie, "Living and Active," 92.

24. BDAG, "ὑπόστασις," 1040. Cf. Köster, "ὑπόστασις," 572–88; Smith, "Faith as Substance or Surety," 381–92.

who is reproduced as the Son (cf. 2 Sam 7:12–16). Further, allowing weight toward a planned endeavor, God as a real person lives with his creation, undertaking plans and projects in his will.²⁵

For God and creation to have a relationship that communicates between both parties in time and space, both must be living in some association to one another.²⁶ Similar to Genesis, the Pastor uses ζαω ("live") twelve times to modify relationships (Cf. Heb 2:15; 3:12; 4:12; 7:8, 25; 9:14, 17; 10:20, 31, 38; 12:9, 22).²⁷ When man was created in the image of God, Genesis 2:7 states, "and man became with the result that a living [ζῶσαν] soul" (Gen 2:7 LXX [Gen 2:7 MT]).²⁸ The term "living" implies animation and interaction with other ontological entities beyond oneself, of which, measurable movements support signs of life. God, in animated life as the promised Son and Christ, continues his servant ministry to sinful people (Heb 2:6). This living assistance commences through incarnation as the person of Jesus, continues in mutual experiences just like other people, encounters fleshly death and judgment before approaching the holy place in common with all people, and since entrance,

---

25. As such, man in God's image as a living soul also does plans and projects in his reciprocal relationship with God. Concerning ministerial accountability, the Pastor shares, "For partners we have become of Christ, if indeed we should hold steadfast the beginning of the substance-reality [τῆς ὑποστάσεως] until the completions" (Heb 3:14). The aorist subjunctive expects the apodosis as true without doubt. As supported in the introduction, in this context, the situation background encourages perseverance in partaking in the reality of the plans in Christ for teaching a proper conversation in his service. Further, he states, "But faith is the substance-reality [ὑπόστασις] of things [plans] being hoped, the evidence of matters not continually being seen" (Heb 11:1). Again, people exercise faith in a reality of plans about matters not yet seen till after death abiding with God in the eternal creation (Heb 11:13–15). The Pastor's faith in Heb 11 is the living out of this substance-reality after one's acceptance in one's plans (cf. Heb 10:38, "But my righteous one will live by faith").

26. Feldmeier and Spieckermann, *God of the Living*, 12–13, 24.

27. Of these, four use a link with God describing predictable interactions with people in blessing or wrath based upon their living choices in relation to his will. In Heb 2:15, the term describes a living relationship in fear of slavery to the devil, who has the power of death. Also, Heb 7:8 speaks of the continued testimony of Melchizedek, who, after receiving tithes from Abraham "he continued living [ζῇ]." In the author's argument this claim supports that Jesus's priestly lineage, like Melchizedek's, was greater than Abraham. This places his priesthood even greater than the Levites, who in Abraham's loins, also experiences fleshly death. Further, in explaining Jesus's priesthood in the order of Melchizedek, Heb 7:25 says, "Therefore, likewise, he is completely able for the purpose to save the ones approaching through him to God, always continually living for the purpose to intercede for them."

28. The MT states, "And the man became a living [חיה] soul" (ויהי האדם לנפש חיה) Gen 2:7c BHS).

offers sinful people a shared holy place at the throne of God (Heb 2:9–18; 12:22–24; cf. Rev 3:21).

GOD SPEAKS AS HOLY

The concept of God's personal holiness is an unstated tenet of the Pastor's theology about God. The typical LXX OT adjective modifier ἅγιος, linked from Hebrew "holy" (קדש), is not attributed to θεός, as seen by God's claims about himself in the Torah (Lev 11:44–45; 19:2; 20:26; 21:8), and spoken later about God (Josh 24:19; 1 Sam 2:2; 6:20; Pss 22:3 MT [21:4 LXX, ἐν ἁγίοις = "in holy ones"]); 89:18; Isa 6:3).[29] Instead of attribution of the modifier ἅγιος directly to God, the Pastor follows the first LXX connection in Exod 3:5 to identify a place of γῆ ἁγία ("holy ground"). He considers God's holiness as an attribute of the creation in the place surrounding his living presence.[30]

The configuration of *aiōn-field* holiness used by the Pastor derives from the movement of the priestly ministers in the tabernacle, "who

---

29. The word "holy" (ἅγιος) occurs 17 times in Hebrews in reference to God the Holy Spirit (Heb 3:7; 10:15), brethren (Heb 3:1; 6:10; 13:24), people in heaven (Heb 2:4; 6:4), the unseen holy place(s) of heaven (Heb 6:4; 8:2; 9:8, 12, 24, 25; 10:19), the holy place of the earthly tabernacle (Heb 9:1–2), holy of holies of earthly tabernacle (9:3), and the holy-*places* of the earthly tabernacle (Heb 13:11). See appendix 2, table 9. It is unlikely that the plural form τῶν ἁγίων (tōn hagiōn) ("holy-*places*," Heb 9:8; 10:19), used in the LXX, infers an abbreviated form of Ἅγια Ἁγίων (Hagia Hagiōn) for the holy holies. The form τῶν ἁγίων (tōn hagiōn) occurs 149 times in the LXX. The holy of holies is usually τοῦ ἁγίου τῶν ἁγίων (tou hagiou tōn hagiōn). In context, it usually glosses either holy-*things* or holy-*places* of the tabernacle ministry and belongs to the Lord as ἀπὸ τῶν ἁγίων μου ("from my holy-*places*," Exod 26:2).

30. In the MT, the first use of the word "holy" (קדש BHS) established, in his meeting with Moses at the burning bush not consumed, that any creation of his presence is "holy ground," (אדמת קדש Exod 3:5 BHS). In previous Sabbath readings of the Torah before this sermon, the returning audience would have heard the required holiness background necessary for any created thing in the presence of God's holiness. Cf. Isaacs, *Sacred Space*, 61–67, 223. Isaacs identifies that the Pastor has a preoccupation with sacred space. He connects this to heaven as a replacement of the loss of the land and Jerusalem in a late 70 CE date for the writing, which is unlikely. Also, for Isaacs, the language of priest and victim, when applied to Jesus, is metaphorical in Hebrews since he was literally neither (223). It is more likely the Pastor's preoccupation is not just toward the space of heaven itself, but any sacred place of creation in the literal presence of the living God. The greater desire, as depicted by the sacrificial system (Heb 11:4), was on approach at judgment for the pleasing reception of access to enter and live with God, more than living in any isolated place without the living presence of God (Heb 7:25; 11:6; 12:23; cf. Ps 89:1 LXX [90:1 MT, "You are our place of refuge in generation to generation"]).

serve as an outline and shadow *ministry* of the heavenlies" (Heb 8:5). His application of this tabernacle "outline and shadow" (ὑποδείγματι καὶ σκιᾷ) suggests a dualism of places that further divides into dwelling levels of holiness in relation to the presence of a holy God.[31] In apocalyptic (*aiōn-field*) language, his descriptions of these separated places imply more significance than a duality of symbolic forensic conditions for a psychological or an ethical fellowship with God.[32] These boundaries of holiness represent ontological real places that are described in dualistic language and continue with time in a linear eschatological history.[33]

---

31. Hayward, *Jewish Temple*, 8–10. Hayward writes concerning the Jewish apologetics of the first century CE, "These forays into apologetics, however, depend on, rather than create, the understanding of the Temple and its furniture as representing parts of earth, heaven, and underworld." Cf. Alexander, "Geography and the Bible," 977. Alexander writes, "*Degrees* of holiness may also function to differentiate space." Cf. Jenson, *Graded Holiness*; Haran, *Temples and Temple Service*, 220–21. Haran recognizes all rites performed in the other areas of the tabernacle are directed towards the true and more perfect room of the holy of holies. Cf. Gorman, *Ideology of Ritual*; George, *Israel's Tabernacle*. Jenson, Haran, Gorman, and George all make contributions to the logical and social organization of tabernacle space within God's creation and open heavens for people in relation to God that is based on the patterns of the tabernacle (cf. Lev 25:8–9, 40).

The apocalyptic literature of the first century CE divides the unseen heavens in multiple ways, most often in the pattern of the tabernacle to demonstrate dwelling levels of holiness created by God due to anticipated sin of the created people and the sin of other beings who previously dwelt in God's holy presence (appendix 1, fig. 4). The previously existing creation of the unsensed place of the substance of the eternal οὐρανός "heaven," as synonymous with the holy-*places* (Heb 8:1–2; 9:12, 24), is an eternal (measureless durative time) dwelling place in God's presence and light of glory. In the visible creation, Gen 1 establishes that the already separated creation from holy space responds to God's spoken fiats. Creation is not itself sinful or corrupted. Creation, in fulfilling God's spoken design, is always good (Gen 1:31; 1 Tim 4:4). Cf. Martens, *God's Design*, 25. Levels of holiness apply not to the attributes of creation itself, as in later gnostic ideology but to the holiness state and separation from God of those dwelling in the respective divided domains.

32. Laansma, "Hidden Stories in Hebrews," 16–17. Cf. Laansma, "Heaven in the General Epistles," 111–18.

33. MacRae, "Heavenly Temple and Eschatology," 190. MacRae, concerning the Pastor's message of hope to strengthen his audience, states, "This he attempts to provide by grounding hope in the Hellenistic, dualist category of the true reality located in the heavenly world of which the earthly represents only inferior copies. He uses the 'vertical' eschatological perspective, in other words, neither to oppose nor to correct the 'horizontal' one, but to reinforce it." Cf. Sterling, "Ontology Versus Eschatology," 210. Sterling finds convincing evidence in Hebrews for platonic language of ontological reality in what might be called "eschatological Platonism." Contrary to MacRae, Sterling finds the eschatology derives from the heavenly realities already present in the Jewish culture of the first century CE, rather than the Platonic language as a later development from eschatology. Cf. Stewart, "Cosmology, Eschatology, and Soteriology," 546. Stewart

For the Pastor, the tabernacle place elements of holiness in estrangement from the place of God's presence involves the problem of sin. The subtopic is found twenty-four times. He begins with this issue in the DI with the understanding that in the previous structural form of the created eternal/perpetual-*places* (Heb 1:2), there exists a necessity for "purification of sins" by the Son (Heb 1:3c). He later speaks of the need of "atonement for the sins of the people" (Heb 2:17) and a requirement for earthly priests "to bring offerings of both gifts and sacrifices for sins" (Heb 5:1). The presence or absence of "sins" determines the confines of holy-*places* in a functional, graded, spatial relationship for people and other created beings in relation to God's holiness.

Further, for the Pastor, this decoupling of God's holiness from the visible temporary dwellings of the earthly eternal/perpetual-*places* probably occurs *before* Adam's sin. The Son's speaking the current visible creation of the temporary decaying "earth" and "world, cosmos" of the "eternal/perpetual-*places*" was "at the beginning" (Heb 1:10–12; 3:3–4; cf. Matt 25:34). Adam is not mentioned in description of the plight of the eternal/perpetual-*place* that was made apart from God's holy dwelling (Heb 11:3). Also, biblical history never connects God's creative acts at "the beginning" to places of holiness linked with people and the inherited sin from Adam (cf. Gen 3:15; Rom 5:12).[34] Even before the Adam's sin, the presence of sin, due to protection of the dwelling place in God's

---

wisely writes, "The author's world view, among other things, includes his perception of the temporal and spatial dimensions of the metanarrative undergirding reality and the unfolding of history. Lack of attention to these spatial and temporal facets of the book of Hebrews can result in misinterpretation." The antithetical tension of these two typical adversarial contrasts by scholarship are likely complementary. Cf. Steyn, "Eschatology of Hebrews," 429–50. Steyn understands Hebrew's eschatology as being both spatial and temporal in nature, against the common adversative frequent practice to contrast the linear view of history in the Bible with the "circular" view of Greek philosophy.

34. Schenck, *Cosmology and Eschatology in Hebrews*, 142–43. Schenck recognizes in Hebrews, "While the author may not tell us of Adam's sin, it is also possible that these characteristics of the created realm served some purpose in God's plan from its foundation, as was the atoning role of Christ as 'high priest' and redeemer." In his conclusion on this observation, he states, "Finally, I speculated on the function and nature of the creation within the purposes of God. Gaps in meaning preclude a full understanding of the author's thought, and it is possible that the author saw Adam as the culprit behind the current state of the created realm. On the other hand, it is also possible that the author believed God had planned the redemption of the creation through Christ from the 'foundation of the world.'" Cf. Lee, *Death Warning*. Lee investigates the probability of mortal death before the sin of Adam and Eve. The availability of the tree of life before sin could support mortality and transformation to heaven as an available option in the separated cosmic design.

holiness, necessitated God's wrath, and hiddenness by divisions of the eternal/perpetual-*places* as later typologically pictured by Israel (Heb 3:11; 4:3; cf. Heb 11:37; cf. Lev 10:1–3).[35]

The Pastor, in the line of noncanonical ST literature, sets culpability and destiny for death, chaos, and decay in dwellings apart from the living God upon "the devil" (Heb 2:14–15).[36] The NT likewise echoes sin by the devil "from the beginning" (John 8:44; 1 John 3:8) before Adam. These observations make improbable the common position that only

---

35. The revealed typology of the antitype of the wilderness experience of Israel fulfilled the type of God's wrath on approach of unbelievers to the eternal/perpetual-*places* in heaven (Heb 3:12, 19). For the concept of God's wrath in relationship to his holiness, see, Feldmeier and Spieckermann, *God of the Living*, 340. Feldmeier and Spieckermann interpret God's wrath as a withdrawal of God's love and revelation to hide himself from a relationship and to allowance of one to follow one's own devices unto destruction. In the modern age, the term is often confused with punishment, due to the dominant collectivist society in loss of the cultural values of honor and shame. Implication of God's wrath results in an increased distance away from the benefits of God's love. Cf. Malina and Pilch, "Wrath of God," 147. Malina and Pilch describe wrath in social context of first century CE. Punishment operates as a legal term for a specific response to a specific transgression of law. However, wrath is defined as the withdrawal of relationship of a person of higher status from a person of lower status when one brings shame or slight by some dishonoring behavior that violates both the person of status and the groups honor. In a first-century CE patron society, any perceived shame was unacceptable and must be avenged in hiddenness of any relationship. In ST and NT culture in the patron model, God is understood in higher status in creation. Any rejection of God's will and provision then brings shame toward God and must be corrected in hiddenness. God's patience in his wrath is not necessarily quick (cf. Rom 2:5) in hopes that the experience of his goodness may led one to repentance (cf. Rom 2:4). The exercise of wrath by God is his withdrawal from a relationship which brings shame upon him by failure to repent of sin with faith in Jesus as Christ.

36. In ST literature, spirits in the lower realms of the heavens were often seen as harbingers of God's judgment (cf. Sir 39:28–31). Also, in the writings of ST Jewish authors, humanity is not responsible for the visible cosmological dwellings apart from God in darkness. The culpability for the divided heavens was charged upon evil spirits. The Book of the Watchers contained in 1 Enoch mentions angels who await execution of judgment (1 En. 10:4–7; 18:14; cf. Jude 6, 13; Rev 12:1, 4), and who are offered no opportunity of forgiveness (1 En. 12:5). Their exit of the highest heaven echoes Jesus's accounting of Satan's fall from heaven (1 En. 12:3; cf. Luke 10:18), and his being bound to earth, never for eternity to return to the highest eternal heaven (1 En. 14:5; cf. Jude 6; 2 Pet 2:4). These writers place this event in the beginning, writing "those are the ones transgressing the commandments of the Lord in the beginning by their rising" (1 En. 18:15; cf. John 8:44; 1 John 3:8). The ST theological view of the origin of sin strongly supports the current temporary creation as a creative response to evil angels before the sin recorded in Gen 3 by Adam. God's same holiness of his dwelling place typologically demanded a response to the sin of people in Gen 3, to reveal heavenly matters in the same way as the tabernacle. It is probable that God made similar dwelling adjustments when angelic sin shamed the holiness of his will (cf. Luke 10:18).

Adam is culpable for the problem of sin in God's *entire* creation.[37] There is also a high possibility that God has been an eternally active creator long before his creation of Genesis and Adam.[38] In fairness, Adam is only responsible for man's inheritance of sin and continuance of death upon *all people* (Rom 5:12), with only minor dwelling changes in an already distant, temporary, and decaying place from the dwelling presence with the living God (Gen 3:14–19).[39] The holiness of God's dwelling places

---

37. E.g., Plummer, *40 Questions*, 152. Plummer ignores precosmic angelic sin in creation, concluding, "From the outset, the Bible establishes that God created a perfect world, humans destroyed that perfection through their rebellion (Gen 1–3)." In relation to the Pastor's typological dualism, this approach escalates the antitype of earthly Eden by ignoring the type of the unseen eternal/perpetual-*places* it portrayed.

38. *Pace*, "What Was God Doing." The authors state, "So before He created the universe, God experienced absolute satisfaction in Himself. God dwelt joyfully alone in eternity as the Trinity. These three were together in fellowship with one another from all eternity. They loved each other. We know at some point they discussed the redemption of mankind (Ephesians 1:4–5; 2 Timothy 1:9; John 17:24), but everything else lies in mystery." Cf. Grudem, *Systematic Theology*, 161. Grudem in review of passages on the eternality of God's existence states, "These passages indicate explicitly what we can learn elsewhere from the doctrine of the Trinity, namely, that among the persons of the Trinity there has been perfect love and fellowship and communication for all eternity. The fact that God is three persons yet one God means that there was no loneliness or lack of personal fellowship on God's part before creation." At some point in temporal existence, it is probable that God existed alone. However, the point of God's first creation of the substance and beings of the eternal/perpetual-*place* of heaven may in space-time views be much farther into eternity than allowed by modern apologetics and theology. Cf. Aquinas, *Summa Theologica*, I, Q. 31, Art. 3. Aquinas asserts the term can only refer to the Trinity as alone.

39. The Genesis cosmogony is "very good" (Gen 1:31) or, in modern terms, "perfect" in the sense that in response to God's speaking, it fulfills God's purposes. However, as a separated temporary creation from the substance of heaven, it still lacked due to darkness and decay any eternal qualities with perpetual living survival (Heb 1:10–12; 11:3). Further, there were substitute lights for God's eternal light (cf. Rev 21:3; 22:5). The greatest evidence against an intended enduring visible creation before Adam's sin is the presence of evil and opportunity of its knowledge to make one wise. This knowledge comes in the form of a persuasive orator, who is allowed in this *perfect* world to make his case in a temptation against the will of God. The evidence for eternal durative perfection of Eden easily fails by these already existing problems in that dwelling location of Eden for Adam and Eve. For a recent scholarly evaluation of proposals to solve this dilemma, see Bimson, "Reconsidering a 'Cosmic Fall,'" 63–81. Solution to the presented tension by expanding the Genesis cosmogony to include unproven scientific claims of evolution, theistic evolution, a "gap theory" between Gen 1:1 and 1:2, or drastic changes in the entire function of everything created does not find traction in the background theology of Hebrews. Also, there is no evidence that anything similar to Eden, with a separation from God's dwelling, has existed before this present temporary heaven and earth creation, with humanity and fallen heavenly beings in dwelling separation from the substance-reality of the heavens. Whether the earth is

in relation to precosmic sin is often not heard, concerning the invisible substance creation and living unseen God, in relation to current places that are separated due to the lack of holiness of dwelling people and other beings therein (cf. Lev 10:9–11).[40]

Inversely, the Pastor exhorts his audience to respond by faith to "approach" (προσέρχομαι) these places of the unseen living God (Heb 12:1–2) like people of the great cloud of witnesses before them, by personal acceptance of the conversation of God's speaking both in life's suffering and their coming deaths. The key subtopic for acceptance of God's calling to invisible heavenly promises is "faith" (πίστις), which is found thirty-one times, second only to "God."[41] In Heb 11, the Pastor

---

relatively young or older, any duration of time does not compare to measureless time of God's creativeness in eternity before the precosmic existence of heaven (cf. Ps 90:1–2).

40. E.g., Beale and Carson, *Commentary on the New Testament*, 867. Cf. Beale, *Temple and the Church's Mission*; Beale and Kim, *God Dwells among Us*; Barr, *Garden of Eden*. Barr proposes Genesis history as a lost chance at immortality from the tree of life, where death is a natural state of Adam even before sin. He dismantles the scholarly antithesis between immortality of the soul and resurrection that was speculated in the early twentieth century and spearheaded by Oscar Cullmann and Krister Stendahl. Cullmann, *Immortality of the Soul*; Stendahl, *Immortality and Resurrection*; Stendahl, "Immortality is Too Much," 193–202. Barr reveals the fallacy of the Jewish and Greek wholistic vs. divisible concepts in anthropology as mainly scholarly bias, in the fallacy of a totality concept of meaning, applied across all uses in the OT. He also negates as fallacy the concept of an *after*life for continued living but still considers death as only fleshly without any consideration as an eternal/perpetual-*place* separation from God. Barr does not consider in biblical texts the background eternal/perpetual-*places* of heaven as the place of possible destiny in Christ. He does greatly add to the conversation by revealing modern, generally accepted fallacies but escalates the antitypes that speak about the eternal/perpetual-*places* over the reality of the types they represent in the eternal/perpetual-*places*.

Beale, Carson, Kim, and Barr represent constricted cosmic-*field* proposals with solutions toward a perpetual return to the original Eden conditions of creation, which is doubtful and unsupported in Hebrews. The creation of the eternal/perpetual-*places* before the sin of Adam and Eve presumes a situation of separation within God's temple that required the necessity of approach even before Adam's sin, while the earthly Eden of Genesis was accessible to him. It is more likely the earthly Eden serves as a revelatory antitype in a situation of precosmic sin that necessitated a separated creation from the space of God's holiness before the fall of Adam and Eve. In antitype fulfillment, once people had sinned, these people had to leave Eden in correspondence to the heavenly type it represented.

41. Gelardini, "Faith in Hebrews," 261–72. Gelardini follows Martin Karrer's remarks concerning the cloud of witnesses in Heb 12:1, writing, "This points upwards to heaven as the goal of the path of faith" (269). Martin Karrer, *Der Brief an die Hebräer*, 2:300. *Contra* Easter, "Faith in the God," 76–91. Easter argues, "God is the object of faith in Hebrews because God is the one who holds the power of resurrection, the eschatological hope of both the faithful one par excellence (Jesus) and those who follow

begins his historical memorial of decisions of faith in life and the heavenly homecoming at death with a spatial definition, stating, "But faith is the substance-reality of things being presently expected, the evidence of things not presently being seen" (Heb 11:1).[42] Faith accepts the speech-action statements about the invisible God in his creation, along with the future unseen promises of access to these places in death, as a certainty of continued living.

The Pastor, in his example of Moses, writes that he "by faith" (πίστει) did not fear the king "because he persevered as continually seeing the invisible *one*" (Heb 11:27). Moses followed others before him in the path of the Christ (Heb 11:26; cf. Heb 6:1–5). Moses's life of faith persevered as if he could see the living God, when he could not in reality see him in earthly life, for he could not see God and live (Exod 33:17–23).

In summation of those who lived and died by faith before Moses, the Pastor writes, "But now they continually desire a better place that is a heavenly place. For this reason, God is not ashamed to be called their God. Because he prepared a city for them" (Heb 11:16). The time for the desire by faith is "now" and the spatial place is "heaven" in a "city" with others. The Pastor mentions neither a timeless "eternal present" nor a prolonged eschatological waiting after death for fleshly resurrection, before beginning of the promises of dwelling with God (Heb 12:22–25).[43]

---

him" (76). The claim of only faith in God in exclusion of Jesus may overreach the whole of biblical text. Jesus said, "Believe in God, also believe in me" (John 14:1). Later Trinitarian debates may have overextended the persons of God, as revealed to creation, away from monotheism, where simply, Jesus is God in flesh (cf. John 1:14). Easter, *Faith and the Faithfulness*. In antithesis, Easter divides faith in life-after-death perspectives into either Jewish or Roman purviews. Easter assumes for the Jewish view that "the body and spiritual natures are so intertwined that to remove the one makes the person no longer human" (64). He further claims, "For Hebrews, to be human is to be embodied. As such, Hebrews does not envision an immortal soul that lives on apart from the body" (69). His evidence against a separable living existence after fleshly death is limited due to space. His position remains unlikely since he bases his examples on a rational speculation of the possibility within Jewish society and a listing of a multiplicity of scholars who follow similar views. In his opinion, faith's conclusion is an unrealized perfection of postmortem enduring life (92) that only becomes perfection at a fleshly resurrection (94). This position escalates the complementary truth of resurrection to match a hope on a the visible cosmic-*field*. Due to rational earthly expectations, it inverts the faith for entrance into the "eternal/perpetual-*places*" and *aiōn-field* expressed in Hebrews.

42. For the lexical evidence for spatial translation of ὑπόστασις as "substance-reality" and ἔλεγχος as "evidence, proof," rather than the classical forensic glosses of Martin Luther as "assurance" and "conviction," respectively, see, Gelardini, "Faith in Hebrews," 269. These referents are explored in context in unit D1ʹ UI/Pt1 (Heb 11:1–2).

43. Eisele, "Bürger zweier Welten," 35–44. Cf. Feldmeier and Spieckermann. *God*

Atonement and the Logic of Resurrection in Hebrews 9:27–28

The renewed holiness of part of God's dwelling place by the Son drives the main thematic unit F of the Pastor's homily (Heb 8:1–2; 9:23). God has spoken direct prophecy of a future time of impermanent return to a temporary Edenic-like ministry in his separated space of the darkness of the "earth" (γῆ) and "world" (κόσμος).[44] Nevertheless, God also had spoken to OT believers of better heavenly promises of dwellings which are holy in his living presence by the ministry of his Son.[45] The Pastor orates that without such faith, it is impossible to live sacrificially as pleasing to God (Heb 11:6). The person of faith seeks the final reward of seeing God in the holy place of his presence (Heb 9:28; cf. Matt 5:8).

GOD SPEAKS BY THE PERSON OF A SON ON BEHALF OF SONS

Just as in the DI (Heb 1:1–4), where the Pastor introduces "God . . . spoke to us in a Son" (Heb 1:1–2), God's speech-action in the interim teaching before Heb 9:27–28, reveals, by Jesus as Χριστός, his "ability" (δύναμις) to bring people to himself.[46] The Pastor does more than speak polemic about who Christ is, as both God and Jesus, in a defense of a high Christology that overshadows later issues. He stresses that there must be congruence

---

of the Living, 109, 404–05, 413; Cody, *Heavenly Sanctuary and Liturgy*, 117–27. Cf. Russell, *History of Western Philosophy*, 206.

44. Cf. Bockmuehl, "Locating Paradise," 207. Bockmuehl observes, "Jews and Christians in late antiquity knew perfectly well how to distinguish terrestrial from celestial realities, however differently or vaguely they may in practice have drawn the dividing line between the two. They merely refused to take for granted what the Enlightenment world would refuse to question: the notion that spiritual and terrestrial truth belong in two incompatible spheres, which must be kept separate and not allowed to 'contaminate' each other."

45. Barth, *Die Errettung vom Tode*. Barth concludes the emphasis in faith in the OT, as expressed in their thanksgiving Psalms, for salvation from death. These OT people of faith evidenced at an individual judgment, desire to see the face of God in the eternal in heaven more than a resurrection to earthly living again. The OT faith for the righteous at judgment embraced continued living without any prolonged experience of death (Pss 9:13, 17; 16:10; 31:17; 56:13; 68:20; 86:13; 89:48; 116:8; 139:8).

46. The Pastor uses two subtopics to delineate these relationships. The first is "Son/son" (υἱός) which occurs twenty-one times. This term of relationship refers either to God in the person of Christ (Heb 1:5) or those who confess Christ in relationship to the Father (Heb 2:10; 12:5–8). The second is "brethren" (ἀδελφός), used ten times. Cf. Schenck, "Keeping His Appointment," 91–117. Schenck is probably correct to state that Christ is the Son before incarnation, as the creator of the heavens and earth, and at exaltation, is enthroned as the Son at his appointment assigned to him.

between the hope of their "confession" (ὁμολογία) and what the Christ, as Jesus, the Son of God, spatially had achieved and is able to continue to achieve, as a person, for sinful people, in the places of God (Heb 3:1; 4:14; 10:23).[47] In their confession, as "holy brethren," his audience are "partners in a heavenly *ministry* calling" (κλήσεως ἐπουρανίου μέτοχοι Heb 3:1). They were exhorted to hold onto a confession in a great high priest, Jesus the Son of God, "who having passed through the heavens" (Heb 4:14), which allows them to have boldness in their own time of need on their "approach" (προσέρχομαι) to the throne of grace (Heb 4:16), since "for he having promised is faithful" (Heb 10:23). This implies his listeners at death will, without doubt, follow the same way through the heavens to God at judgment. The heavenly hope of their confession was previously exampled in those "having confessed that they are strangers and sojourners upon the earth" (Heb 11:13). Confession in the Pastor's exhortation normatively embraces God's heavenly places and confessors receive an inheritance in death of familial sonship in heaven (Heb 2:11–13).

As seen in table 1, "Words in Hebrews Linked with God," many of the terms the Pastor applies to the Son's, exemplary, atoning ability concerning people's sins, have implied spatial movement overtones between the heavens and earth. Most as verbal nouns highlight nodal points along the "way" (ὁδός) of people to the presence of God. The identifier frequency reveals the spatial emphasis and pictures a lively view of Christ.

The Son may now occupy the position of the seat at the throne of God, but he is far from stationary (cf. Acts 7:56).[48] The Son continues as high priest in an active ministry "according to the ability of an endless life" (Heb 7:16). The verbal nouns and activity, combined with his often use of pres. and fut. tense syntax, provide evidence for a continual, vigorous

47. The specific language of the activity of God through the ability of Jesus as the promised Christ and Lord, begins introduction in the DI (Heb 1:1–4). The essential element in this relationship is the confession of his fellow brethren listening to his homily. The subtopic "confession" (ὁμολογία) appears three times. He introduces their confession in the beginning of unit C (Heb 3:1—4:13) with exhortation about ministerial accountability. In the two bookend section transitions of the large, central exposition climax of unit F (Heb 5:1—10:18), the Pastor mentions the "confession" (Heb 4:14; 10:23) in both discourse level summaries of STr1 (Heb 4:14–16) and STr2 (Heb 10:19–25). This common confession in Jesus as apostle and high priest of their heavenly calling unites the Pastor and his audience together in this special Father-Son-sons relationship (Heb 2:10; 3:6; 12:5–6; cf. John 1:12).

48. Delitzsch, *Commentary on the Epistle*, 56–57. Delitzsch comments, "In this created heaven the glorified Jesus presents Himself visibly to those blessed ones who are deemed worthy of the sight, as He does invisibly to the eternal Father in the uncreated heaven." Cf. Crowson, *Epistle to the Hebrews*, 12.

ministry as shepherd to bring his sheep to the Father's heavenly dwelling in a relationship together as his brothers. The aorist syntax implies some force that the sequential action of salvation for some has already begun (Heb 2:9–18; 6:13–15).[49] The Pastor's language of familial relationships illuminates the dwelling nearness to God in heaven through confession in Jesus in his ministry as the Christ, upon approaching in heaven.[50]

The Pastor shares that the Son was saved by the Father after his death at judgment before his flesh resurrection (Heb 5:7). Jesus's prayers and supplications with loud crying were heard by the Father, who was able "to save" (σῴζειν) him at his judgment because of his reverence. Once the process of rising to God completed, he became the source of "eternal/perpetual-*place* salvation" (σωτηρίας αἰωνίου Heb 5:9) for others who likewise approach after death at judgment (Heb 9:27–28).

The Pastor's concern is for his brethren, who may embrace ministry that is incongruent with the present teaching of his listeners confession as sons of God (Heb 5:11—6:8). A previous ministerial choice now contradicts the beginning teaching about the word of Christ, as the Son, to enter only once into God's presence for atonement to receive salvation into heaven for his continued ministry.

Their teaching alternative depicts Christ, and the sons who follow him, as "those having fallen away" (παραπεσόντας Heb 6:6) at "the eternal/perpetual-*place* judgment" (Heb 6:2). This supposition likely occurs after "rising *of* the dead people" (Heb 6:2) concerning "those whom having tasted both the good conversation of God's ability and the present subsequently coming eternal/perpetual-*place*" (Heb 6:5). In the errant teaching about the Christ, neither the Son nor sons remain in heaven after entrance to the Father. As errantly taught, for those who "fall away" at judgment, it is impossible to start again back with the first required step of "repentance of dead works" (Heb 6:1) about the Christ. This teaching would "put Christ to open shame" by crucifying him again (Heb 6:6),

---

49. God's covenant to Abraham begins fulfillment at his death with an assembly of his people and other nations in heaven. Jesus called this place "Abraham's bosom" in reference to the place in heaven. Believers in heaven later, at Jesus's rising to God, followed Jesus as their Shepherd into the presence of God (Heb 2:13; 13:20; cf. Matt 27:51–53).

50. Feldmeier and Spieckermann, *God of the Living*, 89–92. Feldmeier and Spieckermann assert, "The point of Christology is soteriology: in the Son, God as Father places believers as children in a new relationship with himself." Cf. Peeler, "Ethos of God in Hebrews," 37–51; Peeler, *You Are My Son*, 8; Contra Mackie, "Let Us Draw Near," 17–36.

since it would symbolically demonstrate that his previous attempt did not remain in heaven or bring his brethren with him.

Also, the confession by sons of God is not mere magic words, incantations, or formula ritual observances that must be perservered for maintenance of God's familial relationship.[51] The power of one's confession in receiving Jesus as a onetime offering for *all* sin is that even at the reality of God's judgment of his people for sin after death—his people as familial sons and brethren are still his people (Heb 10:26–39). God in his love is jealous for the obedience and will train his sons as a Father (Heb 12:6).

GOD SPEAKS ABOUT HOLY-PLACES, HEAVENLY PLACES AND SINFUL PEOPLE

Current study of the places described by the Pastor conduct under the misleading elevated terms of "cosmology," "mysticism," and more recently, "critical spatiality."[52] Most concepts in these philosophical and

---

51. Bornkamm, *Studien Zu Antike*, 188–203. Bornkamm follows the presuppositions of his Lutheran theology, which connect his biblical interpretation of confession in Hebrews to the symbolic antitypes of the sacraments. This causes him to press the confession too far into congregational sacramental language, which is required for salvific ends, rather than public symbolic testimony in faith of the unseen type in heaven. Cf. Mackie, "Son of God in Hebrews,"114–29. Mackie, by interpreting the Pastor's apocalyptic language of the unseen type in the heavens as divine dramatization in symbolic metaphor, places the confession as faith in imaginary figurative categories, rather than real ontological events. One perseveres by following mystical concepts in architectural psychological mysticism, instead of mimicking the pattern or symbolism that pictures the reality of Jesus's living way in death to resurrection.

52. Adams, *Constructing the* World, 75. Adams finds that even in the LXX, when "world" (κόσμος) is paired with "heaven" (οὐρανός), the meaning speaks of the host of celestial bodies that inhabit the visible sky and never the dwelling of God. In first-century CE sources probable for the Pastor, "world" (κόσμος) as a referent, never refers to the dwelling place of God in heaven. The terms "cosmology," "mysticism" and the newest, "critical spatiality," are words unknown to the Pastor, which are listed in table 6, that have incurred later conceptual weight foreign to him. The etymology of the term "cosmology" naturally limits it to rational study of the visible, sensed creation. The philosophical and theological term "cosmology" serves scholarship as the flagship for discussion of biblical place as delimited space and time. Scholarly use includes the domain of the heaven of God's dwelling. Among modern categories, cosmology often alarmingly expands to include in varying degrees the unseen material creation of God's dwelling place in heaven, even though the first-century CE Greek use of κόσμος uniformly locates the referent only with the visible creation of the earthly, inhabited world. The label "critical spatiality" does improve upon it. Also problematic is the term "mysticism," which has negative connotations of nonreality. The category of cosmology, along with the other later Latin, philosophical, and theological terms, weakens the specificity

Atonement and the Logic of Resurrection in Hebrews 9:27–28

theological categories inherently either flatten or spiritualize the narrative images of the Pastor.[53] He and other first-century CE authors communicate in expressions embracing a duality (*aiōn-field*) of heavenly and earthly places, with each intersecting the other in their own distinct local space-time.[54]

---

of the Pastor's *aiōn-field* apocalyptic language, and enables the more fluid adjustments to subsequent, foreign paradigms unknown by the Pastor (cf. Col 2:8).

Gelardini, "Existence beyond Borders," 187. Gelardini states, "The notion of critical spatiality in New Testament studies and methods reminds Bible scholars that not only time–along with historical and cultural contexts–shaped the minds of the authors of New Testament books, but also space and the different ways of interacting with it." Gelardini recognizes that among many recent "turns," scholarship has made a fresh "spatial turn" in methods that address spatial questions of modern and postmodern culture and scientific relevance in NT studies. Cf. Stewart, "New Testament Space/Spatiality," 139. Stewart acknowledges, "Despite such self-evident truisms, for much of the twentieth century, studies of social phenomena neglected the aspect of space." Cf. Sleeman, "Geography and the Ascension Narrative in Acts,," 79. Sleeman, proposes the entire narrative of Acts as "produced under a Christological heaven." Sleeman comments concerning Luke's "Christological heaven" that "this orientation does not reduce to materialist/non-materialist dualisms, and indeed challenges such categories." Further, that "a place concept . . . is not to be reduced to aspatial, 'spiritual' terms.'"

53. Laansma, "Cosmology of Hebrews," 127. Scholars of Hebrews recognize the first-century CE duality of heavenly and earthly places in the Pastor's language. However, differences arise in either their nature or the rendered destiny of the heavens or earth. Laansma admits in his cosmological analysis a heavy weight of "canonical coherence" from Rom 8, which he interprets as salvation in a visible earthly creation.

54. Philo wrote that the "temple complex" (ἱερόν) was the customary pattern containing the "cosmos, world" (κόσμος) and the "temple building" (ναός), with the latter as "heaven" (οὐρανόν) stating, "On the one part the things upwardly toward the true temple grounds of God, it ought to hold the whole cosmos, on the other part of the temple building having the holiest place of which is the place of substance being part, heaven, but on the first part votive offerings of the stars, on the second part, his underservant priests of capable angels, bodiless souls, not a mixture of rational and irritational nature, of what sort to be our escorts, but having themselves eliminated the irrational part, are through all intelligence, pure reasoning, like the One, but on the other part the things made by the hand of man" (*Spec. Laws* 1:66–67 PAGM). He nests two statements in a A B B´ A´ pattern, with the second μὲν . . . δὲ nested inside his first one, where the "temple complex" contains patterns both for A: "the whole inhabited world," and B: the "temple building" with the "holiest place" (ἁγιώτατον) of the dwelling of God as "heaven" (οὐρανός). Philo further juxtaposes B´: capable "angels" (ἄγγελος) and A´: hand-made things, represents the unseen substance-reality of heaven and (A) the visible reality of the visible κόσμος.

Heavenly Places

In common with Moses's writing of Genesis, the Pastor *speaks* in a narrative that includes topography of places (cf. Gen 1–2). When reading Hebrews, either in his Greek language or by a translation, the topological and typological images spontaneously stimulate mental mapping questions.[55] Some places characterized lack corresponding English word translation equivalents.[56] For assistance, the term "place(s)" in translation of appropriate terms, which have spatial weight, is added to force consideration of its feature of place. It is good to often remind modern readers of these possible place considerations, so as to anchor the spatial sense of the Pastor's overarching faith motif that God speaks through the Son concerning a living relationship with people in the achieved "eternal/perpetual-*places*" (Heb 1:2).

The Pastor speaks about the "ordered dominion" (οἰκουμένη Heb 1:6; 2:5), which is often incorrectly translated "world."[57] He initially

---

55. Casey, *Getting Back to Place*; Casey, *Fate of Place*. Casey outlines the ascendency in the modern era of site-specific models of space and a temporocentrism that draws much of the complex and subtle structure of place into its nebulous embrace. In *The Fate of Place*, Casey concludes, "Instead, it is a matter of realizing that the significance of place has been reasserted on a very different basis from that which it enjoyed in the ancient world, where its primacy was physical, metaphysical, and cosmological (physical and metaphysical in Aristotle; metaphysical and cosmological in Plato, Neoplatonism, and Hellenistic philosophy)" (337). The conception of creation as describable places was common in first-century CE Jewish literature. Cf. Fisher, "Celestial Topography."

56. The Greek dualistic language for translation into Latin, German, and English traditions often followed the theological and philosophical concepts approved by state-churches and now the approval of the current academy. In the state-churches, dualistic language was disapproved and aggressively destroyed, often with martyrdom of their proponents. It is now just ignored in those documents approved and preserved or picked over in one-sided anti-dualistic polemics of like-minded members; e.g., in most English translations, all three Greek words αιων (*aiōn*), οἰκουμένη (*oikoumenē*), and κόσμος (*kosmos*) are translated as "world" (Heb 1:2, 6; 10:5 NASB, ESV, HSCB, KJV, NIV [αιων = "universe"], RSV). This leveling obscures evidence of an open heaven with access by people. Also, the plural syntax of "heaven" (οὐρανός) is regularly translated as singular. Another example is translation of the Greek "holy-*places*" (τῶν ἁγίων) with a transliterated gloss of the Latin translation *sanctum* to English "sanctuary." These alterations miss the point of heavenly divisions and the purpose of the heavenly veil. A dualistic English translation of these Greek terms forces a consideration of the probable intended *aiōn-field* background sense.

57. Scholarly discussion is far from settled concerning the Pastor's concept of οἰκουμένη (*oikoumenē*) in Heb 1:6 and 2:5. BDAG, "οἰκουμένη," 699–700. For Bauer, the term in other biblical contexts than Hebrews usually refers to the inhabited earth, with acknowledgement of one patristic reference to include an "extraordinary use" in 1 Clem. 60:1, that includes "the realm of transcendent beings as well." Cf. Hengel,

references the place of God's ordered dominion at the enthronement of Jesus after his death and follows with God's brethren coming into God's οἰκουμένη at a similar after death transition.[58] His narrative specifies details about bidirectional movement between the holy place of God's dwelling and the earth.[59] These concern interconnecting activities between the heavens and earth for the sacrificial atonement of the sin of the people, perpetual priestly movement of Jesus as the Christ spanning the separated places, and the eternal/perpetual-*place* where God hopes that by faith sinful people after death and judgment, will follow Jesus to

---

Judaism and Hellenism, 19. Hengel writes that in Palestine under Hellenistic rule, the conception was that the whole land was the personal possession οἶκος of the king. As a term often used in the household Hellenistic patron system, Heb in 3:1–6 would expand Jesus's faithfulness in his οἶκος ("house") as greater than Moses in his οἶκος of either the earthly tabernacle or tent of meeting. The statement, "But the builder of all things is God" (Heb 3:4b) alludes to Jesus presently having faithful stewardship over *all* creation as the one building a house (cf. Heb 1:2).

Cf. Vanhoye, *Perfect Priest*, 233–39. Vanhoye identifies the events of Jesus's presentation in the οἰκουμένη in his "triumphant sacrifice." He recognizes the LXX use of οἰκουμένη as a "spiritual reality," in contrast to the "visible, material world" of the κόσμος, rather than including it. Cf. Bruce, *Epistle to the Hebrews*, 58n78. Bruce allows for expansion stating, "For the words would refer to God's bringing his firstborn back from death into the inhabited realm again." Schierse, *Verheißung und Heilsvollendung*, 96; Andriessen, "De Betekenis," 11, 13. Cf. Caneday, "Eschatological World," 28–39; Johnston, "Oikoumenē and κόσμος," 352–60.

58. For the Pastor, like Jesus (Matt 6:9–10; John 12:31) and certain NT authors (Luke 4:6; 14:30; 16:11; Acts 26:18; Rom 8:18–30; 2 Cor 4:4; Eph 2:2; Col 1:16; 1 Tim 6:16; 1 Pet 4:11; 5:11; 1 John 5:19; Rev 13:2), the unseen eternal/perpetual-*places* are considered under the dominion of God, whereas the earth and visible cosmos are under the dominion of the devil (Heb 2:14). The Pastor recognizes God's dominion by enthronement of Jesus Christ but admits not all things are in subjection to him yet (Heb 2:8). By adding spatial weight to αἰών and αἰώνιος as eternal/perpetual-*places*, the current dualistic boundaries of unseen spiritual warfare come into better focus. The recurrent idiom εἰς τοὺς αἰῶνας (τῶν αἰώνων), ἀμήν (Heb 13:20) renders "into the eternal/perpetual-*place* of the eternal/perpetual-*places*," often found in the LXX and NT, suggests the place of the holy of holies as the current location of God's full dominion with all in subjection to him.

59. The Pastor's time narrative functions in relation to either (1) the standard repetitive cycles of other sensed substances of the visible creation, or (2) conceptional degrees in distance units of holiness from the living God dwelling in the invisible space of heaven. For the visible, temporary creation of the distant "world" (κόσμος), God created the heavenly lights as the standards he places for the measure of time by the living in movement through space (Gen 1:14). Hence, he temporally locates earthly matters for his audience with referents: today, day, year, next, now, etc. (see table 2, "Time Referents"). However, in God's measure of time, it was still "today" (σήμερον) during the life of Moses, the life of Joshua, for Jesus at enthronement, and the time of his audience (Heb 1:5; 3:7, 13, 15; 4:7; 5:5; 13:8; cf. Ps 89:2 LXX [90:2 MT]; Isa 60:19–20; 2 Pet 3:8; Rev 21:23; 22:5).

himself, according to the likeness of Jesus's heavenly entrance as God's anointed Christ exemplar (Heb 2:9–18; 11:1, 6).[60]

With an apocalyptic *aiōn-field* lens, the Pastor links in descriptive depth the mystery of the ministry of Christ in atonement for sin as a sacrifice once, then perpetually as an active priest in "the way of holy-*places*" (Heb 9:8–14; cf. Matt 13:11; Rom 16:25; 1 Cor 2:7; 1 Tim 3:16).[61] He

---

60. Laansma, "Cosmology of Hebrews," 127. Laansma comments, "Hebrews' cosmology does enter into open view as an aspect of salvation itself; it is not *merely* among the writer of Hebrews' presuppositions. Salvation in this letter is construed to a significant degree in *local* terms: it is a destination of redeemed humanity, a *place* under the various names" (italics Laansma). Cf. Feinberg, *Four Views on Heaven*. Feinberg documents a scholarly response against views with open heavens now available to believers. In *Four Views*, the open heaven view includes the concept that the spiritual unseen creation as "immaterial," the believer's soul who is in Jesus's presence as "bodiless," no one has "risen" from the dead to God yet until an awaited future event, and eternal/perpetual-*place* life only exists in earthly form of this temporary creation, all of which logically infers that the living soul of the deceased has no "life" until a bodily flesh resurrection back into the temporary creation at Jesus's second coming to earth.

61. E.g., the Pastor proclaims in Heb 9:11, based on the clarification of the Holy Spirit about "the way of the holy-*places*" (Heb 9:8), "But Christ, after arriving himself is a high priest of the good *places* existing, through the greater and more perfect tabernacle not made with hands, that is not of this creation" (Heb 9:11). After the onetime completion of his anointed sacrificial atonement as the substitutionary sacrifice, "through his own blood he entered the holy-*places* he himself finding an eternal/perpetual-*place* of redemption" (Heb 9:12). The Pastor likely refers to access opened by judgment at death into the holy-*places* of God's dwelling in the holy of holies. Christ next, "though a spirit of an eternal/perpetual-*place* offered himself blameless to God" (Heb 9:14) which infers a journeying bodily spirit to God (cf. Heb 9:27–28).

Pace Moffitt, "Blood, Life, and Atonement," 211–24. Moffitt, in a reversal of events of the judgment and rising of the Christ (Heb 6:1–2), ignores the necessity of judgment after death (Heb 9:27) in his option for atonement occurring after flesh resurrection. He states, "Jesus's death on the cross is not the place or the primary means of atonement for the author of Hebrews. Rather, when the writer claims in [Heb] 8:4 that Jesus can only serve as a high priest in heaven, he intends to say that the great redemptive moment of the Christ event occurred not when Jesus was crucified, but after he was resurrected and ascended into heaven" (211–12). His subsequent address of critical questions to this thesis are not satisfying and eventually led in scholarly pushback to a position for the "process" of atonement both on earth and in heaven as depicted in the events of the Day of Atonement. Moffitt, "If Another Priest Arises," 68–79. Here again Moffitt leans heavily in imbalance for all rising to God after death as only flesh resurrection, with no endless life for Jesus until after visible resurrection. Cf. Moffitt's more balanced approach, Moffitt, "Hebrews," 533–36; Moffitt, "Jesus's Sacrifice," 51–68. Moffitt states, "In sum, when one allows that Hebrews works with a notion of sacrifice that is not reducible to a single event, such as the slaughter of the victim, but involves a process that culminates in bringing the elements of the sacrifice into God's presence, it becomes clear that Hebrews does not envision Jesus's death as the sum total of his atoning sacrifice. Rather, Hebrews thinks in terms of Jesus's death, resurrection, ascension, session, and return to his people in sacrificial, high-priestly, and atoning terms" (66).

describes mutually interactive relationships that necessitate the ministry of Christ in a spatial dualism of visible and invisible eternal/perpetual-*places*. Moreover, some eternal/perpetual-*places* are temporary and separated from his living, dwelling presence in a destiny for a catastrophe and end (Heb 11:3; 1:10–12; 12:25–29).[62]

The Pastor deploys "place" (τόπος) on three occasions (Heb 8:7; 11:8; 12:17). Concerning the first in Heb 8:7, modern lexicographers and translators, under the current weight toward a limited future eschatology, lean toward a temporal, "nonliteral" interpretation of τόπος (*topos*) as "occasion."[63] However, the substantial key emphasis of the Pastor's spatial links of typological, antitype to type, priestly movement pressures for a more balanced, spatial-temporal understanding. A heavy temporal gloss ignores the achieved changes in "place" (τόπος) accomplished by Jesus. This thematically includes a transformation from the first to second covenant that offered, at the personal events of death and judgment, a

---

62. Adams, *Stars Will Fall from Heaven*, 182–99. Adams concludes, "The belief that the created cosmos will come to a drastic end does not entail for the writer a repudiation of God's work of creation. The transient created order is subordinated to the eternal God and his unshakeable kingdom, but it is not thereby negated. There is nothing to suggest that it is valued as anything less than good. Although the writer does not explicitly speak of a material re-creation to follow the end of the present cosmos, there is, in my view, good reason to assume that this is what he expects" (199). However, his assertion that nowhere does the "author suggest that the transcendent heaven is a κόσμος νοητός, an 'intelligible world' on which our material world of shadows is modelled" (195), as well as his assumption that the tabernacle only applies to the eternal heaven, weaken under the evidence of the Pastor's description of the ministry of Christ.

63. E.g., BDAG, "τόπος," 1011. Bauer glosses, "Non-literal use οὐκ ἂν δευτέρας (sc. διαθήκης) ἐζητεῖτο τόπος *there would have been no occasion sought for a second (covenant)* Hb 8:7" (italics Bauer). Following this figurative trend, the NASB95 renders Heb 8:7, "For if that first covenant had been faultless, there would have been no occasion sought for a second." Other recent translations with this escalated temporal emphasis include RSV, ESV, HCSB, LEB, CSB. Many simply ignore τόπος, as in the NET, NRSV, and NCV. Those based before the twentieth century's weighted emphasis on future eschatology, which maintain τόπος as "place," are the Wycliffe, Geneva, KJV1900, Darby, ASV, NKJV, NIV, TNIV, and YLT. Some add a presumed sense for τόπος as "to look," as in the ISV and NRSV. See excursus B. Cf. Henry, "Cosmology of the Heaven(s)," 28–62. Both the excursus and chapter discuss how vertical to horizontal figurative leanings, away from heaven as a place of reality for believers after death, took a sharp turn by translation of the plural form of "heaven" (οὐρανός), as singular by Martin Luther. Also, it discusses the final horizontal leveling, in the twentieth century, to nonliteral heavenly places under the influence of Weiss and Schweitzer, combined with Dalman's definition of the kingdom of God as "kingly rule." These two main turns combined to work out against any interpretation of a present, vertical, literal, heavenly fulfillment of faith.

tangible spatial access by transformation of sinful people to enable dwelling with God in heaven (Heb 7:25—8:13).[64]

His second use of "place" in Heb 11:8 speaks of the antitype of Abraham's covenantal calling in Gen 12:7 to a place, declaring, "to a land of promise" (Heb 11:9). The Pastor interprets this promised land of Abraham's covenant typologically as an inheritance in heaven after death (Heb 11:8–16).

The Pastor, in his third use of "place" in Heb 12:17, describes Esau's lack of finding a place in space and time of the actions of his life for repentance of his choices. This led to the loss of Esau's rightful inheritance, as the firstborn to Isaac for being in the direct linage of the promised Christ, even before he was born (cf. Rom 9:10–13).

In his probable MCS, the Pastor infers four places for the movements of the ministry of Christ in relation to the similar movement of living people: (1) the place of living before fleshly death for both Jesus and all other people, (2) the place of personal judgment after fleshly death (Heb 6:2; 4:11–13; 9:27), (3) the place of Christ, appearing to waiting believers to raise them up from the experience of death and judgment to God's presence (Heb 4:13–16; 9:28; 10:37), (4) the "second *place* without sin," where Jesus lives. Christ "from a second *place* without sin" appears for "salvation" of believers for confident rising and entrance to God in heaven, for dwelling in God's presence and rest while awaiting others transformation in spiritual body resurrection (Heb 6:19–20; 7:26; 11:39–40; cf. Acts 7:55–60).

Few NT readers contest the first location of the Son's incarnation and first coming as Jesus in the flesh, as the Christ, while living on earth in the likeness of humanity (Heb 2:9–18). However, resistance concerning open heavens of the other places suggested in Heb 9:27–28 occurs due to two key concerns: (1) tension over concepts of "division" (μερισμός) concerning the people of God's creation, especially the Son's ability to divide people at death into transformed and whole bodily components of "soul and spirit" from the substance features of "joints and marrow"

---

64. The claim of changes in spatial location for believers at death and judgment does not antithetically remove or cancel other future complementary truth about other activities such as later spiritual body return, rewards for service, servant-rule on earth in a temporary ministry to bring other people to God, and finally, residing in God's dwelling at the end of the purpose for the separated holy-*places* in a final transition to one heaven and earth (Heb 12:25–29; cf. 1 Cor 15:24–26; Rev 21–22). It further does not suggest that other complementary truth is less significant to the Pastor since not mentioned thematically in his message.

at their judgment (Heb 4:11–16), and (2) pressures against dualistic suggestions of a common "conversation" (ῥῆμα) by faith, from the times of the elders' testimony, about an eternal ὑπόστασις ("substance-reality") of unseen creation (Heb 11:1–3).

These two issues impede acceptance of a believer's hope as "in heaven" and "to God" (Heb 7:25; 9:14; 11:4–6; 12:23), especially in considerations of the contextual identification of the latter three places mentioned in Heb 9:27–28 concerning (1) the place of judgment, (2) the "from" and the "to where" places of the appearing of Jesus, and (3) the place of salvation rest in God's dwelling presence.

The spatial fullness of the Pastor's apocalyptic (*aiōn-field*) language for the inherited *present* reality regarding heavenly glory and eternal beauty with Jesus at death and judgment often is treated as symbolic metaphor. Most commonly, those who hold such beliefs exchange the Pastor's heavenly spatial hope for flattened symbolism and metaphor with escalation of the complementary truth of a collective temporary return of believers for a future, perfected, Edenic living on earth for ministry.[65]

For the Pastor, heaven, as a place in God's presence, exists as more than just the abstract source of a future *earthly* salvation.[66] It is unlikely that his evidence incorporates disorganized and imprecise thoughts concerning the promised *heavenly* reality. An unorganized mystical approach toward his explanations, both in defense and teaching about Jesus as the

---

65. Schenck, "Archaeology of Hebrews' Tabernacle Imagery," 238–58. *Contra* Stegemann and Stegemann, "Does the Cultic Language," 18. Statemann and Stegemann state, "Our thesis is that the cultic language of Hebrews is not metaphorical and does not substitute for a real meaning of the death of Christ but speaks of Christ as a real high priest and of his death as real sacrifice." Cf. Moffitt, "Perseverance, Purity, and Identity," 357–81. Moffitt options for reality of the language in Hebrews, however he examples a future eschatology that is focused mainly on future flesh resurrection, to be near God on earth at Jesus's second coming.

66. Bultmann set off modern discussion against a structural view of heaven in his attempts to demythologize the Bible, stating, "The cosmology of the New Testament is essentially mythical in character. The world is viewed as a three-storied structure, with the earth in the centre, the heaven above, and the underworld beneath." Bultmann, "New Testament and Mythology," 1. This finally in NT scholarship collapsed heaven as an accessible reality for people in the early twentieth century. Bultmann's ideas dominated scholarship for over fifty years until the latter twentieth century. Many next-generation scholars still follow some variations of his conclusions; e.g., Houtman, *Der Himmel im Alten Testament*, 283–317. In the later twentieth century, scholars acknowledged ancient, Jewish, organized, heavenly concepts based upon heaven serving as the place of postmortem existence over the forces of death; e.g., Stadelmann, *Hebrew Conception of the World*, 169–70; Oden, "Cosmogony, Cosmology," 1162–71; Lucas, "Cosmology," 130–39.

Christ, would cancel his credibility, invalidate the basis of his arguments and encouragement as fictitious, and support later questions against the record in the biblical canon.[67] His excellent Greek prose suggests that his deployments of words in precise grammatical form intend accurate spatial descriptions. His verbal skill contained weighty, deliberate meaning, for both Hellenistic and Jewish listeners, about the literal ministry of Jesus as the Christ, "who having come through the heavens" (Heb 4:14). It does not contain extended metaphoric language intended only to impress them with its grandeur nor to simply to warn them through exhortation. He develops extensive images in a common first-century CE, *aiōn-field*, mental mapping of the unseen heavens as holy and eternal/perpetual-*place*(s) of "substance-reality" for the heavenly inheritance of salvation (Heb 4:14–16; 6:17–20; 7:25–26; 9:24–28; 10:19–23; 11:1).

The Pastor's grammatical syntax in his uses of the singulars and plurals of both "heaven(s)" and "holy place(s)" in his context properly support his parenesis. OT concepts of heavenly places center upon the Hebrew word "heavens" (השמים), which for unknown reasons is in the dual form of things in pairs. Waltke and O'Connor propose that the dual form is incidental due to the final root of the word being weak.[68] Williams and Beckman support the syntactical form as a plural of extension, where it refers to a single object with multiple parts.[69] Thus, heaven is one distinct creation but now is divided into distinct places, where each

67. Young, *Concept of Canon*. This response toward rejection of Hebrews from the canon of accepted Scripture did occur intermittently after the writing of the NT works. In 1522, Luther, in whose time knowledge of Jewish apocalyptic literature had disappeared, found no sense in NT *aiōn-field* language, and so closed the apocalyptic language of heaven by translation of the Greek plural οὐρανός ("heaven") into German as singular. This flattening of the plural heavens explores in excursus B. Cf. Henry, "Cosmology of the Heaven(s)," 28–62. When resurfacing in the eighteenth century, the apocalyptic language of Hebrews was viewed as mystical and outside the rational accepted norms of sensed reality mainly due to the growing influences of Cartesian philosophy with cosmic-*field* constrained concepts for humanity. Bultmann simply drew his mystical conceptions about the NT after these flattened ideas worked out to their ultimate conclusions over several hundred years of the building of straw men antagonists out of Gnosticism, Plato, Philo, Judaism, and outside influences of ancient Near Eastern cosmological thought from comparative religion. These overshadowed, in his own writings, any acceptable probability of tabernacle typological influences as the sacrificial/tabernacle OT background for the movement of both the Christ and his people between earth and heaven.

68. Waltke and O'Connor, *Introduction to Biblical Hebrew Syntax*, 3.

69. Williams and Beckman, *Williams' Hebrew Syntax*, 3. In analogy this would be like a baseball field being divided into the infield and outfield. Both are distinct places but are part of one place, the whole field.

are called heaven within the places of the heavens, or collectively called heaven. Even though there is no direct supportive statement, the dual form of pairs nicely fits the common dualism of the sensed and unsensed heavens found in the OT.

While not denying the possibility of a specific structural existence for creation, many scholars feel there is not enough information given from descriptions in the OT about referents to propose a distinct structure.[70] For example, the translators of the LXX evidently found no consistent number for the translation of השמים (haššāmayim). In classical and secular Hellenistic Greek, the syntactical form for οὐρανός is always singular in number. In the LXX, οὐρανός (ouranos) is used 567 times. Counter to classical tradition, it translates as singular 180 times and plural 453 times, choosing the plural form in 80 percent of the translation.

In Semitic literature beginning in the fourth century BCE, the syntactical form for plural for οὐρανός appears to increase in frequency until it is an established option in the day of Jesus. In his teachings, Jesus at times used plural-singular juxtaposition (cf. Matt 6:9–10; 24:29–31). Pennington recognizes that Jesus would use the plural pattern when speaking to or teaching his disciples, but the singular when speaking to forces of opposition.[71] In the NT, a form of οὐρανός appears 273 times with 90 plurals (33 percent) and 183 singular. The word οὐρανός is noted 10 times in the book of Hebrews, 7 plural and 3 singulars, for 70 percent plurals. In Hebrews, each singular use appears for a particular realm: (1) heaven itself of the holy of holies (9:24), (2) the "the stars of heaven" (11:12), or the temporary visible heaven that can be shaken (12:26). The plural uses refer to all the heavens collectively (1:10; 4:14; 7:26; 8:1; 9:23; 12:23, 25).

Wright considers that the plural forms of the LXX and NT arose from the cosmic influence of other nations during their captivity and later Hellenization.[72] However, the contextual purposes of Judaism and their surrounding ideologies are different. Semitic literature deploys οὐρανός mainly for theological parenesis concerning both approach and relationship of people with the living God, whereas secular use by other nations concerns explanations of the visible cosmos that include speculations in relation to their false gods (fig. 4). Therefore, the OT grammatical syntax of Hellenistic Greek or LXX of οὐρανός alone would probably not

70. Houtman, *Der Himmel im Alten Testament*, 283, 299, 317.
71. Pennington, *Heaven and Earth*, 145.
72. Wright, *Early History of Heaven*, 185–86.

determine for the Pastor a specific spatial background for the ministry of Jesus as the sacrifice/high priest of the Christ. However, when contextually connected with basic OT teaching of sacrificial requirements and tabernacle typology, the referent usually expresses plural holy-*places* in a seen-unseen heavenly dualism (cf. 1 Kgs 8:27; 2 Chr 2:6).

The Pastor's probable orderly arrangement of the heavens as substance-reality falls in line with other possible first-century CE outside influences concerning heavenly contemplation. Edward Adams remarks, "Greek cosmological inquiry, for the sixth century BCE onwards, was based on the recognition that the external universe is a well-ordered system and the conviction that this order is open to rational analysis and explanation."[73] Concerning a difference in Jewish concepts, as including an unseen creation, Adams notes, "Israel's own cosmological thought may have developed, to some extent, in relation to the cult. The structure of creation and that of the temple are correlated in Ps. 78.69: 'He built his sanctuary like the high heavens, like the earth, which he has founded forever.' Scholars have noted correspondences between the priestly account of creation in Gen. 1.1–2.4a and God's instructions to Moses for the construction of the tabernacle in Exod 25–31, suggesting 'a homology of world building and temple building.'"[74] Adams concludes, "God has established a well-ordered and well-regulated creation from Gen. 1.1–2a, and is expressed in passages such as Psalm 104 and Prov. 8.22–31."[75]

Many extant ANE and Hellenistic texts illuminate cultural spatial beliefs, possibly available to the Pastor, that often divided the creation in dualism.[76] Extant Jewish authors, including some which likely appear

73. Adams, "Graeco-Roman," 6.

74. Adams, "Graeco-Roman," 20.

75. Adams, "Graeco-Roman," 20.

76. Kirk et al., *Presocratic Philosophers*, 39, 43–44. Overall, for reasons as noted by Adams above, the extant ANE and Greek stories differ, but basic principles of dualism remain. Commonly, there is existence creation before chaos, invisible creation, and superior gods, with people dependent upon the gods, who may judge their actions. These stories function as attempts to explain the unexplainable about things not seen, by shaping thoughts involving either the observable things of creation around them, or elaborate myths of unseen gods above in heaven. Their gods possessed powers that varyingly interact with nature and people, and who may require entreaty. Schnabel, *Jesus's Atoning Sacrifice in Hebrews*, 64–86. As supported by Moses's history written in the middle second millennium BCE, it is more probable that the one true message of the Christ was changed to the chaotic views of polytheism in the minds of second millennium BCE people, than that the alternate direction from chaotic cosmogony of polytheism to monotheism of the living God. These deviations were explained in the first century CE by Paul in Romans as the result of "worthless minds" given by God to

Atonement and the Logic of Resurrection in Hebrews 9:27-28

shortly after the Pastor's sermon, offer diverse descriptions of the heavens as God's temple. These structurally divide the unseen heavens differently according to authorial desired emphasis and purpose, but the notion of representing distance from God's dwelling of holiness remains the same (fig. 4).[77] The DSS, without likely direct connections, also have similar language and points of contact with Hebrews due to the common OT

---

those who had turned away from acknowledging him (Rom 1:28). Paul's explanation may provide possible explanation for the nonsensical diversity found in extant Hellenistic texts. The Hellenistic cosmogeny probably adapted and transformed the available ancient traditions in the past surrounding the sacrificial ministry of the Christ into mythological legends for earthly gods (Rom 1:18-32). This implies that they neglected the sacrificial ministry of the Christ, which was available since the beginning, by looking for visible solutions.

77. The most to least probable Jewish texts available to the Pastor that provide narrative descriptions of the heavens include Daniel, 4 Ezra, Ezek 40-48, Isa 6:1-11, Revelation, Philo, Josephus, 1 Enoch, 2 Enoch, 3 Baruch, Ascension of Isaiah, Testament of Levi, Apocalypse of Zephaniah, Apocalypse of Abraham, Testament of Abraham, Jubilees, Ezekiel the Tragedian, Sirach, Wisdom of Solomon, 4Q400. In the OT, there is no narrative discourse dedicated to the subject, and only a small portion of text mentions it compared to the whole. However, to claim relative silence as evidence that apocalyptic ideas are late developments commits the fallacy of argument from silence. This common impression of OT relative silence may be only illusionary due to genre, rather than lack of apocalyptic *aiōn-field* concepts in early Israel. Most of the Pentateuch is foundational for history in reference to God's law and establishment of the nation of Israel for provision of the promised "seed" of Christ in the promise of the first covenant. There was no need for a narrative history of the eternal/perpetual-*places* in the contextual purpose of the historical writings. However, on closer inspection, apocalyptic language of plural heavens occasionally does occur in relation to the tabernacle and temple typology. Also, other elements of apocalyptic language occur, such as ascents and descents by men and angels both to and from heaven (Gen 5:15; 28:12).

Scholars often highlight the variance in structure regarding the number of heavens as one, two, three, seven, or ten, as supporting incongruence of early beliefs; e.g., Lincoln, *Paradise Now and Not Yet*, 78-79. However, this varied plural practice likely follows the desired emphasis of the authors for either degrees of holiness or a focus on a subject isolated in particular realm(s) (see fig. 4); e.g., in the genre of history and early mountain typology concerning God's relationship to people, everything above toward God is considered singular, as God's sovereign domain above the people. In matters of death or spirituality, there is an emphasis upon the seen and an unseen accessible God in a duality of places as with Enoch (Gen 5:17). The ancient sacrificial system continued by Israel in the Sinai covenant, which repetitively depicted the sacrifice of Christ for four thousand years, symbolized the dead ascending upwards to God by the rising of the smoke of the burnt offerings as an aroma reaching God in heaven, also supporting the duality of place. In consideration about holiness in link with the First Temple, authors speak of a "heaven of heavens" (cf. 1 Kgs 8:27; 2 Chr 2:6). Regardless of the emphasis, in the OT and all but one extant noncanonical Jewish text, God always dwells at the highest realm in protected holiness from sin in an unseen creation, that is always perceived as accessible reality by angels and people if they are holy. The debate about these observations has existed from the beginning.

exegesis.⁷⁸ Some Qumran documents contain motifs concerning angels in ministry in the unseen heaven of the holy of holies as a "true" realm of God's tabernacle where real worship takes place.⁷⁹ Other available influences possibly upon the Pastor, nurture the same basic ideas of the existence of heavenly unseen substance-reality, based on the tabernacle and temple motif, upon which authors built parenesis and rhetoric with varied theological differences.⁸⁰

The assertion that the Pastor embraces esoteric, mystical, unorganized thoughts by treating apocalyptic spatial language as certainty is implausible. Such claims likely arise from modern bias against the unseen realities described, preconceived Cartesian philosophical outlooks in rationalism and empiricism, and a perceived hope for return to improved earthly conditions. These interpretatively work out biblical promise-fulfillment by orphaned antitype escalation, for realization on earth in rejection of the unseen heavenly types that the typological biblical revelation represents.

For example, the modern lexical semantic meaning of the plural "heavens" (οὐρανῶν) is most often determined as having a purpose for expressing grandeur and majesty about a *singular* heaven of God's sovereign domain.⁸¹ An often-overlooked ST literature and NT view, is that the grammatical plural functionally expresses vertical dwelling levels of holiness, as the current state of the creation, due to the presence of sin in the relationship between God and his created beings.⁸² The Pastor devel-

---

78. Hurst, *Epistle to the Hebrews*, 44–66; Davila, "Heavenly Ascents," 460–85; Davila, "Macrocosmic Temple," 1–19; Gärtner, *Temple and the Community*, 88–99. Gärtner finds a link of "the fellowship of the eschatological community on earth with the community in heaven."

79. Attridge, "How the Scrolls Impacted Scholarship," 208–30.

80. Koester, *Dwelling of God*, 152–82.

81. L&N, "1.11 οὐρανός," 1:2. Louw and Nida comment, "Singular or plural; there seems to be no semantic distinction in NT literature between the singular and plural forms." Cf. Helgeland, "Time and Space," 1285. Helgeland asserts that in the early church, concepts of God transplanted from a "personal, willful, spontaneous image of God, in the Hebrew world to the abstract, distant, metaphysical deity of Greek culture." Helgeland cites the observation of Martin Werner, that "the church traded the historical descriptions of God for some that were timeless." Cf. Wright, *New Testament*, 97. Wright builds his entire series of narrative historical theology on rejection of heavenly categories of ontological dualism.

82. BDAG, "οὐρανός," 738. While admitting he could not find a consistent pattern, Bauer recognized the Semitic view of plural in literature available in the first century CE. In published lexicons from the late nineteenth century, a theological shift can be traced in a movement from possible, to probable, to absolute rejection of plural

ops the common connecting link for apocalyptic thought of plural heavens according to the divisions of holiness designed in the tabernacle.[83] This later choice best harmonizes with first-century CE *aiōn-field* views of the heavens in the eternal/perpetual-*places* of the Pastor. The plural or singular frame for apocalyptic narrative is critical to textual exegesis and exposition of Hebrews.

The recent resurfacing of insights that the Pastor shapes a first-century CE concept of heavenly space as an accessible substance-reality, creates tension with the metaphoric heavenly motifs and cosmic-limited projects about hope for believers.[84] A large lacuna in spatial reflection on a biblical setting of heavenly substance-reality has stimulated recent academy publications that open the door for greater conversation about the spatial possibilities of heavenly places in the message of Hebrews, which counter the inaccessible mirages of metaphoric heavenly symbolism. This first arises from the recognition for the necessity of present heavenly place(s) both: (1) meant for the self-offering of Jesus as human

---

heavens as a semantic option in biblical text. Examples of this trajectory is further discussed in Henry, "Cosmology of the Heaven(s)," 28–62. With the rediscovery and better understanding of apocalyptic literature that was initially viewed as esoteric, the vertical Semitic idea of heavenly substance-reality resurfaced, as noted by Rowland, *Open Heaven*, 2. He recognizes, "Apocalyptic has a vertical dimension which is just as important as any predictions made about the future." It is important to recognize that these vertical dwelling levels do not refer to creation as unholy itself, as in the Gnosticism to follow in the second century CE, but as a temporary decaying situation of created dwellings for sinful volitional creations (cf. Rom 8:18–25; Heb 1:10–12).

83. Charlesworth, "Introduction for the General Reader," 1:xxxi. Charlesworth concludes on STL views of God, "The apocalyptists place him in the highest heaven, far removed from the earth (1En. 1:4; 71:5–11; 2 En. 20:5), but the prayers interspersed through the apocalypses reveal that he is not inaccessible." Evidence of this apocalyptic frame is contained in the ST and NT biblical text in descriptions of both a visible and an invisible divided creation (cf. Col 1:16; 1 Tim 1:7; 6:15). The invisible was further divided due to the presence of sinful creatures (cf. 2 Cor 12:1–4; Eph 6:12). When utilizing an apocalyptic narrative, vertical holiness frame, the singular heaven in singular-plural juxtaposition refers to the highest invisible heaven and the plural refers to all heavens, both invisible and invisible of creation (cf. Matt 6:9–10; Heb 9:23–24). From an apocalyptic view, the highest heaven was not of this creation but eternal, or better, perpetual, in contrast to the temporary situation of dwelling areas less holy (cf. Heb 9:11).

84. Sleeman, "Ascension and Spatial Theory," 160. Sleeman explains the tension in the realization that Jesus's ascension into heaven functions as a "reordering of what kind of space is available for human existence. Furthermore, Jesus remains there, by right of the status given him by God the Father. We cannot go there." He further conceives, "Challenges such as an endlessly delayed eschaton" contrasted with the location of Jesus now safely in heaven. Cf. Berquist, "Critical Spatiality," 181–93; Bryan, "Revised Cosmic Hierarchy Revealed," 61–82.

to God after his sacrifice (Heb 9:24) and designed for his post-judgment enthronement in human immortality at the right hand of God (Heb 1:3, 13; 8:1; 10:12; 12:2),[85] and (2) that these eternal/perpetual-*place*(s) exist simultaneously with the present, temporary, visible "world" (κόσμος).[86]

In recent academic conversation, the suggestion of heaven as a concrete reality is considered by Cynthia Westfall.[87] Even without her discussion about modern social scientific concepts of critical space theory, Westfall convincingly argues that in the narrative of the Pastor, the place where Jesus completes atonement and enthronement for his present mediation from the throne of God must exist as a concrete reality. Additionally, Gabriella Gelardini pushes spatial concepts much further in her consideration of current attempts to balance the Pastor's spatiality with his temporal language in Hebrews. Her recent monograph of essays thematically engages the topic of spatiality.[88] Westfall, Gelardini, and others with similar spatial observations, further open a crack through the ceiling for future discussion about heavenly access for people, particularly in the described heavenly places in Hebrews.[89]

---

85. Anderson, "Lukan Cosmology and the Ascension," 175–212. Scholarly conversation for opening of concrete heavens for Jesus now forms on the complementary truth of his ascension after resurrection as flesh into heaven.

86. Whitlark, *Cosmology*, 120–21. Whitlark identifies (1) that these two places of the κόσμος ("world") and the creation of the "throne," where Jesus sits exist simultaneously, (2) that the eschatological hopes of the patriarchs was already prepared for them (Heb 11:16) as the same place that Jesus entered as forerunner (Heb 6:20), and (3) the place of "rest" for the faithful has existed "from the foundation of the "world" (Heb 4:3). Whitlock concludes, "The fact that the author's eschatological hope simultaneously exists unseen alongside or above the community's present mortal world helps to make sense of the spatial and eschatological tensions in Hebrews" (121).

87. Westfall, "Space and Atonement in Hebrews," 228–48. Westfall reacts to scholarly reduction of the heavenly events into Jesus's death. This reaction against metaphoric language towards acceptance of heavenly concrete reality is correct but application weakens by a remaining conception of the nature of the "heavenly sanctuary," so-called, that maintains closed-heavens for people in a bound future that only connects with a bodily flesh resurrection.

88. Gelardini, *Deciphering the Worlds of Hebrews*. In part 3, Gelardini summarizes in Hebrews spatial concepts concerning faith, living now outside of heaven and the eternal city now in heaven, the eschatological possibility of perhaps entering the heavenly homeland at death as the goal of the earthly pilgrimage, and the principles of the earthly part of that journey. Essays openly address spatial language optional reality for Hebrews.

89. Barnard, *Mysticism of Hebrews*, 171–212. After his discussion of heavenly realities in the message of Hebrews, Barnard provides supporting evidence that the covered heavenly realities "are presently accessible to the author and his community" (171). Cf. Gelardini, "Faith in Hebrews," 269. Gelardini surmises, "And in Hebrews 12:23 there may also be an implication that in heavenly Zion or Jerusalem there is already a

Atonement and the Logic of Resurrection in Hebrews 9:27–28

The Pastor's concept of the tabernacle priestly ministry that functions "to outline and shadow" (Heb 8:5) the organization of God's dwelling in relation to people, had early OT theological roots.[90] According to deSilva, these images go back to 1 En. 14:8—15:2 and early exegesis of Exod 25:9 and 25:40, "stressing the correspondence between the earthly and heavenly."[91] Lewis Ginzberg suggests the general Jewish idea, stating, "The separate parts of the Tabernacle had each a symbolical significance, for to all that is above there is something corresponding below."[92] This purpose of the tabernacle as an outline and shadow would naturally suggest distinctive heavenly places to first-century CE reflection on tabernacle design.[93] The apocalyptic language employed by the Pastor, based in the OT, served as an expression of such meditation about these suggested places, and anticipated both currently available and future activity between these places, by both the Christ and his people of faith.[94]

congregation, an ἐκκλησία, consisting not only of angels and Christ, but also the 'spirits of the perfected righteous'—Perhaps these are simply the ranks of the faithful ones or heroes of faith since Abel." Cf. Bautch, "Spatiality and Apocalyptic Literature," 273–88.

90. Guthrie, *Structure of Hebrews*, 121–24. Guthrie notes that the structure of the letter to the Hebrews is built upon exegesis of the OT as translated in the LXX and in unity with it. As such, any theory suggesting more than common cultural language with other influences is doubtful.

91. DeSilva, "Heaven, New Heavens," 439–443.

92. Ginzberg, et al., *Legends of the Jews*, 648.

93. Cf. Philo's first-century CE concept of tabernacle symbolism in *Spec. Laws* 1:66–67. Cf. Attridge and Koester, *Epistle to the Hebrews*, 222–24. Concerning Philo, Attridge and Koester recognize, "In other contexts Philo works from the more common Jewish notion of a correspondence between earthly and heavenly sanctuaries" (223). They also conclude, "While the 'tent not made with hands' (9:11) and 'pitched by God' (8:2) might be the cosmos, the description of the 'true tent' as being 'not of this creation' (9:11) makes it highly unlikely that the true tabernacle is the cosmos" (222–223). They are correct by a first-century CE definition of cosmos, but incorrect by modern scholarly usage of the term. See table 7. Further, the relationship is neither in a dichotomy of antithesis as only a pattern of the heavens. The Pastor most likely follows near similar language and structure of Philo's first-century CE concepts in the application of the sacrificial/priestly movements, as seen in his description of Jesus in the ministry of the Christ, only without Philo's extended metaphor and allegory.

94. Caird, *Language and Imagery*, 53. Caird affirms the OT basis of the Pastor's apocalyptic thoughts, rather than other outside influences. Cf. Barnard, *Mysticism of Hebrews*, 279. Barnard concludes that apocalyptic literature "exhibits a preoccupation with the realities of the heavenly realm, and the human experience of this realm and its occupants."

Cf. Barrett, "New Testament Eschatology," 154. Can the eschatology of Hebrews be both temporal and spatial? The mediating position of Barrett on the debate between the extremes of "thoroughgoing eschatology" of Albert Schweitzer and "realized eschatology" of C. H. Dodd has merit in the unnecessary horizontal/vertical debate, where he

Even Jesus, according to Luke, while growing up in wisdom and age, viewed his self-purpose in his relationship to the later temple in Jerusalem, as "I must be in the places of my Father" (Luke 2:49).[95] He later also spoke, based on OT dualism and his self-understanding, about his ministerial movements as the Son of Man (cf. Dan 7:13–14) on behalf of other people between the heaven and the earth (John 1:51; 3:13; 6:62; 20:17; cf. Acts 2:34; Rom 10:6; Eph 4:8–10).[96] Scholars interpret Jesus's OT contextual self-understanding, which concerns his sacrificial and priestly ministry as the Christ on behalf of his believers, either in

---

states, "The two schools . . . have each their adherents, but there are also many who take a mediating position, inclined (to speak generally) to the view that the extremists (if so they may be called) are right in what they assert, but wrong in what they deny." Both Schweitzer and Dodd correctly held their respective complementary truth in an incorrect false dichotomy of antithesis. Schweitzer, like many today, due to antitype escalation in earthly fulfillment, denied heavenly fulfillment in exchange for a hope only in earthly ends at the coming of Christ to earth. C. H. Dodd, due to his inherited presuppositions in Cartesian philosophy of timeless heavens, ignored temporal tensions deduced in his study of John toward an "eternal present" hope in heaven. His position, as antithetical to earthly history, denied the future ministry on earth of the coming Christ and considered superfluous the temporal time of living in heaven until he comes. The Pastor's apocalyptic perceptions occupy present and future, and temporal and spatial categories: (1) temporally, the present heavenly "today" (Heb 1:5; 3:7, 13, 15; 4:7; 5:5; 13:8), earthly "at these last days" (Heb 1:2), and the people's nearness of transition from earth to heaven on "that day approaching" (Heb 10:25) of individual death and judgment, and (2) spatially, extending vertically to God "into the inside of the veil" (Heb 6:19), "into heaven itself" (Heb 9:24), and "at the end of the eternal/perpetual-*places*" (Heb 9:26).

95. Bock, *Luke 1:1–9:50*, 270. Bock translates the phrase "I must be in my Father's house," after noting that the prepositional phrase ἐν τοῖς, without an object, functions as an idiom for being in one's house. The idiomatic probability still implies that Jesus associated his experience "in the temple" complex at Jerusalem with the places of his Father. It is unlikely a young man, from the tribe of Judah, had access to the holy place or holy of holies of the "temple" (ναός) or that the comment was limited to it. Jesus implies he was "in" the places/house of his Father. His understanding of the "temple complex" (ἱερόν) as the Father's places/house included the outer court, where he had his experience with the teachers there. Jesus's understanding expands the symbolism of the temple, as the Father's places/house to include the entire temple complex. This may have implications for the Pastor's understanding in Heb 3:1–6 about the "house" of Jesus, as encompassing the entire creation of both seen and unseen of the heavens and earth.

96. In the prophetic vision of Dan 7, it is significant that the Son of Man is pictured in an ascent to God "upon the clouds of heaven" where that "the Son of Man was coming, and that the Ancient of Days was present, and the ones who have stood beside were present with him" (Dan 7:13 LXX). Jesus interprets, probably from this text, that the Son of Man is with others, who are at the place of the Ancient of Days when the Son of Man receives his kingdom of all the people (Dan 7:14). Jesus viewed his Son of Man fulfillment as the bidirectional ability to ascend and descend, with angels assisting, in the movement of the people, who make up the kingdom he assembles (Heb 1:13–14).

a closed- or open-heaven program, according to their biases about the described places for people involved in the provision of salvation.[97]

Open Heavenly Places for Sinful People

A recognition grows regarding the probability that the Pastor conceives of the heaven(s), as both a temporal substance-reality and a dwelling place that both the person of Jesus, and by his ministry, his deceased believers experience. In the Pastor's probable MCS, each believer after death at their judgment waits in a place for the intercessory appearance of Christ and his salvation.[98] The recent spatial proposals to explain Jesus, as a human person in a concrete place in heaven, have bearing on the question of open heavenly access for the already billions of deceased believers.

Does the Pastor, in his direct prophecy of Jesus's priestly enthronement and tabernacle typology about sacrificial atonement, only envision a possible local place "within" a now inaccessible singular "heaven" for people after death? Also, does only Jesus now *live* in the place of heaven and wait for a distant eschatological gathering of people either whom he only *remembers* since non-existent or now are *sleeping* since having lived on earth? Or does the Pastor follow normative first-century CE understanding involving eternal/perpetual-*places* "as" the plural "heavens" and earth for the initial and continual present priestly ministry in the appearance of Jesus for his people, who continue living with him within heaven? Either position indicates a duality of place, with access and later appearance(s) by Jesus, but only the latter option embraces the open-heaven taught in the apocalyptic language of the OT, first-century CE ST literature, and the NT. An open-heaven concept allows six millennia of believers, who

---

97. Rowland, *Open Heaven*. Rowland argues that the vertical dimension of apocalyptic and its mysteries explain human existence in the present heavenly world and are not restricted to future eschatological predictions on earth. *Contra* Pennington, "Dualism in Old Testament Cosmology," 260–77. Pennington assumes, by Isa 55:9, a conclusion without discussion of his evidence, that the contrast restricts the heaven of God's dwelling from containing any material reality, angelic presence, or access by the people of the dead (275).

98. The Pastor syntactically uses the pres. mid./pass. ptc. to imply that the activity of waiting occurs temporally in conjunction with the appearing of Christ and after the ordinal events of death and judgment. From the semantics, the timing of the waiting experience must occur after death and judgment and before seeing Jesus who appears from a different locus and goes to the place of those waiting. The syntax and semantics cannot determine the exact time or location of this waiting, so it must be determined by context.

followed the Christ by faith, to receive entrance to God in heaven after death and judgment, by the present shepherd movement of Jesus (Cf. Matt 25:31–36; Luke 15:1–6; John 1:1–18).[99]

A reading of Hebrews in modern language can miss clues that signal there is probably more for deceased believers than either becoming a mere memory or sleeping unconsciously, waiting dead or in an inferior form to live again as flesh on a transformed earth. If believers are only either memories of Jesus or literally sleeping, in Heb 9:28, *where* do these people consciously wait for salvation in continued living after their deaths? The traditional option only later locates these believers on the earth in a flesh bodily resurrection like that observed of Jesus.

There is evidence for open heavens *now* available to deceased people. Added together, these observations can support a process of substitutionary atonement by the Christ that involves (1) a onetime atonement offering on the cross with rising *of* the dead for judgment at Jesus's fleshly death, (2) confirmation of atonement in heaven by Jesus's salvation in immediate movement as an eternal/perpetual-*place* spirit to God after vindication, and (3) a repetitive mediatory movement in ministry for salvation of people, when they, after death, approach as believers (Heb 6:1–2, 19–20; 9:12–15, 23–24).

The Pastor's support for open heavens with access to God for sinful people comes to light when balancing his contextual spatial weight upon (1) a narrative background *aiōn-field* surrounding deployment of the noun αἰών (*aiōn*) and or adjective αἰώνιος (*aiōnios*) as "eternal/perpetual-*place*(s),"[100] (2) movement emphasis of the activity of "approach,"

---

99. The Shepherd motif of Jesus's teaching reveals, that after giving his life for the flock, he leaves the flock to gather each individual sinner who has repented. Jesus carries them home, where there is rejoicing by others present in heaven and good pasture in continued living. He already sits on the throne as foretold by Jesus (Matt 25:31). Nothing in the motif in Matthew prevents an interpretation of individual judgment and separation of believers and unbelievers at individual death. Cf. Baxter, *Israel's Only Shepherd*.

100. Whitlark, "Cosmology and Perfection," 121n20. After some observations showing that "in Hebrews αἰών can carry a temporal notion (age) as well as a spatial one (world)," Whitlark concludes, "Since the mortal and immortal realms are both spatially related and temporally experienced in Hebrews, the temporal and spatial meanings of αἰών should not be sharply distinguished. The use of the plural in Hebrews 1:2 and 11:3 is then a fitting reference to the totality of creation, the two realms of the creation (mortal and immortal), experienced sequentially by God's faithful" (238). Cf. Stewart, "Creation and Matter," 288–89. Cf. Steyn, "Eschatology of Hebrews." Cf. Lincoln, *Hebrews: A Guide*, 93.

"enter," and the substantive "entrance"[101] (3) typological symbolism using land, mountains, a household, and the tabernacle priestly ministry, (4) frequent restated direct prophecy about the fulfilled place for the person Jesus at the throne of God in the eternal/perpetual-*places* of heaven, (5) spatial understanding of freeing people, from the place under the power of death, in enslavement by the devil,[102] (6) syntactical choices of singular and plural "heaven(s)" and "holy place(s)," (7) repeated extensive narrative for the word groups "bring, carry" (φέρω) and "lead up, bring up" (αγω), implying the travel of the ministry of Jesus as the Great Shepherd of the sheep,[103] (8) implied spatial changes for entry in the eternal/perpetual-*places* by the transition from the first to second covenant ministries, (9) apocalyptic language, in common cultural Hellenistic and Jewish dualism, in spatial matters for conscious activity of people after fleshly death, either to God, or outside of his holy presence,[104] (10) an awareness of the value of the lasting heavenly inheritance given at judgment to believers who serve faithfully in a clear conscience by forsaking sin, (11) identification of Christ with interactive terms in verbal nouns that imply spatial camaraderie by his participation with other people, not only in death, but in continued living,[105] and (12) Jesus's use of familial

---

101. Key terms for understanding the Pastor's conceived movement of the Christ and his people between earth and heaven are "approach" (προσέρχομαι Heb 4:16; 7:25; 10:1, 22, 11:6; 12:18, 22), "enter" (εἰσέρχομαι Heb 3:11, 18, 19; 4:1, 3, 5, 6, 10, 11; 6:19, 20; 9:12, 24, 25; 10:5), and "entrance," (εἴσοδον Heb 10:19). Cf. Barnard, *Mysticism of Hebrews*, 193. Barnard concludes, "As with the previous passages we have discussed in this Chapter, the use of the present tense (ἔχομεν, εἰσερχομένην) suggests that life in the heavenly realm was not simply a future expectation, but also a present reality, the experience of which is encouraged by the author."

102. The place implications of the spiritual warfare of Jesus against people's enslavement to death under the power of the devil (Heb 2:14) is discussed in a later section of this chapter, "God Speaks through Other Eternal Beings."

103. The place inferences of the φέρω (*pherō*) and αγω- (*agō*) word groups, as applied to the Shepherd ministry of Jesus in relationship to his people, surrounding the Pastor's theme of death and judgment, strongly suggest open heavens.

104. McRay, "Atonement and Apocalyptic," 1–9. McRay demonstrates reasons the Pastor expresses the theology of Hebrews in essentially apocalyptic terminology. For an example of apocalyptic spatial dualism and discussion of the Pastor's possible sense of "outside the camp," consider, Gelardini, "Charting 'Outside the Camp,'" 210–37.

105. In appendix 2, table 1, "Words in Hebrews Linked with God," an audience likely would find weight to summarize a personal close interaction and face-to-face experience between God and his people who come by faith in his Son as a pleasing aroma. Each of the Pastor's referents have some level of personal presence and close activity with people. These collectively picture in their surrounding narrative that believers consciously abide near to Jesus after death and during judgment, rather than

terms "sons" and "brethren" in conjunction with heavenly places at his enthronement.

In varying degrees, many of these observations have already been introduced. What remains is to harmonize them together in a narrative of an interconnected path by repetitive realignment, frequent inspection for cohesion with the overall theme, and further identification of propositions often tangentially displaced. The volume of material necessitates the adjustment of some more than others, but what started as a single subtopic about plural heavens, now tracks multiple other intersecting details as evidence.

The terms αἰών and αἰώνιος as "eternal/perpetual-*place*(s)" link with the spatial features regarding the foundation of the beginning teaching about the Christ (Heb 6:1–5). The Pastor reminds his listeners that this teaching since the beginning involves six criteria for the acceptance of a sacrifice as pleasing when rising in approach to God (Heb 6:1–2). The last two include "both of the rising *of* the dead *people* and of eternal/perpetual-*place* [αἰωνίου] judgment" (Heb 6:2; cf. Heb 9:27). Jesus must fulfill, after his death in substitutionary sacrifice on the cross, both criteria as the Christ. In the corresponding pattern of the antitypes of the OT, once the smoke burning from the substitutionary offering(s) arose upward to God, the aroma was judged (Exod 29:18, 25; Lev 1:13; Lev 26:31; cf. 2 Cor 2:14–16). The Pastor perceives, the spatial rising smoke of the offerings represent the rising of *all* dead people to God for his judgment (cf. Heb 9:27). He illustrates expectation of resurrection *of* (all) the dead by the Christ in a scenario stating, "both those whom having tasted the good conversation of God's ability of the subsequently coming eternal/perpetual-*place* [αἰῶνος]" (Heb 6:5). He anticipates, based upon partaking the good conversation of God's ability, at the raising *of* (all) the dead, those tasting God's ability to presently come into the αἰῶνος ("eternal/perpetual-*place*").

In satisfying the pattern of Heb 6:1–5, Jesus as the Christ, at his "eternal/perpetual-*place* judgment" (κρίματος αἰωνίου Heb 6:2), finds αἰωνίαν λύτρωσιν ("eternal/perpetual-*place* redemption," Heb 9:12) while traveling "into the holy place" (εἰς τὰ ἅγια Heb 9:12; cf. 9:27–28), rather than the errant teaching in the Pastor's scenario of "falling away," (παραπεσόντας Heb 6:6). If properly observed in foreshadowing the coming Christ, God upon Jesus's "approach" (προσέρχομαι) promptly at

---

being always considered in some transcendent remote relationship for an unknown existence before finally living again in an eschatological future.

death judges his sacrifice (Lev 9:7; 10:17; cf. Abel's sacrificial death, Heb 12:24; Gen 4:6) concerning both his "gift" of his life that is symbolized by the blood of the earthly sacrifices (Lev 17:11) and his holiness as the offering priest (Lev 10:1-3). If God was pleased, he then extended "atonement" in forgiveness of sin to the offeror (Heb 11:4-6; cf. Lev 4:26, 31; 6:7, 30; 7:7).[106]

Jesus offering of his life was accepted by God on behalf of sinful people, who are invited to receive his substitutionary offering as the Christ by faith. The Pastor proclaims to his audience that Jesus, as a better substitutionary sacrifice according to the OT sacrificial symbols, after suffering sacrificially during his crucifixion, approached toward God by his continued living.[107] When his sacrificial suffering finishes, in fulfillment of OT direct prophecy, Jesus, "through a spirit of an eternal/perpetual-*place*" (διὰ πνεύματος αἰωνίου Heb 9:14) found "eternal/perpetual-*place* redemption" (Heb 9:12) when "he offered himself blameless to God" (ἑαυτὸν προσήνεγκεν ἄμωμον τῷ θεῷ Heb 9:14) for judgment as an acceptable sacrifice (Heb 9:14; cf. Luke 23:46; John 19:30; Rom 1:4; Phil 3:10-11).[108] The sequence events of "rising *from* the dead" (Heb 13:20) for Jesus begins as a bodily spirit with his continued living "through the veil" (Heb 10:20) in being brought up "to God" in the holy of holies (cf. Mark 12:24-27; 1 Cor 15:45).[109]

---

106. Gelardini, "As if by Paul?," 27. Gelardini discusses weight of the "certain place" for atonement implied by the spatial movement of ἱλάσκομαι ("to atone") to the place of ἱλαστήριον ("atonement place") by the offering of Christ for sin.

107. Allen, *According to the Scriptures*, 144-59. The Pastor seems comfortable with several OT lenses of atonement by the death of Christ that form the way of his parenesis and exhortation concerning the OT in Hebrews's passion about the death of Christ.

108. Morales, "Atonement in Ancient Israel," 27-39. On sacrificial atonement, Morales designates the whole burnt offering as an "ascension offering," and comments that it is "a name which reflects not only its root meaning but also a significant aspect of the offering's theology" (28).

109. In the Jewish OT sacrificial system, the burnt offering emphasized for individuals the blessing of rising to the presence of God in his pleasing favor at his judgment more than fleshly resurrection in return to the cosmos. Direct prophecy also emphasized the antitype of God's national return of Israel in the flesh to fruitful living in ministry and service of the Lord in the promised land, with little of any direct conversation about fleshly resurrection; e.g., in Dan 12:1-3, when the spatial force is added to αἰώνιος as "eternal/perpetual-*place*," and ἀναστήσονται as "will stand, rise up," the context, as determined by the Son of Man rising before God after death (Dan 7:13-14), in days of tribulation on the earth, considers during tribulation that some people at death rise to either life or wrath in judgment (cf. John 5:25-30). Daniel states, "And many of the ones presently sleeping [the dead of the tribulation time] in the breath of the earth will stand up, on the one hand those into eternal/perpetual-*place* life [εἰς ζωὴν αἰώνιον], on

Finding redemption and making atonement before God on approach, Jesus, after the onetime experience of "death," then becomes "a high priest according to the order of Melchizedek having moved into the holy place" (Heb 6:19–20; cf. Ps 109:4 LXX [110:4 MT]). As recorded in supportive OT texts in Heb 1:5–14 and 2:9–18, the Pastor speaks about the reception of Jesus as the Son of Man (Dan 7:13–14) by God, angels, and his people with him into the now greater holy place by removal of the veil.

Jesus makes a transition from the completion of the process of atonement as the Christ offering of sacrifice, once at the holy place (Heb 6:1–2), to become a continual priestly mediator when he as the Christ "enters" into "heaven itself" (Heb 9:24) "into the holy place" (εἰς τὰ ἅγια Heb 9:25). On an apocalyptic (aiōn-field) background, this transition would occur after his approval at judgment and before his later fleshly resurrection (Heb 9:23–24; cf. Mark 12:24–27).

An acceptance of the spatial weight of the Pastor's αἰών and αἰώνιος language in the pattern of OT sacrifices, with a connection to death, judgment, and immediate rising to God in Heb 9:27–28, does not lessen the worth of the complementary truth of Jesus's second coming to earth and the transformation of his remaining people. In truth, it is probably part of the Pastor's verbal concept of "to complete" (τελειόω Heb 11:39–40).[110]

---

the other hand those into reproach, even those into dispersion, and eternal/perpetual-*place* dishonor [αἰσχύνην αἰώνιον]. And the ones understanding will shine as the stars of heaven and the ones prevailing my word just as the stars of heaven into the eternal/perpetual-*place* of the eternal/perpetual-*place* [εἰς τὸν αἰῶνα τοῦ αἰῶνος]" (Dan 12:2–3 LXX). The phrase "the ones prevailing my word" (οἱ κατισχύοντες τοὺς λόγους μου Dan 12:3 LXX; cf. Heb 4:12) could very well correspond to the Pastor's theme of judgment after death, with entrance for those prevailing over the Lord's word in judgment into the eternal heaven of heaven. Those who do not prevail at judgment are dispersed in reproach and dishonor (Heb 4:11–13; 9:27–28; cf. Matt 7:21–23; John 5:25–29).

Cf. Barr, *Garden of Eden*, 22–23. Barr observes that the disciples were surprised by Jesus's fleshly resurrection. Also, it is possible, that in 1 Cor 15, Paul is arguing for an individual resurrection of people that has already begun for some in a spiritual body, with the only exception for Jesus, who has completed the process with fleshly resurrection and later fleshly ascension into heaven as proof of rising to God (cf. John 2:18–22; Acts 17:31). He argues for the validity of resurrection in pres. tense action for believers currently rising in Christ at his coming in judgment (1 Cor 15:15, 23, 29, 32, 35–38, 58) to begin the process of events of rising from the dead to God after judgment, that is later confirmed with fleshly resurrection. Paul also writes of judgment as an experience in the past for those who are dead, who would have perished at death if Christ was not raised by God at his judgment (1 Cor 15:18). This implies that some already in death have been judged and are now in heaven.

110. Whitlark, "Cosmology and Perfection," 123. Whitlark for Hebrews postpones

The Pastor likely acknowledges both complementary truths concerning people, where the terms "rise" (ἐγείρω) and "rise up, resurrection" (ἀναστάσεως) both *of* the dead (all people) and *from* the dead (sons) cover a quick judgment-transformation process that promptly for believers completes upon entering heaven in a bodily flesh to spirit transformation (Heb 11:19, 35; cf. Luke 16:23; appendix 1, fig. 2).[111] His main point, as imaged by the OT sacrifices, focuses on the *now* opened

"eternal/perpetual-*place* judgment" to coincide with the removal of the mortal realm of the duality of creation. However, the Pastor does not thematically mention the complementary truth of the direct prophecy of the second coming; rather he focuses on the appearing of Jesus for mediation at death and judgment. The basis of the τελ- word groups in the first century CE has the broad idea of completion in finishing a task or achieving a purpose. For either Jesus or his believers, the context determines what is complete, finished, or achieved by use of the verb τελειόω or the adjective τέλειος. Cf. Carlston, "Vocabulary of Perfection in Philo," 147. Carlston concludes, "To be made perfect, consequently, is either to be translated (by death) into the heavenly realm or to anticipate in this life the benefits purchased in that realm by Christ's death."

Cf. McCruden, "Concept of Perfection," 213–18. McCruden finds in Heb 7:26-28 a connection between the idea of perfection and exaltation. He states, "Hebrews chooses to envision the divine vindication of Jesus more abstractly by construing Jesus's victory over death as a process of completion or perfection whereby the Son is elevated into God's presence (4:14) to serve a priestly role (4:15–16; 7:7:24–25)" (216). Concerning believers, he concludes, "For the believer, perfection has both a future and present dimension. The faithful ultimately experience perfection in the age to come when they inherit an abiding existence in the transcendent glory of God's presence. Even now, however, perfection understood as communion with God is an experiential reality that has been made possible through the personal sacrifice of Jesus that cleanses the believer from within" (229).

Cf. Pester, "Exhortation to Participate," 33–48. Pester writes, "The ultimate goal of the Lord's coming through incarnation and of his ministry in resurrection is the fulfillment of God's eternal will, which is the corporate perfection of redeemed humanity to be an enlarged expression of the Triune God" (33). His observations for believers are probably correct, when he states, "The corporate reproduction of Christ is manifested through His brothers who are being perfected to enter with boldness into the holy of holies and to assemble together in spirit as the house of God (vv. 21–22, 25; cf. 1 Cor. 5:4)" (43). Pester further recognizes, "Christ is not perfecting individuals to be individuals; He is perfecting many into one (John 17:23)" (43). *Contra* Dey, *Intermediary World and Patterns*, 227. Dey's thesis limits believers' perfection to the complementary truth of the here and now. He writes, "The author does not purpose that this will be accomplished in the afterlife or in the eschatological future."

111. Those who were resurrected to fleshly life, died again, even when raised by Jesus. This lessens the emphasis in Hebrews toward a return to fleshly living. Such resuscitations did demonstrate the ability of God (Heb 1:1; 2:4, 11:34). Hebrews has more emphasis on belief in the Son's ability to raise believers from death by shepherding them to the presence of God in heaven, for completion in a substance transformation to a body with eternal spiritual features (Heb 1:3c; 13:20; cf. 1 Cor 15:50; 1 John 3:2). Cf. Harris, *From Grave to Glory*; McKnight, "Nature of Bodily Resurrection," 379–82; *Contra* Geisler, *Battle for the Resurrection*.

heavenly access to God at death. This first access was accomplished by Jesus as the Christ. So now, believers who follow in death, when at judgment, receive intercession by the ministry of Jesus to promptly rise *from* the dead and move to God for a later corporate completion by the living added to the dead now living with Jesus by previous transformation to a compatible "heavenly body" (σώματα ἐπουράνια Heb 11:39–40; cf. 1 Cor 15:40, 47–49; 1 John 3:2; 1 Thess 4:15).[112]

This ability of Jesus allows him to continue as the Great Shepherd of the sheep, to bring other spirits/souls in resurrection to life with God in heaven (Heb 13:20; cf. 1 Pet 2:25), where they await after the corporate

---

112. On multiple occasions, both Jesus and the NT authors use the present tense of the verb "rise" (ἐγείρω) and the noun "resurrection" (ἀνάστασις) about the rising of the dead as a present experience with simultaneous bodily completion (Matt 11:5; Mark 12:26; Luke 7:22; 20:34–39; 1 Cor 15:15, 16, 29, 32, 35, 52; 2 Cor 1:9–10). Other NT authors focus on later-witnessed visible evidence, about completion in rising to God, using Jesus's fleshly resurrection as evidence for his fulfillment of the Christ (cf. John 3:13; 20:17; Acts 2:24; 1 Cor 15:52; 2 Tim 1:10).

John's witness, concerning the response of Mary in John 20:17, does not negate that Jesus in death had already risen to God "through the spirit of an eternal/perpetual-*place*" (Heb 9:14) or that others already had risen into heaven, as Jesus testified in correction of the Sadducees (Mark 12:24–27; cf. Luke 20:34–39). It is clear from the text of John 20:17 that Jesus is in his flesh bodily by his imperative statement, "Stop touching me!" (cf. Luke 24:39). Jesus recognizes and never corrects the existence of spirits of people without flesh and blood or the experience of judgment after death (cf. Luke 16:19–31; 20:35). John makes it clear that Jesus had not yet ascended into heaven *in the flesh*, as Jesus explains, "I have not yet ascended to the Father." Jesus is presently on his way to the Father in the flesh while his brethren share his fleshly resurrection with the other brethren: "I continuously ascend to my Father and your Father and My God and Your God." The implication of the pres. act. tense ἀναβαίνω (*anabainō*), along with the record of other later appearances in the flesh, strongly supports a continual bidirectional movement of Jesus in the flesh to God and in appearance to the disciples after resurrection. Jesus is about to ascend to his Father and does not wait on earth the entire forty days. During those forty days, when ascending and descending, he will be seen at times, and probably ascends repetitively to his Father after each visitation with his disciples. After ascending to the Father in the flesh, even Thomas can touch him (John 20:26–28).

Also, the implications of the Jesus's statement of in John 3:13 do not negate other spirits of people already rising into heaven bodily before Jesus's decent from heaven in fleshly resurrection (cf. Gen 5:24; 2 Kgs 2:1, 11; cf. Heb 11:5; Matt 27:52). According to John's witness, Jesus says, "And no one has ascended into heaven except the one who descended from heaven, the Son of Man" (John 3:13). Whether Jesus intended to reference his incarnation or resurrection from heaven as the Son of Man, either possible event is required before one can ascend "into" heaven (cf. Heb 2:10; 6:20; 9:24; 12:2). Further, even though others had risen to heaven, John shares a statement about Jesus, writing, "No one has seen God at any time" (John 1:18). So, how do people live in heaven after death and judgment and not see God until Jesus makes him known? The tabernacle typology of the unseen plural heavens assists to possibly solve this paradox.

completion, a later future dissolution of the temporary "world" (κόσμος) and "cosmic heaven" (οὐρανός Heb 12:26; cf. Rev 21–22). Jesus continues as a "mediator" (μεσίτης) for others at death, so "the ones having been called may receive the eternal/perpetual-*place* inheritance" (Heb 9:15; cf. Heb 8:6; 12:24; John 5:25; 1 Tim 2:5; 1 Pet 3:18). He now calls those, who are his, "brethren" at their individual judgment (Heb 2:9–18). Adding spatial weight upon the Pastor's verbal narrative with deployment of αἰών and αἰώνιος as "eternal/perpetual-*place*(s)" with an *aiōn-field* background supports open heavens with the probability of a heavenly entrance experienced by believers in faith to see Jesus at their death and then dwell with God (Heb 2:10; cf. Phil 1:20–23).[113]

Another observation that demonstrates open heavenly access by people surfaces in the Pastor's typology. By this hermeneutic, he illustrates intersecting operations involving the current separation of places from the holiness and perpetual eternality of the unseen substance creation in God's presence. He utilizes five main motifs typologically to spatially illustrate his parenesis: (1) Israel's experience in Egyptian deliverance and promise of the land that is integrated with "faith" in "belief," which God requires for access by people to the place of his "rest" in heaven, (2) a patron system of Jesus's/God's house of the heavens and access by confident hope to the secure place of his dominion-rule (Heb 1:6; 2:5; 10:21), (3) the superior king/priesthood represented by Melchizedek (Heb 5:5–10; 7:1–28), to whom Abraham paid tithes after his deliverance of Lot, which symbolizes Jesus's endless life in his royal priesthood ministry to deliver his people from the sin in the place of the cosmos, (4) the tabernacle (Heb 8:5), which symbolizes all of God's creation now separated in levels of holiness, and (5) mountain typology, which symbolizes God's sovereignty above his creation (Heb 12:18–24).[114] Each motif represents

---

113. The Pastor utilizes the corresponding referent "glory" for the presence of God in the holy of holies (Heb 9:5). Applying the spatial weight of αἰών as "eternal/perpetual-*places*" in Heb 13:21, he concludes concerning Jesus Christ, "To whom is the glory into the holy-*place* of the holy-*places*, amen." Some manuscripts omit τῶν αἰώνων but, even so, his point is not affected. Jesus is the glory of the holy of holies of the holy-*places*. Therefore, to be in glory, is to be with Jesus. The Pastor even implies that believers have already entered glory with Jesus in the holy of holies, stating, "having brought many sons into glory to complete the author of their salvation through suffering" (Heb 2:10). The choice of the aorist ptc. has some temporal weight of activity before the main verb concerning Jesus as a suitable author by having experienced the same suffering of death and judgment to a common holiness between Jesus and his brethren (Heb 2:11). This concept further explores in the chapter 4 unit B UC (Heb 2:17–18).

114. Each motif functions as an antitype of the dualistic ontological realities of

distinct aspects about the necessity of (1) separation due to sinful beings enslaved by death in the visible creation (Hcb 2:14), and (2) God's faithfulness through Jesus to enable access to eternal/perpetual-*place* living under condition of faith (Heb 10:23, 38–39).

The Pastor often emphasizes, as another observation, direct prophecy in his narrative about the place of the "throne" (Heb 1:3; 8:1; 10:12; 12:2; cf. Matt 26:64; Eph 1:20; Col 3:1) foretold in Ps 109:1 LXX (110:1 MT). By adding necessary spatial weight to αἰών ("eternal/perpetual-*places*") in the LXX to the location of the "throne" in heaven, God speaking states, "You are a high priest in the eternal/perpetual-*place* [εἰς τὸν αἰῶνα] according to the order of Melchizedek" (Ps 109:4 LXX [110:4 MT]). The access of Jesus to the place of the throne at God's right hand highlights both his position and place for continual priestly intercession. The reduced temporal English translation "forever, eternal, everlasting" when combined with the durative space-time limitation of verse 1, "until I make your enemies a footstool for your feet," creates an illogical tension. His priesthood is only "until" the "enemies" are subjugated and not just "forever." Jesus only temporarily travels from the place of the eternal realms at God's right hand in heaven in the way of the holy-*places* (Heb 9:8; cf. 1 Cor 15:22–26) to shepherd sinful people in need, from the place of the "enemies."

Also, the Pastor's repeated subtopics of "approach," "enter," and use of "entrance" in relation to the "veil" supply language of spatial access to God. People come from the transient, separated creation for an "approach" (προσέρχομαι) to God in judgment. Those in faith "enter" (εἰσέρχομαι) to God's presence (Heb 2:14–18; 7:25–26; 11:6; see appendix 1, fig. 2). In STr2 (Heb 10:19–23), the Pastor begins his conclusion of his S2 main section describing the living movement of Jesus as high priest in the heavens before God. He defines the path to dwelling with God in the holy of holies, "which he inaugurated to us a new and living way through the veil, that is his flesh" (Heb 10:20). The animated path of Jesus becomes the new and living way for those who follow him in faith (appendix 1, fig. 1).

God's seen and/or unseen creation and not the realities of the types they themselves portray. Orphaned interpretation of these antitypes replaces the hope of the invisible ontological reality with the visible tangible reality of that which is now rationally sensed—which is no longer faith (Heb 11:1; cf. Matt 16:23; 2 Cor 5:7; Phil 3:19–20; Col 1:1–4). This chapter and the next focus primarily on Jesus's house, the house of God, and the tabernacle.

Atonement and the Logic of Resurrection in Hebrews 9:27–28

In the same continued living after death, believers enter to Jesus in the eternal dwellings of heaven (Heb 12:22–24).[115] Those who confess him have confidence, due to his imputed holiness/righteousness, to follow his route to enter beyond the veil that separates everything unholy and unclean by sin or by a connection with death from the presence of the living God (Heb 2:11–13; cf. Ps 41:3 LXX [42:2 MT]; John 5:25).[116] This descriptive narrative for the Pastor is more than symbolic metaphor. It is "living," exemplary, coherent language of the spoken words of God in action. The Pastor in his theology expects that people of faith will inherit access and conscious life to dwell with the living God. The nature of God's living way supports access by people to God. By "confession" (ὁμολογίας Heb 3:1; 4:14; 10:23) in Jesus as the Christ, God's sacrifice and high priest in intercession for sin, his people pass through Jesus's "new and living way to us" (ἡμῖν ὁδὸν πρόσφατον καὶ ζῶσαν Heb 10:20) through death to life.[117]

The covenants provide another observation of testimony for heavenly access. The Pastor maintains that the earthly Sinai covenant, as only containing typological shadows of the required law in cultic purity and priestly sacrificial observances for sin involving the tabernacle (Heb 9:1–8), was not by itself able to provide salvation of heavenly access (Heb 9:9–10:25).[118] The LXX "daily sacrifices" (ἡ καθ' ἡμέραν) or

---

115. The pf. act. indic. "you have approached" in Heb 12:22 can carry weight in context of past activity with present continued effects. The believer's faith brings uninterrupted living that begins during earthly life (Heb 12:1–2) and continues in the events of "approach" at death by the "entrance" through the holy-*places* into the presence of Jesus. This concept of continued living after fleshly death was common in the first-century CE literature, some of which was probably available to the Pastor (cf. 4 Macc 7:19; 16:25).

116. The implication of the combined theme of the discourse unit conclusions on the translation of Heb 2:11 follow in chapter 4 unit B UPt2 (Heb 8b–13). The psalmist writes, "My soul thirsts for the living God, when will I come and appear before God?" (Ps 41:3 LXX).

117. *Contra* Mackie, "Son of God in Hebrews," 114–29; Mackie, "Exordium of Hebrews," 437–53; Mackie, "Let Us Draw Near," 17–36. Cf. Wider, *Theozentrik und Bekenntnis*, 179–204.

118. The Pastor declares, "For if the first *covenant ministry* there was faultless, a place should not be sought of a second *covenant ministry*" (Εἰ γὰρ ἡ πρώτη ἐκείνη ἦν ἄμεμπτος, οὐκ ἂν δευτέρας ἐζητεῖτο τόπος Heb 8:7; italics context mine). In context, the range of the fulfillment of the objectless adjectival ordinals of *first* and *second* embraces more than simply differences in party legal status between the two covenants. It must also include the movements and limits of access by priests involved in ministerial places with the substitutionary sacrifices for the parties involved. The covenants symbolically embraced an unseen vertical connection between the heavens and the earth to

the MT "continual, daily" offerings (תמיד Num 4:16; Lev 6:12–16) in the tabernacle only typified fellowship with God in dwelling access to the holy place, on approach to heaven after death, while awaiting the promise of the anointed Christ to access the holy of holies.[119] He prophetically interprets the OT, as foretelling about Jesus, who, both as "the one having brought many sons into glory" (Heb 2:10) and as meeting together with "brethren" (Heb 2:12–14), in a movement to the Father passing those previously waiting in the holy place through the veil before them and their joining him in the holy of holies (Heb 2:9–18).[120]

The Pastor envisions a temporary use and cessation of the functionality of the holy place promise that is symbolized in the daily sacrifices of the Sinai covenant (Heb 8:13; 9:8).[121] The new covenant also embodied

---

demarcate the approved human passage to God's presence by cultic purity, the priests in ministerial activities, and the people making the substitutionary offerings.

119. Edersheim, *Temple*, 132–33. In the daily or continual sacrifices no high priest entered the holy of holies. Edersheim describes how, for all daily offerings except the whole burnt offering, the sacrifice of bulls, goats, or lambs would be killed, and the priest would enter to stand in the holy place between the golden altar and the candlestick. He would then sprinkle the blood, which represented the life of the animal, seven times toward the holy of holies (cf. Lev 4:6). The lobe of the liver and the fat of the kidneys of the sacrifices remained on the altar of fire until the next day (Lev 6:9). The skin and other leftovers were taken and burned outside the camp.

Edersheim follows Philo's first-century CE interpretation that this holy place ministry represented, for the one offering, an assurance of acceptance and atonement by God (Lev 4:20; cf. *Spec. Laws* 1.239–44). It is important to recognize in these daily offerings for this atonement of sin that both the life represented by the blood of the sacrifice, and the flesh eaten by the priest for the person offering, remained separated in the holy place from the holy of holies. The other NT writings and apocalyptic literature, which had a possible influence upon the Pastor, contain examples of the spirits of the dead waiting/living in lesser heavenly dwellings apart from the highest heaven (cf. Luke 16:19–31; 1 En. 3:8; 9:2; 13:2; 22:3–14; Tob 3:6; Wis 3:1; 4:10; 4:14). In a greater degree, the annual "Day of Atonement" included all sins of the people with the anointed priest entrance into the holy of holies (Lev 16:30).

120. Playout, "Lifted Up from the Earth." The Pastor's contextual language about Jesus enduring a human death combined with the deployment of the adjectival aorist act. ptc. "one having brought" (ἀγαγόντα Heb 2:10), as having weight of a past event before the time of the main verb, places the presentation of these brethren before the speaking of his message and probably during the death and rising of Jesus in spirit from the dead to God. The Pastor uses both past and present senses of the αγω– (agō) word group in description of the past and present continual priestly ministry of Jesus as a shepherd in bringing "brethren" to God through his same experience of death (Heb 13:20). He next states, "For both the one continually making holy, and the ones being continually made holy are from one *life-path experience of death*" (Heb 2:11; italics mine from context). The object of "one" (ἑνὸς) of the ordinal is chosen from the Pastor's surrounding context.

121. The "Holy Spirit" has exposed the ineffectiveness of the first covenant by

by the Sinai law appointed an annual sacrifice that symbolically opens and joins the two created places. *Today*, by the ministry of Jesus as the "leader, originator, author, founder" (ἀρχηγὸν Heb 2:10; 12:2; cf. Acts 3:15; 5:31), believers, after approach, (1) can travel within the veil before them in the way of holy-*places*,[122] and (2) into God's subsequently coming "ordered dominion" (οἰκουμένη Heb 2:5; cf. Matt 6:10).[123] The holy place in the heavens, as far as believers are concerned, only functioned till the achievement of the eternal/perpetual-*places*, when it is obsolete (Heb 1:2c).

---

speaking knowledge according to the new covenant fulfilled by Jesus about movement of believers through the way of the holy-*places* (Heb 9:8–9) into the holiest place. The Pastor states, "In that to say a new *covenant/ministry* [Jesus's fulfillment of annual sacrifice] has declared obsolete the first *covenant/ministry* [daily sacrifices of promise]. Since the *first covenant/ministry* is continually aging and growing old near vanishing" (Heb 8:13; italics mine from context). He later asserts, "This *priestly ministry in the first tent of the holy place and second tent of the holy of holies* continually clarifying of the Holy Spirit, has not yet been to reveal that the way of the holy-*places* of the first tent still continually having an existence, which is a symbol for the present time" (Heb 9:8–9; italics mine from context). The Pastor seems to imply some current overlap in the function of the earthy holy place under the new covenant (earthly Temple still functioning) and that it eventually ceases to exist. The anticipated end of the Jerusalem temple may drive his urgency.

122. Gurtner, *Torn Veil*. Gurtner is probably right to recognize, by the ministry of Jesus, both the function and end of the veil "preventing physical and visual access to the holy of holies, and therefore to the God enthroned within" (199) and that "the death of Jesus removed the cultic barriers between the holy (God) and the less holy (humanity)" (200).

123. In the Pastor's context, the οἰκουμένη (Heb 1:6; 2:5) refers to the heavenly eternal/perpetual-*place*, where all is in subjection to God. It is where Jesus was enthroned and where believers come in, following Jesus there. OT Davidic typology supports the movements of Christ, which his people follow. In the triad of Pss 21–23 LXX (22–24 MT), David typologically reveals messianic suffering in life and death, rising to God during death, and enthronement. The prophetic fulfillment of Jesus experientially envisions David as standing in the holy place in an implied judgment before God, waiting to receive the righteousness of God's Savior (Ps 23:5 LXX [24:5 MT]; cf. Heb 5:5–10). David prophetically writes, "Who will ascend into the mountain of the Lord and who will stand in his holy place?" (Ps 23:3 LXX [24:3 MT]). David's contrast of "earth" (γῆ) with the "ordered dominion" (οἰκουμένη) in the first line sets his background in the holy place of heaven after death at his individual judgment. The LXX, which was probably used by the Pastor, contrasts heavily the heavens and earth within God's οἰκουμένη (*oikoumenē*, Pss 88:12 LXX [89:11 MT]; 89:2 LXX [90:2 MT]; Jer 10:12; 28:15 LXX [51:15 MT]). In Ps 89:2 LXX (90:2 MT), Moses places the οἰκουμένη "from everlasting to everlasting" or better, with spatial weight, "from the eternal/perpetual-*place* until the eternal/perpetual-*place*" before the present earth and heavens. The heavens and earth are being shaken with no lasting promise in for the earthly κόσμος (Heb 12:25–29; cf. Hag 2:6; Pss 17:8 LXX [18:7 MT]; 76:19 LXX [77:18 MT]).

Those adhering to cosmic-*field* constrained backgrounds concerning the destiny of the people of God, emphasize God as transcendent and beyond any reach for a personal relationship in dwelling in heaven together, and that no one, yet, or ever, goes "to God" in heaven, except Jesus.[124] In adherents conversation regarding the spatiality of Hebrews, the recent spatial turn often forms on an unstable foundation of several unlikely presuppositions that (1) God's creation consists of a material/nonmaterial duality,[125] (2) Jesus dwells in a local heavenly tabernacle, so-called Sanctuary, at a place "in heaven,"[126] (3) Jesus post-flesh resurrection

---

124. Moffitt, "Jesus as Interceding High Priest," 542–52. Moffitt uses Heb 9:28 for argument that "for Hebrews, the Yom Kippur analogy (and so Jesus's atoning ministry) ends when, like the earthly high priest, Jesus leaves the heavenly holy of holies to return to and be present with his people (Heb 9:28). Only then will his followers receive the salvation for which they are waiting" (542).

125. Claims that first-century CE Platonic language consists of a spiritual (nonmaterial)/material duality is unlikely. Platonism and Philo both understand that the unseen creation is like known substances of the world, which in modern times, would classify the spiritual realm as substance-reality with concrete features. Yet they understood that, as unsensed, this heavenly substance-reality could only be grasped as ideas of the mind. Today, we can do no better. The Platonic claim that the reality of an unsensed creation can only be known in mind differs from the modern allegation that Platonic thought is imaginary, mythical, or ideal, as only existing as a product of the mind. Philo, like the Pastor, learned that evidence was external to his mind, from previous testimonial revelation and concepts known from the historical beginning, and not internal radical nonmaterial thinking of innovative ideas (cf. Heb 11:1–3).

The concept of immaterial or nonmaterial is not used by biblical authors, who speak of the contrasting reality of the earthly and heavenly places as visible/invisible, seen/unseen, natural/spiritual, earthly/heavenly, dishonor/glory, perishable/imperishable, temporary/eternal (perpetual), and mortal/immortal. The biblical term "substance-reality" glosses for the NT ὑπόστασις (Heb 11:1) for creation unseen. As a general broad descriptor, the gloss in English of substance-reality implies identifiable reality of objects in space-time. The term includes objects that God creates that are not sensed by earthly people. The Pastor identifies both the created things seen and not seen as "substance-reality" (ὑπόστασις Heb 11:1–3) in a complementary compatible contrast of temporal duration, rather than the antithetical material-spiritual contrast from Cartesian philosophy. God can speak and the creation will respond to whatever form he desires for his people, according to their holiness (Gen 1–3). The temporary function of the visible creation arises from the holiness of the occupant beings and not any incompatible properties of current opposites of dualistic creation itself (cf. Rom 8:18–22).

126. Modern sense of the term "Sanctuary" or "heavenly tabernacle," which were unknown by the Pastor (table 7) and, when used for a local place in heaven in replacement of the conceptual understanding of an *aiōn-field* of "eternal/perpetual-*places*," hides proper spatial understanding of the pattern of the tabernacle in divided heavens of holiness. Cf. Jenson, *Graded Holiness*, 89–148. Jenson discusses the spatial dimension of graded holiness as demonstrated in the tabernacle and people. The term "sanctuary" developed from the translation of the Latin Vulgate in the fifth century CE with a weight of meaning that was unfamiliar to the Pastor, now limits only to a local place

and ascension begins a ministry of perpetual atonement through a self-offering of his life,[127] and (4) the Pastor's spatial rhetoric of tabernacle divisions of holiness in a flattened, cosmic-*field* constrained eschatology contains no vertical function for access by people.[128] This speculation attempts to satisfy the Pastor's implied necessity for a concrete heaven as only for Jesus without his people.[129]

For example, David Moffitt argues directly against the possibility of the Pastor's tabernacle typology language suggesting a pattern about "all" the plural heavens.[130] He admits the possibility that the earthly tabernacle is a model "about" the heavens, which includes the earth, the probability of plural heavens, and the possible exaltation of Jesus between death and resurrection but rejects these. His evidence includes (1) an allusion to his anthropology, (2) a philosophical distinction between Philo, Josephus, and Middle Platonic tabernacle concepts as metaphor, contrasted with the Pastor as apocalyptic in analogy, and (3) a claim that Moses literally

---

in the holy of holies. It equates with an unlikely concept for the existence of a local tabernacle "in heaven." Christ does sit down in the heavenly substance-reality of the heavenly tabernacle. However, his fulfillment as a sitting intercessory priest, according to the example of the outlined antitype of the earthly-tabernacle sacrificial Christ, occurs at death and rising to God in the place of eternal judgment to open the way of the holy-*places* (Heb 6:1–2). More specifically, Jesus sits down at a particular *place* for intercessory ministry in the true heavenly tabernacle uniting both the holy place and the holy of holies of the eternal heaven, in contrast to the temporary heavens and earth, to literally bring people "to God" (Heb 7:25; 11:6).

127. Moffitt, "It Is Not Finished," 157–75. When worked out in the traditional cosmic-*field* limited hope, the complementary truth of the postresurrection fleshly ascension of Jesus escalates to a ministry of perpetual atonement. Moffitt probably pushes too far his antithetical interpretation of the Pastor's atonement narrative toward an imbalanced, isolated inclusion of postresurrection atonement events that for him integrate with Jesus's fleshly ascension into a perpetual atonement.

128. As Westfall admits, "We have taken what we wanted and left the rest without due reflection." Westfall, "Space and Atonement in Hebrews," 232.

129. The Pastor does acknowledge the typology of the outer court and the holy place. He indirectly references them in the sense that Jesus traveled through the heavens as depicted by the priestly antitype and the place of Jesus's suffering. Jesus's crucifixion on earth as a person was in a particular place, where believers now minister in God's calling "outside the camp" (Heb 2:14; 5:7; 12:1–2; 13:11–13). Gelardini argues several options for this idiom. This phrase may represent Moses as a type of Christ in the tent of meeting "outside the camp" in the presence of God. Another option is outside the gate of the temple in Jerusalem where the bodies of certain sacrifices were burned. Gelardini, "Charting 'Outside the Camp,'" 210–37. The "camp" probably symbolized a place outside either the holy of holies or new Jerusalem where the suffering of death and chaos continues till one enters to Jesus at the completion of one's calling.

130. Moffitt, "Serving in the Tabernacle," 259–79.

saw the complete *source* tabernacle "in heaven" that was used for the analogical model of the earthly tabernacle.

Moffitt's evidence is problematic on several fronts. Moffitt's closed-heaven limitations for people as only flesh explores in the next section of this chapter. Regarding his other evidence, Moffitt and others unnecessarily defend the sensed material creation against later scholarly constructed straw men.[131] Their evidence likewise contains words that incorporate traditional Latin transliterations with later added theological and philosophical freight. Also, they embrace an unlikely first-century CE view of reality, as spiritual/nonmaterial and material dualistic incompatibility, in the antithetical contrast of later Cartesian philosophy concerning the unseen/seen creation.[132] These straw men would include the

---

131. Caird, *Language and Imagery*, 53. Caird speaks of the danger of thinking of Palestinian Judaism and Hellenistic Judaism culture of the first century CE as two homogeneous and contrasting systems with little influence upon one another. He comments, "Now it is generally held that neither was ever homogeneous, and that the contrasts existed as much within the two types as between them." He remarks upon the once held theory for the background of Hebrews as the philosophical Judaism of Alexandria, exampled in the works of Philo, who had expounded the Scriptures considering the teaching of Plato and the Stoics. Caird notes that this theory is precariously founded since the Pastor states that he bases his tabernacle heavenly connections on the OT (Heb 8:5). All that could be said is that the Pastor and other first-century CE Jews used common language of popular vocabulary to communicate their message for understanding, "much as a modern writer might make a reference to evolution without having read Darwin, or to relativity without being able to understand anything of Einstein" (53). The same could be said then of today's counterreaction that there is no common OT background between the Pastor and other first-century CE influences, by presenting Philo's OT background concerning the tabernacle in a complete contrast to the Pastor as a rhetorical straw man of metaphor with only allegorical and philosophical concepts; e.g., Lee, *Jewish Apocalyptic Framework of Eschatology*. Lee, writing under Moffitt, argues for an underlying "Adamic tone" of vertical dualism in an "*Urzeit-Endzeit* eschatology." She builds upon improbable, foundational, background assumptions of the spiritual world as "nonmaterial," a strong antithesis between Platonic and apocalyptic language about the duality of creation, and a closed-heaven conceptual hope to "a fulfillment in the glory of Adam" that is distantly future, rather than at death.

132. Adoption of anachronistic, theologically weighted terms, such as the Latin transliteration "sanctuary," weakens any case for a first-century CE view of the tabernacle symbolism of the Pastor. Further, if Moses had literally seen the "source," in Heb 8:5, of a tabernacle "in heaven" as Moffitt claims, then (1) Moses bodily saw the impossible in seeing creation inhabited by God's dwelling before either his death in judgment or his own later bodily transformation in resurrection to dwell with God (Exod 33:20; cf. John 1:18; 6:46; Col 1:15; 1 Tim 6:16; 1 John 4:12; Matt 5:8). Is it even possible to literally see God's dwelling of the holy of holies of heaven without his presence in his glory and light? Yes, perhaps in visions and revelations as in first-century CE Jewish apocalyptic literature (cf. 2 Cor 12:1–4). However, such separation of God's glory from the reality of his eternal creation is another question. Without God's dwelling presence,

modern spatial understanding about Greek Platonism and later Middle Platonism, Jewish Philo and Josephus, and anachronistic Gnosticism.[133] As previously noted in chapter 2 concerning the possible influence of Philo, it is more likely the Pastor and Philo have complementary *aiōn-field* background views.[134] Similar to recent escalated spatial speculation

---

there would be no light to see (Heb 1:3; cf. Rev 21:23; 22:5). (2) Moses, after a literal vision of eternal reality, would then walk by his sensed experience and no longer by faith in the revelation of the Holy Spirit (Heb 11:24–27; cf. 1 Cor 2:9–10; 2 Cor 5:7). The Pastor later himself places Moses's cognitive view of both God and his dwelling in faith, rather than a sensed reality, stating, "because he persevered as continually seeing the invisible *one*" (Heb 11:27). The adverbial conjunction ὡς (*hōs*), as a comparative, weakens any claim of literally seeing God or his dwelling. Moses was motivated in a faith, as if he in reality had seen the invisible God and the "greater riches" (μείζονα πλοῦτον Heb 11:26) of his dwelling, implying a substance-reality. Upon a mountain on the earth, it is more likely Moses was shown the actual tabernacle outline for his own understanding of things unseen by the senses and understandings within his own fleshly bodily form. However, a distinct vision to Moses for a model about the current divisions of the heavens to reveal typologically the ministry of Christ is more probable (cf. Isa 6:1–6; Ezek 1; 2 Cor 12:1–4; Rev 4–5).

133. Stewart, "Creation and Matter," 284–93. There is a higher probability that the Pastor stands on common ground with Philo, Josephus, and language of Middle Platonism, than the chance that the Pastor stands alone against all of them in later, antithetical, contrastive views with a typology contrary to metaphor. Both typology and metaphor move in the realm of a mental association but with different relationships (287–89). Stewart finds that Plato, Philo, and the Pastor operate in dualistic thinking of two worlds but simply use different terminology that expresses similar meaning. The Pastor's worlds of types/antitypes compare closely with Plato's eternal forms/sensed images and Philo's intelligible/sensed world conceptions. Philo does not easily fit in modern antithetical, philosophical ideas. He embraces elements of a complementary contrast for the opposite creations of the unsensed heavens and the visible sensed world. Philo conceptually held that people would enter heaven (*Praem.* 152, *Spec.* 2:45). His concept would assume some kind of perceivable form for people that is compatible with the spiritual substance-reality of eternal/perpetual-*places* in space and time.

134. Gelardini, "Wir Haven Hier Kine Bleibende Stadt," in Gelardini, *Deciphering the Worlds of Hebrews*, 300. Philo probably viewed the higher space of the heavens as substance-reality through the lens of the temple, much like the Pastor, only with an added preoccupation with allegorical applications mixed with his typological/analogical applications. Gelardini considers that comparable to Philo, the Pastor conceived of an uplifting of the soul to heaven by Jesus, leading into the unshakeable kingdom in heaven. The Pastor and Philo embrace a common similarity with the dualistic language of Plato and previous Greek Presocratic philosophers where the "opposites" referred to contraries mainly in the duration of form in categories of created or uncreated, and destructible or eternal. Other than duration, both the material and non-sensed substance-reality were complementary, resulting from cosmogeny of the temporary visible creation arising from the eternal unseen creation (cf. Heb 11:1–3). Cf. Kirk et al., *Presocratic Philosophers*, 105–40. Kirk and Schofield mention the hotly debated topic by scholars over whether these dualistic worlds are superimposed or successive. Scholars also are far from agreed on Philo's concepts of creation. Several monographs,

about Gnosticism, evidence often develop by mirror reading and by imagining modern ideas upon the background of first-century CE biblical texts.[135] These recent conceptions are accepted without challenge.

For example, Edward Adams rightly pushes back against "pejorative" arguments that the visible creation lacks "inherent good" or is "antithetical" in God's creation.[136] Adams also admits the Pastor's dualism, stating, "The writer distinguishes between the visible heavens, which are part of the created order, and the heaven/the heavens as the dwelling place of God" (131). However, he assumes the unlikely perspective that ancient philosophers held the spiritual creation as *adversative* nonmaterial in contrast to the material of the heavens and earth.[137] As cosmic-*field*

---

articles, and papers focus on the spatial-temporal views of Philo as possibly related to the Pastor. For a summary of this research see, Guthrie, "Hebrews in Its First-Century," 414.

135. Christians in the fourth century CE were familiar with ancient Greek philosophy, as seen in Augustine's reflection on the debate about the nature of time from Aristotle to the Neoplatonists (*Conf.* 11.12.14–11.31.41). Cf. Sorabji, *Time, Creation, and the Continuum*; Turetzky, *Time*. However, the modern terms, "material" and "substance-reality" have different functional domains. The term *material* and its antonym *nonmaterial*, which are not found in the NT, arose out of necessity to describe a general property of physical objects in the visible cosmos of the *natural* world for scientific purposes. Their function introduces into biblical dualism, antithetical contraries, with *material* indicating not spiritual, *nonmaterial*, or *supernatural*, as spiritual substance-reality. In Cartesian philosophy of the modern era, things people physically sense in the *natural* world of the cosmos contrast with the spiritual *supernatural* realm as completely incompatible opposites that include, in their respective places, all aspects of space-time.

E.g., Walter, "'Hellenistische Eschatologie' im Neuen Testament," 335. Walter defines "Hellenistische Eschatologie" as the opposite of "apokalyptischen Eschatologie," which was defined in the phenomena researched by Johannes Weiß and Albert Schweitzer. This clear-cut, adversarial division of Jewish culture which finds the idea of people in heaven as normative across all first-century CE cultures in a variety of ascension motifs, is now heavily challenged. Modern Cartesian lenses often speculate, by systematic theology proof texts, for the Jewish place of the spiritual creation as timeless, occupied only by God, and incompatible with the presence of people or other created beings. The debate over conjectures about eternal time for God before any creation by God, which is considered in the Greek philosophy of Plato's *Timaeus*, with the Eternal Being conceived as timeless before any movement in a created place (*Tim.* 37D–38A), is not found in Jewish history or apocalyptic literature. Jewish cosmogony perceives the cosmos as being created from previous eternal/perpetual-*place* substance, without Jewish culture adopting Plato's philosophical speculation about the time of God before the beginning of any created movement in a place.

136. Adams, "Cosmology of Hebrews," 129, 131.

137. Similarly, several assumptions in Adams's assertions are problematic. He assumes that αιων ("eternal/perpetual-*places*") of space-time equates with the later flattened, fifth-century CE Latin term *universum* ("universe"), which implies only the

limited in destiny in monistic flesh-limited anthropology, the tabernacle as a model about the plural heavens of all creation accessible to people continues rejection to remain in inherited orthodox traditions.[138]

Anthropological Afterlife Options for Sinful People

A great haze envelops the modern background anthropology options that governs the interpretation of the fate concerning those waiting for Christ to appear at judgment after death, which pertains to Heb 9:27–28. Two main antithetical opinions, either a bodiless, incorporeal immortality of the soul or a bodily resurrection of the flesh of the dead, dominate the modern discussion. However, contemporary conversation often overlooks evidence that other first-century CE views concerning the messianic promise of an afterlife for people embrace a different anthropological perspective than the prevailing dominate opinions.

Not a new question in debate among the living in the visible cosmos since before the time of Jesus, the issue remains unsettled without conclusive resolution. For example, STL, in the books of Enoch several centuries before Jesus's ministry, speculates about Enoch's transformation recorded by Moses in Gen 5:22–24.[139] The Pastor in the Letter to the

---

visible creation (124–27). He also uses the later Latin *sanctum* ("sanctuary") for the Greek plural ἁγίων ("holy-*places*," Heb 8:2), which omits visible creation. Transliterated Latin to English terms with their later freight were unknown by the Pastor, foreign to him, and have modern weight difference in meaning from the first century CE. Adams admits in his earlier work on Paul that his analysis involved first-century CE language rather than these later anachronistic categories. Adams, "Cosmology of Hebrews," 124n11. His decisions toward anachronistic language derive confusing conclusions concerning the Pastor's connections between varied forms of ἅγιος (*hagios*) and οὐρανός (*ouranos*) in his descriptions of the movement of the priesthood of Christ in atonement (131). Modern weighted terms also allow bending the text to fit around modern spatial presuppositions.

138. Concerning the negative view of the tabernacle concepts of Philo, Josephus, and contemplations of Platonic philosophy, the separation between ancient tabernacle heaven concepts and Platonic language of Hellenistic culture in relation to the message of Hebrews does not involve the modern vast chasm of adversarial opposites proposed by recent scholarship to shore up problems within traditions. This negative ideological chasm widens in a defense of the long-held narrow cosmic-*field* ideologies that scholars, in bias, often attach to the Pastor. The compiled scholarly version about the Pastor's spatial views relate people only to this visible world, which is really a clue that we have made him like our own traditions.

139. The present extant forms of Enoch are pseudonymous and likely develop as an assembly of several circulated writings in available languages from the fourth to second century BCE as a polemic against the spiritual state of others in a separate orthodoxy.

Hebrews proffers an interpretation that "by this kind of faith, Enoch was changed/transferred [μετετέθη] for the purpose to not see death, and he was not found because God changed/transferred [μετέθηκεν] him. For before the change/transformation [μεταθέσεως], it had been attested he had the result to please God" (Heb 11:5). The aorist and perf. tense support weight for a past historical event where God utilizes Enoch's transformation as revelation of his desired final destiny for humanities place after life on earth. There is no hint that Enoch's pleasing God at judgment merits any kind of inferior, bodiless form or place, when transformed to God's heavenly presence. Such a lessened sense would diminish the purpose of Enoch's illustration supporting the hope of faith as *now* better than his listeners consider.

The Pastor later summarizes his list of elders, which includes Enoch, as "since now they desire a better *place* [κρείττονος], that is a heavenly *one* [ἐπουρανίου]. Therefore, God does not himself shame them [at judgment]; the result God purposes to call to them. For them he prepared a city" (Heb 11:16). Specifically for rhetorical punch in his message, the Pastor considers Abraham (Heb 6:15), David (Heb 10:5), and other deceased brethren (Heb 2:10; 12:22–24) are already with God in heaven at the time of his writing by the present priestly ministry of Jesus. He speaks of no eschatological delay of the promise of a complete life at death.

About thirty-five years before the writing of Hebrews, Jesus's ministry cuts across the debate of ancient afterlife "opinions" (*hairesis*) between the Greeks and the Jewish Pharisees and scribes (the teaching class), the Sadducees (the educated ruling class), and the Essenes (religious monastic groups). Richard Horsley comments, "The Pharisees, Sadducees, and Essenes all originated early in the Hasmonean times, perhaps in response to Jonathan's assumption of the high priesthood."[140] The change from the Zadok to Hasmonaean priesthood generated divided beliefs in Jewish "schools of thought, sects" (αἵρεσις, cf. Acts 5:27; 15:5; 24:5, 14; 26:5).[141]

As other STL which was preserved in later centuries by the state-church, the early Enochic imagination influenced later Christian redactions of Enochic books in line with subsequent developed theology and practice. Cf. Reeves and Reed, *Enoch from Antiquity*, 211–44. Reeves and Reed evaluate passages where Enoch is taken alive either to Gan Eden or the ends of the earth, heaven/paradise, or the fourth, sixth, or seventh heaven. Cf. Esler, *God's Court and Courtiers*. For the relationship of pseudonymity to the NT, see Wilder, *Pseudonymity*.

140. Horsley, *Pharisees and the Temple-State*.
141. Le Boulluec, *Notion of Heresy*.

Atonement and the Logic of Resurrection in Hebrews 9:27–28

A decade or more after the time of the Letter to the Hebrews, the first-century CE historian Josephus regarding these sects describes a common trait of the Essene philosophy with that of the Greeks, stating, "On the one hand those who are subsequently surviving an eternal/perpetual-*place* soul" (μὲν ἀιδίους ὑφιστάμενοι τὰς ψυχάς) before highlighting differences between Jewish and Hellenistic afterlife destinations and speculated experiences.[142] His point is that like the Greeks, the Jewish Essenes had faith for continued living after death. He further comments how Greek philosophy offers that the good virtuous life free from vise is made better in one's lifetime by the hope of reward after death.[143] He compares the monistic Essene afterlife philosophy as like the Greek eternal survival and reward of the soul.[144]

Josephus also describes the Pharisaical school, stating, "And, then again, every soul is immortal, some, the one good only, the result to transfer/change into another body, the one morally base the result to penalize an eternal/perpetual-*place* of punishment" (ψυχήν τε πᾶσαν μὲν ἄφθαρτον, μεταβαίνειν δὲ εἰς ἕτερον σῶμα τὴν τῶν ἀγαθῶν μόνην, τὰς δὲ τῶν φαύλων ἀιδίῳ τιμωρίᾳ κολάζεσθαι).[145] He further contrasts the Sadducean school with the Greeks, Pharisees, and Essenes, saying, "And that continuance of the soul, that according to eternal punishment and honor, they continually condemn *them*" (ψυχῆς τε τὴν διαμονὴν καὶ τὰς καθ' ᾅδου τιμωρίας καὶ τιμὰς ἀναιροῦσιν).[146] Of these groups, Josephus claims that only the Sadducees rejected prompt bodily life after death.

Early twentieth-century scholars translated the commentary of Josephus in line with the common philosophical view of their day as "the doctrine of immortality of the soul," which differently apprehended people's afterlife form as inferior, incorporeal, and awaiting perfection in fleshly resurrection.[147] John Collins writes, "One of the major topics of apocalyptic revelation was judgment after death and the contrasting fates of the righteous and wicked in the hereafter. Belief in life after death was not confined to apocalyptic literature; the immortality of the soul was widely accepted in Greek-speaking Judaism, and the Pharisees, who may have subscribed to apocalyptic ideas to various degrees, believed in

---

142. *WFJ*, 2.154.
143. *WFJ*, 2.156.
144. *WFJ*, 2.156.
145. *WFJ*, 2.163.
146. *WFJ*, 2.164.
147. E.g., *WFJ*, 2:156.

resurrection. But belief in the judgment of the dead and a differentiated afterlife is first attested in Judaism in the books of Enoch and Daniel, and it is the primary factor that distinguishes apocalyptic eschatology from that of the prophets."[148] Collins recognition of immediate afterlife concepts as a common option in apocalyptic literature, so-called, opens opportunities for discussion of the ignored option for prompt and complete afterlife fulfillment.

STL apocalyptic revelation and Josephus's description of the Pharisees as believing that the soul after death changes bodily in perpetual living, against the total opposition of the Sadducees, supports a different take on the first-century CE, often volatile deliberation between Jewish schools of thought (cf. Acts 23:6–10). In Josephus's recollection, the issue focused more on resurrection of the dead as spirits or spiritual bodies than our later anachronistic concepts of incorporeal souls awaiting fleshly resuscitation after the pattern of Jesus's fleshly sign of his accomplished atonement.[149] Jesus's teaching cuts across Sadducean views (cf. Mark 12:24–27) and adopts first-century CE Greek and Jewish afterlife language in his teaching (cf. Luke 16:19–31) with individuals at death rising to God for judgment and continuing bodily in an eternal form and place. It is interesting that the much later opinion that demands fleshly resurrection of humanity, other than that of the Jesus's fleshly sign of atonement (John 2:18–22) by return from the holy of holies after the priestly pattern of Yom Kippur, does not directly appear anywhere in the OT or first-century CE completed NT.

After the obliteration of the Pharisees, scribes, and Essenes in the Jewish Wars surrounding the destruction of the Jerusalem Temple in 70 CE, the Sadducean ruling class outlook for a postmortem closed-heaven emerges uncontested in the revised and rebuilt rabbinic tradition.[150]

---

148. Collins, "Early Judaism in Modern Scholarship," 12.

149. *WFJ*, 2.163. Josephus's counter views of immediate resurrection and transformation bodily to modern traditional concepts since the late second century CE are often challenged by modern scholarship to align with modern controlling ecclesiastical traditions; e.g., Le Moyne, *Les Sadducéen*, 27–62.

150. Cf. *WFJ*, 2.150–55. Josephus comments on the admirable deaths of the Essenes in his account of the Jewish Wars. Horsley, writes, "The Pharisees first emerge as an identifiable group in Judea under the Hasmonaean high priests in mid-second century BCE. They evidently disappear from history after the Roman destruction of Jerusalem temple following the great revolt against Roman rule in 66–70 CE." Horsley, *Pharisees and the Temple-State*, 85 (caps emphasis Horsley). However, scholars commonly recognize that the Sadducees survived in hundreds of thousands; e.g., Le Moyne, *Les Sadducéen*, 19. It appears as the religious educated and moderates, the Sadducees

Atonement and the Logic of Resurrection in Hebrews 9:27–28

When combined with surviving future hope for a fleshly Jewish kingdom, in the early catholic church by end of the second-century CE, Justin and Irenaeus drift toward persecution of those who look for bodily transformation at death in a heavenly hope to God's presence. Alain Le Boulluec documents concerning later first-century CE use of the term *hairesis*, "A position that was simply a rejection of novel aspects in the development of ancient revelation is, in the hands of Christian authors after Josephus, fossilized into an absolute negation."[151]

Le Boulluec demonstrates that by the time of Justin, about 160 CE, there exists a polemically oriented, catechetical tradition held by the ruling class of the educated elders that evaluates *hairesis* pejoratively.[152] For example, Justin, concerning the thousand-year reign of Christ with his church, states, "If you have ever encountered any nominal Christians who do not admit this doctrine, but dare to blaspheme the God of Abraham and the God of Isaac and the God of Jacob by asserting that there is no resurrection of the dead, but that their souls are taken up to heaven at the very moment of death, do not consider them to be Christians."[153]

The Pharisees and Essenes before and Josephus's and Justin's later comments together provide bookends around the Letter to the Hebrews for the existence of people who consider the anthropological end of fleshly life as a rising to God bodily into heaven at the moment of death. Paradoxically, Justin and others held closed-heaven afterlife understandings for people against other aforementioned first-century CE open heaven concepts by the Greeks, Pharisees, Essenes, Philo, and Josephus, even as the Sadducees in the NT (cf. Mark 12:18; Matt 22:23; Luke 20:27; Acts 23:8). By the middle of the second century CE, Justin leads a line of elders that consider the faith for immediate resurrection and transformation bodily into God's presence as demonic. These elders consider the view a rejection of the proper succession concerning the doctrine of the fleshly resurrection of the dead.[154] By the middle second-century CE, the NT afterlife philosophy of the Sadducees that denies prompt heavenly living entrance for the dead, turns on its head, as Christian. Justin's disciple, Irenaeus, takes Justin's pejorative view and assimilates

---

did not fully engage in the war with Rome to the degree of death as the much more conservative Essenes and Pharisees, and thereby survive in great numbers.

151. Le Moyne, *Les Sadducéen*, 68.
152. Le Boulluec, *Notion of Heresy*, 66.
153. Le Boulluec, *Notion of Heresy*, 66–67. Dial. 80.3-4. Translation Le Boulluec.
154. Le Boulluec, *Notion of Heresy*, 66–67.

the belief in a prompt heavenly entrance with other pagan teachings.[155] Irenaeus claims, "For whatsoever all the heretics may have advanced with the utmost solemnity, they come to this at last, that they blaspheme the Creator, and disallow the salvation of God's workmanship, which the flesh truly is."[156]

Notably, the Nicene Creed versions of 325 and 381 by the fourth century CE omit any heavenly expectation apart from the resuscitation of the flesh.[157] By the fifth century CE, a revival of ideology toward spiritual life after death appears in the Apostles' Creed, where believers are rescued from the Roman ideology of Hades, as they wait as inferior souls for later fleshly completion on earth.[158] However, Justin's reinvention of heresy continued to be used for persecution of those who rejected the so-called proper faith for later fleshly resuscitation in an earthly kingdom through the authority and ministry of the state-church.[159]

Later tensions with biblical descriptions related to the afterlife and God's judgment led to gap-filling in doctrines of purgatory, last rites, and indulgences, in order to lessen a conjectured necessary penitence for sin before fleshly resurrection. Many of the reformers, when testing these ideas by statements of Scripture, rejected them as nonbiblical solutions. Many of the educated church elders since, in the inherited traditions and ecclesiastical control since Justin, still deny bodily postmortem opportunities in open heavens, while others surmise either some inferior quality of soul or unconscious sleep until Jesus returns at his second coming. A very small minority, mostly in independent ecclesiastic congregations, consider biblically viable the option for immediate transformation in a complete spirit body to a place in heaven with God.[160]

Recent religious freedom from over a millennium of persecution, by educated elders who view themselves doing God's service (cf. Matt 24:9–12; John 16:2; Rev 16:6; 17:5–6), now opens opportunity in

---

155. Le Boulluec, *Notion of Heresy*, 123.

156. *Haer.* 4. Pref. 4.

157. Schaff, *Creeds of Christendom*, 57–60.

158. Schaff, *Creeds of Christendom*, 45.

159. E.g., Aquinas, *Summa Theologica*, II-II, Q. 11. Art. 3. Aquinas advocated that heretics should be put to death for crimes that murder the soul in the same way a murder commits crimes against the body.

160. Jeremias, "Zwischen Karfreitag," 194–201; Hofius, "Das 'erste,'" 271–77; Hofius, "Inkarnation und Opfertod Jesu," 132–41; Knöppler, *Sühne im Neuen Testament*, 188–219.

a movement away from common, controlled assumptions for dialogue on this unsettled issue in consideration of suppressed first-century CE views.[161]

---

161. Yates, *Between Death and Resurrection*. Yates defends the traditional Catholic dogma of an inferior intermediate state of *animae separata* of the soul until resurrection at the second coming against growing Catholic scholarly views that the NT teaches immediate resurrection. His critical response admits that texts in 2 Corinthians and Philippians confirm this concept through the work of scholars such as Dermot Lane, R. H. Charles, Marray Harris, Anton Van der Walle, and F. F. Bruce. However, Yates after his confirming critical evaluation, still follows the Catholic position of tradition over text. My project proposes to add to the evidence of 2 Corinthians and Philippians the NT text of Hebrews as support for an immediate resurrection after death that includes the full benefits of a spiritual body, without an inferior state, when eternal/perpetual-*place* living. The flipped and delayed presuppositions for the traditions of an earthly kingdom pressure against acceptance of an immediate heavenly hope, and more toward a closure of heaven for people after death. Other presuppositional obstacles follow in footnote discussion.

Cf. Kreitzer, "Intermediate State," 438–41. Kreitzer documents the tensions concerning scholarly attempts to explain a development in Paul's thought between 1 Corinthians and 2 Corinthians from anticipated resurrection at the second coming to earth and Pauline inferences for an immediate resurrection at death. His brief mention of proposed solutions concerning heavenly hope for the dead is unconvincing. However, a review of apocalyptic (*aiōn-field* background) concepts in the first century CE reveals immediate rising to God at death is the normalized eschatology. The NT concept of later resurrection at the second coming for the living has since become imbalanced in limited future eschatology lenses.

Cf. Thiselton, *Life after Death*, 68–88. Thiselton, with presuppositions of soul sleep and general judgment, argues for both immediate rising to Christ and an intermediate state. His approach keeps logic and calculation separate, where believers are immediately with Christ and wait until the second coming to wake up together at a general judgment. His logical separation solves the paradox by the former as an observer with the latter as a participant, with either position having a unique perspective. However, 1 Thess 4:13–18 speaks of two groups as a class—the dead and the those who remain living. As a class, the dead do not all die at the same time. Also, they all do not die together but die over time until the class of the living are added to them by Jesus bringing together the two groups of the dead and living. He brings the dead with him (1 Thess 4:14). The dead rise first as a class (1 Thess 4:16). While the dead are brought with Jesus at the same time, the dead do not die at the same time, and do not have to all rise to Jesus at the same time. They only have to be with Jesus when he comes for those who are living to be together with them. The context does not rule out the possibility of immediate rising to Jesus at death in the first-century CE apocalyptic view. Other footnote discussion briefly provides other NT texts with probable prompt rising to God after death.

Internal Evidence in Hebrews for Waiting a Very Little While for Jesus in the Eternal/Perpetual-*Place* of Heaven

In his probable MCS, the dat. pres. pass. ptc. "to those presently waiting" (ἀπεκδεχομένοις) highlights that people are *presently* waiting in a place after death and judgment *at* the appearance of Christ, for "salvation" by him.[162] The Pastor, in his developed *aiōn-field* (apocalyptic) revelation of the heavens and earth with movement characterized by inseparable elements of space and time, summarizes the consummation of his parenesis as "salvation" in the hope that "Christ . . . will appear" (Heb 9:28).[163] An anthropological question centers on whether the Pastor envisions salvation as either a short wait for Jesus by the people who presently approach after death for judgment similar to the Greeks, Essenes, Pharisees, Philo, and Josephus, or, do all people still wait for a resuscitation of the flesh in denial of prompt bodily rising to God similar to a hope of Sadducees and late second-century CE motifs? Scholars argue for both options. For example, Daivd Moffitt uses Heb 9:28 for argument that "for Hebrews, the Yom Kippur analogy (and so Jesus's atoning ministry) ends when, like the earthly high priest, Jesus leaves the heavenly holy of holies to return

---

162. Consider another angle on the assertion, namely that a reading of Hebrews in modern cultural language can miss many important clues that signal there is more for deceased believers than becoming only a memory or simply sleeping while waiting to live again on a transformed earth. If people are only memories of God "in Christ," without literal conscious existence, or if they are only sleeping in Jesus, until a later fleshly body resurrection on earth, how are people presently aware of God's judgment after death, any waiting for salvation after death, and at that judgment experience their salvation? Both views that concern either non-existence "in Christ" or soul-sleeping create great tension with the Pastor's present reality concerning salvation events involving death, judgment, and the present ministry of Jesus as high Priest from the throne of God to those in need of his service.

163. Visual color illustrations and video are available at www.wmwhenryjr.com. The term *cosmic-field* maps visible, material, spatial-temporal reality and *aiōn-field* includes unseen substance-reality of any *heavenly* invisible movement in space and time narrative. The *cosmic-field* is a subset of the spatial-temporal reality of the Pastor's *aiōn-field* background (apocalyptic) language.

Locative, temporal, and instrumental properties in narrative are naturally complementary, and only adversative when negativized either by a negative particle or a referent/verbal meaning with inherent contrastive properties. The genre of historical narrative mainly emphasizes horizontal eschatology in the OT, but hints reveal a vertical eschatology in heavenly interaction with both God and his created beings, as always present in the background. Also, the study of modern Greek syntax, in teaching separate category choices for time and space, subtly implies to the minds of translators that time and space are divisible. Scholars often argue over enlarged concepts based on one to the exclusion of the other, as seen in examples to follow.

to and be present with his people (Heb 9:28). Only then will his followers receive the salvation for which they are waiting."[164] *Contra*, Martin Karrer contends the believer "strides to God in heaven" and finds a plural of believers in the symbolism of the cloud of witnesses in Heb 12:1.[165]

Concerning the waiting people, the original audience would understand the anthropological interrogatives of this MCS from the narrative of his *previous* context. As a summary UC, Heb 9:27–28 cannot function as a stand-alone proof text for any option, unless the meaning for that option is contained in the previous discourse.[166] The Pastor provides answers about people waiting for salvation after death to audience interrogative categories in the previous narrative concerning this event. Intertextual canonical answers in other messages or church traditions should not be included as choices here.

The modern debate primarily hinges around the spatial-temporal aspects of possible narrative questions. The Pastor, in the spatial *where* exposition about the people, has rhetorically provided directional verbal movement for both Jesus and his people. He provides temporal *when* options for movement to open heavens for access *now* to God (1) by the person of Jesus in an endless life, and (2) for his people who follow him (a) in earthly life by testimonial worship and (b) in reality of an endless eternal/perpetual-*place* life, in death and judgment. The sermon provides *no* mention of the future earthly ministry of Jesus's return to earth for the living and remaining that is supported in other canonical narrative (cf. 1 Thess 4:13–18).[167] Clearly, the possibility of a hope to return to earth is

---

164. Moffitt, "Jesus as Interceding High Priest," 542.

165. *Contra* Karrer, *Der Brief an die Hebräer*, 2:170, 2:300. Cf. Walter, "'Hellenistische Eschatologie' im Frühjudentum," 335. Walter also asserts that Jewish Hellenistic literature emphasizes "the consummation of salvation is in heaven."

166. Treier, "Proof Text," 622–24. If treated as an isolated warrant, with no influence from the rest of his message, then the pres. ptc. "those presently waiting" has a force of contemporary time with the future time of the main fut. verb "will appear." People wait at the same time that Jesus, as the Christ in present priestly ministry, appears. However, the summary text alone does not provide information for the space or time of the verb "appear." The summary text also does not provide the function of the ordinal idiom "from a second . . . " that has adverbial and adjectival properties in modification of both "Christ" and "will appear." The original listeners, as well as those considering this summary text later, must determine available narrative options from the context of the previous message. Options must remain inside the text of Hebrews for an accurate sense of the Pastor's meaning or are a proof text.

167. Paul speaks of two groups as a class—the dead and the those who remain living. As a class, the dead do not all die at the same time. Also, they all do not die together but die over time until the class of the living are added to them by Jesus bringing

not logically supported in Hebrews for narrative summary options by the Pastor. Crucially regarding DUC, other canonical or noncanonical options should only be considered if the Pastor's meaning remains unclear from his previous context.

Answers to the temporal *when* of these options now develop under the label "eschatology," another late philosophical term probably unknown by the Pastor. Among scholars, it carries freight different from the Pastor's rhetorical issues developed from his opening phrase "upon these last days" (ἐπ' ἐσχάτου τῶν ἡμερῶν τούτων Heb 1:2). Gabriella Gelardini provides a history of the term and mentions the debate as to whether it should follow the LXX use "your last things" (τὰ ἔσχατά σου Sir 7:36 LXX) in reference "to death" or the NT cognate "last" (ἔσχατος), used four times in 1 Cor 15.[168]

---

together the two groups of the dead and living who remain. He brings the dead (now living) with him (1 Thess 4:14). The dead rise first as a class as they individually die (1 Thess 4:16). While the dead (now living) are brought with Jesus at the same time, the dead do not die at the same time, and do not have to all rise to Jesus at the same time. They only have to be with Jesus when he comes for those who are living and remaining to be together with them. Further, the term "will be caught up" (ἁρπαγησόμεθα) only applies to the class of those who are alive and remain. The context does not rule out the possibility of immediate rising to Jesus at death in the first-century CE, *aiōn-field* (apocalyptic) view.

168. Gelardini, "Unshakeable Kingdom in Heaven," 308. Cf. Bowman, "Eschatology in the OT," 2:135–40. Bowman asserts the term as a nineteenth-century development. He distinguishes, in the OT, individual (at death) or general eschatology (national future of the chosen people or the whole world). Cf. Charles, *Eschatology*, 1–2. Charles in his work attempted "to deal with Hebrew, Jewish, and Christian eschatology, or the teaching of the Old Testament, of Judaism, and the New Testament on the final condition of man and of the world" (1). He claimed, "From the period of Moses, the religious and political founder of Israel, to the time of Christ, we can with some degree of certainty determine the religious views of that nation on the after-world" (2). However, he admits at the beginning, concerning his after-world conjectures, "But the facts are so isolated, the sources so often defective and reset in later environments that, if we confine our attention to ideas of the after-life alone, it is possible to give only a disjointed statement of beliefs and expectations with large lacunae and unintelligible changes, and lacking that coherence and orderly development without which the mind cannot be satisfied" (2). Charles then proceeded to provide, on this weak foundation of large lacunae, his speculation for the development of afterlife by the rise of the doctrine of immortality. Cf. Rohde, *Psyche*. The problem of "immortality" is another rhetorical straw man conceived by scholars who focus on resurrection as an earthly hope and kingdom like the first-century CE leadership that was holding to an earthly messianic hope. A "now" option for rising at death and entering to God and a kingdom in heaven is unheard. Those who did, as C. H. Dodd, have Cartesian presuppositions of a timeless heaven. All along, the common believer often expressed that they are going to heaven at death.

Atonement and the Logic of Resurrection in Hebrews 9:27–28

Past scholarship's proposals regarding the spatial-temporal message in Hebrews contemplated "now and not yet" solutions, whose speculation was initially based upon now acknowledged missteps about cultural divides of Jewish-Hellenistic (Alexandrian) and Jewish apocalyptic (Palestinian) thinking. These missteps forced, in options for the temporal *when* fulfillment of the future "will appear" concerning Christ, an adversative solution as either within a future eschatology of horizontal time on earth (apocalyptic) or a present eschatology of vertical-space in heaven (Alexandrian).[169] The antithesis of the two lenses spawned other hypothetical tensions over the language in Hebrews.[170] For example, a supposition of early church debate over delay of the Parousia was conjectured under the pressures of an absolute horizontal eschatology of "history" considered under a timeless, transcendent heaven of God's dwelling in

---

169. E.g., Walter, "'Hellenistische Eschatologie' im Frühjudentum," 330. Walter introduced his categories of Jewish Hellenistic eschatology and Jewish Apocalyptic eschatology as containing a great many variations. Since built on "hints," his strong categorical division between the cultural concepts is doubtful. Wisely, he cautions against the rejection of the concepts of individual salvation at death due to a preconceived negation for a collective salvation, especially over negation of the term "individual," because both concepts still involve an individual salvation at the end of judgment. Cf. Steyn, "Eschatology of Hebrews," 429–50. Steyn states, "For many years Scholarship on Hebrews has been divided about whether its eschatology is either vertical-spatial or horizontal-temporal" (431). Steyn contends, in a doubtful solution to the spatial-temporal tension, for a dual spatial and temporal eschatology in Hebrews that flattens together at the second coming of Christ to earth. Cf. Klappert, *Die Eschatologie des Hebräerbriefs*. Klappert traces representatives of the main views of eschatology in Hebrews and presents an attempt to derive a consolidation from them as "rather the testimony of a more radical version of the futuristic-apocalyptic horizontal by means of the vertical Alexandrian." Cf. Klappert, "Begründete Hoffnung und bekräftigte Verheißung," 447–74. Eisele contends by Hebrews's use of Middle Platonic language that the temporal aspects of eschatology are inherently present but deprived of their all-importance. Eisele, "Bürger zweier Welten," 35. His reason for unimportance is that he perceived no time from death to resurrection for the believer, like Earle Ellis, in order to resolve spatial-temporal tensions.

170. Eisele, "Bürger zweier Welten," 35. Eisele identifies the same observed tension between the language in Hebrews and an assumed second coming to earth motif option in Heb 9:28. It is likely both inherent elements of rising at death and subsequent bodily resurrection are inseparable, complementary truths concerning both ends of the process of salvation, without any theoretical Jewish Hellenistic/apocalyptic divide. People who believe and follow Jesus, initially at death in a moment of time, are first assisted in spirit bodies by angelic ministry (Heb 1:13–14), then rise to God by Jesus's shepherding in death at judgment, with later earthly, collective assembly by adding those still living (Heb 11:39–40), in spiritual bodily return for ministerial service in the remaining time of the temporary cosmos (Heb 12:25–29; see appendix 1, fig. 2).

"eternity."[171] The scientific Cartesian timeless solution also was applied to people from death to resurrection in seeking answers to explain the "already and not yet" weight in the adverbial "now" (νῦν) used sixteen times in Hebrews, along with the Pastor's frequent pres. tense constructions in vertical narrative.[172] Further deliberation developed over whether the people waiting represent a continuous entrance of individuals at respective experiences of death or a collective assembly of all the dead for one general judgment.[173] For future, delayed eschatology purists, no one dead, except Jesus, has been able to "rise" (ἐγείρω) or experience "rise, resurrection" (ἔγερσις) from the grave after death to see Jesus.[174] Such rational conclusions, collapse as a house of cards when the evidence of God's salvation has no future delay after death. Such evidence would include Moses and Elijah living at Jesus's transfiguration (Matt 17:1–8; Mark 9:2–8; Luke 9:28–36) or those seen coming from their graves at the time of Jesus's death (Matt 27:52–53). Gap ideology also collapses under the full weight voiced by the Pharisee who we know as the apostle Paul (1 Cor 15:12–58; 2 Cor 4–5; Phil 1:21–24; 3:17–21).

Internal Evidence in Hebrews for Transformation to Spirit Bodies at Death as Complete People into Heaven Just like Jesus Did

In the Pastor's narrative, the question concerning the bodily form in *how* people wait for salvation, now solves according to views of "anthropology."

---

171. Gelardini, "Unshakeable Kingdom in Heaven," 312. Gelardini reviews past scholarly concern over the location of salvation that led to the classical topics of either imminent expectation or the contrary, delay of the parousia. Cf. Grässer, *Aufbruch und Verheissung*, 86–90.

172. Eisele, "Bürger zweier Welten," 35–44. Eisele offers heavenly timelessness as a solution that was asserted by Earle Ellis; e.g., Ellis, *Christ and the Future*, 120–28; Ellis, *Pauline Theology*, 16–17n45.

173. Karrer, *Der Brief an die Hebräer*, 2:170–71. Karrer presents both as a possibility for options but leans toward a traditional option for a collective judgment and resurrection. Eisele supports individual judgment at death in his timeless heaven solution to immediate resurrection. Eisele, "Bürger zweier Welten," 35–44; Eisele, *Ein unerschutterliches Reich*, 85. Cf. Zimmerman, *Das Bekenntnis der Hoffnung*, 201; Gelardini, "Faith in Hebrews," 269.

174. There is intertextual insight that believers have already experienced "rising" (ἐγείρω) to God, as the initial step in the process of "completion" in salvation; e.g., according to Matthew, believers have arisen just like Jesus. If so, *where* are they today and *how* did it happen, before the expected eschaton of Jesus's return to earth (Matt 27:51–53; cf. 1 Cor 15:35–58)? Cf. Allen, *According to the Scriptures*, 65–66.

Based on decades of Jewish-Hellenistic and Jewish apocalyptic cultural partitions, scholars devised two straw men about people in contrastive terms, either as "wholistic," "monistic," and "human" against possibilities for either a "dichotomy," "trichotomy," or "dualism" of the Lord's people with an incomplete eternal/perpetual-*place* spirit/soul.[175] Space does not allow a literature evaluation of the issues surrounding the debate that remains despite crumbling assumptions about the first-century CE Jewish culture.[176] Neither common straw man fits the Pastor's anthropology about people.

The evidence either not considered, or rejected by some scholars, is the Pastor's *comfort* in implementation of a highly descriptive language, without clarification or polemic, that supports *present* spirit bodily access by people rising to God after death and judgment, who are featured as better, complete beings (cf. 2 Cor 5:17). People, in salvation by God's ability and will, participate with Jesus in the substance-reality of the spiritual realm.[177] For example, in Heb 2:4, by addition of *place* for a spatial weight

---

175. Post-Bultmann, there was scant debate in NT scholarship concerning first-century CE views of anthropology, which were dominated by Pauline studies with little consideration for Hebrews. Bultmann, *Theology of the New Testament*, 1:190–352. The modern understanding of anthropology arose primarily with Rudolf Bultmann drawing from his former teacher Johannes Weiss. Bultmann's work, and that of John Robinson, had significant impact. Robinson, *Body*. These works, after World War II, had profound effect on current understanding of anthropology. Their domination is seen in current literature. Scholars often accept this new orthodoxy as warrant with no need for argumentative justification. Dunn, *Theology of Paul the Apostle*, 51–127. A slow advance, in a slightly dissenting option regarding Bultmann's foundations, arose in the work of James Dunn. Both Dunn and Bultmann make claims for OT Jewish against Hellenistic views of holistic vs. partitive views of man. This claim is made without clear evidence in their work. The assumption seems to stem from an antignostic straw man reaction against independence of man's created parts. Cf. Green, *Body, Soul, and Human Life*.

176. Gundry, *Sōma in Biblical Theology*; Cooper, *Body, Soul and Life Everlasting*. Cf. Aune, "Anthropological Duality in the Eschatology," 215–39.

177. Bailey, "Life after Death." Bailey concludes, "The fundamental faith of the NT for a life after death is that it is a life of unending fellowship in and with Christ (resp. God). This is the Christian's life: (1) we live now in Christ; (2) we will, in some way, be with Him after death; (3) we will be with him in full fellowship at the Parousia-Resurrection, 'when our now hidden lives will be revealed (Col. 3:1–4)'" (abstract). He states, "The dead have some physical substance just as they have some conscious existence" (214). He concludes, "While our curiosity regarding the Interim State is not fully satisfied in the New Testament, there is one result that is significant. We may not know with assurance how we shall survive during the Interim, nor know much regarding those 'who have never heard', but the one thing needful' is known. This one thing is that death cannot separate us from God in Christ. We will be with Him and this communion is the vital and essential element of faith and hope. This community

to "holy *place*" (ἅγιος), the Pastor may be referencing the testimonies of God and others, who received gifts in heaven, in correspondence with his later summary of Heb 9:28 (cf. Heb 11:13-16). He rhetorically asks, "How shall we escape after neglecting so great salvation, which after first received through the Lord upon the ones having heard, to us it was confirmed, he of God [the Son] testifying at the same time with both signs and wonders and many abilities, even with distributions of a spirit of a holy *place* [πνεύματος ἁγίου μερισμοῖς] according to his will?" (Heb 2:3-4; cf. Heb 4:12; 6:4; John 3:6).[178] The lexeme "salvation" can locate the subtopic salvation event of Jesus with the first-century CE distribution of his "spirit of a holy place" (cf. Heb 9:14; cf. 1 Cor 15:44-58) at death and judgment, which believers follow in a bodily, spiritual birth (cf. Heb 5:5-7; cf. Luke 23:46; John 3:5-7).[179]

with God and those who are His as the goal of life here and hereafter is another result of importance and abiding worth" (494-95, underline Bailey's). Cf. 1 John 3:2.

178. See appendix 2, table 9 for ἅγιος (*hagios*) as the unseen holy place(s) of the heaven(s) of all creation. The glosses *place*(s) or *tent/tabernacle* are added to ἅγιος, as "holy-*places*/tent" to force consideration of the eternal/perpetual-*place* spatial implications in the context of Hebrews. An exception is when it is used in reference to people, who are "holy ones" (Heb 6:10; 13:24) or places God abides within by his Spirit (cf. Rom 8:16). However, the holiness of people has a spatial weight that is lost in the Latin transliterations of *sanctifico* in the now used transliterated English words "sanctify" for ἁγιάζω (Heb 2:11; 9:13; 10:10, 14, 29; 13:12), "sanctification" for ἁγιασμός (Heb 12:14), and "saint(s)" for ἅγιος (Heb 6:10; 13:24). Sanctification, or holy place dwelling, allows a person into the presence of God's dwelling, both relationally in this life, and literally, by access to the eternal/perpetual-*place* with Jesus (Heb 2:11). This *place* emphasis intensifies when paired in contextual interplay with the place of the "dominion-rule" (Heb 2:5, 11) and *aiōn-field* background theme of "eternal/perpetual-*place*(s)" (Heb 1:2) in Hebrews.

179. Scholars translate πνεύματος ἁγίου (*pneumatos hagiou*) as "the Holy Spirit" with the topic of *spiritual gifts* for ministry in mind, with some light consideration for other options connected with the overarching theme in Hebrews of death and judgment, to which the signs, wonders, and abilities may refer. See Allen, *Hebrews*, 188-201. Concerning "divisions, distributions" (μερισμοῖς), Allen writes, "It is possible that the author had in mind 'a kind of preliminary apportionment of future inheritance' such as in Eph 1:14" (196). Cf. Koester, *Hebrews*, 207. Koester found in P. Oxy. 493.8 and P. Ryl. 65.5, the term "was used for various things, including inheritance." Cf. Kleinig, *Hebrews*, 106n46. Kleinig describes the only two uses for the term in the LXX (Josh 11:23; Ezra 6:18). This included allocation of the land to Israel and the assigned divisions of the Levites with their responsibilities. This would identify with the context of Jesus's inheritance in heaven as well as that of the listeners, who are about to inherit salvation in heaven (Heb 1:2, 4, 14) by the seal of the Holy Spirit as a bodily spirit after death. In the NT era, the ambiguous term "spirit of a holy place" (πνεύματος ἁγίου Heb 9:14), in the different form from the definitive "the Holy Spirit" (τοῦ πνεύματος τοῦ ἁγίου Heb 9:8), may be designed as an idiom to describe the union of the Holy Spirit with the spirit substance of people that together testifies one is now holy and a child of

He closes another, prior UC to Heb 9:27–28, with a warning concerning the example of Jesus's and God's faithful judgment, as historically typified in relation to the antitype of the people of Israel (Heb 3:1–4:13). For the Pastor, the typological events of Israel's deliverance, judgment, and the inheritance of rest in the promised land (cf. Josh 11:21–23 LXX) symbolize the reality of heavenly entrance available "today" (Heb 4:6–10). This includes a "division" (μερισμός) of people by the Son, as the Word of God, for judgment after death into "both soul and spirit, and bones and marrow, even an able judge of intentions and thoughts of the heart" (Heb 4:12). At judgment, when people approach to God in heaven, Jesus can judge the reflections and thoughts of people's hearts, without having to scientifically explain the *how* concerning the people or *where* of the place. The Pastor, like David, accepts by faith the typology of the heavenly access "today" that is symbolized by Israel's inheritance of promised rest in the land, "of heavenly places."

His selection for verbal nouns and verbal activity describes directional movement of people, who are regarded as "partners" (μέτοχοι Heb 3:1, 14) in a heavenly calling of Jesus's house.[180] He comments that his listeners qualify in this partnership with Jesus, by a condition of following a common unseen spatial reality to God's calling in heaven. His condition for partnership states, "If indeed, we should adhere steadfast the beginning of the substance-reality until completion" (Heb 3:14). The context assumes the necessity of a commonly experienced journey of life that begins before death and completes in heaven.[181] His narrative perceives

---

God at judgment (Heb 2:4; 6:4; cf. Rom 8:16; 1 John 4:13). The form πνεύματος ἁγίου is used twenty-three times as unique to the NT. It usually refers to either a filling, faith, renewal, or joy from the Holy Spirit, who is occupying the place of a person as one with the substance of their spirit (Matt 1:18; Luke 1:5, 41, 67; 4:1; Acts 1:2; 2:4; 4:8; 4:25; 6:5; 7:55; 9:17; 11:24; 13:9, 52; Rom 5:5; 15:13; 1 Thess 1:6; 2 Tim 2:14; Titus 3:5; Heb 2:4; 6:4; 2 Pet 1:21).

180. BDAG, "ὑπόστασις," 1040–41. Bauer observes, "The author of Hb 3:14 uses ὑπ. in a way that invites an addressee to draw on the semantic component of obligation familiar in commercial usage of the term . . . an association that is invited by use of μέτοχος, a standard term for a business partner." This language links strongly with the first-century CE patron system and heavenly "dominion rule" (οἰκουμένη).

181. The condition inferred is that if the audience does not travel the entire path Jesus traveled, beginning to end, they will not partner with Christ in their heavenly calling as part of his house. The time range that the audience should hold fast has both individual beginnings and endings, as possibly inferred by "until ends" (μέχρι τέλους), a probable idiom that functions as a marker of continuance in time up to a point. BDAG, "μέχρι," 644. The gen. sg. τέλους (*telous*), could infer either a collective, as "common endings at the same time," or individual, as "common endings at different

that those hearing are in a journey already beginning, with an expected upward rising in death to the eternal/perpetual-*places* (Heb 6:2, 4), toward the unseen ὑπόστασις ("substance-reality," cf. Heb 1:3, 11:1) of faith, with completion at eternal judgment by Jesus appearing for salvation.[182] People either dwell with God or are "turned away" (ἀφίστημι) from God (Heb 3:12; 4:1; cf. Heb 6:5), based upon faith in God's promise of forgiveness and atonement in Christ.[183] The Pastor, based on the symbolism of

---

times" determined by context. Both are probable options since people individually finish in heaven at death and collectively "to complete, finish" (τελειόω) the process of rising to God, all at the same time, when the living people are later added to those deceased, who already live with Jesus (Heb 2:11–13; cf. 1 Thess 4:13–17). Similarly, the verbal activity of "approach" (προσέρχομαι) begins in life at the moment of repentance and faith, realizes at death, and ends in heaven, where all believers "enter" (εἰσέρχομαι Heb 3:11, 19; 4:1, 3, 5, 10, 11; 6:19–20; 9:24–25; 10:5).

182. Käsemann called this heavenward motion of the soul "the wandering people of God" to heaven, after the typology of the journey leaving the exodus into the promised land. Käsemann, *Wandering People of God*. Cf. Johnsson, "Pilgrimage Motif," 239–51. Johnsson asserts this pilgrimage in Hebrews is not realized on earth but "the 'real' city which is 'to come' (13:14) already is, because it belongs to the realm of the invisible, not made with hands, whose builder and maker is God (11:10; 8:1–5; 9:11)" (247–48); Hofius, *Katapausis*, 116–51. Hofius critiqued the idea of "wandering" and pronounced those believers in faith were better described as "waiting."

Laansma, "I Will Give You Rest," 311. Laansma appropriately remarks, "Both of these interpretations—as argued by Hofius and Käsemann—have a direct connection to the respective religious historical hypotheses, for just as the idea of 'waiting' is fitting for the apocalyptically conceived future revelation of the world which is now 'hidden,' so the idea of 'travelling' is suited to the dualistically conceived movement from the created realm to the uncreated."

183. The idea of descent initially was only for those who did not rise up to God at judgment. Cf. Bremmer, "Descents to Hell," 340–57. Bremmer does not find, in the available first-century CE Jewish and Christian apocalypses, the descents to hell with typical features that are mentioned in available Greek literature. The experience of Enoch in 1 Enoch describes a great land of darkness when traveling to the Northwest (1 En. 17–19). However, later writings from the late first- to second century CE of the Latin Vision of Ezra and Greek Apocalypse of Peter reveal descents into hell. These later descents, for *all* people, are probable missteps based upon a change of emphasis by conflation of heavenward hope with elevated antitypes about future available earthly kingdom matters promised to Israel. Earlier Jewish and Christian works, either before or contemporary with the Pastor have close connections with Hebrews in being often composed in the first-person, have angel interpreters, and include the concept of layered heavens. Later Hellenistic Greek explanation turned to downward, earth limited contemplation, whereas it tentatively appears that most Jewish and Christian emphasis in the first century CE was envisioned as a personal ascent heavenward for the righteous with angelic guidance (Heb 1:14; cf. Luke 16:19–31; 23:43).

The first-century CE literary direction of the *ascent* to heaven for the righteous is universally recognized by scholarship. Cf. Bauckham, *Fate of the Dead*, 49–96. Bauckham asserts, in apocalypses that deal with the fate of the dead, that judgment after

Israel's typology, warns that unbelievers are "turned away" (Heb 3:12; cf. Matt 7:21–23; Luke 13:22–35).

He also explains in his UC of Heb 6:11–20 an ontological "better" heavenly access, "as an anchor . . . for the soul" of people, in following Jesus as "the forerunner" (πρόδρομος Heb 6:20). God speaks, he is able, he is faithful, he cannot lie, he provides the heavenly hope promised access, which "presently is entering" beyond the veil—for people as living "souls" after death with a transformed body to eternal/perpetual-*place* spirits just like Jesus did (Heb 9:14; 10:5, 39; 12:22–24; cf. 1 Cor 15:50–58; 1 John 3:2).

The Pastor utilizes fifteen different words to describe features of people in the overarching theme about the priestly intercession of Jesus in death and judgment on approach to God. He especially emphasizes invisible features of people. These include a "spirit" (Heb 2:4; 4:12; 6:4; 9:14; 10:29; 12:9, 23), "heart" (Heb 3:8, 10, 12, 15; 4:7, 12; 8:10; 10:16, 22; 12:3; 13:9), "soul" (Heb 4:12; 6:19; 10:38–39; 13:17), and "conscience" (Heb 9:9, 13; 10:2; 13:18) of both Jesus and people, in connection to the unseen heavenly decisions in judgment about heavenly access.[184] The Pastor's lexical emphasis in language that includes terms to explain the dualism of bodily unseen elements of people in the heavenly places after death is hard to ignore. People after death are still bodily people transformed into another form (Heb 10:5; cf. 2 Cor 5:16–17).

The Pastor further shares in Heb 6:4, that Christ and people share the same spiritual experience in association with death and judgment, which concerns his illustration of the last two basic requirements of Christ, "both of rising of the dead people and of eternal/perpetual-*place* judgment" (Heb 6:2). He reasons, "For it is impossible for the ones having

---

death was an overlapping later development during the first century CE but this probably pushes the limited amount of his evidence too far. Cf. Yarbro Collins, "Traveling Up and Away: Journeys to the Upper and Outer Regions of the World," 135–66. Yarbro Collins provides a brief history of scholarship and recommends general division of the theme of ascents and journeys as a theme of the Bible, post-biblical Jewish and Christian texts, as well as in Greek and Roman works. Cf. Yarbro Collins, "Ascents to Heaven in Antiquity: Towards a Typology," 2:553–72; Segal, "Heavenly Ascent in Hellenistic Judaism," 1333–94; Segal, *Life after Death*; Himmelfarb, "Practice of Ascent," 123–37; Bousset, *Die Himmelsreise der Seele*; Scott, "Heavenly Ascents," 447–52.

184. Burton, *Spirit, Soul, and Flesh*, 141–72. Burton finds no special distinction of the Pastor's use of the terms from other Greek literature of the time (203). In the philosophical and medical writers, πνεῦμα denoted "world-stuff, soul-stuff" (168) with implications of a created element of a human being. The concept enabled the task of denoting the unembodied or disembodied spirit or shade.

once been enlightened, those having tasted of the heavenly gift, those having become a partaker of a spirit of a holy place [πνεύματος ἁγίου], and those having tasted a conversation of God's abilities of the coming eternal/perpetual-*places*" (Heb 6:4–5). This statement links as normative the experience of "a spirit of a holy place" in "the abilities of the presently coming eternal/perpetual-*places*" in his rhetorical illustration of the prerequisites of Heb 6:2.[185] He explains "eternal/perpetual-*place* judgment" in the pattern of the Christ that people follow in "both of rising of the dead and of eternal/perpetual-*place* judgment." The use of the pres. ptc. "presently/subsequently coming" (μέλλοντος) provides force for an available spirit body of substance-reality for the Pastor's *present* expectation of entrance to God.

With words having a dualistic *complementary* contrast, the Pastor's frequent terms of "blood," "body," and "flesh" reference objects in the sensed, visible realm, either the person of Jesus as the Christ, people with sin living in the cosmos, or the symbolic sacrificial offerings portraying the Christ in the OT. This understanding is generally accepted. However, when the seen and unseen language merge in narrative, his message is hard to hear. Many listeners miss how these terms enjoyed a comfortable home in most first-century CE dualistic venues concerning the fate of people waiting after death and already bodily as spirit rising to God from the dead.[186]

The Pastor, in Heb 9:27–28, predicts that Jesus will appear for salvation to those awaiting "for him" (τοῖς αὐτὸν). The location concerning the acc. direct object "him" (αὐτὸν) for the audience of his probable MCS, in his theme about the priestly Christ, has several choices of spatial location for the event(s) where Jesus initially shepherds his sheep together: (1) the

---

185. E.g., the apostles naturally thought due to their concepts about postmortem spirit bodily existence that Jesus appeared to them as an apparition (φάντασμα Mark 14:26; cf. Mark 6:49) in the form of a spirit *body* (πνεῦμα Luke 24:36). Jesus assured them of his flesh resurrection with the logic of their natural concepts that a spirit *body* does not have flesh and bones (πνεῦμα σάρκα καὶ ὀστέα οὐκ ἔχει Luke 24:39). The OT supported substance bodily form for appearance of Yahweh (יהוה Gen 18:1) and angels (מלאך Gen 19:1; cf. Gen 24:30).

186. Bremmer, *Early Greek Concept*. Bremmer states, "It is now generally recognized that the use of modern Western terminology to describe non-Western beliefs influences analysis since it assumes the existence among other peoples of the same semantic fields for modern words, and thus often implies a nonextant similarity" (4). This Western influence colors OT, ANE, and Hellenistic concepts of the afterlife for people by a tradition for only a fleshly bodily rising from the dead in earthly kingdom preconceptions.

place of throne of the holy of holies beyond the veil, (2) the less holy place outside, or (3) the earth of the visible cosmos. In later exhortation, the Pastor shares people bodily enter to a "heavenly place...city" (ἐπουρανίου ...πόλιν Heb 11:16) with other brethren, "an assembly of firstborn having been enrolled in the heavens" (ἐκκλησίᾳ πρωτοτόκων ἀπογεγραμμένων ἐν οὐρανοῖς Heb 12:23), and "spirits of the righteous having been completed" (πνεύμασιν δικαίων τετελειωμένων Heb 12:23).

Contra Claims Against Prompt Resurrection

The Pastor's imagery of people waiting in a place for the appearing of Christ and salvation has bearing on whether God's tabernacle is either a substance-reality "about" the plural heavens with movement of people in spirit bodies by the priesthood of Jesus from the visible realm to God, or only a temple "in heaven," a "heavenly tabernacle" so-called, where *only* the resurrected human person of Jesus enters for offering, atonement, enthronement, and ascension movement. As evaluated above concerning the subsection concept of "Open Heavenly Places for Sinful People," David Moffitt and others reject the proposal that tabernacle symbolism embraces *all* the heavens of both God's seen and unseen creation. Moffit's spatial views are critiqued therein. This section lightly highlights the responses surrounding anthropological questions about the people waiting.

In Moffitt's monograph, *Atonement and Logic of Resurrection in the Epistle to the Hebrews*, he dialogues with Jeremias and Hofius mentioned earlier, who both place emphasis on the approach by Jesus as spirit into heaven for enthronement, after death on the cross, before being rejoined to his fleshly body three days later. Moffitt finds those who follow this first-century CE optional approach as problematic with four main issues: (1) he postulates that the full heavens approach pushes the interpretation of Heb 13:20, as exaltation instead of fleshly resurrection, too far, with no internal evidence in Hebrews to support it; (2) the texts of Heb 1:3 and 8:1–2 may provide for readers "the strong impression that the atoning offering of Jesus and his heavenly 'session' cannot be parsed out as neatly as Jeremias's and Hofius's solutions demand"; (3) the view concerning Jesus's approach as spirit holds less significant Jesus's human body, than does the argument of Hebrews by the author; and (4), in Heb 13:20, it must be admitted that if the traditional language of resurrection does not occur, then the author may steer clear of thinking of resurrection at all.[187]

Regarding Moffitt's first issue, the apocalyptic language employed by the Pastor on his *aiōn-field* of the tabernacle of the heavens easily supports Heb 13:20 as an emphasis about Jesus's salvation when being led by God after judgment at the death of the cross for enthronement and subsequent ministry as the Great Shepherd of the sheep. Further evidence is that Heb 13:20 serves the Pastor as a UC that connects narrowly in stride with his other DUC along the same theme from the DI. Discourse analysis easily demonstrates that the overarching theme, as summarized in Heb 9:27–28, concerns the ministry of Jesus, from the place of the heavenly throne to those recently deceased at the place of judgment for salvation. In Moffitt's assumption for only fleshly resurrection, Heb 13:20 then becomes a tangential proof text about flesh resurrection away from the thematic line. He admits in his logic of flesh resurrection that no one has been saved till Jesus leaves the throne for the second coming to earth. This position suggests that Jesus is a Shepherd, who in personal, near relationships with his people has not shepherded anyone, perhaps at most leaving this work to the Holy Spirit till he can get off his throne. One could ask if Jesus came for Stephen at death when standing at the throne, or does Stephen still wait for the Jesus he saw on that day for his promised salvation in continuous living (Acts 7:55–56)?[188]

The second issue has also been addressed. When the words of these texts and others are stripped of Latin transliterations with sense foreign to the Pastor and are allowed consideration of their spatial weight in context of a first-century CE *aiōn-field*, the specific language of the Pastor more than adequately describes a coherent first-century CE dualism where Heb 1:3; 2:4; 4:12; 6:4–5, 13–20; 9:14; 12:22–24; and 13:20 are the same thematic event of death and judgment as a complete, bodily, holy *place* spirit described herein, rather than Jesus's later "sign" (σημεῖον) of fleshly resurrection (cf. John 2:18–22; 13:31–32).

Moffitt's third issue arises concerning the approach of Jesus in spirit at death for judgment. He views, as opposing rather than complementary contrasts, (1) Jesus's human offering in the pattern of the basic requirements for the OT sacrificial Christ, judgment, rising to God, and

---

187. Moffitt, *Atonement*, 25–26.

188. Urga, *Intercession of Jesus in Hebrews*, 135–42. Urga rightly finds the concept of intercession prevalent in Stephen's vision, even though the text of Acts 7:55–56 does not contain the technical terms for intercession.

his enthronement, and (2) Jesus's human fleshly resurrection. However, both are human and within God's ability for Jesus as human. There is no textual evidence in Hebrews that the change from a fleshly body of Adam to a spirit body of Christ disqualifies a person from the category of being human, no less than losing a limb or an organ makes one less a person (cf. 1 Cor 15:35–57).

Moffitt rightly detects logic about the flesh resurrection of Jesus and that the human factor of Jesus's flesh resurrection carries great emphasis for the Pastor's argument to his audience. However, for the Pastor, the earth and cosmos have no lasting appeal since they are temporary and wearing out in decay (Heb 1:10–12; 12:25–29). Also, the Pastor does not mention in his sermon the direct prophetic fulfillment on earth of OT promises for earthly ministry in a later fleshly resurrection on earth. However, the endpoint of the Pastor's exposition and exhortation easily locates heavenly with God, where the presence of the human Jesus in heaven now testifies, in greater emphasis (cf. John 2:18–22), for the same present ability of Jesus to bring his believers into the substance-reality of heaven at judgment (Heb 2:4; 6:5). Jesus's current ministry anticipates a corporate collection of the living people being added with the dead now living in heaven (Heb 11:39–40). Even then, his message points upward in movement to dwelling with Jesus in the substance-reality of the living God once the temporary heavens and earth are shaken (Heb 12:25–29). In the OT and NT, bodily resurrection is not about the dead joining the living on earth; it is about the living on earth joining the living who died and experience better, complete, and perpetual living with Jesus (cf. 1 Thess 4:17).

In Heb 11:40, by adding the *living* of his audience to the *dead* already in heaven at a corporate "completion, finishing" (τελειωθῶσιν), the Pastor logically supports a rising to God for all believers (cf. Rev 7:9–17) like that of Jesus. His rhetoric does not depend on Heb 13:20 as the events of the flesh resurrection/ascension concerning the later movement of Jesus to God but as his rising to God *at death* and return to earthly fleshly life as proof of completed atonement. Jesus's earthly sign of God's acceptance of his atonement at his death is his fleshly return from the holy of holies in an indestructible life—not his second coming for the living on earth.

The Pastor's use of the αγω– (*agō*) word group (Heb 1:6; 2:10; 8:9; 13:20), as in Heb 13:20, and φερω (*pherō*) word group (Heb 1:3; 9:14, 28; 10:5; 10:18) mainly describe Jesus's ministry in offering, bringing and leading people to God at judgment, and even now shepherding people after the pattern where God brought up Jesus into heaven at his judgment. There is even stronger logical evidence in the τελ- (*tel*) word group (Heb 2:10; 5:9; 7:19, 28; 10:14; 11:40; 12:23) for the process of rising/resurrection *from* the dead into heaven. The Pastor uses the τελ- word group in Heb 11:39-40 to contrast "those, they" (the *dead* in faith), with "us" (the *living* audience), to assure them "that they [the dead in faith] do not finish without us [the living audience]" (Heb 11:40).[189] No believer is left outside of heaven, including those living.

Afterlife concepts surrounding the Pastor in the first century CE were far from monolithic.[190] On approach in judgment, the righteous rise

---

189. The Pastor assures his audience, as living, that they will not be left out of the process of finishing their salvation that includes a collective of the living with the dead, who are already judged and now with Jesus (cf. 1 Thess 4:13-18). This is the inverse of the question "what about the dead?" that Paul answered to the Thessalonians. From the possible observation that all his testimonials of faith did not receive the promises while *living*, but in *death* (Heb 11:13-16), the Pastor anticipates a question "what about us, the living?" The syntax of the aorist prohibitive subjunctive "without us they should not be complete" (Heb 11:40) in context is better considered as a general or customary concept rather than the possible inceptive sense for a statement that implies a completion has not begun for either the dead or living.

A review of the Pastor's use of the τελ- (*tel*) word group supports an application range that includes Jesus's "sufferings" (πάθημα) of his experience of death (Heb 2:10) to his current ministry in the flesh based on his "having been finished" (τελειωθείς Heb 5:9) with the process. Jesus fulfills the word of the law about "a Son, who having been perfected in the eternal/perpetual-*place*" (Heb 7:28), which reveals that his finish, completion, or perfection locates in the eternal/perpetual-*place* and not on earth. Concerning people, the law "perfected" nothing (cf. Heb 9:9; 10:1), but the better hope allowed that "we draw near to God" (Heb 7:19), which implies in context the reality of closeness to the holiness (Heb 10:14) of the living God in heaven as "spirits of the righteous ones having been perfected" (Heb 12:23). By the Pastor's range application of the term, an inceptive sense of the aorist prohibitive subjective would also imply that no one has yet begun to suffer death "with us." For similar findings of the meaning as congruent with the Pastor's contextual use of "entrance" to the holy of holies in the direct and unmediated presence of God, see Scholer, *Proleptic Priests*, 20-30, 185-200. Scholer probably missteps by only finding application of the τελ- word group to believers in this life or a future eschatological gathering by concluding, "The deceased—the first-born who are enrolled in heaven, the spirits of just men made perfect—who are currently gathered around the throne (Heb 12.22-24) have 'entered' into the heavenly holy of holies, i.e., into God's very presence (e.g., Christ: 2:10; 5:9; 7:28; others: 11.40; 12.23)" (201). The Pastor applies the term to people as spirits around the throne with the living God in heaven now, which Scholer forces into a limited future eschatology. Pace Laansma, *"I Will Give You Rest*," 302-3. For a survey of scholarly positions, see Peterson, *Hebrews and Perfection*, 1-20.

190. Bieberstein, "Jenseits der Todesschwelle," 423-46. Bieberstein explores a variety of concepts available concerning the hope of rising after death. He proposes a development of four steps toward a successive formulation of the concept of resurrection of all the dead under the theological force of God's righteousness in the face of innocent

Atonement and the Logic of Resurrection in Hebrews 9:27–28

up from the dead in ascent to God, whereas the wicked descend outside of heaven to remain with the dead, in space labeled by other authors as Sheol, Hades, and the Abyss.[191] For the Lord's partners in his house, the Pastor does not thematically follow Greek or later Jewish Christian cultural options that refer to the movement of the believer in death as descent in going downward to Hades, nor remaining as a wandering spirit in the cosmos in the region of the grave, nor as either asleep or nonexistent to await Jesus in later-resumed earthly living.[192] The Pastor

---

sufferers. These flow from Ps 88 to 1 Cor 15. He observes that the conceptions of hope in resurrection do not provide every detail, and reason no systematically, thoroughly declined conceptions of the fate of body and soul after death. The idea of development of first-century CE afterlife views fails to recognize the genre differences between the history of Israel that has less background of dualism in after death experience and the more apocalyptic perspective-laced genre that includes more heavenly detail. Cf. Hallote, *Death, Burial, and Afterlife*; Katz, *Image of the Netherworld*; Darnell and Darnell, *Ancient Egyptian Netherworld Books*; Cumont, *After Life in Roman Paganism*; Cumont, *Oriental Religions in Roman Paganism*; Garland, *Greek Way of Death*; Fischer, *Eschatologie und Jenseitserwartung*; Suriano, *History of Death*, 53–54. Suriano observes in the ritual of secondary burial with one's collective ancestry and treatment of the dead, that transcended generations, could serve the same purpose to offer hope and security in the afterlife.

191. Cf. Bauckham, "Life, Death, and the Afterlife," 80–95. Bauckham conceives an OT ideology that *all* the dead *remained* in Sheol until a future bodily resurrection and a general judgment. He does not seriously consider the biblical option concerning the righteous expectation for an immediate judgment and rising upward from Sheol to God into heaven of his temple (92; cf. Ps 16:10; 30:3; 31:17; 49:15; 86:13; 139:8, 23–24). Bauckham's preconceptions follow the adversarial rhetorical straw man divide toward either Jewish wholistic or Platonic Hellenistic afterlife possibilities, which has recently been heavily critiqued. Cf. Bolt, "Life, Death, and the Afterlife in the Greco-Roman World," 51–79; Yamauchi, "Life, Death, and the Afterlife," 21–50. Bauckham, Bolt, and Yamauchi provide a balanced evaluation demonstrating a variety of Jewish, ANE, and Greco-Roman beliefs, in concepts that contain similar, spatial, dualistic topography and human afterlife abilities, by which the Pastor claims for the availability of access and entrance into heaven at judgment could be understood.

192. Evidence suggests that the Pastor's emphasis centers more on rising heavenward to God after death for continued life in God's dwelling, than other concepts of bodily return in resurrection for temporary earthly living and ministry with Jesus. Cf. Elledge, *Life after Death*. Elledge provides comprehensive analysis concerning the afterlife in the writings of Flavius Josephus in comparison to other controls of STL. He recognized that Josephus makes no direct mention of the concept of a flesh bodily resurrection of the dead, instead opting in his Hellenistic rhetoric for immortality of the soul. As I have mentioned, Josephus's concept differs from modern partitive or inferior states but possesses complete, bodily features compatible with spirit life. Cf. Farris, *Introduction to Theological Anthropology*, 161–86; Cf. Clark-Soles, *Death and Afterlife*, 61, 102–03. Clark-Soles senses wide variety in NT concepts of the afterlife but pushes in a flattened, future eschatology for NT Christianity, teaching mainly a future, flesh resurrection of believers in a relationship with Jesus in heaven.

does not describe the waiting as for resurrection of the flesh.[193] Neither does his afterlife hope embrace concepts of an "intermediate-state" or the modern straw man of "immortality of the soul."[194] His verbal nouns and activity portray people with hope in Jesus as rising in death to dwell with God as complete.[195]

The Pastor seems uninhibited to speak about humanity either in dualistic, partitive bodily features or wholistic bodily concepts. He fully embraces the necessary language to describe a person's relationship to the invisible/eternal and visible/temporary creation both in and after

---

193. Cf. Friedeman and Overton, "Death and Afterlife," 35–57. Friedmann and Overton explore the scant references of resurrection in the text of the OT in connection with the much greater evidence in Israel's worldview of the existence of an afterlife found in mortuary rites, the netherworld, veneration of deceased ancestors, necromancy, and rising from the dead. They conclude that the history of thought rarely moves in a linear progression toward bodily fleshly resurrection. The evidence supports a focus on what happens to people after death in heaven, with relative silence on fleshly resurrection. Interestingly, Friedmann and Overton find that the priests are less likely to mention life after death and speculate multiple possible reasons. Matters have not really changed; those educated in religion still resist contemplating the afterlife worldview that is held by most of the religious world outside of their small tight circle. Cf. Zangenberg, "Trochene Knochen," 655–89. Zangenberg generally observes that in ancient Jewish funeral practices and in activities surrounding death, from the those on the verge of death, to burial practices, to concepts beyond death and new life, all reflect a perceived understanding of life after death in common with other surrounding people. He chooses not to address the distinct differences. He also notices that, in these practices surrounding death, the NT concept of "resurrection" regarding the flesh was innovative and not found in ancient Judaism.

194. Cf. Cullmann, *Immortality of the Soul*, 48–57. Cullmann's view on immortality of the soul and the waiting of the dead are probably an unnecessary contemplation, especially if believers bodily rise complete to God "now" by Jesus's ministry in death, without an intermediate state. Cf. Buchanan, *Eschatology*, xiv. Buchanan summarizes the modern imbalance of the assumed warrant that drives the concept of the intermediate state and immortality considerations when he says, "The primary event for the Christian faith, then, is not the end which is still to come, but the resurrection which has already occurred and has determined the outcome of future events. Judaism was eschatologically oriented, but in primitive Christianity eschatology was dethroned and the resurrection was given central place."

195. The Pastor's concerns are more toward the rising to God of both Jesus and people in death and at judgment, after the pattern of Jesus's death-to-resurrection experience, than the promised spiritual bodily return to earth. If a person is not with Christ by rising to God after death, then later return in eternal/perpetual-*place* life for future ministry is not an option. Modern thought so focuses on a fleshly resurrection on earth, it diminishes entrance into heaven and afterlife of a present heavenly transformation as nonexistent or perhaps unknowable in God's revelation. The modern concept of later spiritual bodily return to earth is only a final part of the whole first-century CE understanding of rising and resurrection.

visible life. He does not embrace the anachronistic either/or extremes of syncretism vs. disunion, wholistic vs. dichotomy/trichotomy, or dualism vs. monism. His message contains no parenetic correction or polemic reaction to limit his language about people that commonly appears in modern straw men concerning Hellenistic and Jewish philosophy, to regulate the same probable optional understandings of his audience.

The Pastor freely deploys this language without embracing or mentioning any of the collective theological polemic assembled by the speculation of modern theological inquiry. The language of his text in common with STL does not bear the modern weight for either syncretic influence or complete disunion with the then existing language of first-century CE philosophical conclusions or applications. Rather, the Pastor simply uses common Jewish methods and normative language in a first-century CE priestly view that would be understood by his audience for immediate bodily transformation into God's heavenly presence as completion.

GOD SPEAKS AS AN ETERNAL/PERPETUAL-PLACE PRIEST WHO APPEARS AT DEATH AND JUDGMENT

In the probable MCS, the Pastor, by two correlative statements, condenses the entire OT connection of "Christ" with "salvation" for sinful people, who are appointed to experience a personal "judgment" after "death."[196] In a participation of death and judgment himself, Jesus became the "forerunner" (πρόδρομος Heb 6:18–20), as the first person "born" (γεννάω) into the presence of God (Heb 1:5; 12:23; cf. John 3:1–21, esp. 3, 5–7; 2 Cor 4:16–18).[197] The Pastor understands Jesus's actions as "the originator and consummator of faith" (Heb 12:2; cf. Heb 2:10), by his completing the Christ requirements of atonement for the better ministry of the new

---

196. Cf. Attridge and Koester, *Epistle to the Hebrews*, 265–66. Attridge and Koester comment, "The reference to the judgment (κρίσις) that follows death is not specifically to the eschatological judgment of apocalyptic tradition, but to the immediate postmortem judgment that was, in traditional Greek mythology, the fate of the soul." Cf. 1 En. 1:7; 5:6; 50:1–5, 53–56; Dan 7:26; Matt 25:31–46; 2 Thess 2:12; Rev 20:12; (Plato) *Rep.* 10.614b–621d; (Plutarch) *Fac.* 942d–945d. Pace deSilva, *Perseverance in Gratitude*, 315n38.

197. Cf. Jesus, in a first-century CE dualism, explains the experience of rising from the dead as a "birth" in connection with entrance in the spiritual places, "into heaven" (εἰς τὸν οὐρανὸν John 3:13), which also involves "to lift up" (ὑψωθῆναι John 3:14) the Son of Man. This spiritual birth links Dan 7:13–14 concerning Jesus, as the Son of Man, in a necessary upward ascent and entrance with others to God.

covenant (Heb 6:1–2). This section explores specifically what Jesus, as the Son of Man, does *now* and in heaven *today*—since the events of his offering, rising to God, and before his later coming for ministry on earth (Heb 11:39–40; cf. 2 Cor 5:11–21; 1 Thess 4:13–18).

The term "high priest" (ἀρχιερεύς) occurs seventeen times. The Pastor concludes his midrash LXX OT quotations about the speaking of the Father to the Son (Heb 1) and the Son speaking to the Father (Heb 2), with introduction of the term (Heb 2:17). The Pastor also links it with other christological identifications. First, he introduces "a Son" who created access to the eternal/perpetual-*places* (Heb 1:2). He then links that "Son" with the recent humanity of Jesus (Heb 2:9). Next, he links Jesus with people as the "apostle" and "high priest" of their confession (Heb 3:1). Finally, after a warning ministerial challenge, he integrates these three terms together, orating in Heb 4:14, "Therefore, having a great high priest, who having gone through the heavens, Jesus the Son of God, let us hold fast to our confession."

In the Pastor's theology, according to God's speaking in Ps 109:4 LXX (110:4 MT), Jesus, as the Son, was already appointed by God "a priest into the eternal/perpetual-*place*" (ἰερεὺς εἰς τὸν αἰῶνα Ps 109:4 LXX). God fulfills his OT speaking that came "in many parts and many ways" about his eternal/perpetual-*place* appointed priesthood for the sins of the people, by coming in the person of Jesus, who, as a priest, bodily suffers death in the substitutionary sacrifice of himself in completion of atonement and begins provision for his brethren's entrance into heaven before the Father.[198]

The Pastor, in his argument for Jesus as a "high priest," explains the requirements of the law of Moses that the priesthood was not chosen but was appointed by law from the tribe of Levi (Heb 7:13–14). Greater than the line of Aaron from Levi, he maintains that Jesus qualifies as a high

---

198. Smith, "Priest and Sacrifice." Smith explores the textual evidence, in the Fourth Servant Song, concerning the servant as "priest" in both offering himself as a "guilt offering" and becoming a long-lived "offspring" (Isa 55:10). The LXX reads, "And the Lord is pleased to purify him of a blow, if you will give yourself concerning sin, your soul will appear a long-lived posterity" (Isa 53:10 LXX). Yahweh's pleasing response to the servant's self-offering is to purify him of his blow in death so that his soul may appear as a seed who will bring a posterity or offspring. Yahweh's purification likely takes place at his judgment after death and before his resurrection. Jesus is appointed a priest but consummates his priesthood when Yahweh raises his soul up from the dead to himself before his flesh resurrection as the seed who appears that brings others with him in fulfillment of the Abrahamic covenant. For discussion when Jesus becomes a high priest, see Allen, *Hebrews*, 330–31.

priest based on his ability of an endless life that is patterned after the order of Melchizedek (Heb 7:15-17).[199]

This claim for Jesus as both an offering and continual priest in ministry of the Son as Christ is supported by the grammatical evidence of Heb 9:11-12. The Pastor first describes the initial priestly work of Christ, stating, "but Christ after himself arriving a high priest" (Χριστὸς δὲ παραγενόμενος ἀρχιερεὺς Heb 9:11) before the main verb "entered" (εἰσῆλθεν Heb 9:12). He also interjects a complex gen. absolute ptc. clause and two prepositional phrases about this event. The aorist middle adverbial ptc. phrase παραγενόμενος emphasizes the participation of Χριστὸς in the action described. As an aorist tense with weight for verbal action that is antecedent with the main verb, it is grammatically subordinated to εἰσῆλθεν. The verbal action expressed that the ptc. connects is "Christ . . . after appearing himself a high priest . . . he entered." Jesus, in fulfillment of the beginning Christ requirements of Heb 6:1-6, neither fell away nor had to start again his atonement at repentance. He entered heaven as a high priest both who completed his heavenly offering, and who opened to God a path of access through the heavens for ministry of intercession when his believers arrive in need.

Concerning the cultural symbolism of these modifiers, Franz Delitzsch comments, "Παραγενέσθαι is the usual word for appearance or manifestation on the stage of history (comp. Luke 12:51; Matt. 3:1; 1 Macc. 4:46)."[200] Attridge and Koester connect to the previous references about Christ's "becoming" (γενόμενος Heb 1:4; 6:20; 7:26), with a more dramatic nuance for meaning in several NT references "to arrive."[201] Allen comments, "This particular participle, when used with the conjunction *de* at the beginning of a sentence as here, often indicates arrival at a destination."[202]

The subject of the adverbial ptc. παραγενόμενος is ἀρχιερεύς.[203] As a continuance of the Pastor's exposition, this is the fifteenth time the Pastor has used the term, ten times as a type in reference to the Χριστὸς and

---

199. The Pastor possibly takes the position, based upon the eternality of God's substance creativity in relationship with his creation, "for the eternal/perpetual-*place* of the eternal/perpetual-*place*" (εἰς τὸν αἰῶνα τοῦ αἰῶνος Heb 1:8; cf. Heb 13:21), that Melchizedek is the eternal/perpetual-*place* Son before coming into the cosmos as Jesus.

200. Delitzsch, *Commentary on the Epistle*, 75.

201. Attridge and Koester, *Epistle to the Hebrews*, 245.

202. Allen, *Hebrews*, 469.

203. BDAG, "ἀρχιερεύς," 139.

five times in reference to the antitype of the Levitical high priest. After showing the inefficient ministry of a high priest in the Sinai covenant, he now introduces, for the emphatic tenth time, that Jesus as the Christ high priest fulfills the antitype of the Levitical, high-priestly ministry.

The complete adverbial clause then could indicate purpose in intent. If purpose, then the translation "Christ . . . after appearing himself for the purpose of a high priest . . . entered" would be inferred for the action. Since there is not a pres. tense ptc. following the main verb, it cannot be a result participle.[204] Thus, the action described does not result in Christ becoming a high priest but "Christ . . . after appearing himself . . . entered" for the purpose of a high priest in the role he had been appointed.

The main point of the theology of God's speaking in the Pastor's homily is "we have high priest" (ἔχομεν ἀρχιερέα Heb 8:1).[205] A priest intercedes on behalf of another's sin before God (Heb 5:1). As fulfillment of the high priest of Israel's OT typology, Jesus as the Christ both offers himself blameless as a substitutionary sacrifice for the sins of people (Heb 2:17; 9:14) and traverses the separated dwellings of the heavens to minister by intercession on behalf of sinful people who come to God by him (Heb 4:14; 6:20; 7:25–26; 8:1–2; 9:11).

The Pastor's comments suggest, concerning his theology, that God not only speaks by his Son as creator of a new access into the eternal/perpetual-*places* (Heb 1:2c), but also speaks as an eternal/perpetual-*place* high priest and as an apostle sent by God on behalf of people in need at their judgment before himself due to sin and spatial separation.[206] This Son, as an apostle, creator, and high priest, in recent history had become like his brethren in everything, so that, he may be a merciful and faithful high priest (Heb 2:17).[207]

---

204. *GGBB*, 638.

205. BDAG, "ἀρχιερεύς," 139. Bauer notes that the term is used in Hebrews by figurative extension of Christ, who serves as high priest, by atoning for sins of humans (Heb 2:17; 3:1; 4:14; 5:10; 6:20; 7:26; 8:1; 9:11, 14).

206. Cf. Perrin, "Origins," 51–64. Perrin, against the modern *history of religions* tendency toward newly held ecclesiastical concepts in the life of Jesus, finds that the Pastor's concept of Jesus's eternal priesthood rests on the well-established exegetical grounds of Pss 2 and 110. The priestly messianic concept traces back to the beginning by burnt offerings.

207. Feldmeier and Spieckermann, *God of the Living*, 324–27. Feldmeier and Spieckermann discuss forgiveness and reconciliation in Hebrews. Without forgiveness under the law, God is a consuming fire, whereas, through their confession, believers receive sympathetic mediation.

Atonement and the Logic of Resurrection in Hebrews 9:27-28

Jesus's own completed experience of these appointed events and his subsequent personal "appearing" now in heaven at judgment as the Christ make believers holy (Heb 2:9-11; cf. 2 Cor 5:9-10; Matt 16:27; Acts 10:42; Rom 2:16; 14:10-12), and enable a new spiritual birth for the entrance as his brethren into heaven for "eternal/perpetual-*place* life" (ζωὴν αἰώνιον Heb 2:9-18; cf. John 3:15-16; 2 Cor 5:1-8; Phil 3:20).[208] These "brethren," after a very short wait at judgment (Heb 9:27; 10:37-38; cf. 2 Cor 5:10), receive a completed spirit bodily transformation which is fitting for God's eternal/perpetual-*place* dwelling (Heb 2:4; 9:14; cf. 2 Cor 5:17), and Jesus collects them *from* the dead.

The Pastor's use of present tense, temporal adverbs, verbs, and participles in description of Jesus's ministry adds substantial force for his current perpetual ministry. For example, in his statement concerning Jesus as high priest, he states, "And so then now he has attained for a more excellent ministry, as much as also he is a mediator for a better covenant, which has been enacted on better promises" (Heb 8:6).[209] The Pastor later contends, "For Christ did not enter into a place made with hands, but into heaven itself, now to appear in the presence of God for us" (Heb 9:24). His adverb "now" (νῦν) adds present temporal weight to his movement and terms (cf. Heb 11:16). Jesus is already ministering at death, in that, "he is able to assist those presently being put to the test"

---

208. Cf. Gordan, *Hebrews*, 107. Gordan connects Heb 9:28 with the imagery of the Day of Atonement and high priest exiting after atonement once a year in the holy of holies to the people, who were eagerly awaiting outside for the high priest's appearance, which signaled the forgiveness of sins. The verbal "appearing" connects with the high priest exiting from the holy of holies, who was seen by the people after his disappearing from the outer court with the blood of the sacrifice. Pace Allen, *Hebrews*, 487-88. Allen connects the second appearance of the high priest with the earthly second coming and salvation. However, this would mean those "with Jesus" have not yet literally experienced salvation after death. The appearing in Heb 9:28 links with Heb 2:9-18 descriptions in relation to people in heaven or on their way to heaven. Who, when, and where are these "brethren" when presented to the Father? A brief exegesis of Heb 2 follows in chapter 4 in evaluation of the discourse unit B conclusion; e.g., consider Paul's statement, "For our citizenship is really in the heavens, from which also we await a Savior, the Lord Jesus Christ" (Phil 3:20). A large body of evidence suggests that the believer's verbal movement in space and time is not limited to just a second coming to earth.

209. NA28App, 669. The NA28 critical apparatus notes that the adverb in νυν is in $\mathfrak{P}$46 B D and νυνὶ in $\mathfrak{P}$46c ℵ A D1 K L P Ψ 0278. 33. 81. 104. 365. 630. 1175. 1241. 1505. 1739. 1881. 2464 𝔐. Cf. *CNTTS*, "Hebrews 8:6-1.0." The critical apparatus comments concerning the "now" (νυν) reading as, "Orthography, the reading is likely due to vowel confusion or spelling differences." Neither option affects the present temporal force of the adverb.

(Heb 2:18), which speaks of their need after death when facing judgment (cf. Heb 7:25).

The Pastor emphasizes Jesus's *present* ministry as "a high priest in the eternal/perpetual-*place*" (Heb 5:6) and Jesus's achievement of "eternal/perpetual-*places*" (Heb 1:2), where Jesus, as the Son, is now an eternal/perpetual-*place* high priest. In Heb 9:28, Jesus, after the completion of offerings for the sins of the people once, just as the anointed high priest appeared to the people in need in the OT Day of Atonement, as the Christ "he will appear," from the holy of holies at judgment, for salvation. Yet, he also will appear at a second coming, to those living to add them to those now living and complete in heaven, who have already arisen from the dead and only await the finish of those living as flesh.[210]

GOD SPEAKS THROUGH OTHER ETERNAL BEINGS

In the MCS, the Pastor chooses the term Χριστὸς to summarize the activity of God on behalf of people who wait for "him" after death and judgment. In his UC summary, other eternal beings who are not mentioned directly assist in this ministerial process of salvation by bringing sinful people into the presence of God. However, when considering the rest of

---

210. The language of a perpetual ministry indicates that Jesus may appear for judgment either at one's death or to those living before their own experience of death and judgment. In the NT, Jesus's temporal verbal movement for both options approximate due to shortened time differences that are experienced by those deceased now living in heaven, when compared to those now living on earth (Heb 4:6–9; cf. 2 Pet 3:8; Ps 90:1–5 [89:1–5 LXX]). Simply stated, the time (not timelessness), from death to resurrection for the believer in God's eternal presence, does not carry the same measure as time for those on earth. Descriptions of events for believers before rising to God, from an earthly perspective appear to occur distantly apart (e.g., approach, angelic ministry, judgment, Jesus appearing, intercession, rising from the dead, entrance, rest, singing, city life, then corporate resurrection, etc., cf. Heb 11:13–16; 12:22–24). From the spiritual perspective, for those living after death in the eternal substance creation of heaven, these same events before return with Jesus for ministry, occur over a brief period, as if almost all collapsed together. Jesus "comes" (ἔρχομαι/παρουσία), "appears" (ὁράω/φανερόω), and "brings" (φέρω/ἄγω), both during approach to God at his individual death (Heb 1:3c; 10:35–39; 13:20; cf. John 14:1–6; 1 Thess 5:6–11; 1 Cor 4:5; 2 Cor 5:10; Col 3:1–4; 1 John 2:28, 3:1–3) and brings the previous fleshly dead, who are alive in heaven with him by transition to spiritual bodies, to meet in the air all those alive in the flesh at his second coming (Heb 11:39–40; cf. Matt 24; Acts 1:11; 1 Thess 4:13–18; 2 Thess 2:1). Cf. Hendriksen, *Bible on the Life Hereafter*, 73–74. The suggested spatial-temporal distinction suggested by Hendriksen opens an opportunity for further future research concerning NT first-century CE language and concepts that support immediate postmortem resurrection.

Atonement and the Logic of Resurrection in Hebrews 9:27–28

his message, God speaks of other created eternal beings, who "alongside Jesus" are assisting in God's purpose of salvation. Jesus does not minister alone in the logistics of this priestly ministry in the goal to bring people to God as "a source of eternal/perpetual-*place* salvation" (Heb 5:9).[211]

A problem in Moffitt's anthropology in relation to angels, as developed in chapter 2 of his monograph, involves his determination of Jesus's qualification in status above the angels in an opposing polemic contrast of "human" flesh and blood against angelic "spirits."[212] Following Cartesian philosophy, he seems to adversatively pit the "human" Jesus as only qualitatively above the angels because angels are only "spirit" and not "human." This places the better emphasis on Jesus in relation to the earth

---

211. Struckenbruck, *Angel Veneration and Christology*, 148. Strukenbruck notes in Hebrews an appeal "to scriptural traditions and motifs (already in use for some time among Christian circles) to distinguish angels from the nature and function of 'the Son'" (139). Yet, he still speculates for a polemic against a possible threat to the belief in the surpassing exaltation of Christ. However, since, as Struckenbruck admits, there is no evidence, this project section contends that the rhetoric is a positive complementary contrast, as keyed by the term "better" (κρείττων). Struckenbruck provides a comprehensive listing into the late twentieth century of scholars having similar correspondence with basic view presented, that "the inferiority of angels to Christ is a rhetorical or literary foil through which the author argues the superiority of the new covenant over the old" (125n201). Cf. Sullivan, *Wrestling with Angels*. Sullivan discusses scholars who recognize an ST apocalyptic view that humans, in an open heaven, can come into proximity to God in a similar status to the entrance of angels (231). Cf. Heiser, *Angels*, 173–74. Heiser discusses ST literature where the narrative normatively depicts angels assisting the souls of the deceased (T. Job 47:10–11; 52:1–12; T. Ab. 20:10–12); Cf. Dickason, *Angels: Elect and Evil*, 105. Dickason documents texts from the witness of Scripture where angels are attendants upon the righteous dead (Luke 26:22; Jude 9; Dan 12:1–3).

212. Moffitt, *Atonement*, 47–144. Cf. Gleason, "Angels and Eschatology," 90–107. Gleason acknowledges the positive contrast in Hebrews to angels. He comments, "Rather than depreciate angels the writer affirms their traditional role as 'ministering spirits' (1.14), mediating the Law (2.3), visiting the saints (13.2) and worshipping before God's heavenly presence (1.6; 12.22)" (91). However, his thesis speculates the relationship of angels antithetically rather than complementarily. He argues, "The angel-comparison is also intended to caution the readers against a popular hope in angels for national deliverance and personal help. Rather than look to angels for deliverance, the author urges his readers to place their hope in the far greater 'Son' who has come to reign as Davidic king and wage war on the oppressors of God's people" (91). He interprets the angel motif in a limited cosmic field of an extended future eschatology by escalation of the antitypes of future earthly judgment in substitution for the unseen heavenly types. For Gleason, the hope of Christ is salvation on earth, with no thought of the coming judgment after death on approach to heaven. Cf. Cole, *Against the Darkness*. Cole sidesteps Jesus's reference in Luke 16:22 to angelic involvement after death by technical questions of genre (71). He applies Cartesian philosophy in a metaphysics where angels are "spirits" with "nonmaterial" characteristics (50).

and angels on the "form" of the earthly flesh as better than the spiritual.²¹³ However, the Pastor contrasts Jesus and angels by the complimentary ability of a "better" (κρείττων Heb 1:4) two-fold heavenly "ministry" (λειτουργικός Heb 1:14; 8:2) to people by atonement and present intercession. Both angels and Jesus possess the form of substance-reality and could enter God's holy presence (Heb 12:22). However, Jesus could offer himself, in the function of a lower dwelling status, as a human likeness in flesh on earth, in a sacrifice for substitutionary atonement in the place of sinful people, as the Christ (Heb 1:4; 2:9).

For the Pastor, as a warrant for God's nature in his relationships, the lower human form has more value than the higher status (Heb 2:5–18). Why? By becoming the lessor form, Jesus, as the Christ, could bring people into the holy-*places* of "the present subsequently coming place of dominion-rule" (Heb 2:5) by intercession of believers at judgment. The Pastor's language places the contrast as "better" (Heb 1:4) in his sacrificial ministry as servant, "made a little lower" than the angels (Heb 2:7; cf. Heb 3:5; Mark 10:45; Luke 26:25–30; 1 Pet 5:5). He inherited, as a human person in his own death at judgment, the name Son, when entering the dwelling presence of God, by exemplifying this valued servant nature of grace to assist others in need (Heb 1:5–9; cf. Phil 2:3–11).

---

213. Moffitt's approach has much to commend it. However, presuppositions for traditional cosmic-*field* restricted background for people drive his conclusions, such as (1) an earthly salvation hope for a reclaimed earth (Moffitt, *Atonement*, 142); (2) Jesus cannot be exalted till fleshly resurrection (Moffitt, *Atonement*, 228); (3) Jesus later moves downward by the extension of God's glory to the human body, where the holiness of God comes to humans on earth, rather than upward movement to God with people being made holy and coming into the holiness of heaven (Moffitt, *Atonement*, 179); (4) addition to the suffering of Jesus's atonement as a single process on "that day" of the sacrifice to include the events after his fleshly resurrection (Moffitt, *Atonement*, 295). However, in this project concerning the Pastor's *aiōn-field*, with plural heavens, constructed in a gradation of holiness, his argument turns not so much on the difference of angels as "spirit," but that Jesus as human qualified to go where no other human person had gone before. This change in elevation is based more than just upon a state of royal status on the throne for what Jesus is as a person (Moffitt, *Atonement*, 47–52). It is based upon what Jesus has done as a human person in access to a higher level of perpetual eternal/perpetual-*place* living in the holiness of the dwelling of God. Angels, before Jesus's entrance, could only take people to the holy place before the veil. Jesus as the exalted servant, similar in faithfulness to Moses's antitype symbolism (Heb 3:5), by passing through the heavens in type fulfilment, could also shepherd people with him beyond the veil to God's dwelling (Heb 6:18–20). Cf. Harris, "Use of ERCHOMAI." Harris lightly senses the concepts of this project in her work in the noted upward language of Hebrews.

Atonement and the Logic of Resurrection in Hebrews 9:27–28

In the Pastor's narrative, the angelic "spirit," in both substance (form) and ministry (function), is not negativized nor lessened. Rather, Jesus's form and function are elevated, because, as human, he can better serve in sacrificial atonement *and* priestly intercession. The angels participate with joyful observance and worship (Heb 1:6) and bring those people about to inherit salvation (Heb 1:13–14) at death and judgment in approach through the way holy of holy-*places* (Heb 9:28; cf. Luke 16:22). The contrast in exaltation is not only *what* Jesus is as human being, it includes *what he can do* in his "ability" (δύναμις Heb 1:3) as a servant to his fellow human people, to remove the separation from God's dwelling presence due to sin (Heb 2:17–18; cf. Isa 53; John 14:1–7). The greatness and faithfulness of Jesus, as the Son of Man, is not only due to fleshly form in contrast to spirit. It is his ability to humbly serve his people from below in their needs due to sin to shepherd them to God.[214]

The antithetical contrast in the Pastor's homily occurs in relationship to the "devil" (διάβολος Heb 2:14–15; cf. Job 1:7; Acts 26:18).[215] The devil

---

214. It is not faith in God's sovereignty over the cosmos that Jesus shepherds into heaven but repentance of sin and faith acceptance of *what Jesus has done* in substitutionary atonement for personal sin and continues to do in priestly intercession for sinners, who accepted him by faith before approach to God in heaven (Heb 3:6; 4:2; 6:1, 12; 10:22–23, 38–39; 11:6, 13–16; cf. Matt 7:21–23). The theme of freedom from the devil and the state of death is further discussed in the next chapter concerning discourse unit B UC (Heb 2:17–18), in relation to his other DUC, through the lens of the MCS. Atonement is complete in Jesus's death, which enables believers, just like the death of Jesus, to presently rise to God, who is Jesus (Heb 1:3a). For the Orthodox position of Jesus as both human and God, see, Treier, "Mediator of a New Covenant," 105–19. Trier, concerning his exegesis and commentary about Jesus's mediation, states, "Christ perfects pilgrims by taking them on a path he himself walked—without wandering. On this basis, in part, he is the Pioneer of their pilgrimage" (115). However, for Trier, this mediation of Jesus in heaven may be only promised and completed in some future time, meaning that, no pilgrim actually has yet followed Jesus to heaven in the path that he walked. If this is true, then Trier is really saying that Jesus has yet to do any real mediation as the great mediator he eloquently describes. This creates a tension often not addressed about the dead. The offering act of atonement, since satisfied complete by death and sacrifice once, is not perpetually repeated. It is the mediatorial service in Jesus's ministry of priestly intercession that is perpetual, where believers in life are sealed by the Holy Spirit at repentance and acceptance by faith, and then mediation by Jesus is literally experienced at death and one's judgment, which follows, to bring his people to life with God in heaven.

215. Stokes, *Satan*. Stokes summarizes a process of transformation of Satan in literature up to the first century CE. He contends that Satan initially was depicted as an agent of God, as an executioner for those deserving death. Over time, he also was revealed as one who tested the righteous. He, more than just punish the wicked, is transformed in his purpose. He permissively created opposition to God's people in deception and testing. However, Stokes does not take into consideration the changes in genre from mainly earthly history, with little consideration of dualism and the devil's

is spatially separated in the detached cosmos from God's presence, where people now dwell. For the Pastor, God speaks that the devil enslaves people in death all their lives. He portrays the devil as a created being, a hostile force to the living God, and a temporary "power" (κράτος) over "death" (θάνατος). It is the ability of Jesus's ministry in death that renders this power of the devil over death "ineffective" (καταργέω Heb 2:14).[216] The Pastor exhorts believers to follow Jesus's faith in "a pattern of identical repetition."[217] Jesus endures a substitutionary death that is the same fleshly death as any other person, so "he might free those, as many as through fear of death were subject to slavery all their lives" (Heb 2:15).[218]

This includes the same death experienced as Jesus, with both the assistance of his angels and the ability now of Jesus's intercessory mediation on approach, as the Christ. He frees believers from enslavement of the power of the devil in the state of death, by coming to their aid as mediator and shepherding them to eternal/perpetual-*place* life in the presence of the living God in heaven—Jesus himself.

---

role, to more apocalyptic considerations. Chapter 4 suggests concerning the discourse unit C′ UC (Heb 12:12–13), that the permissive presence of the evil power of death and decay in this cosmos is allowed as training to turn people's hope heavenward to Jesus in the eternal/perpetual-*place* of the holy of holies.

216. Bell, *Deliver Us from Evil*, 292–318. Bell notes the same pattern as found in Colossians and Ephesians, where the atoning work of Christ is used in Hebrews for the defeat of the devil (307). This is supported both by the close association of the atonement in Heb 2:17 and the sacrificial understanding of Christ's death throughout Hebrews.

217. Bell, *Deliver Us from Evil*, 313.

218. Attridge, "Liberating Death's Captives," 103–15. Attridge addresses gnostic conceptual language relevant to the early Christian myth of *decendit ad infera* with Jesus descending into hell. The Gnosticism addressed by Attridge has since been largely critiqued as a scholarly rhetorical straw man. The later second-century CE development of some scattered elements using the apocalyptic language in the first century CE, at one time was speculated as early colors of gnostic mysticism. This heavenly conception of salvation, in life after death in accessible heavens, is now considered normative to NT authors. Cf. Gray, *Godly Fear*, 111–55. In the debate over when intercession takes place, Gray makes an excellent observation. He recognizes, concerning freedom from the fear of death, that all benefits take place at intercession. An important fear is judgment after death. Is this freedom from fear *at* death and judgment or only later *in* the eschaton/resurrection with fear of a final judgment? Would the latter mean deceased believers are still under fear of judgment, since they do not yet actually possess salvation with Jesus, and he has not yet actually interceded for them? The latter cosmic-*field* limited position for people creates tension with a believer's benefits and promises that must remain after death until a judgment and intercession in a future distant eschaton.

GOD SPEAKS AN ETERNAL/HOLY PLACE CREATOR

In the proposed MCS, the Pastor possibly speaks that Christ will appear "from a second *place* without sin" for salvation of those waiting for him. His audience likely understood that this idiom, as modified by the adverbial "without sin," designates the purified eternal/perpetual-*place* where Jesus is now enthroned (Heb 9:23).[219] The Pastor states that God speaks to the Son, "Your throne, O God, is in the eternal/perpetual-*place* of the eternal/perpetual-*place* [εἰς τὸν αἰῶνα τοῦ αἰῶνος]" (Heb 1:8). The position of the throne is in the eternal/perpetual-*place* of the holy of holies, which is higher than any other substance-reality of creation. After multiple references to the heavenly position of Jesus on the throne, in his benedictory remarks, the Pastor speaks from his own current perspective to his audience, stating, "Jesus Christ, to whom is the glory in the eternal/perpetual-*place* of the eternal/perpetual-*places* [εἰς τοὺς αἰῶνας (τῶν αἰώνων)], amen" (Heb 13:21; cf. Gen 21:33 LXX; Isa 40:28 LXX).[220]

Extrapolating the durative attributes of God from only a cosmic-*field* window of Genesis constricts God in an anthropocentric view.[221]

---

219. Cf. Bauckham, *Jesus and the God*, 172–81, 233–53.

220. NA28App, 684. Cf. *CNTTS*, 13:21–21.0. The bracketed "[των αιωνων]" is omitted in early manuscripts but serves as a later variation that is likely significant for tracing textual affinities. Still, its presence reveals that later copyists/redactors sensed, from their reading of the context, the plurality of God's created eternal/perpetual-*places* as they sought to harmonize his benedictory statement with Heb 1:8.

221. E.g., Feldmeier and Spieckermann, *God of the Living*, 252–53. Feldmeier and Spieckermann write, "To speculate about God's being and doing before creation is apparently insignificant for God, and, therefore, irrelevant, indeed, as can be read in Gen 2–3, even dangerous for his creatures because then they play with the evil to which God had opposed his creation. Even a text that, on first glance, seems to communicate this very knowledge confirms the avoidance of speculation about God's activity before the beginning: the self-presentation of personified Wisdom and her status with God in Proverbs 8:22–31. The 'before' and 'when not yet' in reference to the creation that dominate this text awaken the impression that the Wisdom speaking here wants to publish knowledge that was available only to her, whom YHWH established from eternity (8:23). She boasts that YHWH acquired/created (*qnh*) her as *rē' šît darkô* 'the beginning of his way' (8:22). Yet, with this, one does not get back beyond the *bĕrē' šît* 'at the beginning' of Gen 1:1. Rather, in her interpretation of Gen 1:1, Wisdom intimates that God's creative work *bĕrē' šît* 'in the beginning' applied to her, to Wisdom. She is not God's companion on the throne, an equal with divine rank, but *rē' šît darkô* 'the beginning of his way,' namely of his walk and work as Creator. Since Wisdom claims this prominent position 'at the beginning,' it focuses not on this beginning, but on its objective." A focus on the objective of this creation is probably correct. However, nothing in either text of Gen 1:1—2:4 or Prov 8:22–31 supports their claim that God had never created before this creation. Such a claim, limits God in an inexperienced and yet

Neither Genesis, nor the other text of the OT stipulate that the current visible creation is all that has ever been created by God. To the contrary, in Hebrews's theocentric apocalyptic view, the presented OT theology of the creation follows a different time duration for God's creativeness than most modern programs. In Jewish apocalyptic literature of ST period, the creation in heaven of God's dwelling is considered an eternal/perpetual-*place* of endless duration.[222] Also, Moses says about God's relationships before this creation, "from the eternal/perpetual-*places* until the eternal/perpetual-*places* you are God" (Ps 89:2 LXX [Ps 90:2 MT]). It seems that the Pastor may follow Jewish ideas of God's experiential relationship to that which is created in the Son, as not infinitely timeless or outside of space-time but as having a possible measureless or endless duration, even before the historical account of Genesis.[223] The cosmogonies of the

unsuccessful relationship to only the present cosmic-*field* of creation of the failures of humankind and that of angels in the unseen creation.

222. In ST literature the creation of the visible heaven (cf. Heb 11:12) and earth and invisible heaven of approach before the veil of separation are temporary when compared to the perpetual eternal/perpetual-*place* of God's dwelling in heaven of the holy of holies. The author of the Book of the Watchers states about some angels, "For that you have left the highest heaven of the eternal/perpetual-*place* of the eternal/perpetual-*place*" (1 En. 15:3 GP). The LXX links the terms "eternal/perpetual-*places*" (αἰών) and "holy place" (ἁγίασμα 2 Chr 30:8 LXX). The Pastor connects "eternal/perpetual-*places*" (αἰών) with "of holy-*places*" (ἁγίων), or together "very holy-*places*; holy of holies" in the context of the location of the holy of holies. The Hebrew OT does not directly connect "eternal/perpetual-*places*" (עוֹלָם) with "heavens" (שמים) but does connect עוֹלָם "eternal-*places*" with other qualities of God in relationships in created space and time (cf. Pss 89:3; 119:89; 136:5; Dan 12:7). Hebrews does state about the holy place, which Jesus enters as high priest, by the emphatic statement "this one is not of this creation" (Heb 9:11). Allen claims this refers to the covenant and others attempt a connection to the body of Christ as a temple, but these are not persuasive. The likely interpretation is local in modification of the holy place in heaven achieved just before Jesus's entrance, which is discussed in the next chapter.

223. Cody, *Heavenly Sanctuary and Liturgy*, 125. Cody comments, "The מֵעוֹלָם of the Old Testament points backwards along the line of time far beyond any definite length of time conceivable." Cf. "You are מֵעוֹלָם" ("You are from the eternal/perpetual-*places*," Ps 93:2 BHS; cf. Gen 6:4; 1 Sam 27:8; Isa 63:16; Pss 25:6; 93:2; 103:17; Prov 28:3). Paul in the NT follows this same Jewish concept of an immeasurable past time trajectory by use of the phrase "before times of the eternal/perpetual-*places*" (πρὸ χρόνων αἰωνίων Titus 1:2; 2 Tim 1:9; cf. Rom 16:25). For Barth, the solution was found in Jesus Christ, as both atemporal God and temporal Jesus. Cf. Cassidy, *God's Time for Us*. Rudolf Bultmann completely stripped away the problem of time by proposing an existential emphasis on "meaning" rather than ontological reality. Cullmann reacted to Barth and Bultmann, by his claim that time in the OT for Jewish people referred to linear time with past, present, and future. Cullmann, *Christ and Time*. Cullmann's idea of Greek time, as timeless, is a probable misstep. Circular motion of the planets meant unending in duration or perpetual, more than timelessness, especially in relation to

Genesis account only refers to God's recent historical creation of man and the narrative history of redemption, by "the seed," through a covenant promise mentioned in Gen 3:15 that is later restated with more detail through Israel. This Mosaic history does not document everything ever created or all the duration of God's creativeness in relationship to that which he creates. The most obvious omission is created angels, whom the

---

linear time, which seemed to have a beginning, present duration, and ending.

The time function of either "eternal/perpetual-*places*" (αἰών) or "time" (χρόνος), is not an object of substance with movement in creation itself or independent in existence from either space or movement. Time does not have concrete existence as does a person, thing, or even God. Time by itself does not move. Time only describes something else moving in space. Time can only exist as either a mental qualitative observation or a quantitative calculated perception about any object or even God, if both space and movement are present. Without either movement or space, there can be no measure of time. In any biblical narrative, time is only a quantitative measure of the standardized distance movement between two objects, at any point relative to an object's standardized movement. Hence, moving twenty miles per hour means an object is moving a standardized distance of twenty miles, relative to the standard of an hour, that is determined by a period of the rotational movement of the earth. When leaving the earth for the substance of the cosmos or unseen heavens, the standards of movement change, causing different experiences of time, that also is determined by adding relative differences in gravity and velocity between the two moving objects. This property explains time differences between the substance of the eternal heavens and the earth. At increased gravity and velocity, the same period of time in heaven that is as a day (the Pastor's "today"), on earth is as a thousand years (cf. 2 Pet 3:8). When all objects in narrative are on earth, differences in gravity and velocity are negligible, so time progresses evenly. In *aiōn-field* dualistic narrative, even when God himself is considered one of the two objects in living movement, if there is another created object besides God present in space in living movement activity—a mental perception of time is present. The mental time perceived calculates a value dependent upon the established standards of the measurement of space and movement. God dwells in heaven in a near relationship to those people and other beings present and abides in time. The contrast of "eternity" as nontemporal against temporal time is another scholarly rhetorical straw man, whose noise distracts from hearing God's speaking about his calling to follow Jesus Christ into open heavens to himself at judgment in living nearness; e.g., Guthrie, "Time and Atonement in Hebrews," 209–27. Guthrie follows Barth in proposing "a wrinkle in time" (210), based upon the long held rhetorical straw man of God as atemporal in heaven. This wrinkle, standing on the claim of God outside of time, who sees time past, present, and future as the same time (God as omniscient and omnipresent can both dwell in time relationships and experience all time), provides his solution to the logical sequence problems of attempting to align Jesus's experience of enthronement after death, with his ascension after resurrection (224–27). His evidential rich history of trajectory of the classical view of time from Augustine and Boethius are likely continued missteps, in closed-heaven paradigms with a destiny away from the presence of the brethren who are now in close relationship with God in the eternal/perpetual-*places*.

Pastor contrasts in a complementary service with the better ministry of Son, saying, "The one making his angels spirits" (Heb 1:7).[224]

Modern theology programs, by rejection of otologic dualism of the seen and unseen creation, presume the Genesis creation cosmogony to include everything the Son has ever created. These often constrict the Son's eternal/perpetual-*place* creativity to only the visible creation, from outside of all space and time, in a remote relationship for a limited period since the near present in the narrative of Genesis.

Contrary to modern space-time Cartesian and timeless conjectures, the Pastor follows an apocalyptic trajectory with an *aiōn-field* background in an ontological dualistic creation of the visible temporary and invisible eternal creation. The former, unlike the eternal/perpetual-*place* stability of the Son, decays in destruction and wears out (Heb 1:10–12). The God who speaks from the heavens will shake the temporary heaven of all substance devoid of God's holiness (Heb 12:25–29).[225] In Heb 11:3, the Pastor states, "By faith we understand the eternal/perpetual-*places* to be put in order by the conversation of God, so that the things being seen to have existed are not from the things being visible" (Heb 11:3). If the Pastor holds by faith to an eternally creative God, then this creation originates from much older creation now unseen.[226] Also, the Pastor philosophically neither pushes beyond the text for creation *ex nihilo*, nor toward a timeless, disconnected concept of God that would follow in later systematic theology and apologetic debates.[227] Rather, the source

---

224. The angels in Scripture seem to preexist the creation of this present, visible, temporary heaven and earth (cf. Job 38:4–7; Heb 1:14; Rev 5:11–14). Cf. Dickason, *Angels: Elect and Evil*, 28. Dickason concludes, "From this we deduce that God created the angels before He created the earth."

225. Feldmeier and Spieckermann. *God of the Living*, 453. They determine that "God does not thereby promise creation eternity."

226. Cf. 2 Pet 3:5 "that the heavens were existing long ago and an earth from water and through water having endured by the Word of God." For Peter, God speaks the current creation into existence. Yet, the creation is from and through water instead of nothingness. Questions about cosmogenic origin that concern modern apologetic debate seem to not come to the minds of first-century CE authors who viewed God as creatively eternal and deal with more than anthropocentric forensic problems in the visible cosmos. In the apocalyptic world view, God's creativity is perpetual and includes other creations such as angels, who also have chosen to sin against the will of God and are in separated dwellings awaiting God's judgment (Heb 2:14; cf. Eph 6:12; 2 Pet 2:4; Jude 6).

227. Oden, "Cosmogony, Cosmology," 1:1162–63. Oden asserts that Hebrew thought does not have a world similar to the Greek *kosmos*, with the idea that the universe has a beginning. However, ideas of cosmogony in early ANE religions, due to recent discoveries and broader definitions, are now better recognized than in the early twentieth

for the visible creation that is seen originates from that creation which is not visible—God's eternal creative dwellings, which are permanent and perpetual without decay and death, and in which he also dwells in living nearness to those who come to him.[228]

CONCLUSION

This chapter explores the Pastor's conversation/biblical theology in Hebrews through the lens of the proposed MCS of Heb 9:27–28 for cohesion and correspondence with the proposed thesis. The overarching "conversation" (ῥῆμα Heb 1:3b) easily tracks on a background *aiōn-field*, in a biblical theology that has strong cohesion with heavenly access for believers by the ability of the Son promptly after death at judgment.[229]

For this project, in evaluation of the suggested ἐκ δευτέρου ("from a second *place*"), several modifications to modern English words help tease out the spatial sense of the Pastor's first-century CE words upon the background of his apocalyptic *aiōn-field*. These adjustments enhance listening ability concerning the Pastor's desired faith about God's speech in Hebrews. To balance modern English sense meaning and common presuppositions to the standards of first-century CE apocalyptic *aiōn-field* concepts of "place," Greek translation and subsequent discussion herein adds consideration of the probable spatial weight by adding the word *place* or *field* to appropriate lexemes. This results in "*aiōn-field*," "*cosmic-field*," "eternal/perpetual-*place*(s)," "holy *place*(s)," "heavenly *place*(s)," "a spirit of an eternal/perpetual-*place*," "eternal/perpetual-*place* judgment," "eternal/perpetual-*place* salvation," "eternal/perpetual-*place* priest," and "the eternal/perpetual-*place* of the eternal/perpetual-*place*(s)." The English gloss "forever, eternal, everlasting" creates tension with the temporal limitation of Jesus's ministry that is only *until* all enemies are placed as a

---

century in which claims were made for a lack of an organized Hebrew cosmogony.

228. Ellingworth, *Epistle to the Hebrews*, 451. Concerning the author's statement in Heb 9:11, "that is not of this creation" (τοῦτ' ἔστιν οὐ ταύτης τῆς κτίσεως), Ellingworth states, "It is impossible to exclude either temporal or spatial elements from the meaning of this phrase. It is both 'the present creation,' that is doomed to destruction in the last time (12:27), and 'the visible world,' that is inferior to the invisible to which it owes its existence (11:3)."

229. Barth, *Der Tod Jesu Christi*, 153. Barth asserts the ministry of Jesus is more than just atonement in his death, but beyond, to the high priestly work of Christ in the way.

foot stool under his feet and misses the spatial positional OT theme in Ps 110 highlighted by the Pastor.[230]

Balancing the concept of place enables a coherent assembly of the functional definition and structure of the Pastor's vertical language. For example, much of the heavenly entrance cohesion of his chosen expressions is lost in modern translations by the collapse of multiple Greek terms to the English word "world." Translation decisions often build on presuppositions of Cartesian philosophy of closed-heavens, with no access by people heard in the Pastor's homily through the way of the eternal/perpetual-*places* by Jesus's ministry.

In this project, Greek to English philosophically loaded words and Latin transliterations, which now have place/field weight of foreign meaning to the Pastor's audience understanding, are stripped away during analysis (fig. 9). These include "cosmology," "sanctuary," "universe," and "session," which often are used as "key" and "title" words in academic discussion. Further, for a greater listening experience in clear hearing of God speaking, the dissonance from multiple unnecessary concept words is avoided by omission of "intermediate-state," "disembodied spirits," "mysticism," "immaterial," "dispensation," "incorporeal," "apostasy,"

---

230. Bauckham, *Jesus and the God*, 252–53. Bauckham elaborates, based upon the ideology of "forever" and systematic category of immutable, the meaning infers that Jesus maintains his identity throughout eternity. Nevertheless, he recognizes, "In the context, a reference to divine faithfulness certainly makes good sense" (253). This implied faithfulness by use of "into the eternal/perpetual-*place*" carries spatial weight in line with the Pastor's heavenly theme for Jesus's ministry for believers. The Hebrew/Greek terminology and concept has no single good English word that reflects its contextual meaning. The translations of "eternal, everlasting, forever" for the Greek concept of αἰών is not so much *forever*, as in our English concept, but perpetual. This description as perpetual is relative to man's temporary experience in visible space and time. The God and his creation continue to exist perpetually, whereas man as temporary ceases to exist. Something may be αἰών ("eternal, perpetual") relative to man, and be limited in duration in God's plan with a prophesized end; e.g., (1) Israel's eternal covenant in the land as "until the eternal/perpetual-*place*" (עַד־עוֹלָם Gen 13:15), (2) the OT place of the dead outside the veil in the holy place "Abraham's bosom" (κόλπον Ἀβραάμ Luke 16:22) waiting for Jesus to enter and follow him inside the veil, or (3) Jesus on the throne of the eternal/perpetual-*place* in heaven *until* (ἕως Luke 16:41–2, italics mine) all his enemies are placed under his feet, when then he gives the kingdom to the Father and where God becomes one again (cf. 1 Cor 15:20–28). These are temporary "eternal/perpetual-*places*" that are often translated as "eternal" or "forever" for temporal emphasis or "world, universe" in a cosmic-*field*, limited, spatial emphasis. These will cease to function in God's purpose for man and even for Jesus's ministry at a time future. The only places that last perpetually, as we use the English eternal/forever/everlasting, are those places of God's kingdom that cannot be shaken inside the veil at the throne of God in his presence (Heb 12:28).

"post-baptismal sins," "sacraments," "reformed," "wholistic," "trichotomy," "dichotomy," and many others that contribute muddled distortions and static to the Pastor's "conversation" (ῥῆμα), and also which falsely color the tone and mood of his harmonious homily.

Further, scholarly constructed speculations toward adversarial straw men are identified that are designed as foils to protect traditional precepts against the tensions created by the Pastor's apocalyptic vertical language. These straw men include (1) the negation of the Pastor's vertical reality by the unavailable second-century CE tenets of later Gnosticism, (2) the negativized common language of Platonic, Middle Platonic, and Philonic influences, (3) the claim for later development and expansion of OT heavenly afterlife concepts (Cf. Matt 11:25; John 3:10; 12:34; 14:1–12; 21:23),[231] (4) the conjecture about divided Platonic Hellenistic spatial versus wholistic Jewish temporal afterlife thoughts about people,[232] (5) the unnecessary Cartesian adversarial problem of "time" and "eternity," and (6) the superfluous debate over "fleshly resurrection" or "inferior immortality of the soul."[233] These oppositional conjectures dull the hearing of God speaking to enable greater emphasis toward dominant closed-heaven prospects for the salvation message.[234]

---

231. The cosmic-constricted views of Israel and the early disciples logically led to incorrect theological conclusions. They are still popular and provide a large reservoir for future research; e.g., Bremmer, *Rise and Fall*. Bremmer finds that ideas of an afterlife between death and resurrection are later developments, which are correctly challenged and fading away.

232. E.g., Kärkkäinen, *Creation and Humanity*, 307. Kärkkäinen makes this observation in his argument for *multidimensional monism* of a whole person against traditional dualism of separate substances of man's creation. He does not accept a "gap" theory that between personal death and the final resurrection that there is "nothing of me" and finds it "problematic from the systematic theological point of view" (349). He concludes the posit of a "soul" is not necessary for God to continue the person in continuity before bodily resurrection. His conclusion is unlikely before biblical and extrabiblical evidence noted in this chapter.

233. Gelardini, "Unshakeable Kingdom," 321. Eisele, "Bürger zweier Welten, " 44 (translation Gelardini). Gelardini comments that Eisele could be quite right with his "Middle Platonic" interpretation, when he assumes, "Since for the individual human being, the transitory world finally passes away at his death, the eternal world of heaven reveals itself to him (i.e., the believer) at this moment, when he meets God as his judge and Christ as his mediator in the heavenly holy of holies."

234. A "see-saw" pattern emerges that needs further research, where first, there is a new proposal. This follows with a period of large acceptance, then with a subsequent rejection and devastation. Finally, in reaction formation, most truth associated with the proposed error of the first proposal is also considered tainted and rejected as a foil for new proposed insights that are out of balance with complete complementary truths of biblical revelation; e.g., Spicq, in 1952, proposes strong background influence of Philo

Also, an awareness of two major missteps in conceptions about the race to Jesus at the throne of God, as reversals toward closed-heaven concepts, is exposed. These include the Pastor as opting (1) for God's living nearness with accessibility in heaven through repentance of dead works and faith in Christ, rather than the misstep of a now distant sovereign God, who chooses and governs from afar, and (2) for emulating God's character of service in a good conscious to come to the aid of others, rather than self-elevation in the desire to rule this temporary cosmos as the completed church and kingdom on earth. For the Pastor, we are called and shepherded by Jesus into heaven, to serve with the serving living God, in his purposes in the needs of the his eternal/perpetual-*places*.

The two correlative statements of Heb 9:27–28 adequately encapsulate his previous exposition. For translation of ἐκ δευτέρου as "from a second *place/position*," the next chapter proposes to add further evidence for meaning cohesion by spatial analysis of the DUC and STr surrounding the Pastor's theme of salvation by Jesus's intercession at death and judgment.

---

for understanding Hebrews. Williamson and Hurst, with others, a generation of twenty to forty years later, reject Philo as the background and propose apocalyptic language in strong association to the LXX OT. Now, fifty years later, the Alexandrian language of Philo is the rejected as an adversarial foil, to press the new Jewish apocalyptic language in Hebrews in-line with current views.

4

Consistent Splint Times
The Place(s) of the Pastor's Discourse Unit Conclusions about Death, Judgment, Intercession, and Salvation

INTRODUCTION

The Pastor encourages his audience, stating, "Let us run through endurance the race being set before us" (Heb 12:1). After the start and initial steps, once a runner reaches a chosen stride, the next analytical measures for improvement in longer races are pace and split times. Just as pace and split-time strategies are modified depending on the race type, in longer discourse, for enhanced communication of their message, successful authors intentionally provide periodic summaries about their thematic subtopics along levels they arrange in their discourse structure.[1] In a well-organized rhetorical discourse, these summaries/conclusions, as planned groupings of text above the sentence level, function to maintain audience orientation and to govern the desired message understanding.[2]

---

1. Grimes, *Thread of Discourse*; Neeley, *Discourse Analysis*, 1, 5, 28; Westfall, *Discourse Analysis*, 73, 77–78.

2. Westfall, *Discourse Analysis*, 29. Westfall comments, "Structures or patterns of organization which cultures and individuals may utilize or create are open-ended in terms of possibilities, but all utilize two essential techniques: the *grouping* of material within the text into units or chunks, and the use of *prominence* to highlight important

A skilled rhetorical author methodically leads his audience through planned thematic content and supported assertions, which link with his supplied introductory topics/subtopics to persuade listeners to accept a strategic conclusion/summary.[3] This chapter traces out the Pastor's discourse unit summary/conclusions about his DI subtopics in relation to Heb 9:27–28 upon his *aiōn-field* background.[4]

Do all the words heard consistently correspond to the perceived intended theme of the other words in the message?[5] This question illumi-

---

material. Detecting an author's groupings of material into units involves looking horizontally at the linear organization of the discourse and detecting the boundaries or shifts in the text that occur in sequence" (italics Westfall).

3. Grimes, *Thread of Discourse*, 323. Grimes states, "Every clause, sentence, episode, and discourse is organized around a particular element that is taken as its point of departure." He calls this phenomenon about how various elements are staged for the hearer's benefit "staging."

4. Van Dijk, *Some Aspects of Text Grammars*, 45. Van Dijk comments, "We touch upon an interesting feature of textual coherence: the establishment of discourse referents, and their ensuing definitivization (and possible pronominalization) is not only based on identical referents but also on 'existence' at the same modal level, that is within the same 'semantic world.'" The Pastor deploys a broad list of related cognates and phrases to topics that track throughout his message. The cognates are found in the word tables of the appendix 2. Translation of the Pastor's words from Kione Greek to English must choose glosses that maintain unity and coherence of thought content, rather than construct an unrelated word salad of favorite glosses for themes from other possibly similar syntax (grammatical function in the sentence), semantics (meaning in relation to other words), and topic referents found in other texts. Cf. Guthrie, *Structure of Hebrews*, 90. Guthrie comments, "Text-linguistic analysis seeks in part to uncover semantic subtopics which relate sections of a discourse. Semantic subtopics in a discourse most often are tracked with the same, or related, lexical items. Such items may be used repeatedly in two or more units, enhancing the semantic relationship between the units."

Contra Moffatt, *Critical and Exegetical Commentary*, xxiii–xxiv. Moffatt claims such division is artificial and deliberately abstains from introducing formal division and subdivision. He contends "The flow of thought, with its turns and windings, is best followed from point to point. So far as the general plan goes, it is determined by the idea of the finality of the Christian revelation in Jesus as the Son of God." Such strategy, as that of Moffatt, misses the purpose for much proclaimed by the Pastor, that is, based upon the revelation of *this* background truth. It is not just who Jesus is, as purported correctly by Moffatt's evidence, but also what Jesus has done and is able to do now as the Son of God for the salvation of people that trust in him, after death and at judgment, to rise into heaven by Jesus's intercessory ministry into the presence of God.

5. Westfall, *Discourse Analysis*, xi. Cynthia Westfall highlights a paradoxical observation, regarding the statements of George Guthrie and David Black, that with Hebrews considered as a literary masterpiece in clear train of thought, then why have scholars, according to Black, reduced it to a collection of memory verses and proof texts, and lack clear hearing of this "symphony in form," so-called by Guthrie? The *functional groupings of text* (FGT) in Hebrews are often used for proof texts to support complementary truth in other topical themes of Scripture or positions without

nates the importance of proper analysis for the purpose of each grouping of text within the Pastor's underlying *macrostructure*.[6] The point concerns the essential linear cohesion of the collective results gained from any methodological approach, particularly in analysis of the discourse *functional groupings of text* (FGT) above the sentence level. Any interpretative result must maintain the constraints of the Pastor's global plan that governs his discourse for it to be correctly understood by later English or other language readers. This necessity was an intuitive limitation applied by the original listeners and later Greek culture that later translators and readers must respect.

Chapter 2 evaluates meanings for the Pastor's words and phrases in Heb 9:27–28 below the sentence level.[7] Glosses are considered from most probable to least possible, but the most probable glosses alone cannot determine the function of Heb 9:27–28 in the discourse.[8] Chapter 3 assesses the most credible word meaning in relation to the Pastor's *aiōn-field*,

---

thoughtful consideration for the Pastor's groupings of contextual summaries that govern his discourse meaning.

6. Van Dijk concerning discourse observes, "Semantic representations and lexicalizations are not only determined linearly, i.e., by immediately preceding sentences. The notions of coherence and continuity are ultimately based on underlying MACROSTRUCTURES, which are global constraints upon the semantic formation rules of the sentences of the text." Van Dijk, *Some Aspects of Text Grammars*. In agreement with the approach of Linda Neeley, in discourse analysis the term "function" refers to structure and not meaning. Neeley, *Discourse Analysis*, 3.

7. Silva, *Biblical Words and Their Meaning*, 10. Silva defines Lexical Semantics as "that branch of modern linguistics that focuses on the meaning of individual words." However, a words referent and sense cannot be determined only by lexical uses in a diachronic review. Semantics must also have concerns about the author's uses of the word in context. Cf. Black, *Linguistics for Students*, 122. Black writes, "Above all, to know what a word means we must consider its context. Meaning is then extracted from the passage in which the work is found. Hence it is not legitimate to say that the 'original' meaning of a word is its 'real' meaning, *unless* that meaning coincides with the usage of the word under consideration" (italics Black). Cf. Louw, *Semantics of New Testament Greek*, 21. Louw shares, "Finally, the insight that it is incorrect to begin with *words* in a semantic analysis, emphasized how semantics is concerned with more than merely the 'meaning' of words. Meaning is what one intends to convey, and words are but one item employed in this process as symbols representing particular features (in fact, a set of relations) of that meaning."

8. Carson, *Exegetical Fallacies*, 128–29. Carson discusses "Fallacies arising from omission of distanciation in the interpretative process." Cf. Trueman, *Histories and Fallacies*, 141–68. Trueman discusses the common "word concept" fallacy that "in a historical text does not mean that the author intended the same concept as someone using the same word today. What the historian has to do is understand how terms were normally used in accordance with the conventions of the period being studied" (156–58).

background theology. God and God's speech emphasizes throughout with concern for the conversation about the Son's ministry as the word of God. How both Heb 9:27–28 and the theology are structurally linked together with other textual groupings at or above the sentence level that function as summaries remain to be evaluated. This chapter explores the Pastor's structural function for Heb 9:27–28 as a UC of his exposition about the present ministry of the Son in relation to his previous units and section transition summaries. This entails evaluation of surrounding exposition that alternates with exhortation to properly hear God's speech about the Son's ministry as the audience's guide to teaching concerning the Christ.[9]

This chapter first introduces the techniques of discourse and thought-structure analysis with a summary of the methodology, concepts, and definition of structural terms. It includes terms from syntax analysis, lexical semantics, rhetorical analysis, narrative analysis, content analysis, and thought-structure analysis.[10]

It next introduces a MCS for God's speech in Hebrews that is illuminated by principles of discourse analysis mapping, thought-structure mapping, and the Pastor's use of chiasm. Mapping guides for FGT and discourse chiastic structure are in appendix 1, figures 12–16. Discourse mapping guides help to maintain the unity and coherence of the Pastor's thought content.

Analysis of Hebrews describes (1) thematic subtopics connected by words, phrases, and cognates that track into a cohesive thematic path from the introduction, (2) threshold indicators that signal the structural boundaries for the functional FGT, (3) overall structural features of each unit or transition, (4) functions of each FGT for each proposed section, transition, and unit, and finally (5), grammatical-historical exegesis of each UC through the lens of Heb 9:27–28 to dynamically compile the Pastor's intended summary conclusion that he wanted the audience to perceive, affirm, and teach.

---

9. Neeley, *Discourse Analysis*, 2. Neeley defines the discourse genre of "exposition" as "a discourse written to explain something" and "hortatory" as "a discourse written to exhort, command, or urge a particular course of action."

10. For the most part, an eclectic technical terminology has been adapted from that used by Linda Neeley, George Guthrie, and Cynthia Westfall, as deployed in Neeley, *Discourse Analysis*; Guthrie, *Structure of Hebrews*; Westfall, *Discourse Analysis*.

Last, a conclusion summarizes the assertions. The footnote discussion explores academic conversation related to the perceived intended meaning.

DISCOURSE ANALYSIS: HISTORY, METHOD, CONCEPTS, DEFINITIONS

Scholars have advanced methods that concern communication theory in relation to the structure of discourse.[11] *Discourse analysis*, as a recent development, mainly arose in text translation. Expanding since its introduction, its principles assist in understanding the meaning of the normative language and the perceptions of information exchange between people.[12] Its focuses above the lexis, syntax, semantics, and pragmatics of the sentence level with added concern for how text organization with FGT may provide weight for specific contextual meaning in communication between individuals.[13]

Another name is *text linguistics*, which mainly concerns the cache of literary devices that authors choose to cohesively connect units and their FGT.[14] Since the technical descriptors are new, with several emerging schools, there are multiple complementary methods, technical terms,

---

11. Coetsee, "Die sprekende God," 2–3n7; 40–80. Coetsee lists in review the common structural approaches for the sermon of Hebrews as (1) structural agnosticism, (2) structural analysis based on the occurrences of OT passages (Caird, Kistemaker, Combrink, France, Longenecker), (3) literary analysis (Büchsel and Gyllenberg–genre differentiation, Nauck–threefold scheme, Vaganay and Vanhoye–literary analysis, Heil–full chiastic structure), (4) rhetorical analysis (Nissillä, Lindars, Übelacker, Koester), (5) linguistic analysis (Dessaut and Neeley), (6) text-linguistic analysis (Guthrie), (7) systemic-functional discourse analysis (Westfall), and (8) thought-structure analysis (Coetsee). Cf. Westfall, *Discourse Analysis*, 1–21; Guthrie, *Structure of Hebrews*, 3–31.

12. For recent attempts at definition, evaluation, and importance of this technique's contribution to NT studies, see Porter, "Defining Discourse Analysis," 194–211.

13. *Lexis* refers to the vocabulary of language involving phonemes, morphemes, and the range of a semantic domain of a form's optional meaning that an author may choose. Choices in *syntax* involve the orderly arrangement of word forms into phrases, clauses, and sentences for meaningful units. *Semantics* comprise determination of the optional meanings for the chosen forms when linked together. *Pragmatics* encompass the meaning of forms in a specific literary context.

14. *Linguistics* is the science of language including phonetics, phonology, morphology, syntax, semantics, pragmatics, and the meaningful links of the text above the sentence level in paragraphs, units, sections, and a complete discourse. Black, *Linguistics for Students*; Black and Merkle, *Linguistics and New Testament Greek*.

and approaches.[15] The competing variances, in overlapping terminology and inconsistent results, challenge research attempts to differentiate an accurate summary understanding.

Standard terms for discussion of Hellenistic Greek σχῆμα ("grammar") concerned structural discourse with the terms περίοδος ("period, rotation") and κῶλον ("colon").[16] The sentence markings, paragraph designations, and chapter and verse divisions found in modern Greek and other language texts are later added conventions to assist modern readers.[17] Creators did not equally realize the Pastor's first-century CE FGT in structural levels.[18] This explains the discrepancy between modern chapter breaks, paragraph indentations, and verse numbers, in comparison with the unit and transition divisions.

Figure 11 illustrates discourse mapping terminology for this project.[19] Also, nomenclature is supplied for identification of the different

15. Guthrie, "Discourse Analysis"; Porter, "Discourse Analysis," 14–35; Westfall, *Discourse Analysis*, 1–87. Westfall, in following Porter, attempts a systemic approach in a comprehensive evaluation of authorial choices that view language as a "tool for communication and social interaction," and which "establishes a reciprocal relationship with its setting and context." Porter, "Discourse Analysis," 20. For a more recent assessment of linguistic schools, see, Porter, "Linguistic Schools," 11–36.

16. Baugh, "Greek Periods in the Book of Hebrews," 24–44. Cf. Nida, *Style and Discourse*. Nida's work emphasizes the rhetorical dimension of colon analysis. Cf. Louw, *Semantics of New Testament Greek*, 95–158.

17. Codex Alexandrinus from the fifth century CE is an example of an uncial text with all capital letters created by a single stroke of the hand in one position by a scribe. The text is in columns with no spaces, sentence markings, paragraph markings, section headings, title, chapter and verse designations, or other devices to assist the modern reader. So how did the Greek literary culture govern and assist listeners and readers understanding of their message intent? They governed meaning by internal groupings of text in structural patterns above the sentence level that functioned to control the interpretation of the text. English readers are not accustomed to sensing these literary indicators and their functions. The methodology of discourse analysis explores these literary devices to assemble this "deep structure" of the author behind the "surface structure" of an author's text or speech.

18. Neeley, *Discourse Analysis*, 18; Westfall, *A Discourse Analysis*, 30. The identifier chosen labels *functional groupings of text* (FGT) for the Pastor's planned collections of text above the sentence level. A *unit* is a cycle of FGTs through a planned introduction, points, and conclusion. Vanhoye and other scholars designate the major division a *partie* ("part"), the next a *section* ("section"), and his groupings above the sentence level as *paragraphe* ("paragraph"). Vanhoye, *Structure and Message*, 53–58. Westfall labels her main groupings of text above the sentence level as units or chunks with smaller units as a paragraph. Westfall, *Discourse Analysis*, 29. George Guthrie utilizes the analysis labels embedded discourse, sections, and subsections. Guthrie, *Structure of Hebrews*, 112–47.

19. Westfall discusses the melting pot of scholarship and techniques working on various aspects under the umbrella of discourse analysis that creates such varied

assemblies of text in the various levels of discourse structure in figures 12–16. In level 3, a *unit* contains FGT above the sentence level that link to an overall introductory topic or the multiple subtopics in the *discourse introduction* (DI) of Heb 1:1–4. A unit may have FGT that function as (1) *introduction* topic/subtopic (UI) (UPt), (2) *points* (Pt) (SbPt) in support or *climax*, and (3) a unit *conclusion* or *summary* (UC).[20] The functional features are fluid, do not have to be used or occur in strict order, and can serve an adjoining unit.

When functioning as introduction, FGT link to later groupings of text.[21] Discourse units can also contain a digression where a new unit completes a cycle of FGT (UI-Pt1-Pt2-UC) within a units sequence of FGT before coming back to the former unit for FGT cyclic completion.[22] A *section* (S) of level 1 discourse contains several units in level 2, and in Hebrews is connected to other level 1 sections by a *transition* summary (STr), which functions for audience orientation about topics both as conclusion for the previous section and introduction for the coming section.[23]

The term *discourse* refers to the entire message that on level 1 contains an DI of thematic topics/subtopics, *sections*, *transitions* between sections, and a *conclusion* (DC). Sections on level 2 are divided into *units*,

---

terminology and techniques. Westfall, *Discourse Analysis*, 23.

20. Neeley labels these units "embedded discourse units" due to "evidence that these sections have their own internal organization that resembles that of a complete discourse; that is, it may have its own introductory paragraph, its paragraphs which develop its theme, and its conclusion." Neeley, *Discourse Analysis*, 3. Also, highlighted discourse climax is labeled "peak." Neeley, *Discourse Analysis*, 24. Cf. Westfall, *Discourse Analysis*, 30. This project purposely avoids the English *paragraph* found in translations since these divisions of text formation are more arbitrary than Greek. Westfall, *Discourse Analysis*. This project follows the standard modern designations of chapter and verse but only to distinguish and highlight portions of text in discussion or example. It should be recognized the English paragraph and chapter/verse divisions of text have little to no bearing on textual meaning and simply assist the reader/student within modern cultures for ease of reading and pointing out particular text in discussion.

21. Some units, such as unit A (Heb 1:5–14) and unit D2′(Heb 11:17–40), inherit FGT introduction topics from previous FGT topics. Unit F contains a MCS of the exegetical and expositional material that is followed by further support and climax to complete propositional argument before a transition unit to S3. The evidence for this observation is provided in discussion of the respective units.

22. E.g., unit D of Hebrews has a digression within unit E before coming back to complete unit D. The Pastor uses this technique for hortatory emphasis of the need for his audience to listen carefully and teach properly the expositional content of unit D and the main thematic content of unit F. This is the only nesting of units within units of the Hebrews discourse.

23. Neeley, *Discourse Analysis*, 8.

which on level 3 have cycles of FGTs positioned for *topic introduction, points, climax,* and *conclusion.* FGTs may also contain *subpoints* in level 4 (see appendix 1, figs. 11–15).

An eclectic array of terminology and methodology is implemented from across the developing schools that describe the observed literary features of Hebrews. Use of these technical terms and concepts indebted this author to the developmental work of many scholars who include a large cross section of NT research. No one system, nomenclature, of method of approach is defended. Each proposed method has its own strengths and weaknesses.[24] The focus of one technique often strengthens the critiqued weaknesses of another when the strengths are integrated together. Attempt is made to remain in an inductive approach behind the Pastor's textual meaning for God's speech and to follow his underlying *macrostructure* to the meaning of his MCS proposed as Heb 9:27–28. This project utilizes a deductive approach in attempts to avoid presuppositions that either carry weighted or confusing difficult technical meaning.[25]

As a general principle, discourse communication in first-century CE Hellenistic Greek, depending on its length, contains multiple levels of organized *groupings* of text above the sentence level. These groupings of text for both the author and audience are part of a *semantic deep structure* "that can 'guide,' in linear production, the selection of lexemes of the subsequent sentences."[26] In the language of Greek culture, by an array of literary devices, these organized, operational groupings are linked together to

---

24. Westfall, *Discourse Analysis,* 1–87.

25. Westfall, *Discourse Analysis,* 7, 28. Westfall defines these approaches stating, "The deductive approach applies the goal and elements of a given genre or form to the text. The inductive approach forms a hypothesis from a close reading or analysis of the text and then forms a hypothesis of how given features relate to the whole." The critique of some scholars against the possibility of outlines defining the meaning of text rather than the text defining the outline is valid. Cf. Neeley, *Discourse Analysis,* 5. Neeley for her proposed "summary" formation, deletes many of the groupings of text functioning as conclusions simply due to her criteria for determination of backbone and support material. If the outline uses the unit support parenesis rather than the unit conclusions, then the main specific thesis of each unit is missed.

26. Van Dijk, *Some Aspects of Text Grammars,* 133. Van Dijk concludes, "This means that in the gradual construction of a semantic deep structure the reader will often be able to predict roughly and hypothetically the further development of a text, such that a progressive increase of informational redundancy is formed." This observation explains the repeated saltatory nature of linked subtopics in the footnotes. The same exposition is redundantly recycled with cognate and related phrases for emphasis.

provide coherent speech.[27] These compilations of text, when received as a coherent structure in sum, form a complete message or *discourse*.[28] By the different chosen literary devices, a speaker organizes distinct levels of text containing subtopics that link related thought by connections with multiple assemblies of other text in groups above the sentence level. This conventional organization follows an intuitive *global plan* that an audience follows for proper language meaning comprehension.[29]

With adaptation and modification, methodology of this project for discourse analysis of Hebrews utilizes a hypothesis about the underlying macrostructure of discourse proposed by Teun van Dijk, whose other work concerning formation of discourse summaries was employed by Linda Neeley.[30] Based on experimental findings concerning communication, van Dijk comments, "A macro-structure is a tentative underlying structure of a summary. The additional hypothesis, however, is that a macro-structure is assigned to a (part of a) discourse, in order to be able to 'control' its complex semantic content, in *all* tasks."[31] Theoretically, the parts of a discourse that function as *summary conclusions* in the units or sections of a discourse are provided by the Pastor to dynamically control

---

27. Neeley, *Discourse Analysis*, 2. Neeley wisely deduces, "The native speaker of a language automatically internalizes the principles of organization his language uses to structure a discourse. The linguistic study of non-Indo-European languages in this century has uncovered principles of organization which can be quite different from those that Indo-European languages use, and even the study of Koine Greek discourse is yielding unexpected insights into that language's discourse structure that could not have been appreciated intuitively by an English speaker. Since we do not perceive intuitively the principles of discourse organization in another language in which we are not bilingual, explicit analysis of these discourses is necessary." Speech communication can range from highly organized coherent rhetoric to schizophrenic word salad in disconnected sentences that is difficult to follow due to the author's failure to provide and follow culturally accepted global plans in language communication that are intuitively learned. Initial discourse analysis studies proposed the control of function and meaning on the literary features that serve as the links above the sentence level, without consideration of the author's global plan or macrostructure that controls the linear coherence of his message to an audience.

28. Westfall, *Discourse Analysis*, 66, 81; Guthrie, *Structure of Hebrews*, 59–111; Neeley, *Discourse Analysis*, 26; Vanhoye, *Structure and Message*, 3–4.

29. Van Dijk, *Some Aspects of Text Grammars*, 133. Van Dijk states, "This global plan may be adjusted during the realization process either by changes in intention or by feedback phenomena from the produced surface structures of sentences" The audience dynamically adjusts their understanding of the semantic deep structure of a text.

30. Van Dijk, "Recalling and Summarizing Complex Discourse," 49–118; Neeley, *Discourse Analysis*, 28.

31. Van Dijk, "Recalling and Summarizing Complex Discourse," 60; italics and other emphasis by van Dijk.

the semantic meaning and audience understanding of the text up to that point.³² An original audience intuitively, in their learned language, mentally compiles these provided summaries together while following the author's discourse until the final MCS concerning the thematic propositions of the chiastic unit F (appendix 1, fig. 16). By tracing the subtopics of the semantic content within the text groupings serving as summaries, this method assembles a MCS that recaps the functional DUC in the discourse units and transitions.³³

---

32. Westfall, *Discourse Analysis*, 73. Westfall, states, "Summaries, conclusions and central sentences tend to offer 'meaningful cumulative thrust' of expository and hortatory discourse. Often such sentences occur with inferential particles and in some way account for the rest of the text in their unit [cf. Levinsohn, *Discourse Features*, 277]. As Levinsohn observes, 'By their nature, summary statements unite together the information they summarize.' Summaries and conclusions may occur at the beginning, middle or end of a unit."

33. This project deploys a *threshold* method to determine divisions of units and sections, which agree with most of Neeley's functional divisions and labels within the units. They are applied in figures 11–16 with only minor change (cf. Neeley, *Discourse Analysis*, 19–20). However, it is unconvincing that a "macro summary," so-called a "summary" by Neeley, can be formed mentally by an audience by such an abstract method that by the methods selective criteria omits groupings of text, admittedly already serving as summary in the discourse units and transitions. This MCS is distinct from the concept about the formation of a *summary* by Neeley, who follows the work of Robert Longacre and Kathleen Callow. Neeley, *Discourse Analysis*, 4, 27–28. Longacre states his work is "non-overlapping" with van Dijk with only slight investigation of semantics or pragmatics of larger discourse structures. Longacre, *Grammar of Discourse*, xvii-xix. He further avers that his investigation focuses on the "notational structures" or literary signals, which glue the internal surface structure of discourse together at the different level units of morpheme, stem, phrase, clause, sentence, paragraph, and discourse. Neeley employs Longacre's methods and divides the text of Hebrews into units that are categorized into "backbone" and "support material" based upon literary notations with some consideration of the text grouping semantic function by the individual units. This semantic function is indicated by her text grouping labels for introduction, support, pre-peak, peak, and conclusion.

However, Neeley comments that her backbone material is determined by an *abstract* use of particles, lack of conjunctions, material supported by γὰρ (*gar*) passages, quotations, or illustrations of significant length. For Neeley, this abstract assembly of backbone material forms a *macrostructure* of Hebrews that she uses to form a *summary* of Hebrews, based upon the work of van Dijk, created by collective assembly of the backbone sentences. Neeley, *Discourse Analysis*, 27–28. The product of this method seems more like an "abstract" of the overall text, rather than a summary meaning of the Pastor's desired thematic conclusion for his audience. Neeley seems to recognize a methodological weakness in formation of a summary, stating, "The claim that a summary is the exact expression of a macrostructure would be an oversimplification. The underlying structure (macrostructure) of a discourse is abstract and involves the interaction of all of it systems of organization" (28). The "all" should include the functional grouping of text in the units and transitions already serving functionally as a summary, of which her backbone often

Identification of the unit and section functional summaries of text groupings greatly aids to maintain focus on the topics and subtopics in the message of Hebrews that track in his sermon content through his DUC and STr. Analysis of these functional units does not eliminate the need for studies concerning external influences but assists to maintain focus on the thematic conclusions the Pastor intends for his audience.[34] These summaries are provided by the Pastor to control intended meaning for his audience and prevent proof texting missteps to other complementary, canonical truth or interpretational missteps.

In the discourse of the language of Greek culture, speakers deploy these FGT in a number of continuous repetitive cycles that primarily function as either (1) UI that connect to the overall theme or other linked subtopics, (2) Pt *support* or emphasis in *climax*, or (3) a UC.[35] A listening audience cognitively assimilates the DUC and STr of distinct signaled discourse levels about the DI topical themes in anticipation for a MCS. In a well-supported discourse, the receivers should find themselves in agreement with the MCS provided by the Pastor.

Modern sentence-to-sentence or point-to-point grammatical-historical studies by their bottom-up nature are easily isolated from the links between the larger FGT in the Pastor's macrostructure or global plan. Readers in English do not innately sense the FGT connections and can often miss linked topics/subtopics due to ill-fitting word glosses by translators.[36] This unawareness or neglect allows a lack of cohesion that can easily lend to proof texts for other complementary truth or error that result from out-of-control comparative observations away from the Pastor's global plan toward meaning.[37]

---

leaves out and deletes, since labeled as support. Neeley does recognize that "a number of different types of summaries can be formed to reflect different aspects of the discourse organization and in differing degrees of detail and conciseness" (28). This observation recognizes the possibility of a MCS of the summaries.

34. While external weight on meaning in discourse carries some level of importance, ultimately the Pastor's groupings of functional summaries govern the meaning of his discourse and intended interpretation of Heb 9:27–28.

35. Cf. Neeley, *Discourse Analysis*, 3, 28. Cf. Heath, "Chiastic Structures in Hebrews," 65–67.

36. Turner, *Christian Words*. Turner demonstrates how many Greek words of the NT due to later religious meanings in Latin, German, and English translation take on new meaning that are often different from the original meaning.

37. Louw, *Semantics of New Testament Greek*, 94–98. Louw stresses the importance of knowing how a text is structured. He further emphasizes that analysis begins with the surface structure to ascertain how the author rendered his thoughts to determine the

The global plan provided by the Pastor for control of discourse meaning is often not considered in studies of Hebrews, where meaning is usually perceived step-by-step by grammatical-historical exegesis.[38] The omission of the semantics of the functional DUC in a top-down approach may explain the often-recognized failure by scholars to unlock the message of Hebrews, since translation from Greek to Latin and subsequently to other languages lacks the identification of innate communication tools of Greek language to govern the meaning of the discourse above the sentence level.[39]

---

deep structural material the author wished to convey in meaningful communication. The surface structure is represented by syntactical relationships that carry weight for meaning. The deep structure is the meaningful units that "flow out of" or "emerge from" the syntactical structures (96). Louw recommends the "colon," rather than the English sentence or paragraph, as his starting point for semantic analysis, which he defines as the basic subject and predicate (97). The cola are clustered by authors into meaningful larger units, "which in discourse have their own semantic content and unity" (98). Louw warns, "To analyze the thematic development of any utterance or discourse, it is, unwise to start with the smallest units, since the resulting segmentations or 'cuts' in the discourse result in too many fragmentary items, and it is extremely difficult to put all of these together in an efficient and convincing manner" (96). Louw also warns about use of larger units of the paragraph or larger sections. The functional groupings of text analyzed with clusters of cola, follow the wisdom of Louw for determination of the deep structure concerning how the Pastor conveyed his thematic meaning to his audience.

38. Longacre and Hwang, *Holistic Discourse Analysis*. Longacre and Hwang caution students against "analytic nearsightedness," where there is a fixation on the smaller parts of a text without consideration of the whole. Longacre focuses on the "paragraph" level of the discourse structure as a grammatical unit (115–54), which is roughly equivalent to the label of FGT, but due to differences from modern English paragraph determination, that choice may lead to confusion. A FGT may contain several natural paragraphs in English or not necessarily form an English paragraph.

39. J. P. Louw wrote nearly twenty-five years ago in his favorable introduction to George Guthrie's double backboned, text linguistic approach, in *Structure of Hebrews*, "When I received the manuscript my first reaction was that this might be yet another of the many relatively futile attempts to unravel the strange flow of the argument in Hebrews." Louw, "Preface," xii. Guthrie's double backbone theory, in separation of expositional and hortatory material, did not correct the detours created by the path of scholar's methods and previous missteps, but he did make a major contribution to understanding the literary devices that connect the discourse units and transitions in Hebrews. Westfall, since her work, has broadened the field of view concerning literary devices in a functional-systemic approach that supports textual meaning above the sentence level. However, she does not connect the meanings of the functional summaries (discourse unit and summary conclusions) together. Their research led to my consideration about functional groupings and transitions that summarize in the overall communication process as the control for the meaning of the narrative, rather than the individual literary devices or systems themselves. Text observations led me to the concept of a *threshold* by use of multiple literary signals to indicate function shifts, both within the units themselves from introduction, then support, followed by a conclusion

The next section explores how the summary language of the Pastor's structured discourse can be analyzed to confirm the functional-grouping of Heb 9:27–28 as his probable MCS of his linear periodic summaries about his developing thematic context. Analysis should be carried out in the same way that an audience, in the innate language of Greek culture, would cognitively listen and evaluate the validity of his final MCS claim. Hearers of Greek language discourse, in a repetitive cyclic manner, cognitively recognize topics/subtopics, then determine a level of soundness of the author's points with provided exegetical, evidential, or hortatory support, and finally either agree, ponder, or disagree with the Pastor's contended UC.

As new spoken FGT follow, the topics continually broaden, change, and condense by the listeners in association with the introduced theme.[40] New speech either deletes, combines, or concentrates with previous conversation. The accepted conclusions at each propositional conclusion repeatedly replace and modify by the addition of new summaries, which combine with subsequent accepted conclusions to dynamically, after the last proposition, form a MCS of the Pastor's discourse.[41] It must be remembered that he attempts in his discourse rhetoric to strategically persuade his audience to agree with his provided MCS or lead the audience to form their own similar summary within the limitations of his previous conclusions. A lack of coherence in proof texting would be rejected by an audience.

Van Dijk concludes that discourse information is kept in short packets or is attached to symbols and concepts to accommodate the limited human ability to remember large messages.[42] Listeners later do not

---

and external shifts to new units or section transitions. Following Guthrie, Westfall, and Neeley, this contribution concerning the MCS of Hebrews is not expected as a magic bullet but only another contribution for consideration along the path to better understanding what God is speaking in the present ministry of the Son.

40. Neeley, *Discourse Analysis*, 1–2.

41. Van Dijk, "Recalling and Summarizing Complex Discourse," 58. Regarding the final structure, van Dijk acknowledges, "Strictly speaking, a definite hierarchical structure may be assigned to a discourse sentence of propositions only after processing of the last propositions. For long discourses this would mean that all other propositions are kept in some memory store."

42. Van Dijk, "Recalling and Summarizing Complex Discourse," 58. Van Dijk found in his experiments that subjects were not able to recall all the propositions of a lengthy discourse. He thereby asserts that recall in discourse comprehension requires "assignment of each proposition into some very complex hierarchical structure." Hence, the longer texts are "reduced" by assigning certain content to "macro-categories." These smaller groupings of text, in their assigned categories of established language patterns, are easier to handle and comprehend by an audience.

repeat the entire discourse communication word for word but synthesize their own cognitively assembled summaries about the topic and concentrated subtopics from the conclusions within the overall theme.

Since in Greek discourse these FGT govern the meaning of the syntactical structure, it is essential that translators and later interpreters consider them for determination of chosen word glosses in the syntactical analysis of grammatical-historical exegesis. The next section discusses the supplied mapping guides.

GUIDES FOR STRUCTURAL MAPPING, THOUGHT ANALYSIS, AND CHIASM

Proposals for the discourse structural mapping of Hebrews are illustrated in figures 11–16. These guides assist readers to maintain linear coherence in the discussion of the suggested DUC and STr that use for analysis and tracking the proposed compiled MCS. This investigation operates on the premise that a formal structure for the message existed in the Pastor's mind while he spoke as moved by God's Holy Spirit. Also, he uses natural features of Greek language communication that his mixed audience would mentally consider, to innately build a MCS understanding of his thematic conclusions.[43]

It must be acknowledged that the structural guides are unsure, since there is no realistic way to accurately ascertain the Pastor's actual discourse levels or FGT in his repetitive cycles of topic/subtopic introduction, supportive evidence, and conclusions. Since these structural guides are greatly distanced from Hellenistic Greek culture and considering the reality of modern interference inherited from Greek to Latin, to German, to English language structural differences in communication, few scholars completely agree on the boundaries of a section or unit, or the FGT.[44]

---

43. Cf. VanderKam, *Introduction to Early Judaism*, 14, 53. VanderKam states that "Ptolemy II and the Greek translation of the Torah . . . gave the Jews of the Hellenistic world who lived outside of Judea access to their scriptures (something that they no longer had because Hebrew was not their native language), but also made those scriptures available to a wider audience." His observation that "a vast and relatively unknown literature has survived from the second temple period—texts written by Jews living in the land of Judah and in the far-flung diaspora" (53) further supports widespread use of consistent and coherent Greek discourse methods.

44. Cf. Lee, *History of New Testament Lexicography*, 3–29. Translators are under heavy influence toward preconceived proof texts for the religious debate of their day. The substantial number of English transliterated words from Latin translations that

In the area of the boundary and function, regarding the determination of the word groupings of Hebrews, this project is greatly indebted to the work of Linda Neeley, whose work is greatly accommodated into the structural proposals. The *threshold* criteria for division that is applied in the analysis discussion of the next section are more comprehensive than Neeley's but nearly in complete agreement on her functional divisions of the discourse.[45] Neeley's structural outlines make sense and have an ease of use in discussion for explaining the functional divisions for a nonspecialist audience.

The analysis, after translation of the UC, composes a *thought-structure analysis*.[46] The thought structure is greatly indebted to the work of

---

were used for over one thousand years requires consideration in the analysis built on English translations. Each must be evaluated for maintenance of first-century CE meaning or trajectories toward later meaning from philosophical and theological divergences away from the Pastor's intention. Readers of Latin translations faced the same problem as English readers today due to Latin glosses by Jerome in the early fifth century CE that evolved in awkward meaning. Also, since other cultures lack FGT, later translators often did not consider these FGT for control of the Pastor's meaning during word-to-word translation and interpretation mainly at the syntactical level. The retention of many proof texts that have evolved illuminate the perception often vocalized by English readers for an incoherent argument in Hebrews, as expressed by J. P. Louw as "the strange flow of the argument of Hebrews"; Louw, "Preface," xii.

45. The functional divisions may be more a reflection of Neely's in-depth familiarity with the Greek language than her absolute criterial determination. The more time one spends in the flow of the Greek text the clearer these functional units of the discourse become. Discourse communication operates more in the environment of an abstract sense than mathematical absolutes based on specific literary devices. This insight also may apply to rhetorical analysis. Cf. Martin and Whitlark, *Inventing Hebrews*, 253. Martin and Whitlark derive the same structural section divisions as Neeley and me (253). Their claim for use of classical rhetorical categories may not be as convincing as their in-depth familiarity with the Greek text to sense the natural rhythm and flow of the discourse. Since the function of the FGT serve a rhetorical purpose, first-century CE classical, rhetorical categories can easily apply.

The differences in the function of text above the sentence level make it difficult for translators from Greek into English to capture for English readers, by isolated methods of historical-grammatical exegesis, the macrostructure that controls the semantic meaning of the functional groupings. The only way to convey the author's global plan in another language is by choosing glosses which reflect it. This is difficult in the age of the concordance and especially the computer age, where comparative connections of every nuance below the sentence level, both internally and externally to other similar text, are available at a moment. Also, in English translations, the translators personal preconceived programs often become highlighted, rather than controlled by the text summaries.

46. The method of *thought-structure analysis* tracks the Pastor's use of his overall topical theme of the ministry of God speaking in the Son through his argumentation. His choice of subtopics, support, and OT quotations, as governed by his DUC and STr,

Albert J. Coetsee for both his contribution to the discussion of structure and his introduction to thought-structure methodology, which tracks the author's thematic thought along the author's literary structure.[47] The thought structure is based upon levels 1 and 2 found in appendix 1, fig. 12.

At the discourse level (level 1), the Pastor appears to have a DI, three S with STr between each section, and a DC. This rendition of the first level of formal textual grouping is favored by typical divisions of homilies found in later rabbinic discourse.[48] Also, the discourse cognate paths track through the topics/subtopics, as governed by the DUC that are reflected in the discourse mapping guides. The mapping is similar to other approaches to Hebrews that Guthrie and Heath provide in comparison charts.[49]

The discourse, topics/subtopics variation and unit divisions occur due to the governing semantic choices that are most often made by the established weight of proof texts, rather than consideration for the Pastor's macrostructure. Another hurdle for mapping analysis is a technical language for Greek communication, which has text organization that is not completely equal to modern English paragraphs, chapter and verse divisions, and subtitles that are found in some modern translations. The English paragraph is more loosely constructed and is based upon less specific linking criteria to previously introduced material, when compared to highly organized and stylistic Greek.

The common use of chiasm in Greek discourse presents another problematic issue, since literary communication in English and other languages do not innately utilize the literary device.[50] In the chiastic

---

strengthens his exhortation about the accountability of conversation in the ministry of the audience.

47. Coetsee, "Die sprekende God," 41–80.

48. In the homily of Hebrews, the extensive Septuagint usage confirms that the unknown author had intensive rabbinic training versed in memorization of the Torah and much of the Old Testament. The author often links contiguous references of LXX Scripture, which includes other books of the Torah, Psalms, and Prophets. Many Jews both in Jerusalem and the diaspora synagogues had received Jesus as the Christ in faith (Acts 6:7; 11:19). By the destruction of the temple in 70 CE, this new christological messianic understanding integrated many synagogues' worship. The NT contains examples of synagogue Scripture reading and commentary by Jesus (Luke 4:16) and the early church (Acts 13:14–31, 42, 44; 17:2–4; 18:4).

49. Guthrie, *Structure of Hebrews*, 22; Heath, "Chiastic Structures in Hebrews," 395–96.

50. Stock, "Chiastic Awareness and Education," 23–27. Stock states, "The case has to be made from a consideration of the history of chiasmus and the system of education that prevailed in the classical world, first in the Greek world and then in the Roman world. If moderns have lost their appreciation for chiasmus it is because they have

structure, the Pastor moves along his propositional path that contains light hortatory application to his audience to a turning point and climax in his expositional argument, then retraces the same concepts through the lens of the climax for hortatory application with light exposition.[51]

---

been educated in a vastly different way" (23). He mentions the work of John Welch, in *Chiasmus in Antiquity*, and avers further that Welch's essays "make it clear that chiasmus was pervasive in antiquity, first as the traditional oral teaching form then as the key structuring device for writings" (23). He later continues, "Chiasmus afforded a seriously needed element of internal organization in ancient writings, which did not make use of paragraphs, punctuation, capitalization and other such synthetic devices to communicate the conclusion of one idea and the commencement of the next" (23). He concludes, "Finally in *Chiasmus in Antiquity* we are shown how chiasmus followed from the most ancient literatures into biblical and western classical literature" (23).

51. Welch, *Chiasmus in Antiquity*, 9–16. For longer discourse arrangements Welch remarks, "An emphatic focus on the center can be deployed by a skillful composer to elevate the importance of a central concept or to dramatize a radical shift of events at the turning-point. Meanwhile, the remainder of the system can be used with equal effectiveness as a framework through which the author may compose, contrast, juxtapose, complement, or complete each of the flanking elements in the chiastic system. In addition, a marked degree of intensification can be introduced throughout the system both by building to a climax at the center as well as strengthening each element individually upon its chiastic repetition" (10).

Cf. Lund, *Chiasmus in the New Testament*, vii, xvi, 40–41. Scholer and Snodgrass, in the "Preface to the 1992 Reprint," based upon scholarly investigations influenced by Lund's work, define chiasmus (or chiasm) as "inverted parallelism or sequence of words or ideas in a phrase, sentence, or any large literary unit" (vii). They go on to write, "Chiasmus involves fundamentally two elements: inversion and balance. . . . Often this leads to a third feature: climatic centrality" (vii). Grounded from years of inductive study of chiasmus in the biblical text, Lund explains so-called laws that govern the form and function of chiasm (40–41). He justifies calling them "laws of chiastic structure" due to the recurrence of certain features that appear in many different combinations. Chiasmus by ancient authors may have parallels based on language, concepts, or content. For unknown reasons, Lund avoids chiasmus in Hebrews, which, like his focus on Revelation, is a complete, oral, structured, rhetorical discourse in the biblical canon. Important for interpretation of Hebrews are Lund's observations concerning the laws covering the central climax and its extremes. In this type of structure, the central climax forms the theological basis of the whole section of propositions from the extreme concepts.

Levinsohn, *Discourse Features*, 277. Levinsohn states, "Chiastic structures indicate that the material concerned forms a self-contained unit, which should be treated as a block over against that which precedes and follows." The Pastor's implementation of chiasmic structure in Hebrews naturally limits the influence of external pressures for text meaning that are not contained within the structure of the chiasm. The chiasm feature protects against proof texting for complementary truth or errant concepts by identifying lack of thematic cohesion and balance within the whole chiastic structure when foreign ideas or concepts are introduced.

Cf. Guthrie, *Structure of Discourse*, 144. George Guthrie proposes two chiastic structures, one for each genre Guthrie gives a double backbone model by separation of the exposition and hortatory genre in Hebrews. The ability to separate the exposition

Several scholars in their research of Hebrews have attempted mapping the chiastic structure.[52] Most of these attempts fail to consider the governing FGT in determination of the main thematic topics/subtopics that derive the parallel concepts required for a coherent chiastic structure. The chiastic mapping found in appendix 1, fig. 16, flows out of the expositional DUC for discourse S1–S2, the unit A to the unit F climax and the MCS, then retraces the hortatory DUC in parallel corresponding concepts through S3.[53]

The guides provided for discourse structural mapping, thought-structure analysis mapping, and chiasm are derived by inductive study of Hebrews. Since the literary work originated in a foreign language and culture, it can only be simply claimed that the offered guides would be recognized as closely representing the logical flow of the Pastor's thought process in the first-century CE discourse to his listeners. Also, it is asserted that the MCS in context has a high probability for being the thematic conclusion that the Pastor wanted his audience to consider in their own ministry decisions as they approached Jesus's ministry as the Christ on the day of death and judgment.

The guides also map the discourse division boundaries at level 1 for an introduction, sections, transitions, and a conclusion. Level 2 mapping provides the unit boundaries within their respective sections. Level 3 maps the unit FGT that are utilized as introduction, points, and conclusions. A discourse unit's FGT may combine other rhetorical devices, including OT quotations, that provide climax or emphasis.[54] These FGT

and hortatory material of the discourse, as in Guthrie's research, does demonstrate the symmetry and balance of the Pastor's sermon.

52. Vanhoye, *La structure littéraire*. Vanhoye senses the presence of chiasmus as a literary device for both the overall external structure and some internal features in Hebrews. He reconstructs the Pastor's chiastic divisions based upon arrangements of perceived concepts (237). His structure is tenuous due to his conceptual topical choices, unit boundaries, and neglect of the function of groupings.

53. Guthrie, *Structure of Discourse*, 139. Guthrie is likely correct in the function of the hortatory units as emotional rather than educational. S3 (Heb 10:26–13:31), with units E′ to A′, primarily challenge his audience to right action based upon understanding of accountability in ministry with the Son, rather than provide more educational material.

54. Dodd, *According to the Scriptures*. Dodd successfully contends that NT use of the OT did not do so "by the postulate of a primitive anthology of isolated proof-texts" (126). Instead, "the *selection* of certain large sections of the Old Testament scriptures . . . were understood as *wholes*, and particular verses or sentences were quoted from them rather as pointers to the whole context than as constituting testimonies in and for themselves" (126; italics Dodd). In agreement with Dodd, it is best to analyze OT

may even divide into level 4 subtopics with a separate layer of FGT cycles. The sections initiate and provide systematic analysis of the DUC. First, it establishes the thematic topics and subtopics from the DI chiastic hymn. Then, four themes are tracked through the FGT of each unit to their thematic links in the UC.[55]

Principles of discourse analysis are used to identify the Pastor's discourse elements that he strategically deploys, which include (1) propositions in a cohesive path containing an introductory and concluding MCS, (2) two transition units that connect three major sections, (3) unit-to-unit shifts that are signaled by threshold changes in genre, lexical syntax, logical particles, connectives, and semantic meaning of his phrases, sentences, and clauses, (4) linear topic connections or thematic strands from unit-to-unit, (5) rhetorical cohesion within the topic introduction, support, and conclusions of each unit, (6) functional-grouping connections by use of a broad cognate word cache to maintain clear word and phrase contextual meaning, and (7) audience mental thematic assembling along new DUC to form a MCS for the message.

HEBREWS 1:1–4: ANALYSIS OF DISCOURSE TOPIC/ SUBTOPIC INTRODUCTION

Discourse Introduction (1:1–4): God Spoke by a Son in Better Ministry than Previous Ministries

> **Topic 1** God spoke long ago in parts and ways through the prophets to the fathers.[56]
> **Topic 2** God in these last days speaks by the Son's ministry to bring sinful people to himself.

---

support in the rhetoric of Hebrews within the context of the OT source. For discussion of the Pastor's OT quotations and his use of their broader context, consider Guthrie, "Hebrews," 919–21.

55. A UC is a FGT that provides summary statements of propositions up to that point in the discourse. Each discourse unit usually has a FGT that serves as DUC (see appendix 1, fig. 11).

56. Introductory topics from a UI are carried through each supportive FGT to the FGT UC to force a normative thinking processing similar to discourse listening by an audience. Bracketed comments are supported by either previous or anticipated propositions to demonstrate that the topic are linked by the author in cohesion so that an audience would follow his rhetoric to his planned summary conclusion.

Subtopic A (2b) God spoke by appointing the Son heir of all things.

    Subtopic B (2c) God spoke through the Son by achieving the eternal/perpetual-*places*.

        Subtopic C (3a) God spoke by the Son who radiates his glory and represents his substance-reality.

            Subtopic D (3b) God spoke that the Son brings all things by the conversation concerning his ability.

        Subtopic C' (3c) God spoke for the Son to make a purification of sins.

    Subtopic B' (3d) God spoke for the Son to sit down at the right hand of the Majesty in the high places.

Subtopic A' (4) God spoke to the Son for inheritance with a better name for ministry than angels.

The DI on discourse level 1 (appendix 1, fig. 12) presents message main topics and subtopics. His main subject is "God," to which is later added the predicate "spoke." This subject and predicate tracks throughout his discourse. The Pastor initiates a complementary contrast for consideration. This establishes the background for God's promised inauguration of the last days that concerns two periods within which God has spoken. The topic concerns God's speaking "in many parts and many ways long ago" (Heb 1:1) to the fathers by the prophets. The second topic announces that God recently "during these last days" (Heb 1:2a) spoke by a Son.

This contrast feature about the speech of God is not antithetical, as if the latter negativizes God's former speech. The Pastor reveals that God's speaking by the Son is "better" (Heb 1:4) than the former way in which he spoke about the ministry of his *promised* Son.[57] It is better because the Son is now able to appear for salvation.

In Hebrews, the referents of the *prophets* and *fathers* serve to initiate a subtopic that links with later discourse. The Pastor attaches propositions to concepts and symbols along subtopics. This practice assists the

---

57. France, "Relationship between the Testaments," 671. R. T. France writes, "Hebrews sets out an extended comparison of all that was best in the old covenant with the 'better' things that have now taken their place with the coming of Christ. Its theology is often described as 'supersessionist': Jesus supersedes the OT, his church supersedes Israel. Such language must be used with care; its potential misuse to fuel anti-Jewish prejudice is clear. The more positive term 'fulfillment' is more typical of the NT perspective. For all his dismissal of aspects of the old covenant (especially its priesthood and sacrifices) as no longer relevant, the writer of Hebrews is second to none in his love for the OT and his desire to do justice to its role in the ongoing purpose of God."

audience in remembering them as they periodically form condensed and combined summaries for contemplation and application. This subtopic relates to the former covenant relationships in the past between God and others. Other former ways that testify God's speech about the true, heavenly, covenant relationships by the Son, include *angels* (Heb 1:5–14), *brethren* (2:8b–13), *Moses* and *Israel* (3:1–19), *Joshua* (4:1–13), *Melchizedekian* priesthood (5:1—7:28), *Aaronic* priesthood (4:14—10:18), and the *fathers* (11:1–38).

The referent *Son* also starts a subtopic that connects multiple related referents, which relate to the Pastor's contrast of *better* covenant relationships. These include *the living God, Jesus* in promise-fulfillment as the *Word* and the *Christ*, who first completes an entrance into heaven with God as the first human *originator* and *consummator* of salvation, his exalted position as *Lord*, his ministry as *high priest*, his leading of believers to heaven as *Shepherd*, and his antithesis to the place of the devil, unbelievers, and temporary creation outside of heaven that can be shaken.

After establishing his complementary contrast, the Pastor's DI continues with a list of subtopics related to the activity of the Son.[58] This announces seven relative and participial dependent clauses that form linked subtopics to outline a path and explain the Son's present new covenant ministry.[59]

---

58. Meier, "Structure," 168–89. Meier observes, "All the clauses following *huiō* depend directly or indirectly upon it, and all these clauses are linked to *huiō* by either a relative pronoun or a participle. The natural thing to do, therefore, is to count as a unit of Christological designation each clause linked to *huiō* by a relative pronoun or participle" (171–72). He adds in his reference, "Strictly speaking the participles modify *huiō* through the relative clause introduced by *hos*. But the rhetorical arrangement and thought content show that each clause forms a distinct unit expressing a distinct aspect of the Son's nature or work" (172n22). The division herein of the clauses followed this natural positioning before finding this structural agreement in the work of Meier concerning the numerical and theological symmetry of Heb 1:1–4 with 1:5–14. Beyond Meier, the symmetry of Heb 1:2b–4 contains an *inclusio* for a possible chasmic hymn consisting of the seven dependent clauses that function as introductory subtopics in the Pastor's discourse to govern his meaning for his audience.

59. Black, "Hebrews 1:1–4," 175–94. Cf. Davies, *Letter to the Hebrews*, 19–20; Bruce, *Epistle to the Hebrews*, 3. Contra Meier, "Structure," 174. Meier strongly argues for one designation by the Pastor's use of either a relative pronoun or participle to signal a new subtopic. Also, the structure provides interlocking links for both predicate nominatives by the connective καὶ ("and") with the final emphasized αὐτοῦ "of his" in reference to God. It is possible to attempt division of Heb 1:4. However, as recognized by Meier, it is an example of *synkrisis*, where both statements in comparison are either equal or greater to one another and form one complete thought. Meier, "Structure," 173.

Each subtopic concerning the Son's ministry focuses upon subtopics concerning intercession and salvation at death and judgment regarding either the Son or the sinful people in need.[60] The Pastor's seven thematic subtopics about God's recent speaking by the Son easily form a chiasm (Ch. 4 p. 204-5).[61] Subtopic A (Heb 1:2b) and A′ (Heb 1:4) recognize God's judgment of the Son at death resulting in his being appointed an "heir" (Heb 1:2b). This initiates a subtopic (cf. Heb 6:17; 11:7) that connects with the verb "inherited" (Heb 1:4; cf. Heb 1:14; 6:12, 17; 11:7; 12:17) found in subtopic A′ (Heb 1:4). These terms would be understood by an audience as part of technical legal language, which both links with the Jewish concepts of covenant and an OT narrative motif that describes heavenly access as an "inheritance" (Heb 9:15, 11:8).[62] This

---

60. Meier, "Structure," 177. Meier contends strongly that the immediate context and general thought of Hebrews "identifies the decisive act of redemption with the death-exaltation of Jesus. Indeed, the whole central section of the Epistle (8,1–9,28) is dedicated to explication this pivotal event of bloody sacrifice and triumphal entrance into the heavenly sanctuary [holy-*places*]." By removing terms such as "sanctuary," it is easier to see the strong possibility for the Pastor's language to apply to events after death in Jesus's rising to God from the dead to eternal/perpetual-*place* life before his later bodily resurrection and ascension. The latter is not part of the Pastor's rhetoric and only implied indirectly by Jesus's presence bodily on the throne in heaven as evidence for God's ability to bring believers into heaven at death. This event is discussed among scholars under the philosophical terms "exaltation" and "enthronement."

61. Cf. Rhee, "Role of Chiasm," 84–108. Rhee's chiasm combines two separate FGT, the DI and unit A, to form one large chiasm. Cf. Scholer and Snodgrass, "Preface to the 1992 Reprint," xxi. The scholars warn, "The fact of the matter is that if a person wants to find chiasmus, he or she probably will." They further wisely comment, "Ultimately, one can do only what Lund himself did—carefully analyze the text and identify the structures that are revealed in the text. No value is to be found in forcing texts to conform to structures with which one is enamored. Chiasmus is a functional and artistic literary device and a frequent method of human expression. One will understand texts only where the text reveals structure, not where it is imposed."

62. Harris, "Eternal Inheritance in Hebrews," iv, 282–83, 288, 298–99. Harris understands the Pastor's inheritance language as beyond history "to point to a heavenly, eternal reality." She states, "The pivot of this worldview is God's final Word, Jesus Christ, now seated in heaven at God's right hand." She is likely correct in accepting a connection for the Pastor's use of the inheritance motif with the OT promises to Abraham, the Sabbath, rest, and God's holy mountain, that all point to fulfillment in the heavenly, eternal reality. However, Harris limits fulfillment to an eschatological "world to come" that is remotely future, only at bodily resurrection of the flesh in a new heaven and earth, and without any present fulfillment for the dead in heaven.

Harris is probably correct that the Roman, legal, testator language and a requirement of a testator death for inheritance as problematic. She rightfully rejects inheritance language in terms of "a legal, testamentary model" due to "apparent logical incongruities." Harris's logical incongruities include the following: (1) How can Christ inherit that which he created in Heb 1:2? (2) If God is the apparent testator, then why

event of inheritance includes for the Son, who is the heir, a bequest, as stipulated by a "covenant," which in Hebrews concerns positions and rights of heavenly access to "the eternal/perpetual-*place* inheritance" (αἰωνίου κληρονομίας Heb 9:15; cf. 11:8). The Son's inheritance is executed by God's judgment after death (Heb 9:16–17). He is the designated person, who is "called" at the legal judgment of the matter to receive the "promise" (Heb 9:15). In the same way, believers are called to receive an inheritance when judged by God through the mediation of Jesus (Heb 3:1; 8:6; 9:15; 12:24; cf. Eph 1:18; Phil 3:14; 1 Tim 2:5; Rev 3:8).

The subtopic concept of inheritance occupies the first prominent place at the chiasmic extremes of subtopic A and A′ in the Pastor's descriptions of the ministry of the Son. Looking ahead through the MCS lens of Heb 9:27–28, this subtopic about an heir tracks through DUC to the more general subtopic term "salvation."

In subtopic B, the Pastor affirms that the Son "achieved the eternal/perpetual-*places*" (Heb 1:2c).[63] He launches his sequence of propositions from the subtopic context for the initial extreme propositions of subtopics A and A′ that contain inheritance language surrounding Jesus's

---

must the Son as *heir* die to obtain inheritance (instead of the testator)? (3) How can Christ be both the testator who dies and the heir of all things? (4) It is nowhere evident that the author himself intended inheritance language to be understood along a testamentary model. (5) The author's use of "firstborn" (πρωτότοκος) and "covenant" (διαθήκη) do not fit the testament model. She concludes, "Appeal to the testamentary model obscures this background [OT background], and hence, the coherence of the author's argument" (299). Her choice for Hebrews's use of "covenant" as restricted in reference to the Sinaitic covenant is likely correct (288). Also, Harris argues that the Pastor links "covenant" with the requirement of the death of sacrificial animals of the first covenant to the death and mediation of Christ, in Heb 9:14–22, which logically embraces a requirement of death for execution of the promised eternal inheritance of the new covenant. Unit F explores this link for the inheritance requirement of death, for both Jesus and his believers (Heb 9:27), and *eternal*/perpetual-*place* inheritance with Jesus in heaven Cf. Hahn, "Covenant," 65–88.

63. Grässer, *An die Hebräer*, 1:47, 59–60. Grässer argues for a conceptual spatial meaning for αἰών in reference to the creation of the visible and invisible worlds. He aligns the statements more toward the old scholarly straw man of Alexandrian cosmology and explains the plural form of the term from rabbinic Judaism. Grässer asserts the lack of use of the traditional formula for creation of the "heaven and earth" in the OT supports a lack of interest in a positive theology of creation. The earth is devalued where believers are only "guests and strangers" (Heb 11:13). These believers expect an exodus from the world (Heb 13:13). *Contra* Karrer, *Der Brief an die Hebräer*, 1:117–120. Karrer acknowledges that both propositions in Heb 1:2c and 1:3c "hang together" but he ignores the cohesion and options for a strict temporal interpretation regarding the phrase as a tribute to "history" as the passage of time, which was a favorite scholarly straw man in his generation.

death and judgment. This launching point sets the contextual stage for subtopics B and B′ as salvation at death and judgment, from which Jesus enters heaven, as confirmed in subtopic B′. The creative activity of this linked proposition would likely describe the Son's recent opening access into the eternal/perpetual-*places* of God's presence to both himself and other people (Heb 2:11–13; cf. Matt 27:52–53; Luke 23:43; John 14:1–6), rather than the complementary truth of a statement about his creation involving the separated and temporary Genesis heavens and earth (Heb 1:10–12; cf. Heb 4:3c–4). The use of "do, make, create, achieve" (ποιέω) in subtopic B is probably like subtopic C′ where the Son "after achieving a purification of sins" (Heb 1:3d) sits down. In both B and C′, the Pastor's intent is likely what the Son does surrounding the events of inheritance in heaven and not a digression to his initial creating, as God, of the temporary visible world.

Several observations support a postmortem application for the Pastor's creative comment, in subtopic B (Heb 1:2c), about "the eternal/perpetual-*places*." The focus of his chiasmic propositions and homiletic expositional material, in units A–F, is upon the outcome of God's judgment at death concerning both Jesus (Heb 1:8–9) and people (Heb 9:27–28), in relation to the audience's teaching about the now open heavenly access enabled by Jesus's intercession in the way of the eternal/perpetual-*places* (cf. Heb 9:8).[64] The Pastor's linked, propositional subtopics in sermon introduction, function as more than a systematic theology or philosophical list of tangential proof texts about remotely disconnected activities under the topic of the Son. Further, this official ministerial position of the Son in access to the right hand of God on the throne is not inherited by Jesus until after his experience of death and judgment (Heb 1:5–12; cf. John 14:1–6). Also, when the Pastor does refer to creation of all things, his referents are "God" (Heb 1:9; 3:4; 4:3–4) and "Lord" (Heb 1:10–12) in agreement with the Greek LXX (cf. Gen 1:1; 2:8; Ps 102:22

---

64. For the Pastor, the preexistence of heaven is supported by the OT claim that God rested there on the seventh day after creating the temporary creation (Heb 1:10–12). He says concerning God's rest, "And yet his works being existent from the foundation of the world" (Heb 4:3). The Pastor asserts that place of rest, where God rested, which the promised land to Israel symbolized, is not temporary as the land and exists from the foundation of the world. Just as God could provide Israel with the opening access to the land that was promised, he can open heaven and bring people, who accept by faith the conversation of his ability to bring them into heaven to himself. This further explores in analysis of unit C.

LXX).⁶⁵ Additionally, the relationship of DI subtopic B (Heb 1:2c) with subtopic B´ (Heb 1:3d), in a probable hymnic chiasm, supports the probability that this parallel assertion in subtopic B concerns midrash about the Son's creation of heavenly access, by events that are occurring after Jesus's death and before his later bodily ascension in the flesh.⁶⁶

The ministerial focus upon the Son's more recent actions after death in connection to making of the eternal/perpetual-*places* is not antithetical to the Son's preexistence or past eternal activity as God but emphasizes what the listeners are to emulate about Jesus's ministry in their own teaching about the Christ in his Melchizedekian priesthood (Heb 5:11—6:20; cf. unit E to follow). In the lens of the MCS in Heb 9:27-28, the subtopic B and B´ track to the phrase "from a second *place* without sin." This translation has a high probability for audience understanding in relation to the subtopics involving eternal/perpetual-*place* access related to the sufferings of death further discussed in discourse unit F.

---

65. Cf. Costley, *Creation and Christ*, 80. Costley's thesis focuses on "the Epistle's use of references to the creation of the world, not Hebrew's world view, even if the two topics are intricately connected." It is problematic that in the NT and LXX, when the title "Christ" is used, the term refers in all cases to what Jesus as the Lord and God does in the gospel events in creating access for believers into heaven and not the Genesis creation (e.g., "according to a plan of the eternal/perpetual-*places*, which he did in Christ Jesus our Lord" [Eph 3:11]). Costley forces the connections of "Christ" and "make, do" in "conceptual" Genesis applications even though she admits that there is no lexical cohesion with the Genesis creation account texts. This limitation of "Christ" does not limit the human Jesus from preexistence as the Greek Lord God in the LXX or OT Yahweh.

66. *Contra* Meier, "Structure," 178, 181-82. Meier follows an extended horizontal eschatology position where the plural αἰῶνας could reference the present creation contrasted with "the future heavenly world which lies before humanity as the goal of its pilgrimage." He presents the common position that Heb 1:2c represents a reference to the Genesis creation in a backward move to "timeless preexistence." (182). Meier pushes the Pastor's links with the visible Genesis creation represented, in Heb 1:10-12; 4:3; 11:3, too far by his misrepresentation of the Pastor's dualism about the nature the invisible creation and accepts modern, Cartesian, metaphysical views of timelessness in heaven. (181-82).

Meier avoids conflict with Albert Vanhoye's position that Jesus will only obtain his inheritance of all things at the last judgment. Cf. Vanhoye, *Situation du Christ*, 291. Meier takes the position for both realized and future eschatology proposed by Graham Hughes. Cf. Hughes, *Hebrews and Hermeneutics*, 66-74. Meier, "Structure," 177-78. Meier, in agreement with Hughes, asserts, "The Christological-doctrinal sections of the Epistle tend to stress realized eschatology, while the ecclesiological-paraenetic sections tend to stress futurist eschatology." Meier, "Structure," 182. Meier contends that the "world to come" and "lasting city ... is already present in heaven (13,14 [*sic*, 11:13-16] and 12,22)." However, believers do not enter there until a supposed last judgment.

Subtopic C focuses upon *who* the Son embodies by his ministry of death and judgment. The Son's ministry radiates God's glory and represents his "substance-reality" as the living God. The Son is God himself from the glory of heaven, who ministers in the person of the Son (Heb 2:7, 9–10; cf. Gen 3:15; John 1:14; 17:5, 24). The Son tracks through words, phrases, and cognates to connect, by the lens of the Heb 9:27–28 MCS, with "Christ," the Pastor's loaded term describing the ministry of God as the Son, which surges in unit E (Heb 5:11—6:18) and peaks in unit F (Heb 5:1–10; 7:1–28).

Subtopic D initiates the topic of the Son's capabilities, by his experience of death and judgment, for ministry to people who suffer the equivalent. In a chiasm, subtopic D would form the basis for the theological propositions at the extremes of both subtopics A and A´. In subtopic A, Jesus's inheritance is all things, whereas in subtopic A´, he is the first at death and judgment to inherit a "name" as the Father's Son in the eternal/perpetual-*places* (Heb 1:5–6, 8). In subtopics B and B´, inheritance is described as heavenly access. In subtopics C and C´ the inheritance of heavenly access occurs by God himself in purification of sins. The climax and theological basis for his sequential propositions A–C, and in turn, C´–A´ are that the Son "brings" all things to God in heavenly access (subtopic B/B´) by (Heb 1:3b) conversational witness about God's speaking through Jesus's ministerial "ability, capability" (Heb 1:3b), as God in heaven, to purify sin (subtopic C/C´). The referent "conversation" (ῥῆμα) introduces the audience conversational witness about both Jesus's personal experience in human death, judgment, intercession, and salvation for entrance into heaven at God's dwelling presence, and by this, Jesus's ability to bring all things to God.

Cognates related to "bring, carry" (φέρω) and Jesus's "ability, capability" (δύναμις) track through the lens of Heb 9:27–28 to "Christ . . . will appear" (ὁ Χριστὸς . . . ὀφθήσεται), which references the moment of a literal salvation experience by Jesus for believers who are waiting after death at judgment. In the context of death, judgment, intercession, and salvation, this claim by the Pastor does not refer directly to the complementary truth in other promises concerning his second coming to earth but his shepherd ministry in bringing his believers to God's dwelling presence in heaven (cf. Heb 2:11–13; 6:19–20; 13:20). Neither does subtopic D simply express the Son's ability to preserve the world that he created nor only function as a general statement about the obedient faithfulness of the Son.[67] Subtopic D, at the center of a hymnic chiastic structure, introduces the Pastor's climactic subtopic, which later concerns the ministerial teaching of his audience about the Christ ministry of the Son in units D–F (appendix 1, fig. 16).

Subtopic C′ for the Pastor concerns how God spoke for the Son to make a purification of sins. This begins the path of Christ's activity as God for the substitutionary atonement of sinful people before himself. In the lens of Heb 9:27–28, this subtopic tracks through the Pastor's summary propositions to "who being offered for the purpose of bearing the sins of many people." The purification of sins again concerns the context of the Son's death, judgment, intercession, and salvation for the sins of people, who will all suffer death and then judgment before God. This position, in a chiastic structure, runs parallel with subtopic C for emphasis that the work of atonement is carried out by God himself. Also, as the launching point for subtopic B′, C′ links atonement for sin with the Son's enthronement as high priest for approach in heaven.[68]

---

67. Meier, "Structure," 182–83. Meier unfortunately, without considering the Pastor's distinction, combines "conversation" (ῥῆμα) and "word, speech-action" (λόγος) with both having glosses of "word" in a totality transfer fallacy. Meier also interprets δύναμις by the more general concept for "power" as God, rather than the Pastor's more specific intention in context for the Son's "ability" or "capability" in bringing believers to God in heaven. Ironically, in an attempt for symmetry, he examples non-cohesive interpretation and exegesis of the seven dependent clauses, in Heb 1:2b–4, more toward popular, christological proof texts for complementary truth or common misconceptions toward issues not intended in the context. He comments, regarding subtopic C′ (Heb 1:3c), "Strangely, this is the only clause in the exordium which touches upon this main doctrinal theme of Hebrews: the redeeming work of Christ the high priest in offering himself once and for all as a sacrifice for sins (see especially 4,14–5,10; 7,1–18)." (183). This is problematic and accepts incohesive introductory statements as normative. This type of distraction misses the full beauty of the Pastor's exposition about the believer's gospel hope in Christ at death by Jesus's ability to mediate and lead his brethren into heaven that introduces in Heb 1:1–4, tracks through units A–F, and peaks in Heb 9:27–28. Cf. Rowlands, "Faithful Son," 699–716. Rowland omits the specific, recurrent, context of the αγω- and φέρω word groups for only the local more general context of the introduction. The Pastor introduces more than general faithfulness as the Son but more specifically what the Son does faithfully as the main theme of his entire exposition and exhortation.

68. Hay, *Glory at the Right Hand*, 143. Hay writes, "Temporally, the reader is clearly meant to regard the acts of purifying and sitting as sequential. Further, these two clauses announce the chief themes of the epistle's Christology, i.e., atonement and exaltation." This sequential link is further elucidated in Heb 10:12 and 12:2. Joachim Jeremias argues strongly that this connection found throughout the message of Hebrews occurs in relation to Jesus's death. Jeremias, "Zwischen Karfreitag," 198–99.

In subtopic B´, the Pastor introduces that God spoke for the Son to sit down at the right hand of the Majesty in the high places.⁶⁹ The good news is that the Son made it as the first person into heaven to God's presence by overcoming the sin problem and people's lack of holiness. This path provides the initial link with the OT promise of Ps 110 that frequently appears in support of the present king-priest ministry of the Son in heaven.⁷⁰ The antitype-type links found in Ps 110 support heavenly rather than earthly fulfillment.⁷¹ It provides the background spatial path for all previous subtopic themes. In the lens of the MCS, this spatial heavenly destiny tracks to the phrase "from a second place without sin"

69. Westfall writes about *linearization* and *staging* in the production of discourse. Westfall, *Discourse Analysis*, 29. She comments, "An author must choose a beginning point that influences the reader's interpretation of what follows in the discourse. Part of intentional discourse production involves *staging* where the author uses the point of departure to effectively provide the context for the message that follows. However, each section, unit and sentence has its own point of departure in which the author is able to give the discourse a particular spin" (italics Westfall). Westfall quotes Grimes's observations about how each division level of text is organized around a particular element that is taken as a "point of departure" that through which, the speaker presents what he wants to say from a particular perspective. Grimes, *Thread of Discourse*, 323.

70. Hay, *Glory at the Right Hand*, 25–26, 33, 50–51. Most scholars assert that the Greek Ps 109 LXX was originally written in Hebrew (Ps 110 MT) to authenticate the monarch as a king-priest with the authority of Yahweh himself. When Christians applied Ps 109:1, 4 LXX (Ps 110:1, 4 MT), they consciously compared the Davidic priestly kingship with that of Jesus's greater fulfillment. This Greek text is the most quoted Scripture of the OT in the NT, which reveals the importance in NT understanding.

71. The earthly events involving David's Lord, the people of Israel, Mount Zion, and the foot stool symbolize as antitypes present unseen events of the substance-reality in heaven. In messianic light, NT writers develop the links from Ps 110 to the unseen heavenly types, rather than earthly connections. Jesus now rules over his enemies who come to him in death and intercedes as priest-king for his people to bring them into heaven. *Contra* Orr, *Exalted above the Heavens*. Orr builds on the foundation that believers are not bodily united with Christ until his second coming return to earth. He concludes, "For Paul death and the parousia will mean being with Christ. In the intervening time, though, having an individual body that is distinct and distinguishable from the bodies of believers means that Christ is located elsewhere from believers. This other place is at the right hand of the Father (Rom. 8:34) in heaven (e.g., 1 Thess. 1:10). It is only when he comes at this parousia that he will be with them (1 Thess. 4:17). In the meantime, Paul expresses his longing to be with the Christ (Phil. 1:23) from whom he is absent (2 Cor. 5:6–8)" (132). Orr acknowledges in the biblical texts no difference in the "epiphanic" presence of Christ between the living believer and the deceased believer. This epiphanic presence is pass. as an object rather than act. For Orr, in closed-heaven view, believers wait for salvation for judgment until the Parousia, which he equates with Heb 9:28 (195). Cf. MacLeod, "Present Work of Christ," 184–200. MacLeod works out all of the Pastor's vertical descriptive terminology in Hebrews either as present benefits for the living on earth or an eschatological benefit at the second coming, even though that coming is not mentioned in his message.

(Heb 9:28) to further support more specifically the implied heavenly place of the Son's current ministry to people. In its position within a chiastic structure, it runs parallel with subtopic B for emphasis upon the place of the ministry of the Son and for the believer's entrance to God in the eternal/perpetual-*places*.

In subtopic A´, the Pastor closes with a statement that again concerns the Son as heir in inheriting a better name.[72] This name is "Son," which supports a tight focus in the hymn for all points, including subtopic B, on the themes of death, judgment, intercession, and salvation in heaven.[73] With the introduction of his last subtopic, he announces his subtopic link with unit A (Heb 1:5–14) by a comparative referral of the Son's ministry with the complementary ministry of angels. In the lens of the MCS this path links again with the salvation of access to heaven for those waiting for the Son.

The complete hymnic chiasm functions as the subtopic UI for the propositions in unit A. The DI boundaries are well-marked by the Pastor's beginning statement and signals for shifting to the first unit.[74] These include (1) the end of the linked chiasmic propositions with the subject of God's speaking by a Son in ministry, (2) the closure of the initiation for the introductory contrast for the sermon of the former and recent ways for God speaking, (3) the announcement of the ministry of angels, and (4) the particle "for, because" (γὰρ) to signal the announcement of a new subtopic statement. A Hellenistic Greek audience would anticipate and recognize the Pastor's movement toward support of his introductory contrast and subtopics.

---

72. Meier, "Structure," 188–89. Meier proposes a ring structure with the understanding that the purpose of the introduction is to describe the Son from the viewpoint of exaltation as the starting point and exaltation as the goal. However, he senses the Pastor's goal as emphasis on a flow of retrogressive and progressive designations of his christological thoughts. His proposal does indirectly link subtopic A to A´, but problematic is his admission that only subtopic C´ parallels the Pastor's exposition in units A–F. As Jeremias notes concerning Hebrews, these subtopics and subsequent teaching place an emphasis on "obedience" in what the Son does more than his "nature" about who Jesus is as the Son. Jeremias, "Zwischen Karfreitag," 187.

73. Meier, "Structure," 187. Meier comments, "The main point for us though is that v. 4 speaks of the event of becoming superior at or immediately following upon the exaltation, an event connected with a name (*onoma*)." He lists other scholars who favor the name as "Son."

74. Meier, "Structure," 169. Meier claims, "There is both a numerical symmetry and a symmetry in the movement of theological thought between 1,1–4 and 1,5–14."

The FGT of the DI (Heb 1:1–4) is well-marked. First, it introduces his listeners to his topical complementary contrast about the ways of God's speaking, where the more recent ministry is better than the past. This contrast in covenant inheritance language of promise-fulfillment, peaks in the unit F upon the propositions in units A–D. Second, it supplies a hymnic chiasm about the Son's current ministry in the new covenant. These propositions initiate by the Son's death and judgment for sins and complete by God's salvation of the Son. The Son's sacrificial offering is transmitted to sinful people, who now can by faith rise to God in heaven along the same way of Jesus (Heb 2:11; 9:8).

The final task is the provision of introduction of his discourse units to follow. Discourse units A, B, D, and F, as mainly expositional in function, link with introductory propositions. For example, his A (Heb 1:2b) and A′ (Heb 1:4) subtopic propositions function to announce the exposition of unit A (Heb 1:5–14) introduction subtopic (see appendix 1, figs. 13, 14). The B (Heb 1:2c) and B′ (Heb 1:3d) subtopics introduce the subtopic of discourse unit B (Heb 2:1–18), C (Heb 1:3a) and C′ (Heb 1:3c) subtopics introduce discourse unit D (Heb 5:1–10; 7:1–28), and the D (Heb 1:3b) subtopic introduces discourse unit F (Heb8:1–10:18). Discourse units C (Heb 3:1–4:13) and E (Heb 5:11–6:20) are mainly hortatory with a focus on the audience. Figure 13 maps the level 1 discourse units of S1, level 2 unit boundaries, level 3 unit FGT, and the DUC before a return to a level 1 discourse STr to summarize the previous exposition and introduce the next section.

HEBREWS 1:5—4:13: SECTION 1 INTRODUCTION

Section 1 Structural Map: Listen Carefully to God's Speech to be a Proper Example of the Son's Ministry, since You Will Be Judged in Accordance with Your Conversation about the Word

The Pastor continues to compare the two traditions in which God has been speaking in the promise-fulfillment covenant relationships. He provides the difference between that which only promises a relationship with himself and the reality of Jesus's fulfillment in a dwelling relationship with God. The key concept of his central subtopic D concerns the "conversation, testimony" (ῥῆμα Heb 1:3b) about the Son's "ability" (δύναμις Heb 1:3b). The Pastor offers exposition and exhortation, both extrapolating and applying the covenantal differences for his audience to consider in the examples of their own ministries. God is personally about ministry to others as a servant (cf. Heb 3:1); the audience should be about modeling his ministry.

The Pastor's audience can in their ministerial teaching either continue exampling God's former speech about future promises contained in the past covenant relationship or embrace God's new speech in the new covenant relationship that was exampled by Jesus and is currently being implemented by Jesus to complete the promised hope in heaven for people by faith. The Pastor exhorts an audience, who he surmises as being dull of hearing about God's speaking, to carefully listen to the differences and consider their own teaching concerning Christ. The conversation of the ministerial teaching of his receptors will be judged and those teaching error concerning the work of Christ will suffer loss.

Figures 13 and 16 show the background structure that governs S1 (Heb 1:5–4:13). S1 provides biblical warrant and supportive exposition for the propositions delivered in the DI (Heb 1:1–4) and listener exhortation. The Pastor's main theme centers on the audience "conversation" (ῥῆμα Heb 1:3b) about the Son's ministerial ability, by which the Son brings to God all things into heaven and God's presence. In S1, he develops this ῥῆμα (*rhema*) theme through three units, two with exposition (unit A–B), and one with exhortation (unit C), with a trailing STr (Heb 4:14–16) for summary/conclusions and introduction concerning the Son's ministry for salvation on approach to God in heaven for judgment.[75]

HEBREWS 1:13–14: ANALYSIS OF DISCOURSE UNIT CONCLUSION A

Unit A Structural Map (1:5–14): The Son's Ministry in Heaven is Better than God's Ministry by Angels

Figures 12 and 13 illustrate mapping of the FGT. The UI for the unit A links from the introductory subtopics in Heb 1:2b–4 concerning the Son.

---

75. *Contra* Mackie, *Eschatology and Exhortation*, 199. Mackie follows Jewish apocalyptic versus Platonic philosophy, largely optioning for a hypothetical Jewish temporal focus (114–15; 160–64). He proposes to stretch the temporal divide of salvation in Heb 9:28 across two ages, "where the access imagery is transformed: salvation is depicted as a rescue from the present evil age, and conveyance into the coming age." Following this now heavily challenged straw man, he rejects any vertical eschatology participatory element in the Pastor's encouragement of his audience by opting for a flattened cosmic-*field* fulfillment of salvation at only the second coming.

The inherited ministry of the Son appears in the first and last lines of the subtopic hymnic chiasm in A (Heb 1:2b) and A′ (Heb 1:4). The Pastor supports the introductory subtopics A and A′ assertions in discourse unit A with two FGT points before closing with a UC. Unit A develops a complementary comparison of the current angelic ministry with the ministry of the Son.

Figure 16 demonstrates chiastic structure and relation of unit A with unit A′. Both units contain a complementary contrast concerning the subtopic of ministry by "minister" (λειτουργός Heb 1:7) and "ministering" (λατρεύω Heb 13:10). The focus in unit A is centered upon the introductory subtopics of A and A′ about the better inherited ministry of the Son. This follows unit propositions to the main unit F, where "minister" (λειτουργὸς Heb 8:1) occurs again in the unit F UI. Unit A′ concerns the better ministry of the audience as partakers with Christ in his heavenly ministry, rather than their continuing in the obsolete earthly altar of former service (Heb 13:10).

Discourse Introduction (1:2b–4): The Son's Speaks by Ministry (Subtopic A–B–C–D–C′–B′–A′ in DI)

The introductory FGT chiasm serves as the unit A UI/Pt introduction. DI (1:2b–4) subtopics A (Heb 1:2b) and A′ (Heb 1:4) provide the subtopics of unit A.

Unit Point 1 (1:5–6): The Son, Who Ministers as God, is Worshiped by Angels

The opening support for the Pastor's DI subtopics arises in unit A UPt1. The Pastor initiates his exposition with three OT quotations of Ps 2:7; 2 Sam 7:14; and Ps 97:7. The first quotation discloses a declaration of Yahweh's judgment from his heavenly throne concerning the installation of his promised messianic king.[76] It states, "The Lord said to me, 'You are my Son to me, today I have begotten you'" (Ps 2:7 LXX/MT).

---

76. Andriessen, "De Betekenis," 1–13. Andriessen, in discussion of Heb 1:5–14 concerning the Son's heavenly entrance, supports that the Heb 1:6 prophesized event occurs between death and bodily resurrection. Cf. Jipp, "Son's Entrance," 557–75. Jipp fruitfully argues that unit A "depicts a hymnic celebration of the Father's declaration of Jesus's sonship and his royal enthronement to the heavenly world, is critical for the entire logic of the author's argument and the symbolic world which the text creates. At

The Psalm shares the people's rebellious response to the "Christ" (Ps 2:2 LXX/MT) and their impending judgment. Yahweh will install his King as his Son and will give him an inheritance in heaven from the earth. The Son's inheritance in heaven, rather than the bricks and mortar of the temporary earth most likely refers to the people who receive God's invitation to pay homage to the Son that they may not perish "from the way" (ἐξ ὁδοῦ Ps 2:12 LXX) to him at their judgment from heaven (Ps 2:4). With the selection of this OT quotation, the Pastor reminds his audience about the promise concerning God's judgment from heaven and subsequent enthronement of the Christ Messiah, where he becomes the promised Son and inherits people who choose to do homage to him, from the ends of the earth at the speaking of his judgment.

The second LXX OT quotation in Heb 1:5 that is taken from 2 Samuel 7:14 announces, "I will be to him for a Father, and he will be to me for a Son." God promises a Son from David's linage, for whom God says, "I will establish his throne into the eternal/perpetual-*places*" (2 Sam 7:13 LXX). This language likely assumes both spatial and temporal duration about a kingdom *in heaven* that Jesus receives at enthronement, rather than the complementary truth for the antitype in an extended future form as a kingdom on the temporary earth (Heb 1:8; cf. John 8:23; 18:36).

The Pastor's third OT quotation in Heb 1:6 is taken from Ps 97:6 MT (96:7 LXX). He follows the LXX translation, which states, "Worship him! All his angels" (Ps 96:7 LXX). Celebratory worship follows at Jesus's enthronement at death and rising to God, which included the angels. The Psalm predicts Yahweh's reign in heaven for the righteous people of the earth.[77]

The Pastor's identification of the Son's enthronement described in his OT Scripture is designated by the Greek οἰκουμένη ("God's rule, dominion, government" Heb 1:6). In the heavenly setting, this does not yet include the κόσμος (*kosmos*, cf. Heb 2:8) but encompasses the Son's government in the unseen creation of the eternal/perpetual-*places* in heaven.

---

the very least, the Son's exaltation, depicted in Hebrews 1.5–14, functions as the means whereby God secures his promises to humanity (2.5–18), is the basis for the argument that Jesus is humanity's Melchizedekian high priest (5.5–6; 7.1–28), and establishes the narrative goal or pattern which God's children follow (12.1–3)" (558–59).

77. Schenck, "Celebration of the Enthroned Son," 469–85.

Unit Point 2 (1:7–12): The Son, as Righteous and Upright in His Ministry, at His Death and Judgment Inherited with God in Heaven an Eternal/Perpetual-Place Kingdom That Remains, in Contrast to the Temporary Heavens and Earth Creation

UPt2 affirms UPt1 about the Son's better ministry by providing evidence about the visible realm of creation and its duration. The Pastor chooses two OT texts. The first is the quotation of Ps 104:4 MT (103:4 LXX) in Heb 1:7, which emphasizes that angels were created. Angelic creation contrasts with the Son, who is not created; he is God, which makes what he does in his ministry better than the angels.

The second in Heb 1:8–9 comes from Ps 45:6–7 MT (44:6–7 LXX), which concerns the King's qualities that merited God's endorsement and enthronement in his heavenly domain. First, his throne, as God, is "into the eternal/perpetual-*place* of the eternal/perpetual-*place*" (εἰς τὸν αἰῶνα τοῦ αἰῶνος Ps 44:6 LXX).[78] This phrase used by the Pastor possesses both temporal and spatial weight in reference to the holy of holies or heaven. The rule of the Son's kingdom is based upon his love of uprightness and righteousness with hate for lawlessness. This quality inspired God's choice to joyfully anoint him above his "partners" (Heb 1:9). These partners in context are probably angels, since the Pastor is speaking about ministry to sinful people. Sinful people would not quality for consideration of a Christ work status in substitutionary atonement. The use of "oil" provides a messianic weight to the enthronement language. The Pastor chooses this OT text to base Jesus's appointed ministry as better than the angels due to better qualities.

The second OT quotation in Heb 1:10 comes from Ps 102:25–27 MT (101:25–27 LXX), which records the troublesome complaint of an afflicted person, who is enduring the death and decay of the temporary heavens and earth in contrast to God, who "abides in the eternal/perpetual-*place*" (Ps 101:13 LXX [102:12 MT]), also called "heaven" (οὐρανός Ps 101:19 LXX [102:19 MT]). In Ps 102 MT, the complainant recognizes

---

78. The phrase "into the eternal/perpetual-*place*" (εἰς τὸν αἰῶνα) functions as a thematic phrase used seven times by the Pastor in his message. It is both temporally and spatially weighted to mean the now existing perpetual place of the holy of holies of heaven (Heb 1:8; 5:6; 6:20; 7:17, 21, 24, 28; 13:8, 21; for "into the eternal/perpetual-*places*," cf. Ps 109:4 LXX [110:4 MT]). Lexicographers and translators antithetically flatten the meaning, with major emphasis toward glosses of either the temporal features as "forever," "everlasting," and "eternity" or the spatial visible world features as the glosses of "world" and "universe."

that Yahweh, as God, at the beginning had thrown down the heavens and earth that perish and become old like a garment, which like a robe is rolled up and changed.[79] Yahweh, as God, remains the same and his years do not run out. The Pastor uses the psalmist understanding of the complainant to show Jesus's ministry as better than the angels because he can provide access to the eternal/perpetual-*place* where God perpetually dwells in heaven that abides and remains. This access contrasts with angelic ministry of the first heavenly covenant in the temporary heavens and earth.[80]

Unit A Conclusion (1:13–14): The Angels Minister to People About to Inherit Salvation

The UC is signaled by δέ (*de*). This particle introduces a final emphatic and summarizing contrast between the ministry of the Son and angels. The Pastor's OT quotation of Ps 110:1 connects back to the subtopics B and B´ in the DI chiasm concerning the eternal/perpetual-*places* of heaven. No angel even once had been given a throne for ministry. The Son's throne, where he now ministers, is not located on the temporary earth but in heaven, where the Son now abides until his enemies are made a "footstool" for his feet.

The footstool imagery links with OT typology concerning the function of the ark of the covenant. It is there that Jesus judges his enemies, who must after death remain outside of heaven, due to sin and rejection

---

79. A tension arises with the Pastor's language when the antitype of the promised conditions in a future earthly rule are escalated to the final type of his spatial heavenly hope to God (Heb 12:23). Mainly, the created "eternal/perpetual-*places*" by the Son are presently divided into three major realms of (1) the temporary "cosmos, world," (2) the unseen eternal/perpetual-*place* of approach and judgment, and (3) the end at the eternal/perpetual-*place* of eternal/perpetual-*places* of "heaven." In the Pastor's narrative, the place of the material "cosmos, world, universe" is (1) new with a known beginning, (2) temporarily exists in a limited duration in decay and chaos as destined for fire and shaking of destruction, (3) contains plural heavens as typified in the tabernacle with both visible and invisible regions in levels of holiness with the earth distant from God, (4) resides in darkness of substituted light, (5) remains under the slavery of the devil, and (6) is not worthy of the people of faith (cf. Heb 1:10; 4:3; 9:26; 10:5; 11:7; 11:38).

80. *Contra* Goldingay, "Death and the Afterlife," 61–84. Goldingay argues that the Psalms like Proverbs, Job, and Ecclesiastes as "strands of Israelite faith implicitly or explicitly opposed belief in a positive afterlife." In his argument he presumes the hope and fate of the outer person is the same as the inner person (2). Upon this foundation he applies all observations about the fate of the living body to the soul.

of God's salvation in his ministry as the Christ.[81] Further, his rhetorical question about the angels is meant to be answered in the affirmative. He expects listeners to agree that the complementary ministry of the angels is "ministering spirits for service, ones being sent for the sake of the ones continually coming to inherit salvation" (Heb 1:14).[82]

The Pastor expects by his rhetorical question, several summary points of agreement with his audience before he precedes to his next unit B. His audience should agree: (1) angels are "ministers" (λειτουργικὰ) from the unseen reality who serve in the eternal/perpetual-*places* of the heavens and earth,[83] (2) angels are "presently being sent for service" to

---

81. Vaillancourt, *Multifaceted Saviour*," 98–99. Vaillancourt finds that the frequent use of enemies, by the Pastor's chosen Pss 2 and 89 MT, peaks in Ps 110 MT for "the enemies will be the footstool of David's lord, and—later in book 5—in Ps. 132.7 the people worship at the footstool of Yhwh, which presumably refers to the ark of the covenant." He references, Hal 239 "הֲדֹם." Koehler states with the gloss "footstool" that the Hebrew term always pairs with רַגְלַיִם ("feet") as a footstool for a king (Ps 110:1) and links with the people of the earth in relation to the ark of the covenant (Isa 66:1; 1 Chr 28:2; Ps 99:5; Lam 2:1). Vaillancourt also mentions VanGemeren, "Psalms," 814. To make one's enemies a "footstool" is an ancient Near Eastern metaphor for absolute control. Originally the victorious king placed his feet on the neck of his vanquished foe (cf. Josh 10:24; 1 Kgs 5:3; Isa 51:23). From this practice arose the idiom of making one's enemy one's footstool.

82. A syntactical cadence of present tense emphasis rings noteworthy for an audience to signal that the ministry of angels is viewed as a presently occurring activity for those awaiting salvation. The adjectival pres. pass. ptc. "ones being sent out" (ἀποστελλόμενα) carries weight for a present ministry at the time of the main pres. act. verb "they are," (εἰσὶν Heb 1:14) and modifies "ministerial spirits" (λειτουργικὰ πνεύματα Heb 1:14). The adjectival pres. act. ptc. "the ones about to come to" (μέλλοντας) as object "on account of" (διὰ) in the acc. implies both a continual present spatial and temporal force in relation to the event of salvation to those waiting and establishes activity as the time of the main pres. act. indic. verb "they are," (εἰσὶν Heb 1:14). Also, the pres. act. inf. "to inherit" (κληρονομεῖν) suggests that the event of salvation inheritance is a repetitive recurring event at the time of the Pastor's question.

The temporal tension created by modern theological paradigms finds expression in comments regarding the present heavenly high priestly work of Christ, where Robert Culver writes, "Yet we know our Lord in heaven does not spend his time (Is there time in heaven?) merely receiving praise from the 'innumerable company of angels' and 'the general assembly and church of the firstborn (Heb 12:22, 23 KJV) who dwell there, to the neglect of his permanent work as Mediator." Culver, *Systematic Theology*, 629.

Jesus's eschatological ministry in occurring while the Pastor is speaking to those waiting and not just at some future eschatological completion. His syntax infers angelic activity at the time of the Pastor's question. There is no evidence for a postponement or delay of this angelic ministry only at some future eschatological event.

83. The term λειτουργικός (*leitourgikos*) has weight for cultic service in God's temple that is patterned typologically in the tabernacle and temple. This depiction of angels serving in the holy-*places* is part of the décor on the veil and ark of the covenant. Cf. Himmelfarb, *Ascent to Heaven*, 15. Himmelfarb notes how cherubim were woven

people in God's present economy, and (3) angels minister to people presently about to inherit salvation.[84] The present, heavenly, high-priestly ministry of Christ still involves the ministry of the angels from the first covenant. The Pastor's link of the DI subtopic about inheritance with salvation connects the events concerning the people who receive this angelic ministry with the requisite experience of death and judgment. He infers the conclusion that angels assist the Son in his better ministry from heaven, for the inheritance of salvation access by people into heaven at death and judgment.

Dynamic Conclusion A in Lens of Hebrews 9:27–28

The unit A conclusion about the Son, as sitting at the throne, and his complementary ministry with angels from heaven to people about to inherit salvation, provides the Pastor's first conceptual link from the introductory subtopics to the MCS of Heb 9:27–28. The expected event described from the introductory subtopics A–A′ through the DUC A–F is that Christ will appear from a second place without sin to those people waiting for him by faith for salvation at death and judgment.

Unit A concludes that the Son inherited, during his own death at judgment, this better ministry to people about the receive salvation to himself and away from his enemies. The subtopic of the Son's enemies thus far includes (1) sin, for which he had made purification (Heb 1:3c), and (2) heavens and earth qualities of perishing and growing old, which heaven has changed (Heb 1:2c; 9:23), and the cosmos will be changed (Heb 1:12). People appear as a subcategory of recent creative events in a temporary dark decaying cosmos (Heb 1:10–12). The Pastor does not speak directly of human creation or of an "original" sin.

The unit A UC (Heb 1:13–14) syntactically characterizes the time frame for the ministry of the Son and his angels as ongoing at the time

---

into the walls of the tabernacle (Exod 26:1, 31; 36:8, 35) or engraved in the walls of the temple (1 Kgs 6:29; 2 Chron 3:7; Ezek 41:15–26). Also, Rowland, *Open Heaven*, 219. STL, often in overreach of this teaching about their protection of God's holiness, in discussion of ascents into the heavens by angelic escorts speculates about groups of angels being stationed at heavenly levels of God's holiness for his protection from exposure to evil. The role of angels through the plural heavens in relation to STL and first-century CE normative concepts is a subject for future research.

84. DeSilva, *Letter to the Hebrews*, 118n21. In his discussion, deSilva recognizes in scholarly analysis of Heb 1:14 that there is a neglect of the present tense concerning salvation.

of the Pastor speaking. Salvation was future for the audience, but how far future? Unit E' UC suggests believers enter heaven a very little while after death (Heb 10:37). In unit D2' the Pastor comments about the completion of salvation concerning the living, who are added to those now with Jesus (Heb 11:39–40). However, his assertion does not negate his overwhelming present tense language that maintains believers are already experiencing the beginning of the promises by entrance into heaven soon after death by the present shepherd ministry of Jesus (Heb 13:20). He creatively describes this saving event in his coming discourse units B–F and discourse sections 1–2 to follow.

Thus far in the Pastor's context, the key events, for the Son or people, are cognate subtopics from the introduction subtopics about (1) death (Heb 1:3c), (2) judgment (Heb 1:5–7, 8–12), (3) intercession (Heb 1:3bd, 6, 14), (4) salvation (Heb 1:2bc, 4, 13–14), (5) ministry (Heb 1:3c, 9b, 13–14), and (6) the throne in heaven (Heb 1:3c). The cognate words and phrases contained correspond with the main unit F MCS of Heb 9:27–28 as oratory descriptions of the same salvific event ongoing at the time of the Pastor's speaking.

HEBREWS 2:17–18: ANALYSIS OF DISCOURSE UNIT CONCLUSION B

Unit B Structural Map (Hebrews 2:1–18): The Son is Able in Ministry to Bring Salvation to People at Their Time of Need Before God at Testing

The Pastor provides literary signals that he shifts to his next cycle of FGT, which function as introduction, support, and conclusion.[85] His signals and changes in emphasis would cognitively meet the threshold for a unit shift when any one of them alone usually would not. No one inferential

---

85. These signals include (1) the idiom "for this reason" (Διὰ τοῦτο Heb 2:1), (2) the verbal shift from third person to first person with the new subtopic (we) in reference to himself and his audience, (3) the exhortation to pay close attention to what they had heard lest they should drift away (Heb 2:1), (4) a cognate shift of focus from inheritance to exhortation and exposition of the topic of salvation at judgment that was introduced at the end of unit A (Heb 1:14; 2:2), (5) a cognate shift from "conversation" (ῥῆμα) about the "Word" (λόγος) of God's speech to exposition about the activity detail by the actual "Word" (λόγος) that God spoke in Jesus's actions (Heb 1:3c; 2:2a), (6) a rhetorical question to consider the example of judgment under the first covenant (Heb 2:2–3a), and (7) a contrast shift from the angel's current ministry to their former ministry of the "Word" (λόγος) in the first covenant (Heb 1:14; 2:2) of promise.

conjunction, syntactical lexical form, or marked structural feature signals a unit shift. The speaker/author must provide a *threshold* of indicators for his audience to sense a new unit shift.[86]

Figure 13 supplies the discourse structural mapping of the FGT that illustrates the Pastor's second unit B (Heb 2:1–18). The introduction subtopics for the FGT track from both the introductory subtopics B (Heb 1:2c) and B´ (Heb 1:3d) provided in Heb 1:2b–4 and shifts in focus concerning previous referents, phrases, and cognates from unit A. Previous introductory details of the Son's activities as the λόγος (*logos*) appear in the subtopic hymnic chiasm of the DI. The introductory subtopics B and B´ highlight the *aiōn-field* place background for salvation at death and judgment as the Son's achieving of the eternal/perpetual-*places*, which is where he sat by the God's throne. The topic changes in unit B introductory assertions are supported by three points before the Pastor closes with a UC.

Figure 16 demonstrates the discourse chiastic structure and the relation of unit B (Heb 2:1–18) with unit B´ (Heb 12:14–29). Both units contain exposition concerning the subtopic "salvation" (σωτηρία) in heaven. Unit B describes the salvation of the Son, with his brethren who follow him, at the celebration of his enthronement in heaven. Unit B´, after an evangelistic concern for an acceptance of God's grace, provides a descriptive contrast between only one of two possibilities, either for overwhelming fear on approach of God for judgment or the heavenly blessings of salvation for those meeting Jesus as their mediator of the new covenant.

Westfall proposes alternate unit A boundaries and functions for the FGT between unit A and B. She contends that the FGT of Heb 2:1–4 functions as the conclusion for unit A and shifts the FGT of UPt1 as introduction for unit B.[87] The FGT of Heb 2:1–4 functions as UI for an

---

86. Westfall, *Discourse Analysis*, 78. Westfall comments concerning prominence in background or support material determination, "There must be a confluence of indicators that indicate discourse motifs, topics and themes, and if it supports a more prominent topic or theme, it is still background." This same principle of a "confluence of indicators" also applies to audience detection for a unit shift to mentally begin a new cycle of FGT.

87. See Westfall, *Discourse Analysis*, 93–99. However, Westfall's argument for Heb 2:1–4 as conclusion that based upon the cohesive use of God's speech in the Son is not persuasive. Her focus on the general commentary truth of the Son as the "ultimate messenger" that should be heard misses the actual particular activity of the Son's salvation in heaven that is represented within God's speech in the Son.

application of the propositions in the unit A UC concerning the present activity of salvation in heaven.

Unit Introduction (2:1–4): Do Not Neglect the So Great Salvation, and as God Has Revealed, Was First Received by Others Who Having Heard and Is Now Confirmed to Us

The Pastor claims that the evidence and conclusion supplied in unit A (Heb 1:5–18), which concerns the Son's present, better ministry in salvation into heaven at death and judgment, should cause both he and his receptors to pay closer attention to what has been heard concerning God's speech (Heb 2:1). Not paying attention could cause them to "drift away" from what truly has been said by God in what he had done by the Son. The referents "pay close attention" and "drift away" continue with other later words and phrases to form a path that concerns the "conversation" (ῥῆμα) of the audience's own ministries that tracks through the hortatory path about Jesus in heaven.

In the DI, in the central main point of the subtopic hymnic chiasm, the Pastor states the Son brings all things by the "conversation" (ῥῆμα) of the Son's ability (Heb 1:3b). This conversation about God's speech must be accurate for people to believe and to achieve God's desired goal of bringing people to himself.

Support for the concept of accountability in conveyance of the "Word" (λόγος Heb 2:2) of God's past speech-action during his first covenant is illustrated in the angel's provision of God's speech in intermittent revelations and the law. According to Jewish tradition, the law was given by angels. The angels in unit B serve as a cognate with prophets and other messengers of the "Word" (λόγος).[88] When the revelations or the law were incorrectly exampled by Israel, every transgression and disobedience received a just recompense in judgment from God or his representatives. Their judgment under the first covenant experience served as a typological example of impending judgment on approach to God after death. Based upon the warrant of accountability by Israel for actions concerning their execution of the λόγος (*logos*) of God's speech-action, the Pastor asks his audience to reflect in their own ministries upon how they would escape God's judgment in similar offenses after neglecting so great a salvation (Heb 2:3). In relation to salvation, the "escape" that the Pastor

---

88. Westfall, *Discourse Analysis*, 91.

implies refers to God's judgment after death. Salvation involves following the path of the Son to God into the eternal/perpetual-*places* by the Son's cleansing of sins. His implication is they will not escape judgment for such errant teaching, even as Israel did not before them.

He reminds his audience that this salvation was first spoken through the Lord (Heb 2:3). The Pastor's transition from the referent υἱός (*huios*) to the semantic cognate of κύριος (*kyrios*) is significant. The Greek κύριος was used to translate the Hebrew "Yahweh" in the LXX. The Pastor's use of "speak" (λαλέω) refers to God's fulfillment of the salvation activity of the promised messianic Christ, where Yahweh himself would come in this role as both the anointed offering and priest. The Lord himself was the first person after his fleshly death to receive salvation at judgment with subsequent entrance into heaven of God's dwelling. This reception of salvation in heaven through the Lord was first received "upon the ones having heard" (ὑπὸ τῶν ἀκουσάντων Heb 2:3; cf. Heb 2:9–13; Matt 27:52–53) at the time of Jesus's entrance into heaven, then it was confirmed by revelation to those in the audience still living. Witnesses, who heard God's speech concerning the Son's salvation into heaven supplied corresponding testimony with God by signs, wonders, many abilities, and "distributions of a spirit of a holy place" (πνεύματος ἁγίου μερισμοῖς Heb 2:4; cf. Heb 6:4; 9:14) according to his will. The Pastor suggests that such a large testimonial witness about salvation to distributions of a "spirit of a holy place" would be hard to neglect. This phrase is likely a NT idiom for the spiritual body given to people.[89]

The UI of unit B (Heb 2:1–4) turns to the subtopic about God's speech in a testimonial witness that concerns the salvation of three groups at judgment. These are (1) the Lord, (2) those who heard and who are now in heaven in complete spirit form, and (3) the Pastor with his listeners. This expectation of salvation includes accountability for individual attentiveness toward the proper witness of God's speech in the ministry that God has revealed. The Pastor's use of the particle "for" (γὰρ) signals a transition to the first of three FGT points of exposition concerning God's speech about the salvation of the Lord and other brethren in heaven at judgment.

---

89. See chapter 3 section "Internal Evidence in Hebrews for Transformation to Spirit Bodies at Death as Complete People into Heaven Just like Jesus Did," esp. 157n179 [XREF].

Unit Point 1 (2:5–8a): Salvation Is in the Realm about to Come That Is Now in Subjection to the Son of Man

Figure 13 shows the mapping of three FGT points that support the Pastor's introductory assertions concerning so great salvation after death at judgment for the Lord and people who hear. His UPt1 considers "the present subsequently coming dominion-rule" (Heb 2:5) that "subjects, subordinates" (ὑποτάσσω Heb 2:5) to the Lord in the location of his enthronement after his salvation. The pres. act. ptc. μέλλω caries weight for a possible present availability of this dominion-rule to the author and listeners at the time of his main pres. act. indic. verb "we speak" (λαλοῦμεν).

His OT quotation of Ps 8:4–6 MT (8:5–7 LXX) shares a contemplation about the present creation that stimulates an irony for its author regarding God's remembrance of man in contrast to his consideration of the Son of Man, who receives glory, honor, and all things in subjection under his feet (Heb 2:6–8a). The Pastor interprets the psalmist's observation as occurring at the Lord's salvation and his enthronement over the heavenly government that is now in subjection to him. His point is that the so great salvation occurs in the place of the realm of the presently coming rule of God that is now in subjection to the Son of Man in heaven and not the realm of the ministry of the angels on earth.[90]

---

90. Cf. Dan 7:13–14 and other sources where the Son of Man ascends upwards to receive the inheritance of his dominion at a heavenly court of judgment. Cf. Son of Man, see Nickelsburg, "Son of Man," 137–50. Using the unfortunate term mysticism and a late date for Daniel, Nickelsburg discusses the conceptual dualism involving conflicts between those in the heavens and those on the earth in the OT apart from Dan 7, 1 En. 37–71, Wis 1–6, 4 Ezra 11–13, and 2 Baruch. In these writings, the conflict with Roman oppression of Israel likely symbolized typologically God's conflict with the evils of the world system and promised judgment by a Davidic king, Righteous or Chosen One, figured as a man. He would receive a kingdom that he would give to his people of holy ones (Heb 2:11; cf. Dan 7:18, 22, 27). This heavenly inheritance involves his suffering of death and rising to God in heaven (Heb 2:9–10; cf. Dan 7:13–14; Mark 8:31; 9:9–12, 31; 10:33–34, 45). Also, this kingdom he receives at his judgment locates in heaven (Heb 1:7) for both the Son of Man and his people, with an anticipated destruction of the earthly world oppressive systems that correspond with unseen evil powers and dominions which function as an enemy of God due to death on both micro and macro levels (cf. Heb 1:10–12; 2:5–18).

Unit Point 2 (2:8b–13): The Son through his Death, by the Same Holifying Salvation Experience, Brings Many Brethren to God in Heaven by Their Being Made Holy because of Their Trust in Him

The Pastor's Upt2 in unit B highlights a contrast in the present situation of people. Up until the salvation that was accomplished by the Son of Man in ascending into the presence of God, people while living dwell in a realm that lacks subjection to the Lord (Heb 2:8b; cf. Matt 6:10). The Pastor then interprets the Lord and Son of Man, as Jesus, who was made lower than the angels, and because of the suffering of "death" (θάνατος) was crowned with glory and honor. Both "glory" and "honor" (Heb 2:7) function as cognates in the Pastor's subtopic about salvation with connections to Jesus residing in heaven (cf. John 17:5, 22, 24). In his experience in route back to heaven, by the grace of God, Jesus through his suffering tasted death for all people (Heb 2:9).[91]

The Pastor's use of "for" (γάρ Heb 2:10) signals an explanation concerning the outcome of Jesus's enthronement after death (Heb 2:5–8b) in the realm that is now in subsection to him, in contrast to people now living in the realm lacking subjection to him (Heb 2:8b). The result is for Jesus, as the one for whom all things are and through whom all things are, who having carried many sons into glory, to complete through sufferings the "originator, author, consummator" (ἀρχηγός Heb 2:10; cf. Heb 12:2) of salvation.

The referent "sufferings" (πάθημα Heb 2:10) joins the author's thematic subtopic concerning his experience of death that tracks to the unit B UC (Heb 2:17–18). The aorist act. ptc. "having brought" (ἀγαγόντα) many sons into glory carries weight that the enthronement completes Jesus as the originator/author of salvation and implies that he has already carried many sons to glory in heaven at the time the Pastor speaks.[92]

---

91. Cf. Williams, *Jesus's Death as Saving Event*. Williams argues the hypothesis, by connections of Romans with 4 Maccabees, other Jewish writings, Greek, and Hellenistic literature, that the idea of human death as being beneficial to others was a common Greek-Hellenistic tradition in the first century CE.

92. The Pastor's choice of "having brought/after bringing" (ἀγαγόντα) may be significant regarding the *aiōn-field* context of Jesus's present ministry under consideration throughout his discourse. He does not choose the noun "rising up, resurrection" (ἀνάστασις Heb 6:2; 11:35), the verb "rise" (ἐγείρω Heb 11:19), or "ascend" (not in Hebrews) (ἀναβαίνω cf. Rom 10:7). These referents carry an OT emphasis centered more on rising up to God at death than fleshly bodily resurrection. The Pastor's choice of "having brought/after bringing" (ἀγαγόντα) avoids this ambiguity by cohesion with Jesus's present ministry at judgment after death and subsequent completion after the

This assertion follows the main introductory subtopic in Heb 1:3b that the Son brings all things by the conversation of his ability. Jesus by his ability, which is defined as sufferings in death and rising in salvation to glory, now opens the way for him to bring all things to God in heaven. If past deceased believers are not yet already in the glory of heaven, then Jesus has not yet originated or authored salvation in his primary task of bringing many sons into glory but only able so far to enter himself into heaven. The conclusion that Jesus has yet to begin his ministry to bring sons into glory is problematic for the Pastor's rhetoric about the Son's ability in bringing people to God.

Another "for" (γὰρ Heb 2:11) continues exposition concerning both Jesus and other sons entering glory after death. Both the one holifying and the ones being holified are "all from one," (ἐξ ἑνὸς πάντες Heb 2:11).[93] The combination of the pres. act. and pres. pass. ptc. of "holy" (ἁγιάζων) provide more force for a present ministry of Jesus to people at judgment on approach to heaven. The Pastor points out that the ones being made holy, which is a requirement for dwelling in God's presence, "are all from one." One what? A more general term is required that embraces the contextual referents and verbal activities involved by both Jesus's *experience* in sufferings from death to enthronement and the *experience* of the sons carried by him into glory. The Pastor does not mention the complementary truths of the source of the Father (Heb 1:5) or God (Heb 13:20) that

---

pattern of Jesus with eventual addition of the living to those now with Jesus (Heb 11:39–40). Cf. Jeremias, *New Testament Theology*, 308–11. Jeremias states, "Judaism did not know of any anticipated resurrection as an event in history. There is nothing comparable to resurrection of Jesus anywhere in Jewish literature. Certainly, there are mentions of raising from the dead, but these are always resuscitations, a return to earthly life. Nowhere in Jewish literature do we have resurrection to δόξα as an event of history. Rather, resurrection to δόξα always and without exception means the dawn of God's new creation. Therefore, the disciples must have experienced the appearances of the Risen Lord as an eschatological event, as the dawning of the turning point of the worlds." Jeremias mentions the tension of Matthew's claims of people already experiencing resurrection by observation of "many bodies of the saints," who had gone to the holy city, and were seen. In the NT, after Jesus's fleshly resurrection as visible proof of his having risen to God to receive a pleasing judgment, these terms expanded in semantic meaning as reference to both his rising at death from the dead to God in heaven and his later proof by visible fleshly resurrection (cf. John 2:18–22; Acts 17:31).

93. Otto, *Idea of the Holy*. Otto argues against ideas that holiness only rationally defines as "moral perfection" but includes as religious categories, a pointing to the mystery of concepts of man in relation to God. Also, that ancient man's conceptions of holiness as a mystery of myth, symbol, and allegory should not be considered as irrational or infantile since these are rational conceptions. He finds that these are "unrationalized" expressions to an encounter with the mystery of God.

are commonly supplied in translations. The Pastor concludes that because of the common experience of moving from earth to heaven through the suffering of death, Jesus is not ashamed to call those he makes holy as his "brethren" (ἀδελφός Heb 2:11).

The Pastor then provides from the OT quotation of Ps 22:22 MT (21:23 LXX) support for this common experience of entering heaven together with is brethren, saying "I will proclaim your name to my brethren, in the midst of the assembly I will sing to you" (Heb 2:12). The Pastor interprets this event to have already occurred and begins a path that follows to a point in unit B´ (Heb 12:18–27) that believers are already in heaven with Jesus as part of a kingdom that cannot be shaken. He completes his support for this heavenly assembly with the OT use of Isa 8:17–18 that concerns the proper response to Yahweh's instructions for the people of Israel to look to him for their needs in the chaos of the land. The Pastor exhorts the same response to his audience, stating "I will be one who has dependence on him" (Heb 2:13). This statement likely functions as an emphatic statement to his audience in a hortatory manner for them to join him in following the same experience as Jesus. He then quotes Yahweh's observed outcome of that dependence for Israel in Isaiah, stating, "Behold, I and the children that God gave to me" (Heb 2:13). The outcome for trust in the Lord at death and judgment is beholding other children of God in his presence. His point in this functional unit is that the Son through his death, by the same salvation experience of being made holy, brings many people to God in heaven by their being made holy, due to their trust in him.

Unit Point 3 (2:14–16): The Son Endured Death and Experienced Salvation to Free People from the Realm of the Devil

UPt3 offers more evidence for a present salvation of brethren in heaven through the suffering death of Jesus and his own heavenly entrance. First, Jesus shared the same flesh and blood as the children so that through death he might render powerless the devil and his power of death (Heb 2:14). In paradigms with closed-heavens, the beginning of evil and its persistence in the realm of the earth before human sin create spatial-temporal tensions that are difficult to resolve.[94] In open-heaven, *aiōn-field*

---

94. Cf. Levenson, *Creation*, 19. Levenson deals with OT Jewish ideas regarding the solution for the tension between "God's absolute sovereignty and the empirical reality

concepts, the complex speculative solutions resulting from the tension of the presence of evil are unnecessary.

Second, by the event of the devil's defeat, the Son frees people from fear of death, who were enslaved by it all their lives (Heb 2:15). Finally, the Pastor notes that it is not angels that God helps into heaven and God's presence but the seed of Abraham, which references the messianic seed promised to him. In the OT period, the fear of death centered more on an adverse response in judgment, so as to remain in Sheol or the Pit, rather than an idea that death constitutes only a permanent silence away from God.[95]

UPt3 asserts that the Son endured death and salvation to free people from the realm of the devil, whose realm is outside and away from the realm of God's rule. The three FGT points together indicate that those who trust in Jesus already have heavenly access after fleshly death, even as the Son, away from the realm of the devil, which currently lacks subjection to the Son. Transition from his evidence to his conclusion on the subtopic of salvation in heaven for both Jesus and his brethren is signaled by the particle "for which reason" (ὅθεν Heb 2:17).

Unit B Conclusion (2:17–18): In the Ministry of Salvation as the Son, Jesus, as a High Priest, Capably Atoned for Sins and Can Now Assist in Need at Testing

The unit B UC highlights the ministerial work of Jesus to offer himself in atonement of sins, to subsequently enter heaven for enthronement, and to by intercession carry others into heaven. This salvation is through the Son, by his being made like his brethren in all things, which included a

---

of evil triumphant and unchecked." He recognizes how the author/redactor in Ps 74 "acknowledges the reality of militant, triumphant, and persistent evil, but he steadfastly and resolutely refuses to accept this reality as final and absolute. Instead, he challenges YHWH to act like the hero of old, to conform to his magisterial nature: Rise O God, champion your cause; be mindful that You are blasphemed by the base men all day long. (Ps. 74:22)." Levenson argues that "Genesis 1 does not describe the banishment of evil but the attempt to contain the menace of evil in the world, a struggle that continues today" (cover).

95. Backhaus, "Zwei harte Knoten," 198–217. Backhaus states concerning Jesus's death, "His death opens the gate into eternity" (206) in consideration of vertical eschatology. He wrestles with the debate of his day over the eschatology behind death and judgment within Heb 2:14–15 as either freedom from the tension over the expectation of the parousia or individual judgment in the afterlife and finds inconsistencies with both.

Atonement and the Logic of Resurrection in Hebrews 9:27–28

common experience of death and judgment before his heavenly entrance. Jesus endures this experience of death to become a merciful and faithful high priest, and make atonement for the sins of the people (Heb 2:17).

The referent "high priest" (ἀρχιερεύς) and verbal activity of "to atone" (ἱλάσκομαι) continue the language of the subtopic cognate path about intercession at judgment before God (Heb 1:3c) for salvation and freedom from the fear of death in the realm of the devil.[96] Since Jesus was tested in the things that he suffered, he can provide aid "to those who are presently being put to the test" (πειραζομένοις). The verb "test" (πειράζω Heb 2:18) follows the path toward judgment that began in the DI with the language describing activities of the Son's in relation to the Father's judgment (cf. Heb 4:15).[97] The pres. pass. ptc. "to those who are presently being tested" (τοῖς πειραζομένοις) implies ongoing and current testing. This would consist of testing by judgment after death on approach to heaven, rather than the complementary truth of daily experiences of testing while living upon the earth (cf. Jas 1:2–4).[98] Also, the term "aid"

---

96. Knöppler, *Sühne im Neuen Testament*, 188–219. Knöppler argues that atonement in Hebrews occurs on Karfreitag (Good Friday) and יום כפרים (Day of Atonement) (200). His position links Jesus's atonement with Jesus's death against the more common view of atonement at his later fleshly body resurrection or at his ascension into heaven.

97. Each of the activities of the Son in the introductory subtopics of Heb 1:2b–4 describe events during the process of God's judgment of the Son upon his approach to God in heaven after rising *of* death (all people) that include Jesus's entrance to him in rising *from* the dead. In Heb 4:15, The Pastor states Jesus "had been tested" (πεπειρασμένον) the same way anticipated by the audience and found "without sin" (χωρὶς ἁμαρτίας). A wide range of cognates for "testing" (πειράζω) spoken in Heb 2:18 were available in the first century CE. Cf. L&N 1:329–331. These cognates along with other metaphoric language often appear in STL and the NT to describe expectant judgment after death that involved the ministry of angels; e.g., the cognate δοκιμάζω (*dokimazō*, "learn genuineness by examination or testing") occurs in the Testament of Abraham in description of judgment after death. It states, "And the fiery angel, the one holding the fire tested the souls" (T. Ab. 12:14 *OTGP*). In chapter 13 the author writes, "But if the fire tests the works of anyone and it does not burn him, this one is justified, and the angel of righteousness receives and brings him up to be saved in the lot of righteous ones" (T. Ab. 13:13 *OTGP*). Charlesworth comments, "Fire as a means of testing, as distinct from being the means of punishing sinners, is not so common a judgment theme as weighing and recording. It is, however, indicated in such passages as Ps 66:10–12 (65:10–12 LXX): 'You tested us, God, you refined us like silver . . . but now the ordeal by fire and water is over.' Here 'test' is dokimazō, the word used in TAb. So also, Zech 13:9; Jer 6:29; Wis Sol 3:6. For refining by fire, see Mal 3:2. The image of testing (dokimazō) by fire is picked up by Paul (1 Cor 3:13–15) and in 1 Pet 1:7 (cf. also 1 Pet 4:12, 'for a test,' peirasmos)." Charlesworth, *OTP*, 1:889–90,

98. The Pastor's uses forms of "test" (πειράζω) five times in his message. Heb 3:9 and 11:17 occur in his historical accounts of antitypes concerning both the failure of Israel

(βοηθέω Heb 2:18) links as a cognate with the topic of salvation that introduced in the introductory subtopic D (Hcb 1:3c) and continues in the unit B UI (Heb 2:3).

Dynamic Unit Conclusions A–B in Lens of Hebrews 9:27–28

The Pastor's unit A discourse conclusion summarizes that the angel's minister to people in the temporary heavens and earth who were about to inherit salvation, but that the Son's ministry in heaven at the throne, as God, is better. The listeners, at this point would add more summary from unit B that concerns exposition about the Son in relation to the angelic activity in salvation. The Son, as God, Lord, and Jesus, in the ministry of salvation was capable to atone for the sins of the people. The Son now assists as a merciful and faithful high priest in heaven before God at their need of salvation from sin at testing during their common experience of death and judgment.

The unit B UC continues using thematic referents, related phrases, and cognates in the human events of death, judgment, intercession, and salvation in heaven that coherently track from the introductory subtopics

---

and the success of Abraham in providing proper examples of faith for unseen typological events surrounding judgment on approach to the eternal/perpetual-*places* (Heb 9:27–28). The Pastor states that in Jesus's testing at judgment after death, he was without sin (Heb 4:15). He later asserts in unit E´ (Heb 10:26–39) that his listeners need "perseverance" (ὑπομονῆς) in a proper faith example that expects similar testing results at death and accountability regarding rewards that accompany salvation (cf. Heb 6:9). His challenge implies living out their faith example as what Jesus will do and not just gratitude for what he has done. The verbal form is "to persevere" (ὑπομένω Heb 10:32; 12:2, 3, 7). Perseverance is not necessary to either receive nor to not lose Jesus's intercession for salvation at judgment (Heb 10:39). Perseverance in salvation is totally by God's enablement and not dependent upon gratitude, however the setting of this enabling perseverance that begins with the believer's choice in faith is often transferred incorrectly from the situation of judgment in heaven after death to daily earthly experience in examples of faith while bodily living. This transfer puts undue pressure for a believer's continual performance due to a constant tension in relation to the reception of salvation, rather than the Pastor's exhortations for believers to be the example of that salvation that God provides at judgment. Perseverance at judgment in Hebrews, like Romans, is not a day-to-day mandate to keep one's eternal/perpetual-*place* salvation in this world but the need only for Jesus to know us for his intercession at the moment of our need in salvation at but one judgment. Jesus does not judge us day-to-day determining if our faith perseveres enough to merit his grace in atonement. Nor is God's salvation totally without a necessary choice by faith (Heb 11:6). There is but one judgment to fear and that judgment is after death. Believers do not merit salvation but by faith find grace and freedom from the realm of death now occupied by the devil in time of need. This distinction often becomes muddied in numerous ways; e.g., Whitlark, *Enabling Fidelity to God*.

of the DI (Heb 1:2b–4) to the MCS in unit F (Heb 9:27–28) before turning and making by chiasm more specific application to the audience in units E′–A′. In UC B, the cognates and expressions "to be made like his brethren," "high priest," "to atone for the sins of the people," "having endured after testing," and "able to help" (Heb 2:17) connect with "Christ," "salvation," and intercession. The phrase "he having endured after being tested," "the ones being tested," have correspondence with "death" and "judgment." The main emphasis of unit B corresponds with the introductory subtopics B and B′ where God spoke that the Son achieved the eternal/perpetual-*places* by his sitting at throne of the Majesty in the high places. Unit B locates the expected salvific event of the audience in heaven.

The Pastor exhorts his audience to consider their accountability regarding their handling of the "Word" (λόγος) in the UI of unit B (Heb 2:1–4). However, in unit B, he did not address this accountability at judgment in detail but chose first to address the element of heavenly salvation. In his next unit he again picks up the topic of ministerial accountability. As noted in figure 12–13, even though unit C does not embed as a digression within unit B, as unit E embeds in within unit D1–2, the Pastor makes a hard link from the UI subtopics of unit B to unit C that continues to serve his main DI subtopic D (Heb 1:3c) concerning the Son, who brings all things by the conversation of his ability.

HEBREWS 4:11–13: ANALYSIS OF DISCOURSE UNIT CONCLUSION C

Unit C Structural Map (3:1–4:13): Jesus Faithfully Ministers as a Capable High Priest at Judgment and Provides Rest in Heaven to His Brethren, Who are to Properly Confess and Testify about Him by Faith, before Entering into Rest from their Works even as God Did from His

The Pastor provides signals indicating a unit shift to his next cycle of FGT in unit C (Heb 3:1—4:13).[99] This unit offers eight FGT functioning

---

99. His unit shift indicators for his audience include (1) the adverb "therefore, hence, from the place where" (Ὅθεν), which in context at a sentence beginning can indicate a move to a new distinct discourse structure that is based on the discourse up to this point (Heb 2:17; 3:1), (2) a vocative of address of "holy brethren" and their metaphorical identification as the Son's "house" (οἶκος), which stresses their expected eternal/perpetual-*place* domain (Heb 3:1, 6), (3) a subtopic connection with "high priest"

as two UI/Pt about DI subtopics, support for each SbPt proclamation, a SbPt1c climactic emphasis, and a UC. Figures 12 and 13 map the new unit C discourse. The first UI/UPt topic reaches a FGT climax of hortatory emphasis before turning to a closely related second topic. After UPt of support, unit C ends with a UC to complete the S1 (Heb 1:5—4:13).

Figure 16 shows the discourse chiastic structure and the relation of unit C (Heb 3:1—4:13) with unit C′ (Heb 12:1–13). Both units contain hortatory challenge concerning the subtopic of a life of approach that looks forward to the ministry of Jesus in death at judgment. The focus in unit C is on Jesus's role as a faithful high priest in judgment at death of his people's ministerial example of faith. Unit C′ concentrates on looking to Jesus's example of faith to follow during the difficult training of a life of approach.

Unit Introduction/Unit Point 1 (3:1–6): Jesus in his Faithful Ministry as High Priest is Better than Moses's Faithful Ministry in his Testimony of God's Speech

The adverb "therefore" ("Ὅθεν) marks the beginning of unit C.[100] The Pastor carries his undeveloped introductory subtopic of the ministerial accountability of his audience in judgment (Heb 2:1–3a) from unit B into the introduction of unit C (Heb 3:1–6). The vocative "holy brethren," signals a link for the identification of his audience with both Jesus and those brethren already in heaven. As outlined in unit B (Heb 2:10–13), the Pastor first applied the terms to those who, through the common experience with Jesus for death and judgment, entered together with him

---

(ἀρχιερεύς) and "Jesus" (Ἰησοῦς) from unit B for the ministry of the Son (Heb 2: 9, 17; 3:1), (4) the new subtopic cognate "apostle" (ἀπόστολος) added to the subtopic regarding God's messenger in the ministry of the Son (Heb 3:1), (5) a new subtopic cognate for the path referencing ministers of God's speech that adds Moses and Israel with the prophets, angels, and "we," (6) the new cognates "confession" (ὁμολογία Heb 3:1) and "testimony" (μαρτύριον Heb 3:5) to the subtopic regarding people's "conversation" (Heb 1:3b), as a faith expression for sole dependence on Yahweh's ability to provide salvation at the judgment of people (Heb 2:13; 3:1), and (7) the subtopic concept of "heavenly calling" (κλήσεως ἐπουρανίου) to confession and testimony about Jesus's service (Heb 3:1; 5:4–6). Collectively, these new subtopics combine with an expansion of those subtopics already introduced and developed thus far, to reach a threshold for an audience to recognize a move to introduction of a new cycle of exposition and exhortation in further support of the DI topic concerning God's speech.

100. Cf. BDAG, "ὅθεν," 692–93; *EDNT*, "ὅθεν," 2:493. The *EDNT* notes that at the beginning of sentences the adverb usually takes the meaning "therefore."

at his enthronement (cf. Matt 27:52-53; Luke 23:43). He led brethren, who he had made holy into the presence of God in heaven and exhorts the Father to behold them. Jesus now continues this shepherd ministry (Heb 13:20).

The acknowledgment by listeners of this common way into God's presence with Jesus into heaven condenses to the referent "confession" (ὁμολογία Heb 3:1). As brethren, united by this communal confession, they are "sharers in a heavenly calling" (Heb 3:1; cf. Heb 1:9; 2:11). The "sharers, participants" (μέτοχος) would function, as a general category in complementary contrast with Jesus, to identify the prophets from the DI (Heb 1:1), the angels as "ministers," (λειτουργοὺς Heb 1:5) from unit A, and the audience as "we" in unit B, who are confirmed as part of this group in Heb 3:1.

All are involved in the heavenly calling of God for conveyance of God's speech. This expression indicates a sharing of participation in a ministerial calling from God in heaven regarding their "conversation" (ῥῆμα) about the ability of the Son, Jesus, who purposes as God's "apostle" (Heb 3:1) being sent, to bring sinful people to himself at their death and judgment. The Pastor further explains the heavenly calling of his listeners by pointing out Moses "being faithful to the one having created him" (Heb 3:2) for his ministry of service to Israel. These shifts indicate the subtopic has moved from the exposition describing salvation in heaven in unit B to an accountability at judgment for the quality of believer's confession in their call for the purpose of a testimonial ministry of God's speech about that salvation in Jesus as the Son.

The first main UI/Pt1 of unit C (Heb 3:1-6) introduces a complementary contrast of Jesus's example of faithfulness, as the Son in his house, with the testimony of Moses in his house that he was appointed to serve. The referent "house" semantically joins the spatial referents of "eternal/perpetual-*places*" (Heb 1:2) and "rule, dominion, government," (οἰκουμένη Heb 1:6; 2:5) for the thematic contrast with the temporary "heavens" and "earth" first developed in UPt2 (Heb 1:7-12) of unit A.

In the continuance of the spatial contrast, Moses's house represents the antitype, earthly, covenant relationship as executed in the temporary visible creation (fig. 5), whereas Jesus's house represents the real type of heavenly covenant relationship in the eternal/perpetual-*places* (Heb 1:2c) that is further explained in unit F. The Son inherited at his enthronement an eternal/perpetual-*place* kingdom with God in heaven that remains, in contrast to the temporary heavens and earth creation

(Heb 1:8). Moses's ministry over Israel served as an example in antitype of the type in the heavens (cf. Heb 8:1–5) that Jesus has inherited and is presently building in the unseen substance-reality out of all the things God made (Heb 3:3–4, cf. Matt 16:18; 1 Pet 2:4–5). Jesus's present construction, as the builder, is a better enduring house, which makes the faithfulness of Jesus better with greater honor.[101] His observation "But the one having built all things is God" (Heb 3:4) implies Jesus's divinity during the building of his house. The Pastor states that his audience represents the Son's house "if we should hold fast to the confidence and boast of hope" (Heb 3:6). The Pastor's faith emphasis concerning the Son is not on Jesus's attitude nor on his being as God but on what Jesus faithfully does in building a house of people in heaven. The bricks and mortar of Jesus's house are the people who hold fast to their confidence and boast of hope in his present ministry.

Moses's faithful service provided an example of Christ to Israel "as a servant for a testimony of things that will be spoken" (Heb 3:5). The referent "testimony, witness" (μαρτύριον) continues with the cognate "confession" (ὁμολογία) and "conversation" (ῥῆμα) about Jesus's ability as the Son to bring all things to God (Heb 1:3b). The fut. pass. ptc. "of those things that will be spoken" (λαληθησομένων Heb 3:5), functioning adjectivally, provides a force that God's speech-action in Christ during Moses's service to Israel was both still future and the aim or object of Moses's testimony (cf. Heb 11:24–27).[102]

---

101. Cf. Still, "Christ as Pistos," 746–55. Still properly perceives in the NT textual references which possibly involve the πίστις Χριστοῦ (*pistis Christou*) antithetical debate, that the message of Hebrews explores Jesus's faithfulness (subjective genitive reading) more than any other NT author, who usually lean semantically toward a faith in Jesus meaning (objective genitive reading). The open-heaven, *aiōn-field* background substantially changes the balance of the scales toward a sematic meaning that includes both options. Believers by faith confess in Jesus and his faithfulness to bring them as righteous to God in a mutual relationship of activity. Cf. "But a righteousness from God through faithfulness of Jesus Christ for all the ones believing" (subjective genitive) and/or "But the righteousness from God through faith in Jesus Christ for all the ones believing" (objective genitive) (Rom 3:22). Faith is believing what Jesus has faithfully done in rising to God as the Christ during death and judgment, rather than only who he is as the Lord God (Heb 11:6; cf. Matt 7:21–23).

102. Cf. *GNTG*, 202. Blass comments indirectly on the future participle, stating, "The future infinitive, which like the participle and the optative of the future, expresses the time-notion relatively with reference to the principal action, has disappeared from the popular language, and is found only in the Acts and the Epistle to the Hebrews." He further notes that the fut. ptc. is "used as the complement of the principal verb (to express the aim or object)."

The UI/Pt1 to unit C in the minds of the audience serves to (1) maintain the complementary thematic contrast of the DI of the Son's ministry and other ministries, (2) continue his spatial dualism of the eternal/perpetual-*place* reality (type) and temporary creation (antitype) where these ministries are based (fig. 5),[103] (3) expand the umbrella of partners who minister underneath the better ministry of the Son in heaven, (4) and reinforce God's calling and accountability of the audience at judgment as to the content of their conversation about God's speech in their ministry in building with the Son. The main unit C SbPt that follow support the need for the audience to consider Jesus's ministry and their own accountably of their confession and calling for participation in his ministry.

Subpoint 1a (3:7–11): The Example of Israel's Confession is that God in Judgment Denied the Potentially Available, Conditional Entrance into His Rest Due to Unbelief

The Pastor's support for his first SbPt1a FGT in unit C begins with "therefore" (Διό Heb 3:7), which functions as an inferential conjunction to signal the addition of support for his assertions provided thus far about Jesus's faithfulness in building his house as better than the house of Moses's ministry. It is likely the audience would feel tensions between long held traditions for emulation of Moses's ministry in the earthly Sinai covenant (antitype) and their need to focus on Jesus's ministry in the new covenant (type). The Pastor now continues along his path about the consequences of ministerial failure to motivate his audience toward a proper choice that is pleasing to God. He modifies the OT quotation with the introductory phrase, "the Holy Spirit says" (λέγει τὸ πνεῦμα τὸ ἅγιον Heb 3:7). The pres. act. indic. "says" (λέγει) continues his view that the OT Scripture from Ps 94:7–11 LXX (95:7–11 MT) is God's present speech to his listeners.

---

103. De Vos, "Hebrews 3:7—4:11," 169-83. De Vos applies to Hebrews concepts about mental time-space landscapes with their four dimensions of height, length, width, and time that also perceives of the here and now for position and orientation of an individual or group in respect to sacred space. Mental space-time landscapes enable individuals and groups to locate themselves within the cosmos. De Vos concludes that the mental time-space landscape in Heb 3:7—4:11 combines the four meanings for rest in the LXX for comfort and security to reassure the audience that by faith "they are in fact on their way to God/his realm" (181).

Ps 95 MT, as a psalm of David, contains a warning that is directed to God's people who are in his pasture as his sheep in his hand, to hear the voice of God, and not to harden their hearts after the example of unbelief as Israel. By proper faith in listening, the wilderness generation would have inherited the promised land that typologically represented God's ability to provide a dwelling with himself in the unseen eternal/perpetual-*place* in heaven by the ministry of the Christ.[104] This decision of unbelief in Israel's hearts failed testing in comparison with the speech of God, who intended a positive testimony about his ability to bring his people into unseen heavenly realities. Israel's unsuccessful

---

104. Backhaus, "Das Land der Verheißung," 171–88. Backhaus discerns that Hebrews "develops a theological topography in which conventional biblical goods are desanctified by means christological reorientation. The 'land of promise' (11:9), the promised rest, the sanctuary of the first covenant, Mount Sinai, are left behind in the shadows of earth whereas all light is shed upon their counterparts in God's heavenly realm, which turns out to be the faithful's true fatherland" (171). He proposes a vertical realistic typology for hope in heaven, rather than the more common earthbound hope. Cf. Pate et al., *Story of Israel*, 253. The authors state, "The restoration of Israel in Hebrews is seen more as a spatial ('heavenly') and as atemporal ('rest', Jer 29). He argues that the church is already experiencing in Christ at least some of the eschatological blessings of the restoration, although he does not forsake an eschatological consummation which is still imminent (Heb 9:28; 10:13, 25, 36–37; 13:14)." Their "spatial" and "heavenly" sense of Hebrews is commendable but there is no biblical merit for an "atemporal" hope in the promised "rest." Cf. Wenell, *Jesus and Land*. Wenell addresses the relationship between Jesus and the land promised to Abraham that involves communication concerning sacred space. She finds a positive relationship where Jesus taps into the land promise but only did so symbolically by offering an alternative to the present structures of society in himself. She mentions Jesus's heavenly priesthood and the promise of an inheritance in Heb 1:14 only to point out the diversity of attitudes about the land (2). Wenell concludes with generalities, which she asserts makes the power of future hope stronger, rather than specifics in the connections of Jesus's vision for "new sacred space." She casts Jesus's relationship to the land as more symbolic within a millenarian attitude in contrast to Hebrews's substance-reality of sacred space as Jesus's focus of future hope.

Contra Moffitt, "Wilderness Identity and Pentateuchal Narrative," 153–72. Moffitt correctly observes the Pastor's intended identification of his audience with the wilderness generation. He explores a possible blurred distinction in the message of Hebrews between covenant inauguration in Jesus's Passover-like death and the covenant maintenance of his continual ministry in a local *heavenly tabernacle/Temple* not found in Hebrews. Moffitt rightly senses how the audience must live and wait for Jesus's return to obtain their inheritance. However, he links Jesus's return in Heb 9:28 to only his eschatological return to earth that is not found in the message of Hebrews or the wilderness motif. Israel is led by Moses from Egypt and by Joshua into the land—not rescued while wandering away from Egypt. Moffitt ignores the possible covenant maintenance by Jesus's continual returns in his intercessory work at the present common experience of death and approach to God for judgment that is found throughout the message (Heb 7:25; 11:6).

testimonial conversation about God's promised speech in Christ, regarding "my ways" (ὁδούς μου Heb 3:10), failed emphatic fulfillment due to their unbelief, just as it does in unseen spiritual reality for unbelievers on approach to God after death for judgment.

In God's anger over their flawed testimony, he swore, "If they shall enter into my rest" (Heb 3:11).[105] Rather than a positive outcome to enter his rest as symbolized in the land, God makes the outcome conditional, to delay the wilderness generation to "enter" (εἰσέρχομαι) his "rest" (κατάπαυσις Heb 3:11).[106] The Pastor's SbPt1a emphasizes that a rest in God's presence was still available to those in unbelief. He also highlights ministerial accountability for the believer by understanding that Israel's error, by modeling hardened hearts in unbelief of God's intended speech-action in Christ, brought accountability in judgment.

As a condensed metaphor of Israel's typological experience, the referent κατάπαυσις ("rest") and verbal activity of "to enter" (εἰσέρχομαι) unite with the thematic subtopic of salvation at judgment in the hope of the Son's high priest intercession in heaven. These propositions were introduced in the DI topics A–A′ that govern the discourse and were just described in unit A (Heb 1:5–14) and unit B (Heb 2:1–18).[107] In the

---

105. McKay, "Jesus as Faithful in Testing," 12–18, 155–216. McKay argues convincingly that the open-ended conditional clause leaves the question of entering rest as potentially available and neither an emphatic negation nor emphatic truth. The state of unbelief while living leaves entrance into heavenly rest undecided but potentially still available on the condition of faith, as seen in the pages to follow. The Greek syntactical form occurs as a protasis of a conditional clause without an apodosis. Lacking the apodosis would require the context to determine the meaning of the conditional statement, "If they will enter into my rest." Translators often follow proposals for an unlikely Hebrew idiom that would make the form an emphatic negation, as "They shall not enter my rest" (Heb 3:11, e.g., KJV, NASB, ESV, NET, HCSB, NRSV, CSB). For over one thousand years, before German and English translations, the Latin Vulgate translated the Greek text correctly as *si introibunt in requiem meam* ("if they shall enter into my rest," Heb 3:11 VUL).

106. Gleason, "Old Testament Background," 281–303. Cf. Thiessen, "Hebrews and the End," 353–69.

107. Baxter, "Whether the Souls Departed," 94–96. Baxter solidly argues the evidence for the souls rest at death of the flesh. Cf. Delitzsch, *Commentary on the Epistle*, 198. Delitzsch comments, "Like the rest of God after the work of creation, it is a rest of man from his works, that is, his daily labor here below: it is therefore a rest above in heaven." Cf. deSilva, *Perseverance in Gratitude*, 35. DeSilva concludes that God's rest was not merely the land of Canaan but some primeval creation of God; Lincoln, "Sabbath, Rest, and Eschatology," 197–220. Lincoln views the typology of Israel's promised land and the Sabbath of the Lord after creation, in Heb 3:1—4:13, as "rest" (κατάπαυσις) that is now available to believers. He states "Though the epic-making significance that in the process of fulfillment the old categories are reinterpreted and transformed"

first century CE, the available use of "rest" (κατάπαυσις) in Greek and Jewish literature often expresses a metaphorical link with commonly articulated conceptions about a person's experience in death.[108] By use of Israel's failed exemplary experience, the Pastor continues to highlight the consequences of both unbelief and failure of his people by improper modeling (antitype) of God's provision of salvation (type). God expects not only to be heard and believed but also to be repeated correctly in his chosen revelatory antitypes about his ability in Christ to bring people to himself.[109]

Subpoint 1b (3:12–15): Look at the Ministerial Example of the Confession of your Heart

In his SbPt1b FGT, the pres. act. impv. "*Please* look!" (Βλέπετε Heb 3:12) entreats his audience to evaluate whether their ministerial example about the confession of their heart is one that "departs, falls away" (ἀφίστημι Heb 3:12) from the living God. The repeat of "partners" (μέτοχοι Heb 3:14) and unit theme of accountability at judgment carries over from the unit B UI (Heb 2:1–4). This contemplation would indicate checking for a misstep that portrays of an example about Christ which departs or falls away at judgment from the living God, rather than enter heaven. This speculation about errant conversation about God's speech begins a

---

(181), where rest is available both now on earth and "a present heavenly reality entered by believing and ceasing from one's own works the salvation rest of the true Sabbath" (182). Cf. Hofius, *Katapausis*, 116–51. Hofius soundly contests the gnostic source proposed a generation before him by Käsemann in *The Wandering People of God* by revealing the common first-century CE usage of rest in connection with either a future end-time resting place of the blessed dead, a final beyond-time resting place of the soul, or a between-time resting place of the soul. These uses were not antithetical options but complementary metaphorical descriptions about people in death. Pace Laansma, "I Will Give You Rest," 305.

108. E.g., Sir 38:23 links rest with death, stating, "When the dead is at rest, let his remembrance rest too, and be comforted for him when his spirit is departed" (Sir 38:23 NRSVApo). Cf. Hofius, *Katapausis*, 59–74. Hofius provides a large list of Greek and Jewish examples. Cf. Wray, *Rest as a Theological Metaphor*. Wray follows the work of Otfried Hofius and builds her own commentary upon his work citations that reference examples of the use of rest in Jewish and Christian literature written about the second century BCE through the early second century CE.

109. One would expect God neither to be "pleased" (εὐαρεστέω cf. Heb 11:5–6; 13:16) with ministerial depictions of his revelatory speech (Heb 1:1–2; 5:22–24) by an errant sacrifice (cf. Gen 4:3–7) nor an errant priest (cf. Lev 10:1–2), no more so than the nation of Israel in their unbelief or Moses in striking the rock (Num 20:11).

subtopic theme concerning a possible depiction about salvation that has Christ and his believers falling away rather than entering heaven (Heb 2:3; 3:8, 9, 10, 12). This issue arises again in Heb 6:6 of the Pastor's unit E digression concerning the beginning teaching about Christ.

The Pastor further asserts a warrant that "for we have become partners with Christ, if indeed we should adhere steadfast the beginning of a substance-reality until completion" (Heb 3:14). Ministerial participation with Christ is contingent upon proper expression of a continued faith in the concrete reality of God's promises for entrance into the unseen substance-reality of heaven (cf. Heb 11:1). The audience had begun with this faith and the Pastor raises the question whether they would continue to adhere steadfast in it until completion of their ministries.

In the context of not falling away or departing from the living God in heaven, the "completion, finish" (τέλος) would likely refer to the completion of their beginning belief that they would enter the substance-realty of the living God in heaven. No longer teaching this confession in ministry would nullify their participation with Christ in his ministry. SbPt1b closes in Heb 3:15 with a repeated quotation of Ps 94:7 LXX (95:7 MT) in Heb 3:7 as an exhortation from God to not follow the example of Israel in hardened hearts and to hear the voice of God speaking.[110]

Subpoint 1c Climax (3:16–19): Compare your Ministerial Confession with Israel's Example of Unbelief That Received God's Judgment Not to Enter the Land

The final SbPt1c FGT forms a third climactic point for his assertion about accountability for ministry at judgment. A series of rhetorical questions that highlight previous exposition concerning Israel's disobedience and not believing the things they heard from God's speaking about the promise of the land. His analysis states, "And we see they were not able to enter on account of unbelief" (Heb 3:19).

The Pastor maintains by the typological example of the people of Israel, who died in the wilderness, that God's judges his people, who both do not listen and convey alternative speech in unbelief of God's promises. God desired to speak through the positive actions of Israel to by faith enter the land (antitype), which typologically represented to the world

---

110. Löhr, "Heute, wenn ihr seine Stimme," 226–48.

his provision through the work of Christ for an access to the eternal/perpetual-*place* of heaven with himself to those who believe in the Son's ministry (type). However, the desired symbolism fulfilled negatively to covey a response of God's wrath due to unbelief. By placing this outcome in the minds of his audience, the Pastor next turns the experience of Israel more pointedly toward them.

Unit Introduction/Point 2 (4:1–5): Fear Being an Example, in Confession about Jesus's Ministry, That Falls Away in Unbelief, Rather Than Enters by Faith into God's Place of Rest

The Pastor supplies signals for a minor shift in emphasis for his unit C UPt2 subtopic, from God's judgment concerning other's ministry for Jesus, Moses, and Israel, toward the "outline, example, model" (ὑπόδειγμα Heb 4:11) reflected by the ministry of the audience.[111] The second UPt2 subtopic signals by "therefore" (οὖν) and centers on the concept of "rest" (κατάπαυσις Heb 4:1, 3, 4, 5) that is previously mentioned in unit C concerning Israel (Heb 3:11, 18).[112] Israel's model in response to God's speech about rest in the promised land typologically functions as a cognate in path from the DI about salvation into heaven.[113] Since the promise remains for the audience to enter by faith into the typological fulfillment of

111. These markers include (1) the inferential particle "therefore, consequently" (οὖν Heb 4:1) that implies an introduction in a link with what proceeds, (2) a verbal shift to the first person hortatory subjunctive "let us fear" (Φοβηθῶμεν Heb 4:1), which turns the subtopic attention toward the audience, (3) an assertion, by the adjectival pres. pass. ptc. "a promise of which is presently remaining" (καταλειπομένης ἐπαγγελίας Heb 4:1) to enter into God's rest, for current obtainability to the audience, (4) a new cognate "fail to reach" (ὑστερέω Heb 4:1; cf. Heb 2:1; 3:12; 4:1; 6:5; 12:15) in the conceptual subtopic for a conversation about the ministry of Son by the receptors that possibly conveys an example of falling away at judgment, rather than entrance to God in heaven, (5) a new verbal cognate "to proclaim good news" (εὐαγγελίζω) in the conceptual subtopic about conversation, which is heard by the listeners about the "Christ [speech-action]" (ὁ λόγος) that fulfilled in the Son's ability to enter heaven, (6) a new cognate "to believe" (πιστεύω) in the conceptual subtopic about "confession" among the audience for the faith acceptance of the substance-reality for the ministry of the Son in heaven as a prerequisite for entrance into God's rest (Heb 4:3; cf. Heb 11:6), and (7) a spatial connection by the metaphor for access to the promised place of rest, which is available for the audience, in connection with the location of God's presence, both when and where he dwelled after he finished the foundation of the temporary "world" (κόσμος Heb 4:4).

112. Cf. BDAG, "οὖν," 736.

113. Backhaus, "Das Land der Verheißung," 178. Backhaus concludes that rest or place of rest is "metaphor for the heavenly home."

this rest, the listeners should fear that their confession concerning Jesus's ministry examples falling away in unbelief, rather than enters by faith into God's place of rest.

The Pastor reminds his listeners that Israel had failed to enter God's rest because when they heard the proclaimed good news of the word of God's speech, just like the audience, "those people had not been united by faith after hearing" (Heb 4:2). Since God intends Israel's speech-action as an antitype in earthly testimony about entrance by faith to himself in heaven, when they harden their hearts in unbelief, God swears in his wrath against them that his entrance into his rest is based upon the condition of faith. This statement is not a negation but a positive reinforcement of a mandatory condition of faith for heavenly entrance. Rather, Israel by unbelief in God's speech typologically outlined failure to enter heaven by unbelievers about the ministry of the Son.

The Pastor asserts, based upon a logical reversal of God's speech in Ps 94:11 LXX (Ps 95:11 MT) and by use of the pres. tense in the first per. pl. "we are entering" (Εἰσερχόμεθα), that "the ones having believed" (πιστεύσαντες) in the audience "are presently entering" that promised rest (Heb 4:3).[114] Believers presently at death go to God in heaven. The Pastor's language for rest includes weight for a thick spatial emphasis as a place, rather than only a forensic or emotional state of mind or heart during living and worship upon the earth. In the Pastor's examples about Jesus and Moses with Israel, both left one dwelling place for another dwelling place. Moses and Israel left Egypt for the promised land of rest (antitype). Jesus left the earth to sit at the throne in heaven and takes his people with him at death to rest (type). Hearing the spatial language in God's speech-action emphasizes a call to ministerial conversation about the Son's ability that is more than only analogical, with no heavenly

---

114. Barrett, "Eschatology of the Epistle," 153. Cf. Moore, "'In' or 'Near'?," 186–98. Moore senses the future weight of the promise of entrance into rest and that the present tense regarding "enter" and "approach" usually should be taken as a futuristic present. However, he pushes the future weight too far. The futuristic present when describing action in a large group can encompass an activity that is available now but with possible random occurrence in the near future, i.e., the expectation of approach and entrance into heaven at death is both presently available as believers randomly experience death and still future until each individual death occurs. Neither the distant collective future expectation nor the theme of worship carries the weight Moore desires in order to reject a heavenly entrance for believers at death and to preserve antithetical presuppositions concerning only the complementary truth of a general future judgment; Moore, "Heaven's Revolving Door?," 187–207. To separate vertical and horizontal eschatology is a misstep that creates much of the current scholarly debate.

reality for dwelling in God's presence.¹¹⁵ The message of Hebrews has a very timely warning for believers to not harden their hearts in rejection of the Son's ability to shepherd his people at death and judgment into the substance-reality of the presence of God's rest in heaven.

As evidence for rest existing in the presence of the living God, the Pastor identifies the place of this promised rest from God as synonymous with the location of God's rest in Gen 2:2, where God rested from all his labor (Heb 4:4). The living God rested in heaven of the eternal/perpetual-*places* and not on the earth. He then warns his listeners again with the quotation of the OT speech of God in Ps 94:11 LXX (Ps 95:11 MT) concerning God's conditional response to Israel's errant example for an evil heart of unbelief in his spoken promises, stating, "If they will enter into my rest" (Heb 4:5). The conditional statement implies the option for rest in heaven was still available and not absolute, as in the situation of unbelieving hearts.

In this UPt2 introductory FGT, the Pastor directs his audience to fear following the same example as Israel in judgment. If, in the conversation in their ministry of the Son, they example a falling away from the living God, rather than a ministry that projects entrance by faith into heaven by the ministry of the Son, there are consequences of accountability for such errant examples both now and at judgment after death.

Subpoint 2a (4:6–8): An Entrance for the Audience to God's Place of Rest Mentioned by David Still Remains Today, Conditional upon Jesus's Provision on Another Day

The Pastor offers to his audience two FGT points to support the need for serious reflection about God's judgment upon his people who participate with him in the ministry of his speech. SbPt2a recognizes that the entrance into God's rest mentioned by David still remains "today" (σήμερον Heb 4:7) for the audience after David's day, because that rest was conditional upon Jesus's provision on another day, after that day.¹¹⁶ The Pastor's

---

115. E.g., Moore, "Heaven's Revolving Door?," 187–207," 15. Moore states, "I will seek to show that approach denotes a privileged proximity to the heavenly realm which is an innovation on the author's part, yet *without* transition from one part of the cosmos to another" (199; italics Moore).

116. McKay, "Jesus as Faithful in Testing," 7–11, 89–154. McKay's discusses the christological interpretation of Ἰησοῦς. His arguments for the link between Heb 3:1–6 and Heb 3:7–4:13 are solid, which supports the cognate subtopic of Ἰησοῦς in Heb 4:14 as having an implied semantic meaning for Jesus in correspondence with Heb 3:1 in

conditional statement says, "For if Joshua [antitype]/Jesus [type] rested them, he would not speak about another day after that day" (Heb 4:8). His first-class condition assumes the protasis is true that Jesus has given rest to David and others on another day. Also, he has already mentioned the Son with other brethren in heaven (David et al.) in unit B. His further evidence for current heavenly accessibility is that David while living had spoken during his ministry about the availability of God's rest for his people of his pasture, saying "Today, if you will hear his voice, do not harden your hearts" (Ps 94:7 LXX [95:7 MT]; cf. Heb 4:6–8). Further, if Jesus had given them rest during their ministries, then David or others during those ministries would not have spoken of another day when God will give rest to them.[117] The day that one receives rest equates to salvation at death.

Subpoint 2b (4:9–10): The Rest of Jesus and His People is the Same Place as God's Rest from His Work of Creation

SbPt2b (Heb 4:9–10) emphasizes that the location for the rest of both Jesus and his people is at the place where God rests from his works on the seventh day.[118] The pres. pass. indic. syntax in the statement "consequently, there is remaining a Sabbath rest for the people of God" (Heb 4:9) rationally implies a force that no one in the audience had not only not yet achieved that promised rest, but also had not completed the prerequisites of death, judgment, and salvation by the Son. They were not impervious to these preconditional experiences required before entering that rest. However, once the opportunity availed with the completion of death and judgment, the one who entered his rest would rest from his works just like God did from his (Heb 4:10).[119]

The Pastor's second point provides two details that support an entrance to rest of salvation into God's presence in heaven. First, this rest still remains to be experienced by the audience with availability today when the opportunity for need avails itself as expressed in unit B. Second, the rest promised is in the same place as the rest of God with his cessation

---

the unit C UIPt1 introduction.

117. McKay, "Jesus as Faithful in Testing," 7–11, 89–154. Cf. Whitfield, "Pioneer and Perfecter," 80–87; Whitfield, "Three Joshuas," 21–35; Ounsworth, *Joshua Typology*.

118. Attridge, "God in Hebrews," 199–200.

119. McKay, "Jesus as Faithful in Testing," 11, 155–216. Cf. Moore, "Jesus as 'the One,'" 383–400.

of work on the seventh day after completion of the visible creation. With his evidence completed, he ties off his assertions thus far by a ΓGT that functions as the UC.

Unit C Conclusion (4:11–13): In Your Confession During Ministry, Diligently Example/Outline an Entrance by Faith into Rest at Judgment and Not Falling Away in Unbelief, since the Word of God [Jesus] is a Capable Judge to Decern the Thoughts and Intensions of the Believer's Heart until the Division of Soul and Spirit and Joints and Marrow [Death Transformation to Spirit Life]

The Pastor accumulates the necessary literary indicators to merit a threshold shift by the audience for an anticipated UC.[120] He concludes unit C and S1 with "toward whom the Word *is* with us" (Heb 4:13). The statement, translated in its simplest form, presumes that judgment is located in the literal presence of the Son's "eyes."[121] Throughout the

---

120. These markers include (1) use of the particle "therefore" (οὖν Heb 4:11), (2) a hortatory subjunctive "let us be eager, zealous" (Σπουδάσωμεν) in exhortation of the audience about the unit subtopic concerning a remaining rest for them, (3) a summary phrase "to enter into that rest" (εἰσελθεῖν εἰς ἐκείνην τὴν κατάπαυσιν Heb 4:11) as a cognate concept linked with in the subtopic about salvation, (4) a warning reminder about the subtopic concerning falling away at judgment similar to the antitype of Israel by the statement "so anyone should not fall in the same example [outline] of disobedience" (ἵνα μὴ ἐν τῷ αὐτῷ τις ὑποδείγματι πέσῃ τῆς ἀπειθείας Heb 4:11; cf. Heb 2:1; 3:12; 4:1; 6:5; 12:15), (5) the new use of the cognate phrase "the Word of God" (ὁ λόγος τοῦ θεοῦ) in the path to describe the ministry of the Son, which stresses that he is the functional equivalent for God's speech (Heb 4:12), (6) a new cognate phrase "is piercing until division of soul and spirit until joints and marrow" (διϊκνούμενος ἄχρι μερισμοῦ ψυχῆς καὶ πνεύματος, ἁρμῶν τε καὶ μυελῶν Heb 4:12) in the subtopic of death, and (7) the role of the Son as "capable Judge" (κριτικὸς) that continues the subtopic of judgment in complete exposure of the thoughts and intentions of the heart upon approach when seen by him (Heb 4:13). These markers would likely meet the threshold by the audience for a shift to the next anticipated conclusion to the Pastor's lengthy unit of discourse about ministerial accountability, by judgment after death, before entering into the rest of salvation in heaven.

121. Eklund, "To Us, the Word," 101–15. Eklund thoroughly evaluates interpretative options for this phrase, of which a majority consider a context of accountability in judgment. Few consider the simple syntactical options for the preposition πρός with the acc. relative pronoun ὅν. Cf. *GGBB*, 300. In the *aiōn-field* background context about individual judgment by the Word of God, before one enters into their heavenly rest, the Pastor envisions himself and his audience as literally before the eyes of the Lord with his eyes toward them. There is no indication in the metaphoric language describing this judgment context for audience consideration that the event is only mythical with no real factual connection. Jesus's judgment of his people is more than a mental forensic

discourse so far, the Pastor heavily emphasizes the Son's ministry is in heaven to those before his throne, with minimal reference to any earthly activity (cf. Heb 5:7–8). In unit C, he desires for his audience a "confession" (ὁμολογίας Heb 3:1) and "example, outline" (ὑπόδειγμα Heb 4:11) in ministry as "partners" (μέτοχοι Heb 3:1) in the heavenly calling with Jesus that eagerly examples for believers "to enter" (εἰσέρχομαι Heb 4:11) rest by faith at judgment and not a pattern of ministry that falls away in unbelief.[122] An *aiōn-field* background for the Son's ministry is definite.

In summarizing his subtopic of ministerial accountability, which he establishes in the introduction of unit B and develops throughout unit C, he reminds his listeners that the Son, as the Word of God, is living, active, and sharper than a double-edged sword.[123] Smillie, in discussion of the multiple options for the meaning of "the Word of God" (ὁ λόγος τοῦ θεοῦ) in Heb 4:11–12 writes, "The author identifies the Word of God addressed

---

exercise or change of emotional feelings while living on earth. Judgment is presented as a real experience for the people of God that occurs after the ordinal event of death (cf. Heb 9:27; 10:29–39).

122. Moore, "Heaven's Revolving Door?," 189–96. The collective syntax of the Pastor's seventeen uses of "enter" (εἰσέρχομαι) alone cannot answer the who, where, and when questions about entry, as adequately demonstrated by Moore; e.g., the Pastor syntactically chooses the aorist act. inf. εἰσελθεῖν four times (Heb 3:19; 4:1, 6, 11), an aorist ptc. εἰσελθών (Heb 4:10) once, and an aorist indic. (Heb 6:20; 9:24) that provide no special aspectual emphasis and must determine the who, where, and when by context. He chooses the pres. tense four times (Heb 4:3; 6:19; 9:25; 10:5) that is probably a fut. pres. in the context in relation the audience and the fut. tense four times (Heb 3:11, 18; 4:3, 5). The semantic solution for the contextual meaning of the who, where, and when concerning "enter" (εἰσέρχομαι) can be better confirmed by considering the governing subtopics in the Pastor's discourse FGT above the syntax and sentence level. Moore mainly analyzes only the isolated syntactical usage between the heaven and the earth and four other passages in the context of OT and ST period texts concerning "approach" (προσέρχομαι) and "enter" (εἰσέρχομαι). He correctly asserts, as a limit of his methodology rather than the implications of the letter itself, an "imprecision and lack of explanatory power with respect to the entrance passages in the letter" (1). Moore is likely correct "that it is more coherent in cosmological terms to regard approaching and entering as separate rather than identical movements" (1) but interpret the language as a literal, spatial entrance into heaven for believers against his contention "that means actual heavenly entrance now is unnecessary as well as uncountenanced by Hebrews' author" (24). The introductory cognate tracks through the Pastor's FGT in his discourse units strongly support a realized heavenly entrance after a literal heavenly approach to Jesus.

123. The "sword" (μάχαιρα) is commonly associated in the OT with death and judgment. Isaiah states, "My sword is intoxicated in the heavens, behold it will descend upon Edom and the people of destruction with judgment" (Isa 34:5 LXX; cf. Jer 32:31 LXX [25:31 MT]). The OT concept language involving judgment by God's sword infers more than just bodily death but includes an anticipated heavenly judgment after death.

to his people so closely with the divine person speaking it that it is nearly interchangeable with the person of God himself. The Word of God in Hebrews is not a figure of speech or a circumlocution for the Old Testament; it is the word that God speaks to those who hear, whether through Scripture or through the Son or through those who are sent by the Son to proclaim the Word. It is the personal word of that personally-addressing God that is the focal point of both verses 12 and 13 of Hebrews four."[124] It is not a mere historical biblical record by which God discerns the thoughts and intents of the heart, but rather God's own direct speech/action that speaks even in the present to those who will hear and that should be their confession and conversation by faith.[125]

The phrase "the Word/word of God" (ὁ λόγος τοῦ θεοῦ) has been interpreted in several ways due to disconnection from the governing introductory subtopics of the discourse in correspondence to each previous UC.[126] The Pastor in units A–C weaves a proposal that Jesus's

124. Smillie, "Living and Active," 170. Cf. Allen, *Hebrews*, 284. Allen asserts most of the church fathers and medieval theologians saw ὁ λόγος τοῦ θεοῦ (*ho logos tou theou*) as referring to Jesus the Son. Since the Reformation, the phrase has usually been interpreted as the written word of God due to apologetic issues.

125. The Pastor's concern appears to be a mismatch between the actual speech-acts events of the "logos" and the contemplated "conversation" of his listeners in teaching about the logos. This misstep becomes clearer in analysis of the rhetoric of unit E (Heb 5:11—6:20).

126. E.g., Wider, *Theozentrik und Bekenntnis*, 72–87. In his section for Heb 4:12–13, Wider follows the hermeneutic of the overall letter context to interpret the phrase ὁ λόγος τοῦ θεοῦ as an objective genitive for "the speaking God" as Jesus, rather than the post-reformation subjective genitive "word from God." In his exegesis of subsection "2. Deadly Judge or Superior Revelation," Wider attempts to justify this hermeneutic choice by claiming the subjective comes from a corrupting influence, where it is viewed as that of a mere legend of God's past record of speech to the author. However, the subjective genitive does not satisfy the intention of the author's intent in the context. Some modern exegetes take verse 12 as the written word and verse 13 as a switch to Jesus. Wider argues that the parallelism of the two verses, along with the fact, that in order to position the word of God in the appropriate context, one must view the text from God the creator (88). However, this complementary truth is not supported in the discourse context.

Cf. Griffiths, *Hebrews and Divine Speech*, 163–64. Concerning the concept of a defined *logos*, Griffiths finds evidence of an implicit *logos* Christology, but avers that Christ is not directly referred to as *logos* in the text. Griffiths concludes the term ὁ λόγος τοῦ θεοῦ (*ho logos tou theou* Heb 4:12, 13:7) does not identify Jesus in Hebrews, but in forms of divine speech. Also, the term ῥῆμα (*rhema*) with the gen. θεοῦ (*theou* Heb 6:5, 11:3) is best understood as subjective genitive thereby making its divine origin explicit (163). In comparison, he thinks each term bears a distinctive significance within the writer's presentation of divine speech, with λόγος mostly used for communication of information and ῥῆμα chosen for physical manifestation of God speech in particularly

Atonement and the Logic of Resurrection in Hebrews 9:27–28

exemplary path in his own death, judgment, and entrance into heavenly rest qualifies him as a capable heavenly Judge. The Pastor's unit C UC (Heb 4:11–13) in the path from the introductory subtopic D (Heb 1:3b) declares that it is belief in Jesus's speech-action that determines one's entrance into his heavenly rest of his house.[127] The Pastor's metaphoric imagery describes how Jesus's abilities involve piercing the division of people until soul and spirit and joints and marrow to allow entry. This description likely designates the natural state of existence after death in Jesus's house of all creation, in the realms of heaven and earth, whether visible or invisible (cf. Col 1:13–23).[128]

Jesus judges candidates for entrance into God's heavenly rest. The pres. middle/pass ptc. "while himself presently penetrating/who is presently penetrating" (διϊκνούμενος) offers added weight that this capable position as Judge is a current activity for the Son with his people who approach for his judgment (cf. 2 Cor 5:6–10). As God, the Son is able to create the necessary piercing until division of the soul and spirit of people and to leave behind only the joints and marrow as earthly evidence of their lives.[129] He is a capable Judge of the preserved soul and spirit-heavenly body (Heb 10:5, 39; cf. 1 Cor 15:42–49) to decern the thoughts

---

as the created order. The "word of God" references both what God says and does and "conversation" references words in witness about what God says and does. Griffiths finds a lack of conclusive evidence from the text that the term λόγος in Heb 4:12 refers to Jesus as the personalized Word. He takes the combined language of Heb 1:2 and 11:3 as the author's view that Jesus is the Word by whom God created the world. See introductory subtopics B (Heb 1:2c) and B´ (Heb 1:3d). Griffiths further asserts that the divine speech of Heb 12:24 of Jesus's blood "speaking" within the frame of God's speech in Heb 1:1–4 combines to reveal the Son's person and work are presented as the means by which God has spoken his eschatological word. Likewise, the author may access a word stock of common concepts, vocabulary, and images with Philo, yet there is no evidence that demonstrates literary dependence. Thereby, for Griffiths, the Pastor does not share a common view of the *logos* with Philo as God.

127. In consideration of Jesus's justice, scholarship often disregards the present function of Jesus as divine Judge on approach to heaven after death; e.g., Nardoni, *Rise Up, O Judge*. Nardoni writes from the Catholic perspective of the establishment of God's kingdom on earth that expects a final consummation (322). He acknowledges the apocalyptic reality of a heavenly kingdom (169). However, he ignores the message of Hebrews concerning Jesus's heavenly ministry and kingdom building. He focuses on Jesus's earthly ministry as an introduction into society of an expected radical change of divine dominion over the world (196). This early misstep escalates the complementary truth about antitypes concerning future earthly promises to Israel that correspond as revelation to heavenly types.

128. Robinson, "Hebrew Psychology," 353–82.

129. Backhaus, "Zwei harte Knoten," 198–217.

and intensions of the believer's heart as they rise and stand before him to determine rewards that accompany salvation by proper ministerial conversation about the Jesus in his ministry as the Christ (Heb 6:9–10; 1 Cor 3:9–15). These rewards are further discussed in unit E (Heb 5:11—6:18).

Dynamic Unit Conclusions A–C in Lens of Hebrews 9:27–28

The combined DUC A–C continue the introductory subtopic concerning the ministry of the Son observed in units A from the DI introductory subtopics (Heb 1:2b–4). The unit A UC (Heb 1:13–14) condenses to the Son's ministry concerning his inherited kingdom that is better than the present angelic ministry to people presently about to inherit salvation. The unit B UC (Heb 2:17–18) added exposition that the Son, as the Lord who became Jesus in the ministry of salvation, was capable to atone for the sins of the people and to now assist from heaven in their need of salvation. In unit C (Heb 3:1–4:13), the Pastor explains how God speaks through the antitype of Israel in the exodus motif and emphasizes his spoken contingency of the requirement of faith for entrance into the promised land. In correspondence with the pattern, the Son now functions in his role of Judge and conducts the judgment of his people, who await by faith the expectation at death for the hope of salvation into heavenly rest by the Son appearing from his throne (cf. Heb 11:6). The unit C UC (Heb 4:11–13) now exhorts his audience to consider accountability at the testing of judgment regarding their own confession and conversation about the "Word of God" when they stand, with him looking directly upon them, before they enter his heavenly rest.

The unit C UC continues the DI subtopic themes that consistently track to the MCS of Heb 9:27–28 that include death, judgment, intercession, and salvation in heaven. The cognate phrases "to enter his rest" and "enter that rest" (Heb 4:11–12) positively link with "salvation" (Heb 9:28) in conjunction with "an example with the result to fall from disobedience" (Heb 4:11) negatively expressing the lack of salvation. The "Word of God," "judge," and "piercing" link thematically with the referents for "judgment" and intercession of "Christ" (Heb 9:27–28). The expressions "piercing until both a division of soul and spirit and joints and marrow" and "open and laid bare to the eyes of him" (Heb 4:12–13) connect with "death" and "judgment" (Heb 9:27). This correspondence makes it highly probable that the A–C DUC thus far relate to the same expected event in heaven as the MCS of Heb 9:27–28.[130]

HEBREWS 4:14–16: ANALYSIS OF DISCOURSE SECTION TRANSITION 1

The Pastor advances his message with a discourse transition between discourse S1 and S2 to maintain orientation, clarification, and understanding in harmony with his introductory propositions in Heb 1:1–4. Multiple literary markers signal a threshold for a discourse level transitional FGT.[131] It provides both a summarizing conclusion of his first three units and introduction to his next three units.[132] It condenses the A–C

---

130. The chapter 4 unit C UC (Heb 4:11–13) infers that the phrase "Word of God" (Heb 4:12) references the speech-action of the priest Jesus, as the Christ, in judgment of people at the time of fleshly death enroute to God. It corresponds with the MCS unit F UC (Heb 9:27–28) as an *inclusio* for the contained parenesis regarding Christ's ministry at death and judgment.

131. These include (1) the phrase "therefore having" ("Ἔχοντες οὖν), which is repeated in a corresponding section transition at the end of S2, to designate forthcoming summary oratory and conclusion about propositions asserted to this point that will be emphasized in greater detail in coming units to follow, (2) a condensed reemphasis of his utilized language indicating the spatial destiny of believers for "approach" (προσέρχομαι) "to the throne" (τῷ θρόνῳ Heb 4:16) that follows Jesus through the heavens for entrance into sacred space, which introduces the main exposition to follow in unit F (Heb 8:1—10:18), (3) recall of "high priest" (ἀρχιερεύς Heb 4:14–15) twice, which provides head-tail linkage for introduction to his next subtopic of his exposition in unit D (Heb 5:10–6:20) to follow concerning the ministry of Jesus as high priest, who is able provide suitable assistance for their weaknesses exposed at judgment, (4) connection of "high priest" directly to "Jesus" with the vocative "Son of God" from the DI (Heb 1:1–4) to reemphasize the endpoint for messianic fulfillment for a kingdom in heaven, rather than a kingdom on earth, (5) reminder concerning the spatial and salvific elements of the audience "confession" (ὁμολογία) that they should hold fast to (Heb 4:14), which introduces an issue with the audience that is disclosed in unit E (Heb 5:10—6:20), (6) reiteration of the main proposition in the introductory subtopic D (Heb 1:3b) concerning "conversation" about the Son's "ability" (δύναμις Heb 1:3b) that is again verbalized with the verbal cognate "able" (δύναμαι Heb 4:15), and (7) from the same main introductory point, a ministerial correspondence between the "bring" (φέρω Heb 1:3b), "bring" (ἄγω Heb 1:6; 2:10), "assist" (βοηθέω Heb 2:18), and "assistance" (βοήθεια Heb 4:16) during judgment, which reintroduces forthcoming high priest ministerial conversation in units D–F concerning the φέρω and αγω- semantic field.

132. Guthrie, *Structure of Hebrews*, 117. Guthrie labels the transition material as having an "opening" and "closing" function in relation to the expositional material. This observation maintains its purpose for providing a link that contains both conclusion and summary for his previous three discourse unit conclusions and introduction for his three coming discourse unit conclusions. As summation, this FGT is added at

DUC within the main introductory subtopic D (Heb 1:3b) about the listeners' "conversation" (ῥῆμα) concerning the Son's "ability" (δύναμις Heb 1:3b; cf. Heb 4:15, δύναμαι [able]) to bring all things, as their "confession," (ὁμολογία Heb 3:1; 4:14). The Pastor continues ὁμολογία (*homologia*) in STr 2 (Heb 10:23), which has strong parallel correspondence.[133] The issue is conversation to confession cohesion. Does your ministry teaching equal Jesus's ministry?

The content of STr1 summarizes the Son of God's abilities. The Pastor's use of the negated adjectival pres. mid./pass. ptc. "who is not himself enabling/who not being able" (μὴ δυνάμενον) implies that the audience confesses a present ongoing ministerial activity, which they now receive when approaching the throne after death. The audience holds these abilities in a confession that affirms Jesus as a great high priest, "who having passed through the heavens" (διεληλυθότα τοὺς οὐρανούς Heb 4:14).[134] Just as in the antitype of the earthly Levitical ministry that necessitated high priest movement through sacred space, Jesus, in fulfillment as the type, did as well. The perf. act. ptc. "who having passed" (διεληλυθότα) suggests completed passage to God through the sacred space of the heavens with continued effects. Jesus made this journey in sympathy for the weakness of the people whose sins are exposed when tested before God while attempting his same journey to God after death. Jesus, by his entrance, is presently able to bring those who believe into the heavenly rest.

This summary declaration connects with introductory subtopics (Heb 1:1–4), about which the Pastor provides exposition in units A–C in S1 (Heb 1:5—4:13). This movement through sacred space into heavenly entrance also introduces Jesus's ability to stand before God as a high priest in intercession for salvation. The Pastor is not just concerned about who Jesus is as the Son but also where he went and what he is doing there. Jesus sympathizes with the weakness of people due to their sin before God by making it possible for believers to enter heaven by his own

---

this point to mentally govern the understanding of the audience.

133. Nauck, "Zum Aufbau des Hebräerbriefs," 201–3; Guthrie, *Structure of Hebrews*, 18.

134. The first-century CE conception of God's creation includes a topography of plural heavens in a gradation of sacred space. Cf. Kohler, "Heaven," 298. Kaufmann states, "The conception of a plurality of heavens was evidently familiar to the ancient Hebrews (see Deut. 10:14; 1 Kgs 18:15; Ps. 148:4; comp. Ḥag. 12a); while rabbinic and Apocryphal literature speaks of seven or of ten heavens." Other OT references for plural heavens include 1 Kgs 8:27; 2 Chr 2:5–6; 6:18; Neh 9:6.

completely similar experience when tested in judgment after death, even when he himself had no sin (Heb 4:15).

The Pastor introduces the term "approach" (προσέρχομαι Heb 4:16) in summation of this expected similar experience.[135] His use of the hortatory pres. subjunctive "let us approach" (προσερχώμεθα) carries aspectual weight in this context for ongoing action that is not completed or perfective. As just summarized, listeners should expect to stand before Jesus as high priest after death at their judgment before entering into heavenly rest. As emphasized in unit C, by meeting God's contingency requirement of faith in the Son's ability, they should approach with confidence to the throne of grace, so that they may receive mercy and find grace "for a suitable assistance" (Heb 4:16).[136]

The noun "assistance" (βοήθεια) links as a cognate in the same semantic field with the verb "to help" (βοηθῆσαι Heb 2:18) in UC B. As the great high priest, Jesus at the throne assists believers when they approach after death for judgment. This concept further delineates his main introductory subtopic D (Heb 1:3b) that the Son brings all things by the conversation of his ability.

---

135. Scholarly analysis of "approach" (προσέρχομαι) in Hebrews often limits to local syntactical conclusions and uses in other OT and ST literature; e.g., Moore, "'Heaven's Revolving Door?," 199–207. Moore links "approach" in Hebrews with either "conversion" (Heb 12:18-24) or "worship" (Heb 4:14-16) until an eventual horizontal "entrance" into a later renewed "cosmos" (207). Moore's statement, "there is no suggestion of a transition on the community's part into that heavenly space" (200) is more a reflection of his syntactically limited methodology and his presuppositions for cosmic-*field* constricted theology than the overall FGT above the syntactical level that governs the meaning of the text. The language in Hebrews easily supports the assertion that the community expected a spatial transition into heaven at death just like Jesus did. The Pastor first suggests this transition by the subtopic from the introduction main point (Heb 1:3b) and tracks the proposition throughout the discourse through each UC. The term "approach" summarizes the spatial language in S1 (Heb 1:5—4:13) that continues in forthcoming exposition through S2 (Heb 5:1—10:18) and then applies to the current situation of the audience in unit S3 (Heb 10:26-13:30).

136. Collins, "Throne in the Heavens," 43–58. Collins notes, "The notion of the ascent of the visionary appears in Judaism in close proximity to the notion of heavenly afterlife" (47). He documents STL embracing this connection with enthronement of the righteous that is also found in the NT.

Dynamic Conclusion of Transition 1 in the Lens of Hebrews 9:27–28

The transition summary and introduction contain high correspondence with the unit F MCS (Heb 9:27–28) by reaffirming his exposition in S1 concerning death, judgment, intercession, and salvation in heaven. The Pastor's described journey "through the heavens" on "approach" "to the throne" after death for judgment has topographical cohesion with an *aiōn-field* background. The audience's "weakness" arises when they stand before God after death at judgment due to the problem of sin, for which Jesus as Christ has offered himself to bear the sins of many. As the Christ, in the function of a high priest, Jesus, the Son of God, appears to those waiting for him. He will assist those who have placed faith in his ability to bring all things to God for salvation.

HEBREWS 5:1—10:18: SECTION 2 INTRODUCTION

Section 2 Structural Map: Take Care to Properly Teach about the Son's High Priest Ministry as God has Spoken

Figures 14 and 16 show the structure that governs S2 (Heb 5:1—10:18). S2 provides further exposition for the propositions in the DI (Heb 1:1–4). It structurally supplies two exposition units (D, F) with a digression for listener exhortation (E) within the first unit. S2 continues the Pastor's main DI thematic subtopics C and C´ (Heb 1:3a, c) in unit E (Heb 5:10—6:20) that concerns the Son of God's offering for sins, and thematic subtopic D (Heb 1:3b) in unit D (Heb 5:1-10; 7:1–28) that centers on the audience "conversation" (ῥῆμα) about the Son's ministerial ability, by which the Son brings to God all things into heaven and God's presence. STr2 (Heb 10:19-25) follows S2 for further summary introduction and conclusions that functions to turn the audience toward his chiasmic exhortation through S3 (Heb 10:26—13:21).

HEBREWS 7:25-28: ANALYSIS OF DISCOURSE UNIT CONCLUSION D1-2

Unit D1-2 Structural Map (5:1-10; 7:1-28): Jesus Ministers as God and High Priest after the Order of Melchizedek, Which is Greater Than the Levitical Priesthood Ministry

The Pastor provides signals for a shift to next cycle of FGT.[137] His audience would recognize a threshold shift by several literary signals.[138] Figure 14 maps the new unit D discourse. This unit contains six FGT, with two as topical UI, three FGT for support, and a UC, that emphasize the DI subtopics C and C´.

Figure 16 demonstrates the discourse chiastic structure and the relation of unit D (Heb 5:1-10; 7:1-28) with unit D1´ (Heb 11:1-16) and unit D2´ (Heb 11:17-40). These units contain exposition concerning the subtopic of the Son of God's intercession as a high priest in the eternal/perpetual-*places*. Unit D provides biblical warrant for the high priest ministry of the Son as the Christ and God. In application to the audience, units D1´ and D2´ support the necessity of a faith reception of Jesus's ministry for purification of personal sins and entrance into the substance-reality of the eternal/perpetual-*places* with Jesus.

Unit Introduction (5:1-10, 7:1-3): God Calls Every High Priest

The Pastor's high priest motif tracks through the message from the DI subtopic C (Heb 1:3a) and C´ (Heb 1:3c) in the subtopic path that concerns God's personal intercession for sins. Jesus, as the Christ, as God,

---

137. Kurianal, *Jesus Our High Priest*. Kurianal successfully uses the "paragraph" (FGT) level of discourse analysis to successfully argue that Heb 5:1—7:28 is an embedded discourse unit. He views Heb 5:11—6:18 as parenthetical parenesis that is structurally unrelated but important to the argument. In the next section, unit E functions as a coherent embedded discourse inserted within unit D.

138. These signals include (1) the particle "for" (γὰρ Heb 5:1) to indicate the reasoning for assertions summarized to this point, (2) the verbal shift from first person back to third person away from the subtopic "we" in reference to himself and his audience, (3) the return to expositional genre to signal completion of his exhortation unit and transition, and (4) a cognate shift of focus from the activity of the believer's inheritance of heavenly rest and ministerial accountability at judgment to exposition on the subtopic of high priest that was introduced at the UC of unit B (Heb 2:17) and twice in STr1 (Heb 4:14-15).

and who is the radiance of glory and representation of his substance-reality, made a purification of sins in priestly actions.

The Pastor begins his introductory FGT of unit D by reminding his audience about the present ministerial and intercessional function of a high priest.[139] A high priest is enabled to deal gently, with those unknowing and misguided about their actions before God, by offering gifts and sacrifices on behalf of the sins of the people and himself.

The Pastor next emphasizes the priesthood significance. In matters before God, a priest is called by God like Aaron. He then introduces a complementary contrast, stating, "so also the Christ" (Οὕτως καὶ ὁ Χριστὸς Heb 5:5). His support for a link to a christological priesthood deploys again the two OT texts used for bookends (Heb 1:5, 13) in his OT textual support of unit A.[140] These OT texts provide correspondence between the ministerial function of the Christ as a high priest to bring

---

139. Cf. Perrin, "Origins," 51–64. Against a post-Easter novel concept, Perrin asserts that Jesus's eternal priesthood rests on the well-established exegetical grounds of Pss 2 and 110. The sacrificial priesthood, by the promised Christ for entrance into heaven, temporally projects back to Genesis from the beginning of God's revelation concerning removal of the judgment of sin to the burnt offerings and priestly function of family heads. Contra Horton, *Melchizedek Tradition*, 153–60; Leschert, *Hermeneutical Foundations of Hebrews*, 202–3. Horton and Leschert assert the Pastor chose Melchizedek because he is the first priest mentioned in the Torah. The fact of first mention may be true but there is no evidence concerning the thinking of the Pastor as motivated by it. The heavenly force of Pss 2 and 110 link with Gen 3:22, 24. For general understanding surrounding the first-century CE discussion that Hebrews addresses, see Ribbens, *Levitical Sacrifice*. Ribbens primarily addresses the first-century CE issues regarding the efficacy between the earthly Levitical sacrifices and the heavenly ministry of Christ. He attempts to outline the first-century CE Levitical theology that the Pastor interacts to better delineate the contrast between what understanding both the earthly first covenant and heavenly second covenant sacrifice do for people. Cf. Torrance, *Royal Priesthood*, 15–22. Torrance develops the priestly terminology surrounding the argument in Hebrews as the foundation for ordained ministry as symbolic of the ministry of Jesus for the church in heaven; cf. Lookadoo, *High Priest in the Temple*, 74–77. Lookadoo contrasts the distinct roles emphasized concerning the role of Jesus as the high priest in relation to Yom Kippur between Hebrews and Ignatius in *Philadelphians*. He concludes the different emphasis is not incompatible. Both portray Jesus's priesthood as better than the Levitical priesthood. Hebrews contains more details about the effects of Jesus ministry upon the audience, whereas Ignatius focuses without Hebrews's details on how Jesus is the only high priest who entered the holy of holies.

140. DeSilva, "Invention and Argumentative Function," 300. The Pastor links the two OT texts by the Jewish interpretational method of *gezera shawa*. David deSilva perceives, "Psalm 2:7 is reintroduced here (see Hebrews 1:5) as a supporting proof, linking the 'you' addressed in the more familiar text (Jesus as the Son of Ps 2:7) with the 'you' of the more novel text (Jesus as the promised 'priest after the order of Melchizedek' of Ps 110:4)."

believers into heaven.[141] He then adds historical testimony about Jesus's fulfillment of these evidential OT texts.

The first OT text once again employs Ps 2:7 LXX/MT. The Psalm reminds his listeners concerning the judgment by God in heaven upon those who reject the way of the Messiah when God installs his king as his Son.[142] Yet those who do homage and take refuge in God's Messiah and Son will not perish "from the righteous way" (ἐξ ὁδοῦ δικαίας Ps 2:12 LXX [דרך ("way," Ps 2:12 BHS)]; Heb 3:10; 9:8; 10:20; cf. John 14:6) when they are judged.

The Pastor's second OT text reintroduces Ps 110:4 MT (109:4 LXX), which links the enthronement of the Lord with his priesthood ministry after the order of Melchizedek.[143] The Psalm forecasts a ruler from Zion amid Yahweh's enemies. This ruler in the day of his ability will offer his people to Yahweh in the splendors of the holy place.[144] This fulfills by Jesus bringing people as a free will offering to God at his enthronement (cf. Heb 2:10-13). God made an oath, in which he would not change his mind, that the Lord as a youth of the morning dew "from a womb" (ἐκ γαστρὸς Ps 109:3 LXX) is brought forth, which foretells of God's own fleshly incarnation. Concerning the purpose for this begotten Son, the

141. DeSilva, "Invention and Argumentative Function," 295-323. In discussion concerning the function of the priestly argument in Hebrews, DeSilva traces the priestly discourse throughout the argumentation of Hebrews for the conceptual goal "to perfect/complete" (τελειῶσαι Heb 2:10). He observes, "The word group is also used repeatedly in Hebrews to express transfer to the divine, permanent realm, a use that also belongs to priestly discourse since that realm is conceived, inter alia, as a heavenly sanctuary in Hebrews (8:1-2; 9:11-12, 23-24). Jesus is 'perfected' as he is brought before God in the heavenly Holy of Holies, a move for which his suffering and death . . . was the necessary prerequisite. . . . The author establishes a relationship between the 'perfecting' of Jesus and the incorporation of the 'many sons and daughters' into their heavenly destination, hinting here at something he will make explicit in Hebrews 12:1-11, namely that the many, like the One, will enter glory through suffering. The language of perfection and its particular link to entering the heavenly sanctuary (which is the believers' destination as much as it was Jesus'; Hebrews 6:19-20) thus contribute to the normalizing of the experience of hostility and suffering and thus the major paranetic [sic] purpose of the sermon" (298).

142. See previous discussion unit A UPt1 (1:5-6).

143. Kurianal, *Jesus Our High Priest*, 199-219.

144. The MT reads, "Your people are a free will offering in the day of your ability in the splendors of the holy place" (עמך נדבת ביום חילך בהדרי קדש Ps 110:3 BHS). Greek translation in the LXX states, "With your rule in the day of your abilities in the splendor of the holy-*places*" (μετὰ σοῦ ἡ ἀρχὴ ἐν ἡμέρᾳ τῆς δυνάμεώς σου ἐν ταῖς λαμπρότησιν τῶν ἁγίων Ps 109:4 LXX). The psalm prophetically foretells that the enthroned priestly ministry of the Lord involves bringing his people before Yahweh in the holy-*places* as a free-will offering.

Hebrew text reads, "You are a priest for the eternal/perpetual-*places*" (אתה כהן לעולם Ps 110:4 BHS). The LXX Greek translation reads, "You are a high priest into the eternal/perpetual-*places* according to the order of Melchizedek" (Ps 109:4 LXX).[145] The Pastor underscores that the promised enthroned Lord serves as a priest to his people as they approach the eternal/perpetual-*places* of God's dwelling. This OT textual selection by the Pastor counters the dominant kingly view of most messianic paradigms of the first century CE that persists throughout church history.

Apart from another scant reference in Gen 14:18 and Ps 104, little is known about the priesthood in which Melchizedek served. In the ST period and the high speculation about Melchizedek, his OT historical reference and part in Abraham's life likely serve as a literary antitype of God's speech about the promised high priest. He is used as part of God's speaking in the past that the Pastor contrasts with the Son (Heb 1:1).

The Pastor next adds support by historical testimony about the Son's fulfillment and experience regarding these stressed OT texts. As God in flesh, Jesus's passionate requests "before the one being able to save him from death" (Heb 5:7) were heard due to his obedience and reverence

---

145. The Pastor deploys the term 7 times (Heb 1:8; 5:6; 6:20; 7:17, 21, 24, 28). The idiom appears 309 times in the LXX with both spatial and temporal force; e.g., in God's assessment of Adam's sin in relation to the tree of life, the Greek LXX translation states, "And now he perhaps might stretch out the hand and take of the tree of life and eat and he will live in the eternal/perpetual-*places*" (καὶ νῦν μήποτε ἐκτείνῃ τὴν χεῖρα καὶ λάβῃ τοῦ ξύλου τῆς ζωῆς καὶ φάγῃ καὶ ζήσεται εἰς τὸν αἰῶνα Gen 3:22 LXX). The Hebrew MT has the conjunction "otherwise" (פֶּן) with the imperfect "stretch forth" (יִשְׁלַח Gen 3:22 BHS). Cf. *CHAL*, "פֶּן," 293. Holladay states, "W. impf., prevention of an otherwise predictable event." No negation by God is implied in his observation, but only a predictable outcome from Adam and Eve eating of the tree of life, which would allow living in the eternal/perpetual-*places*. By this reference to possible activity of Adam and Eve after their sin, the statement reveals God's recognition that access to eternal/perpetual-*place* life was now contingent upon the possible event of people taking and eating from the tree of life (cf. Rev 2:7; 22:14). With balance of the spatial and temporal forces of the idiom within a background of plural heavens in a gradation of holiness, the statement falls in line as an affirmative gospel promise with Gen 3:15, for God's personal provision of his final location of salvation in the eternal/perpetual-*places*. By eating of the tree of life that God provides himself, Adam and Eve contingently would live in the eternal/perpetual-*places*, rather than negation/prevention by God to remove *all* access to the tree of life. God's personal provision of access into the eternal/perpetual-*places* by the tree of life metaphorically represents "the way" (τὴν ὁδὸν Gen 3:24 LXX) that God himself would provide into heaven (cf. Heb 9:8; John 14:6). The way to God into heaven receives angelic protection and assistance like the cherubim over the mercy seat of the holy of holies in the tabernacle, rather than "the way" as a return to Edenic-like conditions, which typologically portrayed heavenly access through Christ (cf. Rev 2:7; 22:2).

Atonement and the Logic of Resurrection in Hebrews 9:27-28

during his own suffering.[146] The Pastor then states, "And after being finished, he became to all the people presently obeying him a source of eternal/perpetual-*place* salvation" (Heb 5:9). In a few sentences, the Pastor combines the finishing experience of Jesus's own salvation through the suffering of death to the presence of God in heaven, with the anticipated experience of believers receiving salvation in heaven through Jesus's ministry as a high priest after the order of Melchizedek.[147] The present location of Jesus's present priestly ministry is not on earth but in heaven for those who have obeyed him.

So, what does this required obedience look like to receive Jesus's intercession for salvation at judgment? The Pastor's use of "obedience" (ὑπακοή Heb 5:8) and "to obey" (ὑπακούω Heb 5:9) concerning both Jesus and his brethren link in a path from unit C with the referents of "faith" (πίστις Heb 4:2) and "to believe" (πιστευω Heb 4:3).[148] Just as "dis-

---

146. Bertolet, "Obedience of Sonship." Cf. Bertolet, "Hebrews 5:7," 9. Bertolet rightly concludes, "Hebrews sees Jesus as the David Messiah who, like the Davidic figure in the Psalter, trusts his Father into and through his death ordeal. This righteous servant's trust rewarded by exaltation." Exaltation is part of the events of Jesus's death ordeal at the transition from a death sequence of events to a rising sequence of events. Exaltation occurs before both his fleshly resurrection, as proof of the unseen events of entrance to God, and later ascension to continue his intercessional ministry already begun when rising from the dead. (cf. John 2:18-22; Acts 17:31).

147. Cf. Nelson, "He Offered Himself," 253-54. Nelson rightly perceives the Heb 5:7-10 hymn as Phil 2:6-11: obedience that involves first a downward then an upward movement, whereby "Christ thus partakes in the same sequence of 'first death and then judgment' common to all humanity. But, for him, this sequence is transformed by Jesus's 'having been offered' (*prospherō*, the sacrificial act in its entirety) to bear sins (LXX Isa 53:12) and then returning a second time to save (9:27-28)."

148. Due to failure to track the linked referent paths of the FGT, it is not uncommon for scholars, by proof texting in theological missteps, to view Jesus's intercessional priestly work only in relation to the believer's encouraged pursuit of moral and legal "obedience" before death, i.e., perseverance. The more sacramental the theology in requirements to meet a level of obedience for salvation by ordinances and other religious rights, the more pressure occurs for an elevated theology of a continual earthly intercession by Jesus before death, rather than at death; e.g., both H. Windisch and E. Käsemann agree upon Jesus's appointment as priest at his ascension but hold that his actual intercession for people occurs on earth in relation to Heb 5:7-9 by his priestly offering of himself as the personal sacrifice that is described in Heb 10:5-14; 13:11-12. Cf. Windisch, *Der Hebräerbrief*, 42; Windisch applies the OT quotation to Ps 2:7 LXX to Jesus's obedience in earthly life as a Son and Ps 109:4 LXX to Jesus's exaltation. Cf. Käsemann, *Wandering People of God*, 219-23. Käsemann, following Rafael Gyllenburg, divides Jesus's saving work into two trains of thought. One is a heavenly atonement for sin and the other is the earthly conquest of death. Cf. deSilva, "Invention and Argumentative Function," 305n40. However, the Pastor establishes a path of referents regarding Jesus's intercession that stress the only "obedience" requirement for Jesus's

obedience" (ἀπείθεια Heb 4:6, 11) and "unbelief" (ἀπιστία Heb 3:12, 19) example a failure to enter God's heavenly rest, so obedience fulfills by faith acceptance to follow the path of Jesus as priest and shepherd to lead believers into heaven during their similar sufferings of death and consequent judgment. The statement, about God "having heard" (εἰσακουσθεὶς) Jesus's appeals by faith (cf. Heb 2:13), joins the path of subtopic themes that track from the DI concerning Jesus's judgment, such as "to atone" (ἱλάσκεσθαι Heb 2:17) in unit B that requires a possible verdict by God's judgment. The subtopic paths of death, judgment, intercession, and salvation into heaven permeate every chosen word from the DI in a highly coherent message.

After a digression in unit E, which is separately addressed after completion of this unit, the Pastor returns to complete his unit D high priest motif with a midrash concerning Ps 104:4 MT (103:4 LXX).[149] He reintroduces the high priest subtopic in Heb 7:1–3 with brief exegetical history and asserts that "had been similarly made like the Son of God, to remain a priest for a continuous *ministry*" (Heb 7:3).[150]

---

intercessional salvation experience after death into God's heavenly rest is faith in God's provision of salvation in Jesus as Christ in his suffering of death, and in offering himself for the sins of the people. He does not mention the later church issues that surrounded obedience to church ordinances or other religions rites for participation in a later kingdom on earth but only faith in Jesus's ability to bring others with him to God and his kingdom in the heavens.

149. Kurianal, *Jesus Our High Priest*, 85–160.

150. The syntax of the prepositional phrase with the arthrous adjective διηνεκής (*diēnekēs*) suggests that it modifies the thematic context. The phrase εἰς τὸ διηνεκές is a restatement of εἰς τὸν αἰῶνα ("into the eternal/perpetual-*places*" Heb 1:8; 5:6; 6:20) that is found in the midrash text of Ps 103:4 LXX. Both terms contain some degree of spatial force since there is no measure or existence of time without activity in space. In the later prepositional phrase, the spatial weight in translation is exaggerated to force a balance in the spatial-temporal consideration of the context. However, the emphasis of the former adjective is not so much upon the place, as it is the continual nature of the priestly ministry of Jesus in heaven. Cf. Neyrey, "'Without Beginning of Days or End of Life'" (Heb 7:3), 439–55. Neyrey successfully asserts that the descriptions in Heb 7:3 correspond with Greek Hellenistic philosophical requirements of a deity, to support that Jesus, rather than Melchizedek, is God the Son. The Pastor's purpose for this deification of Jesus is more than just who Jesus is as God but what he does as God incarnate in human flesh now in heaven in a priestly ministry for sinful people in line with intercessory promises first revealed in Gen 3:15 that continue through the biblical testaments.

Unit Point 1 (7:4–10): A Melchizedekian Priesthood is Greater than the Levitical Priesthood

After introduction of Melchizedek, UPt1 relates that the Melchizedekian priesthood is greater than the Levitical priesthood. His evidence for this claim logically encompasses how Levi was still technically in the loins of his father Abraham when Abraham paid tithes to the king/priest Melchizedek. The traditional transfer of a blessing from the greater to the lesser meant that the Melchizedekian priesthood was greater than the Levitical priesthood of Aaron that would follow from the linage of Abraham. This observation also implies that the Melchizedekian priesthood linage ministered as a symbolic antitype of heavenly matters long before the priesthood established by the law of Moses. The latter priesthood did not replace or supersede the promised typology of the former that had ministered God's revelation for over 2,500 years before Moses.

Unit Point 2 (7:11–19): Jesus Is a Melchizedekian, High Priest Successor

The Pastor begins UPt2 with a summation by "perfection, completion" (τελείωσις Heb 7:11) that tracks from the DI subtopic of salvation in heaven. His previous syntactical use, until now, has been verbal forms of the τελ– (*tel*) word group (Heb 2:10; 3:14; 5:9, 14; 6:1, 8, 11; 7:3). This verbal activity concerning completion now summarizes in a verbal noun as a concept related to an expectation to experience salvation at judgment. Salvation is a process of living events, that expects above all else, to finish at death in heaven in the presence of God.

A key term with some spatial weight concerning the ministry of "another priest" is "to arise" (ἀνίστασθαι Heb 7:11, 15). In ministry, the priest stands between the people and God as a mediator with the expectation that those delivered from judgment will arise to God in salvation. This rising *from* the dead occurs in the same way that Jesus arose *from* the dead to the presence of God in heaven. Also, three days later Jesus arose in fleshly resurrection as proof of his having been allowed in the heavenly presence of God at judgment (cf. John 2:18–22; Acts 17:31). Jesus exceptionally arose three days later in the flesh, which is unnecessary for believers.[151]

---

151. The term "to arise" (ἀνίστημι) links with the dat. phrase "from the dead" (ἐκ

Also, the concept of perfection/completion in relation to the law of Moses forms an *inclusio* (cf. Heb 7:11, 19). Hebrews 7:19 reconfirms, as already hinted by Heb 6:19–20 in the digression of unit E, that the Aaronic priesthood of the law could not bring perfection. DeSilva states, "'Perfection' is here understood as 'consecration' and as the process by which the people would be brought to their final destiny, the very presence of God."[152] The Pastor closes the FGT by stating that the law on

τῶν νεκρῶν) twelve times in the NT (Mark 9:9, 10; 12:25; Luke 16:31; 24:46; John 20:8; Acts 10:41; 13:34; 17:3; 17:31; Eph 5:14; 1 Thess 4:16) and in other syntactical forms thirty times. In the NT text, the dat. phrase also twice links with "to raise up" (ἐγείρω 1 Cor 15:20; 1 Thes 1:10). The NT links "from the dead" (ἐκ τῶν νεκρῶν) and "the third day" (τῇ τρίτῃ ἡμέρᾳ) only once. Jesus statement, "In this way, it has been written, that the Christ for the purpose to suffer and to arise from the dead the third day" (ὅτι οὕτως γέγραπται παθεῖν τὸν χριστὸν καὶ ἀναστῆναι ἐκ νεκρῶν τῇ τρίτῃ ἡμέρᾳ Luke 24:46), can be problematic for the concept that rising to God in heaven begins as a sequence of events at death, rather than a later singular fleshly resurrection similar to the visible pattern of Jesus's proof of rising to God (cf. John 2:18–22; Acts 17:31). In Luke 22:46, the syntactic construction of the dat. phrase "the third day" (τῇ τρίτῃ ἡμέρᾳ) has several semantic options in context. It is most translated ("the third day") as a dat. of direct object (NASB, HCSB, KJV) or dat. of time (ESV, NET, NRSV, VUL) with minor difference in meaning. It functions as an adverbial modifier of the adverbial infinitive of purpose ἀναστῆναι ("to arise") in modification of Christ. The dat. phrase "the third day" (τῇ τρίτῃ ἡμέρᾳ) appears eleven times in the NT (Matt 16:21; 17:23; 20:19; Luke 9:22; 18:33; 24:7; 24:46; Acts 10:40; 1 Cor 15:4). In every case it emphasizes the third day after death of the visible proof of Jesus fleshly resurrection. On the third day the disciples received visible proof of Jesus rising from the dead by seeing him in his flesh after being fleshly dead. In Luke 22:46, Jesus was speaking in his fleshly presence on the third day after his death with the disciples on the Emmaus Road, but that does not negate spiritual bodily rising to God before the third day that could not visibly be seen in this cosmos (cf. 1 Cor 2:9). Luke also records that Jesus foretold his presence in heaven would be several days prior to fleshly resurrection (Luke 23:43). Also, God's judgment after death and salvation of Jesus into heaven must proceed Jesus's fleshly resurrection in rising from the dead as the proper pattern argued in Hebrews for those who follow in salvation after death and judgment for all people (Heb 9:27–28). Further, consider that at the martyrdom of Stephen, as he gazed into heaven, he saw Jesus standing at the right hand of God, rather than sitting. Luke's use of the cognate "stand" (ἵστημι) may infer Jesus's expected ministry before God for Stephen at his death.

The timing of modern cosmic-*field* controlled views reverses this order and has Jesus's visible proof of rising from the dead before God's salvation judgment, which in these views, occurs at his later ascension into heaven to offer himself. Further, the Son of God goes missing from death to resurrection without continuous living after fleshly death as the living God. The problematic three-day speculated interruption of the Son of God's "indestructible/endless life" (Heb 7:16) speaks volumes against temporal delays away from rising to God on the day of death. The reason there is no biblical discussion of an intermediate state, is that the philosophical contemplation does not exist, except in the logical missteps of flattened paradigms of cosmic limited concepts for people.

152. DeSilva, "Invention and Argumentative Function," 303.

the one hand perfects/completes nothing, "on the other hand is an introduction of a better hope by which we presently draw near to God" (Heb 7:19). His choice of "draw near, come near, approach" (ἐγγίζομεν) joins a cache of αγω– (*agō*) words and the summary term "to approach" (προσέρχομαι) that describe the believers experience of salvation into the heavenly realm.

Further, since the law requires that only Levitical priests are eligible for ministry and Jesus descends from the tribe of Judah, the Pastor argues in this FGT for the necessity of a change of law to the superior Melchizedekian priesthood. He contends that Jesus's qualification corresponds with the symbolism of Melchizedek as "according to ability of an endless life" (Heb 7:16).[153] Jesus's life continues endlessly at his judgment after fleshly death when God raises him up into the eternal/perpetual-*places*.

Unit Point 3 (7:20–24): Jesus's Melchizedekian Priesthood is Continual and Perpetual

UPt3 conveys another reason for the superiority of the Melchizedekian priesthood as God's "oath" (ὁρκωμοσία Heb 7:20, 21, 28) that guarantees his intercession for sin. The Aaronic ministry did not have this oath from God (Heb 7:21). As OT support for this claim, he quotes again Ps 110:4. Because ὁ κύριος ("LORD," Ps 109:1 LXX; יהוה ["Yahweh," Ps 110:1 BHS]) has sworn concerning David's κύριος ("Lord," Ps 109:1 LXX; אָדוֹן ["Lord," Ps 110:1 BHS]) and will not change his mind, the promised Lord will advantageously locate his priestly ministry "into the eternal/perpetual-*places*" (εἰς τὸν αἰῶνα). The Levitical ministry of the law on earth is merely symbolic and only introduces those receiving that ministry to their need of God's own intercession as high priest when they approach the holy-*places*. The OT often expresses faith in God's character and ability to faithfully intercede for sin at judgment before him for those who put their trust in him (Num 23:19; 1 Sam 15:29; Pss 6; 9; 18; 23; 56).

The advantageous, heavenly position places Jesus between God and people when they approach him for judgment after death. Jesus is properly positioned by God to be at the right place at the right time

---

153. Cf. Kibbe, "God-Man's Indestructible Life." Kibbe discusses the theological tension in the Son of God as both dying in an offering of atonement and at the same time endless in living. Like others in similar paradigms, his options remain inconclusive and end with only remaining unanswered questions due to a flattened anthropology that disregards continued living after death, except only in a fleshly resurrection.

when one needs his priestly ministry.¹⁵⁴ In this position Jesus guarantees a "better covenant" (κρείττονος διαθήκης Heb 7:22) relationship between God and people than previously possible.¹⁵⁵ The point concludes with a comparison to the temporary nature of the many individual Levitical priests, stating, "On the other hand because he continues to abide in the eternal/perpetual-*places* he presently has a permanent priesthood" (Heb 7:24). The predication of the pres. tense emphasizes the present ongoing nature of his ministry providing continual access at the time of the Pastor's message, not that Jesus never leaves his throne.¹⁵⁶

Unit D Conclusion (Heb 7:25–28): As High Priest, Jesus Is Able to Save Those Approaching God

The Pastor accumulates the necessary literary indicators to establish a threshold for a shift to an anticipated UC.¹⁵⁷ The UC centers on a pres-

---

154. The omission of spatial consideration in open heavens misses this critical point about Jesus's intercessory location and fails to explain why Jesus does not personally carry out his priestly ministry now on earth. If salvation entails only a legal change in status of people before a distant inaccessible God, then why must Jesus abide in heaven? Surely, God can hear the Son's present continual intercession on earth. The reason for the particular location is that judgment for sin takes place in heaven after death.

155. The Pastor expands his description of this new, mediated, covenant relationship in unit F by comparison to the older model of God's previous covenant relationship as depicted by the tabernacle in the covenant at Sinai. In unit F UPt1 (Heb 8:7–13), the antitype of the first covenant outline is introduced by Moses (Heb 8:5–6) in comparison to the true heavenly realities they represent for people upon entrance into the eternal/perpetual-*places*. The first and new covenant concept are not new to Moses and Israel as represented in the law, but further describe the transition realities in heaven from the first covenant that existed from the beginning foundation of the world to the new covenant inaugurated by the death of Christ.

156. The pres. tense of the adverbial inf. phrase "because he continues to abide" (διὰ τὸ μένειν) carries casual weight. Cf. *BNTS*, 264. The pres. tense infers progression and repetition of the priestly activity where Jesus abides, which is in the eternal/perpetual-*places* of heaven. *BNTS*, 221–24. Also, the pres. tense "presently has" (ἔχει) adds further force to a present, continuous, repetitive, ministry in heaven for each believer who approaches at death.

157. These markers include (1) use of the particle "therefore also" (ὅθεν with καὶ), which suggests a change in the unit D FGT cycle to a new FGT with a soon expected conclusion by the audience, (2) the correlative adjective "such as" (τοιοῦτος Heb 7:26) in modification of "high priest" (ἀρχιερεύς), which signals that the current FGT content summarizes the previous unit context up to this point, (3) close repetitive use of the particle "therefore" (γὰρ Heb 7:26, 27, 28), which lists a set of conclusions based upon previous support, (4) repeat of the concept summary referent "approach" (προσέρχομαι Heb 7:25) from the first discourse transition (Heb 4:16), which summarizes the

ently available salvation by Jesus's high priest ministry as the Christ.[158] Jesus intercedes before God to save those who are presently approaching. Since always living in heaven, when the day comes to approach God, Jesus will faithfully perform his ministry to sinners who come to God through him.

The unit D UC contains three rapid explanatory "for" (γὰρ) statements to concisely clarify the intended meaning of the unit D UC content. The first clarification is that Jesus is a suitable high priest for their needs. Along with his character of holiness, innocence, and ceremonial cleanliness, he was separated from sinners and exalted above the heavens. Jesus was able to enter through the heavens where no person had gone before, due to having no personal sin (cf. Heb 4:15). After God's judgment on the cross just before approach, Jesus was able to instantly enter the holy of holies into the eternal/perpetual-*places* in fulfillment of God's oath in Psalm 109:4 LXX (Ps 110:4 MT).

The Pastor's second clarification summarizes another difference between Jesus and the Levitical priesthood. Jesus does not have the daily need to offer up sacrifices, both for himself and the people, as the Levitical priests did. He only sacrificed himself for sins once when he offered up himself to God in the suffering of death. Jesus's advantage is that his onetime offering for atonement has been completed for the sins of the people; an offering does not need to be repeated as did the Levitical annual and daily sacrifices.[159]

---

contextual timing and location of Jesus's intercession in relation to believers, (5) application of the Son's ability of the main DI subtopic (Heb 1:3b) with "to save" (σῴζειν Heb 7:25) in the subtopic path of salvation for people that was the same salvation experience of Jesus (Heb 5:7), (6) use of the cognate phrase "for all completeness, quite complete" (εἰς τὸ παντελὲς) for "into the eternal/perpetual-*places*" (εἰς τὸν αἰῶνα Heb 7:28), used already eight times to designate the location and duration of salvation, (7) introduction of a new term "to intercede" (ἐντυγχάνειν) as an adverbial inf. of purpose to summarize, on the subtopic path from the DI, the function of the ministry of high priest in intercession for sins of the people when standing for judgment before God, and (8) use of the term "always living" (πάντοτε ζῶν Heb 7:25) to summarize Jesus endless purpose life (Heb 7:16) that has never had exceptions or interruptions. These markers together would likely meet the threshold by the audience for a shift to the awaited conclusion to the Pastor's unit of discourse about Jesus's high priest ministry for believers, at judgment after death, before entering near to God in the eternal/perpetual-*places*.

158. The pres. mid./pass. tense pct. "those who are presently approaching" (προσερχομένους) and pres. act. ptc. phrase "always living" (πάντοτε ζῶν) suggest that Jesus's ministry is available at the time the Pastor speaks.

159. In the language of this clarification, the Pastor implies that Jesus's advantage over the Levitical priesthood is that his atonement offering for sin is complete and perpetually effective for those who come to God through him. However, the atonement

In his third clarification, the Pastor again distinguishes Jesus's priesthood with the weakness of the Levitical priesthood. Concerning Jesus's advantage, he states, "But the word of the oath, of which after the law, he having been completed the Son into the eternal/perpetual-*places*" (Heb 7:28). The logos, who is God, in fulfillment of his own oath, is now the expected Son in heaven and acts according to his spoken promises.

The unit D UC continues the unit A–C subtopics concerning death, judgment, intercession, and salvation into heaven that were introduced in the DI subtopics. Death continues in the discussion of Jesus's offering up of himself (Heb 7:27). Intercession at judgment persists in the Pastor's purpose statement for Jesus's ministry as always living to make intercession (Heb 7:25). The goal of salvation on approach to God into heaven maintains by verbal descriptions concerning Jesus's ability and purpose for always living as both exalted above the heavens and into the eternal/perpetual-*places*.

In his explanatory midrash concerning Ps 109:4 LXX (Ps 110:4 MT), the Pastor reveals how God, according to his oath, strategically places himself as Son and high priest in the eternal/perpetual-*places* to save those who come through faith in his ministry for atonement of sin. With his midrash completed, the Pastor next begins his main discourse unit F along the same thematic course. However, analysis of the unit E digression that he inserted in the UI of unit D has not yet been provided. He expresses concerns about the audience ministry in their conversation about Jesus's fulfillment as the Word of Christ.

Dynamic Unit Conclusions A–D in Lens of Hebrews 9:27–28

As the audience mentally assimilates the DUC A–D and STr1, definite coherent paths track though the DI subtopics of death, judgment, intercession, and salvation into heaven toward the anticipated message MCS of Heb 9:27–28. It becomes clear from unit A that Jesus's ministry is better than the angelic ministry, by providing an inheritance of salvation. Having the same personal experience of salvation into the eternal/perpetual-*places*, from unit B the audience would surmise that Jesus can in mercy meet their need. When tested before God in judgment against

---

activity of Jesus's suffering in atonement for sins should not be viewed as a perpetual atonement of self-offering.

ATONEMENT AND THE LOGIC OF RESURRECTION IN HEBREWS 9:27–28

his enemies of sin and the devil that enslave them in the temporary cosmos, Jesus is a faithful high priest in things pertaining to God.

Concerning faithfulness in ministry, in unit C, the listeners would understand that in Jesus's house there is ministerial accountability for their conversation concerning their confession of God's speech. They also know that their ministries self-fulfill, either as examples of unbelief in Jesus's onetime atonement, or as examples of faith in his spoken word. Those who live life in a pattern of faith demonstrate the joy of entrance into the heavenly rest that Israel failed to symbolically demonstrate when not believing God could keep his promise about the land. Jesus, as the Word of God, will judge all, as he looks upon them in the day of their death, to discern every matter of the heart.

STr1 (Heb 4:13–16) summarizes units A–C by linking the audience confession, in Jesus as the Son of God who has passed through the heavens, in the same personal testing of God's judgment since being found without sin. He also again mentions Jesus's high priest ministry that can sympathize with grace when seeing the people's weaknesses and need as they are tested, so that they can approach God's throne with confidence.

Unit E completes before transition back to unit D. Unit E would be considered in the minds of the audience as they create mental summations thus far. It confronts the audience about their teaching impossible things and readdresses their need to be taught again the milk of the beginning sayings of God and the beginning word of Christ. The Pastor suggests that the audience have been lazy listeners of God's speech, which influences them to perceive the meat of Christ's priesthood in heaven as hard to explain. The message is not hard to understand; they are hard of hearing.

In summary, the unit D UC explains the meat of the word of Christ that builds upon the milk of the beginning of the word of Christ. It concerns the superior priesthood of Jesus in heaven over that from Aaron on earth. Jesus's position in heaven, as the Son of God, both fulfills God's oath of Ps 109:4 LXX (Ps 110:4 MT) and strategically allows Jesus to make priestly intercession when believers approach to God after death into the eternal/perpetual-*places*. His onetime offering is sufficient; he will always be there when their moment of judgment comes. Unit E makes this expectation certain.

All exposition concerning the Son and believers encompasses upward movement through unseen heavenly space and displays concern about rising to God in heaven. The Pastor has only lightly stressed the earthly ministry of Jesus, and only then so in qualification for his entrance to God in heaven. There is no mention or hint thus far of a downward return for the audience to consider in his rhetoric. Before coming back to these DUC again, the unit E discourse and its conclusion first need examination. The unit E digression, during the introduction of unit D, provides the issue behind the Pastor's stress upon ministerial accountability when judged before God.

HEBREWS 6:11-20: ANALYSIS OF DISCOURSE UNIT CONCLUSION E

Unit E Structural Map (5:11—6:20): The Audience Must Have True Teaching about God's Speech Concerning Christ's Offering and Priesthood to Receive Reward at Judgment

The Pastor provides signals that he shifts to the next cycle of FGT, which function as topic introduction, support, and conclusion. His audience would recognize a threshold shift for a digression by multiple literary signals.[160] Unit E contains four FGT, one functioning as a topic introduction about DI subtopics, two FGT for support of each subtopic proposition, and a conclusion. Figures 12 and 14 map the unit E discourse. These FGT emphasize the DI subtopic C and C′ (Heb 1:3a, c) and the beginning teaching about the word and sayings of God and Christ in his offering for sin. Following the completion of unit E, the FGT further develops the theme of unit C about the audience accountability for their "conversation" ($ῥῆμα$) in their ministerial confession about the Son's ministerial ability, by which the Son brings all things to God into heaven and God's presence (Heb 1:3b; cf. Rom 10:17).

Figure 16 demonstrates the discourse chiastic structure and the parallel relationship of unit E (Heb 5:11–6:20) with unit E′ (Heb 10:26–39). Both units include an exposition concerning the subtopic

---

160. These signals include (1) the idiom "concerning which things" ($Περὶ οὗ$ Heb 5:11), (2) a verbal shift from third person to first and second person with readdress of the subtopic "we" and "you" in reference to himself and his audience, (3) introduction of a new subtopic concerning the audience issue of making the teaching about the priesthood of Melchizedek hard to explain due to the audience laziness in hearing God's speech, (4) new commentary about the audience need to be taught the beginning basics of the sayings of God, (5) new commentary about the audience lack of training to discern good and evil regarding teaching about the word of righteousness, since in need of milk and not strong meat.

of accountability and rewards for ministry that accompany salvation at judgment in heaven. Unit E describes the beginning word of the Christ. Listeners should conclude that both Christ and his people rise from the dead at eternal/perpetual-*place* judgment, enter heaven, and cannot fall away. In personal application to the audience, unit E´ encourages continued perseverance in the knowledge of the truth that the listeners had in the beginning, to be pleasing to God at their judgment and to receive reward for good ministerial teaching.

Scholars propose multiple meanings for the unit E discourse.[161] Some in the audience for Hebrews, regarding their teaching, majored on an incomplete version of the priesthood of Christ that focused only on Jesus as a sacrificial offering according to the law. They did not hear in God's speech the present ministry of Jesus's intercession at an individual's death and judgment as a Melchizedekian priest.

Unit Introduction (5:11–14): The Audience Teaching Situation Concerns an Impossible Logos Teaching about God's Speech that Needs Remediation about the Beginning Sayings of God

The Pastor's unit D UI thoughts concerning the high priest ministry of Melchizedek prompts a digression that alters the placement of unit E within unit D. He transitions into unit E during his unit D introduction about Jesus's Melchizedekian priesthood, declaring, "Concerning which great things to us, the word, also so as to say, hard to explain things, because you have become lazy to hear" (Heb 5:11). The Pastor asserts that the audience only hears part of God's speech and considers his speech hard to explain due to their laziness in listening. The remainder of unit D, which concerns Jesus's present priesthood, describes the missing "word/message of righteous" (λόγου δικαιοσύνης Heb 5:13) that they do not hear, dismiss as difficult, and repeat incorrectly in conversation. The Pastor breaks off his unit D exposition to also include an issue about "the

---

161. Bateman, *Four Views*, 74–83; 108–18; 149–54; 176–87; 272–80; 352–63. Cf. Toussaint, "Eschatology of the Warning Passages," 67–80. Toussaint takes a position that is *contra* to either a loss of salvation by the audience or the audience never having salvation. Based upon the context of the subtopics that track from the DI, the placement within the unit D concerning the Pastor's exposition about the Melchizedekian priesthood, and the Pastor's description of the issue about his listener's teaching in relation to the word, this project builds upon the loss of rewards view as explained by David Allen. Allen, *Hebrews*, 332–405.

beginning basics of God's sayings" (Heb 5:12). He confronts his audience on these two issues.

The Pastor illuminates the audience situation with a complementary contrast between two layers of God's speech. The first is metaphorically classified as "milk" (γάλακτος) and second "solid food" (στερεᾶς τροφῆς), which respectively pair with "infant" (νήπιος) and "mature" (τέλειος Heb 5:13–14). He emphasizes the obvious, where the infant can only tolerate milk; solid food is for the mature.

In the next FGT, the Pastor links the milk/infant metaphoric categories to the beginning word of Christ and the audience need for remediation and correction in their testimonial conversation about the milk of God's speech. His UC following highlights ministerial accountability and reward regarding their personal ministerial conveyance about the milk of the beginning word of Christ. This leaves his meat/mature metaphoric connection for his return to the interrupted unit D expositional theme that generated his unit E digression about this need of his listeners.

Analysis prior to unit E observed that the split unit D (Heb 5:1–10; 7:1–28) concerns Jesus's ministry after the order of a Melchizedekian priesthood in heaven. It builds upon "the beginning word of Christ" (Heb 6:1) contained in God's OT earthly covenant speech that the Pastor insets into the UI of unit D.[162] In unit E (Heb 5:11–6:20), the Pastor announces his return to the metaphoric meat of unit D for those mature, stating, "Therefore, having left the beginning word of Christ, we should be moved to maturity" (Heb 6:1).[163] However, he does not immediately transition back to the unit D high priest ministry theme. Ironically, while stating, "not presently laying down again a foundation" (Heb 6:1) regarding the milk of the beginning word of Christ, he continues with the milk metaphor of unit E with extended exposition in completion of the UPt1

---

162. The Pastor's word choice of "beginning" (ἀρχή Heb 1:10; 2:3; 3:14; 5:12; 6:1) in modification of his subtopic theme surrounding God's speech of the "word" (λόγος Heb 5:12; 6:1) likely infers some weight for a connection to the initial speech of God concerning Christ that tracks through the OT to fulfillment by Jesus (cf. Gen 3:15; 2 Sam 7:14; Ps 110:4). While mainly applying to (basic, elementary, principles of teaching, doctrine, instructions, and message) as translated in the NASB, ESV, NET, HCSB, KJV, NRSV, these options lose the link to the beginning origins that the Pastor intends to convey in support for both the continuity and significance of God's speech as the Word in redemptive speech-action from the beginning.

163. The term "maturity" (τελειότης Heb 6:1) is a cognate in the semantic domain of his subtopical theme surrounding "perfection" (τελείωσις) by entrance into heaven. This play on Greek words connects mature ministerial conversation of God's speech with the endpoint of perfection/completion by entrance in heaven.

FGT, addition of the UPt2 FGT, and the UC, before returning to the mature expositional teaching of unit D.[164]

The Pastor will complete in unit D the meat metaphor about God's speech that is heard by those mature, after the closing FGT UC of unit E, by which his audience "on account of the skill has been training the faculty for the purpose of continually discerning both good and evil" (Heb 5:14). The Pastor maintains that the skill of listening to God's speech concerning the Jesus's Melchizedekian priesthood mentally enables his ministers to consistently better discern whether their testimonial conversation is good or evil. The implication is that attentive hearing of God's speech (cf. Heb 2:1–4) concerning Jesus's offering and intercessory priesthood becomes their discerning test for good and evil testimonial conversations about God's speech by his ministers.[165]

All "good" (καλός Heb 5:14) teaching builds upon the foundation of the word of Christ found in unit D and unit E that concern the elements of Jesus's christological offering and his present ministry of priestly intercession. The Pastor considers any other ministerial teaching deviance as "evil" (κακός Heb 5:14). His next UPt2 FGT reveals that such evil teaching has no value for believers at judgment.[166] His audience ought to be

---

164. By the distant head and tail linkage with the subtopic of unit E, the Pastor keeps unit E in the minds of his listeners while he completes his supportive exposition and conclusion of unit D. This device supports the continual connection of these two units about milk/meat and infant/mature before moving to the main themes of unit F.

165. Jesus's offering as the beginning word of Christ and his subsequent intercessory priesthood in heaven are foundational for all other ministerial teaching (cf. 1 Cor 3:11). Improper hearing of God's speech in these two concepts distorts the testimonial conversation about God's word/speech that is built upon this foundation and renders alternative content as evil (cf. Gal 1:6–10). All derived concepts of biblical and systematic theology should be governed by the exposition milk and meat contained in unit D and unit E, rather than arise from proof texting apart from that which is good. This may provide solemn warning to those theological paradigms that add required sacramental "dead works" to the offering of Christ for salvation from sin or that omit Jesus's expected heavenly intercession at death for believers, in distant eschatological options that focus only on varied conjectures about earthly kingdoms and endpoints. Such alternative distortions in earthly focus have been rejected by God from the beginning as evidenced in Cain's first misstep (cf. Gen 4:3–7; 1 John 3:12; Jude 11). Unit D1′ SbPt1b (Heb 11:4) further explores the rejection of Cain's offering as proper symbolism about the Christ.

166. Cf. Matt 10:15; 1 Cor 1:8; 3:10–15; 4:5; 1 Thess 1:7–10; 2 Tim 1:12, 18; 4:8. In later discussion of STr2 (Heb 10:19–25), the context of Hebrews addresses that places the timing of "the day" (Heb 7:25) as a shortened reference to the day of Jesus's appearing after death at judgment, rather than some distant future eschatological point. The NT exception about the gathering of living believers remaining at Jesus's second coming is not directly addressed by the Pastor in this message but finds some indirect

teachers that lead others beyond the beginning of the word of Christ to the meat he introduces in unit D about the present priestly intercession of Jesus. However, he charges that they need someone again to teach them (Heb 5:12) the milk, rather than strong meat. His UPt1 FGT explains to them, again, the milk of the teaching about Christ's offering.

Unit Point 1 (6:1–8): The Pastor Reminds his Audience Concerning the Beginning Teaching about the Word of Christ and Illustrates Impossible Teaching, where Christ and Others Fall Away after Entering Heaven

They were to avoid evil teaching, i.e., where Jesus and other people would after entering heaven experience a "falling away" (παραπεσόντας Heb 6:6).[167] The sermon encourages rejection of a temptation, which would result in their improper instruction of others in the speech of God's "word" (λόγος Heb 6:1), that renders their teaching "conversation" (ῥῆμα Heb 6:5) "unable . . . to again renew people into repentance" (Ἀδύνατον . . . πάλιν ἀνακαινίζειν εἰς μετάνοιαν Heb 6:4–6).[168] The listeners' enticement describes a possible errant theological "confession" (ὁμολογία Heb 4:14), which involves a practice in ministry, that portrays a message "continually crucifying again to themselves the Son of God and disgracing

---

traction in the promise of not being left out in Heb 11:39–40. The day of the Lord references for earthly events are recurring antitypes for the unseen judgment of God upon those who reject his offering for sin and intercessory ministry as the Christ. These recurring earthly judgments self-fulfill, just as with Israel in the wilderness, to symbolically teach the world about eternal/perpetual-*place* unseen truth.

167. The failed maturity as teachers is commonly accepted. Daniel Trier writes, "Hebrews measured spiritual formation by capacity to receive and pass on biblical teaching." Treier, "Speech Acts," 344. Issue surrounding teaching explores in chapter 4 unit E (Heb 5:11—6:18) analysis. The conjectured conversation that symbolized falling away likely concerns former teaching antitypes of the first covenant that are linked to events after judgment and approach to God in heaven after death. Jesus's first covenant fulfillment as Christ makes some features of the former OT antitypes errant. There is no mention of the verbal noun "rebellion, apostasy" (ἀποστασία cf. 2 Thess 2:3).

168. This builds upon exegesis of David Allen. See Allen, *Hebrews*, 344–93. Sandwiched in the middle of this lengthy sentence, the Pastor makes grammatical use of the five interval participles. Beyond Allen's assertion, it is probable that all five phrases consistently function as substantive participles in the sentence, and these should interpret as descriptive of the current expectation of the recipient's applied teaching experientially in relation to the basic requirements of the Christ listed in Heb 6:1–2. This interpretation is supported by the compilation of the discourse unit conclusions later discussed in chapter 4.

him in shame" (Heb 6:6; cf. 10:18). The sacrificial repetition feature of their teaching error had no ability to renew listeners in repentance once judged after death by the powerful exposing "Word of God" (λόγος τοῦ θεοῦ Heb 4:12–13) and effectually could not properly portray the path of the harvest God seeks (Heb 6:7–8), in salvation at judgment (Heb 9:27–28; 10:26–39; fig. 3). The Pastor warns for the believers to maintain their previous foundation of repentance "from dead works" (ἀπὸ νεκρῶν ἔργων Heb 6:1; 9:14) in a ministerial teaching service congruent with an effective confession of God's specific speech concerning the basic requirements of the teaching of the Christ, which those who enter to God's presence must follow.[169]

The UPt1 supports UI assertions about his listener's laziness in hearing God's speech regarding their teaching. The Pastor begins by challenging them, stating "Let us lead to completeness [heaven]" (Heb 6:1; cf. Heb 1:3c). He then provides both exposition concerning the beginning word of God's speech and illustration regarding an impossible teaching under contention, where Christ and people leave heaven after entrance.

In his audience confrontation, the Pastor first reminds his listeners about the foundational milk of the beginning word of Christ. In the first century CE, the term "Christ, anointed one" (Χριστός) carries heavy messianic weight in two main promised features. One is that of a divine priest, who is both the offering and intercessor for sin. The second is that of a divine king, who is a son of David and serves his people in their needs. After signaling his teaching topic of Christ, the Pastor outlines the fundamental, christological activity symbolized by the OT sacrifices. The sacrificial background clarifies the first-century CE overarching issue

169. As an early equivalent issue, Paul's letter to the Galatians mirrors the Pastor's situation, where some believers had, due to external pressures of false teachers, turned to a message of merit-based salvation by keeping the law. Paul labels this alternative message "a different gospel" (ἕτερον εὐαγγέλιον) and then states, "Which is not a different one" (ὃ οὐκ ἔστιν ἄλλο Gal 1:6–7), demonstrating its ineffectiveness. These express similar negative demands as the Pastor upon those who proclaim a message other than what God has spoken. *Contra*, Lewicki, *"Weist nicht ab den Sprechenden!"* Lewicki follows the mainstream modern thought that the listeners temptation was rejecting Jesus as the Christ, rather than possible corruption of their teaching about the Christ. (cf. Matt 24:5). As compelling evidence against Lewicki and others, Heb 6:6 does not center the issue on the *who* of Jesus as "the Son of God" (τὸν υἱὸν τοῦ θεοῦ) but on the *what* in their ministerial practice of their faith concerning Jesus, which would depict ἀνασταυροῦντας repetitive crucifixion and openly shamed Jesus's ability as the Son of God in a onetime offering as the Christ. The temptation to return to repetitive sacrifices of the Sinai law that the Pastor argues as obsolete by Jesus achieved changes in the holy-*places* has strong cohesion with his rhetoric.

over whether Jesus is the hope in fulfillment of the Christ pictured by four thousand years of sacrifices. The foundation elements listed for the teaching about the Christ (Heb 6:1) correspond to OT requirements for a sacrifice, in a sacrificial substitutionary death, to be pleasing to God at judgment in atonement for sin.

Historically, this warning about teaching interprets through the issues of later church debate. David Allen summarizes the later interpretations about the instructional problem as "(1) post-baptismal sins, (2) sins requiring extreme discipline, (3) high-handed apostasy, and (4) the unpardonable sin or the 'sin unto death.'"[170] These later church proposals neglect the possible authorial/audience context concerning foundational teaching of Christ in sacrificial prerequisites to be pleasing to God that both the audience inherited and followed as fulfilled in Jesus (Heb 1:1–4). After listing these prerequisites, the Pastor states, "And this we will do, if God should permit" (Heb 6:3). He expects both himself and his audience to experience these elements of the beginning word of Christ as represented in sacrificial acceptance by God.

The Pastor reveals that for God's acceptance, a sacrifice must affirm (1) repentance from dead works, (2) faith in God, (3) ceremonial cleanness, (4) laying on of hands, (5) rising of the dead, and (6) eternal/perpetual-*place* judgment. If properly executed, the substitutionary sacrificial act typologically testifies, for each of these listed elements, about an expected, heavenly, experiential reality by both the Christ and for those who follow him.[171] These steps consist of (1) repentance of dead works by complete reliance upon God's provision for heavenly entrance (Heb 5:5–10; cf. Luke 23:46),[172] (2) faith in God's acceptance of

---

170. Allen, *Hebrews*, 354. The collapse among recent scholarship on Hebrews of an early church anti-Semitic purgation against first-century CE sacrificial practice and law invites a possible parenetic solution within early Jewish-Christian sacrificial teaching concerning the Christ.

171. The reach of the exhortation to follow Jesus expands well beyond this life to include a similar experience with Jesus in presently rising *of* the dead and eternal/perpetual-*place* judgment (Heb 6:3; cf. John 21:19).

172. Cf. Heb 9:14 analyzed in unit F. The phrase "dead works" (νεκρῶν ἔργων) likely refers in context to seeking salvation through personal obedience to the law in the sacrificial system without recognition of the unseen realities it symbolizes. For the Pastor, obedience is belief in God's provision of salvation that only requires an acceptance without human works. Dead works in principle can also generally include any other inaccurate teaching concerning God's speech that adds criteria beyond the reception of God's personally provided salvation. This would include moral or ceremonial choices that only symbolize both one's recognition of need before God due to sin, and by a turn to the patterns of heavenly living, a demonstration of the better way of Christ.

the Christ sacrifice for atonement for sin (Heb 2:3; 11:6, 13–16), and (3) God's cleansing for holy living (Heb 1:9; 11:7), (a) which is enabled by a onetime transfer to Jesus's bearing of sin (Heb 7:27; 9:28), (b) before rising *of* death as pleasing to God (Heb 11:19, 35; 13:20),[173] (c) in a personal eternal/perpetual-*place* judgment (Heb 9:27–28).

The Pastor's illustration to follow, in Heb 6:4–6, lists five aorist substantival participles that demonstrate an "impossible" (ἀδύνατος Heb 6:4) completion of the way of salvation that was being taught about these OT to NT sacrificial Christ requirements.[174] His exemplification portrays a path that is not acceptable teaching about a believer's intercession by Jesus at eternal judgment and subsequent entrance to God into the eternal/perpetual-*places*. These foundational elements and adjectival participles correspond to a path as follows:

1. repentance from dead works = those once being enlightened
2. faith in God = and those tasting themselves of the heavenly gift
3. teaching of ceremonial washings = those partaking of being born of a spirit of a holy place
4. laying on of hands = and those tasting a good conversation of God

---

Repentance does not infer living sinless, which is not yet possible while believers are in the flesh (cf. 1 John 1:8–10). The law was effective for its purpose, which is to reveal the foundational elements of the Christ; it was unable to enter people into the completion of the presence of God in heaven (Luke 10:1). Likewise, religious observance of worship symbolizes faith in the acts of God that bring heavenly entrance.

173. In Heb 11:35, the Pastor testifies, "Women received their dead because of resurrection" (Ἔλαβον γυναῖκες ἐξ ἀναστάσεως τοὺς νεκροὺς αὐτῶν Heb 11:35). In context of proof for resurrection from the dead into heaven, the aorist act. indic. likely references a reunion of women with their dead loved ones in heaven that has already taken place at their own resurrection in death. This context is developed in the analysis of unit D2′ of this chapter.

174. The use of the particle τὲ . . . καί ("x, x, and," Heb 6:4–6) signals connection of members in a series. See BDAG, "τέ," 993. This series of five aorist participles is inserted in the sentence "for it is impossible . . . to renew again into repentance, while continually crucifying and disgracing to themselves the Son of God" (Ἀδύνατον γὰρ . . . πάλιν ἀνακαινίζειν εἰς μετάνοιαν, ἀνασταυροῦντας ἑαυτοῖς τὸν υἱὸν τοῦ θεοῦ καὶ παραδειγματίζοντας Heb 6:1, 6). The implication is that it is impossible to start the salvation series events over again at the first member of repentance of dead works once a person has risen to the dead in approach of the eternal/perpetual-*places*. People cannot come back for a do-over and the moment a person stands before God is too late (cf. Matt 7:21–23).

5. rising of the dead = those abilities of the presently coming eternal/perpetual-*place*[175]

6. eternal/perpetual-*place* judgment ≠ those falling away, i.e., do not stay in heaven[176]

In a contextual link with the Christ sacrificial motif, the considered path demonstrates the impossibility for the last conjectured step. This step proposes an incorrect teaching about substitutionary sacrifice of the Christ that suggests either a need for repetitive sacrifices of Christ or later opportunity after death by an option for renewed repentance once God's eternal judgment has taken place. Once inside of heaven, one does not leave to start over again at their initial step of repentance. If left outside of heaven at judgment, there is no way or new sacrifice to get inside. The conjecture is impossible. Any teaching that implies a repetitive entrance is impossible because one cannot fall away from heaven once tasting the abilities of God's intercession to lead them in rising to God at judgment (cf. Heb 10:39). God cannot lie and entrance by faith in Christ is based upon the stability of his oath and the believer's personal acceptance of God's provision of salvation. Consequent, a teaching act that symbolically crucifies Christ again, even in a sacrificial demonstration of his fulfilled promise, puts him to open shame (Heb 6:6).

In a summary clarification of his UPt1 FGT that is signaled by an explanatory γὰρ "because," the Pastor illustrates with an analogy about values of two classes of watered vegetation produced by the earth, the

---

175. The pres. act. ptc. phrase "the presently/subsequently coming eternal/perpetual-*place*" (μέλλοντος αἰῶνος Heb 6:4) reflects the Pastor's context about the present availability of entrance into heaven by Jesus's ministry. This occurs by Jesus's ability and presence at the throne to intercede for his believers in his offering upon their approach after death.

176. There is no internal support in Hebrews for treating the last aorist ptc. "ones falling away" (παραπεσόντας Heb 6:6) conditional as many translators surmise (e.g., NASB, ESV, NET, KJV, NRSV, HCSB, and LEB translates adjectively in a consistent list). In context, the speculated situation implies teaching about activity that might occur after entrance into the eternal/perpetual-*places*. There is no evidence for this possibility as an earthly option, while living, for either the believers or unbelievers in the audience before entrance into God's presence. The Pastor links, by the particle idiom τὲ ... καί ("x, x, and"), the acc. verbal adjective of the aorist act. pct. "ones falling away" (παραπεσόντας Heb 6:6) with the acc. adjective "impossible" (Ἀδύνατον Heb 6:1). He uses the impossibility of falling away from heaven as support mainly against teaching that involves repetitive sacrifices of the law. The context has nothing to do with either not being saved or a risk of losing salvation for lack of personal perseverance as found in many paradigms.

different values of God concerning good and evil teaching (Heb 6:7–8). Good teaching, like the useful watered vegetation produced by the earth, receives a blessing from God, whereas the vegetation from the earth of thorns and thistles is worthless and near cursed. His phrase "of which the end is the result for burning" (ἧς τὸ τέλος εἰς καῦσιν Heb 6:8) links with the cognate path concerning the "end" (τέλους) at judgment for the believer (Heb 3:14). The person engaged in evil teaching fails, as a partaker in ministry with Jesus, in faithfulness concerning their conversation about God's speech (Heb 3:14). The path of falling away does not illustrate concerns about a falling away from salvation by apostasy but an unproductive teaching that receives loss of reward at eternal judgment when rising to God after death in the pattern of sacrifices that are pleasing to God (Heb 9:14; 10:1–2, 22, 39; 13:18). With such impossible teaching of falling away from heaven after entrance, God does not get the harvest he desires by proper faith in Christ's onetime offering. After introducing the meat of Christ's intercessory ministry, having defined the valuable milk of the beginning word of Christ, and addressing the impossibility of a teaching that reflects a falling away after entrance into heaven, the Pastor continues more support with his next point for accountability for ministerial teaching.

Unit Point 2 (6:9–10): At Judgment, God has Reward for Good Productive Teaching about His Speech Concerning Christ but Loss for Evil Unproductive Teaching

UPt2 reinforces God's conditional blessings upon those engaged in good teaching. His conjunction δὲ (*de*) signals contrast with the evil teaching concerning falling away from heaven. He states, "But we have been persuaded, brethren, those better things also presently ourselves possessing, which is part of salvation, if also in this manner we continually speak" (Heb 6:9). His language continues his concerns about his audience's ministerial accountability and God's rewards upon those who remain faithful in their speech about the beginning word of Christ. This topic adds weight for the gen. sing. as a partitive gen. "which is part of salvation" (σωτηρίας Heb 6:9). The reward by God for faithfulness in teaching is an expected part of salvation-inheritance in Christ at judgment.

The Pastor's support about this contingent reward, as part of salvation, is backed by God's character. God is not unjust to forget their work and love for his name. He specifically, points out their teaching ministry stating, "having served to the holy *ones* and presently serving" (διακονήσαντες τοῖς ἁγίοις καὶ διακονοῦντες Heb 6:10). His listeners serving in good teaching to the holy ones the foundational milk and meat of Christ will bring reward from God at judgment. Based upon the prospect of these contingent rewards for good teaching at the inheritance of salvation, the Pastor next completes his thoughts about the content of ministerial accountability with a summary of the expectation of hope contained in good teaching and a challenge to his listeners.

Unit E Conclusion (6:11–20): Imitate, in Teaching, Abraham and Those Who Follow the Promise inside the Veil about God's Speech Concerning Christ

The Pastor accumulates the necessary literary indicators to reach a threshold by the audience for a shift to an anticipated UC.[177] This unit E conclusion centers, in imitation of Abraham and those who entered heaven before them, on the proper content of their own ministerial teaching for which they will give account.

With an epistolary we, the Pastor shares with his audience his desire for their ministerial message "to demonstrate" (ἐπιδεῖξαι Heb 6:17) to the heirs of the promises the unchangeableness of God's purpose that is guaranteed with an oath. Their conversation should be directed "to the certainty of hope until the end" (Heb 6:11). His initial summary statements join his past thematic subtopics in unit C regarding the expected

---

177. These markers include (1) use of the contrastive conjunction "but" (δὲ Heb 6:11) to continue contrast with the impossible teaching, (2) The pres. act. indic. "we desire" (ἐπιθυμοῦμεν Heb 6:11), which announces the Pastor's desires for his audience in the teaching situation, (3) the choice of "to yourselves demonstrate" (ἐνδείκνυσθαι) as an expression for the desired result for content with good ministerial teaching, which is "to the certainty of hope until the end" (πρὸς τὴν πληροφορίαν τῆς ἐλπίδος ἄχρι τέλους Heb 6:11), (4) the repeat of the thematic subtopics "end" (τέλος Heb 6:11; cf. Heb 3:14; 6:8), and "hope" (ἐλπίδος Heb 6:11, 18, 19; cf. Heb 3:6), and "promise" (επαγγελια Heb 6:12; cf. Heb 4:1) regarding the destiny of believers at judgment into heaven, (5) the repeat of the thematic subtopic "lazy" (νωθρός Heb 6:12); cf. Heb 5:11) regarding the undesired situation and teaching of the believers, (6) the repeat of "faith" (πίστις Heb 6:12); cf. Heb 6:1) regarding belief in God's perseverance in his salvation provision, and (7) introduction of a new referent "patience" (μακροθυμίας Heb 6:12) regarding the audience wait for inheritance at their entrance into heaven. The continued contrast, personal desire, repeated subtopic themes, and reminder about God's provision by faith should easily meet a threshold for a UC by an audience.

heavenly "rest," "end" (Heb 6:11; cf. Heb 3:14; 6:8), "hope" (Heb 6:11; cf. Heb 3:6), and "promise" (Heb 6:12; cf. Heb 4:1). The contextual path of his repeated referents suggests that their ministry should be certain about an inherited heavenly destiny in nearness to God to those with faith in God's salvation provision, rather than continued "laziness" (Heb 6:12; cf. Heb 5:11) in not listening carefully to God's speech, claiming the promises are hard to explain, and leaning to other impossible teaching.

The Pastor's main example, of whom his audience should become "imitators" (μιμηταὶ Heb 6:12), is Abraham. The Pastor finds support for Abraham after death receiving the promise for continued bodily living in heaven from the LXX textual promise in Gen 22:7, which declares, "For the purpose of continual blessing, I will bless you, and for the cause of continually increasing, I will increase you" (Gen 22:7 LXX).[178] In the first century CE, the common understanding in harmony to this promise of God views Abraham as bodily alive as a spirit in heaven, even as the Pastor states, "And so having persevered he received the promise" (Heb 6:15).[179] The Pastor is certain that Abraham now lives in heaven.

---

178. For the meaning of εἰ μήν as "certainly, surely" with weight with the indic. mood as toward the assumption that the statement is true, see BDAG, "εἰ μήν," 279. This Greek translation by use of the pres. act. pct. "continually blessing" (εὐλογῶν) and pres. act. pct. "continually increasing" (πληθύνων) implies certainty of a continual action without interruption. The LXX translators chose this syntax to express the *piel* intensive "to bless," (ברך Gen 22:17 BHS) and *hiphil* והרבה ("cause to be numerous," Gen 22:17 BHS). The *piel* stem is understood in the LXX as iterative or repetitive action. See Gesenius, *Gesenius' Hebrew Grammar*, 141. The Hebrew *hiphil* stem suggests causative or declarative action by God upon Abraham. Gesenius, *Gesenius' Hebrew Grammar*, 144–45. Gesenius provides optional semantic meanings, stating, "Hiph'il stems which express the obtaining or receiving of a concrete or abstract quality . . . the entering into a certain condition and, further, the being in the same . . . express action in some particular direction." The Pastor interprets this syntax as support that Abraham continued after death in blessing and increasing in heaven.

179. The Pastor omitting the "seed" of the promise in Gen 22:7 may be significant. His focus is certainty on Abraham's continued destiny and reception of the promise after his patient wait during earthly living. The aorist act. indic. "received" (ἐπέτυχεν) carries weight for promise of a completion, specifically, for Abraham. This involves more than just hope completed by the coming "seed" of the Christ in the promise but Abraham's own entrance into the presence of God, following with the entrance of Jesus as the Christ as forerunner. The contrast between "sands" of the earthly seashore and "stars" of heaven, regarding those blessed by the promise, may reflect heavenly transition from earth to heaven for those holding on in confession to Abraham's received promise.

Cf. Luke 16:22. Jesus only indirectly defends his statement that links the described destiny of Lazarus with Abraham. The Sadducees disagreed with bodily rising in spirit to God after death. Jesus's speech supports that bodily existence after fleshly death was

The Pastor further states that because of God's guarantee by an oath (Heb 6:17) that this promise for Abraham could never change. There could be no interruption or delay of God's promise, even after death, because God's purpose for this promise is unchangeable; it is impossible for God to lie (Heb 6:18; cf. Rom 8:38–39). The Pastor counters the impossible teaching that demonstrates falling away from heaven by Christ with the truth that it is impossible for God to lie; God does what he promises.

The Pastor also applies the promise that Abraham received both to himself and his audience, saying "the ones taking refuge should have strong encouragement to hold onto for hope set before themselves" (Heb 6:18 cf. Heb 4:14; 8:6). The subst. ptc. "the ones taking refuge" (οἱ καταφυγόντες) stresses again his already mentioned heavenly place of rest and protection from the dangers of sin before God in unit C (Heb 3:1–4:13).[180] The verbal infinitive "to hold fast" (κρατῆσαι) links back to

---

understood and accepted by those listening, including many of the religious teachers of the law other than the Sadducees. This conceptual understanding of Abraham, as living bodily in heaven after his death, agrees with descriptions in the LXX, NT, and STL using Hellenistic referent of "Hades" and Jewish referent of "Abraham's bosom." In both the NT and STL, the death of one blameless in righteousness pre-certifies a different spiritual body destiny than the unrighteous. In 1 En. 22:3–14, the author writes about "the spirits of the souls of the dead" (τὰ πνεύματα τῶν ψυχῶν τῶν νεκρῶν 1 En. 22:3 *OTGP*) and describes an explanation of heavenly separation based upon righteousness. In Tob 3:6, there is a possible anthropologic dualism where Tobit asks for "my spirit" (πνεῦμά μου Tob 3:6 *OTGP*) to be released "into the eternal/perpetual-*place*" (εἰς τὸν αἰώνιον τόπον Tob 3:6 *OTGP*) from his fleshly body (cf. John 14:2). Tobit's body will die and become dust (1 En. 3:6). There seems to be continuity of bodily consciousness after death in a temporary dwelling location of God called "Hades" (1 En. 3:8; 13:2; cf. Luke 16:19–31). It is a place of "darkness" away from the light of God himself in his holy of holies presence or the lights of the created cosmos, i.e., sun, moon, stars, fires, etc. (1 En. 3:10). It has degrees in comparative or superlative states of darkness inferred by "deepest Hades" (1 En. 3:19; cf. Luke 16:23). The wicked go "into eternal/perpetual-*place* darkness" (εἰς τὸ σκότος τοῦ αἰῶνος 1 En. 14:10 *OTGP*). This region for unrighteous death is theologically set more distant than the earth in relation to God's immediate presence of fellowship dwelling for the righteous. In Wisdom of Solomon, the author deals with post-Hades afterlife destinies as typically blessed in the presence of the Lord for the righteous and the wicked separated in sufferings away from God (Wis 3:1–13; 4:10; 4:14; etc.). Hades for the author is not on the earth (Wis 1:14), no one returns (Wis 2:1), and is powerless in the affairs of men (Wis 17:14).

180. Cf. Gordon, "Better Promises," 434–49. Gordon connects the verb καταφεύγω (*katapheugō*) with the cities of refuge (cf. Num 35:6–28) in the LXX OT against the nautical metaphor associated with the term "anchor" (ἄγκυραν Heb 6:19). When combined with the present tense movement of "for presently entering into the inside of the veil" (Heb 6:19), the Christian hope reaches right into the holy place of God. The Pastor may be using both the nautical metaphor and correspondence with the cities of refuge for added weight of the surety of the believer's hope in their confession of Jesus as their offering for sin and intercessor on arrival at judgment. By faith in the abilities Jesus's

the Pastor's STr1 (Heb 4:14–16) discourse transition summary about the audience "confession" (ὁμολογίας Heb 4:14). They confess that Jesus can bring all things to God by his ability to enter near God.[181] Also, just as Abraham has entered heaven, so also those who hold this confession can be strongly comforted by God's oath. Their soul has hope of continued living in heavenly access after death.

The Pastor finishes his unit D conclusion with a parenetic description of the "hope" (Heb 6:18) of Abraham and themselves that he emphasizes throughout this long UC. The length rhetorically reinforces and emphasizes his surety. He adds to his lengthening list of cognates, related words, and phrases about this guaranteed heavenly destiny, the adjectival participial phrase "even which is presently entering into the inside of the veil" (Heb 6:19).[182] This specifically locates the destiny of the heirs of salvation in the expanded holy space of God's immediate presence by the tearing of the veil, which opens at Jesus's entrance for others to follow.[183]

---

ministry, believers hope after death to enter a safe haven where they are anchored from the storm of God's judgment and enter into a city of refuge in heaven where they are protected from their sin.

181. See the audience confession that summarizes in STr1 (Heb 4:13–16).

182. The Pastor's spatial language of cognates, referents, and phrases involving the spatial heavenly destiny of the audience's salvation continues to grow. For a full listing, see spatial referents in appendix 2, table 2, "Words in Hebrews Linked with Creation."

183. Cf. Gane, "Re-Opening *Katapetasma*," 5–8. Gane argues that the language of Heb 6:19 by employing the modifier "inside" (ἐσώτερον) specifies the inner veil due to the ambiguity of the LXX translation of καταπέτασμα and scholarly views that the term metaphorically applied to the entire temple complex. Cf. Gurtner, "Καταπέτασμα," 105–11. Gurtner, in support of the observations by Roy Gane, provides evidence that the language Heb 6:19 can only refer to the inner veil; Gurtner, "LXX Syntax," 344–53. Gurtner shows that scholars cannot presume that variances in word choice employed by the LXX translators of veil language necessarily results in ambiguity regarding which curtain or veil was in view. He asserts that translators have consistently used καταπέτασμα as the default translation "inner veil" (פרכת).

Contra Rice, "Hebrews 6:19," 65–71; Rice, "With Which Veil?," 20–21. Rice observes how the Pastor dropped the specific language of the tabernacle topography of "the holy place" (τὸ ἅγιον, cf. Lev 16:2 LXX) that specifies the inner veil. He then concludes that the veil language of Heb 6:19 can only metaphorically reference the blessings of the Abrahamic covenant and options for tabernacle inauguration background, rather than the Day of Atonement. Cf. Young, "Where Jesus Has Gone," 165–73. Young provides pushback that the contentions of Rice cannot be sustained in reference to the texts. He argues for the Day of Atonement background for Jesus's entrance into the inside of the veil.

The positions of Gane, Gurtner, Rice, and Young operate within the Adventist presupposition that there is a "last judgment," which includes Christians and that Christians' lives are accessed prior to the second coming to earth. This concept was retained by early Adventist theologians, whose early education embraced endpoints with

His description of this hope as a "certain" (ἀσφαλῆ), "firm" (βέβαιος), and an "anchor" (ἄγκυρα Heb 6:19) links to the contested teaching illustrated in UPt1 about Jesus and others "falling away" (Heb 6:6) from heaven after entering, that errs from teaching the beginning of the word of Christ, where the dead rises for eternal/perpetual-*place* judgment (Heb 6:2). Souls of people who enter heaven after death, remain in heaven, by the unchangeable guarantee of an oath spoken by God (Heb 9:14; 10:39; 12:22–24).[184]

His readers conversation about heavenly entrance after death, in continued living like Abraham, should be certain, secure, and teach

---

closed-heavens. Common missteps include a last judgment concept for believers after death. However, it should be remembered that in the Heb 6:19–20 context, the Pastor argues both Jesus and Abraham are now in heaven as support in his rhetoric against the impossible teaching of falling away and for his audience' hope to enter into heaven at death. This common first-century CE understanding is problematic, if Abraham after fleshly death enters into the holy of holies of heaven before the forerunner of Heb 6:20 on the Day of Atonement (cf. John 1:18). One must not forget that since the inner veil of the tabernacle patterned temple tore asunder, many years after the death of Abraham at Jesus's death, the two areas of the holy place and holy of holies are now one common place, with Jesus at the right hand of God. At the time of the Pastor's writing, the inner veil no longer plays a part in separation of the holy-*places* of the heavens. Understanding the change in heavenly topography, the Pastor drops the specific OT veil meaning found in either inauguration or the Day of Atonement LXX texts because they no longer apply, and he revises the OT quotation for application to his listeners in line with the changed topography by Jesus's entrance.

184. *Contra* Cortez, "Anchor of the Soul." In a focus on Jesus's ascension after fleshly resurrection, Cortez omits discussion of continuous living, after either Jesus's death until fleshly resurrection, or the death of people until an unspecified future time when Jesus comes out of heaven at the completion of the Day of Atonement, which for Cortez is not finished yet (21–22). Instead, for the present-time benefits in Hebrews, he proposes a "theological redescription of time and space" (441). For Cortez, the Pastor only creates a "Scriptural World" (441) of the present speech of God in the Son about the hope in Jesus as the Anchor of the soul. However, the language in Hebrews has shown the Pastor's expectation is more than just for the soul's imaginative presence of God through contemplations about OT Scripture, as only speaking in the present. Just as Jesus is in heaven as their Anchor, so also those who believe in Jesus's ability to bring them into heaven should have hope to bodily enter heaven themselves after death at judgment.

Contra Moore, "Heaven's Revolving Door?," 14. Moore against Mackie's strong realized eschatology view presently on earth for the living, argues for a future eschatology view, in which it is only the hope that enters, i.e., Jesus, and application to community unjustified. Moore only evaluates the local syntax in grammatical-historical exegesis without following the FGT discourse subtopics that govern the meaning of who or what enters within the veil. In the view of perpetually realized eschatology, the souls of believers, who transform into eternal/perpetual-*place* spirits, follow Jesus into heaven after death at judgment, just like Jesus did.

that believers follow Jesus as "forerunner" (πρόδρομος Heb 6:20) due to his high priest ministry after the order of Melchizedek "into the eternal/perpetual-*places*" (εἰς τὸν αἰῶνα Heb 6:20).[185] The term forerunner strongly implies others follow Jesus to the place he abides; without such following by others, the Pastor's choice is nonsensical. The phrase "having himself become a high priest after the order of Melchizedek into the eternal/perpetual-*places*" (Heb 6:20) transitions the audience back to his incomplete unit D about the meat of the ministry of Jesus as the Christ.

Dynamic Unit Conclusions A–E in Lens of Hebrews 9:27–28

Unit E completes before unit D and merges within it. Now that the analysis of both units D–E is complete, the Pastor's intended audience mental summary of the exposition and exhortation to his rhetoric in DUC A–E that is heading on a well-defined summary path toward the MCS of Heb 9:27–28 can be integrated. Each unit adds concepts concerning the ministry of the Son that the audience should confess in their ministerial conversation with others. Following the path of the introductory subtopics of death, judgment, intercession, and salvation into heaven in the lens of God's speech introduced in the DI, the Pastor adds (1) in UC A, the complementary angelic ministry in assistance with the ministry of the Son for those about to presently inherit salvation, (2) in UC B, the ability of the Son to meet listener needs after death, just as he has already brought

---

185. Cf. Davidson, "Christ's Entry," 175–90. In an argument for OT veil background of tabernacle inauguration, Davidson follows William Shea, in his adaption of the chiastic structure of Vanhoye, with an attempt to assemble a chiastic structure connecting the veil in Heb 6:19–20 with the veil in Heb 10:19–20. His linked chiastic subtopics seem forced to the forefront of the textual divisions. Vanhoye and Guthrie support a close connection but do not press an independent chiastic structure between them. Vanhoye, *La structure littéraire*, 45, 228–29. Vanhoye finds Heb 6:19–20 as the final formula for the preamble and Heb 10:19–20 as the initial formula for the exhortation. Guthrie, *Structure of Hebrews*, 99–100. Guthrie joins hortatory blocks placing Heb 6:19–20 at the end of the first hortatory section and Heb 10:19–20 at the beginning of the final hortatory section. These veil subtopics are connected, however the link that connects them are their position in summary FGT of the overall chiasm that demonstrates in appendix 1, fig. 16. Hebrews 6:19–20 provides summary exposition in UC E and Heb 10:19–20 summarizes the unit conclusions A–F concerning the same event. The latter is a reworded summary of the former. Cf. Heike and Tobias, *Day of Atonement*; Davidson, "Inauguration or Day of Atonement?," 69–88. Since the specific location of the veil is the same in both the tabernacle inauguration by Moses and the typological imagery of the Day of Atonement, the choice of either background for Heb 6:19–20 is a moot point. The point is that Jesus has entered inside of the veil, and that his entrance made its function obsolete to the audience and those who believe.

brethren into heaven in freedom from the enslavement of the devil in the cosmos, and (3) in UC C, the matter of ministerial accountability for the audience about their conversation concerning their confession that he illustrates by the self-fulfilling example of Israel in relation to the expectation of heavenly rest for believers. In ST1, he summarizes DUC A–C as their reception of a great high priest, who has passed through the heavens, who is Jesus, the Son of God. He reminds them about Jesus's testing, in relation to their own anticipated testing at God's judgment upon their approach after death, that enables him to sympathize with their weaknesses and provide confidence to receive grace and help in time of need.

In S2 (Heb 5:1—10:18), the Pastor continues the DI subtopics, for which they have ministerial accountability at judgment, concerning their teaching both (4) in UC D, the meat of the priestly intercession of Jesus on approach at death for salvation, and (5) in UC E, the milk of the sayings of God and word of Christ in the priestly offering of the Christ that they follow by faith into heaven. His UI during unit D stirs a digression to unit E, which reviews again to his audience the milk, opposes a situation of milk intolerance with infantile colic due to laziness in hearing God's speech concerning teaching that violates the surety of heavenly entrance, and desires the demonstration of their confession as an unchangeable entrance by the purpose of God into heaven by imitating both Jesus and Abraham.

In the lens of Heb 9:27–28, the milk exposition in unit E corresponds with the statement in Heb 9:28 concerning "Christ, who being offered once for the purpose to bear sin of many people" (Heb 9:28). The meat exposition in unit D corresponds with "Christ . . . from a second *place* without sin, will be appearing for salvation to those eagerly themselves awaiting him" (Heb 9:28; italics mine). These two main concepts regarding the teaching of Christ prepare the audience for the final exposition of unit F and a deeper dive into the Pastor's support for the proper milk and meat of their confession concerning death, judgment, intercession, and salvation in heaven.

HEBREWS 9:27-28: ANALYSIS OF DISCOURSE UNIT CONCLUSION F MACRO SUMMARY

Unit F Structural Map (8:1—10:18): The Son Fulfilled the High Priest Offering of the Christ by His Death at His Judgment and Now Promptly Intercedes in Heaven at Death and Judgment on Behalf of Approaching Believers to Provide a New Covenant Ministry/Relationship into God's Presence in Heaven

The Pastor provides signals that he shifts to his next cycle of FGT, which function as topic introduction, support, climax, and conclusion. His audience would recognize a threshold shift by several literary signals.[186] Unit F offers twelve FGT. Figures 12 and 14 map the structure of the unit F discourse. It contains three FGT operating as subtopic introduction. The unit F three main topics include in UPt1 the Son's high priest ministry in the heavens within the promise of the new covenant, in UPt2 the Son's spatial elimination of the holy place of the heavenly and earthly tabernacle ministry, and in UPt3 the Son as mediator of a new covenant relationship in heaven itself of the holy of holies.

The exposition of these UI subtopics overlap the DI introductory subtopics, previous unit subtopics, and discourse transition subtopics. The FGT introductions of these three topics each have FGT points for support. Also, UPt2 functions as a pre-climax and UPt3 a climax UPt of the rhetoric. An embedded UC peaks as the MCS of units A–F before completion of the unit with several more FGT UPt to support it. A second discourse transition of STr2 (Heb 10:19–25) closes the S2 exposition (Heb 5:1—10:18).[187]

---

186. These signals include (1) the connective "but, as for, and, now" (δὲ Heb 8:1) to join the unit D conclusion to the unit F introduction FGT, (2) the term "main point" (Κεφάλαιον Heb 8:1) to communicate transition to a unit summary, (3) the phrase "upon to which is being spoken" (ἐπὶ τοῖς λεγομένοις) that connects his previous message content to his coming message content, (4) the phrase "we have a high priest such as this" (τοιοῦτον ἔχομεν ἀρχιερέα Heb 8:1) that links the subtopic of high priest with his previous exposition and exhortation to this point.

187. Attridge, "Uses of Antithesis in Hebrews," 5, 8. Attridge, against Vanhoye's discourse unit divisions of Heb 8:1—9:28 and 10:1–18, comments regarding the last several FGT, "The exposition concludes with a rhetorical flourish explicitly recalling the beginning of the unit (10:11–18)." Concerning Heb 10:1–10, he states, "The final segment of the exposition (10:1–10) serves not as an appendage or separate repetitive comment, but as the climatic point in the author's argument." The rhetorical flourish of recall is probably correct but would assign Heb 10:11–18 to unit F UI/Pt1 (Heb 8:1–13) about OT support for the priestly ministry of Christ and label Heb 10:1–10 as recall

Figure 16 demonstrates the discourse chiastic structure of unit F (Heb 8:1—10:18) in relation to the other units and sections. Unit F serves as the message thematic climax of the expositional material in proclamation of the Son, as Jesus, as the speech-action of God as the Word of Christ. Jesus is recognized as both the onetime offering for the sins of the people, who at death rose to God like all men for judgment. He passed through the heavens to the throne of God, and became the agent of high priest intercession in mediation for people who approach after death at judgment for entrance by faith into heaven. Unit F summarizes the DI introductory themes contained in A–B–C–D–D′–C′–B′–A′ (Heb 1:2b–4) and serves to bring all subtopics of the exposition together in one coherent message about the better present ministry of Jesus as the Christ.

Unit F provides more supportive exposition about the milk-like teaching outlined in unit E (Heb 5:11–6:18), which primarily concerns Jesus as the beginning Word of Christ that strategically positions him in the place of people's need before God at eternal/perpetual-*place* judgment (Heb 6:1–2). It also shares more detailed exposition about the meat-like teaching outlined in unit D (Heb 5:1–10; 7:1–28) concerning Jesus's strategic position in heaven for priestly intercession to believers after death at judgment that enables the guarantee for a better covenant relationship into the heavenly presence of God (Heb 7:22). The Pastor condenses the discourse S1–2 exposition with the MCS of Heb 9:27–28, which contains the subtopics of death, judgment, intercession, and salvation in heaven.

As noted in appendix 2, table 9, the unit F exposition about the better ministry of Christ is antithetically compared in numerous ways to the earthly ministry of the tabernacle. The Pastor informs his audience that the typological ministry depicted by the daily sacrifices is no longer valid due to the spatial changes achieved by Jesus's entrance into the holy of holies of heaven after the annual pattern of Yom Kippur. Since fulfilled, he also argues that Yom Kippur observance is no longer appropriate due to its repetitive practice, possibly suggesting repeated cycles of atonement by the Christ.

---

with about the law in UI/Pt2 (Heb 9:1–14) in connection with the earthly tabernacle exposition. The difference lies in methodology. Attridge focuses only on the literary device of antithesis to determine what he calls "segments." This project applies a much broader array of literary devices that meet a threshold for determination of FGT within each unit to increase thematic control in authorial intent.

Unit Introduction/Point 1 Introductory Topic (8:1–6): The Son's High Priest Ministry in the Holy-Places of the Heavens, after His Onetime Offering, Is Typified by the Outline and Shadow of the Tabernacle Service

After describing Jesus's high priest ministry in unit D, the Pastor, in his unit F first UI/UPt1 topic about the Son's high priest ministry, declares, "And so, the main point on the basis of which is being spoken, we presently have such a high priest" (Heb 8:1).[188] Drawing on the high priest promissory oath and guarantee of God's speech shared in unit D (Heb 5:1–10; 7:1–28), he affirms that this priesthood ministry, of which God speaks, is both spoken now and presently available.[189]

The Pastor begins by adding more OT supportive midrash regarding Psalm 109:1–4 LXX (110:1–4 MT) to his claims about the Melchizedekian high priest ministry just described in unit D. He elevates three LXX phrases: (1) "sit by my right hand" (Κάθου ἐκ δεξιῶν μου Ps 109:1 LXX), (2) "of the holy-*places*" (τῶν ἁγίων Ps 109:3 LXX), and (3) "into the eternal/perpetual-*places*" (εἰς τὸν αἰῶνα Ps 109:4 LXX). The Pastor, concerning the Son as a "minister" (λειτουργὸς), in Heb 8:1–2 expands the three LXX phrases into three spatial descriptions that summarize the Lord's present place of ministry as (1) "at the right hand of the throne of the Majesty" (ἐν δεξιᾷ τοῦ θρόνου τῆς μεγαλωσύνης),[190] (2) "in the

---

188. The term Κεφάλαιον (*Kephalaion*) is best glossed as "main point, main thing, subject" to fit the rhetorical position of the unit F discourse as the climatic exposition of the Pastor's message. Less persuasive are other Greek gloss options such as "source" that might be applied to other NT writers. The phrase ἐπὶ τοῖς λεγομένοις (*epi tois legomenois*), containing the preposition ἐπὶ (*epi*) with the dat. ptc. τοῖς λεγομένοις (*tois legomenois*), should be taken as causal, where God's speech heard so far logically causes the pres. indicative statement that follows. The pres. tense ptc. and pres. indic. verb signal that God's continued speech-acts, in the form of the priestly ministry of Jesus, are presently available when needed at the time of his message for their approaching need.

189. The Pastor divides the new covenant ministry of Christ into two aspects expressed in units D and E. The milk of unit E centers on the initial onetime offering. The meat of unit D focuses on Christ's perpetual priesthood. These ministerial distinctions of the Christ have cohesion with use of aorist tense in relation to Jesus's onetime offering of atonement for sin and the pres. tense in relation to Jesus's present ministry after death at judgment. The syntax adds support for a perpetually realized eschatology. The future tense applied to the living on earth correctly points an audience ahead to an anticipated day of death and the moment of Jesus's appearing at judgment for his believers.

190. The Pastor changes the possessive genitive "by my right hand" (ἐκ δεξιῶν μου Ps 109:1 LXX) in the LXX to the dat. of place "at the right hand of the throne" (ἐν δεξιᾷ τοῦ θρόνου Heb 8:1). This emphasis on Jesus's heavenly place carries heavy weight in

heavens" (ἐν τοῖς οὐρανοῖς),[191] and (3) "of the holy-*places* . . . and the true tabernacle" (τῶν ἁγίων . . . καὶ τῆς σκηνῆς τῆς ἀληθινῆς).[192]

In the Pastor's latter ministerial description, the referent "holy-*places*" (τῶν ἁγίων) and "tent, tabernacle" (σκηνῆς) are in parallel construction allowing most to equate the two in hendiadys.[193] Since there are multiple semantic options in unit F (Heb 8:1–10:18) within the complex spatial ideas introduced by the Pastor for the paired ἅγιος (*hagios*) syntactical choices, later readers catalog multiple interpretative views.[194]

the Pastor's message for rhetorical support that the Son's ministry is where people need him most, which is during approach to God for judgment after death.

191. The concept of plural heavens is normalized in first-century CE, dualistic, apocalyptic views. Jon Levenson demonstrates multiple OT texts from the beginning that in context apply the temple as a common spatial pattern of God's domain, which includes the heavenly creation. Cf. Levenson, "Temple and the World," 283. Levenson summarizes, "In short, the Temple is a visible, tangible token of the act of creation, the point of origin of the world, the 'focus' of the universe." The speaking by God about the coming Christ through tabernacle symbolism occurs at least 2,500 years after the whole burnt offerings in Gen 4, and the later temple system arises nearly 3,500 years later. For his ministerial comparison, the Pastor chooses to go back to the connection of temple ministry with the law instructions about the tabernacle, since in principle, the basic tabernacle ministry was still being practiced through the temple and continued the whole burnt offerings from the beginning. For discussion about absence in Hebrews of a direct connection with the Second Temple, see Lindars, "Hebrews and the Second Temple," 410–33. Lindars highlights the importance of the Second Temple on the Jewish religious consciousness up to the end of its service in 70 CE. Lindars's support for indirect Second Temple presence in Hebrews through the continued symbolism from the tabernacle contains several of the straw man argument assumptions of his day (e.g., delay of the parousia, concern about apostasy, concern about how to cope with present guilt in the audience conscience over sins after salvation). However, Lindars's line of argument about an exhortation for the audience to make a complete break with former repetitive, Jewish, sacrificial practices has strong coherence with the impossible errant teaching described in unit E (Heb 5:11—6:18).

192. Hebrews 8:2 is the Pastor's first spatial sense for "holy-*places*" (ἅγιος). For cohesion of the Pastor's nomenclature for spatial infrastructure of all creation in Hebrews, see appendix 2, table 9.

193. E.g., Hughes, *Commentary on the Epistle*, 283–90. Hughes offers a full discussion of other optional interpretations. He writes, "It is our understanding, then, that the author of the Epistle to the Hebrews means here not two things but one; that is to say, that the sanctuary [holy-*places*] into which Christ has entered is the same as that tent which is described as 'true' and 'greater and more perfect'" (289).

194. E.g., Hughes, *Commentary on the Epistle*, 282. Hughes comments that "The phrase τῶν ἁγίων λειτουργός (*tōn hagiōn leitourgos*) is susceptible of a variety of interpretations. A number of patristic authors treated the genitive τῶν ἁγίων (*tōn hagiōn*) as masculine and accordingly interpreted the phrase to mean 'a minister of the saints,' which in itself is appropriate enough. Alcuin explains that 'the souls of the saints are this tabernacle in which he ministers with eternal joy.' If, however, the genitive is understood as being neuter, then two other possibilities arise: either 'a minister of holy

The corresponding referents "holy-*places*" and "tabernacle" can spatially index either (1) the holy of holies linked with a true and more complete tabernacle 'within' heaven, (2) both holy-*places* of the unseen spiritual realm linked with the unseen spiritual portion of the true and more complete tabernacle "in the heavens," or (3) both unseen holy-*places* linked with the entire tabernacle representing all creation.[195] Claims for the first option usually limit τῶν ἁγίων (*tōn hagiōn*) to only the holy of holies in a conceptual pairing with the unusual first-century CE concept of a tabernacle "within" or "in" heaven. These maintain the shortened form does not necessarily imply reference to the holy place because, in the Hebrew language, the text in Leviticus 16 arranges this shortened single word form to designate the holy of holies.[196] This shortened form was kept in the LXX, which was heavily used by the Pastor.[197] However, the LXX support for the syntactical abbreviated form using τῶν ἁγίων (*tōn hagiōn*) as the holy of holies does not in itself confirm that "and the true tabernacle" (καὶ τῆς σκηνῆς τῆς ἀληθινῆς) has an intentional sense meaning for the Pastor's listeners about a place of only in holy of holies. The isolated "holy of holies" link is only partially correct due to the creative spatial changes and necessary cleansing in the unseen heavenly realm achieved at the entrance of Jesus that the Pastor rhetorically leverages in unit F to hedge the temptation to embrace now false impossible teaching by continuing OT sacrificial daily and annual Day of Atonement offerings.

---

things,' which is how Luther took it—and it is worth remarking that Philo uses the same expression, in the order λειτουργὸς τῶν ἁγίων (*leitourgos tōn hagiōn*), of the Levitical priest in this sense (*Legum Allegoriae* iii.135; cf. *De Fuga* 93); or 'a minister of the sanctuary,' which is the accepted interpretation today, the sanctuary intended being the heavenly holy of holies. The justification for this conclusion is our author's repeated designation of the wilderness holy of holies as τὰ ἅγια (*ta hagia*, 9:8, 12, 24, 25; 10:19; 13:11; in 9:2 it is used of the holy place; cf. also τὸ ἅγιον [*to hagion*] in 9:1 and ἅγια ἁγίων [*hagia hagiōn*] in 9:3). It can hardly be doubted that this usage, within the immediate context, in which Jesus is conceived as having entered as our High Priest into the heavenly holy of holies, determines the authentic understanding of the expression here." The plurality of semantic options points to the importance of the context for each use. The referent τῶν ἁγίων (*tōn hagiōn*) in Heb 8:2 contextually refers to the unseen holy-*places* of the heaven(s) of all creation. See appendix, 2 table 9 contextual uses.

195. Allen, *Hebrews*, 458–59. Along with referenced scholars, Allen concludes, "The author's reference to the 'sanctuary' indicates the entire tabernacle and not just the inner sanctuary."

196. Delitzsch, *Commentary on the Epistle*, 66. Delitzsch writes, "In the Old Testament, likewise, הַקֹּדֶשׁ, τὸ ἅγιον, is not infrequently the abbreviated term for קדש הקדשים (Lev. 16:16, 17, 20, 23, 27), as being the holy place κατ' ἐξοχ."

197. Isaacs, *Sacred Space*, 48.

Since this is his first introduction of the spatial concept about the "holy-*places*," had he meant to distinguish a specific nuance about one of the two referents, then he likely would have included the more exact referent for the holy of holies in the discourse.

Table 11—Psalm 109:2-3 LXX Semantic Spatial Correspondence with Hebrews 8:1-2

ῥάβδον δυνάμεώς σου ἐξαποστελεῖ κύριος ἐκ Σιων, καὶ κατακυρίευε ἐν μέσῳ τῶν ἐχθρῶν σου (Ps 109:2 LXX)	("the LORD sends out from Zion a scepter of your ability, and he will rule in the midst of your enemies")	ὃς ἐκάθισεν ἐν δεξιᾷ τοῦ θρόνου τῆς μεγαλωσύνης (Heb 8:1)	("who sits at the right hand of the throne of the Majesty")
μετὰ σοῦ ἡ ἀρχὴ ἐν ἡμέρᾳ τῆς δυνάμεώς σου ἐν ταῖς λαμπρότησιν τῶν ἁγίων (Ps 109:3 LXX)	("after your beginning in the day of your ability in the brilliance of the holy-*places*")	τῶν ἁγίων ... καὶ τῆς σκηνῆς τῆς ἀληθινῆς (Heb 8:2)	("of the holy-*places* ... and true tabernacle")

Finally, semantic meaning in context always trumps syntactical use when ambiguous meanings are an option.[198] The Pastor's spatial terms in Heb 8:1-2 have strong correspondence with the Ps 109:2-3 LXX phrases, which support the OT text as his source from which spatial terms are probably derived (see table 11).

The phrase "The LORD sends out from Zion a scepter of your ability, and he will rule in the midst of your enemies" (Ps 109:2 LXX) conceptually links with "who sits at the righthand of the throne of the Majesty" (Heb 8:1). The phrase "after your beginning in the day of your ability in the brilliance of the holy-*places*" (Ps 109:3 LXX) corresponds with "of the holy-*places* ... and true tabernacle" (Heb 8:2). This connection strongly supports that the spatial listing in Heb 8:1-2 condenses the place location described in the LXX. He interprets by midrash that the referents in the LXX Ps 109 symbolize the unseen heavenly types. In unit F, the Pastor develops how Jesus's heavenly entrance and enthronement

---

198. The tabernacle details of the Pastor's second main rhetorical point UPt 2 (Heb 9:1–14) best determine the specific spatial meaning for syntactical uses of ἅγιος (*hagios*).

spatially created and purified the previously divided spiritual creation into one consecrated realm.

In Heb 8:1–2, location of the first spatial phrase "at the right hand of the throne of the Majesty" (ἐν δεξιᾷ τοῦ θρόνου τῆς μεγαλωσύνης) is generally uncontested as ministry with God in heaven. However, the location represented by the phrases "in the heavens" (ἐν τοῖς οὐρανοῖς) is heavily contested. Many have *singularized* the glosses of the latter two options to match the location of the first option as "in heaven." This view commits missteps away from the semantic intentions of the text (1) by use of the modern Latin transliterated gloss "Sanctuary," which misses the creative spatial changes achieved by Jesus's movement "through the heavens" as an offering, and "in the heavens" as a minister,[199] (2) by understanding the plural heavens as metaphor for simply heavenly grandeur,[200] (3) by the true tabernacle as only a local structure "in heaven," rather than "in the heavens,"[201] (4) by use of the Latin transliterated term "universe," a gloss

---

199. The Pastor would likely follow the first-century CE common conception of the σκηνῆς (*skēnēs*) as the complete tabernacle complex that typologically and spatially represents the entire structure of the seen and unseen creation of God discussed above, which modern scholars incorrectly label the "cosmos" in the study of "cosmology." Cf. Keene, "Heaven Is a Tent" 50–137. Keene lists scholarly conversation about Heb 8:2 that embraces a structural view of the true tabernacle. Cf. Michel, *Der Brief and die Hebräer*, 311; Andriessen, "Das Grossere und vollkommenere Zelt," 76–92; Michaelis, "σκηνή," 368–81, esp. 376–77; Héring, *Epistle to the Hebrews*, 66; Lane, *Hebrews 9–13*, 228–36; Koester, "Outside the Camp," 309. Keene does agree with the conception of a duality of the eternal and temporary creation in Hebrews (111–12). However, he rejects the structural application of σκηνή (*skēnē*) in Heb 8:2, based upon perceived (1) imprecision of the spatial language of Hebrews, (2) inability to answer questions raised about the spatial structural view, (3) distortion of the metaphoric language by precise structural views, (4) disharmony with the statement "this one is not of this creation," interpreted as the true tabernacle is in the "transcendent" creation, (5) epexegetical connection between ἁγίων "Sanctuary" ("holy-*places*") and σκηνῆς ("tent, tabernacle"), and (6) tension with a redemptive-historical position and Christology. Keene's negative perceptions about the spatial structural view are attenuated herein in discussion to follow.

200. Manuscript evidence, concerning Heb 8:1, shows later redaction of οὐρανοῖς from "heavens" to υψηλοις for the sense of "high places" by Eusebius and some Latin translators that may reflect fourth-century CE theological changes from Christ's *heavenly* ministry expectations to a delayed end in an earthly kingdom hope. Modern English translations vary with plural "heavens" (KJV, ASV, NKJV, NASB, HCSB, NRSV) and singular "heaven" (RSV, ESV, NET, NIV, NLT, LEB).

201. MacRae, "Heavenly Temple and Eschatology," 172–96. MacRae incorrectly assumes that both views were available in first-century CE ST theology. MacRae's heavily challenged notion for an antithesis between a Hellenistic Platonic and a Jewish apocalyptic view influences the weight of his claim; he has no tangible evidence for a tabernacle "within heaven." Cf. Klawans, *Purity, Sacrifice, and the Temple*, 109–44.

Klawans also supports that both views were available and not contradictory. However, his analysis has several weaknesses. The "in the heavens" view is considered as temple = cosmos, whereas in the first century CE the heavens and cosmos are distinct spatial areas that do not overlap. Also, his evidence for a temple/tabernacle "within heaven" is both weak and anemic. He stretches the evidence for a tabernacle/temple "within heaven" by weakening his criteria for such a view as primarily an analogical correspondence of events involving worship in heaven with similar events on earth. What is described by Klawans's criteria, is more likely activity of worship *in a part* of the overall structure of the seen and unseen creation and not an independent tabernacle/temple "within heaven" itself. Further, in his evidence, the location of this worship is not actually called a "temple" or "tabernacle," except perhaps in the Qumran document Songs of the Sabbath Sacrifice. However, Klawans admits that the documents are so poor preserved, any analysis remains provisional and tentative. This observation for the activity of worship in heavenly structures as part of the whole of all creation probably applies to Klawans' evidence in the pseudepigraphic literature of 1 Enoch and the Testament of Levi. Klawans evidence for a tabernacle as "in the heavens" contains strong affirmation in the company of Philo and Josephus. This project considers the addition of Hebrews. *Contra* Calaway, *Sabbath and the Sanctuary*, 98–138. Calaway claims, "While there is increased speculation in the Second Temple period on the heavenly temple, Hebrews provides only the second occurrence for the concept of the tabernacle as the heavenly sanctuary. The first was the Songs of the Sabbath Sacrifice, which, like Hebrews would, used the 'pattern' Moses saw as part of its basis" (99). Calaway builds his thesis on an idea that is at most provisional and tentative against Hebrews's syntactical language and solid evidence of structural correspondence with other ST literature.

The presuppositional concept concerning only a local tabernacle "within heaven," which is now closed for believers until an age to come, creates difficult tensions for scholars who evaluate the places of Hebrews. The assumption embraces a house of cards as the foundation for salvation theology by cutting across the more common position of "in the heavens" conveyed in writings by Plato, Philo, Josephus, and the ST pseudepigraphic descriptions that contain visions concerning material plural heavens. In these literary works, the syntactical choice for either singular or plural heavens is authorily determined by their chosen genre and context. For Plato's material conception of heaven, see Vlastos, *Plato's Universe*. For Josephus, see *Ant.* 3:180–1; *Ant.* 3:123.

The "within/in heaven" view for the tabernacle is unintelligible; e.g., Ellingworth comments concerning spatial views in Hebrews, "Since, therefore, the author so seldom pauses to make explicit cosmological statements and is never sufficiently interested in the subject to draw a comprehensive picture of the universe as he sees it, it is not surprising that this aspect of his thought presents obscurities and apparent contradictions." Ellingworth, "Jesus and the Universe," 338–39, 345. He further states, "Hebrews is full of such gradual transitions. It is a question of deciding which line of interpretation causes the least problems" (345). Ellingworth recognizes one of the important causes for disagreement about the spatial aspects of Christ's priesthood, averring, "As for the distinction between central and peripheral teaching, this must be made on the basis of the epistle as a whole, not the individual verses or passages, still less on the basis of grammatical criteria" (338). However, he analyzes eight patterns in his spatial discussion of Hebrews rather independently with only light connection between them and without consideration of their governing FGT. He concludes by light of his limited methodology, there are two types of spatial language, which he finds difficulty harmonizing. He rejects, because of perceived distortion, a possible solution by flipping his so-called horizontal pictures vertically. Tracking the Pastor's thematic subtopics of the

that typically limits to the visible creation,[202] (5) by application of the Greek "cosmos" and "cosmology" to include the unseen creation of the heavens, and (6) by rejection of the tabernacle link with plural heavens based upon the variance in number of heavens in other ST literature.[203]

The linked phrases, τῶν ἁγίων ... καὶ τῆς σκηνῆς τῆς ἀληθινῆς (tōn hagiōn ... kai tēs skēnēs tēs alēthinēs), containing two descriptors linked by καὶ ("and"), should be considered as epexegetical, with each phrase describing the spatial domain covered by the ministry of the Son from his positional location in heaven. These two forms need not be the same spatial territory but do require correspondence with the spatial ministry of the Son. He ministers (1) in the heavens, which includes not only the invisible area of his throne but also the distant location of his enemies in the visible realm where people by the conversation of his ability believe his sacrifice for sin and promise of salvation, (2) in the unseen holy-*places* where the Son saves his believers on arrival by angelic ministry after death for judgment, and (3) in the true tabernacle, which encompasses all the seen and unseen creation (see figs. 1–2).

The adjective "true" (ἀληθινῆς), in modification of "tent, tabernacle" (σκηνῆς), does not assume that the former ministry in space and time

---

governing FGT through each unit within God's design for a tabernacle-based typology of plural heavens greatly removes the distortion that Ellingworth perceives.

202. The Latin transliterated gloss "universe" confuses the semantic meaning of the eternal/perpetual-*places*; e.g., Trotter, "The Jerusalem Temple in Diaspora," 195–200. Trotter claims that Philo considers the "universe" as a temple of God. He translates τὸ μὲν ἀνωτάτω καὶ πρὸς ἀλήθειαν ἱερὸν θεοῦ νομίζειν τὸν σύμπαντα χρὴ κόσμον εἶναι as "one must recognize that the highest and truly sacred temple of God is the entire universe." He overlooks Philo's syntactical comparison for a description of the "temple complex" (ἱερόν), not the κόσμος, which he translates as "universe." The κόσμος never in Greek literature contains the unseen heavens. Philo provides two statements in a A B B′ A′ pattern, with the second μὲν ... δὲ (*men ... de*) nested inside his first one, where the "temple complex" (ἱερόν) contains patterns both for A, "the whole inhabited world" (κόσμος), and B, the "temple building" (ναός) with the "holiest place" (ἁγιώτατον) of the dwelling of God as "heaven" (οὐρανός). Philo further juxtaposes B′, capable "angels" (ἄγγελος) and A′, hand-made things. B represents the unseen substance-reality of heaven and A the visible reality of the κόσμος (*kosmos*).

203. Collins, "Seven Heavens," 59–93. Collins comes to several solid conclusions after analysis of the ST literature that describes seven heavens, rather than the biblical three heavens based upon the OT phrase "heaven of heavens" and NT 2 Cor 12:2. He finds (1) no indication of a link between the seven heavens and seven known planets, (2) the motif was probably borrowed from Babylonian tradition, (3) the motif was added to the Testament of Levi by a Christian redactor, (4) it does not appear until the late first century CE, and (5) in later comments, it only appears in reference to the teaching of others.

was false but that the seen and unseen realities of God's domain symbolized are the original for determination of the earthly teaching image.²⁰⁴ The earthly tabernacle was, before the entrance of Christ, a useful ministry for God's purpose (cf. Heb 5:4; 9:1–10). The antitype ministry of earthly tabernacle outlines the type of the true ministry of the tabernacle in the heavens, where Jesus as an exemplar was able to pass through the heavens into the presence of God.

The Pastor's comments about this organization, stating, "Which the Lord pitched, not people" (ἣν ἔπηξεν ὁ κύριος, οὐκ ἄνθρωπος Heb 8:2) likely do not reference an unrelated proof text about the original Genesis creation but continue reflection about the recent spatial changes to the unseen creation regarding the present arrangement of the true tabernacle that are achieved by Jesus in rising to God from the dead.²⁰⁵ A tabernacle or temple typologically testifies about how one may approach a deity in

---

204. The Pastor's use of "true" provides an interpretative key for the audience. Burrows claims that the ancient traditions, concerning the heavenly forms of the archetypal temple cosmology, passed down by Babylonian influence on NT philosophy about the heavenly sanctuary, and came to be called "the 'true.'" Burrows, "Some Cosmological Patterns," 46. However, ideological patterns, about the seen and unseen holy-*places* of God, historically have passed down from the early typology of Eden that represented features about access to the unseen, "true," holy space of God's dwelling in heaven. The creative change in the true unseen realities indicates the old examples in the OT tabernacle were no longer valid and outdated.

205. See DI subtopic B (Heb 1:2c), where God spoke through the Son by "achieving the eternal/perpetual-*places*," which likely refers to the newly created heavenly entrance by a refinement of design with change achieved by the Son (cf. Heb 10:19). For the Pastor, God's eternal/perpetual-*place* domain underwent creative changes to the design of the current heavens and earth at the beginning (Heb 1:8–10; 11:3), then the eternal/perpetual-*places* experienced a creative change at Jesus's entrance (Heb 6:19–20; 10:19–20), to await a future creative change by removal of that which is temporary (Heb 12:25–29).

Cf. Levenson, "Cosmos and Microcosm," 78–99; Levenson, "Temple and the World," 275–98. Levenson shows that the temple symbolizes the present ideal creation, which is the result of God's labors as sovereign over it. He rightly remarks, "It is God's authorship *of* the world that establishes his sovereign independence *from* the world and demythologizes all human efforts to enthrone him *within* the world" (237; italics Levenson). The temple/tabernacle testifies that people, beginning with Jesus as the forerunner, enter the dwelling of God, not that God perpetually enters the present visible work of his hands to dwell with people. The ministry of Jesus's entrance into heaven of the Genesis creation attained a change in the first covenant design of the tabernacle in the heavens. The rhetorical point is that God's physical changes in his tabernacle outline about the macrocosm necessitate changes in teaching by those called to a teaching ministry, not that the place of the invisible heavens were created at a different time from the visible heavens and earth.

heaven.[206] The Son's creative change in the true tabernacle that symbolizes all creation, by removal of the inner veil, now enables approach for people and entrance into God's presence to those who believe in Jesus's offering for sin that was not previously available in the teaching of the tabernacle ministry copies.[207] The Pastor's main point is that the Son has

---

206. Lundquist, "Common Temple Ideology," 55–57. Lundquist organizes the typological features concerning the common language and praxis that centered around the ANE temples until approximately late Hellenistic times. The ordinary understanding outlined by the tabernacle would be familiar to the audience of Hebrews. Some of the important features expressed by the Pastor, concerning the tabernacle, include "an architectural embodiment of the cosmic mountain," "build on separate, sacral, set-apart space," "a copy or counterpart of a heavenly model," "express successive ascension toward heaven," "plans . . . revealed by God," "associated with the realm of the dead, the underworld, the afterlife, the grave," "God's word is revealed in the temple," "close relationship between the temple and law," and "a place of sacrifice." Modern study of Hebrews that flips the believer's heavenward momentum to God toward earthly fulfillment concepts, which ideas have persisted since the beginning from the misstep of Cain to modern times, often misses ancient understanding. Cf. Patai, *Man and Temple*. Patai writes, "The Temple was regarded as a miniature picture of the world, and at the same time the centre, the Navel, of the earth. The welfare of Israel, nay, of the whole world of seventy nations, was dependent on the proper performance of the service in the Temple, each state and each moment of which had a closely determined effect on some corresponding state or moment in the beneficial working of the force of nature" (132).

207. The design change upon God's invisible creation in relation to people that Jesus's heavenly entrance achieved, supports the true tabernacle under consideration by the Pastor as "in the heavens" of all visible and invisible creation (cf. Col 1:16), rather than only "within/in heaven" where people cannot enter due to theological tensions requiring closed-heaven concepts. The tabernacle in the heavens and superior design changes created by Jesus are repeated again in UPt2 (Heb 9:11) and UPt3 (Heb 9:24). In the former, the Pastor exclaims, "But Christ, after arriving is a high priest of good-*places* existing, on the basis of the greater and more perfect tabernacle not made with hands, this one is not of this creation" (Χριστὸς δὲ παραγενόμενος ἀρχιερεὺς τῶν γενομένων ἀγαθῶν διὰ τῆς μείζονος καὶ τελειοτέρας σκηνῆς οὐ χειροποιήτου, τοῦτ' ἔστιν οὐ ταύτης τῆς κτίσεως Heb 9:11). The διὰ is probably instrumental. Yet as attempted in scholarly debate, the instrumental implication by the Christ event occurs in the greater and more perfect tabernacle, rather than the first tabernacle, does not remove the spatial structural changes under consideration. Jesus arrived a high priest in the tabernacle in the heavens which resulted in creation no longer existing as the Genesis creation design. His point is that Jesus's entrance redesigned and created a way into the holy of holies of heaven for people. In Heb 9:24, the Pastor states, "For Christ did not enter into holy-*places* made with hands, antitypes of the true ones, but into heaven itself, now to appear before the presence of God for us" (οὐ γὰρ εἰς χειροποίητα εἰσῆλθεν ἅγια Χριστός, ἀντίτυπα τῶν ἀληθινῶν, ἀλλ' εἰς αὐτὸν τὸν οὐρανόν, νῦν ἐμφανισθῆναι τῷ προσώπῳ τοῦ θεοῦ ὑπὲρ ἡμῶν Heb 9:24). The Pastor, for emphasis, restates the ministry of Christ, as not in the earthly tabernacle that functioned as an antitype of the true tabernacle places of Heb 8:1, but heaven itself of the true tabernacle in the heavens. Jesus's accepted offering at God's judgment, and rising from the dead to God, opened a way for others to

built a lasting entrance and has a priestly ministry in the heavens that is now available.[208]

In unit F, this better location of heaven that is highlighted within the true tabernacle begins the Pastor's antithesis with the place of the earthly tabernacle, where he contrasts the present heavenly ministry

---

follow through the heavens inside the veil, creating "the way of the holy-*places*" that left the design of the first tabernacle ministry obsolete (cf. Heb 9:8).

208. Cf. Torrance, *Space, Time and Resurrection*, 102. Torrance reacts to the modern independence of scientific geometry of space with dualistic forms in concern regarding its projection about knowledge of God that easily caused his contemporaries to think of resurrection and spiritual bodies as lacking concrete ontological reality. He interlocks together, for his study, the incarnation of God and his/believers' resurrection in spiritual bodies and treats them "as the same nature, in the integration of physical and spiritual existence, as his birth and death" (xv). However, Torrance rejects an individual completed resurrection at death (35) and attempts philosophical explanation for the uninterrupted life grounded in the biblical promise while retaining his inherited theological traditions for a general resurrection at the *parousia* of Christ (italics Torrance). He recognizes, "When the believer dies, he goes to be with Christ and in his immediate presence, participant in him and made like him. That is to each believer the *parousia* of Christ to him." Torrance then adds, "Yet when this is regarded on the plane of history and on the on-going processes of the fallen world, the death of each believer means that his body is laid to sleep in the earth, waiting until the redemption of the body and the recreation of all things in the final *Parousia*. Looked at from the perspective of the new creation there is no gap between the death of the believer and the *parousia* of Christ but looked at from the perspective of time that decays and crumbles away, there is a lapse of time between them." Torrance recognizes the tension he creates by his antithetical constructions and asks, "How do we think these together?" His solution is found in the philosophical straw man of different no time-form for the world and philosophizes a Christology of "*in Christ*." The problem of Torrance's tension is not in his perception of a present parousia of the individual to Christ at death, but in the elevation of the missteps of traditions with closed-heavens until the parousia.

However, many scholars assert Jesus's spatially created way to God's presence in heaven is still closed until a future time or does not exist as a reality at all; e.g., Craig Keener notes parallels between the earthly and heavenly temples in relation to the whole cosmos (all creation) and that Jesus as forerunner "always signifies that the rest of the company is coming afterward." Keener, "Hebrews 8:1–5." Cf. Moore, "True Tabernacle," 49–71. Moore agrees with the linear future eschatology views of Hurst and Church, where the true tabernacle represents God dwelling with his people still future. Yet, he disagrees with their omission of the spatial aspects of the tabernacle and temple by pushing a temporal interpretation heavily over the top of the myriad of spatial language instances in Hebrews. Moore defends the heavenly tabernacle, so-called by modern scholars, in Hebrews as "a pre-existent, cosmological, spatial reality" (55), while opting for integration of both spatial and temporal language for proper understanding of Hebrews. Moore's defense of the spatial language is commendable but any delay of the promised salvation event for believers after death does not appear in Hebrews. God *now* dwells with his people in heaven of the present tabernacle of God's tent/house of all creation, rather than a local heavenly tabernacle, a term which is not found in Hebrews.

of Christ with the ministry of the earthly priests (Heb 8:3–4).[209] Just as the earthly high priest offers gifts and sacrifices, so also Christ as a high priest must have something to offer. The Pastor later affirms what Jesus offers in UPt4 (Heb 10:5–14). Further, the Christ does not qualify as an earthly replacement for the high priests that served in the earthly tabernacle according to the law. Rather, the earthly tabernacle priests "serve to outline and shadow *places/ministry* of the heavenlies" (ὑποδείγματι καὶ σκιᾷ λατρεύουσιν τῶν ἐπουρανίων Heb 8:5).[210]

The Pastor provides OT evidence from Exod 25:40 by linking "the tent, tabernacle" (τὴν σκηνήν) Moses was about to build with the true reality of the heavenly places. In his commission, Moses was warned by God, "'For see!,' he says, 'you shall make everything according to the type having been explained to you in the mountain'" (Heb 8:5). Moses created the earthly tabernacle as an antitype of the type that he was shown on the mountain.[211] Mountains typologically symbolized the high presence of God above the view of the people in the creation. The Pastor's word choice of "type" (τύπος) links with the phrase "to outline and shadow" (ὑποδείγματι καὶ σκιᾷ) both signals and supports his interpretative method of typology that would be familiar to his audience.[212]

---

209. Attridge, "Uses of Antithesis in Hebrews," 1–9. Attridge uses the literary device for his segmental divisions of the unit without weight for consideration of other devices. He rightly recognizes there are multiple spatial, temporal, and other categorical comparisons ongoing at the same time in the well demarcated unit.

210. The subject for the plural adjective "heavenly . . . s" (ἐπουρανίων) must be supplied by the listeners from the context. Most English translations ignore the context and supply the generic subject "heavenly *things*" (KJV, NASB, ESV, HCSB, LEB), or choose perceived contextual glosses of "heavenly sanctuary" (NET, NABRE, RSV), "heavenly *one*" (NRSV), "of what is in heaven" (NIV, NCV), and "of the real one in heaven" (NLT). Except for the generic gloss of "heavenly *things*," the other translations ignore the plural number that links back to the UPt1 introduction subtopics and links with the places of the Son's *ministry*, as "in the heavens" (cf. Heb 8:1–2, 6). Τὰ ἐπουράνια in the NT is usually "heavenly-*places*" (Eph 1:3; 2:6; 3:10; 6:12 ['heavenly-*things*']; John 3:12; Phil 2:10; Heb. 9:23). Westcott suggests "heavenly order." Lünemann supplies ἁγίων as ("*sanctuary*"). Westcott, *Epistle to the Hebrews*; Lünemann, *Epistle to the Hebrews*.

211. The verb δείκνυμι (*deiknymi*) can gloss as something apprehended by the senses, as "show, make known," or something made clear by evidence or reasoning, as "explain, prove." Cf. BDAG, "δείκνυμι," 214. It is unlikely Moses literally sensed the true heavenly reality of both the seen and unseen creation itself that was typologically symbolized by the tabernacle that he made for the people according to the law. It is more likely Moses received a vision of the true tabernacle in accordance with his prophetic office like other visions and revelations that the Pastor refers to as "in many parts and in many ways" (πολυμερῶς καὶ πολυτρόπως Heb 1:1) of God speaking in the past.

212. These terms are often linked with some level of influence from Philo or

Hebrews 8:6 serves to conclude the topic A UI FGT by again supporting the accomplished structural changes by Christ that position him as a "mediator" (μεσίτης Heb 8:6; cf. Heb 9:6; 12:24; Gal 3:19–20; 1 Tim 2:5) in heaven. This verbal noun joins the path from the main introductory topic D (Heb 1:3b) regarding the Son's ability to bring all things to God. Jesus mediates better promises in a better "covenant" (διαθήκη) that involves ministry in a better relationship and place.[213] The term tracks as a conceptual path from the introductory subtopics of A (Heb 1:2b) and A´ (Heb 1:4). Regarding Christ's more excellent ministry, the syntax of the perf. act. indic. "has attained" (τέτυχεν) and perf. pass. indic. "has been legislated" (νενομοθέτηται) specify that the better promises and better covenant relationship/ministry of this structural change have already

---

Platonic ideas. Cf. Girdwood and Verkruyse, "Hebrews 8:5." Girdwood does not find influence of Philo or Platonic ideas, as perceived by scholarly misunderstanding, in the OT quotation and midrash of this unit F topic A UI.

213. The term "covenant" (διαθήκη) is a subtopic of the priestly "ministry" (λειτουργία) of the Christ, which the audience would understand by considering the antitype of the Sinai covenant and OT promises such as Ps 2 and Dan 7:13–14. In this understanding, God's covenant refers to a promise/oath made by God in his relationship with people that is executed at the death of both the Christ and his believers for an inheritance in heaven.

The term "covenant" (διαθήκη) introduces in Heb 7:22 of unit D (Heb 5:1–10; 7:1–28), which concerns the high priest ministry of the Son. It appears seventeen more times in the message. After the unit D UPt3 introduction in Heb 7:22 concerning Jesus's guaranteed better covenant relationship by his Melchizedekian ministry in heaven, the term διαθήκη (*diathēkē*) appears thirteen times in unit F to describe the better spatial relationship and personal transformation features of believers in the eternal/perpetual-*places* by current his ministry, one time in the S2 for summary-conclusion covering unit F, one time in unit B´ UPt1 for encouragement, and one time in the unit A´ conclusion. the Pastor's unit F Pt3 topic C (Heb 9:15–26) has three FGT which focus heavily on the attributes of covenant execution in connection with death.

In his unit F comparison of the priestly earthly ministry and Jesus's ministry in the heavens, The Pastor also on multiple occasions simplifies his oratory by use of the ordinal "first" (πρῶτος Heb 8:7, 13; 9:1, 2, 6, 8, 15 [with διαθήκη], 18; 10:9), "second" (δεύτερος Heb 8:7; 9:3 [with καταπέτασμα], 7, 28; 10:9), the adjective "new" (καινός Heb 8:8 [with διαθήκη], 13), verbs "make old" (παλαιόω Heb 1:11; 8:13) and γηράσκω ("grow old," Heb 8:13). When these terms are deployed without a modifier or subject, the modified object must be understood by the context.

These terms emphasize the spatial and personal transformational change by Jesus's new ministry from a former relationship in the first ministry located in the holy place of heaven that included a veiled separation from God by angelic beings to a heavenly relationship located anew in the holy of holies with God. In topic B of unit F (Heb 9:1–14), the Pastor links these ordinal terms to the holy place and holy of holies, which he uses to support the structural changes in heaven by removal of the veil. The location of the holy place is now obsolete after Jesus's entrance into heaven. This event allows believers at judgment after death to enter heaven itself.

occurred as a reality with a present prospect for this audience at their time of need. In the remainder of his unit F main exposition, the Pastor explains more features of this current, better expectation at death and during judgment that results from the Son's entrance into the holy of holies. In his next FGT of UPt1 (Heb 8:7–13), the Pastor describes the transitional changes in the true heavenly realities, represented by the antitype of the earthly covenant outline introduced by Moses (Heb 8:5–6), about people upon entrance into the eternal/perpetual-*places*.

Subpoint 1a (8:7–13): The OT Supports That the Son's Priestly Ministry Currently Mediates a Better Covenant Relationship at Judgment and Personal Transformation into Heaven with God after Death, Rather than Earthly Promises

UPt1 introduces the boundaries of the contrasting spatial locations of the two priesthood ministries. The priests of the law serve on the earth. The Lord, as a priest, is a minister of the holy-*places* and the true tabernacle in the heavens. The Pastor concludes that, by this ministry, the Lord brings a better covenant relationship between God and people based upon better promises. He next, in SbPt1a provides OT support for these promised transformational changes in the features of people after death that enable living in God's presence at their new location in heaven.[214]

Concerning the Son's ministry in the newly, created, structural opening in heavenly places, the Pastor concludes, "For if that first *covenant ministry* was a faultless one, then a place should not be sought of a second *covenant ministry*" (Heb 8:7, italics mine from context).[215] His choice of

---

214. The temporal window of nearly all expositional material in Hebrews centers on the either the experience of Christ as offering in death and judgment (unit E) or the priestly ministry of the Christ to believers at death and judgment (unit D). The offering as the Christ nearly exclusively focuses on Jesus's approach after death and the outcome of his judgment as subsequent enthronement for a priestly ministry after the order of Melchizedek. The priestly intercessory work focuses on the same temporal window for believers, which describes Jesus's mediation after death on approach at judgment with subsequent entrance and transformation for entrance to God. This provides contextual weight for the temporal markers that relate to believers as reference to the day of death and judgment, rather than some common distant day in an eschatological future that only applies to the addition of those living at the time of Jesus's return to earth.

215. The topic "first ministry" from the introduction FGT to the topic A UPt1 FGT best describes God's salvific activity within his "covenant" relationship to people. Because the referents of the ordinals "first" and "second" are not supplied by the Pastor, the audience must supply the implied ordinal events from the message context. The introduction

"place" (τόπος) serves as the subtopic of the apodosis of the conditional statement, which assumes the location for the heirs the first ministry had faults concerning the place of its endpoint. Since the ministry of the law was limited to priestly intercession concerning outward testimonial matters on earth about what God would do himself, its observance could not cleanse the inward conscience of sin that is required for entrance to God at judgment before him in heaven after death (cf. Heb 9:9, 14; 10:22). This inward cleansing of the conscience of sin is provided by the second better ministry of the Lord, which enables a better covenant relationship into the very presence of God in heaven. The subject of "place," related to the Pastor's OT quotation to follow, illuminates the spatial benefits of this second ministry and transformational changes in the features of people that occur on the day of death with subsequent entrance into heaven.

FGT theme of the UPt1 topic (Heb 8:1–6) defines a contrast between the locations of the Lord's "ministry" (λειτουργία Heb 8:6) as a "minister, servant" (λειτουργὸς Heb 8:2) and that of the priests in the law, who on earth outline and shadow the Lord's ministry.

The Pastor adds the new term "covenant" (διαθήκη Heb 7:22; 8:6) to his list of thematic subtopics about God's activity regarding salvation for inheritance in heaven, his promise, his oath, his rest, and his ministry. The subtopic of "covenant" (διαθήκη Heb 8:6) is mentioned in a head-tail linkage within the next UPt1 FGT (Heb 8:7–13) and several times in unit F. A covenant refers to a binding agreement between two parties, which in Hebrews would be between God and people. The Pastor later adds explanatory details about God's covenant with people that describe a binding agreement where property transfers to heirs (cf. UPt3a–b Heb 9:15–22). This covenantal inheritance is transferred from God to eligible parties upon death, with those receiving those benefits designated as heirs.

Jesus's ministry of mediation in the new covenant relationship between people with God takes place after an individual's death at judgment for those who choose to believe in his ability to provide salvation from sin. Modern usage of the term covenant within closed-heaven paradigms often inflates and distorts the covenant relationship beyond the Pastor's original intensions as one-sided and away from a mutual relationship for the mediatorial ministry of Christ between God and people. God provides through Christ a new relationship in his presence and allows a decision by people to receive it. However, the biblical view of this mutual covenant relationship can become imbalanced toward a sovereign determinism that is limited only in a distorted form of God's covenant election and omits all people's relationship opportunity and responsibility to choose by faith to believe God's ability to remove the consequences of sin by God's own offering in a substitutionary experience of death and judgment. The concept of covenant in Hebrews refers to an agreement between God and his people about his ministerial responsibilities that concern salvation of an inheritance in heaven after death at judgment to those *who chose* to believe. During the first/old, heavenly, covenant ministry symbolized under previous earthly covenants before the law, people by faith in Christ entered heaven of the first tabernacle (Abraham's bosom) to await second tabernacle entrance by the promised Christ's new, heavenly, priestly, covenant ministry.

The Pastor's OT support for a current transformation into the place of God's presence arises from Jer 31:31–34. Jeremiah's prophecy begins with the statement, "Behold days presently coming, says the Lord" (Heb 8:8). The syntactical combination of the plural "days" (ἡμέραι Heb 8:8; cf. Heb 8:10) with the pres. act. ptc. "coming" (ἔρχονται) suggests that Jeremiah's listeners should watch for the coming of continually occurring events over a period of days. This observation, when added to the Pastor's weight for a ministry that is available now for his audience, supports a present, complete, recurring fulfillment of the "new covenant" (διαθήκην καινήν) relationship described in Jeremiah's prophecy, rather than only a onetime event in "the" day of Jesus's return to earth.

The Pastor's contextual temporal window for this prophetic fulfillment is during the Son's better ministry of priestly mediation after death at judgment to those who believe. The prophecy of Jeremiah again reminds listeners about UPt3 (Heb 3:1—4:13) concerning the failure of Israel to typologically demonstrate the blessings of eternal/perpetual-*place* rest in heaven by faith in God's promise during the wilderness disobedience.[216] The subsequent first covenant at Sinai is fulfilled by the new covenant that is carried out over days. This fulfillment makes the typology of the first covenant obsolete (Heb 8:13).

The believer's transformation by Jesus's priestly mediation at judgment is described in Heb 8:10–12. The syntactical description of this new relationship with the previous contextual support that the Word of God is at judgment "presently giving" (διδοὺς Heb 8:10) people his mind, laws, heart, personal relationship, common citizenship with other brethren, mission teaching change, and mercy with no memory of iniquities and sins.[217] Jesus now intercedes at death and judgment to bring into heaven those who believe in his offering for sin, in the same way that God raised him from the dead into heaven. This change in location requires creative bodily changes for continued living in God's presence after death. There is

---

216. God's promise, "I will accomplish" (συντελέσω), in reference to Israel and Judah does not limit the promise only to Israel and Judah but indicates the promise is accomplished through Israel and Judah. The expected "seed" of the promised Christ would come through them.

217. The pres. act. ptc. διδοὺς (*didous*) has weight for each of the subsequent features that he lists to occur in the temporal window under consideration. It is beyond the scope of my work to detail the changes in the spiritual body that are given by the Son as the "Word of God" at judgment to his people (cf. unit C conclusion Heb 4:11–13). The Pastor's OT support for a possible present transition to a spiritual body at death is a topic for later investigation. This evidence in this project finds the concept based upon UPt5 (Heb 10:5–14) corresponds well with all NT teaching.

no intermediate-state. After supporting this present availability of salvation promises, the Pastor continues with more comparison of the unique endpoints of earthly and heavenly ministries revealed by the tabernacle.

Unit Point 2 (9:1–5): The Earthly Tabernacle Ministry, with the Regulations of Service and the Earthly Holy Place as the First Covenant Relationship, Is Not by Parts to Now Speak

UPt2 shifts to the Pastor's second main topic (Heb 9:1–14) of unit F that mainly concerns the heavenly changes by Christ exampled in the earthly tabernacle. His focus is upon the recent creative consequences by the offering of Jesus upon the spatial area of "the holy place" before the "holy of holies."[218] The syntax in his LXX is ambiguous since each

218. Cf. Young, "Gospel According to Hebrews," 198–210. Young attempts to ascertain the use of τὰ ἅγια in Heb 9. He states that the acc. neut. sg. τό . . . ἅγιον (*to . . . hagion*, Heb 9:1) "clearly refers to the whole sanctuary" (198). Building upon this premise, he follows the general agreement of commentaries that the neut. pl. τὰ ἅγια (Heb 9:8, 12, 24, 25), which is syntactically "the holy-*places*," is a reference only to the holy of holies; e.g., Westcott, *Epistle to the Hebrews*, 254. Westcott states, "The comprehensive sense which has been given to τὰ ἅγια, as including both the Holy and the Most Holy place, explains the use of ἡ πρώτη σκηνή." His position purposely changes the Pastor's chosen syntax in Heb 9:1 and his second main point FGT to a perceived theme almost entirely about the Day of Atonement and the holy of holies.

However, even though the priestly action of Yom Kippur in the holy of holies that is antithetically contained in the Heb 9 contextual argument as better, his chosen syntax for Heb 9:1 should remain unchanged as acc. neut. sg. *noun* τό . . . ἅγιον ("the . . . holy place," Heb 9:1) in agreement of case, number, and gender with its acc. neut. sg. adj. "earthly" (κοσμικόν), in reference to the first area under the tent. This corresponds to the nom. fem. sg. Ἅγια ("holy tent," Heb 9:2) and nom. fem. sg. ἡ πρώτη σκηνή ("the first tent") before the nom. fem. sg. adj. and gen. fem. pl. adj. Ἅγια Ἁγίων ("most holy tent," Heb 9:2). The uncorrected syntax provides three references to the *holy place* as the topic of the UPt2 FGT introduction (Heb 9:1–5) before a reference to the holy of holies.

The confusion comes by attempts to determine infrastructure sense by forcing the Pastor's syntactical choices as controlled from the LXX. The Pastor's Greek syntactical choices are governed by rules of grammar that require agreement in case, gender, and number between adjectives and their either provided or implied substantive nouns in context. The syntax of the LXX and the Pastor should not be corrected by English speaking scholars to say what is perceived said, rather than what is said. The scholars seem to know better what the authors are saying more than the authors themselves when bending grammatical rules for predetermined applications. Also, semantics from the Pastor's LXX Ps 109 contextual usage trumps LXX Lev 16 optional syntax. See table 11 regarding Heb 8:1 with Ps 109:2–3 LXX in the UI/Pt1 FGT introduction (Heb 8:1–6).

Young and other commentators correctly regard "the way of the holy-*places*" (τὴν τῶν ἁγίων ὁδὸν Heb 9:8) as a path involving both the first and second tent of the whole complex. Yet, a fourth UPt2 subtopic about the holy place is εἰς τὰ ἅγια (Heb 9:12), which likely is acc. fem. sg. adj. "into the holy *tent*." The phrase designates (1) the place

Atonement and the Logic of Resurrection in Hebrews 9:27–28

area of the earthly ministry is treated as distinct with the ministry for both designated as εἰς τὸ ἅγιον ("into the holy place").[219] The Pastor adds σκηνή ("tent, tabernacle") to further distinguish these compartments as separate parts of God's speaking.

opened by Jesus's judgment on the cross before rising to God in heaven of the holy of holies, (2) the place that Jesus found eternal/perpetual-*place* redemption (Heb 9:12), (3) the place Jesus offered himself to God as an eternal/perpetual-*place* spirit (Heb 9:14), and (4) the place Jesus now in ministry cleanses the conscience of sin for his believers by mediation after death (Heb 9:14) in execution of the new covenant (Heb 8:7–13), after the pattern of Heb 9:28 summarized in the macro conclusion. Further, the phrase εἰσῆλθεν ἅγια Χριστός (Heb 9:24) is also likely acc. fem. sg. as "Christ entered a holy *tent*," since at Christ's entry, it references the combined space of both the holy place and holy of holies by removal of the veil upon his entry of his eternal/perpetual-*place* spirit (Heb 9:14) in heaven itself (Heb 9:24). The holy place was cleansed, and the previous designed separation in the true tabernacle was removed. Finally, the phrase εἰς τὰ ἅγια (Heb 9:25) is also likely acc. fem. sg. as "into the holy *tent*" in agreement with the context concerning an antithesis with the priestly entry of Yom Kippur. From the observations, it becomes apparent that the Pastor is true to his Greek syntax as he contemplates the spatial changes created by Jesus's entry into the holy of holies after his death and at his judgment in the holy-*places*. This entry, as symbolized by the tearing of the earthly veil, occurred without delay, simultaneously with Jesus's death and departure of his spirit to God, and was open before him at his rising to God.

219. In the spatial nomenclature of Exodus, the acc. neut. sg. phrase "into the holy place" (εἰς τὸ ἅγιον) appears four times (Exod 28:3, 29, 30, 35). The contextual language is nonspecific and conveys a cultic infrastructure that can apply to either area of the holy place or holy of holies. The acc. neut. sg. adjective "holy *thing*" (ἅγιον) appears five more times (Exod 30:10, 13, 24, 35; 38:25). It modifies ointment, work, and shekel. In Leviticus, the spatial nomenclature is also nonspecific. The phrase "into the holy place" (εἰς τὸ ἅγιον) may refer to either to the distinct "holy place" (Lev 10:18) or the "holy of holies" (Lev 16:2). The phrase εἰς τὸ ἅγιον (Lev 16:2) is linked with the phrase "in the holy place" (ἐν τόπῳ ἁγίῳ Lev 6:9) as a referent to the holy of holies. The phrase "in the holy place" (ἐν τόπῳ ἁγίῳ Lev 6:9, 19, 20; 7:6; 8:3; 10:13, 14, 17, 18; 14:13 [twice], 16:24; 24:9) designates the areas consecrated for specific ministry in the required cultic observations of the respective sacrificial offering discussed.

Cf. Gelardini, "Inauguration of Yom Kippur," 233–35. Gelardini correctly concludes, "Hence, none of the relevant passages contain a term referring to the sanctuary as a whole" (233). The Pastor supplies "tent" (σκηνή) to maintain the separation of the spatial areas for the respective, required, ministerial activity in connection to the first and second covenants. Gelardini limits her attempt at interpreting the spatial nomenclature of the tabernacle vocabulary in Hebrews from the LXX and Lev 16 regarding the Day of Atonement due to preconceptions that "past and present scholarship has sufficiently acknowledged the fact that Yom Kippur is of major if not fundamental importance for the interpretation of Hebrews" (227). Her listing of scholarly agreement enables the claim that the phrase τό . . . ἅγιον (*to . . . hagion*) indicates the holy of holies. She pushes this partial LXX interpretation upon Hebrews to the distortion of the Pastor's syntax about the spatial revelation indicated in the text that the audience would follow in his excellent Greek. It is unlikely the Pastor, in a mixed audience, would use inappropriate LXX nomenclature in incorrect grammatical syntax without either authoritative direct quotation from the OT or explanation.

As a rhetorical piece of his climactic argument, his exposition emphasizes the spatial adjustments resulting from Jesus's heavenly entrance were typified in "even the earthly holy place" (τό τε ἅγιον κοσμικόν) of the tabernacle "regulations of ministry" (δικαιώματα λατρείας Heb 9:1).[220] He states, "for the first tent/tabernacle was prepared" (σκηνὴ γὰρ κατεσκευάσθη ἡ πρώτη Heb 9:2).[221] The Pastor uses an unusual syntactical form to create possible dual meaning that can connect either specifically with "the holy place" of the tabernacle or the general unseen whole of the earthly tabernacle ministry.[222] However, his use of "even" (τε) stresses a

220. The misstep by Latin transliteration of ἅγιον κοσμικόν as "earthly sanctuary," (NASB, NET, HCSB, NRSV, LEB, KJV [worldly sanctuary]), or an "earthly place of holiness" (ESV) falsely supports the concept of a tabernacle "in heaven" and obscures the second major thematic point that the Pastor asserts in unit F. The errant concept misses the spatial changes by Jesus in the heavens that render obsolete the first covenant sacrifices as "dead works" (Heb 6:1; 9:14) with fault. The former symbolism of the daily priestly ministry in the holy place could no longer demonstrate the true tabernacle reality after God's removal of the veil. Since Jesus's entry, the holy place no longer exists. Also, once Jesus entered the holy of holies and remained seated on the throne, there was no need for symbolism that might suggest his offering of atonement is repeated. As a basic principle, symbolic antitypes that are observed by believers as a demonstration of faith about accomplished unseen realities are only publicly observed once; e.g., baptism (an event symbolic of a personal faith to follow Jesus in his accomplished death, burial, and resurrection from the dead to God for sin). Those antitypes that are anticipated by faith and forward reaching can be repeated; e.g., Lord's Supper (an anticipated congregational event in the unseen kingdom in heaven with Jesus and other believers that will recall the body and blood offered by Jesus for sin). The Pastor seems concerned that repetition of Yom Kippur could be interpreted as if Jesus, or others who follow him, were falling away after entrance into heaven to create an impossible teaching situation that implies starting again at the beginning of God's requirement of repentance. As noted in unit E (Heb 5:1–10; 7:1–28), the Pastor claims the concept that anyone can fall away from heaven once they have entered as impossible teaching, because of the oath and guarantee of the promise of God, who cannot lie.

221. Not all scholars accept the reality of the tabernacle existence in the history of Israel. Cf. Liss, "Imaginary Sanctuary," 663–89. Liss follows Wellhausen in an ideology that embraces the tabernacle text as fictional and never constructed, but "a splendid faking" (668). He further attempts to classify the text speaking about the tabernacle of Exod 25—40 and Lev 8—9 as fictional attempts by post-exilic author(s) from older oral and written traditions to explain loss of the land. However, Lipschits ignores the authorial confirmation upon the text on the OT as the word of God speaking. The Pastor and those who accept by faith that "God is" (Heb 11:6) should also accept the biblical record as inspired (Heb 9:8) and inerrant from God, who cannot lie or break his oath in promises (Heb 6:17–18).

222. This semantically could mean the whole of the tabernacle in the wilderness or the first holy place. The Pastor does not use the usual terms "temple" (ναός, holy place and holy of holies) or "temple complex" (ἱερόν) that includes the outer court. The separation of the nom. adj. ordinal "the first" (ἡ πρώτη), without a subject, from the nom. subj. σκηνὴ (skēnē) by the verb κατεσκευάσθη (kateskeuasthē), is unusual. The

distinctive emphasis between his topic about "the holy place" in relation to the other ministerial area of the "holy of holies" that foreshadowed respectively both the old and new heavenly covenants.[223]

Listeners must avoid an unifocal emphasis on the Day of Atonement typology and not ignore the Pastor's full rhetoric regarding the holy place and subsequent outcome rendered upon it by the entrance of the Christ. For example, Paul Ellingworth comments concerning possible errant discrepancies in the Pastor's Day of Atonement theology, "The author is concentrating in the Day of Atonement, as the lesser counterpart of Christ's sacrifice, all his thinking about sin and forgiveness under the old covenant."[224] However, the Pastor illustrates the creative changes brought about by the entrance of the Son into heaven that renders obsolete the symbolism of the holy place with its daily sacrificial typology in relation to their current ministry in teaching conversations (cf. Heb 8:13).

In a very brief review, the Pastor reminds his audience about the distinctive divisions and furnishings of the tabernacle (Heb 9:2–5a). His brevity signals that his point of exposition is not centered upon all details of the many *parts* contributing to God's speech in the earthly tabernacle ministry. Instead, he highlights two fixtures related to the holy of holies. The first is the altar of incense that represents people's prayers ascending to the presence of God in heaven, which parallels the ascent of the smoke of the burnt offerings.[225] The second is the ark of the covenant and

---

grammatical structure may support special emphasis and provide weight for keeping in the audience mind two concurrent comparisons. The first comparison is the earthly first area of the holy place (Heb 9:1, 2, 6, 8) as the subject of UPt2a–b (Heb 9:1–10) as distinct from the second area of the holy of holies (Heb 9:3, 7). This comparative form seems to place emphasis on the spatial creative adjustment involving the holy place of the greater tabernacle itself in the discussion. The second comparison is that of the earthly tabernacle changes as the subject of Pt2a–b (Heb 9:1–10) in rhetorical application to the heavenly true tabernacle (Heb 9:11–10:18).

223. BDAG "τε," 992. Bauer speaks of this use providing ascensive stress and serving without a copulative force. Cf. appendix 2, table 9, "Spatial Syntax Cohesion in Hebrews" for syntactical and semantic relationships to other adjectival uses determined by the UP2 FGT subtopics.

224. Ellingworth, *Epistle to the Hebrews*, 435–36. Cf. Loader, *Sohn und Hoherpriester*, 171–72. Loader comments that the Day of Atonement typology by no means dominates the argument of the entire section. See also, Allen, *Hebrews*, 489–90; Bruce, *Epistle to the Hebrews*, 207–8, 213–14; Koester, *Hebrews*, 121–22; Lane, *Hebrews 9–13*, 223; Ezra, *Impact of Yom Kippur*, 180; Gane, *Cult and Character*, xxi; Moffitt, "Blood, Life, and Atonement," 211–24; Jamieson, "Hebrews 9.23," 569–87.

225. This may refer to the golden censor for burning incense that was carried by the high priest into the holy of holies and left there as his third event. Cf. Gelardini, "Inauguration of Yom Kippur," 243, 246. This symbolism in the altar of incense or

its contents. He especially notes the position of the cherubim of glory overshadowing above the "place of propitiation, mercy seat [novel German/English term]" (ἱλαστήριον Heb 9:5).[226] This verbal noun symbolizes the place, before the observing angels in the presence of God, where the offering of the Christ would complete atonement for sin in the holy of holies.[227] Jürgen Roloff rightly ascertains that "the center of the typology

---

incense censor carried by the high priest tracks with the smoke of the burnt offerings that ascends upwards and represents, if God is pleased at judgment by the offeror and gift offered, the bodily soul approaching and entering the holy of holies. The Pastor expresses major concern for his audience to have a clear conscience regarding sin, esp. errant teaching, so that God may be pleased with them upon presentation before him for judgment after death (cf. Heb 11:6; 13:21).

226. Roloff, "ἱλαστήριον," 2:186. Cf. MM, 303. Moulton and Milligan comment, "It should be added, however, that, whatever view is taken of Rom 3:25, in Heb 9:5, the only other place where the word occurs in the NT, ἱλαστήριον must mean "place of propitiation" or "mercy seat," as in the LXX of the Pentateuch."

This meaning was unfortunately distorted in English translations as "mercy seat," even though the contextual intent was not mercy and there was no actual seat but only intent to symbolize the place of the priestly ministry of the promised Christ after sacrificial death, when by transformation, his soul life symbolized by the blood carried by the priest (Lev 17:11) ascends for judgment before God. The Greek OT of the LXX translated the term as ἱλαστήριον (hilastērion) with preserved meaning. The Latin Vulgate OT later in 405 CE glossed proper meaning with *propitiatorium*, which literally means "atonement place." Luther substituted the German *Gendenstuhl* meaning "mercy seat" in Heb 9:5 for Greek ἱλαστήριον for his 1522 CE September New Testament. He and those who assisted him in translation of the OT in 1534 CE also substituted the German *Gendenstuhl* meaning "mercy seat" for Hebrew *kappōret*. Later English translations used Luther's German Bible for English translations. For similar unique translation changes effecting meaning by Martin Luther concerning the Greek word for "heaven," see excursus B. For the present role of angels in salvation, see previous discussion about unit A, esp. UC A (Heb 1:13–14).

227. In English translation of the Hebrew OT and Greek NT, the gloss "atonement" or more specific sub meanings often appear according to the weight of the context. As common in all languages, specific words rarely keep their original meaning. Over time and varied usage in different people groups, the referents get freighted with additional semantic meaning or changed altogether. Proper biblical understanding of atonement must begin with the first use of the Hebrew verb *kāpar* and its parent verbal nouns *kōper*, *kippūr*, and *kappōret*. When Moses spoke these terms in the fifteenth-century BCE, the verb *kāpar* refers to the general activity of providing a ransom or gift to secure favor (e.g., Gen 32:20). The verbal nouns infer either a general use or added specific surrounding details about the verbal activity. *Kōper* provides understanding of the general verbal meaning of the act of a ransom or gift for favor (e.g. Lev 17:11). Both *kippūr* and *kappōret* include understood specific details. The former alludes to the Day of Atonement events (e.g., Lev 23:26–27). The latter refers to the specific place and activity in the holy of holies, where the high priest on the Day of Atonement sprinkled the blood of the proper symbolic sacrifice before the cover layered in gold on top of the ark of the covenant to obtain a hopeful judgment of pleasing acceptance for purification of the sins of the people (e.g., Exod 25:17; Num 7:89).

is not the literal ritual of expiation by sprinkling of blood, but rather the establishment of a new *place* of expiation to surpass the former one" (italics Roloff).²²⁸ The Pastor previously introduces the Son's activity of atonement for sin that is needed by people in the unit B UC (Heb 2:17–18).

After briefly reminding his audience about features of the distinctive areas of the first ministry, the Pastor comments, "Concerning which, it is not to speak now by part" (περὶ ὧν οὐκ ἔστιν νῦν λέγειν κατὰ μέρος Heb 9:5).²²⁹ His use of the phrase "by part" (κατὰ μέρος) links back with his first word "many parts" (Πολυμερῶς Heb 1:1) concerning God's speech-action in the past under the promise in the first covenant ministry. The

---

The revelation about the fulfillment of the OT symbolism regarding atonement by God himself as Christ records in the common language of first-century CE Greek. The Septuagint (LXX) OT with added Apocryphal writings served as the common Bible recording the speech of God's revelation in the first century CE, since most Jews no longer spoke Hebrew but Aramaic or Greek. The Greek gloss chosen for the Hebrew OT context, in the second-century BCE by the translators of the Greek LXX, included the cognate verbs *exilaskomai* and *hilaskomai* and the verbal-noun *hilastērion*. The verbs usually referenced the action of seeking the good will of another, or to appease. Other later English glosses for this activity include propitiate and conciliate. The verbal noun carried two semantic meanings of the place of atonement and the means of atonement. The LXX OT only considers the place of atonement to reference the place for priestly ministry in the holy of holies on the Day of Atonement. Common first-century CE Greek usage had two contextual semantic meanings depending on the view of either the person seeking to be appeased (expiation) or God being sought out to appease (propitiation)

In the NT, the OT and LXX described atonement activity above adds semantic meaning of either expected promise (Luke 18:13) or completed fulfillment (Heb 2:17) by Jesus's ability as the Christ to appease God by his substitutionary death for the sins of the people in the true tabernacle of the heavens that the OT tabernacle symbolized (Heb 9:15–28). The sense meaning of atonement maintains a strong spatial force for the place of the holy of holies in which atonement by the high priest takes place (Heb 9:5), even when testifying about the means of Jesus's ability (Rom 3:25) as the source of atonement. If Jesus does not enter the holy of holies after death, then he is not the promised Christ in the activity of making atonement. The ability in fulfillment to enter the holy of holies after death as an eternal-spirit and living soul is critical to the complete meaning of atonement in both the OT and NT. There is no source for removal of personal sin of the people without entrance by Jesus after approach to God at death for judgment as the Christ on the cross.

228. Roloff, "ἱλαστήριον," 2:186. Roloff comments, "God has publicly set him forth as the place of expiation through faith in his blood."

229. *GGBB*, "κατὰ," 377. Wallace, concerning κατὰ in the acc., provides the semantic option, "Distributive: 'indicating the division of a greater whole into individual parts.'" The Pastor negates the continued speaking of the first ministry of the tabernacle service by parts, since Christ has now spoken in fulfillment of the whole of the symbolic meaning. Cf. BDAG, "κατὰ," 511. BDAG provides the sematic distributive meaning option as a "marker of division of a greater whole into individual parts" that are not indications of place and time.

audience should listen to the Son and not the distinct parts of the tabernacle ministry, because with the spatial changes achieved, the former symbolic teaching parts of the tabernacle is now faulty. The part of the ministerial function and the holy place itself no longer exist due to Jesus's entrance. The daily sacrifices, if continued now, typologically present an incorrect conversation about unseen realities. Also, since Yom Kipper is now fulfilled, the symbolic meaning of this ministry to foreshadow the Christ is now obsolete. In his next FGT, the Pastor compares the symbolism of these two ministries and applies the outcomes of their fulfillment to the present time of his speaking.

Subpoint 2a Pre-Climax (9:6–10): The Continual Earthly Ministry by Priests in the First Ministry Was Symbolic and Enforced, until the New Order for the Present Time That Opens the Way into the Holy-Places

SbPt2a continues the subtopic of the first holy place and contrasts the earthly daily ministry with the annual ministry with the Day of Atonement. The Pastor first relates that the priests continually enter the holy place (Heb 9:6). However, their ministry into the holy of holies occurs only once a year (Heb 9:7). Also, he emphasizes a feature about the Day of Atonement that the high priest does not enter without blood, which is offered both for himself and the sins of the people committed in ignorance.[230] The subtopic of blood links back to unit B (Heb 2:1–18)

---

230. Gilders, *Blood Ritual*. Gilders in analysis of OT texts finds that from an ancient perspective, blood is identified with animation of the body, as in Lev 17:11. Gilder's strength is that he identifies scholarly conclusions beyond the basic observations of the text without support as "conceptual gap-filling." His observations reveal that more is said in the OT about manipulation activity with blood in either the ministry or social prohibitions, than exposition about the symbolism behind the instructions provided. He finds more meaning from "indexes" connected as facts in association to the social functions of blood manipulation than the very limited OT teaching concerning symbolism from the lone text of Lev 17:11. However, his adoption of the multiple sources of the Knohl-Milgrom hypothesis, that the OT text first consisted of a holiness code with further development by later redaction of priests, rather than accepting the OT text as a cohesive record of God's speech, as the Pastor, is problematic for his antithetical conclusions. Gilders advances the conceptual meaning of the blood manipulation activity by investigating "latent functions" surrounding it that "establish and define social-cultic relationships, status, identity, as well as serve in the construction and maintenance of sacral space and of its boundaries with nonsacral space" (187). He works hard only to in the end to agree with the Pastor in his conceptual recognition in the areas of latent function mentioned. The Pastor in the NT era claims that the blood of the sacrifices

about the necessity of the bodily, animated humanity of the Son, in common with people, that is required to render powerless the devil's power of death (cf. Heb 2:14–15). The Son, by the sacrifice of his life for the atonement of sin, now brings those who believe in his ability into God's presence at judgment to free them from the devil's domain. The Pastor, from this point, will heavily stress the fleshly offering of the animated life of Jesus before God for sin by referring to the significance of sacrificial blood nineteen more times in his message.

The Pastor next returns to the spatial aftermath established by the priestly ministry in each separate holy place of the tabernacle (Heb 9:8). As clarified by the Holy Spirit, the tabernacle functioned as a "parable" (παραβολὴ Heb 9:9) concerning the differences in the offering of Christ in the new heavenly covenant of the holy of holies compared to the many offerings of the earthly covenant in part.[231] The priests continued offering

---

represented symbolically the flesh sacrifice of the living animated body of Jesus (cf. Heb 10:4–10). The latent functions derived from Gilders' observations surrounding cultic blood manipulation apply perfectly to Jesus's sacrifice, as the Son of God, high priest, and offering, both spatially on the nonsacral earth and then as an eternal/perpetual-*place* spirit (Heb 9:14) in the sacral heaven. As animated flesh, Jesus gave his life sacrificially for removal of the sins of the people. He then approached God as an eternal-place spirit for judgment, just as appointed for all people (Heb 9:27). In God's pleasure, at judgment on the cross, the Son found redemption at death and was enthroned to serve as a high priest in the sacral holy-*places* on behalf of those who accepted him by faith as their sacrifice for sin (cf. unit C).

231. Caneday, "God's Parabolic Design," 103–24. Caneday correctly states, "Because these uses of τύπος contribute to a cluster of other terms—τύπικως, ἀληθινός, ἀντίτυπος, σκιά, ὑπόδειγμα, παραβολή—they provide significant insight by which one can discover and explain numerous other OT prefigurements of Messiah and his kingdom" (104). He further states, "The Creator designs shadows within the natural realm to instruct us concerning earthly shadows of heavenly realities" (105). However, Caneday omits the present, tangible, heavenly spatial realities to believers at death in his vertical considerations. He considers that Israel's "covenant promises established them as participants in a grand earthly drama, a symbolically-laden allegory which for them anticipates the latter days when the promised Messiah will fulfill God's covenant promises by bringing heavenly realities to earth so that at last heaven and earth become one (cf. Eph 1:10; Rev 21:1–3)" (106). His theology inverts the endpoint from expectation of the perpetual heaven to the temporary earth and God's presence in a future eschatology. Caneday does admit, "To explain biblical types by focusing upon the temporal-historical axis fails to do justice to the multidimensional nature of all the Bible's types which derive their typological forward looking function from their spatial relationship to heavenly realities, namely their divinely authorized revelatory functions. It is biblically shortsighted to restrict one's definition of typology to the temporal-historical axis" (106). His essay attempts "to demonstrate that the coherence and complementarity of these two axes, the revelatory-spatial and the historical-temporal, is essential to how all biblical types function" (106). Caneday follows the scholarly straw man of revelatory (nonhistorical, transcendent, spiritual, intangible, inaccessible God) against

daily the burnt offerings that demonstrated only the promised offering of the Christ. This sacrifice of the burnt offering had been observed from the beginning of man's sin. In the burnt offering, after the life blood of the animal was offered on earth, then specific sacrificial portions were placed on the altar so that smoke would ascend into heaven. This offering symbolizes Christ rising upward to God for his judgment and atonement of the offerers' sin. The same life, blood, sacrificial symbolism was representatively depicted in the inauguration of the tabernacle, ordination of the priests, the offering of the red heifer, as well as other gifts and offerings to God. Other offerings in part by additional symbolism also collectively foreshadow the offering of Christ.

Once a year, on the Day of Atonement that prefigures the new and better covenant, several variations occur.[232] Two rams are pictured, with one offered and one released. Also, the high priest travels through the holy place and the veil into the holy of holies to sprinkle blood on the place of atonement ("mercy seat") before the onlooking angels. The Day of Atonement events depict the journey of Christ's transition from the heavenly first covenant to the new covenant, as symbolized by earthly approach at the holy place and entrance into the holy of holies.[233] The

---

historical-temporal, tangible, natural existence on earth. In this view the vertical is only revelatory without historical-temporal reality. Caneday's misstep in philosophy causes him to disregard the biblical concept of the material, tangible reality in heaven. He does state, "Christians need to keep in mind that the earthly is the analogy of the heavenly"(118, italics Caneday). Ironically, he warns, "The temptation may be to invert the analogy by forgetting that the earthly Most Holy Place is only the copy of that the true, the original, is the heavenly tabernacle, the habitation of God's presence" (118).

232. For a recent listing of scholarly discussion and comparison of the OT Day of Atonement priestly actions in Lev 16 and those actions highlighted in Hebrews, see Gelardini, "Inauguration of Yom Kippur," 242–47.

233. Cortez, "From the Holy," 527–47. Cortez highlights multiple inconsistencies in the context of Hebrews against a strict Day of Atonement theme. These are (1) the more general term offered rather than sprinkled in Heb 9:7, (2) mention of sprinkling of blood with the inauguration of the covenant in Heb 9:15–23, (3) the mention of "goats" (τράγοι), which are not associated with the Day of Atonement, (4) possible reversal about the order of purification of sin by Christ before entering the holy of holies rather than a condition for entry in Lev 16, (5) the description of Christ's death in Heb 9:11–23 conflates multiple offerings of Yom Kippur (Lev 16), red heifer (Num 19), covenant institution (Exod 24), and priestly ordination (Lev 8), and (6) ratification of the covenant rather than the Day of Atonement as the primary typology to describe Jesus's death. Cortez classifies Heb 9:6–10 as a Greek "period" that in the first century CE mainly indexed either poetic material or a long sentence constructed for rhetorical punch (529–32). Many scholars continue to conflate the term period with Greek FGT or English paragraphs. Cortez argues convincingly that the Greek period of Heb 9:6–10 explains how the two areas of the tabernacle function as a parable, with explanation by

Pastor asserts that the "way of the holy-*places*" (τὴν τῶν ἁγίων ὁδὸν) had not been revealed while the holy place still stood (Heb 9:8). God's elimination of the holy place at the completion of Jesus's atonement for sin allows Jesus's revelation as "the way" into the presence of God.

He emphasizes that the spatial changes accomplished by Jesus traveling through the heavens apply as a "parable for the present time" (παραβολὴ εἰς τὸν καιρὸν τὸν ἐνεστηκότα Heb 9:9) of his speaking about the ineffectiveness of the daily gifts and sacrifices observed in the holy place "to complete the conscience" (συνείδησιν τελειῶσαι Heb 9:9) of those worshiping God.[234] The daily ministry in holy place could not prevent the continued painful awareness of sin by its removal at judgment in the needed transformation for entry into the holy of holies (cf. Heb 8:12; 10:2). This temporary flaw, with the daily sacrifices only serving the flesh without any effect on the people's spiritual need at judgment, serves "until a time being imposed of a new order" (μέχρι καιροῦ διορθώσεως ἐπικείμενα Heb 9:10). This SbPt2a FGT functions as a pre-peak and sets up his SbPt2b climax FGT regarding the Pastor's transition to Christ's

---

the Holy Spirit, like Jesus's explanations of parables in the gospels.

Cf. Caneday, "God's Parabolic Design," 112. Caneday is correct that the section is not only about Day of Atonement typology regarding Jesus's sacrifice as much as exposition about the changes achieved in transition from the first to second heavenly covenant. By replacing his philosophical terms "sanctuary" and "ages" with "holy place(s)" and where syntactically appropriate "eternal/perpetual-*places*," Cortez's assertions support an expositional antithesis in Heb 9:6–10 for spatial changes from limited access into heaven by the old heavenly covenant to only the heavenly holy place (Abraham's bosom) to the new covenant access to the heavenly holy of holies that is inaugurated by Jesus's entrance. *Contra*, Gelardini, "Inauguration of Yom Kippur," 225–54. Gelardini argues against successionism of the covenants but rather for "the destruction of the earthly holy, and with it the entire temple . . . to make way for a new way of perpetual access by God by means of the one remaining celestial sanctuary" (243).

234. The concept for completion or perfection of the believer at entrance into the holy of holies tracks from the main introductory subtopic Heb 1:3d through the τελ- (*tel*) word groups. For the Pastor's use of συνείδησις, (*syneidēsis*) see Selby, "Meaning and Function of Συνείδησις," 145–54. Selby rightly analyzes συνείδησις as one's personal, painful awareness of sin before God, particularly at judgment, which awareness would exclude entrance into God's presence. The term is used three times in main topics of unit F (Heb 9:9, 14; 10:2), once in the transition 2 summary conclusion (Heb 10:22) and in his closing unit A′ for an application in an exhortation to loving conduct in all things. Selby shows in the Pastor's argument that the first covenant ministry in the holy place blocked entrance into the holy of holies by increasing an awareness of sin. The second covenant ministry in the holy of holies is better, in that it removes a consciousness of sin so that the one approaching in worship may enter to God. The first covenant preveniently allowed sinful people into heaven of the holy place pending Jesus's changes and cleansing forgiveness by atonement of sin.

new covenant that both fulfills the many parts of the collective first covenant symbolism and the new covenant symbolism of the annual Day of Atonement ministry.

Subpoint 2b Climax (9:11–14): Christ, Who Entered the Holy-Places to Obtain Eternal/Perpetual-Place Redemption as an Eternal/Perpetual-Place Spirit When Offering his Own of Blood, and Who Achieved the Now Greater and More Perfect Tabernacle in Heaven, Should Better Cleanse the Conscience in Order to Serve the Living God from the Now Dead Works of the Earthly Tabernacle Ministry That only Outwardly Cleansed the Flesh

SbPt2b signals a climactic fact in his ongoing unit F comparison by beginning with "but Christ" (Χριστὸς δὲ Heb 9:11). The referent signals to his audience that he is about to describe the transitional spatial events and holy place changes accomplished at the moment of salvation by the promised offering of Christ depicted by the earthly sacrifices. His content tracks the vertical path for the fulfillment of the beginning teaching about the Christ "of both rising of the dead and eternal/perpetual-*place* judgment" (ἀναστάσεώς τε νεκρῶν καὶ κρίματος αἰωνίου Heb 6:2) outlined in unit E (Heb 5:11—6:20). The Pastor now focuses on the instant of Christ's completed sacrificial salvation by the blood of his animated life, his nearly concurrent experience of rising of the dead, and his subsequent eternal/perpetual-*place* judgment (Heb 9:14, 27; cf. Luke 23:46). These elements occur in the temporal space of a flash of time.

God judges the sacrificial offering of the blood of Jesus's animated life (Heb 9:12; 1:8–12; cf. John 19:30) at the temporal point of his death as the Christ in atonement for sin just before he journeys "through the greater and more complete tabernacle/tent" (διὰ τῆς μείζονος καὶ τελειοτέρας σκηνῆς Heb 9:11).[235] The Pastor's account highlights in Jesus's offering

235. The OT and ST expectation in the first century CE included views for the dead to rise to God in spirit after death, more than the lesser consideration of flesh resurrection; e.g., consider the preacher in Ecclesiastes as he metaphorically explains the vanity of the experience of aging. He comments, "Man goes into his eternal/perpetual-*place* home.... The dust may return upon the earth, as it was, and the spirit should return to God, who gave it" (Eccl 12:5–7 LXX). For Hebrews, evidence supports that once in heaven, Jesus at his entrance becomes a continual high priest. The Pastor describes the travel of the Christ as not in the movements of the sacrifice and priest of the earthly tabernacle but first as sacrifice in death and judgment, then as priest through the heavens (cf. Heb 4:14). Both the anointed Christ as sacrifice and priest involve "the way of

an achievement of creative changes to the first tent of the holy place mentioned in his SbPt2a FGT (Heb 9:6–10). He states, "But Christ, after himself arriving is a high priest of the good *places* themselves existing" (Χριστὸς δὲ παραγενόμενος ἀρχιερεὺς τῶν γενομένων ἀγαθῶν Heb 9:11). In his declaration, the nominative referents "Christ" and "high priest" are likely either an implied predicate nominative "Christ is a high priest" or a parenthetic nominative linking the subjects in the two participial phrases.[236] The aorist mid. ptc. "after himself arriving" (παραγενόμενος) and "after themselves occurring" (γενομένων) carry weight for antecedent time for actions before the implied main verb "is" in reference to the salvation event under consideration. The syntax implies that the first tent of the holy place is already obsolete, at the moment of completed atonement, *before* Jesus's rises to God in death (Heb 10:19–20) for his continued participation in his high priest ministry, which the Pastor previously outlined in unit D (Heb 5:1–10; 7:1–28).

In a split-second, as Jesus's dismisses his spirit into the hands of the Father for judgment (Heb 1:5–12; 5:7; 10:7; cf. Luke 23:46; 1 Tim 3:16b; 1 Pet 2:23), the Father approves the atonement for sin, and opens access into the holy of holies for Jesus's approaching soul of his eternal/perpetual-*place* spirit (Heb 6:19–20). Jesus, upon his arrival into heaven, "enters once into the holy *tent*" (εἰσῆλθεν ἐφάπαξ εἰς τὰ ἅγια Heb 9:12), which the Pastor describes as now a greater and more complete tabernacle/tent "not made with hands" (οὐ χειροποιήτου Heb 9:11).[237] The

---

the holy-*places*" (Heb 9:8). As a subst. aorist mid. gen. pl. neut. ptc. phrase modifying "Christ, a high priest," his crafted phrase "of the good *places* having existed," probably specifies the place of the ministry of Jesus as the Christ and references back to "the way of the holy-*places*" of the tabernacle of the heavens (Heb 8:1, 5; 9:23), to reinforce the ability of Jesus as Shepherd to lead believers to God, believers who follow the same experience as his own death and judgment to himself and the Father (Heb 11:6).

Some scholars attempt to make the described tabernacle as only symbolic of Jesus himself without any application to the heavenly creative changes to the holy place. The gospel of John does link Jesus with the temple. Also, the term "flesh" in Heb 10 could be taken as his literal fleshly body rather than sacrificial language for Jesus's atonement at death. However, the extensive, descriptive, local language and verbal movement by the Pastor make this application unlikely.

236. *GGBB*, 40–48, 53–55. Here, the two nominatives as a parenthetic nominative are translated as an implied equative verb with supplied "is." However, other options do not change the semantic meaning.

237. The comparative language references the former, unseen, divided holy-*places* in the first covenant in comparison to the undivided heavenly reality of the new covenant for believers who approach God for judgment after death. For scholarly discussion of the spatial interpretative views regarding Heb 9:12, see Laub, "Ein für allemal hineingegangen," 65–85. Laub attempts to harmonize the language of Hebrews between

Pastor exclaims, "This one is not of this creation" (τοῦτ' ἔστιν οὐ ταύτης τῆς κτίσεως) to distinguish the creative changes from the previous reality in heaven that required separation of people from the dwelling of God.[238] The veil is gone (cf. Matt 27:51; Mark 15:18; Luke 23:45), with the boundaries of the holy place no longer in existence when Jesus's rises to God for judgment in the pattern of the OT sacrifices (Heb 10:19–20).

In contrast to the endpoint depicted by the inefficient substitutionary animal sacrifices, the Pastor further declares about Christ, "But by his own blood he entered once into the holy *tent* after finding eternal/perpetual-*place* redemption" (δὲ τοῦ ἰδίου αἵματος εἰσῆλθεν ἐφάπαξ εἰς τὰ ἅγια αἰωνίαν λύτρωσιν εὑράμενος Heb 9:12).[239] The referent antecedently found before "Christ entered" the holy *tent* is "eternal/perpetual-*place* redemption" (Heb 9:12). The term λύτρωσιν (*lytrōsin*) refers to a release or deliverance from a captive situation.[240] In the Pastor's exposition, the

---

Jesus's offering on the cross and his entrance once into the spatial reality of the holy of holies. He admits the presence of first-century CE apocalyptic language but his vocabulary cohesion in the spatial language of Hebrews is hampered by Greek translation with preconceived vague philosophical terms such as "sanctuary," errant Greek syntactical spatial applications for "holy place" (ἅγιος), and history of religions philosophical features, such as influence of Platonic or Philonic sources. He further, regarding the veil and blood, integrates links with salvation and the Lord's supper with later church, traditional, sacramental concepts. Hebrews must stand on its own merits in syntax, semantics, theology, and meaning of groupings of text above the sentence level that govern the message for proper understanding. When outside influences are stripped away, the spatial beauty of the atoning ministry of God as the Son better comes to full light, where after the example of Jesus, believers are bodily in spirit led after death at judgment by his present priestly mediation into the holy of holies of God's dwelling.

238. The "eternal/perpetual-*places*" (αἰών) of the material unseen reality in heaven are not stagnate. Eternal/perpetual-*place* creation does not infer that it is unchanging, but perpetual, durative, and lasting. For the Pastor, the fathers by faith recognize the visible creation derives from things not seen in reference to the perpetual eternal/perpetual-*place* creation (Heb 11:3). Sin in the creation and the power of the devil in this temporary realm over death necessitate changes that allows access into God's dwelling in heaven by sinful people through repentance and faith. The perpetual creation undergoes cleansing and restructuring, before the arrival of Jesus in the eternal realm, immediately after death. It will again experience change in the future when God's removes all temporary creation under the dominion of death and decay (Heb 12:25–29).

239. The spatial creative changes achieved by the Son in his death renders argument over the semantics of the syntax of "into the holy *tent*" (εἰς τὰ ἅγια Heb 9:12, 24) a moot point.

240. For translation of λύτρωσιν as "redemption," see BDAG, "λύτρωσις, εως, ἡ," 606. Bauer defines the term as the "experience of being liberated from an oppressive situation" with glosses of "ransoming, releasing, redemption."

Atonement and the Logic of Resurrection in Hebrews 9:27-28

term continues in the track from the DI and each UC in the language about the subtopic of salvation at judgment before God (Heb 1:3c).

The aorist mid. ptc. "after *himself* finding" (εὑράμενος) can infer that Jesus is either the subject or object of release before entering. If objective, what is it that Jesus must be released from? There are several options for which Jesus may need deliverance at the point of entering the eternal/perpetual-*place* at death. First, is the consequence of the sins of the people in making atonement. Second, is the heavenly boundaries and limitations for people concerning the holy place that existed before Jesus's atonement for sin and subsequent entry into God's dwelling. Both are probably inferred since Jesus is considered a "forerunner" (πρόδρομος Heb 6:20) and "originator, author" (ἀρχηγός Heb 2:10; 12:2) for other people to follow his example of finishing into heaven.

If Jesus had to continue suffering the consequences of the sins for either himself (he had no sin) or others beyond the event of sacrificial atonement of the cross, then in death, at his ensuing judgment, he would not have been ceremonially clean to enter either the holy place or holy of holies for priestly ministry in mediation. Atonement must be finished on the cross as implied by Jesus's dying assertion (cf. John 19:20). This claim, by the Pastor, for Christ finding redemption, likely represents cleansing language that required priestly preparation before entering a holy place (cf. Lev 10:1–3). The purification language continues in his next conditional sentence with the terms "defile" (κεκοινωμένους Heb 9:13),[241] "purity" (καθαρότητα Heb 9:13),[242] "cleanse" (καθαριεῖ Heb 9:14),[243] and "blameless" (ἄμωμον Heb 9:14).[244] Jesus, at his judgment by God at death, was ceremonially clean, as blameless from sin for himself or others. Only after his completed effective atonement for the sins of others on the cross could he enter for priestly ministry the refashioned holy *tent* prepared for him by God after his sacrificial death. Any ritual uncleanness at his judgment would prevent his ministry in heaven. This included any contact with the dead in heaven, who were still without atonement (cf. Heb 7:26), and who would need cleansing (Heb 10:9) before their own experience

---

241. BDAG, "κοινόω," 552. Bauer glosses the term stating, "Most freq. in the sense of κοινός 2 **make common** or **impure, defile** in the cultic sense" (italics and bold Bauer).

242. BDAG, "καθαρότης," 490. Bauer glosses, "State or condition of being ritually cleansed, purity."

243. BDAG, "καθαρίζω," 488. Bauer glosses, "To purify through ritual cleansing, make clean, declare clean."

244. BDAG, "ἄμωμος," 56. Bauer glosses the term, stating, "Pert. to being without defect or blemish, unblemished of the absence of defects in sacrificial animals."

of the remodeling of the holy place by its merger into the holy of holies (cf. Heb 2:8b 18; 12:22–24) that the Pastor summarizes again in unit F SbPt3b (Heb 9:23–26).[245]

The problem of sinful people in the holy place of heaven raises a second subjective option, for Jesus as the one providing redemption, concerning the spatial limitations and boundaries symbolized in parts by the tabernacle ministry. Jesus, as a priest and the God-man, needed deliverance or release from the restrictions of the location of the holy place in the heavens. A continued journey "passing through the heavens" (διεληλυθότα τοὺς οὐρανούς Heb 4:14) to the holy of holies of God's presence was limited by an angelic veil in separation. Therefore, before Jesus's death, it is likely that the holy place restricted the souls of the righteous dead from God's dwelling presence. Redemption then also speaks of a subjective reference to Jesus in the salvation of others (Heb 2:11; 9:13; 10:10, 14, 29; 13:12). Since Jesus, as Christ, is holy and clean from any hinderance before he entered, he already had found "eternal/perpetual-*place*" (αἰωνίαν) deliverance from the temporary holy place. Symbolically, the earthly veil was torn while Jesus is on the cross promptly at death, signifying God's judgment for Jesus's salvation. Jesus, as the Christ, can then immediately pass through the former holy place bordered by the veil (cf. Heb 6:18–20). He, in his journey through the heavens, creates a durative entrance and way into the holy of holies that makes the holy place no longer functionally active (Heb 9:8). This deliverance is eternal and perpetual in comparison to the temporary earthly sacrifices that needed repetition. Jesus, as a forerunner in the way to God, by one sacrificial offering, also found redemption for those who would by faith follow him in death to where he now abides.

The three aorist participles "after arriving" (παραγενόμενος), "having existed, occurred, happened" (γενομένων), and "after finding" (εὑράμενος) grammatically occur in contemporary time antecedent to the time of the main verb "entered" (εἰσῆλθεν Heb 9:12) and implied verb "is" in his

---

245. The Pastor's understanding about needed cleansing of the heavens that is symbolized by the necessity for items being made holy when used in the earthly covenant ministry, becomes clearer when it is recognized that at the time of Jesus's death, there were sinful people on earth, and in the holy place in heaven, whose sins had not yet been atoned. By faith in God's promise, people were consciously awaiting the sacrificial offering and intercession of the Christ for their salvation at God's judgment after death (Heb 2:8b–13; cf. Ps 16:10; Matt 17:3; Mark 9:4; Luke 2:29–32; 16:23–31). This cleansing of people for heavenly entrance is further discussed in unit F Pt3b (Heb 9:23–26) to follow as part of the Pastor's subtopic theme of salvation.

parenthetic nominative referents "Christ" and "high priest" (Heb 9:11). Before "Christ entered," he is already at his dying moment on the cross, a high priest who created the existence of good *places* in the heavenly eternal/perpetual-*places* (cf. Ps 109:4 LXX [110:4 MT]) and found redemption for himself from the restrictions of the holy place that is extrapolated to others. Collectively, these imply the effectual atonement was complete at sacrificial death on the cross, before "Christ entered," without later necessary manipulation of literal blood, his later multiple ascensions to the Father between witnessed earthly visitations, or the promised second coming in other NT text. The description "Christ entered" is the event of salvation tightly linked to the instant of Jesus death as "the way" of atonement that would be applied to others who follow in confession by faith. With a veil gone, and the opening of a way established, there is no longer a distinction between the holy-*places* that are now "a greater and more complete tent" (Heb 9:11) by Jesus's finished atonement and arrival in heaven itself.

The Pastor completes his climax FGT about the moment of salvation with another distinction between the offering of Christ and the earthly sacrifices in a conditional sentence spanning Heb 9:13–14. The apodosis immediately contrasts the sacrificial death of the animals mentioned in the protasis with Christ's sacrificial death, stating rhetorically "how much more the blood of Christ" (πόσῳ μᾶλλον τὸ αἷμα τοῦ Χριστοῦ Heb 9:14). Again, the blood, by use as shorthand sacrificial language, points the audience to the event of Jesus's offering in death.

The Pastor's better offering, by the blood representing the animated life of Christ, is followed by an apodosis statement that is formatted in a relative clause. Due to a long history of presuppositions, this clause is perhaps one of the most difficult syntactical challenges of the NT. The masc. relative pronoun "who" (ὅς) modifies Christ. Next the Pastor states that Christ "through a spirit of an eternal/perpetual-*place* offered himself blameless to God" (διὰ πνεύματος αἰωνίου ἑαυτὸν προσήνεγκεν ἄμωμον τῷ θεῷ Heb 9:14). Yet this translation is not without other syntactical choices that must be considered and evaluated.

First, διὰ (*dia*) with a genitive has several syntactical choices. As agency, it can translate "by the spirit" or as means, then "through the spirit." Those who introduce the Holy Spirit prefer that the intended meaning refers to Jesus's empowerment by the agency or means of the Holy Spirit as the implied variance in the rhetorical, earth-heavens, offering contrast.²⁴⁶ This position is not without exegetical problems that are next noted regarding the preposition διά with the object "spirit, Spirit" (πνεύματος) and gen. adj. "of a holy place" (αἰωνίου).

Second, "spirit, Spirit" (πνεύματος) has several choices. The three options are human spirit, Holy Spirit, or a human spirit that is filled with the Holy Spirit. The author uses πνεῦμα (*pneuma*) twelve times in his homily. He uses the term to refer to (1) "angels" (Heb 1:7, 14), (2) a transformed "human spirit" at death (Heb 2:4; 4:12; 6:4; 10:29 [Jesus?]; 12:9; 23; cf. 1 Cor 15:44–45; 1 Pet 3:18),²⁴⁷ and (3) the "Holy Spirit" (Heb 3:7, 9:8, 10:15). In every use, where the context is clearly the Holy Spirit, an adjectival form of "Holy" (ἅγιος) is included. In nearly all other instances where πνεῦμα is used without ἅγιος, the context clearly refers to either spirits of angels or men. The two interrogative clauses with πνεύματος in Heb 9:14 and 10:29 have strong evidence toward Jesus's as a conscious, human, spirit form in his immediate self-offering after death before approach to God (cf. Luke 23:46, appendix 1, fig. 1, nos. 2–4).

In Heb 10:29, in a warning exhortation of S3 unit E′ UI (Heb 10:26–31), the phrase "spirit of grace" (πνεῦμα τῆς χάριτος) is in apposition with "the Son of God" (ὁ τὸν υἱὸν τοῦ θεοῦ) and the sacrificial language of Jesus's death of "the blood of the new covenant" (τὸ αἷμα τῆς διαθήκης κοινὸν Heb 10:29). The temptation of the audience is not a direct rejection of the Holy Spirit in some quasi link to blasphemy, but a teaching choice that distorts the heavenly reality of Jesus's gospel priestly ministry that created the greater and more complete tent, completed atonement, and presently continues intercession in making believers holy for entry to God.

In Heb 9:14, the idiom "a spirit of a holy place" (πνεύματος αἰωνίου Heb 9:14) modifies "πνεῦμα" (*pneuma*) with genitive "αἰωνίου" (*aiōniou*) as "an eternal/perpetual-*place* spirit." This combination in extant Greek texts is found only in Hebrews. It is not in the LXX or other Judeo-Hellenistic noncanonical works. Even the Hebrew, עוֹלָם (*ʿōwlām*), which is

---

246. When worked out logically the meaning would imply that the animal sacrifices had no empowerment by the Holy Spirit. Since commanded by the speech of God to Moses, the concept that the animal sacrifices had no Holy Spirit empowerment is problematic. These sacrifices did have faults by inability to clear the conscience of the believer at judgment but were used for nearly 1,500 years by the Holy Spirit (Heb 9:8) to teach in a parable the necessary atonement event in heaven by the Christ for sin.

247. See chapter 3 section "Internal Evidence in Hebrews for Transformation to Spirit Bodies at Death as Complete People into Heaven Just like Jesus Did," esp. 157n179 [XREF]; chapter 4 unit B UI (Heb 2:1–4).

translated Greek αἰώνιος, is never found as a description of who God is but only what God does.²⁴⁸ The Greek αἰώνιος is difficult to translate in English due to its combined temporal and spatial qualities.²⁴⁹ The adjective αἰωνίου applies a durative descriptive quality to πνεύματος. Therefore, it likely does not refer to the Holy Spirit, as God who is beyond time and space, but God who works within time and space of his creation. Also, to prevent confusion the Pastor adds "himself" (ἑαυτὸν) to clarify Christ as the subject under consideration in the antitype of the apodosis statement. Christ is durative and perpetual in spiritual bodily form necessary for dwelling in a perpetual creation without decay or chaos.

A better option is that in the Pastor's sacrificial, contrastive context, πνεύματος αἰωνίου (*pneumatos aiōniou*) describes Jesus's human "eternal/perpetual-*place* spirit," who is blameless, and without exception, is filled with the Spirit of God. Several evidence support this choice. First, for God to be fully human in flesh, he must have a durative human spirit. Jesus, as the God-man, becomes human in space and time having flesh and spirit. Flesh without the durative spirit exitance is a quality of death (cf. Jas 2:26). Second, atonement in death requires Jesus's tasting death for every man. There must be a potential for both death of flesh and spirit or the cross is a fake-out with no significant meaning. For atonement, Jesus must die in the flesh and at least could potentially die in spiritual separation from God as spirit just as any other man (fig. 3).²⁵⁰ Otherwise, judgment of the Son by God is only for dramatic purposes without real possible consequences of other people. The Pastor even proceeds to speak, in the next UPt3 FGT introduction (Heb 9:15–18), about the requirement of death for the new covenant, to support the death of the Son as a required reality, even if it was only a moment between the removal of Jesus's spirit and God's verdict of judgment before entering the holy-*places*.

Without exception Jesus's human spirit was continuously filled with the Holy Spirit without blame in judgment of his life after death. The biblical text has no hint of division of Jesus's God-man person from the will of the Father or the empowering agency of the Holy Spirit. Without this blamelessness, the God-man incarnate atonement is not possible. In

---

248. Compton, *Psalm 110*, 124–26. See esp. section "Excursus 7: πνεῦμα in Hebrews 9:14." He finds αἰώνιος in the LXX in reference to God's actions (Isa 40:28, 57:15). Actions of God implies a relationship with creation beyond himself.

249. Allen, "Forgotten Ages," 144–51.

250. Kibbe, "God-Man's Indestructible Life."

comparable manner to Jesus, the created substance form of the human spirit of believers is sealed by the indwelling agency of the Holy Spirit (Eph 1:13–14, 4:30; Rom 8:16; 1 John 4:13). This empowers the spatial substance of the Holy Spirit–indwelled spirit of believers to durative eternal/perpetual-*place* living by the present agency of the Holy Spirit in following the pattern of Jesus in conscious active living beyond death of the flesh. This interpretative position, if sustained with proper exegetical evidence, would further affirm the Christian confession that deceased believers abide in a conscious, heavenly, living presence, with Jesus before their return with him for raising the remaining living at the second coming to join with them in Jesus's earthly ministry.

In the Pastor's argument, his protasis concerns the old animal sacrifices that were only beneficial for the cleansing of the flesh in an outward testimony of inward realities. This overt cultic demonstration of outward cleansing only symbolized the inward cleansing of the conscience of sin required at approach for judgment to enter to God in heaven after death. This conscience cleaning would have to be provided by God himself and accepted in faith by the listener. It could not occur by the "dead works" of the sacrificial system of the first covenant that only publicly revealed one's acknowledgment of sin and realized necessity for God's provision in Christ for forgiveness in a clear conscience before God at judgment after death.[251]

---

251. For discussion of the scholarly interpretive options for "dead works" in Heb 9:14, see Gordon, "Better Promises" 434–49. He options (1) the Jewish law, (2) moral offenses or pre-Christian experience before baptism, and (3) his most favored option of works that lead to death as a link between sins of ignorance for which the earthly sacrifices enabled forgiveness and premeditated sins that only incurred a remedy of death. The option for moral or pre-Christian experience provides an excellent example of proof texting beyond the meaning of the text. The first and latter explanations do address the context but miss the overall point of the recurrent antithesis between the Christ offering and the offerings specified in the law, which included the daily and annual Day of Atonement sacrifices mentioned by the Pastor. The point is that the former ministry of the earthly covenant sacrifices, including the Day of Atonement, are dead as far as ministry is concerned since fulfilled by Christ once due to Jesus's achieved spatial changes in heaven.

For description of the Day of Atonement ministry of the high priest, see Edersheim, *Temple*, 319–23. On the Day of Atonement, the high priest to fulfill all the commands of Scripture actually enters the holy of holies four times and offers the sprinkling of blood forty-three times. Since both daily and annual sacrifices after Jesus's fulfillment errantly teach about the unseen realities, they have no value when ministerial teaching is judged. The topic of ministerial accountability at judgment tracks from the beginning of the Pastor's message. It is developed in the unit B UI (Heb 2:1–4), unit C (Heb 3:1–4:13, and unit E (Heb 6:11–18).

The apodosis of Jesus's sacrificial death allows Jesus, as an eternal/perpetual-*place* spirit, to approach God. It must be remembered in a first-class condition both statements of the Pastor's earth-heavens rhetorical contrast are true. Christ not only completed priestly work in the flesh for fleshly cleansing of sin in the cross, but also continued with priestly work in an "a spirit of an eternal/perpetual-*place*" that is necessary to complete the way to God with his subsequent flesh resurrection as proof of his heavenly provision of salvation.

There are several reasons the referent πνεύματος αἰωνίου (*pneumatos aiōniou*) does not directly refer to the Holy Spirit alone without human spirit presence. First, the phrase is unique only here in description of Jesus's after death in atonement. Thus, it would more likely depict a unique situation of Jesus's human death than an introduction of direct solitary Holy Spirit participation. Second, the relative pronoun ὅς (*hos*) that introduces the dependent clause modifies Χριστοῦ, continues a focus in both the FGT and unit on Jesus's better sacrificial offering and priestly ministry over the Sinai covenant animal sacrifices.

Third, when the author speaks of the third person of the Trinity, he uses a designation of some form of "Holy Spirit." Fourth, the adj. term "eternal/perpetual-*place*" (αἰώνιος) always biblically designates ontological durative space-time. It is never used as a modifier of Divinity, either in the NT or LXX. Divinity is beyond space and time, yet as God, always works in space-time creative relationships. God's preferred location is the better eternal/perpetual-*places* until his enemies of sin and death in the temporary creation are removed. The Holy Spirit is never described as αἰώνιος (*aiōnios*) as a person of the Trinity of God. Fifth, Jesus, as the incarnate God-man, must possess a durative human "spirit" (πνεῦμα). What is not assumed is not covered in expiation when Jesus tastes death for every man. Jesus must be incarnate as a durative full man in every respect.

Sixth, penal substitutionary atonement of Jesus's death for all humankind requires fleshly death which separates the material πνεῦμα (*pneuma*) from the fleshly body just before prompt bodily resurrection. If there is no separation of the πνεῦμα (*pneuma*) in death for Jesus, there is no immediate atonement at his death on the cross but delay to an unspecified time of personal offering after fleshly resurrection. This spatial-temporal separation by current scholarship of Hebrews concerning Jesus's death and atonement in providing salvation does not exist in the context of either the OT or NT. The evidence in context overwhelmingly supports that πνεύματος αἰωνίου (*pneumatos aiōniou*) can only describe Jesus's human spirit as "a spirit of an eternal/perpetual-*place*" (Heb 9:14).

The Pastor uses his contrast to motivate his audience toward a proper choice in their teaching about the Christ, by declaring concerning his offering, "It cleanses our conscience from dead works for the purpose to minister to the living God" (Heb 9:14). The temptation for continuance of the earthly covenant sacrifices, either the daily or annual Day of Atonement, due to their inaccurate portrayal of the current topographical change in the heavenly realities, was judged by the Pastor as a dead work where those so engaged possessed a conscience that needs cleansing to serve the living God.

In exhortation to his audience about their ministerial service of the living God, the Pastor highlights the better teaching concerning the sacrificial value of "the blood of Christ, who through a spirit of an eternal/perpetual-*place* offered himself blameless to God" (Heb 9:14). The reference to the blood of Christ continues the Pastor's two prong connection about the moment of salvation. The sacrificial death of Christ solidly links with Christ's entrance into the holy place in heaven, after the pattern of the high priest on the Day of Atonement, which exemplified the promise of the new covenant. Jesus's onetime offering is superior and better than the earthly priest by providing access to God's presence.

The Pastor's comment about Christ "after finding eternal/perpetual-*place* redemption" (αἰωνίαν λύτρωσιν εὑράμενος Heb 9:12) tracks in the path about the Son's inheritance of salvation received from the DI and DUC subtopics up to this point. The Son in his ministry, as the Christ, became heir of all things, made the eternal/perpetual-*places*, radiated God's glory and represented his substance-reality, brings all things by the conversation of his ability, made a purification of sins, sat down at the right hand of God's throne in the high places, and received a better inheritance than the ministry of angels. The Pastor, in his next FGT, doubles down by further cementing together the connection of death with a heavenly inheritance in the eternal/perpetual-*places* by means of the present mediation of Christ for fulfillment of God's covenant promise regarding his people's own moment of salvation.

Unit Point 3 Introductory Topic (9:15–18): The Son Is Mediator of a New Covenant Relationship by Redemption through the Necessary Blood Offering of His Death, So Those Called at Judgment Should Receive the Promise of Eternal/Perpetual-Place Inheritance

The unit F UPt3 topic (Heb 9:15–26) has three FGT, which continue development of his first two main points in the unit concerning the Son's high priest ministry in heaven and the now obsolete teaching of the parts of the earthly tabernacle ministry. The UPt3 FGT topic focuses heavily on teaching features about the new covenant inauguration by the Son as Christ. For the Pastor, the second covenant proclaims more than a metaphoric promise about a new legal state of salvation from sin before a distant, oblique, nebulous God, who is worshiped overhead from afar. Rather, he highlights a promised oath for a new relationship in transformation of believers at death into an eternal/perpetual-*place* inheritance for dwelling with the living God.

The Pastor continues his parabolic interpretation of the earthly tabernacle typology for a present heavenly application to his audience (cf. Heb 9:9). In his first FGT topic introduction (Heb 9:15–18), he points out the "necessity" (ἀνάγκη Heb 9:16) that the Son had to die, since at his moment of dying, the new covenant inaugurated. Likewise, the new covenant is only effectual for people at death. His second supportive FGT (Heb 9:19–22) strengthens his first feature about the necessity of death by providing parabolic evidence from the Mosaic covenant in all typological activities about the sacrificial blood requirement for forgiveness and holiness before God. His third FGT (Heb 9:23–26) declares the efficacy of Christ's onetime cleansing over the whole temporal multitude of animal sacrifices offered before God from the foundation of the world. These three FGT, with his previous two main points in unit F (Heb 8:1–10:18), prepare for his final UC (Heb 9:27–28) and expositional MCS as the focal point of his message.

Several indicators signal a new topic that links as further explanatory support to his first two main points of unit F concerning the Son's present priestly ministry and the spatial changes achieved by his entrance into heaven at the moment of his offering.[252] The Pastor's use of the pres.

---

252. These signals include (1) the connective "and" (Καὶ Heb 9:15), (2) the demonstrative phrase "for this reason" (διὰ τοῦτο Heb 9:15), (3) repeat of "mediator" (μεσίτης Heb 9:15), which appeared in his first main point (Heb 8:6) as a verbal noun

act. indic. verb "he is" (ἐστίν) with the antecedent as Christ, adds evidence that his exposition continues his parabolic descriptions of a current ministry of the Son (Heb 9:9) that was developed in the pre-climax SbPt2a (Heb 9:6–10).

He again connects the verbal noun "mediator" (μεσίτης Heb 9:15; cf. 8:6) to explain the present "new covenant" (διαθήκης καινῆς Heb 9:15) ministry of Christ, as a high priest before God, who is now available to the people at their time of need (Heb 2:17–18; 7:25–28). He further concretizes the link of "death" (θάνατος Heb 9:15; cf. Heb 2:9–15; 5:7) with the Son's accomplishment of "the eternal/perpetual-*place* inheritance" (τῆς αἰωνίου κληρονομίας Heb 9:15) promised in his concept of "first covenant" (πρώτῃ διαθήκῃ Heb 9:15).[253] The new use of the verbal noun "inheritance" (κληρονομία Heb 9:15) summarizes his previous descriptions of the "heir" κληρονόμος (Heb 1:2b) and the verbal activity "to inherit" κληρονομέω (Heb 1:4) in the DI (Heb 1:1–4) chiastic subtopics A (Heb 1:2b) and A′ (Heb 1:4).[254] His link of the concept of covenant with death

that summarizes the present ministry of Christ, (4) a continued focus on the "death" (θάνατος Heb 9:15) of the Son, (5) a continued contrast with "the first covenant" (τῇ πρώτῃ διαθήκῃ Heb 9:15), and (6) a continued subtopic about the promise of eternal/perpetual-*place* inheritance that designates salvation in heaven in God's dwelling.

253. The Pastor mainly focuses on inheritance at death of both Jesus as the Christ and his believers. However, he does mention that Jesus's ministry providing completion in heaven should not cease without the later addition of those living in his audience (Heb 11:39–40). In his context, this does not infer that the expected finishing in heaven must occur for all at the exact same time (i.e., at the second coming) but only that all believers will finish with no believer left out. This concept is further discussed in the UC D2′ (Heb 11:39–40) in this chapter.

254. Cf. Hahn, "Covenant," 65–88. Hahn offers a solution to the perplexity of the Pastor's argument in Heb 9:16–17, by application of the Sinaitic covenant, as the necessity of death of the covenant-maker when the first covenant is "violated" or "broken" by one of the covenant makers. He assumes the first covenant was "broken," which necessitated the second. However, the concept of a broken covenant mentioned about Israel in the OT does not apply here. In each case where the covenant is broken, Israel looked to other gods for redemption, rather than God of their covenant (cf. Lev 26:15, 44; Deut 31:16, 20). Nothing in Heb 9:15–22 describes a failure of Israel or broken covenant as the reason for the second covenant. In truth, the second covenant was outlined within the Sinaitic covenant in the Yom Kippur annual sacrifice and planned from the beginning of the teaching about Christ before the law at Sinai (Heb 5:12; 6:1); e.g., the symbolism provided by Melchizedek, developed in unit D (Heb 5:1–10; 7:1–28), existed before the Aaronic priesthood of the law and Sinai. The earthly covenant provides only an outline of the promise of God and symbolically reminds Israel about the transgressions that needed atonement by the death of only God himself as a person (cf. Heb 10:1–3). It was weak, by not being able to bring people into God's presence. Hahn's speculation for further research, that the death of Israel was delayed until Christ's substitutionary death (87–88), does not apply. The individual Israelites

continues from unit D (Heb 5:1–10; 7:1–28) his exposition regarding the better promises enacted by Jesus more excellent ministry (Heb 7:22).[255]

The application of Christ's inheritance that runs to believers connects back to his UC A (Heb 1:13–14) concerning the angels, who minister "for the sake of those who subsequently are presently about to inherit salvation" (διὰ τοὺς μέλλοντας κληρονομεῖν σωτηρίαν Heb 1:14). The inheritance by heirs of salvation path picks up again in Heb 6:12, 17 within the warning about accountability for teaching in unit E (Heb 5:11—6:20). The unit reveals that a believer's inheritance includes more than just a qualitative entrance into heavenly access but also quantitative blessings. Now in unit F, the Pastor states about his subtopic of the mediation of Christ, "So that of a death occurring for redemption of transgressions over the period of the first covenant, the ones having been called should receive the eternal/perpetual-*place* inheritance" (Heb 9:15). In contrast to the lesser access into the holy place for the righteous by the first covenant ministry before the veil, those embracing by faith the second covenant outlined by Yom Kippur can now journey beyond the veil for an inheritance in the eternal/perpetual-*place* (cf. Heb 6:19–20).

---

did physically die, just as all men have been appointed, which is the first part of the Pastor's MCS (Heb 9:27). The sacrifices concerning Christ that were demonstrated by the commandments of the earthly covenant revealed how one could in death approach God through faith in Christ's substitutionary offering and priestly intercession, rather than somehow not physically die at all or have death delayed till Christ comes. However, the execution of the penalty of eternal/perpetual-*place* death was delayed until Christ's entrance as forerunner at physical death, but this is probably not the spiritual death that Hahn has in mind.

255. Gorman, "Effecting the New Covenant," 26–59. Gorman connects "covenant" and "atonement" to suggest a new model of atonement. He comments, about the scriptural overtones that connect these concepts, "Furthermore, the implicit or explicit (in Matthew) connection to forgiveness of sins suggests that Jesus's death fulfills both the Day of Atonement in Lev 16 (plus perhaps the atoning sacrifices more generally [e.g., Lev 4:1—6:7]) and inaugurates the new covenant promised in Jer 31:31–34, which (as we will see below) includes liberation and forgiveness" (29; brackets in the original). He properly identifies an early connection to Jer 31:31–34 without recognition of the Pastor's understanding of even earlier second covenant language in the outline of tabernacle and the burnt offerings in the Melchizedekian priesthood before Aaron's priesthood in the law at Sinai. In evaluation of the link of atonement and covenant in Hebrews, Gorman chooses "to consider not the *mechanics* of the new covenant in Hebrews but the *effect*" (52; italics Gorman). This allows overreach in escalation of the feature of "permanence" of the connection his presuppositions about the possible loss of salvation, if the audience does not remain permanently faithful. This common presupposition is invalidated by proper governance of the FGT for meaning in discourse analysis of unit E (Heb 5:11—6:20) concerning accountability in teaching about the beginning sayings of Christ.

The substantive perf. pass. ptc. "the ones having been called" (κεκλημένοι) highlights both the literal event and the timing for this new covenant inheritance of salvation, as at judgment after death, even as Jesus's own inheritance (Heb 2:11; 3:1). Christ will call his believers by name upon their approach of their spirit and soul to God for eternal/perpetual-*place* judgment (Heb 4:11–13) and subsequently shepherd each of them into the holy of holies (Heb 8:8–12; 13:20).

The remaining portion of the UPt3 topic introduction (Heb 9:15–18) emphasizes three warrants about the new covenant. It (1) requires the necessity of the death of the one who made it (Heb 9:16), (2) effectually validates when people die (Heb 9:17), and (3) mimics the inaugural pattern of the first covenant ministry that when symbolizing the new covenant requires the offering of the blood from an animated life. Patterned after God's furnished legal design in his first covenant relationships, the Son, as Christ, had to die by offering the blood of his animated life for it to be implemented (Heb 10:5–10; cf. Mark 14:24; Matt 26:28; Luke 22:20; 1 Cor 11:25; 2 Cor 3:6).[256] Further, in extrapolation of this earthly outline to other people, the second covenant mediatorial priestly intercession is a "valid *covenant*" (βεβαία Heb 9:17) upon the death to those eligible. For the Pastor, the earthly sacrifices not only represented the death of the Christ but also the death of the individual, who after

---

256. The OT to NT second covenant concept does not slavishly follow the patterns of other ANE covenants and does not claim to be influenced by them. While there are covenant similarities with other ANE cultures and common legal language that enabled conceptual understanding, the covenant revelation from God to Moses, as original from God himself, further explains the beginning teaching about the Christ regarding the absolute necessities that are required in order to establish an eternal/perpetual-*place* covenant relationship with the living God in heaven. In this sense, the revelation about the covenants (cf. Rom 9:4) is progressive. The second improves the heavenly access of the first. This unique purpose to establish a perpetual heavenly relationship with people after death separates the purpose of the first and second covenant from other covenantal interpretations that focus on legalities of continued earthly relationships with God; e.g., Paul's concept of second covenant ministry in 2 Cor 3:6 propels his thoughts to look towards eternal/perpetual-*place* things (2 Cor 4:18) and a walk by faith until absence from the body to be at home with the Lord in 2 Cor 5:7–8. The modern misstep of progressive covenantalism inverts the heavenly hope for legal restoration to earthly Edenic relationships that is similar to other ANE cultures with an earthly focus, by elevation of the antitype of Eden to the heavenly Eden type itself. The application of historical conclusions about ANE culture to the parts of the first covenant revelation on earth erects a philosophical straw man not found in Gods speech. God has not spoken concepts of unconditional covenants and other rational conclusions in reformed theology from the "many parts" of his revelation about the first covenant of promise.

death would ascend up to God for his judgment.[257] He reinforces this connection of the offering of blood between with the two covenants in his next UPt3a FGT.

Subpoint 3a (9:19–22): After the Pattern of the First Ministry, the Son's Offering of His Blood by Death Was Required by God's Judgment for Cleansing in Forgiveness of Sins

The use of "for" (γὰρ Heb 9:19) signals explanatory support for the Pastor's last warrant concerning God's covenantal requirement for the offering of the animated life of the Son. He lists three groupings, which include (1) Moses's use of blood in commandments (Heb 9:19), (2) Moses's words in Exod 24:8 at the inaugural agreement of Israel to obey all the commands of the first covenant outline, and (3) the logic that since nearly all things are cleansed in the first covenant pattern by blood, then "without the shedding of blood, forgiveness does not occur" (χωρὶς αἱματεκχυσίας οὐ γίνεται ἄφεσις Heb 9:22). These facts concerning the first covenant outline provided to Israel prepares the ground for application to the realities by Christ in the next FGT.

Subpoint 3b (9:23–26): Christ's Onetime Cleansing of Things in the Heavens Is Better Than the Earthly Covenant Ministry, since He Did Not Enter into the Outline of the True Holy-Places but into Heaven Itself, to Now Appear in the Presence of God for Believers

The Pastor once again moves the thoughts of his audience from the "outlines of the *ministry* in the heavens" (ὑποδείγματα τῶν ἐν τοῖς οὐρανοῖς Heb 9:23) to the reality of Christ. The outlines of the earthly tabernacle suggest to the Pastor another ἀνάγκη ("necessity") concerning "purification" (καθαρίζω Heb 9:23) in the heavens. This necessity of purification in the heavens completes upon entry by Christ into heaven itself with his better sacrifice than those of the earthly covenant that the Pastor previously described in his SbPt2b FGT climax (Heb 9:11–14).[258] It is likely

---

257. Weiss, *Die predigt Jesu*, 135–36. Weiss suggests that modern Christians reinterpret the end of the world in terms of the end each one of us must face, namely, death.

258. The holiness of creation in relation to dwelling presence with God is directly related to the sinful state of the created creatures who dwell in that creation. The people defile creation from God's presence in levels of holiness, and nothing innate in the creation itself. The decay of sin and death are God's enemies that he now patiently is

that the necessary purification concerns the problem of the sins of those people in the holy place awaiting forgiveness. The Pastor gives no indication about sinful defilement with the creation itself but that the separated territory of creation accommodating sinful people, needed reclaiming. In first-century CE apocalyptic (*aiōn-field*) concepts about heavenly realities, the celestial holy place provincially allowed sinful people and angels temporary residence in lower divided levels of heaven. For the Pastor, this defilement of the space in the true tabernacle of all creation awaited Jesus's purification by forgiveness of sin in the promise of the new covenant. Once sins had been atoned and the veil of separation removed, the people could enter with Jesus into God's presence.

The Pastor again claims the ministry of Christ as not an entry into the earthly tabernacle "made with hands" (χειροποίητα Heb 9:24), which was an "antitype of the true *tabernacle*" (ἀντίτυπα τῶν ἀληθινῶν Heb 9:24) but into heaven itself. The implication is that Christ enters the current space of heaven itself that has been cleansed, and to which a way is

---

eradicating (Heb 12:25–29; cf. Rom 8:18–25). For recent summation of the scholarly theories concerning the relationship of the earthly ministry purification in relation to purification in heaven, see MacLeod, "Cleansing of the True Tabernacle," 60–71. MacLeod provides light discussion of nine views.

Cf. Ribbens, *Levitical Sacrifice*, 119–27. Ribbens addresses three main interpretative options for (1) purification of the heavenly tabernacle, (2) purification of the conscience in a metaphorical implication about the defilement of people, and (3) purification as inauguration of the heavenly sanctuary for ministry. He recognizes the connection of "cleanse, purify" (καθαρίζω Heb 9:23) with "inaugurate" (ἐγκαινίζω Heb 9:18) and the listed sacrificial examples which indicate the inaugural purification of the tabernacle for ministerial service. He further comments, "While inauguration of an earthly temple was an action prerequisite to the ability to offer a sacrifice within it, the inauguration of the heavenly sanctuary is subsumed in Christ's sacrifice. He does not purify the heavenly sanctuary and later offer himself. Rather, in one offering Christ consecrates the heavenly sanctuary, inaugurates the new covenant, and atones for sins" (123).

Cf. Jamieson, "Hebrews 9.23," 569–87. Jamieson recognizes a pattern concerning rites of purification that also arises in the text of Heb 9:23. He states, "Cultic inauguration or consecration is a multi-stage process in which the cultic implements are first cleansed of impurity, changing their status from impure to pure, and then consecrated, changing their status from common (or profane) to holy" (585). He concludes, "Given that the cleansing of the tabernacle is a major focus of Lev 16, and that the author sees the Levitical cult as in some sense patterned in advance on Christ's offering, perhaps readers of Hebrews should be rather less surprised than we tend to be when we find the author stating that the heavenly tabernacle itself needed to be cleansed. Further, far from being removed from the pressing concerns of its recipients, the idea that the heavenly tabernacle is cleansed from defilement both agrees with and advances the letter's central hortatory motif. Because the record of human sin has been removed from God's presence, God's people can draw near to him, approaching the very Holy of Holies in heaven with confidence, a true heart, and full assurance of faith (4.16; 10.22)" (587).

created for him by God instantly at his offering of atonement, just like the high priest annually entered beyond the veil. The space of the former holy place is now reclaimed to form the greater and more complete tabernacle (Heb 9:11).

From this newly expanded space, Christ operates his ministry "now to appear before God for us" (νῦν ἐμφανισθῆναι τῷ προσώπῳ τοῦ θεοῦ ὑπὲρ ἡμῶν Heb 9:24). By the aorist pass. inf. ἐμφανισθῆναι ("to appear"), the Pastor charts a general mission statement. Outside of the indicative and participle, there is no aspect of time for the aorist infinitive.[259] Wallace states, "The aorist normally views the action as a whole, taking no interest in the internal workings of the action. It describes the action in summary fashion, without focusing on the beginning or end of the action specifically."[260] Any detail about the action implied in the verb must come from the context. The context indicates Jesus's ministry includes appearing "now," "in the presence of God," "in heaven," and "for us" (Heb 9:24).

In distinction with the annual Yom Kippur offering, where the high priest often entered with the blood of another, the Pastor further asserts that in Christ's priestly ministry, while Christ appears "often" (πολλάκις) after the pattern of the priestly sacrificial offering, he suffered but "once" (ἅπαξ Heb 9:25). The Pastor rationally concludes that if there were an equivalent between Christ's atonement sacrifice and his current and frequent intercessional ministry, he would have needed to suffer often from the foundation of the "world" (κόσμος Heb 9:26). Atonement in suffering for sin only occurred once at Jesus's death on the cross, whereas individual mediation after death at judgment occurs "now" at the time of his writing.

The Pastor's final statement of the SbPt3b FGT (Heb 9:23–26) encapsulates both the enabled spatial and personal changes for people by

---

259. *GGBB*, 555.

260. *GGBB*, 557–58. Wallace describes several other semantic options for the aorist infinitive. For the gnomic aorist, he states, "In this respect it is not very different from a customary present, but is quite different from a customary imperfect. The gnomic aorist is not used to describe an event that 'used to take place' (as the imperfect does), but one that 'has taken place' over a long period of time or, like the present, does take place" (557). For the ingressive aorist, he states, "The aorist tense may be used to stress the beginning of an action or the entrance into a state" (558). In this usage, there is no suggestion that the action is repeated. However, The Pastor's context suggests repeated action. The Pastor's point from this FGT that carries over into his unit F UC in Heb 9:27–28 MCS concerns Jesus's present ministry of appearing from heaven since the moment of his entrance from the cross.

Jesus's onetime sacrifice. He states, "But now, once, upon the completion of the eternal/perpetual *places* for removal of sins through his sacrifice he has been revealed" (Heb 9:26). The Pastor claims Christ "now, once ... has been revealed" (1) upon completion of the eternal/perpetual-*places*, (2) for removal of sins, and (3) through his sacrifice. The perf. pass. indic. "has been revealed" (πεφανέρωται) suggests a past event with present effects. As introduced in the DI subtopic D (Heb 1:3b), these accomplished features continue to reveal the Son's current ability by "conversation" (ῥῆμα) to bring people to God. This ability of the Son shared in conversation in teaching to others includes his heavenly purification in the completion of the eternal/perpetual-*places* and removal of the barriers of personal sin for an open entrance into the eternal/perpetual-*places* for those who believe (Heb 9:28; 13:20; cf. John 14:1–6).

The Pastor maintains that a ministerial conversation in the earthly antitypes of the continued sacrifices portraying the heavenly first covenant promises distorts the Son's accomplished message. The tent of the lesser holy place no longer exists and Jesus's removal of sin at judgment allows him by his priestly mediation to now shepherd people into the presence of God. The previous works of the earthly covenant are now dead teachings without a heavenly correspondence. So now they are without eternal/perpetual-*place* value at judgment concerning the inheritance that accompanied salvation.

His next FGT serves as a UC and MCS about the ministry of Christ to those who approach God for judgment after death. It summarizes his previous expositional conclusions in unit A through F. Unlike Paul's conversation with the Thessalonian believers, the Pastor does not distinguish between salvation by Jesus at his appearing for intercession of the those who have died and those living. He focuses on Christ's present ministry at death with a promise that the group living should not be complete without them (Heb 11:39–40; cf. 1 Thess 4:13–18). This is discussed further in unit D2´.

UC A/B/C/D/E/F Macro Conclusion/Summary (9:27–28): Christ, after Offering Himself Once to Bear the Sin of Many People, Will Appear from a Second Place without Sin for Salvation to Those Waiting for Him after Death at Judgment

At this point, the Pastor accumulates the necessary literary indicators to suggest an easily recognized threshold by the audience for a shift to an anticipated UC that serves as a both conclusion and summary for his accumulated expositional material about the two-fold ministry of Christ thus far through unit F (Heb 8:1–10:18).[261] After this MCS, in a chiastic point structure, he will later provide three more FGT UPt in support of his propositions (see appendix 1, fig. 14). However, the current breadth of his rhetoric is pregnant with great anticipation for delivery of a peak summation in his main unit F exposition, which drives home the proper teaching that the Pastor expects from his audience in their conversation about the Christ.[262] This syntactical structure recaps his conversation to his audience. Christ fulfills the onetime, sacrificial offering to bear the

---

261. These markers include (1) the Pastor's use of the idiomatic phrase "and in accordance with this" (καὶ καθ'), (2) the placement of clauses with the correlative conjunction "just as . . . so" (ὅσον . . . οὕτως) as the object of καὶ καθ', indicate that these devices function together to frame his summary explanations of the correspondences within his previous parenesis, (3) the reemphasis of the topic of "Christ" (Χριστός Heb 9:28) as the highlight of the summary comparison in relation to "people" (ἀνθρώποις Heb 9:27), (4) use of words to specify the correspondence between Christ and people in the tracked subtopics from the DI and other UC A/B/C/D/E of "to die" (ἀποθνῄσκω), subsequent "judgment" (κρίσις), the sacrificial ministry of Christ "to offer" (προσφέρω) himself once in bearing the sins of many, the continual ministry of Christ "to appear" (ὁράω) to those waiting for "salvation" (σωτηρία), and the expected location as "from a second place without sin" (ἐκ δευτέρου χωρὶς ἁμαρτίας) that was prepared. These should easily meet a threshold for a UC by a first-century CE Greek audience.

262. Runge, *Discourse Grammar*, 307–8. Runge demonstrates the Pastor's use of the "pro-adverb οὕτως to form a left-dislocation," which "introduce the most important information of the clause." He further writes, "Christ is portrayed as performing a task comparable to doing one thing followed by another. In the same way that people are destined for death and afterward prepare for judgment, Jesus accomplishes a comparable activity. The first activity is framed as a circumstantial participle, backgrounding it to the main action of 'appearing.' Being offered up to bear the sins of many enables his second appearance to bring about salvation instead of judgment. Most all of this information has already been introduced into the discourse, but the comparison of similarities and differences has not been made explicit. Restating the relevant information provides an important frame of reference for the clause that follows. The pro-adverb οὕτως signals the end of the dislocation and rhetorically promotes the information. Stating the information in two clauses would have significantly reduced the rhetorical impact of the comparison. The book of Hebrews contains many such comparisons, but most are executed using simple frames of reference without dislocation."

sin of many people. He appears from the second place without sin after death at judgment and provides salvation to those awaiting him.²⁶³

The Pastor's syntactical choice of an aorist inf. of purpose "to bear" (ἀνενεγκεῖν Heb 9:28) joins his other cognates from the φερω (pherō) word group to express the present ministry of Christ. In a contextual connection with the aorist inf. "to be appearing" (ἐμφανισθῆναι Heb 9:24), the aorist tense signals another general mission statement to review an additional feature about the purpose of Christ's current activity that trails from the main chiasmic subtopic D (Heb 1:3b) of the DI toward his last UC (Heb 13:20–21). These verbal nouns describe how Jesus now shepherds his brethren to God.

His choice of the fut. pass. indic. "will be appearing" (ὀφθήσεται) adds more weight to the expectation of the audience for validation of this second covenant promise at death (Heb 9:17, 27), rather than simply the provision of a metaphor for a state of access in worship by the living audience for God's approving notice from heaven.²⁶⁴ The verbal infinitives "to die" (ἀποθανεῖν Heb 9:27) about people and "to bear" (ἀνενεγκεῖν Heb 9:28) about the sins of people link in parallel in the MCS, further

---

263. Cf. Cullman, *Christology of the New Testament*, 101–33. Cullman comments, "Jesus the High Priest thus fulfils a double office: that of the once-for-all act of atonement, and that of the extension of this work continued into eternity" (101). However, in his discussion, he limits the present work of Christ in Hebrews as only intercession for the living. This interpretative move then allows Cullman, regarding the concept of Jesus's high priesthood, to speculate "a third aspect, the *eschatological* side, of his work as the New Testament understands it" (103). He then aligns Heb 9:28 as a reference to the "second" coming of Jesus, even though recognizing no context in Hebrews supports it. He comments after his claim, "Hebrews does not further explain the particular meaning of the high priestly work of Jesus at the end of time; it only indicates its nature with the words 'not to deal with sin'" (103). Cullman negates both offices in his commentary about the Pastor's summary statement: the once-for-all sacrifice and the present intercession for believers after death at judgment by removal of sin. Cf. Cervera i Valls, "Jesús, gran sacerdot i víctima," 477–502. Cervera i Valls concludes, "The letter works through a Christological consideration of two inseparable themes: to affirm the divinity of Jesus (his role as mediator) and to set out the meaning of his death of the cross (his role as expiator of sin)" (502); Ounsworth, *Joshua Typology*, 117n57. Ounsworth, in a realized eschatology view, states, "Jesus is the one whose journey is re-enacted, or re-capitulated, by the Christian pilgrimage."

264. Worship by those living among the audience is important to the Pastor, as seen in discourse S3 unit A´ (Heb 13:1–21) with chiasmic application of his expositional teaching. This further explores in unit A´ (Heb 13:1–21) analysis. However, worship is only another earthly outline of heavenly realities when properly observed. Therefore, the audience could no longer accurately teach proper worship of God in their ministerial conversation if continuing the now faulty outlines of the law due Jesus's achieved covenantal and heavenly changes for people in their relationship with God.

Atonement and the Logic of Resurrection in Hebrews 9:27–28

connecting the timing of Jesus's ministry for the salvation of people as after death and at judgment (see appendix 3).

In Hebrews, the direction of the priestly ministry of Christ with his people at death is upward and heavenward by provision of open access to God.[265] Nothing is mentioned in the Pastor's message about the second coming with his people that is found in other NT letters (1) to gather the living, (2) to judge, in earthly realization of the day of the Lord prophecies that symbolize God's heavenly judgment after death, and (3) to temporarily minister on earth with promised blessings to symbolize his goodness. His nested frequent use of "once" (ἅπαξ) concerning Christ (Heb 9:26–28) links with his suffering offering of atonement and not his current ministry in priestly activity regarding appearing to believers after death at judgment.[266]

---

265. For introductory discussion of the different lines of STL tradition of Merkavah mysticism concerning an anticipated, active, upwards movement of the righteous to God in divided heavens of God's house against a passive, downward movement of God to the righteous on earth, see Nickelsburg, "Enoch, Levi, and Peter," 575–600. Nickelsburg suggests the correspondence of this long standing Merkavah tradition posits from possible authorial reaction to priestly corruption and pollution at Jerusalem in support of the later cultic ministries in the environs of Tel Dan in upper Galilee. The message of Hebrews has correspondence with the Merkavah STL along these lines. The upward movement of believers to the unseen eternal creation of God's dwelling set against the downward movement of God to the temporary creation stimulated debate long before, during, and after the days of Jesus since the beginning of the building his church in heaven (John 18:36; Acts 7). Nickelsburg reveals possible early connections between Petrine and Enochic traditions in rejection to the priestly authority of Jerusalem. The later elevated earthly ministry of Peter toward an earthly kingdom provides another area of further research along these lines.

266. The link of the idiom ἐκ δευτέρου, with "once" (ἅπαξ), with sense as "a second time" in limitation to his second coming for the living in application to the ministry of Christ for believers, neglects the very teaching the Pastor emphasizes, and logically works out where no one is yet saved. The connection of "second" (δεύτερος) with "once" (ἅπαξ) is awkward. He does not speak about Jesus's coming into the κόσμος ("world," Heb 10:5) as a "first coming" (πρῶτος εἰσερχόμενος) and his ordinals deal with either space, or the inauguration and execution of covenant relationships, rather than coming for an Edenic earthy kingdom. Besides, the Pastor's kingdom theology resides spatially in heaven, even as Jesus stated (Heb 1:8; 12:28; cf. John 8:23; 18:36).

The common anachronistic solution is to locally assume the ordinal idiom is only adverbial in connection to the ordinal "once" (ἅπαξ), for a common assumed sense for "a second time," without consideration of the inherent spatial weight of the idiom toward a presently available place option at death and judgment. A spatial *present* option was normative in apocalyptic language and thought. Cf. Dov, "Apocalyptic Temporality," 289–303. Ben-Dov claims, "In fact, readers of Daniel and members of the Yahad experienced a 'thick' present, with the dimension of time playing a crucial role in the fabric of reality" (289). He also states, "I believe, in contrast, that apocalyptic writings attest to a substantial concept of time, which constitutes more than a mere continuum

Neither does the Pastor provide exposition for a philosophical intermediate-state, which from the beginning has persistently developed alongside heavenly kingdom teaching. By elevation of antitypes, outlines, and shadows to the level of the promised truth and types of heavenly realities themselves, various forms of afterlife speculation rationally surface within the misstep of an upside down, earth rather than heaven, delayed kingdom theology. Even after Jesus's enthronement in heaven, this worldly mistake was retained and corrupted by later state-sanctioned churches and traditionally held by the educated separatists of the Reformation as the catalyst for the later conflicts over the true church.[267] Yet because of the promises of God, who cannot lie, the elementary believer has always hoped by faith to see their Savior at death and enter with others into heaven.

---

of appointed moments" (290). Ben-Dov dismantles the adversarial rhetorical straw man in Western ideas that OT Jewish concepts of time were considered abstract, and lacking importance in the traditions in Semitic languages (290–91). Ben-Dov provides a major contribution with the recognition that in apocalyptic literature, time is not a phenomenon that exits by itself but rather "a fundamental entity which exists regardless of the phenomena and serves as their cause" (291). He concludes, "In apocalyptic literature, and more profoundly at Qumran, time carried a heavy burden alongside an enormous potential. It was experienced both as *kairos* and as *chronos*, and was expressed in elaborate literary and scholarly media. Eschatology revolves around a very powerful *kairos*, the moment of redemption. In turn this *kairos* concludes a very long *chronos* that precedes it. The now derives its meaning from the continuous past, as the two form a lively dialectic. This dialectic yielded in apocalyptic circles a 'thick' present" (303).

In contrast, in the dominant view of future eschatology, interpretation of the idiom "from a second . . . " by scholars today, universally and without question, connects in an isolated future temporal application with the canonical complementary truth of the second coming to earth in contrast to Jesus's first coming. However, this futuristic leap ignores the spatial-temporal context of the entire message to determine the Pastor's intentions building up to this summary. Also, "once" does not refer to Jesus's coming to earth but more specifically to his one-time offering as the Christ sacrifice on earth *and* in heaven. Further, the adverbial phrase "without sin" always modifies the word it follows. This creates, in a strictly future temporal application, the awkward phrase "at a second *time* without sin" that is very unlike the Pastor's previous highly sophisticated Greek. The issue in context harmonizes better with imputed holiness like Jesus's innate holiness that is necessary to enter the place of the holy of holies of heaven, as "from a second place/position without sin," where Jesus is now in position at the right hand of the throne of God. It is not the time that is without sin or the people, but the person of Jesus and the cleansed place from where he comes (cf. Heb 4:15).

267. Based upon the Pastor's exposition contained in Hebrews, an intermediate state does not exist in the NT and that rising to God by Jesus's present ministry in fulfillment of the second covenant occurs for the believer after death at judgment. This assembly of believers in heaven is the true church that Jesus is now building by his shepherd ministry. None of the earthly churches as assemblies of baptized believers have ever been the true church but only symbols, when properly mirroring the true heavenly church.

After his delivery about the two-fold ministry of Christ, the Pastor next provides three more FGT to reinforce his MCS. These continue his antithetical comparison of the earthly ministry with the heavenly ministry.

Unit Point 4 (10:1–4): Since the Law Is Only a Shadow, the Priestly Sacrifices for Worship Could Not Remove a Consciousness of Sin at Judgment before God

UPt4, concerning the Son's ministry, additionally adds support to the Pastor's MCS that the sacrifices specified in the law could not "make complete, finish" (τελειῶσαι) the journey by people into heaven when approaching God for judgment. His categorization of the law as a "shadow" (σκιά Heb 10:1) joins in unit F, "type" (τύπος Heb 8:5), "parable" (παραβολή Heb 9:8), "outline" (ὑπόδειγμα Heb 9:23), "antitype" (ἀντίτυπος Heb 9:24), "true" (ἀληθινός Heb 9:24), and "image" (εἰκών Heb 10:1) regarding his hermeneutical interpretation of all earthly ministry beyond that of Christ himself as only a typological representation of unseen, true, heavenly realities. This typological hermeneutical method is reinforced in his statement that the law is a shadow "of the present subsequently coming good things, not itself the image of the events" (Heb 10:1). The "image" (εἰκών Heb 10:1) denotes the good things the audience should expect in the realities of heaven above after death.

Since the law of the Sinai covenant with Israel only symbolizes the true heavenly realities, its observance either before or after Christ's fulfillment cannot complete the entrance of people into heaven (Heb 10:1; cf. Rom 9:31). The transition completed by the sacrificial offering of Christ is not a change from earthly ministerial reality to a heavenly ministerial reality ("lower to higher") but a change within the coexisting heavenly ministerial reality.[268] The law, as a *shadow*, revealed God's

---

268. Scholars often reject the simultaneous validity of the priesthood of the Jewish law and that of a heavenly ministry running concurrently before the priesthood of Jesus as the Christ; e.g., Koester, *Hebrews*, 359. Koester argues that Jewish tradition only allows one priesthood at a time, rather than Greco-Roman practice of multiple priesthoods. However, he fails to view the Jewish priesthood typologically, which can provide multiple earthly viewpoints of one concrete reality in heaven. Cf. Issacs, *Sacred Space*, 146. Issacs argues against application of temple imagery to the church, stating, "For the author of Hebrews, the cult has not been replaced by the church, but superseded altogether, and re-located in heaven." His rationalization is problematic on several issues due to his initial faulty premise that could not be further from the truth. The earthly tabernacle and temple only provided symbolism of the transitions achieved by Jesus in the heavenly realities.

ability to complete in Christ, as an *image* of the *true* heavenly reality, the prospect of the illustrated, covenant relationship changes in the heavenly priesthood that by faith bring people now to God (Heb 7:12; cf. Rom 8:2-4, 9:31-33; 10:4). Believers today at death enter God's spiritual reality of the holy of holies, a better access described in UPt2 (Heb 9:1-14), than just the now no longer existing holy place before the veil.[269]

Contra Thiessen, "Hebrews and the Jewish Law," 183-94. Thiessen correctly rejects that the Pastor considers the law as abolished by Christ. He supports this conclusion with examples where the Pastor continues to apply some aspects of the law as valid with areas of continuity and discontinuity. He further supports his conclusion by demonstrating "in his belief in two distinct, yet simultaneously valid, priesthoods and cultic systems, the author of Hebrews explicitly depends on Exod. 25:8-9. . . . The earthly structure is a model of that heavenly temple in which God himself dwells" (188). However, Thiessen further avers, "Hebrews claims that the cultic regulations have changed because there has been a change in location—from terrestrial to celestial" (191). Based upon the Pastor's conception of a preexisting heavenly priesthood before Jesus's priesthood, the change in location is not earthly to heavenly but the change occurs, as pictured in the daily and annual sacrifices, from the previous celestial ministry administered by angels in the holy place to a new celestial ministry mediated by Jesus into the holy of holies. The earthly ministry, including Siani, has never been the truth or realty but only copies of ministry in the heavens (Heb 9:23).

269. The first and new covenant traditions, as typologically represented by the law in the Sinai covenant, are not new to Moses and Israel; e.g., the Melchizedekian priesthood symbolized the new covenant before the law at Sinai and the change to the Aaronic priesthood on earth typified the change in the law to Jesus. The Pastor previously describes the "change, transition" (μετάθεσις Heb 7:12) of the priesthood realties in unit E (Heb 5:1-10; 7:1-28). Yet, he also in unit F (Heb 8:1-10:18) describes the transition in heaven, from the first, heavenly, covenant relationship after death that existed from the beginning foundation of the world in access to the holy place before the veil, to the new, heavenly, covenant relationship after death inaugurated by the death of Christ in access to the holy of holies.

In proper observance, the law was not impossible to keep in blameless, righteous living by use of the sacrificial system for both personal and public testimony in outward purification of personal sins (cf. Phil 3:6). A common misstep is escalation of the law itself, as the heavenly required reality, and pursuit of righteousness by the works of the law (cf. Rom 9:30-33). The law, even as the observed previous priestly services before it, did not demand or declare righteousness before God at judgment as by either sinlessness or works, but by its required sacrificial reminders facilitated recognition of personal sin and God's remedy by faith in Christ's sacrifice for sin. Also, keeping the law symbolically testified to a person's faith in Christ (cf. Rom 4:1-8). In this understanding, Christ fulfills the law but does not do away or negate the law's main point of the need for faith in Christ.

The difference in the transition from the first to new covenant is that of promise and fulfillment. Nevertheless, the different heavenly access between the experience of the holy place by the first covenant, and the guaranteed access to the holy of holies by the new covenant promise, renders the first covenant teachings in the law as now obsolete and necessitates change in teaching (Heb 7:12). This teaching by the priesthood ministry about the spatial changes in the heavenly ministry from the first to new covenant is often overlooked by scholars, who either ignore the heavenly ministerial realities

By a rhetorical question, the Pastor logically concludes that if the law could function to cleanse the conscious of the worshipers of their sins before God at judgment, then its requirements would never need to be repeated (Heb 10:2). He signals a logical contrast by use of "but" (ἀλλά Heb 10:3), stating the law's typological purpose as "in these rites is a reminder of sins year by year" (Heb 10:3; cf. Rom 5:20; 7:7; Gal 3:24). His contextual conclusion of this UPt4 FGT (Heb 10:1–4) affirms that it is impossible for the law's sacrifices to remove sins before God at judgment (Heb 10:4) and prepares the audience for what God does require for forgiveness of sin in UPt5.

Unit Point 5 Climax (10:5–14): In God's Desire, He Provides a Body after Death to Jesus, as the Christ, Who Made a Self-Offering That was Sufficient to Make People Holy by Removal of Sin

With quotation of Ps 39:7–9 LXX (Ps 40:6–8 MT), through King David, the Pastor allows God to speak for himself as to what constitutes his desire for an acceptable ministerial sacrifice, which could take away the sin

---

depicted by the earthly or fail to recognize the heavenly spatial transition as part of the teaching of the law in the tabernacle priesthood.

E.g., Joslin, *Hebrews, Christ, and the Law*, 133, 171, 237. Joslin correctly surmises a "change, transition" (μετάθεσις Heb 7:12) in priesthood implied in the Pastor's rhetoric (133). He rightly concludes, "To follow the same priesthood and to sacrifice animals for sin is now to go against the work of God and not to hear his speaking in the son" (133). He then advances the change in the priesthood from that specified in the law back to the Melchizedekian priesthood promise that Jesus now fulfills in heaven in Ps 110. However, he overlooks the heavenly change and distinctions in the heavenly holy-*places* that was already being taught within the requirements of the law by the daily and annual sacrifices, which represented the first and second covenants. Later, Joslin writes, "The final sentence of Hebrews 9 (vv. 27–28) asserts the axiom that men die once, thus Christ could only offer himself once 'to bear the sins of many' (briefly citing Is 53:12). Judgment follows death, yet salvation awaits those who await the return of Christ. Christ entered the holy place and will return from that holy place, appearing a second time (δευτέρου ὀφθήσεται). The second appearance (9:28) that is anxiously anticipated by his people (τοῖς αὐτὸν ἀπεκδεχομένοις) is likely analogous to the Yom Kippur ritual when the priest returned from offering the sacrifice for the people" (237). Christ in his current ministry leaves the ninety-nine and comes to every individual sheep after death at judgment (Heb 13:20; cf. Matt 18:12; Luke 15:4), with *ek deuterou* (ἐκ δευτέρου Heb 9:28) in context representing the Son's present priesthood in appearing from heaven. This does not negate his later addition by gathering those believers still living while coming during the day of the Lord judgment upon the earth (Heb 11:39–40; cf. 2 Thess 2:1) that again symbolizes God's judgment in the heavenly realities.

of people and prepare them bodily for heavenly entrance. The Psalm of David shares his patient trust in God as his deliverer for salvation from his iniquities in the face of his accusers who seek to nullify his hope in continuance of life. The Pastor may find a link with David's cries to the Lord similar to Jesus's petitions at the end of his offering of his fleshly life (Heb 5:7; cf. Matt 27:46; Luke 24:39). David's heavenly anticipation, originally expressed in Hebrew language, is translated in the LXX within the αγω– (*agō*) word group to describe his expected movement to God by his Lord's salvation. David says, "And he brings me up from a pit of distress and from a muddy clay" (καὶ ἀνήγαγέν με ἐκ λάκκου ταλαιπωρίας καὶ ἀπὸ πηλοῦ ἰλύος Ps 39:3 LXX [40:2 MT]). The Greek LXX αγω– word group links to the DI main subpoint about the ministerial ability of the Son to bring people to the firm stable ground of God's presence in the eternal/perpetual-*places* (Heb 1:3b). The imagery suggests external circumstances that involves more than a difficult life situation, but an anticipatory concern against his enemies' predicted failure for continued living after death in the presence of his God. David's prideful enemies, who know the sin of his life, lapse into falsehood about God's abilities of salvation for those who put their trust in him and seek to establish that David will not continue living in God's presence (Ps 39:4–5 LXX [40:5–6 MT]).

The Pastor prefaces the OT LXX quotation of Ps 39:5–7 with "therefore, he says while presently coming himself into the world" (Διὸ εἰσερχόμενος εἰς τὸν κόσμον λέγει Heb 10:5). Commentators universally interpret the Pastor's statement as a reference to the incarnated, fleshly, bodily life of the Son, as Jesus, coming into the world. However, (1) the syntax of the pres. mid. ptc. "while presently coming himself" (εἰσερχόμενος Heb 10:5), (2) the context, in unit D (Heb 5:1–10; 7:1–28) and unit F (Heb 8:1–10:18), of the Son's present ministry from heaven of the new covenant, and (3) the Ps 39 LXX (Ps 40 MT) background imagery regarding death and David's trusting hope for restoration of a body, may provide significance for the Son's current bodily ministry from heaven after death at judgment more than an outlier topic about Son's incarnation and life on earth.[270] In this setting, the Pastor continues to place emphasis upon the Son's current role as the Christ in doing the will

---

270. Concerning the Pastor's exposition about the ministry of the Christ, the temporal-spatial boundaries in Hebrews limits in narrow margins between his offering on the cross, with immediate subsequent enthronement in heaven, and his current ministry from heaven to those at death and judgment. Neither the complementary truth of the Son's incarnation for earthly ministry nor the second coming to earth for future ministry that are found in other NT texts enter the emphasis of the Pastor's message.

Atonement and the Logic of Resurrection in Hebrews 9:27–28

of the Father both after his onetime sacrificial offering for the sins of the people and currently in his priestly intercession for believers after death at judgment in his unit F UC (Heb 9:27–28).

Based on textual criticism, the most probable *Vorlage* for Ps 39:7 LXX is "but a body you restore to me" (σῶμα δὲ κατηρτίσω μοι Ps 39:7 LXX [Ps 40:6 MT]).[271] In the ST period, most would likely assume the Hebrew "ear" or Greek "body" as a literary devise, where David anticipates a whole, eternal/perpetual-*place*, spiritual body, rather than a later return to earthly flesh and blood creation (Heb 9:14; cf. Luke 16:19–31; Rom 8:1–17; 1 Cor 15:45, 50; 1 John 3:2).[272] David by faith expected to

---

271. Cf. Bergh, "Textual Comparison," 353–82 for recent comparison. Bergh argues convincingly that "body" (σῶμα) represents the better LXX reading from an original translation for meaning by interpreting "ears" (אזנים Ps 40:7 BHS) as *pars pro toto* in metonymy or synecdoche, rather than "ear" (ὠτία) that is found in Rahlfs' Göttingen edition and based upon weak evidence of a couple LXX textual branches. It is likely that in the LXX translators' venue, if David has "ears" (אזנים), then rationally he has a body that is functionally present in his judgment and restoration of life before God. Cf. Kraus, "Ps 40(39)," 119–31. Kraus argues all variances in Hebrews were part of the LXX text tradition and not original by the Pastor. Kraus concludes, "The earthly death of Jesus is at the same time understood as a heavenly event." Cf. Johnson, "Hebrews 10:5–7," 53–57. Johnson's observations about Jewish authors lack of concern to follow verbatim their OT quotations has recently been challenged. However, his reflection concerning the necessity of understanding the interpretative method of typology for proper interpretation of Ps 40:5–7 in Heb 10:7–9 remains essential for the Pastor's rhetorical context. Cf. Jobes, "Function of Paronomasia in Hebrews," 181–91. Jobes speculates that the Pastor's textual exchange of "you do not ask" (οὐκ ᾔτησας Ps 39:7 LXX) to "you do not delight" (οὐκ εὐδόκησας Heb 10:6) is influenced by God's ministerial approval recorded in the gospels. However, in the context of judgment, the concept of pleasing God may typologically correspond to the smoke that arises from the burnt offerings and altar of incense up to heaven.

272. Jeremias, "Flesh and Blood," 151–59. Jeremias contends that the context of 1 Cor 15:50 is about the change of the living at the parousia and not the resurrection or rising of the dead previously discussed, in 1 Cor 15:12–49, by Paul (158). He avers, "It must be said that the misunderstanding of the first half of 1 Cor. xv. 50: 'flesh and blood cannot inherit the kingdom of God' as speaking of the resurrection has played a disastrous role in the New Testament theology of the last sixty years until the present day" (157). The dead do not have flesh and blood bodies at the moment of inheritance no longer having any need for change since they have already transformed to the superior form of spirit bodies. In 1 Cor 15, the verbal change is not linked directly with the dead but the living. The contextual topic and language concern the necessary change of the living, before they sleep in death, to agree with the state of the dead, who have risen to be with Jesus, and already have victory over death and the necessary change to be with God (Phil 1:21–24; 3:20–21). Cf. Eberhart, "Characteristics of Sacrificial Metaphors," 37–64. Eberhart demonstrates that the cultic terminology "flesh," "body," "blood," "sacrifice," and "offering" evoke metaphors in reference to the life and events surrounding the crucifixion of Jesus. *Contra* Johnson, "On Removing a Trump Card," 175–92. Johnson argues against the modern Cartesian philosophy containing the spiritual and

continue living bodily after death in the presence of God in heaven (Heb 4:7; 11:32; cf. Ps 16:10–11; 23; 95:7).²⁷³ The Pastor follows the LXX translators and interprets David's anticipatory statement as an antitype of the promised messianic Davidic king, with correspondence to the present coming of the "body" (σῶμα Heb 10:5) of the Son to meet the dead coming from the "world" (κόσμος) to the "eternal/perpetual-*places*" (αἰών cf. Heb 9:8).²⁷⁴ This concept of immediate rising to God for the righteous

---

material anthesis of the resurrection body but contends that fleshly material is capable of participation in the coming kingdom of God.

For Jewish STL that engages concepts of antithetical dualism concerning the interior dimension of human nature in socioreligious battles against perceived evil, see Stuckenbruck, "Interiorization of Dualism," 145–68. Stuckenbruck pushes the event of God's judgment too far by assuming, "The 'flesh' itself re-emerges cleansed and purified from divine judgment" (165). The author of 1QS IV, 18–26 envisions God's removal of all spirit of injustice at God's judgment and purification of the inner person to prepare the person to live in an eternal/perpetual-*place* covenant.

273. Cf. Stemberger, *Der Leib der Auferstehung*. Stemberger evaluates ST concepts of life after fleshly death in the apocryphal and pseudepigraphic literature. He summarizes, stating, "In this thinking, all being is necessarily corporeal, God and his heavenly world, Sheol and the dead are all somehow bodily, material. There is no soul existing independently of the body. One therefore cannot speak of soul in our sense" (115). He recognizes that even in death, people are viewed as a whole corporal being with preserved individuality. He further concludes, "The development of opinions about the relation of the grave to the realm of the dead or that of the corpse to the dead or to the resurrected, questions that are not yet known in the OT, is relatively slow in our time, i.e., up to about 100 AD, and not at all straight ahead. Many problems are reserved for later time" (115).

For optional Greek semantic meanings for "body" (σῶμα) that includes the dualistic concept of a spirit body, see Schweizer, "Σῶμα, Σωματικός, Σύσσωμος," 1024–94, esp. 1057–59. When stripped of the straw men from the history of religions school that assumed Hellenistic influence upon Jewish concepts concerning the Greek text when dealing with the body in relation to the soul, heart, mind, flesh, etc., Schweizer properly recognizes the term refers to people in totality of their individual members. He also identifies the first-century CE dualism of the body of visible creation and spirit of the eternal/perpetual-*place* creation (cf. 1 Cor 15:40).

274. Nichols, *Death and Afterlife*, 55–75. Several anachronistic presuppositions hinder Nichol's conclusions, including the soul's postmortem survival (1) as a bodiless separation, rather than an immediate whole complete transition, (2) as nonmaterial, rather than a spiritual body consisting of eternal/perpetual-*place* material, and (3) as awaiting the eschaton for a fleshly resurrection before transition to a glorified spiritual body. Cf. Nickelsburg, *Resurrection, Immortality, and Eternal Life*. Nickelsburg's strength is that his assertions are based on the STL text. However, he fails to distinguish between a spiritual or fleshly body and adopts an anachronistic assumption for only a fleshly resurrection from post-NT concepts back onto STL textual references. Further, he assumes the failure to mention a "body" in a ST text as bodiless existence and a later idea of an inferior form of a spirit or soul. Cf. Cavallin, *Life after Death*. Cavallin broadens the same ground as Nickelsburg by allowing the context of STL to presuppose a belief in bodily

after death enjoys common acceptance in the first century CE.[275] The tradition of a flesh and blood resurrection for believers appears as later development and is often confused with the spirit-resurrection to God at death due to totality transfer of meaning for all resurrection or rising as a reference to flesh and blood.[276]

---

life after death. However, he follows the same anachronistic straw man assumption that resurrection must refer only to fleshly resuscitation from the dead, and that bodiless life after death supports the straw man concept of immortality of the soul, which causes him to conclude either concept was not established until some decades after Paul (195). This now traditional view of the NT concept of resurrection was not fully developed until the late first century CE. Cavallin is probably correct in his thesis that "'the Jewish doctrine of the resurrection of the dead'—more particularly 'of the body'—is indeed a 'myth'" (200). The NT concept more aligns with the concept of transition from the flesh body to a spirit body at death. Cavallin concludes, "The motif of a common end of history does not at all exclude but may very well include the hope of immediate salvation for the righteous after death. In most cases this does not imply a doctrine on the intermediate state between the two 'dates' of final salvation and judgment. Both aspects seem to be accepted side by side without any need of harmonization" (201).

275. In first-century CE resurrection conceptions, the rising of the fleshly body was unnecessary. Just as the OT and STL, in the NT, the dead are not considered bodiless but transition to a complete, material, spiritual body in a continued whole individual existence provided by God that is compatible with the unseen eternal/perpetual-*places* (cf. 1 Cor 15:35–58). Cf. Collins, "Afterlife in Apocalyptic Literature," 129. Collins concludes, "It is often claimed that Jews believed in resurrection of the body, while Greeks believed in immortality of the soul. Such a claim fails to do justice to the books of Enoch and Daniel. What we find is these apocalypses is the resurrection of the spirit. It is not the Greek idea of the soul, but neither is it a physical body. In the terminology of St. Paul, it might be described as a spiritual body (cf. 1 Cor. 15:44). Ideas of physical resurrection also gained currency in Judaism in the second century B.C.E., as can be seen in the account of the martyrdoms in 2 Mac. 7." Collins conclusion greatly weakens by the text stating later about the Maccabean martyrs, "For our brethren, now on the one hand having endured brief affliction, by covenant of everflowing life of God, have fallen" (οἱ μὲν γὰρ νῦν ἡμέτεροι ἀδελφοὶ βραχὺν ὑπενέγκαντες πόνον ἀενάου ζωῆς ὑπὸ διαθήκην θεοῦ πεπτώκασιν 2 Macc 7:36 LXX); i.e., these brethren have fallen into the blessings of God's covenant to eternal/perpetual-*place* life after falling into affliction.

276. Nickelsburg, "Judgment," 141–62. Nickelsburg posits later development of afterlife concepts in Jewish writings. He applies the recently contested separation of Jewish bodily resurrection against Hellenistic beliefs concerning the immortality of the soul in an afterlife. Also, he bases his conclusions upon the scant available sources, in multiple genres, over a broad period, that reveal diverse positions in the early debate. The proposition collapses by removal of the anachronistic definition of resurrection as a return for people to the obsolete body of flesh and blood. Cf. Goodman, "Paradise, Gardens, and the Afterlife," 57–63. Goodman assumes the supposed silence about details concerning an afterlife, in Josephus's large volume discussion, supports infancy and development of the concept in the first century CE. However, his anachronistic criteria about afterlife expectation, lack of consideration for common assumptions understood in spatial and people dualism, and argument from silence greatly hinder his claim.

The Pastor concludes that by God's desire and pleasure, "we have been made holy" (ἡγιασμένοι Hcb 10:10) in removal of sin, not by the sacrificial offering of animals or grains according to the law but by the self-offering of the body of Jesus Christ to do God's will once for all and please him (Heb 10:5–10).[277] Concerning Jesus's sacrificial self-offering, the Pastor again reminds his audience about his previous three unit F points (Heb 8:1—9:26) concerning the transitions accomplished by the heavenly entrance of Jesus regarding both heavenly space and the hearts and minds of his believers by saying, "He takes away the first *heavenly covenant ministry* in order to establish the second *heavenly covenant ministry*" (ἀναιρεῖ τὸ πρῶτον ἵνα τὸ δεύτερον στήσῃ Heb 10:9).

In contrast to the daily ministry and repeated offerings of the earthly ministry, Jesus's onetime sacrifice removed sin for all time (Heb 10:11–12). The Pastor, then yet again, reiterates with his audience about Jesus's current ministry at the right hand of God until his enemies be made a footstool for his feet (Heb 10:12–13). In further support of his MCS (Heb 9:27–28), the Pastor finishes his second FGT, about completion in heaven, by affirming, "For by one offering he has completed for all time the ones who presently are being made holy" (Heb 10:14). For the Pastor, there is but *one offering* that by God's approving judgment allows Jesus's movement from the cross to immediate heavenly access, rather than separate offerings on earth and a later offering in heaven.[278] Also,

---

The theological transition from concepts regarding a whole, spiritual, corporal existence after death to the inferior quality of an independent soul, in breaking apart body from soul, follows later tradition that rationally builds upon theological delayed expectations for only a final kingdom on the present earth in return to a fleshly existence. While dominating the theology of the Christian educated for over last 1,800 years, the philosophy reaches back through the NT era and the Sadducees to earlier OT and STL debates.

277. Use of the modern transliterated Latin terms *sanctify* and *sanctification* are avoided due to modern theological force toward concepts beyond the text of Hebrews with loss of the implied spatial weight of "make holy" (ἁγιάζω Heb 10:14).

278. Modern discussion concerning the "one offering" (μιᾷ . . . προσφορᾷ Heb 10:14) of Jesus as the Christ has diverse levels of temporal, spatial, descriptive disjunction between the sacrificial event of the cross and subsequent heavenly entrance. Temporal separation of these events requires some redefinition of Jesus's relationship to the cross and heavenly entrance, to qualify the Pastor's "one offering" assertion as either on earth or in heaven, but at the same time, somehow related to both spatial areas. The pressure for separation comes from several presuppositions already addressed: (1) God's kingdom building mission by Christ involving a tabernacle within heaven, rather than "in the heavens," (2) rejection of God's ability to separate the members of people's bodies and presently transition a change to a complete, perpetual, spiritual bodies a very little while after death at judgment, (3) placement of hope for eternal life on a future restored earth, rather than in a present, coexisting, perpetual heaven, and (4)

believers are presently made holy after death to enter the holy of holies, rather than still waiting for Jesus's intercession for salvation on earth.[279] His claim, about Jesus's escort of believers into the holy of holies to begin permanent eternal/perpetual-*place* life without interruption, once more cuts across the contested impossible teaching in unit E (Heb 5:11—6:18) about the audience possibly of teaching an error of falling from heaven after entrance. With this understanding, the Pastor now supports his unit F MCS (Heb 9:27–28).

---

perception that the present "coming" into the cosmos in Heb 10:5 must refer to the Son's incarnation in Jesus's life on earth, rather than surrounding context about his present priestly ministry in coming to meet his believers and shepherd them after death at judgment into heaven.

E.g., Moffitt, *Atonement*, 229–56; Gäbel, *Die Kulttheologie des Hebräerbriefes*, 185–202; Jamieson, *Jesus's Death and Heavenly Offering*, 71–94. Moffitt argues for Jesus's offering after fleshly resurrection during ascension in a local heavenly tabernacle. Gäbel, like Moffitt, follows the same timing but claims Jesus's offering occurred during his earthly life. Jamieson takes a mediating view and attempts, at the same time, to keep Jesus's death as what was achieved but restrict Jesus's offering, as his "achievement" in death, after fleshly resurrection. All three representative views to some degree, either temporally or spatially separate, separate Jesus's onetime offering from either the cross or heaven.

Commonly, these positions lack discussion about the requirement of God's judgment after death for all people, including Jesus, before rising from the dead. At what point does God judge the efficacy of Jesus's life blood sacrifice found in the Pastor's FGT subtopics? If judgment and offering occur in heaven at ascension, then Jesus arose from the dead before either God's judgment or Jesus's self-offering. A major hurdle for redefining Jesus's offering, so as to exclude the event of the cross as an offering, occurs in Heb 9:28. In his macro conclusion of unit F, the Pastor summarizes two aspects of the expected Christ. The first, regarding his sacrificial offering, states, "After being offered once for the purpose to bear the sins of many people" (Heb 9:28). The second concerns his present priestly ministry, which states, "He will appear from a second *place* without sin to the ones who are waiting for salvation by him" (Heb 9:28). Jesus's judgment by God as an acceptable offering for sin finishes just before death on the cross, with subsequent immediate entrance of his bodily spirit into heaven for inauguration of the new covenant, without either a temporal delay or technical exclusion of his sacrifice by the cross as Jesus's offering. Regarding the latter proposal, the exclusionary definition, against the earthly cross as an offering, cuts across the natural first-century CE usage of "offering" (προσφορά). Cf. Nelson, "He Offered Himself," 252. Nelson comments, "The verb 'offer' (*prospherō* and *anapherō*), used frequently in Hebrews, does not mean narrowly 'kill as a sacrifice' (even in 9:28), but rather describes the whole complex act of sacrifice, of which death is only the first element."

279. There is no bodily intermediate state described in the speech of God's word, but simply spatial transitions for believers with reception of spiritual bodies into God's presence with eventual removal of all God's enemies of sin and death.

Unit Point 6 (10:15–18): The Scripture and Holy Spirit Confirm the Present New Covenant Relationship on Approach after Death at Judgment

The final UPt6 FGT of unit F (Heb 8:1—10:18) circles back to the Pastor's strongest evidence to support his MCS and to complete his exposition regarding the one offering and present ministry of Christ that renders any other offerings as obsolete. Before he quotes again Jer 31:33, he prefaces the OT quotation, saying, "But also the Holy Spirit testifies. For after that *testimony* to have said . . ." (Μαρτυρεῖ δὲ ἡμῖν καὶ τὸ πνεῦμα τὸ ἅγιον· μετὰ γὰρ τὸ εἰρηκέναι Heb 10:15). The perf. act. inf. construction εἰρηκέναι with "to after have said" (μετὰ τὸ) indicates God's speech in the OT quotation occurred before the present testimony by the Holy Spirit that the Pastor interprets as a present promise-fulfillment for his audience of believers.[280] For the Pastor, according to the present speech of the Holy Spirit, the new covenant promise contained in Jeremiah 31:33 presently transpires in the experience of believers for salvation after death at judgment.[281]

---

280. *GGBB*, 594.

281. Cf. Brandon, *Judgment of the Dead*. Regarding Christianity, Brandon highlights the discrepancy evident in the creedal statements of the church about Jesus's different and logically contradictory roles as Savior and the Judge of people on earth (98). He develops early concepts of individual judgment as later products of Pauline eschatological reinterpretation against the early church Jewish apocalyptic visions about judgment of the world (105–111) that included recognition concerning NT teaching about an "immediate or particular judgment" (110–114). He then highlights "the absolute emphasis laid upon baptism as an essential prerequisite of salvation" rationally motivated later teachings where "instances of special *port-mortem* treatment arise . . . out of the Church's theology and feelings of justice and humanity" (116). The positions of this rational development are an area of needed future research. The formal state-church, by only earthly, kingdom focused understandings, and escalation of the antitype of baptism as sacramental for salvation, reduced Jesus's two separate roles into only the eschatological role of the promised second coming as Judge. This overemphasis for only a general final judgment often included eradication and persecution against teaching about Jesus's present fulfillment of salvation in heaven at individual judgment for the dead and baptism as only symbolic of faith in immediately following in Christ's death, burial, and resurrection from the dead into heaven (Heb 6:2; 9:10; cf. Rom 6:4–11; Col 2:12). Brandon documents the developments of Christian teachings based on these positions.

Most present scholarly work expects a final delayed judgment in connection with the promised seconding coming to earth but in varying degrees tolerates biblical teaching about immediate individual judgment; e.g., see discussion, Travis, "Judgment," 408–11. Travis concludes, "Jesus rejects speculation about many aspects of final judgment and its outcome. He is silent about the geography of God's kingdom or of Gehenna" (410). The Son, as Jesus, speaking in the text of Hebrews, counters Travis's claim. Further,

The present fulfillment of Jer 31:33 entails transitioning believers bodily at judgment to God's laws put on their hearts and written on their minds (Heb 10:16). Also, after judgment, God will not again remember their sins and lawless deeds that required Jesus's mediation (Heb 10:17). Further, in their new location, since there is forgiveness, there is no more offering for sin (Heb 10:18). The Pastor's midrash interpretation once again negates the errant impossible teaching considered in unit E (Heb 5:11—6:20), regarding the implication of continued repetitive sacrificial teaching that both Jesus and his believers repeatedly fall from heaven necessitating repetitive crucifixion of Jesus and continually renewed repentance by people.

Dynamic Unit Conclusions A–F in Lens of Hebrews 9:27–28

In summary, unit F structurally forms a chiasm with three preparatory unit points before the MCS of the Pastor's exposition and three supplementary unit points after it (see appendix 1, fig. 14). The Pastor antithetically and typologically compares the earthly daily and annual ministries with the transitional changes after Jesus's onetime offering regarding both individual believers and the heavenly ministry (see table 10). The two earthly ministerial operations of the Sinai covenant of the daily and annual sacrifices reveal the two unseen ministerial operations of the former and new heavenly covenants that is validated in death by continued bodily living a very short while into God's presence.

In the UC of Heb 9:27–28, the Pastor voices his understanding of the unseen events regarding the outcome for believers by Jesus's present

---

many texts, in which readers assume a final judgment, can easily apply to Jesus's current individual judgment at death as depicted in Heb 9:27–28. Nothing in the NT text about judgment demands only a delayed final judgment of all people at the same time. The imbalance toward final judgment perceptions rationally grows as the product of antitype escalation into earthly kingdom expectations with closed heavens for people at death. Cf. deSilva, *Perseverance in Gratitude*, 221. DeSilva rationalizes, based on earthly kingdom and general judgment premises, that salvation is future having no security until Christ's second coming to earth. However, the "day" implied in most references for judgment better applies in the context of the day of death and approach to God (Heb 10:25). This corresponds with other text referencing the final corporate execution of punishment that is already determined at an individual judgment at death and the coming day of the Lord earthly judgment that typologically portrays the current invisible judgment shortly after death. It is the people already shaken outside of heaven in death and Hades who are completely removed from God's presence in judgment (Heb 12:18–29; cf. Rev 20:13–14). Salvation comes by belief in Jesus as mediator when before God in an individual judgment of sin at death.

priestly ministry after death and at judgment. He rhetorically constructs his conclusion as rational interpretation of OT text of God's speech that he traces from his DI topics/subtopics (Heb 1:1–4) through six DUC (see appendix 1, figs. 12–14). He tracks the main DI subtopics of death, judgment, intercession, and salvation into heaven. The literary operations of his FGT in these units govern the understanding of his exposition to this point of his MCS.

In S1 (Heb 1:5–4:13), beginning in UC A (Heb 1:13–14), the Pastor concludes that the Son's new inherited ministry at death is better than the former heavenly ministry of angels when bringing those who are about to subsequently inherit salvation to God. UC B (Heb 2:17–18) reveals that the Son himself by his death made atonement for sins and will meet peoples' need at the testing of judgment. Jesus's faithfulness as a Judge during his complete evaluation of individual ministerial accountability to provide rest at the division of both soul and spirit, and joints and marrow closes his UC C (Heb 4:11–13).

The Pastor's STr1 (Heb 4:14–16) again highlights Jesus, as the Son of God, who passed through the heavens at his experience of judgment. Now as a high priest, believers can have confidence on approach after death to receive mercy and find grace at their time of need before God, when facing the Son's same experiential circumstances.

S2 (Heb 5:1–10:18) dives deeper with more exposition about the previous and present two-fold ministry of the Son. UC D (Heb 7:25–28) provides OT justification for Jesus's present priestly ministry for salvation by intercession in heaven for those who approach through him after death at judgment. His introduction FGT of unit D, at Heb 5:10, interrupts with insertion of UC E (Heb 6:11–20) concerning ministerial accountability for conversation about the Son's ministry as the offering of Christ. Finally, his UC F (Heb 9:27–28) summarizes thorough exposition about both the Son's offering achievement in relation to his present ministry for salvation after death at judgment, within the heavenly personal and spatial changes of the promised new covenant.

This complexity of information through S2 demands in the minds of the audience a discourse summary for clarification of his assertions presented to this point. The Pastor's STr2 discourse provides both a summary conclusion of units A through F and prepares the listeners to anticipate exhortation based upon his expositional teaching.

HEBREWS 10:19-25: SECTION TRANSITION 2 DISCOURSE ANALYSIS

The Pastor offers an expected transition between S2 (Heb 5:1—10:18) and S3 (Heb 10:26—13:21) for further orientation. Multiple literary markers signal a threshold for a discourse level transitional FGT.[282] In the form of *shorthand language*, STr2 supplies both conclusion and summary about his previous exposition of the DI (Heb 1:1-4) through the first six discourse units. This FGT also introduces his next six units of exhortation. In a broad application, the Pastor challenges his audience to live with expectation and anticipation to personally experience the ministry of Jesus.

STr2 transitions a chiastic turn that parallels in reverse his previous units through the lens of hortatory anticipation and application concerning Jesus's priestly intercession (see appendix 1, fig. 16). Units of A to F systematically laid out propositions in midrash exposition of the OT LXX to support the christological completion of the forgiveness of sin before God by Jesus's bodily offering in death of the flesh to inaugurate the expectation for a new and living way through the veil at God's judgment. Jesus, by intercession for "those who are presently approaching" (τοὺς προσερχομένους Heb 7:25; 10:1) by faith (Heb 4:3), will lead them into the eternal/perpetual-*place* rest for salvation (Heb 9:27-28). Jesus's atonement offering, as pleasing to God in the pattern of the promised Christ (Heb 6:1-2), is not perpetually repeated, but Jesus's intercession is lively now (Heb 7:25; 10:20).

---

282. These include (1) the repeat of the phrase "therefore having" (Ἔχοντες οὖν Heb 10:19) which corresponds to the section transition at the end of S1, to designate forthcoming summary oratory and conclusion about propositions asserted to this point that will be applied to the audience in greater detail in coming units to follow, (2) the literary device of "brethren" (ἀδελφοί Heb 10:19) to capture the attention of the audience and to signal an emphasis for a new FGT, (3) a condensed reemphasis of his utilized language indicating the spatial destiny of believers as "into the entrance of the holy-*places*" (εἰς τὴν εἴσοδον τῶν ἁγίων Heb 10:19), "which he inaugurated to us a new and living way through the veil" (Heb 10:20), "the house of God" (Heb 10:21), and exhortation concerning his previous movement language of "approach" (προσέρχομαι Heb 10:22), (4) the use of the shorthand phrases "by the blood of Jesus" (ἐν τῷ αἵματι Ἰησοῦ) in reference to his sacrificial offering for the sins of the people immediately before his entrance into the holy-*places* and "great high priest" (ἱερέα μέγαν) concerning his continued ministry at the throne in heaven, (5) another reconnection for the reminder concerning the spatial and salvific elements of the audience "confession" (ὁμολογία Heb 10:23), which they should hold fast to (cf. Heb 4:14), and which counters the teaching issue with the audience that is disclosed in unit E (Heb 5:10—6:20), and (6) shorthand language for the need to properly reflect for judgment (Heb 10:22).

Each statement of STr2, again summarizes both the DI (Heb 1:1-4) topic of the better ministry of the Son over the former Aaronic ministry and the chiastic subtopics listed that track to this point. Subtopics A (Heb 1:2b) and A′ (Heb1:4), about the Son's appointed inheritance and better name for ministry than the angels, correspond to his abbreviated statements concerning the believers' material access to "the holy-places" (τῶν ἁγίων Heb 10:19) and clearance of the obstacle of the "veil" (καταπετάσματος Heb 10:20) in the "house of God" (οἶκον τοῦ θεοῦ Heb 10:21). Subtopics B (Heb 1:2c) and B′ (Heb1:3d), about both the Son's achieving the eternal/perpetual-*places* and now sitting down at the right hand of the Majesty in the high places, correspond to his condensed statements concerning "for an entrance" (εἰς τὴν εἴσοδον Heb 10:19) and "which he inaugurated to us a new and living way" (ἣν ἐνεκαίνισεν ἡμῖν ὁδὸν πρόσφατον καὶ ζῶσαν Heb 10:20). Subtopics C (Heb 1:3a) and C′ (Heb 1:3c), about both the Son's glory as God's substance-reality and his purification of sins, correspond to his shorthand declarations concerning "by the blood of Jesus" (ἐν τῷ αἵματι Ἰησοῦ Heb 10:19), "this is his flesh" (τοῦτ' ἔστιν τῆς σαρκὸς αὐτοῦ Heb 10:20), and "a great high priest" (ἱερέα μέγαν Heb 10:21).[283] The climax introductory subtopic D (Heb 1:3b),

---

283. By neglect of the contextual tracks through the discourse that are governed by the FGT, when the interpretative ceiling is limited to only grammatical historical exegesis, the Pastor's shorthand term of "flesh," in reference to the sacrificial offering of Jesus, expands to his visualized body of the resurrection of his flesh either in incarnation or ascension; e.g., Jennings, "Veil," 85-97. Jennings argues unsuccessfully for the veil as a metaphor for Jesus's incarnation. The necessary context for this view is a major problematic hurdle. The metaphor better links with the context of his sacrificial offering on the cross. Cf. Moffitt, "Unveiling Jesus's Flesh," 71-84; Moffitt, in reaction to Hofius' view of incarnation, writes, "What Hofius missed is that Hebrews 10:20 refers neither to the incarnation per se (as he tried to argue), nor to the separation of Jesus's spirit from his body when he died (as many others maintain), but rather to Jesus's bodily ascension into heaven as a glorified human" (72). Hofius is correct, but the conception of a glorified human in first-century CE is a material, bodily, eternal/perpetual-*place* spirit, rather than a flesh and blood body (Heb 4:12; cf. Jub. 23:31). Similar debate by early Christian leaders and transition to fleshly resuscitation/resurrection exposes an area for further research.

The phrase "this is his flesh" (Heb 10:20) is a condensed literary device that refers to Christ's sacrificial offering in the flesh and not the complementary truth of Jesus's fleshly resurrection, which functions as visible proof of his rising to God at the invisible events of death and judgment with completion of atonement immediately at death on the cross. In Hebrews, proper conversation about the beginning teaching of the sacrificial offering of Christ dominates unit E (Heb 5:11—6:20) and codominates unit F (Heb 8:1-10:25) in conjunction with Jesus's present priestly ministry. The STr2 FGT, functioning as a transition, do not follow strict grammatical rules but connect back as a summary statement to the previous context or to introduce new context. The

about the Son bringing all things by the conversation of his ability, corresponds to the audience "approach" (προσέρχομαι Heb 10:22) at death and judgment with "confidence" (παρρησία Heb 10:19). This cohesion supports a contextually narrow message that centers around the unseen event of salvation by intercession after death at judgment.

The Pastor's use of the verbal subjunctive mood in both STr, rather than the absolute truth sense of the indicative mood, assists a shift to a heightened listener anticipation and expectation for the experience of Jesus's ministry. When fulfilled, the new covenant promises that are accomplished by Jesus's sacrificial offering, apply to the believers in the audience both internally and externally, and personally and spatially. The effect is for more than only a present ethical challenge toward an acceptable earthly worship that is pleasing to God. Their earthly worship activity in assembly with other believers, for acceptance must properly portray the heavenly expected changes that the audience should encounter when the day their death and judgment comes (Heb 9:27; 10:25).

Both STr significantly deploy the *present* subjunctive verbal aspect. In the NT, hortatory ethical subjunctives are usually aoristic in aspect.[284] It is at times good to go back to the Greek basics. William Mounce speaking on the hortatory subjunctive, reminds, "Just because a verb is first person subjunctive does not mean it is necessarily hortatory. Context will decide."[285] The aorist carries no temporal weight and is viewed from outside the verbal action.[286] In contrast, the present imperfective aspect views verbal "occurrence from the inside, focusing on its internal

---

antecedent of "this" (τοῦτ' Heb 10:20) functions as a shorthand link with the context of Jesus's fleshly offering highlighted in the previous exposition, rather than local connection with the referents of the "veil" or "way" (Heb 10:20). The καὶ (kai Heb 10:21) then links a statement about Jesus's present ministry, stating "A great high priest over the house of God" (ἱερέα μέγαν ἐπὶ τὸν οἶκον τοῦ θεοῦ Heb 10:21). Neither incarnation nor ascension appears in either direction of the message from this point. Hoffius is likely correct on the instrumental use but chose a contextual topic not found in the Pastor's previous or consequent FGT. Moffitt does the same to support his thesis concerning placement of Jesus's offering completion later at his ascension after fleshly resurrection.

284. Robertson, *Grammar*, 889. Robertson notes, "The aorist is used as a matter of course here unless durative action is to be expressed."

285. Mounce, *Basics of Biblical Greek*, 295.

286. Campbell, *Basics of Verbal Aspect*, 69. Campbell writes, "The use of the present subjunctive reveals regular expressions of imperfective aspect, viewing the action internally. Some common implicatures of imperfective aspect within present subjunctives are activities that are conceptually unfolding, temporally ongoing, stative, or personally characteristic." Cf. MHT, 3:74–78; Fanning, *Verbal Aspect in New Testament*, 393–95.

make-up without regard for its beginning or end."[287] The syntactical choice of the present subjunctive, within the context of death, judgment, intercession, and salvation, has better semantic meaning as a customary or gnomic sense.[288] Listeners customarily experience the ministry of Jesus when they face judgment after death. As such, the Pastor expects his audience to properly "to observe, reflect" (κατέχωμεν) their "confession" (ὁμολογία Heb 10:23) in their life-worship about the anticipated event of Jesus's intercession to salvation.

So, what does the present experience of salvation at death and judgment by Jesus's ministry look like that believers should confess and reflect in living assembly of worship until that day (Heb 10:25; cf. Luke 20:34–40)? The remaining STr2 text introduces and restates subtopics that are expanded in S3 (Heb 10:26—13:21). These include (1) a true heart (unit E′ Heb 10:26–39), (2) a certainty of faith (unit D1–D2′ Heb 11:1–40), (3) a clean conscience and body (unit C′ Heb 12:1–13), (4) confession in an unwavering hope in a faithful God (unit B′ Heb 12:14–29), and (5) love and good deeds unto others with exhortation in assembly (unit A′ Heb 13:1–21).[289] These new covenant features outlined in STr2 (Heb 10:19–25; cf. Heb 8:7–13), which track through the six discourse units of S3 (Heb 10:26—13:21), offer a good topic for future research to further consolidate the message cohesion of Hebrews.

---

287. Fanning, *Verbal Aspect in New Testament*, 390–93. Fanning lists several possible durative categories of present subjunctives.

288. Fanning, *Verbal Aspect in New Testament*, 392. Fanning defined this sense as "an activity which continues in some way over a period of time, or it may involve multiple repetition of the occurrence (perhaps in a distributive sense: each individual in the plurality does the action once)."

289. Ignoring the context of literal heavenly access rationally leads to sacramental interpretation of the Pastor's metaphorical summations concerning the ministerial worship activity of believers in baptism and assembly that picture expected heavenly realities; e.g., Leithart, "Womb of the World," 49–65. Leithart argues that Heb 10:19–22 states precisely that baptism confers priestly privileges (51) and qualifies a people to draw near to the heavenly sanctuary (53). His observation is likely correct that the language probably represents the religious rite of baptism observed by the audience and carried over from the OT cleansing rites though the ministry of John the Baptist, which publicly express faith and repentance. However, the context more properly supports that the audience's literal, earthly baptism symbolizes heavenly access by Jesus's literal ability of rising from death to indestructible life with God, which cleanses the sins of his believers when experiencing similar heavenly approach at death and judgment for entrance into the promised new life. The literal experience, regarding transition to a spiritual body by Jesus's intercession, fulfills the new spiritual birth requirement to enter the kingdom of God (Heb 10:5; 12:22–24; cf. John 3:1–21; 1 Cor 15:29; Titus 3:5).

Based upon his completed exposition about the ministry of Jesus, as the Son and Christ, the Pastor now turns to exhort his audience through corresponding propositions to A–E in units E′–A′ (see appendix 1, fig. 15). Since not directly related to the thesis claim, these units are only lightly examined to demonstrate correspondence with both the STr2 and their respective mirror units of exposition in chiasm (see appendix 1, fig. 16). This cohesion further supports the discourse analysis and thought-structure analysis derived.

HEBREWS 10:26—13:21: SECTION 3 INTRODUCTION

Section 3 Structural Map: Live by Faith, Hope, and Love during and until Approach of the Son's Ministry That God has Spoken

Appendix 1, figures 15 and 16 map the background FGT structure that governs S3 (Heb 10:26—13:21). S3 mainly provides listener exhortation with some further biblical warrant and supportive exposition for audience practice motivated by expectation for the propositions delivered in the DI (Heb 1:1–4). S3 continues the Pastor's main theme that centers on the audience "conversation" (ῥῆμα Heb 1:3b) about the Son's ministerial ability, by which the Son brings to God all things into heaven and God's presence. It develops through six discourse units before closing with the DC (Heb 13:22–25).[290] The six discourse units E′–A′ mirror in reverse order the subtopics of discourse units A–E, with a focus on exhortation in application of his expositional DUC about the Son's mediation for salvation in expectation for approach to God in heaven for judgment after death.

---

290. Crowther, "Rhetorical Function of Jesus's Session." Crowther provides excellent evaluation of the rhetorical function of Ps 110 MT in Hebrews. He finds the Ps 110 MT text supports the twin ministry of Jesus as the Christ concerning his exaltation and session. However, he applies the ministry only to the living in salvation and perseverance through earthly trials until the end at the second coming in a closed heaven paradigm. The contextual themes of death and judgment on approach to heaven in Hebrews, which apply to believers, and which believers follow for entrance into heaven after death at judgment are unnecessary due to his isolated earthly focus upon the living audience.

HEBREWS 10:35-39: ANALYSIS OF DISCOURSE UNIT CONCLUSION E´

Unit E´ Structural Map (10:26–39): Approach God with an Expectation for the Reality of Judgment after Death

The Pastor provides signals that he shifts to his next cycle of FGT. The unit has three FGT that function as introduction, support, and a conclusion. His audience would conceptually recognize both an expected threshold shift and chiastic turn by numerous literary signals.[291] This unit considers future anticipation of the believer, in relation to the DI subtopics of death, judgment, intercession, and salvation, and the STr2 outline. Figures 15 and 16 map the new unit E´ discourse.

Figure 16 demonstrates the discourse chiastic structure and the link of unit E´ (Heb 10:26–39) with unit E (Heb 5:11—6:20). The introduction subtopic is outlined in STr2 (Heb 10:19–25). The parallel correspondence, which is previously discussed in unit E and the STr2 analysis, in the former, provides exposition about the beginning teachings of the Christ. The audience should consider accountably for ministry in conversation involving errant teaching. Such teaching has no eternal value but teaching in the will of God has reward at judgment. The Pastor affirms that such ministerial conversation portrays the

---

291. These signals include (1) the particle "for" (γὰρ) to indicate the reasoning for assertions up to this point in the discourse (Heb 10:26), (2) the personal pronoun "we" (ἡμῶν) to indicate personal application of the assertions to the situation of the audience, (3) a return to the theme of unit E (Heb 5:11—6:20) about their temptation for errant teaching conversation concerning Christ, which activity the Pastor now directly identifies as "while intentionally presently sinning," (Ἑκουσίως . . . ἁμαρτανόντων Heb 10:26), (4) a summation of his previous exposition as reception of "knowledge of the truth" (τὴν ἐπίγνωσιν τῆς ἀληθείας Heb 10:26), (5) a connection of the themes of sin in teaching with "certain expectation of judgment" (τις ἐκδοχὴ κρίσεως Heb 10:27–28, 31) before witnesses with the Lord as Judge of his people (Heb 10:30), (6) an identification of those embracing the sinful conversation as "opposition" (ὑπεναντίους Heb 10:27), who insult the spirit of grace, treat the new covenant as unclean, and trample underfoot the Son of God (Heb 10:29), (7) recognition of the theme of accountability for errant teaching at judgment by the term "punishment" (τιμωρίας Heb 10:29) and a "terrible" (φοβερὸν Heb 10:31) experience before the living God, who is not pleased by those who "hesitate" (ὑποστολή Heb 10:38), (8) a call to remembrance about their former teaching conversation when enlightened in the knowledge of the truth that resulted both in earthly persecution and heavenly reward (Heb 10:32–33), (9) encouragement to endure in proper conversation to receive the rewards promised when the Lord comes after their death at judgment (Heb 10:36–37), and (10) reassurance that those who hesitate to teach the truth that he has developed do not receive destruction at judgment, since those who with faith have preservation of the soul (Heb 10:39).

promised "true heart" (Heb 10:22b) on account of their faith in the new covenant relationship Christ provides.²⁹²

Unit Introduction (10:26–31): God Will Judge the Willful Ministerial Sin of a Continued Sacrificial Activity by His People

The UI returns the audience to the themes of unit E (Heb 5:11—6:20) concerning ministerial accountability after death at judgment for teaching conversation about the Christ. The topic readdresses the audience temptation for errant teaching conversation concerning Christ that likely by sacrificial repetition, symbolizes Jesus as repetitively crucified again and falling from heaven. The Pastor labels errant ministerial activity as "while intentionally presently sinning" (Ἑκουσίως ... ἁμαρτανόντων Heb 10:26a). He identifies the summation of his previous exposition about Christ as reception of "the knowledge of the truth" (τὴν ἐπίγνωσιν τῆς ἀληθείας Heb 10:26b). The errant teaching away from the truth about Christ onetime offering and continual ministry in heaven establishes a situation where a sacrifice for sins no longer remains (Heb 10:26c). Rather, the repetitive sacrifices continually emphasize the expectation of judgment (Heb 10:27a) and zeal of fire on the altar that consumes God's adversaries (Heb 10:27b).²⁹³

The Pastor supports God's judgment by acknowledging the OT practice of putting to death without mercy those who invalidate the law (Heb 10:28; cf. Heb 2:2; Deut 17:2–6).²⁹⁴ He rhetorically asks, "How much do you think worse he will consider worthy punishment the one who trampled underfoot the Son of God, and himself regarded profane the blood of his covenant, in which he is made holy, and insulted the spirit

---

292. Truth points to the features of the unseen perpetual creation that believers enjoy at death in execution of the new covenant relationship. In cosmic-*field* constricted paradigms, truth is downgraded to biblical tradition and practice perceived as approved by God. Such tradition and practice often have little connection to the unseen spiritual realities they should represent due to loss of the heavenly connection. In pride and exercise of power, adherents of these traditions often compete and war against one another for the position of being the *true* faith and the *true* church. None of these assemblies of believers are the true church; they only, at most, represent on earth the features of the true church that Jesus is now building in heaven (Heb 12:22–29; cf. Matt 24:4–14).

293. McKay, "God's Holy Temple Fire." McKay explores the imagery of temple fire as God's judgment of his people.

294. This statement has cohesion with other NT statements where the law is not invalidated or done away but fulfilled by Jesus as the promised Christ (cf. Heb 9:22; 10:10; Matt 5:17; Luke 24:44).

of grace?" (Heb 10:29). The Pastor further supports God's judgment with an OT LXX quotation from Deut 32:35–36 (Heb 10:30), where God will avenge and repay when judging his people. He expects the experience of the living God's judgment upon the false teaching as frightening (Heb 10:31).

Unit Point 1 (10:32–35): Remember That Suffering in Conflicts against Faith and Hope in Christ Has Great Reward after Death at Judgment

UPt1 supports ministerial accountability by directing the audience to remember their previous enlightenment, when their ensuing ministerial conversation brought endurance in many struggles of suffering (Heb 10:32).[295] They had been publicly humiliated in their treatment (Heb 10:33a) and sharers with those treated in the same way (Heb 10:33b). They had sympathized with those who were prisoners and accepted the seizure of their property, because they knew they had a better and lasting possession in heavenly reward at judgment (Heb 10:34). The FGT closes with an aorist act. sub. "you should not throw away" (Μὴ ἀποβάλητε) their "outspokenness" (παρρησίαν), which has great reward when facing judgment (Heb 10:35). These comments prepare the Greek-speaking audience for an expected UC concerning how an anticipated time of

---

295. Young, "Suffering," 47–59. Young argues that the context of suffering supports a Jewish background second-generation Christians somewhere in the ethnic diversity of the Graeco-Roman world. However, it is more probable that the background concerns first-generation Christians who are tempted to return to the earthly Sinai covenant ministry that is now obsolete due to Jesus's fulfillment as the Christ. It is doubtful second-generation Christians would have the priestly training or authority to offer sacrifices. The offerings designated by the law in the tabernacle symbolized both the first and second heavenly covenant. Jesus's entrance into the holy of holies removed the veil of separation, which made both the daily sacrifices and the annual Day of Atonement obsolete. Continuing obsolete ministry would be a misstep with no eternal/perpetual-*place* reward at judgment. Unit A′ UPt3 compares the former and new covenant ministerial options for the listeners. Cf. Dyer, *Suffering*, 125–26. Dyer comments, "A function of both the temporal and spatial eschatology in Hebrews is to encourage the audience to think beyond their present situation. As with apocalyptic literature, Hebrews' eschatology offers its audience hope beyond death and this earthly existence. . . . Such an eschatological vision encouraged those marginalized or persecuted that their present reality did not reflect the true state of affairs. They could look to a future time and another world as a source of hope in the midst of despair. . . . For a community facing active suffering, the author encourages them by placing them within a cosmic drama that promises salvation to those who endure in faith (Heb 10.36, 39). This should calm any fear since death, it is shown, is not the end."

ministerial accountability in their teaching about Christ should work out for them.

Unit E´ Conclusion (10:36–39): Confidently Persevere as an Example of Faith to Receive the Promised Rewards That God Has Spoken

The Pastor accumulates the necessary literary indicators to imply a threshold by the audience for a shift to an anticipated UC.[296] In reflection on the current ministerial differences from their beginning enlightenment, the Pastor asserts his listeners need "perseverance" (ὑπομονῆς), so that when they do the will of God in following Christ in death, at judgment they should receive "the promise" (τὴν ἐπαγγελίαν Heb 10:36).

He uses an OT conflation of Isa 26:20 and Hab 2:3–4 LXX to assure the audience that the time after death to judgment is but a moment, which should motivate them against timidity or hesitation in their teaching conversation about Christ.[297] The Pastor does not anticipate a long delay after death and judgment for Jesus's expected coming presence (Heb 10:37).[298] The fut. act. indic. "he will come" (ἥξει) has weight of nearness of distance into the presence of the one coming.[299] The contextual background pictures Jesus, for intercessional ministry, coming into the presence to those who by angelic escort are approaching in the way of the holy-*places*.

---

296. These markers include (1) an OT LXX quotation of Hab 2:3–4 (Heb 10:37–38) for connection with the MCS and the coming of the Lord for the audience after death at judgment. The OT quotation also addresses important themes regarding judgment. This includes the righteous living by faith and the Lord's displeasure in the timid. Also, (2) recurrent use of "we" (ἡμεῖς) for a unit *inclusio* indicating closure of the unit (Heb 10:26, 39), and (3) an expositional statement concerning the limits of timidity among those who have faith in conversation about Christ when at judgment only to a point that still preserves the soul (Heb 10:39).

297. Gheorghita, *Role of the Septuagint*, 149–231.

298. The context surrounding the MCS specifies, for the Pastor, that the future appearing of Jesus for waiting believers to presently receive this already existing place of rest with him at this throne occurs at individual death and judgment. A onetime exception occurs when Jesus appears on earth for a temporary future servant-rule, which involves a gathering of living believers to those already with him (1 Thess 4:13–18). During Jesus's rule on the temporary earth, people still endure death and judgment (Isa 65:20), with believers transformed at death for continued service on earth (Rev 14:14), until the removal of that which can be shaken (Heb 12:25–29; cf. Rev 21:1).

299. BDAG, "ἥκω," 435.

The Pastor summarizes the unit with exposition about this anticipated judgment experience that includes ministerial accountability. He establishes both the criteria for life and the limits of God's displeasure at judgment (Heb 10:39). First, the righteous individual will live by "faith" (πίστις). His use of faith introduces the theme outlined in STr2 (Heb 10:19–25) concerning "certainty of faith" (Heb 10:22c). His next unit D1ʹ and D2ʹ reflect what certainty of faith looks like. If the righteous draw back, God will voice his displeasure.[300] However, that displeasure is not to the point of destruction since those of faith have promised preservation of the soul after death at judgment.

Dynamic Unit Conclusion Eʹ in Lens of Heb 9:27–28

Unit Eʹ (Heb 10:26–39) begins the Pastor's exhortation in application of his exposition that he expects his audience to properly "observe, reflect" (κατέχωμεν) in their life-worship regarding their "confession" (ὁμολογία Heb 10:23) about the anticipated event of Jesus's intercession to salvation. He demonstrates what the present experience of salvation at death and judgment by Jesus's ministry should look like that the audience should confess and reflect in living assembly of worship until that day (Heb 10:25; cf. Luke 20:34–40). His outline in the STr2 (Heb 10:19–25) identifies the unit topic as "a true heart" (Heb 10:22b). In an apocalyptic context, the referent "true" reflects congruency with the unseen heavenly realities that one confesses. A "true heart" begins with living that includes acknowledgment of the reality of judgment by God after death. Those of faith will live and cannot draw back to destruction. However, those of faith who live out their ministerial confession in timidity, rather than outspokenness, or who adhere to missteps about the onetime offering

---

300. Lewis, "And if He Shrinks Back," 88–94. Lewis counters the common interpretation in the commentaries for apostasy as the meaning of "be timid, hesitancy, timidity" (ὑποστολή Heb 10:39) in relation to the "coming" (παρουσία) to earth, which is not found in the message of Hebrews. Lewis follows presuppositions about the language of Heb 10:37–38 and the Pastor's modifications. He states, "It has long been recognized that the quotation from Habakkuk appears in Heb. x. 37–38 is a significantly modified form of the LXX text. . . . By the deliberate insertion of the definite article the one referred by ὁ ἐρχόμενος ἥξει is clearly the Christ in his second advent" (90). However, the context about the intercession of Christ at death and judgment and ministerial accountability in relation to future reward makes this proof text conclusion for the second coming improbable. The implication is the righteous ones will stand before the Lord at judgment without delay after death and face his displeasure if they are timid in their conversation about the present ability of Jesus the Son.

and continual present ministry of Christ highlighted in the MCS will experience fear at judgment with loss of reward due to God's displeasure. The Pastor in his next unit provides examples of those who reflect the proper confession in the certainty of the knowledge of the faith.

HEBREWS 11:13-16: ANALYSIS OF DISCOURSE UNIT CONCLUSION D1´

Unit D1´ Structural Mapping (11:3-12): Approach in Faith to the Heavenly City of the Fathers That God Promised

The Pastor provides signals that he shifts to the next cycle of FGT. His audience would cognitively recognize a threshold shift by multiple literary signals.[301] This unit contains nine FGT functioning as introduction about DI and STr2 subtopics, support for subtopic assertions, and a conclusion. Figures 15 and 16 map the new unit D1´ discourse.

Figure 16 demonstrates the discourse chiastic structure and the relation of unit D1´ (Heb 11:1-16) and D2´ (Heb 11:16-40) with unit D (Heb 5:1-10; 7:1-28). The parallel correspondence, previously discussed in unit D analysis, summarizes as the audience need to approach the heavenly city where the fathers now live, by following others example of faith at death in the high priest intercession of Christ for people into the unseen eternal/perpetual-*places*. These units follow the outline of the STr2 (Heb 10:19-25) for an expected ministerial confession that reflects a "certainty of faith" (Heb 10:22c) in the ministry of Jesus as Christ after death at judgment.[302] The unit confirms that people of faith anticipate

---

301. These signals include (1) the connective "now" (δὲ) that can reflect a transition to a new unit segment, (2) a link to the previous subtopic issue addressed with the audience concerning proper "conversation, testimony of God" (ῥήματι θεοῦ Heb 11:3) in ministry about the actual "Word" (λόγος Heb 2:2); 4:2, 12; 5:11; 6:1; 7:28) that God spoke that should be heard in Jesus's actions (Heb 1:3c; 2:2a), (3) the literary head-tail linkage of the referent πίστις ("faith," Heb 10:39; 11:1), rather than rational conclusions from empiric evidence, (4) use of the verbal concept of "were approved" (ἐμαρτυρήθησαν Heb 11:2) as a link to the outward activity of the elders expected ministerial confession while anticipating Jesus's ministry at death and judgment, (5) apocalyptic language that positions the "evidence" (ἔλεγχος Heb 11:1) of faith as completion in the unseen, heavenly "substance-reality" (ὑπόστασις Heb 11:1) of the "eternal/perpetual-*places*" (τοὺς αἰῶνας Heb 11:3), rather than that which is seen on earth.

302. *Contra* Schoonhoven, "Analogy of Faith," 92-110. Schoonhoven interprets the faith in Heb 11 as future earthly reward that is secured only if one perseveringly obeys. For Schoonhoven, the Pastor's threats warn about the outcome for a lack of obedience with endurance that results in irremediable judgment in God's wrath. However, the

that the promises in Christ fulfilled into heaven a very short while after death at judgment.³⁰³

Unit Introduction/Unit Point 1–2 (11:1–2): Hope by Faith in the Reality of Unseen Things, by Which Hope the Fathers Received a Good Report after Death at Judgment

The UI/Pt1–2 FGT begins by defining "faith" (πίστις Heb 11:1a). It doubles as a UI for both unit D1′ (Heb 11:1–16) and unit D2′ (Heb 11:17–40). Faith is "substance-reality of things being presently expected" (Heb 11:1a). He clarifies this present prospect of substance-reality as "evidence of things not presently being seen" (Heb 11:1b). The two adjectival pres. pass. ptcs. add force for faith having the intrinsic feature of accessibility to the present existence of an unseen reality.

The Pastor maintains that "by this *kind of faith*" (ἐν ταύτῃ) the elders "were approved" (ἐμαρτυρήθησαν Heb 11:2). This desired approval links with both unit E (Heb 5:11—6:20) and unit E′ (Heb 10:26–39) about ministerial objective at judgment "to please" (εὐδοκεῖ) God (Heb 10:38).³⁰⁴ The approval received would be understood, as from God, during the context of death and judgment.

Subpoint 1a (11:3): Faith Conversation Understands the Eternal/ Perpetual-Places Were Made Out of a Substance-Reality Not Visible

The Pastor links his explanation about faith in Heb 11:1 to Heb 11:2 by his pronominal phrase "by this *kind of faith*" (ἐν ταύτῃ) and continues

---

context of the exposition in the ministry of Christ and audience calling for proper ministry that is accountable when before Christ at judgment cannot support the weight of his supposed rational conclusions.

303. Bulley, "Death and Rhetoric," 409–23. Bulley comments, "Whatever decisions are finally made about the rhetorical species of Hebrews, it is apparent that descriptions of death and suffering run throughout the document. . . . A more careful examination of the themes and language of death and suffering will very likely help to illuminate the connection between the exposition and paraenesis of Hebrews, and may afford further insights into the rhetorical situation of the argument." Four themes run concurrently in the Pastor's words, phrases, and OT quotations from the DI. These are death, judgment, intercession, and salvation in heaven, which draw the exposition and exhortation in tight cohesion together as Bulley mentions.

304. The verbal concept of ministry to please God at his judgment extends back in the LXX to Enoch as developed in unit D′ Pt1c (Heb 11:5–6) with corresponding links to the offerings of Cain and Abel in unit D′ Pt1b (Heb 11:4).

this link in units D1′ and D2′ with the dat. shorthand πίστει eighteen more times. In each use, he provides evidence from previous confession of other people in ministerial conversation that reveals the hope of access into the substance-reality of the unseen eternal/perpetual-*places* after death at judgment.

He begins with the ordinary understanding for both himself and his audience, in their conversation of God, about the heavenly unseen creation. He comments, "By faith we understand the eternal/perpetual-*places* in conversation of God to have been made, with the result to occur that the things presently being seen are not from the things presently appearing" (Heb 11:3). Rather than an outlier subtopic serving either as a rhetorical proof text about creation *ex nihilo* or defense of the Genesis creation as by the fiat of God, the statement more likely links with the Pastor's previous rhetoric about Jesus's recent transformation of the eternal/perpetual-*places*. The heavenly creation of the greater and more complete tent not made with hands that is now only seen by faith in the speech of God (cf. 1 Cor 2:9–10) was creatively achieved by Jesus's recent entrance through the veil after his judgment at death.

The Heb 11:3 statement, considering the Pastor's previous FGT unit exposition and discourse chiastic application, specifies in proper conversation of God that what is seen now, regarding access into the eternal/perpetual-*places*, no longer links to the conversation seen that is represented by the previous and continued sacrifices in the earthly covenant of the law. The priestly sacrificial offerings, still observed at the time of the Pastor's message (Heb 13:10), are both obsolete and errant teaching conversation that no longer accurately portray God's current speech regarding either the current status of the holy-*places* or Jesus's present priestly ministry (cf. unit F UPt4 Heb 10:1–4).

Subpoint 1b (11:4): Abel by Faith in the Reality Not Seen Offers a Better Sacrifice than Cain

The Pastor continues, in unit D1′ (Heb 11:1–16), his evidence concerning ministerial conversation by elders before the offerings required by the covenant of the law at Sinai. His first contrast explores the respective offerings of Cain and Abel (Gen 4:1–16). Cain was comfortable and content with God's blessings upon him in the temporary decaying world. In his offerings of the first fruits from work with his crops, he worshiped with offerings in gratitude to God during approach before him. However, Cain only rationally knew, through the testimony of Adam and Eve and Eden's remote closed existence, the contrast between the antitype of earthly Eden against his present surroundings resulting from sin. In his way of worship, he did not portray the faith in the unseen substance-realities nor the necessary offering requirement for heavenly access. His ministerial conversation, in offerings and worship, did not reveal a faith in heavenly expectation to the unseen kingdom by God's promise (cf. Gen 3:15), for which Eden was an antitype.

Abel's sacrificial offering provided testimonial conversation that, in the OT, initiates the beginning sayings of the Christ (Heb 6:1–2) and worships by revealing need for a sacrificial atonement that ascends upward to God for his approval and access into God's presence (Heb 13:10). Cain's displacement and reaction of anger, at the offering rejection by God and Abel, reveals a heart of pride in his earthly work under God's blessings that grows into murder of Abel. Cain's faith rests in the realities of earth and not the unseen substance-realities of heaven that God provides in the promise of Christ.[305]

Subpoint 1c (11:5–6): Enoch Pleases God, So God Took Him, without Him Seeing His Own Death, to the Reality Not Seen, without Which Similar Faith, No One Can Enter to God

As his next evidence, the Pastor includes Enoch with the elders for expectation by faith in God's provision of heavenly substance-realities in relation to death and judgment. The STL about Enoch is highly developed in the first century CE from multiple theological points of view and later receives an explosion of speculation in support of perceived orthodoxy by diverse Christian redaction.[306] The Pastor concentrates upon the language of the second-century BCE Greek OT LXX for his thoughts about "transfer" (μεταθέσεως Heb 11:5) to heavenly realities for those "to have pleased" (εὐαρεστηκέναι Heb 11:5) God.

His midrash commentary focuses on the text concerning Enoch in the LXX, which states, "And Enoch pleased God and he was not found, since God transferred him" (Gen 5:24 LXX). In correspondence to

---

305. Cain demonstrates that the misstep for earthly hope has been embraced by the ministries of people since the beginning (cf. 1 John 3:12; Jude 11).

306. See chapter 3, 159n183 [XREF].

common first-century CE tradition, the Pastor apocalyptically applies this LXX translator understanding to his message context about God's judgment of people after death at approach to God's presence. He emphasizes, "For he had been approved before the transfer to God to have pleased" (Heb 11:5). The perf. act. inf. adds weight that Enoch's offerings symbolically refer to an expected realistic completion. The Pastor suggests that God's pleasure in judgment of Enoch's symbolic offerings was confirmed by his later completed transfer to heaven.

The LXX translators gloss the Hebrew *hithpael* syntactical form "walked himself" (ויתהלך Gen 5:24 BHS) with the aorist act. indic. "pleased" (εὐηρέστησεν Gen 5:24 LXX). This links the metaphoric concept of Enoch walking with God to the previous dialogue about Cain and Abel (Gen 4:1–10). God's response to their respective worship indicates narrow requirements for proper sacrificial offerings that please God when ascending before him in heaven. The allusion to the previous Gen 4 text indicates that Enoch offers proper sacrifices, even as Abel, which upon ascension of the smoke of his sacrificial burnt offerings pleases God by demonstration of faith in expectation to later follow the promised sacrificial Christ into heaven.

The LXX translators continue apocalyptic interpretation by translating the Hebrew "took, grasped" (לקח Gen 5:24 BHS) with the aorist act. indic. "transferred" (μετέθηκεν Gen 5:24 LXX). The result of Enoch's pleasing sacrificial expressions of faith results in Enoch's transfer by God into his presence. He did not see death and was not found, because God transferred him to himself in heaven.

The Pastor emphatically states, "But without faith one is not able to please. For it is necessary the one approaching to God to believe that he is, and he becomes a rewarder to those seeking him" (Heb 11:6). The Pastor links expectation of the substance-reality not seen with belief in both God's existence and reward at God's judgment on approach to him.

Subpoint 1d (11:7): Noah Examples Salvation by Faith in God's Speaking about Things Not Seen Regarding Judgment to Come after Death

Noah serves as the Pastor's next evidence for an elder who exemplified faith in an expected substance-reality of things not seen. The Pastor highlights the correspondence between Noah's warning from God "concerning the things not yet presently seen" (Heb 11:7) to continue a connection with faith in Heb 11:1. Noah's reverent preparation of the ark resulted in the salvation of his household, condemned the "world" (κόσμος Heb 11:8), "and of that righteousness according to faith became an heir" (Heb 11:7). Noah's obedience to God's warnings concerning judgment of the world with the flood typologically demonstrated that the endpoint of his faith, as an heir, was not this world, but salvation in the substance-reality of things not seen (cf. 1 Pet 3:18–22).[307]

Subpoint 1e (11:8) Abraham Examples Faith in God's Speaking of a Land Not Seen

Abraham hears God's call and obeys by going out to a "place" (τόπος Heb 11:8), which he was going to receive as an inheritance. He went out not knowing where he was going. In this response to God, Abraham symbolized faith in the substance-reality of the eternal/perpetual-*place* creation not seen.

---

307. The apocalyptic language in Hebrews about unseen creation, in relation to Noah, sheds light on the typology exploited in 1 Pet 3:18–22. For Peter, Jesus "having been made alive in spirit" (ζωοποιηθείς ... πνεύματι 1 Pet 3:18) corresponds in Hebrews with Jesus's "spirit of an eternal/perpetual-*place*" (πνεύματος αἰωνίου Heb 9:14), who instantly enters to God after death in the flesh (cf. unit F Pt2b Heb 9:11–14). The spirits in prison metaphorically refer to those transitioned to spiritual bodies at death who are still under the dominion of the devil in the "world" (κόσμος) or abyss outside of heaven (cf. unit B Pt3 Heb 1:14–16). Peter's language exploits the apocalyptic first-century CE Enochic worldview that commonly considered that the disobedient in the days of Noah remain outside of the holiness of God's spatial presence in the realm assigned to the fallen angelic spirits and their demonic offspring due to their relations with earthly women. Like Enoch, Christ preaches to those fallen beings without accomplishing for them the opening of the gates of heaven for entrance (Heb 2:16; cf. 1 Pet 1:12; 2:4). However, like Noah and the ark, those who listen and obey God's speech while living concerning faith in Christ are brought at death through the chaotic waters of the κόσμος and surrounding abyss outside to salvation in heaven. Peter shares that baptism is an "antitype" (ἀντίτυπον 1 Pet 3:21) of this same heavenly typology claimed in Enoch. Peter validates the typology, rather than the unseen reality of the Enochic claims that likely originates as Samaritan polemic against the Jerusalem priesthood in the second-century BCE. Like the typology in Enoch regarding Noah and the flood judgment, for Peter, baptism does not remove the problems of the flesh in relation to the heavenly reality but demonstrates an appeal to God for a good conscience when approaching him as a bodily spirit at judgment after death through the same rising experience by Jesus as the Christ; i.e., heaven opens for Jesus and those who obey him. Jesus both enters into heaven to the right hand of God with all angels, authorities, and powers of the typified Enochic worldview subjected to him (cf. Luke 8:31) and enables entrance to God for those who obey by belief in him.

Subpoint 1f (11:9–10): Abraham Examples Faith, Not in This World, but in a City of the Unseen Reality Which God Spoke and Built

Abraham further examples an expectation for entrance into the substance-reality not seen, rather than a later return to the visible, provisional world (cf. Heb 7:6). He was a foreigner in the promised land that typologically represented the unseen heavenly promise. He dwelled in temporary tents with Isaac and Jacob, who were fellow-heirs of the eternal/perpetual-*place* promise (cf. Heb 7:6; 8:6; 9:15). Rather than the earthly land of promise, Abraham "was expecting" (ἐξεδέχετο) the permeance of that city having the foundations, of which, God is architect and creator. The Pastor claims "so after persevering he obtained the promise" (Heb 6:15). The promise fulfills after Abraham's death.[308]

Subpoint 1g (11:11–12): Sarah Examples Faith in God's Speaking in a Miraculous Conception to Maintain the Promise of Many Descendants in That City

For the Pastor, God's blessings in the miraculous conception and continuance of the seed of Abraham through Sarah suggests that she considers God faithful in the promise to her husband and surmises his seed as involving heavenly eternal/perpetual-*place* expectation. Abraham's descendants, as the stars in heaven and the sand of the seashore, indicate both immediate transformations linked at death with anticipation for reception of spiritual bodies that brilliantly shine and a large number of spiritually born offspring (cf. Dan 12:3). At this point in the Pastor's growing list of elders, after comments on the faith of Cain, Abel, Enoch, Noah, Abraham, and Sarah, the audience awaits a FGT UC about the common features that he desires to underscore.

---

308. For the Pastor, the expectation by Abraham links to the creative changes achieved by Jesus, as the Christ, in the foundations of the eternal/perpetual-*places* upon entry through the veil. God instantly transforms the creation at Jesus's death, enables him to bodily rise as an eternal/perpetual-*place* spirit from the dead on the cross, allows him travel through the now cleansed temple of the heavens from the sin of the people waiting there, and enthrones him for ministry in the now created greater and more complete tabernacle; e.g., Moses and Elijah speak with Jesus after their deaths about his anticipated death that would open access into heaven for himself and those who trust in the seed from his linage (Matt 17:2; Mark 9:4; Luke 9:30–31; Heb 4:1; 6:17; 10:36).

Unit D1´ Conclusion (11:13–16): All the Examples of the Fathers Died without Receiving the Promises in This World That God Spoke but Received Them in the Heavenly City of Reality Not Seen, Which God Prepared

The Pastor reaches an early climax in unit D1´ (Heb 11:1–16) with his listing about the faith of the elders that is pregnant with expectation of an UC for audience summation. At the end of his unit D1´ discourse, the Pastor accumulates the necessary literary indicators to imply a threshold by the audience for a shift to an anticipated UC.[309] The UC has cohesion with the provided outline topic "certainty of faith" (Heb 10:22c) in STr2.

The elders' choices, for a heavenly, rather than an earthly completion concerning their faith, provides ample cohesive, rhetorical evidence for his proposed explanation of faith in Heb 11:1, as expectation for the unseen substance-reality of heaven.[310] The Pastor's evidence through the testimony of the elders establishes a compendium of support in his D1´ UC for heavenly fulfillment of the promises. He highlights that (1) they all died without receiving the promises, (2) what they saw on earth is not what they later saw and greeted, (3) they confessed themselves foreigners and sojourners upon the earth, (4) they continually speak about desire to another homeland in heaven, (5) they could have returned to what they remembered but did not, (6) they aspired a better heavenly place, and

---

309. These markers include (1) the phrase "all these people" (οὗτοι πάντες Heb 11:13), (2) repeat of the subtopic "according to faith" (Κατὰ πίστιν Heb 11:13) in relation to each of the elders mentioned, (3) a common verbal action for all the listed elders, as all these people "died" (ἀπέθανον Heb 11:3) that tracks from the exposition MCS subtopics in Heb 9:27–28, and (4) use of the summary terms "promise" (ἐπαγγελία), "receive" (λαμβάνω), "see" (εἶδον), "admit" (ὁμολογέω), "foreigner" (ξένος), "exile" (παρεπίδημοί), "better" (κρείττων), and "heavenly" (ἐπουράνιος Heb 11:13) in the language surrounding the main subtopic path of salvation for confessed believers as a transfer to the unseen eternal/perpetual-*places* that tracks from the DI (Heb 1:1–4) through the discourse exposition in sections 1 and 2.

310. Niederwimmer, "Vom Glauben der Pilger," 121–31. Niederwimmer recognizes that "the goods of hope to which the believer directs themselves is already reality, what is to come is already anticipated reality" (124). He further states, "Faith is thus a reality contrary to the evidence of empiricism of the finite, geared to the fact that what can be experienced proleptically finally becomes the definitive object of experience" (124). He concerning the timing finds, "Faith is here exodus. Certainly, an exodus of a special kind. It has nothing to do with utopian departures into the future" (127). He perceives from Heb 11 that "an exodus is letting to, detaching, dying" (127). Niederwimmer concludes understanding the home of the believer is the heavenly Jerusalem available now to the pilgrims and strangers upon the earth.

(7) at their judgment after death, God is not ashamed of them to be their God and prepared a city for them together.

The Pastor's use of the aorist and present tenses syntactically treats the people in this unit about the elders as if they have already received and continue to enjoy the promises, rather than still awaiting them at the time of his writing (cf. Heb 6:5; cf. Deut 32:39; 1 Sam 2:6; 2 Kgs 2:11; Isa 26:19; Prov 12:28). In the first-century CE apocalyptic (*aiōn-field*) lens, as read in the extant STL and the NT, these elders a very little while after death should approach God and bodily enter heaven (cf. Matt 27:51–53; Luke 23:43; 2 Cor 5; Phil 1:20–23; 3:20–21; 1 Thess 5:1–11; John 3:2).[311]

Dynamic Unit Conclusions E′–D1′ in Lens of Hebrews 9:27–28

The Pastor's STr2 (Heb 10:19–25) outline projects application of his expositional material about the sacrificial offering and present ministry of Jesus as the Christ. He has considered a "true heart" (Heb 10:22b) in unit E′ and "certainty of faith" (Heb 10:22c) in unit D1′–D2′ (Heb 11:1–40). In unit D1′ (Heb 11:1–16), he challenges his listeners to model perseverance in the knowledge of the truth concerning the unseen realities regarding Christ. Maintaining their first witness would result in great reward when receiving the promise. He introduces the topic about the righteousness of faith in the E′ UC (Heb 10:36–39). In unit D1′, after defining faith as an expectation for the unseen substance-realities, the Pastor documents midrash about the elders who demonstrate what the certainty of faith looks like. The endpoint of faith is not here; it is there in heaven in a city with others who have already received and greeted their destiny when they died.

Yet, the Pastor is not done yet. In the nearly four thousand years of history about people before the time his message, there are many more, who in many ways reflect the same "certainty of faith" (Heb 10:22c) with an expectation for entrance into the eternal/perpetual-*places*.

---

311. For recent comprehensive study concerning STL afterlife concepts, see Sigvartsen, *Afterlife and Resurrection Beliefs*. The contributing scholars recognize interpretative assumptions about continuance of life after death underlie the text of the OT and STL (1). However, their anachronistic presupposition that all bodily resurrection concerns only living in the flesh with the promised spiritual bodies as inferior and incomplete, hampers contextual interpretations of early references to resurrection. The concept of immediate, unseen, complete, continued living of the righteous in heaven, due to lack of articulate and consistent burial rites in the OT, is often incorrectly interpreted as a lack of interest in the afterlife among religious leaders (1–2).

HEBREWS 11:39-40: ANALYSIS OF DISCOURSE UNIT CONCLUSION D2´

Unit D2´ Structural Map (11:17–40): Live By Faith by Imitating Others Who Had Faith in the Son to Bring Believers into the Substance-Reality of Things Not Seen

The Pastor provides signals that he shifts to next cycle of FGT. His audience would conceptually recognize a threshold shift by several literary signals.[312] This unit contains thirteen additional FGT functioning as unit subtopic, support, and a conclusion to the unit D1´–D2´ UI (Heb 11:1–2). Figures 15 and 16 map the new unit D2´ discourse. The unit continues new covenant features "certainty of faith" (Heb 10:22c) from STr2.´

Figure 16 shows chiastic structure and the link of unit D1´ (Heb 11:1–16) and D2´ (Heb 11:16–40) with the two parts of unit D (Heb 5:1–10; 7:1–28). The parallel correspondence, that is previously discussed in unit D analysis, summarizes as the need to emulate the faith of the elders, who had expectation for the offering of the Christ and his high priest ministry to bring them into the eternal/perpetual-*places* at death.

Unit Introduction/Unit Point 1–2 (11:1–2): Hope by Faith for the Substance-Reality of Unseen Things, by which the Fathers Received a Good Report

The UI (11:1–2) functions as an introduction for both unit collections about the kind of faith that anticipates the unseen substance-realities. Believers should find encouragement for ministry, since by this kind of faith, they like the elders and those after them, "were approved" (ἐμαρτυρήθησαν Heb 11:2) when judged by the Lord after death (Heb 9:27). The Pastor continues in unit D2´ more midrash about just what a ministry of faith in the new covenant promise looks like that the audience should emulate.

---

312. These signals include (1) the resumption after a FGT UC (Heb 11:13–16) of the shorthand term Πίστει "by this *kind of faith*" in connection to his introductory definition in Heb 11:1–2, (2) the resumption of listing people as examples of his proposed definition, and (3) the resumption of features about Abraham that completed the first list in unit D1´ (Heb 11:1–16).

Subpoint 2a (11:17–19): Abraham Was Willing to Offer Up Isaac Due to Faith That the Dead Rise to the Unseen Substance-Realities that God Speaks

The Pastor returns to Abraham, after using him as an example in unit D1′ SbPt1e, SbPt1f, and SbPt1g (Heb 11:8–12). Abraham was willing to offer Isaac as a sacrificial burnt offering "because reasoning himself the ability of God to raise up from the dead" (Heb 11:19). In the first century CE, the view of the OT thought of rising from the dead suggests, for those judged as righteous, a transfer of the deceased soul from a fleshly body to a whole living spirit body in the unseen eternal/perpetual-*place* realm.[313]

The Pastor interprets the events in Gen 22:1–19 regarding God's provision of a sacrificial ram and Isaac's continued living in return to Abraham after testing as a "parable" (παραβολή Heb 11:19). The spiritual lesson derived from the visible earthly events teach about God's ability

---

313. In unit F UPt5 Climax (Heb 10:5–14), the Pastor has previously stated that he considered David had expectation for a "body" (σῶμα Heb 10:5) prepared for him by God at death, which the Pastor typologically applied to Jesus as the Christ. Also, Jesus is judged as an offering without blemish as an "eternal/perpetual-*place* spirit" (πνεύματος αἰωνίου" Heb 9:14). The Pastor further comments that Enoch "was transferred" (μετετέθη Heb 11:5) to the God's presence without seeing death in unit D1′ Pt1c (Heb 11:5–6). To testify of God's ability, the transfer from flesh to spirit occurs untimely without death in the usual fleshly decay that is left behind. The OT supports "transfer" to the unseen spiritual realm, rather than earthly resuscitation. In the NT, Paul shares the same idea by classifying the spiritual body now available as superior to the fleshly humble body of current life (1 Cor 15:35–58; Phil 3:17–21), with Jesus's purpose as "for a life-making spirit" (εἰς πνεῦμα ζῳοποιοῦν 1 Cor 15:45). Peter follows the same intent by stating "being made alive in spirit" (ζῳοποιηθείς ... πνεύματι 1 Pet 3:18) as complimentary with "being put to death in flesh" (θανατωθεὶς σαρκί 1 Pet 3:18). These two statements occur concurrently on the cross, just after Jesus's statement of trust to his Father for judgment, when he states into your hands I entrust "my spirit" (τὸ πνεῦμά μου Luke 23:46). This highly suggests that Luke may have in mind this same concept of transfer to a spirit body before the Father.

Also, first-century CE Enochic STL provides possible background available to the Pastor for fulfillment of God's promised seed through Isaac in the concept of a transfer to a spiritual body that God provides after death of the flesh. In the second century BCE, 1 Enoch offers further speculation about possible procreation of angelic beings with earthly women. This assertion is unconfirmed in the accepted canonical documents written by Moses in the middle of the second millennium BCE. One would assume speculation about postmortem life in the unseen eternal/perpetual-*places* of heaven in the time of Abraham would not be monochrome but much like all other times even through today. However, Jesus refutes this speculation by the Sadducees by stating the categories of male and female in marriage are not part of the features of the spiritual domain (Matt 22:29–30). From 1 Enoch's context in elevation of Mt. Horeb near Dan and Enoch as not a priest but a scribe, the document is a probable second-century BCE polemic against the Jerusalem priesthood.

to provide a sacrificial offering of his promised "seed" in the Son (Heb 11:17), who by atonement for sins enables eternal/perpetual-*place* living.

Subpoint 2b (11:20) Isaac by Faith in the Substance-Realities Not Seen Blessed Jacob and Esau Regarding Things to Come

The Pastor continues with the example of Isaac (Gen 27:27–29, 39–40), who blessed Jacob and Esau "on behalf of present subsequently coming *substance-realities*" (περὶ μελλόντων Heb 11:20).[314] The pres. act. ptc. caries weight for a current anticipated future fulfillment of the promise in the "seed" (Gen 22:17–18), which passed down from Abraham, at the time of the blessing pronounced before Isaac's death.

Subpoint 2c (11:21): Jacob by Faith in the Substance-Realities Not Seen, as He Was Dying, Blessed the Sons of Joseph

Jacob follows the same pattern of conveyed blessings upon those left behind associated with his death (Gen 48:1–20). In Joseph's presence, Jacob recounted the promise God has given him (Gen 48:4). The Pastor considers the double meaning in the antitype-type promise "even to your seed after you for an eternal/perpetual-*place* possession" (Gen 48:4 LXX). The dat. sg. "seed" (σπέρματί) continues the oath of the Christ from the lineage of Abraham. Jacob's prophecy concerning Israel's earthly inheritance in the land typifies the eternal/perpetual-*place* possession that Jacob by faith in the Christ was about to enter at death.

Subpoint 2d (11:22): Joseph Exampled Faith to Enter the Promised City Not Seen by Having Israel Take His Bones Out of Egypt in the Exodus

The Pastor continues the timing of death in relation to reception of the promises in the request of Jacob for his bones related to an exodus of the sons of Israel. Israel's movement of Jacob's bones functions as an antitype

---

314. In the context of passing blessing from Isaac to Jacob and Esau, the gen. preposition περὶ (*peri*) has powerful force expressing a current personal advantage more than only reference to probable future benefits delayed after death. The blessing was the opportunity to place faith in God's promised "seed" for perpetual blessings that continue beyond death.

of the hope for transfer after death into the rest of heaven.³¹⁵ The Pastor provides extensive exposition in unit C (Heb 3:1—4:13) in his theme of ministerial accountability and Israel's failure to enter due to unbelief.

Subpoint 2e (11:23): By Faith in the Substance-Realities Not Seen the Parents of Moses Hid Him Alive Rather than Fear the Edict of the King

Moses's parents demonstrate faith in realities not seen when hiding Moses for three months in disobedience to the edict of the king for all male children to be put to death (Exod 2:2). The parents understood with no male children in Israel, eventually both the antitype of the nation and the type regarding the promised linage in the Christ would cease. Their faith in the unseen substance-realities, as they beheld the beauty of the child Moses, simulate actions to keep him alive that God prudentially blessed. As the Pastor expounds in unit C UI/Pt1 (Heb 3:1–6), the child by his faithfulness becomes an antitype of the faithfulness of Christ over his house symbolized by the tabernacle.

SbPt2f (11:24–26): By Faith in the Greater Riches and Rewards of the Substance-Reality Not Seen in the Christ, Moses Refused to Be Called a Son of Pharaoh

Moses, by faith in the promise of Christ, "was thinking about" (ἀπέβλεπεν Heb 11:26) the greater rewards of unseen riches in realities not seen, which his Egyptian peers consider "the reproach of Christ" (τὸν ὀνειδισμὸν τοῦ Χριστοῦ Heb 11:26; cf. 2 Cor 4:16–18).³¹⁶ He chooses his brethren, rather than to live under the linage of Pharaoh, as a son of Pharaoh's daughter, for an inheritance of earthly treasure (Exod 2:10–14). Moses's experience

---

315. *Contra* Pulse, *Figuring Resurrection*. Pulse interprets the antitype symbolized by Joseph's bones as the final type itself to support fleshly resuscitation. Rather, the land motif typologically demonstrates the bodily rising of the dead in spirit to enter heaven, while the bones are in the grave. Joseph, understanding the land-heaven link, wants Israel to see his hope rests in the unseen substance-reality of heaven.

316. D'Angelo, *Moses in the Letter*. D'Angelo investigates "Moses-Christology" in an understanding of the relationship to Moses in the formation of NT Christology. She presumes the views about Moses by either the Pastor and/or his community determines a major portion of Hebrews's Christology. Moses becomes more than just a role model of Christ mentioned in Heb 3:1–6. In Hebrews, the Pastor speaks that Moses's actions live out a faith as a participant in the ministry of Christ that he models.

illustrates another feature of faith, which sees the unseen in Christ, as considered a reproach of little value to those only attentive to riches and rule in the visible cosmos (cf. 1 Cor 2:14; 3:18–19).

The Pastor explains ministerial accountability in unit E (Heb 5:11—6:20) and, by chiasm (see appendix 1, fig. 16), applies it to his audience in unit E ′ (Heb 10:26–39). Only ministerial conversation that is congruent with the beginnings of the sayings of Christ, consistent in approach to Jesus in a true heart, and corresponds with the knowledge of the truth concerning the unseen changes achieved by Jesus as the Christ to enable a heavenly entrance for believers will receive reward at judgment. All cosmic-*field* constrained philosophies with its rulers of authority, future sought after kingdoms, sacramental controlling concepts, and visible wealth in earthly treasures have no lasting value in the eternal/perpetual-*places* for believers. Moses exemplifies upward contemplation in all areas of life.

Subpoint 2g (11:27): By Faith in the Substance-Realities Not Seen, Moses Left Egypt, Not Fearing the Wrath of the King, but Looking to One Not Seen

Moses left Egypt (Exod 2:15; 12:50), not because of his fear of the king's wrath (Exod 2:14) but because he persevered as one continually seeing the *one* not seen (Exod 10:28–29). The pres. act. ptc. ὁρῶν (*horōn*) carries weight for a current continuous faith that governs Moses's decisions. The Pastor's context from the introductory FGT subtopics contained in Heb 11:1–2 supply the interpretative options for the audience about what is not seen concerning the adjective ἀόρατον (*aoraton*). As the focus of Moses's contemplation, ἀόρατον can gloss as a masc. sg. "invisible *one*" in link to θεός ("God" Heb 11:2). Moses fulfills the formula in Heb 11:6 of pleasing God by both believing that God exists and that he is a rewarder of those who seek him.

SbPt2h (11:28) By Faith in the Substance-Realities Not Seen, Moses Kept the Passover to Keep the Firstborn from Being Destroyed

The Pastor again links the elements in Moses's ministry for evidence of faith in the unseen substance-realities that is approved by God in judgment. The events of the Passover kept by Moses and the people of Israel powerfully reveal unseen realities (Exod 12:21–50). The features Moses "had accomplished" (πεποίηκεν Heb 11:28), in the preparation and eating of the sacrificial lamb and "the spreading of the blood" (Heb 11:28) in order that the one destroying the firstborn should not touch them, and journey from Egypt, compellingly testifies about God's promise of salvation into heaven at judgment through faith in the offering of the Christ.

Subpoint 2i (11:29): By Faith in the Substance-Realities Not Seen, as an Example, Israel Passed through the Red Sea on Dry Land, Whereas the Egyptians Were Drowned

The Pastor also adds the events of the Red Sea (Exod 14:22–31) to the evidence. Israel crosses the Red Sea as through dry land, which after an attempt, the Egyptians drown. God's unseen provision of the dry land and the drowning of the Egyptians symbolize the journey to heaven by faith in the offering and ministry of Christ.

Subpoint 2j (11:30): By Faith in the Substance-Realities Not Seen, the Walls of Jericho Fell by Simply Marching around the City Seven Times

The Pastor further includes the miracle at Jericho (Josh 6) to the evidence. After Israel encircles the city seven times, the walls of Jericho fall before them. Israel's access, by the power of God, into the impregnable space of Jericho evidentially supports God's ability to also provide entrance into the unseen holy-*places* on approach after death at judgment.

Subpoint 2k (11:31): By Faith in the Substance-Realities Not Seen, Rahab the Harlot Did Not Perish and Welcomed the Spies

The foreigner Rahab from Jericho (Josh 2:1–24) serves as an example of faith. Based on the conversation about the Lord's previous victories and purpose for Israel in giving the land, Rahab assists the spies. Rahab's inclusion reveals even foreigners who place faith in God's heavenly provision receive the blessing of entering the land. Access is open to anyone upon belief in the offering and ability of the priestly ministry of Christ.

Subpoint 2l (11:32–38): By Faith in the Substance-Realities Not Seen Others Became Examples of Approach to God in the Face of Death in a World Unworthy of Them

In a final support before his UC, the Pastor lists multiple other scenarios symbolizing the diverse experiences of people who provide evidence for faith in the unseen substance-realities. In his wide-ranging list of the varied ways in which people died, he connects the event of fleshly resurrection in resuscitation (Heb 11:35a; cf. 1 Kgs 17:17–24 MT; 1 Kgs 4:18–37 MT) with the first-century CE concept of resurrection by rising to God in heaven at death (Heb 11:35b; 9:14, 28; 10:5; cf. Dan 12:1–3). In the former, people who experienced fleshly resuscitation all died again in the flesh. In the latter, these people recorded by either the rejection of continued fleshly life during persecution or endured forced loss of life in martyrdom, "so that they may experience of a better resurrection" (ἵνα κρείττονος ἀναστάσεως τύχωσιν Heb 11:35).[317] The conjunction ἵνα (*hina*) best functions with a subjunctive verb, in the topic context concerning the experiences of those at death, as a marker of objective "that" with verbs of sense.[318] The conjunction "so that" links the genitive phrase as the objective, "so that, of a better resurrection" (ἵνα κρείττονος ἀναστάσεως), to point the audience back to *that* faith in his unit D1′–D2′ topic concerning the expectation of the unseen substance-reality at death. The Pastor

---

317. Cf. Cockerill, "Better Resurrection," 215–34. Cockerill argues that the references in Heb 11 to resurrection are central to the structure and argument of the chapter. However, he posits the later view of a future fleshly resuscitation, rather than rising shortly in a spiritual body from the dead. His assertions for the rhetorical function of resurrection in Heb 11:17–19 and Heb 11:35 in major sections have strong merit. When adapted to their position in the discourse FGT of unit D2′ (Heb 11:17–40), the two resurrection texts form an *inclusio* before the UC (Heb 11:39–40) to bracket his list with clear examples concerning faith to rise to God a very little while after death (Heb 10:37). Cf. Lane, "Life in the Face," 247–69. Lane also considers resurrection in Hebrews as only hope for a future fleshly resuscitation in the face of death. He acknowledges that all the exemplars of faith link in some way or other with death. Lane recognizes, "This capacity to endure suffering and death presupposes a relationship to the unseen world" (257). However, he does not look upwards to heaven in the first-century CE view of rising upward to God. For similar traditional interpretation about resurrection, see Levenson, *Resurrection and the Restoration*. Levenson presses later popular rabbinic conceptions upon life-after-death issues in the Hebrew Bible that reject an antipode to Sheol and consider Sheol as dying with an unfilled personal life and family. For Levenson, God is known as the God of the living, who will bring life in resurrection back to corpses. However, the NT and Jewish STL teaching tradition consider the functions of the flesh obsolete in kingdom conditions (cf. 1 Cor 15:50).

318. BDAG, "ἵνα," 476–77.

closes this heavenly expectation with an observation about those listed by stating, "Of whom the world was not worthy" (ὧν οὐκ ἦν ἄξιος ὁ κόσμος Heb 11:39). Better life is rest in heaven and not in the temporary world.

The contrast of the temporary fleshly resurrection of resuscitation with the better resurrection of faith expectation into the unseen eternal/perpetual-*places* eludes cosmic-*field* limited kingdom traditions. Earthly desires apart from faith begins with Cain in contrast to Abel (Heb 11:4). The worldly resurrection of the flesh with expectation for return to Eden, rather than the expectation of the unseen eternal/perpetual-*places* continues domination of church scholars since long before the first-century CE.

Unit D2′ Conclusion (11:39–40): By Faith in the Substance-Realities Not Seen, All These People Did Not Receive Themselves the Promise, but He of God Provided Himself Something Better, That Should Not Complete without Adding the Living with All Believers Now in Heaven

At the end of his unit D2′ discourse, the Pastor accumulates the necessary literary indicators to suggest a threshold by the audience for a shift to an anticipated UC.[319]

The adjectival aorist pass. ptc. "who having been approved" (μαρτυρηθέντες Heb 11:39), in reference to his subtopic about approval at judgment, supports that the Pastor considers those in his catalog of faith have already been judged. This would not only include literary judgment by the audience of other people about their witness but also by God upon approach to the eternal/perpetual-*place* substance-realities after death (Heb 9:27). This approval, as pleasing to God at judgment, occurs

---

319. These markers include (1) the opening phrase "and all of these" (Καὶ οὗτοι πάντες Heb 11:39) to indicate an expected summary statement in a FGT UC about the people he has listed as evidence with the features of faith, (2) the aorist pass. ptc. "having been approved" (μαρτυρηθέντες Heb 11:39) in reference to the thematic topic about approval at judgment, (3) the repeat of the unit D′ subtopic of faith, (4) the cognate "the promise" (τὴν ἐπαγγελίαν) and "better" (κρεῖττόν) that tracks in the topic of salvation in heaven (Heb 11:39–40), (5) the negation of the personal effort of people with the aorist mid. indic. "receive themselves" (ἐκομίσαντο) in contrast with the aorist mid. ptc. about God "having himself provided" (προβλεψαμένου Heb 11:40) regarding the source of salvation in heaven, (6) the application to the audience with "without us" (χωρὶς ἡμῶν Heb 11:40) and, (7) the repeat of the concept of completion in heaven with the aorist pass. sub. "they should not be complete" (μὴ . . . τελειωθῶσιν Heb 11:40).

"through faith" (διὰ τῆς πίστεως Heb 11:39; cf. Heb 11:6), suggesting faith is how they could enter to God's presence.

By the adjectival aorist mid. ptc. phrase "who having not received themselves the promise" (οὐκ ἐκομίσαντο τὴν ἐπαγγελίαν Heb 11:39), the Pastor clarifies that this faith in salvation at judgment is not in themselves. The phrase has coherence with the Pastor's stress upon the abilities of the Son to bring people to the presence of God. In context, the claim is not that these people have not received the promise yet, but that they did not receive it on account of faith in themselves (cf. Heb 6:15). The next phrase further supports a contrast for these people having faith in God's ability in the Son, rather than faith in themselves, by stating, "Because he [the Son] of God providing himself concerning us something better" (Heb 11:40). God through the Son provides believers after death at judgment something better than what people could accomplish for themselves in this world.

The final phrase "so that they should not complete without us" (ἵνα μὴ χωρὶς ἡμῶν τελειωθῶσιν Heb 11:40) reassures the audience, who is still living on earth apart from the promises, that they should not be without completion in heaven. The interpretation, as a proof text, for general judgment of all believers at some future time with a final endpoint on earth has no contextual support in the message of Hebrews. The inference of this position puts the Son in a situation where while sitting on the throne in heaven, he has never yet saved anyone in promise-fulfillment, no one has entered into heaven, and the dead are still in their sins since still awaiting judgment, which would be very similar position to Paul's rhetorical exposition in 1 Cor 15:12–58.

Dynamic Unit Conclusions E´–D2´ in Lens of Hebrews 9:27–28

In STr2 (Heb 10:19–25), the Pastor provides for his audience an outline about expected ministerial conversation in an anticipatory approach to Jesus that is in line with his previous exposition concerning the offering of Christ and his continual ministry of intercession. In unit E´ (Heb 10:26–39), he expects his listeners to embrace the quality of a "true heart" associated with "the knowledge of the truth" concerning heavenly matters. Such a heart pleases God in judgment but all else should expect no loss of reward. His midrash in unit D´1–2 (Heb 11:1–40) suggests a large cache of people with features that witness the quality of "certainty of faith" (Heb 10:22c) in the promise of salvation into heaven by the ministry of Christ. He closed unit D´1-2 (Heb 11:1-40) with reassurance that God's plan includes a community finish of all believers. In his next unit C´ (Heb 12:1-13), the Pastor tenders that this heavenly expectation of salvation should motivate believers to receive training of the Father as a son in purity of holy living during anticipated sufferings.

HEBREWS 12:12-13: ANALYSIS OF DISCOURSE UNIT CONCLUSION C´

Unit C´ Structural Mapping (12:1-13): Lay Aside Sin During Approach Looking to Jesus and Enduring God's Difficult Training

The Pastor provides signals that he shifts to next cycle of FGT. His audience would recognize a threshold shift by multiple literary signals.[320] Unit C´ contains four FGT that function as introduction about DI and STr2 subtopics, support, and a conclusion. Figures 15 and 16 map the new unit C´ discourse. Figure 16 establishes the chiastic structural relationship of unit C´ (Heb 12:1-13) with unit C (Heb 3:1-4:13). Both units include exhortation concerning the necessity of holiness in respect to sin (Heb 3:13; 12:1). Unit C´ also links with the S3 outline in STr2 (Heb 10:22-25) regarding *"believers* having been sprinkling the hearts away from an evil conscience and having been washing the body with pure water" (Heb 10:22d). The priestly language concerns external rights of ceremonial cleanness that are required before ministerial offerings. The

---

320. These signals include (1) use of the particle and conjunction "therefore also" (Τοιγαροῦν καὶ Heb 12:1), (2) an introductory summary phrase of unit D´1-2 evidence with the substantive pres. act. ptc. phrase "we presently having so great" (ἡμεῖς τοσοῦτον ἔχοντες Heb 12:1), (3) a summary metaphor regarding the spiritual effect of the evidence on the listeners, stating "a cloud of witnesses presently itself surrounding us" (περικείμενον ἡμῖν νέφος μαρτύρων Heb 12:1), (4) use of an aorist mid. ptc. "after we ourselves laying aside" (ἀποθέμενοι) to specify desired qualities for the audience in response to the witness of the faith of those listed, (5) connection with the STr2 (Heb 10:22-25) outline introducing the expectation that the ministry of Christ produces living in ceremonial cleanness with purity of the conscious and body from "sin" (ἁμαρτίαν Heb 12:1), (6) a repeated link with the unit E´ UC (Heb 10:35-39) exhortation to the audience concerning "perseverance" (ὑπομονή Heb 10:36; 12:1), (7) and a summary about the example of Jesus that the listeners should emulate (Heb 12:2-3).

Pastor metaphorically links the ceremonial cleansing law in relation to the hearts and conscience of his listeners.

Believers should follow the path of Jesus during testing and approach, while living through the experience of death. Unit C develops the necessity for belief in God's speech concerning Jesus for entrance into God's heavenly rest. Unit C′ encourages the listeners to live out the expectation of their faith with a witness that includes ceremonially clean consciences and bodies during the training of life that includes suffering.

Unit Introduction (12:1–3): Run Your Race Set before You like the Cloud of Witnesses by Laying Aside Sin, with Eyes Fixed on Jesus, Who Ran It First, Endured the Cross, and Joyfully Sat Down at the Right Hand of the Throne of God

In the UI, the Pastor encapsulates the people in his examples of faith by a metaphor to illustrate the unseen effect of God's spoken evidence. He visualizes his OT inventory "a cloud of witnesses presently itself surrounding us" (Heb 12:1).[321] The imagery recalls past occasions where the glory of God fills the temple and surrounds the ministerial priest as they carry out their duties (cf. Exod 40:34–35; Num 9:15–23; 1 Kgs 8:10–11). The intent is not so much that these witnesses are watching them, but that they should be inspired by the faith of the great cloud of witnesses in their ministerial calling.[322] The holy decisions of these past people, with expectation for the unseen substance-reality in God's true tent of all creation seen and unseen, should encourage ministerial purity (cf. 1 John 3:2–3). He adds a running metaphor about "perseverance" (ὑπομονῆς) in

---

321. Baugh, "Cloud of Witnesses," 113–32. Baugh correctly rejects the glosses of conviction, assurance, being, actualization, and realization for ὑπόστασις (*hypostasis*) in Heb 11:1. He senses the English term "substance" best fits the sematic context and commends William Lane's translation as "substance reality" (117–18). Baugh further examples scholars, who due to tension of presently available heavenly substance realities slip back to the more comfortable language of assurance and conviction but in his conclusion does the same. When combined in context with Heb 11:2, he concludes, "The OT saints believed the 'realty' and 'evidence' of eschatological events, but their faith itself rested upon divine testimony of these things" (118). This testimony emanated from the witnesses about things not seen. He concludes the cloud of witnesses in Heb 12:1 point to the unseen, hoped for realities of the world to come. The subtopic of death can be added as the common event encountered by the witnesses that enables immediate rising to the substance-reality of their world of faith in the likeness of Jesus as the author and consummator of heavenly access.

322. Allen, *Hebrews*, 572.

"a race" (ἀγῶνα Heb 12:1).³²³ A minister, as a properly prepared runner, should lay aside sin that entangles while waiting for Jesus to appear in his expected ministry.

The Pastor again recapitulates the two-fold ministry of Christ, once as an offering for sin and continually in intercession, that the audience should expect imminently with eyes fixed looking for him. He exhorts his listeners they should be "presently looking for Jesus, the author and consummator of the faith" (Heb 12:2).³²⁴ The pres. act. ptc. "presently looking" (ἀφορῶντες Heb 12:2) provides more syntactical weight for a presently available, rather than delayed expectation. In correspondence with the context of his previous exposition in S1 and S2, the imagery suggests that the audience should expect Jesus's priestly ministry at death in transfer to his kingdom to be with him.

The UI (Heb 12:1–3) closes with the aorist mid. impv. "*please consider!*" (ἀναλογίσασθε Heb 12:3). The Pastor reckons that contemplation upon the suffering experience of Jesus, for the joy of now providing the path open for his brethren to follow to the Father after death and judgment, encourages believers to not grow weary or lose heart in the forsaking of sin. Yet, believers are not left on their own in a calling to pure living. In this unit about ceremonial cleanness from sin, in his next

---

323. See Croy, *Endurance in Suffering*, 37–76. After analysis of athletic imagery in Heb 12:1–3 as a paradigm of behavior for others to follow, Croy concludes, "Hebrews 12:1–3 presents Jesus not so much as a martyr or a model of self-renunciation, but as the paradigm of faithful endurance who has completed the course in advance of others" (76). In the Pastor's imagery, Jesus opened the way by completion of the course to heaven, so that the audience should endure ministerial suffering by anticipatory joy in following his path to heaven at death with rising to God at judgment.

324. Croy, "Note on Hebrews 12:2," 117–19. Croy comments that scholars typically consider τελειωτήν as a hapax legomena in the NT and often a term coined by the Pastor. However, he quotes a parallel from the rhetor and historian Dionysius of Halicarnassus, who in the opening line of his essay writes, "He was neither the inventor of an individual style . . . nor the perfecter of styles" (118). Croy concludes, "The significance of the latter term in Dionysius is clear. A τελειωτής is one who perfects, refines, or brings full flower the work of others. The work of both 'pioneers and perfecters' is commended" (118). He further comments about the Pastor's overarching expression in application to Jesus, "He, according to the author, is both the originator and consummator of faith. He is the 'prototype,' but not the one to be transcended by subsequent improvements, for he is also faith's paragon" (119). By supplementation of Croy's insights with faith defined as an anticipation for the unseen substance-reality in God's presence, Jesus not only originated the unseen substance-realities of the eternal/perpetual-*places*, but also refined his creation by his offering of atonement on the cross to be the first to enter through the obstacles into heaven.

Unit Point 1 (12:4–6): God Trains His Children along the Race to Jesus in Heaven

support FGT, he reminds his listeners about the new covenant relationship they have with the Father.

UPt1 addresses a group in his audience, stating, "The ones who are presently struggling, you did not yet resist without blood against sin" (Heb 12:4). Those addressed forgot the OT LXX exhortation in Prov 3:11–12, which addresses them as sons and speaks of the Father's love in training every son that he receives. The language of present suffering by the audience again underscores the probable pressures to conform with the traditional ministerial teaching of the Sinai covenant, from which their discontinuance early on in their ministry, they had suffered (cf. UPt1 Heb 10:31–35).

The new covenant accepted by believers operates under a relationship with God as a Father and the believer as a son. In the former covenant, Israel typologically serves as an example of a chosen people, who live out on earth their relationship with God as an antitype to the nations in emulation of the unseen truth in heaven.[325] Due to their covenantal reception to abide by the law that pointed to the salvation promise in Christ, righteous living receives earthly good, but evil living receives earthly wrath. The receipt of this new relationship by faith, by God's oath, guarantees forgiveness of sin for perpetual eternal/perpetual-*place* living at death by the ministry of Jesus. However, this new covenant does not imply that the believer, until the time of their salvation, is free to sin in impurity without God's intervention. God still expects his sons to live in purity of conscience and body while waiting for Jesus. In his next FGT UPt2, the Pastor's understood expectation in the areas of purity from sin stimulates further exposition about the Father and Son relationship under the new covenant.

---

325. Thiessen, "Hebrews 12.5–13," 366–79. From both from the athletic imagery and language that links with Israel's wilderness period, Thiessen senses in Hebrews that the audience is living in a positive period of discipline. He concludes, "The fact that the readers of the epistle to the Hebrews find themselves in the gymnasium of the wilderness should encourage them since it demonstrates the legitimacy of their sonship and socializes them for their imminent entry into the promised rest" (379).

Israel's faced the negative outcomes of disobedience for not properly exampling a people looking to God's provision of heaven. The spiritual outcome links with unit C and rest in heaven at death. See appendix 1, fig. 16. Those who are sons should receive training during approach to God by looking to Jesus's race to God.

Unit Point 2 (12:7–11): Since God Trains as Father Does, We Should Endure the Sorrowful Training to Yield the Peaceful Fruit of Righteousness along the Race to Jesus in Heaven

Perseverance during suffering and training on earth during one's ministerial calling is a major topic in the Pastor's message. He supports the inevitability of suffering as part of the Father's training for his coming heavenly relationships to his children. Those without such training are "illegitimate" (νόθος Heb 12:8). However, those who receive training do so for good, to share in his holiness, and to yield fruit of righteousness. As one submits to an earthly father, the Pastor rhetorically asks, "On the other hand, how much more rather we are subject to the father of spirits, and we will live?" (Heb 12:9). The question, taken under the assumption of first-century CE beliefs, assumes both he and his audience will live as spirits with the father.

Unit C′ Conclusion (12:12–13): Strengthen Your Weaknesses by God's Training in the Race to Jesus in Heaven

At the end of his unit C′ discourse, the Pastor accumulates the necessary literary indicators to imply a threshold by the audience for a shift to an anticipated UC.[326] His *inclusio* about the running metaphor integrates the language for treatment of running injuries, weaknesses, and course obstacles to holiness in ministerial purity.

By the Father's training and with the audience assisting others who are struggling (Heb 12:4), he through them strengthens the weak hands and feeble knees that represent the believer's ministerial service to others in the race before them. He uses them along their running in approach to the throne of Jesus, to make the running paths straight in removal of obstacles and to heal the lame limbs out of joint. The Pastor's aorist act. impv. "*please* restore, rebuild, straighten up" (ἀνορθώσατε Heb 12:13) and pres. act. impv. ποιεῖτε ("*please* make, do") pictorially accentuate his entreaty for audience rectification of their ministerial conversation about the beginning sayings of Jesus as the Christ in his sacrificial offering and

---

326. These markers include (1) use of the particle "therefore, for this reason" (διό Heb 12:12), (2) an *inclusio* closure of the running and training metaphor to purity and holiness with application to treatment of injuries and course obstacles (Heb 12:12–13), and (3) strong exhortation by the imperative ἀνορθώσατε (*anorthōsate*).

Jesus's continued ministry from the throne.³²⁷ As trainers assist their runners, believers should entreat others in the proper message of Christ.

Dynamic Unit Conclusions E´–C´ in Lens of Hebrews 9:27–28

During approach to Jesus, from God's speech in unit C´, believers should recognize in ministerial earthly sufferings their sinful impurities in conscious and body. Believers should strengthen weak areas and make straight the things that do not imitate the cloud of witnesses, who continue to witness the feature of certainty of faith in Jesus's offering and present ministry. As encouraged in A´, believers should emulate the "knowledge of the truth" in the feature of a "true heart" that reflects the substance-realities of the unseen heavens described by God's word. Believers should strengthen the weakness of others and make straight the errant conversation that has no eternal/perpetual-*place* reward.

The Pastor continues his outline from STr2 (Heb 10:22–25) in exhortation in unit B´ (Heb 12:14–29) concerning the feature of a confession with "an unwavering hope" (Heb 10:23) for eternal/perpetual-*place* fulfillment. In this unit he shares more details about what believers hope for when seeing Jesus for prompt transfer to spiritual bodies and following Jesus as shepherd into the unseen eternal/perpetual-*places*.

HEBREWS 12:28–29: ANALYSIS OF DISCOURSE UNIT CONCLUSION B´

Unit B´ (12:14–29) Approach Expecting to See Jesus as Mediator and the Blessings of the City of the Living God

The Pastor provides signals that he shifts to next cycle of FGT. His audience would recognize a threshold shift by his literary signals.³²⁸ This discourse unit offers three FGT that function as a basic introduction

---

327. The movement from the aorist to the present imperative intensifies the climax of the unit C´ FGT UC from an urgent command without regard to frequency that is a good general rule to a command with continuous action that should be repeated in a particular situation.

328. These signals include (1) another entreaty with the pres. act. impv. "*please pursue!*" (διώκετε Heb 12:14) and (2) a list of several positive and negative effects with all relationships to illustrate correctly or incorrectly the confession of their unwavering faith introduced in STr2 (Heb 10:22–25) about the corresponding unit B (Heb 2:1–18) exposition on the salvation of Jesus into heaven at death.

about DI and STr2 subtopics, support for each subtopic assertion, and a conclusion. Figures 15 and 16 map the new unit B′ discourse.

Figure 16 demonstrates the discourse chiastic structure and the relation of unit B′ (Heb 12:14–29) with unit B (Heb 2:1–18).[329] The parallel correspondence, which is previously discussed in unit B analysis, in unit B recaps as the audience need to live in expectation of the mediation of Jesus in heaven described and, in unit B′, live with anticipation for an entrance into the heavenly city as other brethren have previously experienced. Unit B′ also links with the S3 outline in STr2 (Heb 10:22–25) regarding believers exhibiting the feature of the confession of an unwavering hope for the salvation provided by Jesus because the one having done the promising is faithful (Heb 10:23).

Unit Introduction (12:14–17): Pursue Peace and Holiness with All Relationships, by Which One Sees the Lord, Making Sure No One Falls Short of the Grace of God, by Avoiding Bitterness and Immorality That Defiles Others

The UI of unit B′ begins his application of his unit B (Heb 2:1–18) description of salvation by Jesus in heaven with more imperative entreaty for the audience to exhibit the confession of an unwavering hope of their salvation. His pres. act. impv. "*please* pursue!" (διώκετε Heb 12:14) links with multiple reinforced and negated actions expected for them in the unseen substance-reality of heaven from his previous discourse that they already should now repeatedly pursue in their earthly relations.

The Pastor specifically entreats his audience about their ministry with others to *please* pursue (1) peace with all relationships, (2) the holiness without which no one sees the Lord, (3) not lacking the grace of God, (4) no root of bitterness that would defile many, and (5) not as a sexually immoral, worldly focused person like Esau. The Pastor expounds on the features in God's OT speech about Esau's worldly immoral fixation in the loss of his birthright as part of the linage of Christ in exchange for a single meal and his inability to repent when he desires to inherit the blessing. The implication for mentioning Esau's situation as part of the Pastor's plea is that his listeners now experience a similar crossroads in

---

329. Cf. Stolz, *Der Höhepunkt des Hebräerbriefs*. Stolz argues for this unit as the structural and theological climax of the letter to the Hebrews. By rhetorical analysis, he associates the unit as the end of speech (peroration) of the writing of the sermon. However, the unit better fits the chiastic structure of a discourse.

their future ministry. Will they follow worldly, sensual, bitter pursuits in loss of heavenly rewards or approach seeing Jesus in peace, holiness, and grace? In his next UPt1 FGT, the Pastor provides exemplary inspiration for proper elements in their relationships with others from God's speech about the expected heavenly realities.

Unit Point 1 (12:18–27): You Have Not Approached to the Fearful Situation, as Moses and the People at Sinai, but to the Blessings of Mount Zion in the City of the Living God

The Pastor provides added typological support from Israel to illustrate the motivating impetus behind his plea for pursuit of his requested conduct related to others in unit B′ UI.[330] As a mirror application of his unit B (Heb 2:1–18) exposition about the salvation experience of Jesus after death by God's judgment, in chiastic correspondence, unit B′ entreats for the audience salvation in heaven to be like Jesus (see appendix 1, fig. 16). The Pastor first shares negated typology of what his listeners should not encounter, then lists what they will find on approach after death at judgment.

The negated perf. act. indic. "for you have not approached" (Οὐ γὰρ προσεληλύθατε Heb 12:18) provides illustration about what believers do not encounter at death (see fig. 3).[331] The Pastor's listeners do not endure the unseen heavenly events symbolized by Israel's failure at Mt. Sinai, where God illustrated his holiness in relation to sin at the giving of the law.[332] The unseen descriptors that believers do not endure in God's

---

330. Levenson, *Sinai and Zion*, 140. Levenson concludes, "In short, what we see on earth in Jerusalem is simply the earthly manifestation of the heavenly Temple, which is beyond localization. The Temple on Zion is the antitype to the cosmic archetype. The real Temple is the one to which it points, the one in 'heaven,' which cannot be distinguished sharply from the earthly manifestation."

331. The Pastor's syntactical choice of the perf. act. indic. concerning his context of approach to God after death properly supports his previous exposition and exhortation about a present, ongoing, immediate judgment after death corresponding to his MCS UC of Heb 9:27–28. At the time of his sermon, some, with Jesus as the first, have experienced approach to God under the new covenant promise. The opportunity for approach by the audience to God in the future is still available to each believer at the event of death. The Pastor's pres. tense syntactical choices throughout his exposition further support immediate rising to God, rather than delay (Heb 10:37).

332. Kibbe, *Godly Fear or Ungodly Failure*, vii. Kibbe recognizes how the Pastor exploits Israel's experience at Sinai to maintain distance from the presence of God due to fear, which was commended (Deut 5:28). Israel requested a mediator, which

judgment include a place (1) presently being touched, (2) burning with fire, (3) include darkness, gloom, and whirlwind, and (4) hears a trumpet sound and voice of conversation. The Pastor highlights from God's OT speech the responses of both the people and Moses to the visible symbolic gesture demonstrating God's unseen judgment. The people who having heard requested a word to not be spoken further to them and could not bear the command that if an animal touches the mountain, it must be stoned. Moses even said, "I am terrified and trembling." Understanding such great salvation from the outcome of God's judgment upon sin intensifies the Pastor's entreaty in his unit B´ UI (Heb 12:14–17) for his audience in all relationships to model grace, holiness, and peace, with repentance from worldly, sensual, bitter pursuits.

The perf. act. indic. "but you have approached" (ἀλλὰ προσεληλύθατε Heb 12:22) illustrates the Pastor's predicted salvation encounter for the believers in his audience at Jesus's intercession by his ability to bring all things to God (Heb 1:3b). The Pastor illustrates their heavenly expectation by again drawing upon Israel's earthly typological relationship in God's speech in correspondence to Mt. Zion. He continues with extrapolation about the destiny of believers now in the heavenly unseen type with the descriptors (1) to the city of the living God, (2) to a heavenly Jerusalem, (3) to a myriad of angels, (4) to a festal gathering, (5) to the assembly of the firstborn of those who having been registered in the heavens, (6) to God, the Judge of all people, (7) to the spirits of the righteous of those who have been completed,[333] (8) to Jesus, mediator of the new covenant, and (9) to blood of sprinkling presently speaking better than Abel.[334] These unseen

---

"demonstrates that true covenant mediation in Jesus brings two parties into a single space rather than perpetually crossing the gap between them."

333. The Pastor connects the "spirits of the righteous" with the concept of completion in heaven. This follows the first-century CE concept of transfer at death to a whole spiritual body, rather than ideas of some inferior, incomplete, intermediate state waiting for return to the obsolete fleshly body. The concept of heavenly completion tracks from the DI subtopic Heb 1:3d.

334. The sprinkled blood functions in this list about the unseen heavens as shorthand for Jesus's sacrificial offering of his life on the cross that was accepted by God at judgment in atonement to immediately open the veil of separation between the holy-*places* and create the greater tabernacle not made with hands. Abel's martyrdom, because of his worship that portrayed his faith in God's sacrificial provision of Christ, in traumatic loss of blood by the hand of Cain in reaction to that testimony, allows his entrance near to God in heaven but did not open entry into the holy of holies. The sprinkled blood of Jesus on the cross of the new covenant is better, in that it purifies the sin of those awaiting entry into the holy of holies from Abraham's bosom of the first heavenly covenant. Jesus's offering of the blood of his life continues to be efficacious for

images from his previous exposition portray the present substance-reality for those who see Jesus promptly after death at judgment.

After comparing the expected list of promised blessings with the differences of God's judgment, the Pastor again confronts his listeners with symbolism from the disobedient choices of Israel at Sinai. The pres. act. impv. "*please* see!" (Βλέπετε Heb 12:25) begins yet another entreaty. Just as Israel did not escape when they refused to listen and believe the warning speech of God regarding their call to mirror the destiny of the promise in Christ for those who believe, those who turn away, like Israel, will also not escape God's judgment of their ministry.[335] He quotes God's speech in Hag 2:6 LXX, stating, "Yet once more I will shake not only the earth but also the heaven" (Heb 12:26).[336] Worldly, sensual, and bitter pursuits in accord with things that can be shaken will have no reward at judgment (see unit E and unit E'). The stern warning should cause the Pastor's audience to anticipate a UC to summarize his hortatory encouragement.

Unit B' Conclusion (12:28–29): Since You Receive a Kingdom [at Death/Judgment] That Cannot be Shaken, Show Gratitude and Offer Acceptable Service, because God is a Consuming Fire

At the end of his unit B' discourse, the Pastor accumulates the necessary literary indicators to imply a threshold by the audience for a shift to an anticipated UC.[337] He uses the broad referent "unshakable

---

those in the audience who believe in him. No NT text considers a delay in atonement waiting for blood carried by Jesus before the mercy seat at some later time. In such a case, God's judgment would also be delayed. For previous discussion of shorthand terms loaded with broader meaning, see STr2 (Heb 10:19–25).

335. See chapter 4 unit B UI (Heb 2:1–4); unit C (Heb 3:1–4:13); and unit E UC (Heb 6:11—20) for the Pastor's exposition about ministerial accountability concerning their conversation about the beginning sayings of Christ and his continual present ministry from the throne to bring those who believe into heaven.

336. The juxtaposition of the sg. "heaven" (οὐρανόν Heb 12:26) that God shakes and the pl. "heavens" (οὐρανῶν Heb 12:25) of God's warning concerning οὐρανός ("heaven") provide important understanding for the tabernacle of God's creation. The pairing for his support in unit B' UPt1 further confirms the Pastor's apocalyptic first-century CE views with negative expectation toward the visible "cosmos, universe" (κόσμος) that consists of the heaven and earth, in respect to the perpetual heavens of his dwelling from which God warns people about his judgment after death.

337. These markers include (1) use of the inferential conjunction "therefore, for this reason" (Διὸ Heb 12:28), (2) the referent "kingdom" (βασιλεία Heb 12:28) in summation

kingdom" (βασιλείαν ἀσάλευτον Heb 12:28) to encapsulate the present heavenly expectation of their confession of hope that they should hold without wavering. The present receiving of this heavenly kingdom at death and judgment along with understanding the consuming fire of God upon errant ministerial conversation should inspire gratitude and acceptable service.

Dynamic Unit Conclusions E´–B´ in Lens of Hebrews 9:27–28

The earlier STr2 (Heb 10:22–25) hortatory outline suggests for the audience an expected exhortation to hold firmly the confession of hope without wavering (Heb 10:23). In the unit B´ UC, the causal pres. act. ptc. "since presently receiving" (παραλαμβάνοντες) that links with the unshakable kingdom of the heavens and the adjectival pres. act. ptc. "who is a consuming" (καταναλίσκον) that links with God's fire restates the MCS in Heb 9:27 concerning death and judgment. Judgment of the ministry of believers is immediate at death. Even though Jesus faithfully mediates for all who believe and receive his offering for sin, errant confession in ministry that mirrors any other hope but the knowledge of the truth about the unseen substance-reality of the heavenly kingdom is still accountable. Just as Esau, any worldly focused, sensually based, bitterly driven service away from a clean conscience and body in a confession of hope, which in gratitude, reverence, and awe portrays the peace, holiness, and grace of God's heavenly kingdom, has no eternal/perpetual-*place* reward.

With one more chiastic link left to apply in exhortation to his audience, the Pastor now continues his theme of ministry in relation to the ministry of the Son. He will close with one last cycle of FGT to press more details about proper ministerial service.

---

of his listed heavenly descriptors, (3) the adjective "unshakable" (ἀσάλευτος) in continued description of God's kingdom in heaven, (4) the causal pres. act. ptc. "since ones presently receiving" (παραλαμβάνοντες Heb12:28) in association with himself and the audience in relation to God's kingdom, (5) the hortatory encouragement for the audience to have gratitude (Heb 12:28) due to their participation in the ministry of the kingdom, (6) the renewed subtopic of "ministerial service" (λατρεύω) acceptable to God (Heb 12:28) to remind again of ministerial accountability, (7) the features "with reverence and awe" (μετὰ εὐλαβείας καὶ δέους Heb 12:28) for ministry to have profound respect for God's speech, and (8) the adjectival pres. act. ptc. "who is a presently consuming fire" (πῦρ καταναλίσκον Heb 12:29) to recall the quality of God in relation to ministerial disobedience.

HEBREWS 13:20-21: ANALYSIS OF DISCOURSE UNIT CONCLUSION A´

Unit A´ Structural Mapping (13:1–21): Approach by Living That Loves the Brethren as God Loves

The Pastor provides signals that he shifts to his last cycle of FGT. His audience would mentally expect a threshold shift by his literary signals.[338] This unit offers seven FGT, which function as introduction about DI and STr2 subtopics, support for each subtopic assertion, and a conclusion. Figures 12 and 15 map the new unit A´ discourse.

Figure 16 diagrams the discourse chiastic structure and the relation of unit A´ (Heb 13:1–21) with unit A (Heb 1:5–14).[339] The parallel correspondence that is previously discussed in unit A analysis, summarizes as the audiences need to live by loving others even as Jesus's did. The STr2 (Heb 10:22–25) outline suggests to the audience the theme of love and encouragement in faithful assembly together as one anticipates the day approaching for the inheritance of the promise in Christ.

Unit Introduction/Point 1 (13:1–6): Love of the Brethren Should be Modeled in All Things Done

The UI sets the theme as love of the brethren. Such love works out by (1) the show of hospitality to strangers, (2) the remembrance of the prisoners, (3) marital fidelity rather than conduct that God will judge, and (4) contentment with God's provision and protection. His next FGT further supports special relationships among brethren.

---

338. These signals include (1) the pres. act. impv. "*please* continue!" (μενέτω) linked with the new theme of brotherly love consistent with his outline in STr2 (Heb 10:22–25) and (2) a broad exemplary catalog for how the audience illustrates brotherly love.

339. Filson, "Yesterday." Filson finds unity in the form and structure of Heb 13 as vitally linked with Heb 1–12. He presents a four-fold pattern with common themes with Heb 1–12 to support this claim. An insight of this investigation comes from the use of FGT in discourse analysis to form a chiasm. Hebrews 13 as unit A´ and unit A (Heb 1:1–14) corresponds thematically in relation to the rest of the discourse (see appendix 1, fig. 16).

Unit Point 2 (13:7): Love Those Who Are Leading, Who Spoke the Word of God, by Remembering the Result of Their Conduct and Imitating Their Faith

The Pastor singles out leaders in Upt2 for special consideration in relationships highlighted by love among brethren. His pres. act. impv. *"please remember!"* (Μνημονεύετε Heb 13:7) entreats the audience about the substantive pres. pass. ptc. "those of you who are leading" (τῶν ἡγουμένων ὑμῶν Heb 13:7). Two relative clauses further define these leaders for his audience to love.

First, these are leaders "who spoke to you the word of God" (Heb 13:7). The Pastor's choice of the αγω- (*agō*) word group, with the speech-action context of the word of God in Jesus as the Christ, adds weight for how those leading, who deserve brotherly love, do so. The Pastor's previous use in correspondence to ministerial conversation tracks back through his message to the DI main theme of unit A (Heb 1:5–14) regarding how the Son brings all things by the conversation of his ability (Heb 1:3b). These leaders speak about Jesus leading believers to heaven at death by his ministerial ability as the Son. Leaders therefore speak what God speaks in the ability of Jesus as both sacrificial offering for sin and continual ministry as priestly intercessor.

Second, the Pastor's next clause, "of whom, continually considering the outcome of their conduct" (Heb 13:7), further identifies the leaders. The implied outcome of their speech in all they do concentrates upon a heavenly outcome by the great Shepherd Jesus to bring them at death to God, even as God raised up Jesus to himself (Heb 13:20).

The pres. mid. impv. *"please* imitate the faith!" (μιμεῖσθε τὴν πίστιν) entreats the listeners to follow the faith of those who led in this manner. The audience in unit D1–2´ (Heb 11:1–40) would understand faith as hope of the elders at death to see the unseen substance-reality of the eternal/perpetual-*places*. The Pastor indicates this love is more than affection of emotion but includes speaking the same conversation about Jesus's ability as Christ to bring believers to heaven. The audience loves their leaders by imitating their speech and conduct. The imitation of faith-centered speech in content and conduct that looks to see Jesus in heaven introduces the Pastor's next support FGT concerning love of the brethren.

Unit Point 3 (13:8–14): Jesus [as the] Christ Is the Same Yesterday [First Covenant] and Today [New Covenant] in the Eternal/Perpetual-Place, so Do Not Follow Strange Teachings Different from His Altar as You Minister Outside the Lasting City to Come

UPt3 further highlights brotherly love associated with the steadfast ministry of Jesus, as the Christ in the eternal/perpetual-*places*, rather than embracing those who persist in varied and strange teachings. His statement in Heb 13:8 serves as more than a theological proof text for the changelessness of Jesus as the Christ. He states, "Jesus [as the] Christ is yesterday [first covenant] and today [new covenant], the same into the eternal/perpetual-*places*" (Heb 13:8). The claim connects with "the faith" (τὴν πίστιν) in Heb 13:7, as the object of imitation that the Pastor describes in his S1 and S2 exposition and evidence by the elders in unit D1–2´ (Heb 11:1–40). The emphasis in context falls not on the unchanging nature about who Jesus is, as the Christ, but about what Jesus continues to do now and where he does it for his brethren on approach to the throne of God after death at judgment.

The remaining discourse of UPt3 continues to contrast the ministry of the former heavenly covenant of promise with the ministry of Jesus in the new covenant. Those who minister under the old covenant that the Pastor entreats his listeners about (1) are carried away by many strange and various teaching, (2) occupy themselves with foods with no eternal/perpetual-*place* benefit, (3) presently minister at the altar of the earthly tabernacle, and (4) daily offer bodies of animals brought into the holy place by the high priest for sin that are burned outside the camp.

However, in following the new covenant, the Pastor entreats his brethren (1) to occupy themselves with the strength of grace, rather than the foods good for the heart, (2) to eat and minister with the body of Jesus, by right of his altar of the cross in the tabernacle of the heavens,[340] (3) to bear Jesus's reproach by going out to the same place where Jesus suffered outside the camp to make holy a people through his blood offering,[341] and (4) to seek the present subsequently coming city.

---

340. The Pastor deploys the altar, which is a place in the tabernacle outside the holy-*places* in the outer court, as shorthand for the area of the cross outside of the heavens. Cf. STr2 (Heb 10:19–21) and the Pastor's shorthand deployment of body, blood, and flesh for broad concepts regarding his previous exposition about Jesus as the onetime sacrificial offering on earth and continual high priest in heaven.

341. The link of Jesus's offering of blood with the phrase "outside the camp" and his suffering "outside the gate" supports a connection by both illusions with the cross.

The Pastor symbolically uses the gate of the Jerusalem and the camp outside the earthly tabernacle ministry as antitypes of the unseen types in heavenly realities. In his *aiōn-field* view with the tabernacle representing the heavens, outside the camp would symbolize the regions of God's creation outside of the unseen holy-*places*. In Jerusalem typology, outside the gate corresponds to created regions outside the invisible heaven. The adjectival pres. act. ptc. "the present subsequently coming *city*" (τὴν μέλλουσαν Heb 13:14) provides weight that the Pastor considers the heavenly Jerusalem in existence at the time of his writing. By both analogical examples, he exhorts his listeners to follow Jesus in suffering for ministry outside of heaven, where there is no lasting city, while seeking the present subsequent coming city of the heavenly Jerusalem.

Unit Point 4 (13:15–16): Live Loving the Brethren as God Loves by a Sacrificial Life with Praise, Confession of His Name, Doing Good, and Sharing

UPt4 continues the new covenant ministry of the audience in the love of the brethren that follows the sacrificial example of Jesus. He exhorts that "through him" (Δι' αὐτοῦ Heb 13:15) his listeners should (1) offer sacrifices of praise to God through everything and (2) the fruit of their lips confessing his name. The adjectival pres. act. ptc. "continually confessing" (ὁμολογούντων Heb 13:15) in modification of the fruit of lips links as a verbal noun with his main thematic DI subtopic concerning their conversation about the ability of the Son to bring all things to God (Heb 1:3b).

The FGT concludes with further allusion to the anticipated experience of pleasing God in relation to his judgment. The pres. pass. indic. "for God is being pleased with sacrifices" (γὰρ θυσίαις εὐαρεστεῖται ὁ θεός Heb 13:16) corresponds with the LXX language of acceptable offerings. Enduring sacrificial living with praise, confession, and doing good pleases God.

Aitken, "Body of Jesus," 194–209. Aitken by correspondence with the Exodus tabernacle, links the space outside the camp "as the place of assembling with Jesus prior to entering with Jesus into the holy of holies" (200). She connects this space with the altar and Jesus's suffering on the cross. She further connects the itineraries at work in Hebrews with Jesus's journey to open a way for believers to follow into heaven and the space of the holy of holies (202). Cf. Koester, "Outside the Camp," 299–315.

Unit Point 5 (13:17): Live Loving the Brethren as God Loves by Following Your Leaders Who Give an Account, so They Can Minister with Joy and No Grief

UPt5 returns to the loving relationship "to those of you who are leading" (Heb 13:17) introduced in Heb 13:7. His pres. pass. impv. "*please* be sure!" (Πείθεσθε) and pres. act. impv. "*please* submit!" (ὑπείκετε) entreat his listeners to evaluate and submit to the Word of God being spoken (Heb 13:7) by leaders. The entreaty is not either for blind submission or independent service but listening in brotherly love to leadership with the intent to submit to speech from God that the audience affirms.

He closes this FGT entreaty by again explaining ministerial accountability. A proper relationship with leaders occurs with joy and not that which is continuously grieving as if in separation. Grieving relationships are unprofitable to the listeners.

Unit Point 6 (13:18–19): Live Loving the Brethren as God Loves by Praying for Other Ministers to Have a Good Conscience in Honorable Conduct and Opportunities of Fellowship Together

In UPt6, the Pastor requests specific prayer that they all have a good conscience, which again in his context links with the awareness of sin with loss of reward at God's judgment after death. In love of the brethren, each prays "continuously desiring good to be conducted in everything" (Heb 13:18). He strongly encourages his audience to such prayer that he might be quickly restored to them. The form and content of this request suggest that the Pastor at the time of his speaking lovingly leads his listeners from a distance in a written document.

Unit A´ Conclusion (13:20–21): The God of Peace, Who Brought Up [into Heaven] the Shepherd of the Sheep through the Blood of the Eternal/Perpetual-Place Covenant [at Death/Judgment], Will Equip You to Please Him and to Do His Will in Love of the Brethren as God Loves through Jesus Christ, to Whom Is the Glory into the Eternal/Perpetual-Places of the Eternal/Perpetual-Places

At the end of his unit A´ discourse, the Pastor accumulates the necessary literary indicators to imply a threshold by the audience for a shift to an anticipated final UC before his DC.³⁴² He summarizes his application and entreaty about love among brethren with God's relationship with others by his love.

First, he addresses the relationship of God relative to his audience as the God of peace. Even though God will judge sin after death, he provides peace in his relationships. The Pastor shares in his exposition the details concerning how God through the Son offers a peaceful new covenant relationship through his ministry. The Pastor entreats leaders and their fellow brethren to imitate this relationship of peace among themselves in all they do.

Second, God facilitates this dwelling relationship. He enabled a peaceful relationship as "the one who having raised up from the dead" (ὁ ἀναγαγὼν ἐκ νεκρῶν Heb 13:20). Death and sin, as enemies of God, need atonement before this peaceful relationship could be established. The adjectival aorist act. ptc. ὁ ἀναγαγὼν (*ho anagagōn*) suggests the peaceful relationship for people with God is already established. The use of "rise up" (ἀνάγω) is significant. The semantic use of "lead, rise up" (ἀνάγω) more narrowly focuses on living things, i.e., people. The Pastor does not choose the noun "resurrection" (ἀναστάσεώς Heb 6:2; 11:35) the verbs "stand up, rise up" (ἀνίστημι Heb 7:11, 15), or "ascend" (ἀναβαίνω) (not in Hebrews). His choice continues the αγω- and φέρω (*agō-* and *pherō*) word groups to describe the ministry of the Son, who is Jesus, as the Christ and Lord—the Great Shepherd who leads his sheep to the presence of God in heaven.

The theme tracks from the DI main chiastic point in Heb 1:3b. The semantic use of "bring, carry, lead" (φέρω) broadly encompasses all things. The force includes his purification of the holy place regarding the heavenly access available by the first covenant (unit F SbPt3b Heb 9:23–26). The righteous awaited the Christ before his traveling through the holy-*places* to sit on the throne. By his ability to overcome the barriers to

---

342. These markers include (1) use of the particle "now" (δὲ Heb 13:20), (2) the new summation topic of "but the God of peace" (Ὁ δὲ θεὸς τῆς εἰρήνης) to affirm his theme about God's desire for peace through the offering and priestly ministry of Jesus as the Christ, (3) the new summation of his thematic topic about the completed offering of Christ concerning God as the one who rose up from the dead, (4) the new summation of his thematic topic about the present ministry of Christ concerning the Great Shepherd of the sheep, (5) the source of peace as by the blood of the eternal/perpetual-*place* covenant, (6) the God of peace as Jesus, our Lord, (7) God's desire to restore in all good things and make us pleasing in his sight, and (8) observation that Jesus receives glory in the eternal/perpetual-*place* of the eternal/perpetual-*place*.

open access to God in heaven, he leads all things and his brethren with him into the domain of the holy of holies (unit B Heb 2:9–18).

The Pastor in his exposition shares details about how God provides a body, in continuous living after death, with features of an eternal/perpetual-*place* spirit. Leaders and their fellow brethren imitate this peace by unity in their conversation about the ministry of Jesus, as the Christ, who in a very short time brings all things to God in heaven by raising believers up from the dead.[343]

Third, God operates this his relationship with his brethren by the Son in ministry as the Shepherd of the sheep. The Pastor in his exposition shares details about Jesus present ministry to lead his sheep to a peaceful relationship in the presence of God in heaven after death at judgment. Leaders and their fellow brethren follow a heavenly calling to share their confession in the ministry of the Son to bring peace with God. They also love others in the same way God has loved them in all that they do.

Fourth, God guarantees this relationship of peace through the blood of the eternal/perpetual-*place* covenant. The Pastor in his exposition shares details about the sacrificial offering of Jesus as the Christ to atone for sin and open an entrance into the unseen eternal/perpetual-*places*. Leaders and their brethren guarantee peace with each other in the same way God enables peace with him. They sacrificially offer themselves in ministry to others.

Fifth, God equips his brethren for a pleasing relationship with him. The Pastor in his exposition shares details about God's ability to provide all good things needed to maintain a peaceful relationship with God. Leaders and their brethren look to Jesus as the author and finisher of their faith, in God's ability to provide good things needed for ministry with him.

Sixth, God shares the glory of his presence in peace through Jesus as Christ. The Pastor in his exposition shares details about the Son exhibiting and opening peaceful access to the presence of God's glory in the

---

343. The phrase "the one having risen up from the dead" expands beyond fleshly assumptions to include the God of peace having raised up the Great Shepherd of the sheep to himself at judgment after his fleshly death as a complete, bodily, eternal/perpetual-*place* spirit before his fleshly resurrection as proof of his entrance to God (cf. John 2:18–22; Acts 17:31). Also, the shepherd motif implies that Jesus does the same for others in his intercession to do God's will, to bring both peace with God in salvation and entrance to God, when a believer rises in spirit to judgment. This is developed in the final UC in chapter 4.

eternal/perpetual-*place* of the eternal/perpetual-*places*. Leaders and their brethren follow Jesus in anticipation and imitation of his glory.

By the model of God's relationship to his people, the Pastor summarizes both his positive and negative entreaty concerning the features of love among the brethren. He entreats leaders and their people in a few obvious specifics in unit A´, however his UC turns the audience attention to God's relationship with his people as a standard to follow for achievement of the love of God among themselves.

Dynamic Unit Conclusions E´–A´ in Lens of Heb 9:27–28

The unit A´ UC topical content summarizes both his exposition and exhortation about his discourse thematic subtopics from the DI that track through the DUC and STr. The main DI subtopics in his exposition include death, judgment, intercession, and salvation into heaven. The broad supportive detail delivers significant explanation concerning God's speech-action about the Son's ability in both his sacrificial offering and his continual shepherd ministry to lead all things to the place of God's glory in the eternal/perpetual-*place* of the eternal/perpetual-*places*.

Following the outline offered in STr2 (Heb 10:22–25), the Pastor applies to his listeners the anticipated ministry of the Son that he affirms from God's speech in his previous six units of discourse exposition. In chiasm corresponding to his previous unit themes, he encourages his listeners in the desired features of a true heart, a certainty of faith, a clean conscience and body, a firm confession in an unwavering hope, and love and encouragement in their assemblies until the day approaches for Jesus's intercession after death at judgment (see appendix 1, fig. 16).

CONCLUSION

Often, the application of modern structural methods can result in thematic incoherence or incompleteness with missing or unused discourse fragments.[344] David Black wrote over three decades ago acknowledging

---

344. E.g., Westfall recognizes the incompleteness of spatial studies in Hebrews, stating the conclusion, "We have taken what we wanted and left the rest without due reflection." Westfall, "Space and Atonement in Hebrews," 232. This phenomenon of spatial cherry picking explains the scholarly generational shifts in rising new paradigms from classical . . . to revised . . . to progressive . . . etc. Observed incohesive and incongruent gaps in the message create new questions that require constant revision by the next

a probable coherent literary structure for the message of Hebrews exists but that it had not been determined by scholars.[345] Even with all the new methods of structural analysis posited since, of which each often contribute new and helpful observations, nothing has changed. Why? The problem may not be the methods. It may be that scholars, when listening to God speaking in Hebrews, are pressing the text into either incorrect traditional themes or new novel ideas for publication that have been shaped into a worldview like that which Jesus opposed in the first century CE (see fig. 4). In line with inherited educational training within long held theological positions, modern readers attempt to deductively interpret the Pastor's address toward a presuppositional explanation that only brings God to people on earth, rather than Jesus literally bringing people from earth to himself in heaven.

The question remains, which offered, alternative, literary background field is really portrayed by all the words of the discourse of Hebrews? Does all the spatial-vertical language mean believers really go to heaven or not? If not, what should be made of all the heavenly dialogue that the Pastor shares as substance-reality? As documented in the extensive footnotes, the educated have wrestled with these questions for a long time with myriads of twists and turns of the pieces of Hebrews's puzzle in search of thematic links to build a coherent structure. Maybe it is time to consider a different approach and overall perspective—a heavenly one.

The next chapter serves as a conclusion of this long segment of the race set before you. As runners do in fellowship after a race, it shares an assessment and highlights.

---

generation of scholars. A structural method that properly interprets concepts of biblically defined space (1) fits easily into first-century CE apocalyptic concepts without imbalance toward other traditional or new philosophical concepts, (2) does not require strained, unique, grammatical-historical exegesis in a force-fit for later traditional or modern preconceived views, (3) chooses commonly understood first-century CE lexical meaning in contextual correspondence with the author's governing functional groupings of text, (4) avoids proof texting for other truth or later issues not addressed, and (5) enhances determination of the biblical theology of the original author.

345. Black, "Problem of the Literary Structure,"163–77. At the time of this writing, he introduced and greatly favored the progress made by the structural approach of Albert Vanhoye. Vanhoye, *La structure littéraire*. Vanhoye's conclusions have been challenged since but his contribution for the recognition of structural links above the grammatical and lexical level remains the starting place for modern discourse analysis.

5

Finish Well

Prompt Completion of God's People in God's Place
in the Pastor's Main Conclusion of Hebrews 9:27–28

INTRODUCTION

When runners finish, the awards reinforce past efforts in discipline and training as they replenish and rehydrate during pleasant conversation about their present and past races. The endorphins provide a feeling of euphoria that overcomes the pain and motivates future planning.

With the finish of this marathon effort, this chapter engages light conversation about findings, calculates the evidence for the thesis considered, makes some observations about insights discovered along the way, and offers suggestions for further research. Last, it also restates the Pastor's invitation to hear God's voice. Since people are now probably meeting in heaven, he would appropriately agree in desiring those who read his work to receive God's salvation in Jesus, as Christ, to join those there.

This project completes but one leg of the race set on a course already attempted by many in a large conversation that grows exponentially. Of those who have previously run their race toward Jesus, at the day approaching when people complete their journey into heaven, those who enter call past, present, and future fellow runners in the study of Hebrews brethren. Such brethren look forward to singing and conversing together in fellowship over God's speech in the Letter to the Hebrews.

SUMMARY OF THE FINDINGS

The research appraises the thesis that Jesus now intercedes a very little while after death at judgment to bring into heaven people who believe in his offering for sin, in the same way God promptly raised him in salvation from the dead into heaven, recaps Heb 9:27–28, as the true conversation of the exposition, exhortation, and rhetoric.

Overall, this project strongly affirms a high probability for the thesis proposition proposed for evaluation.

The analysis senses authorial coherence for cohesive DUC and STr concerning spatial language upon an apocalyptic, *aiōn-field* background. By use of the methods of lexical semantics, biblical theology, discourse analysis, and thought-structure analysis, the work looks through the lens of Heb 9:27–28 as the MCS of the sermon. By study of the FGT above the sentence level, it becomes obvious that the Pastor deploys a broad list of cognates, related words and phrases, and OT LXX midrash, in a tight thematic structure beginning with a chiastic outline in the DI and tracking though cycles of FGT in units, sections, and transition summaries. His topics and subtopics narrowly summarize events surrounding death, judgment, intercession, and salvation for both Jesus, his people into heaven, and the purification and reclaiming of the holy place. These major themes track along a path through two sections of exposition. Then, in a chiasmic relationship, the Pastor back tracks through corresponding units of FGT of a third section in application of the anticipated ministry of Christ to the present desired conversation of an audience.

The discourse units and sections assist the audience to cognitively process the message with FGT conclusions/summary introductions that track through the exposition to the MCS. Rather than an outlier subtopic about the NT alternative truth of the second coming, the two correlative statements in Heb 9:27–28, in tight coherence and correspondence, summarize the two-fold ministry of Christ promptly after death at judgment. In the new covenant, Christ offers himself once to bear the sins of many people and presently continues in his ministry from the throne to appear to those awaiting him after their death at judgment. Jesus, as the Great Shepherd of the sheep, leads those who believe into heavenly eternal/

perpetual-*place* rest. The Pastor envisions this wait for Jesus coming as a very little while (Heb 10:37). He describes the promise of hope, for those who believe in Jesus as Savior for personal sin, as a bodily transformation with new features into a perpetual eternal/perpetual-*place* kingdom in the inheritance of a city with other brethren that cannot be shaken.

The two main topics underlying the entire discourse are the heavenly covenants of God's speaking. The older heavenly covenant of promise has been fulfilled by the new heavenly covenant in the speech-action of the Son, Jesus, as the Christ. The Pastor delivers exposition about these two heavenly covenants by the hermeneutic of typology in a first-century CE apocalyptic view. As such, his chosen earthly counterparts are antitypes that provide revelation of God in speech-action about his desires in Christ for a better dwelling relationship for sinful people who live as flesh in the temporary creation.

For the Pastor, the new covenant does not replace the earthly Sinai covenant, or the multiple previous related versions similar to it that only symbolically illustrate both the former and new heavenly covenant relationship. The Sinai covenant of the law typologically illustrates both the first and new heavenly covenant relationship between God and the sinful people about the current separated creation in a gradation of holiness. The fulfillment of the new covenant by Jesus as the Christ made the former ministerial speech representations obsolete due to old and new covenant typological depictions, of which parts of the old covenant relationship are now errant regarding heavenly truth.

Jesus's entrance and enthronement into heaven, as the first human person beyond the veil, by bodily transformation to an eternal/perpetual-*place* spirit at death and judgment, achieves creative spatial change resulting in the greater and more perfect tabernacle. By Jesus's onetime atonement at death on the cross, the consciences of sinful people in heaven are cleansed, which allows reclamation of the space of the holy place that is separated from the presence of God by a veil. By heavenly veil elimination, Jesus presents his brethren before the Father on arrival and sings with them in worship.

The Pastor stresses that to continue or return to the ministerial conversation and teaching about either the daily or annual offerings of the Sinai covenant has no value at judgment on approach to the Lord. Such teaching is impossible, since it implies one must repent again and requires crucifixion of Jesus afresh in open shame. He addresses this underlying problem and ministerial accountability about the conversation of this obsolete ministry of the Sinai covenant in his exposition and exhortation. Acceptable ministerial worship portrays accurately that which presently occurs in the truth of the unseen substance-realities of heaven while following Jesus in suffering outside the gate until the day approaching of death and judgment.

Finally, those believers who anticipate the ministry of Jesus should live in a confident approach to the throne of grace. Consistent with that hope, the believer's life ought to exemplify a true heart in knowledge, certainty of faith, a clear conscience and pure body, an unwavering confession of hope in God's faithfulness, and love with encouragement in assembly together.

EVIDENCE SUPPORTING SALVATION A VERY LITTLE WHILE AFTER DEATH

The first spatial issue attempted by this author in a seminary paper over ten years ago investigated a question about plural heavens to address an observed realization commonly assumed by the academic literature of required reading in seminary texts—that no people traveled to heaven at death to be with Jesus. However, common singing, teaching, and preaching hears in God's speech a narrative about deceased believers in heaven as encouragement, comfort, and hope to see Jesus at death. After listening to the spatial-temporal clues in the message of Hebrews, a question surfaced: why do published scholars often not hear the biblical melody of believers now in heaven as complete in Jesus? The answers have substantially increased from a solo, to a band, and now an orchestra full of muted and distorted speech often not heard regarding deceased believers now in heaven with Jesus, since unclear in our languages and distorted by traditions.

Subsequent inquiry found evidence that translations, articles, books, and commentaries make multiple steps away from a straight path to Jesus and either muffle or mute hearing of clear teaching about prompt access after death at a short immediate judgment to Jesus at the throne in heaven. A short list includes (1) transliteration of Latin Vulgate terms to English with altered semantic meaning to support presuppositions for only a future, visible, earthly kingdom, (2) assimilation of multiple lexemes with dualistic first-century CE invisible/visible meaning by flattening translation of several Greek words as only the visible "world,

Atonement and the Logic of Resurrection in Hebrews 9:27–28

universe," and (3) collapse of the grammatical syntax of plural heavens and holy-*places* to a singular place of history, upon an incomplete cosmic background field, with a transcendent closed-heaven where people are not allowed in the presence of the living God.

Further evidence encompasses (4) flattening of the *aiōn-field* by an impossible antithetical contrast of space and time in support of future eschatology and rejection of continually realized eschatology, (5) ignoring the weight of both human spirit and the Holy Spirit within people that enables prompt spirit, bodily, transition to living in a better, perpetual, heavenly place, (6) proof texting of other issues in the DUC of Hebrews that miss the tight overarching theme of the Pastor's rhetoric in the parenesis of Jesus's present ministry in death at judgment, and (7) elevating or flattening the revelation of earthly antitypes to orphaned, final earthly types in promise-fulfillment.

Additional data involves (8) turning topsy-turvy the hope of a present heavenly dwelling for only a distantly future reclaimed earth, (9) placing God at a distance as a dictatorial sovereign rather than hearing the people's desire for living with the sovereign, living, servant God in a perpetual substance-reality of heaven, (10) turning up the volume by antithetical faulting between adherents of early church heretical issues to reject heavenly destiny for support of a desired perpetual, earthly, fleshly hope, (11) inventing first-century CE straw men, as conversation partners, for adversarial contrast to dismiss the impure Jewish Hellenist from the pure Jewish apocalyptic, and (12) imagining that the "now" and syntactic present tense language must have created a first-century CE tension by delay of the parousia, instead of realizing the heavenly promises are presently available, now, in death at judgment.

Extra support comprises (13) envisioning the people waiting as either asleep, wandering their tombs, or nonexistent, for an unknown eschaton instead of being passed without delay from death to eternal/perpetual-*place* life, (14) flipping verbal activity of "approach," "enter," and "entrance" to only worship by the inner man while alive on earth rather than the reality of heavenly truth that worship should imitate in conversation, (15) leaving Jesus stuck on his throne with no active shepherd ministry to carry and lead those in need at death, (16) ignoring the devil and his place of enslavement, outside the holy dwelling of God, (17) pitting Jesus in opposing contrast against the angels as lesser inferior beings since not human, and (18) rejecting apocalyptic, *aiōn-field* language in common cultural Hellenistic and Jewish dualism in spatial matters for conscious activity of waiting people after fleshly death either to God or outside of his holy presence.

Actions also comprise (19) pushing the implied presently available spatial comradery by Jesus participation with other people as his "brethren" and the Father's "children" to some future time on this earth, (20) missing the Holy Spirit indicated spatial changes achieved by Jesus's entry in the eternal/perpetual-*places* by the transition from the first to second heavenly covenants that made both the Sinaitic covenant daily and annual offerings obsolete, (21) limiting the temple spatial typological language as only Jesus, without his people, "within" heaven, rather than both Jesus and people "in the heavens," and (22) reversing the heavenly reward of eternal/perpetual-*place* inheritance for a claim only to a distant, rerouted, future salvation on this earth instead of immediately at death.

This orchestra of contrasting evidence in the setting of Hebrews, which is highlighted in academic conversation of chapters 1–4, composes a paradigm shift and necessitates the theses/dissertation length chapters that include lengthy footnotes and a large bibliography for interaction with both the text and momentous scholarly conversation surrounding the issues. The evidence considered, if properly accomplished, covers a mountain of information by scholarship and educated church elders about the first-century CE message of Hebrews.

The lexical semantics demands checking of the extant, first-century CE, conversational strides from most probable to least possible concerning the Pastor's intended meaning of his summary words of Heb 9:27–28 (fig. 9). This thesis length effort requires stripping away anachronistic glosses, expanding flattened glosses that reduce multiple cognates and related words into the same English word, and eliminating Latin transliterations connected to derived theological concepts in the traditional, cosmic-*field*, constrained paradigms. The weight of space and time in English glosses balances by adding the spatial weight of *place*(s) and *field* to appropriate terms. Many referent meanings in context require a spatial force consideration since the Pastor's conversation is about faith in unseen, material substance-realities, rather than philosophical, timeless nonmaterial ideas, metaphors, or mysticism.

The second thesis length chapter concerning the Pastor's background biblical theology must embrace a long-forgotten culture in apocalyptic thinking and typological interpretation of the LXX as God's speech that does not easily fit the long traditional empiric and rational organized norms of modern traditional Christianity. The Pastor accepts the MT, LXX, and midrash interpretation as God's direct speech-action. Further, he seems to embrace a theology where all people promptly rise to God for judgment after death, into an unseen substance-reality of faith. Both David and Abraham are considered already in heaven along with others of faith. The Pastor's concern is the different rising *from* the dead by the ministry of Christ and change in heavenly destiny from the first heavenly covenant to the second heavenly covenant. Further, he accepts that earthly events about people, places, and institutions represent in greater correspondence the truth of heavenly unseen substance-realities. The unsettled newness of apocalyptic, typological, revelation interpretation concepts and recent challenges against inspiration of God's word demand definition and characterization for proper interaction with other scholars.

The communication approach of Greek discourse and chiasm that governs meaning with literary elements in functional features above the sentence level greatly differs from the modern language paragraph and below sentence analysis elements. A third dissertation level discourse analysis of the entire work of Hebrews is essential to provide coherence to the communication structure and to avert interpretative errors of uncontrolled grammatical-historical exegesis, scholarly favoritism of syntactical choices, and bias of semantic meaning in proof texting toward presuppositions of tradition that may be against authorial intent. Evaluation of the individual cycles of FGT introducing and supporting the DUC and STr maintain message cohesion and topical correspondence during tracking of the paths of the main subtopics from the DI through the message exposition to the MCS and then turn back for corresponding application.

The answer against the charge of allowing outside structure to influence and control the meaning of the text is a positive affirmation since the text original designs accommodate these natural devices much more than modern paragraphs with chapter and verse divisions that clumsily provide similar influence upon exegesis. The comfortable fit for message coherence without forced exegetical gymnastics in backbends and contortions to accommodate the optional tradition of renewed cosmic hope greatly validates the chosen methodology in evidence accrual.

OBSERVATIONS AND FUTURE RESEARCH

This work is the first known dissertation level investigation about believers promptly entering heaven in immediate rising of the dead since Hebrews circulation. Others have held this view, but none have applied it fully to Hebrews. The first is always a rough start. Prayerfully, others who choose to follow the same conversation will smooth the course laid out with improvements.

There were multiple surprises in the investigation. Most of these are written either in the body or footnotes. They mostly arose when maintaining word correspondence for message cohesion along the cycles of FGT. A couple of observations are notable. One concerns proof texting about creation. Topics about the Son's creating in context better refer to the changes achieved by Jesus's entry into the holy place through the removed veil by God that makes holy the heavenly realm, purifies the people there, and creates the more perfect tent. The second notable discovery involves the distinction in all people at death experiencing rising *of* the dead but only those with Jesus's mediation rising *from* the dead. While compiling appendix 1, fig. 1–3, initial perceived duplicates required erasing one or the other of these respective events until the difference was heard in an "ahhh!" moment.

Two areas of important dissertation length research were reduced into two excursuses from this work. The first excursus centers on NT and other first-century CE postmortem views that are only lightly alluded to in the body and footnotes, with a more developed example for research in excursus A.

The second reduced chapter research covered the period between the early churches and the modern era (see fig. 4). Once hope inverts from heaven to dominant cosmic-*field* limited tenets, elders rationally derive creedal statements of the classical concept where all the dead enter Hades and Jesus descends into hell to rescue the dead to resuscitate them into heaven. When the reformers reject these conjectures, other missteps in translation transpire to maintain traditional, cosmic-*field*, endpoint ideals. Just after the five hundredth anniversary of Luther's September Testament, Luther's syntactical error documents in excursus B.[1] Perhaps further research will find completion in the future, or possibly by supervision of a graduate student or two before my day before the Lord.

---

1. This initial research originally appeared in Henry, "Cosmology of the Heaven(s)," 28–62.

INVITATION

Now the final and most important part. This invitation one day may be located where people sneak a peek to know how this work ends. At races someone usually passes out race fliers announcing the next race opportunities. I, also, close with a flier with an opportunity in your final race to finish well. Jesus now lives at the finish in heaven ready to complete the final segment on the day of your approach by his intercession at death and judgment. After addressing personal sin, he will come to you and bring you through the entrance into his eternal/perpetual-*place* kingdom as pleasing to God the Father, with no consciousness of sin. This salvation with eternal/perpetual-*place* inheritance comes to those waiting for Jesus to appear for them. In his new covenant relationship, you will receive a new mind and new heart to keep God's law in righteousness in the joy of eternal/perpetual-*place* service.

This final segment opportunity to run the race that finishes well in heaven is available by reservation today if you will hear God's voice. Please listen. It must be received in a prayer with God like that of Jesus, who offered up prayers and supplications with loud crying and tears to the one able to save him from death. He was heard because of his reverence to God and his offer of salvation. To qualify and reserve your position, you must first by faith in unseen substance-realities believe God is, and that he is a rewarder of those who seek him. Salvation is available to those who first take a step of repentance in an acknowledgment of sin before God. We must see our need before a holy God. The next step is faith in God's provision by Jesus. He is able by his offering to open the way of the holy-*places* to God in heaven. A third step is transference of sin to Jesus, so we can be made holy before God by his substitutionary offering.

The Pastor invites all today to accept the Christ of faith in preparation for the day of salvation when rising *of* the dead, so that Jesus appears and brings you up *from* the dead to eternal/perpetual-*place* living. He describes this hope in the promise to believers as heavenly rest, light, peace of God, joy, reward, inheritance, blessing, a city of the living God with other believers and angels, and most of all "better" thirteen times. I hope you receive him today for anticipation of Jesus's intercession for salvation into heaven.

Excursus A

Other Runners' Corresponding Place(s) of Other NT Gospel Sequences
A Nodal Example and Area for Further Research

INTRODUCTION

One of the measures that a serious runner uses for personal assessment of progress concerns evaluation and comparison with other runners. The Pastor mentions "having a cloud of witnesses surrounding us" (Heb 12:1). A little comparison in competition stimulates better running. Analysis of the races by other participants provides methodological insight into technique and strategic choices for training, running gear, running locations, venues, opportunities, and common maintenance issues in a range from injury treatment to healthy eating and rest. Runners learn from the experience of others.

    Similarly, proper hearing of Hebrews's message necessitates comparisons with other canonical and noncanonical textual usage and meaning during the interpretative process (Heb 1:1; 2 Tim 3:16–17; 2 Pet 1:20). A complete comparison must include analysis of the spatial-temporal background in the deep structure that governs each author's message, without syntactical proof texting. This especially includes other authorial conversations related to the speech-action about the anticipated Son of

God, as the Word and Christ, in both his substitutionary sacrifice and present intercessory ministry.

Chapters 2–4 analyze Heb 9:27–28 as a MCS of the expected conversation of the Letter to the Hebrews. These chapters explore the Pastor's (1) probable to possible optional meanings for his chosen words, (2) his spatial-temporal background theology through his lens about the revelation of God speaking, and (3) his controlling discourse conclusions that govern the spatial-temporal understanding. Further testing of other first-century CE biblical texts also evaluates if I have adequately supported the thesis.

The evidence gleaned by the assessment validates the thesis with compelling force that the spatial-temporal place envisioned by the Pastor, where salvation occurs for those waiting for Jesus's appearing, occurs at death and judgment during approach to heaven (appendix 1, fig. 1, no. 7; fig. 2, no. 2). It is highly probable that promptly at judgment, Christ will appear "from a second *place* without sin" (Heb 9:28) to those waiting for him. Jesus's shepherds each of his brethren through the way of the holy-places that he created, to enter God's presence. These spirits made righteous by the blood of the eternal-place covenant now form a city of God's people with Jesus, who is the mediator of their new covenant relationship. They enjoy God's rest, God's laws in their minds and written on their hearts, personally know the Lord, and await a corporate completion when those still living will be added with their forming church in Jesus's inherited kingdom in heaven. These brethren will continue service with Jesus in the eternal-places until all enemies are placed under his feet and the final shaking of all temporary things.[1]

Do other writings of other extant first-century CE authors envision the same hope of salvation? An area of needed dissertation level research focuses on the spatial-temporal features of other first-century CE canonical and noncanonical texts possibly available to the Pastor. An analysis should explore the language of other first-century CE texts for spatial-temporal markers to determine information about the anticipated intercessory ministry of Jesus.

---

1. The Pastor's thematic focus of his parenetic sections is on Jesus's onetime ministry of sacrifice in atonement of sin and the personal ministry of his perpetual present intercession in this new covenant fulfillment. However, the Pastor does not develop themes that deal with a future ministry after rest either before all enemies are eliminated or afterwards. One would commit the fallacy of an argument from silence to deduce from his silence that he either does or does not support the future prophetic events written by other canonical authors.

Possible key questions concern how other authorial special-temporal language links with the topics of death, judgment, intercession, and salvation. Is their conception of salvation a continued living for those who believe in Christ? If yes, is this promised eternal life either (1) only an idealistic feature to influence current restful living before fleshly death, (2) an expected future nodal event sometime after death, (3) a delayed future general event for all believers at once, (4) or a process that is now ongoing that continues through the individual events of death and judgment, with a corporate completion in the future?

Exploration should also investigate these background markers to determine whether the destiny of the believer's hope for continued living in "eternal-place life" is available (1) now in heaven at death, (2) only by a resuscitation on the earth at some point future, or (3) both now at death by spiritual transition to Jesus for rest with later ministerial service at his coming to earth until all enemies are placed under Jesus's feet.

As an example of this future research, a small NT assessment regarding the present activity of the Son's second covenant ministry in heaven is offered by analysis of four NT gospel sequences.[2] Space will not allow exploration of the entire NT and available noncanonical texts or all points of contact with the proposed conception in Hebrews. So, it provides one nodal sampling of these texts for evidence that gospel fulfillment contains spatial-temporal language for salvation activity in heaven, in spirit form, promptly after death and judgment for both Jesus as the offering of the Christ and those believers who follow him in the same sequence of dying and rising events for entrance to the Father (see appendix 1, fig. 10). This sampling includes 1 Cor 15:1–8; Rom 1:1–6; 1 Tim 3:16b; and 1 Pet 3:18–22; 4:5–6. Does other NT narrative contain similar *aiōn-field* heavenly themes with possible spiritual access as the conversation in Hebrews?

GOSPEL ACCOUNTS WITH SIMILAR LANGUAGE

The nodal point of contact for evaluation of these NT sequential gospel accounts for similar language with Heb 9:27–28 concerns the meaning of Jesus's continual living in transformation as "a spirit of an eternal-place"

---

2. For gospel activity perceived by Paul in a sequence of events, as evidenced in his use of the idiom "first in sequence" (ἐν πρώτοις), see Fredericks, "Question of First Importance," 165–81. Fredericks by first-century CE evidence strongly supports ἐν πρώτοις as an idiom with weight meaning first in a sequence of events.

(πνεύματος αἰωνίου Heb 9:14). The increasing number of deaths of the first generation of Christians influenced the writing of biblical sequential gospel narratives of Jesus's death with similar language as Heb 9:14. These possibly describe the flesh-spirit activity of Jesus in atonement. The four major NT sequential gospel accounts are 1 Cor 15:3–5 (Mid-50s CE); Rom 1:3–5 (Mid-50s CE); 1 Tim 3:16b (62–65 CE); and 1 Pet 3:18–22; 4:5–6 (62–65 CE).[3] Each contains a flesh-spirit pairing with Heb 9:13–14 in gospel descriptions. The exception is Corinth which initially simply speaks that Christ ἐτάφη ("was buried," 1 Cor 15:4), but later enjoins in the teaching on resurrection the σαρκὸς-πνεῦμα language.

1 Corinthians 15:1–8

The first sequential gospel narrative to consider in relation to living as "spirit of an eternal-place" (πνεύματος αἰωνίου Heb 9:14) is the subunit of 1 Cor 15:1–8. It focuses on the earthly view of the gospel from an eyewitness perspective. Paul first states what is known rationally. First, Christ "died" (1 Cor 15:3). Second, "he was buried" (ἐτάφη 1 Cor 15:4), which verified the fleshly death of Jesus. Third, "he was raised the third day" (ἐγήγερται τῇ ἡμέρᾳ τῇ τρίτῃ 1 Cor 15:4).[4] Jesus's dead flesh body remained in a tomb until the third day. This period provides adequate time for a possible unseen sequence of "spirit of an eternal-place" dying and rising events before his bodily resurrection (appendix 1, fig. 10). Finally, "he was seen" (ὤφθη 1 Cor 15:5) as visible proof of his rising to God (cf. John 2:18–22).

It would seem this presentation thematically concentrates on visible actions without mention of the referent "spirit" (πνεῦμα). In the simplest

---

3. First Corinthians and Romans are from the mid-fifties and undisputed letters of Paul. First Peter and 1 Timothy are likely from the mid-sixties before Peter and Paul's deaths. Peter's ministry overlaps in same relative time and locale as Paul.

4. The verbal ideas of "to rise" (ἐγείρω) and "stand up, resurrect" (ἀνάστασις) with the source genitive "from the dead" (ἐκ νεκρῶν [used forty-six times in the NT]) describe sequential events from the locations of a transitioning to a spirit body from a flesh body. These terms usually function with an earthly perspective for living people in the *effective aspect* with emphasis on the end of the action in returned resuscitation with breath of the flesh as proof of unseen spiritual resurrection. However, when used in discourses containing a heavenly eternal-place perspectives to explain the work of the gospel in invisible creation, the *constative aspect* in reference to all the events of the whole action may be contained in the meaning. Resurrection as a verbal noun is as the term "surgery" or "game." Each describes a collection of narrative activities done in sequence.

form, the section reduces Jesus's gospel sequence events to nodal points of death, burial, resurrection *from* the dead, and his appearing to living people (1 Cor 15:1–8). He on the third day according to the Scriptures appears in witness bodily as living proof of having been to God in death and judgment with a good outcome (cf. John 2:18–22; Acts 17:31). There is a visible dying sequence and rising sequence in this gospel rendering of the Christ offering event.

A look at this gospel sequence in the light of the entire pericope of 1 Cor 15:1–58 however does find hints of possible invisible "spirit" life intercession that is not part of the visible earthly witness. Paul, while arguing various aspects of the resurrection in his Adam-Christ contrast of the resurrection body composition, states, "Thus also it has been written, the first man Adam became the result of a living soul, the last Adam the result of a life-creating spirit" (1 Cor 15:45). The acc. preposition εἰς can have several syntactical meanings. The historical narrative in discussion in association with the gospel and the resurrection body favors the acc. of result.

Both statements have positive inference about people in Christ. Adam's sin is not in focus but his body. The first man Adam contributed the result of the living soul to the body of flesh. Man became an animated fleshly being in God's plan. Christ, the second-Adam, contributed the result of the "life-achieving, -creating spirit" (πνεῦμα ζωοποιοῦν). In context, Christ, on the path of the gospel as the life-creating spirit after death to resurrection (appendix 1, fig. 1), provides a way for transformation from Adam's likeness of weak, corruptible, fleshly, soulish bodies to durative, incorruptible, spiritual, heavenly bodies (fig. 2). Therefore, it is highly possible that this phrase "life-achieving, -creating spirit" may have a strong thematic nodal connection to Heb 9:14 "spirit of an eternal/perpetual-*place*" (πνεύματος αἰωνίου) with prompt enthronement of Christ in heaven as part of the gospel dying and rising sequence (appendix 1, fig. 10) and example that believers now follow in Heb 9:28 (appendix 1, fig. 2).

Romans 1:1–6

The next sequential gospel account that may have possible nodal contact with πνεύματος αἰωνίου (Heb 9:14) as Jesus's prompt continued living in a spiritual form of "a spirit of an eternal-place" is Rom 1:1–6. This description matches more closely Hebrews and the others in 1 Timothy and 1 Peter. Paul introduces Romans by sequentially listing five relative clauses that each modify "gospel of God" (εὐαγγέλιον θεοῦ Rom 1:1). The second and third clauses contain a "flesh-spirit" (σαρκὸς-πνεῦμα) language pairing, which may easily link the phrases "a spirit of a holy place" (πνεύματος αἰωνίου Heb 9:14) and "a spirit of holiness" (πνεῦμα ἁγιωσύνης Rom 1:4) for Jesus and a comparable state in Heb 9:27–28 for his believers when seeing Jesus appear for their salvation. Some translations recognize the possible meaning.[5]

The second clause states that Jesus is the seed of David "according to the flesh" (κατὰ σάρκα Rom 1:3). This again, like the context behind *pneumatos aiōnio* (πνεύματος αἰωνίου) in Heb 9:14, infers Davidic King-Priest language. The third clause states, "Who being appointed a Son of God in capability according to a spirit of holiness from this point resurrection from the dead" (τοῦ ὁρισθέντος υἱοῦ θεοῦ ἐν δυνάμει κατὰ πνεῦμα ἁγιωσύνης ἐξ ἀναστάσεως νεκρῶν Rom 1:4). The acc. *kata* (κατὰ) with *pneuma* (πνεῦμα) has the standard force meaning of "in accordance with" or "concerning." It modifies the subst. ptc. "who being declared a Son of God" (τοῦ ὁρισθέντος υἱοῦ θεοῦ). The unique gen. modifier hagiōsynēs (ἁγιωσύνης) then becomes an attributive gen. to *pneuma* (πνεῦμα) for likely the meaning of "spirit of holiness."[6] In its limited use and meaning, it would be an awkward reference for the Holy Spirit. It references the result of dedication or consecration to God's use, which is tenuous for describing the Holy Spirit. Can the Holy Spirit as God do anything else? While long debated, at least the humanness of Jesus as God-man has possibly the potential of unholiness in being tempted in every way as his brethren (cf. Heb 2:17).

The combination phrase *pneuma hagiōsynēs* (πνεῦμα ἁγιωσύνης) is rare and only used twice in the Pauline NT and once in STL. The Pauline use refers to the influence of continual mature holiness before God upon the ethical attributes of people.[7] The phrase has strong correspondence

---

5. NASB: Spirit (n), or spirit; ESV: Spirit; NET: Holy Spirit (n), inner spirit; HSCB: Spirit (n), or the spirit of holiness, or the Holy Spirit; KJV\RSV1901: spirit of holiness; RSV1971\DARBY1890: Spirit of holiness; Luther 1545: *Geist* in German translated "Spirit or spirit" determined by context. (n) = note with "spirit" option.

6. L&N, "53.45 ἁγιωσύνη," 1:537. It glosses the word, "*f*: the state resulting from being dedicated to the service of God—'dedication, consecration.'"

7. It occurs twice in the Pauline corpus (2 Cor 7:1; 1 Thes 3:13). In the former, he infers an ethical characteristic for the dual nature of "flesh and spirit" (σαρκὸς καὶ πνεύματος 2 Cor 7:1). In the latter Paul infers the anthropological aspect of the καρδίας

both linguistically and thematically with T. Levi 18:7.[8] In a Jewish text with clear messianic expectation, the phrase "spirit of understanding and holiness" refers to the one coming as Christ. The term indicates the expectation of dedication in holiness.[9] Several other thematic linguistic and contextual evidence could support a possible Pauline allusion to the text for the phrase πνεῦμα ἁγιωσύνης.

In the context of the gospel of God, the complete phrase κατὰ πνεῦμα ἁγιωσύνης is more likely a reference to Jesus's quality of holiness in his human spirit nature. His mandatory prerequisite for resurrection *from* the dead, during his experience regarding the rising *of* all the dead for judgment, demands holiness in both his human natures of flesh and spirit when his offering is judged by God (cf. Col 1:22, 1 Cor 15:21, Rom 9:5).

The expression "according to a spirit of holiness" (κατὰ πνεῦμα ἁγιωσύνης) precedes "from this point to resurrection of dead *people*" (ἐξ ἀναστάσεως νεκρῶν). If a temporal gospel sequence, then it would possess a temporal force for the semantic meaning for the preposition ἐκ as "from this point to."[10] The language proclaims that it was Jesus's spirit of holiness that enables both his declaration as a Son of God and the temporal point from which he begins his continued movement of rising from the dead (cf. Acts 13:34–35, appendix 1, fig. 1, no. 3). Further, "of the dead *people*" (νεκρῶν) as an gen. pl. adj. could have a syntactical meaning of possessive and source with the implication that Jesus's spirit in death was with other dead humanity (appendix 1, fig. 1, no. 2). Jesus as a person does taste death for all people (cf. Heb 2:9, 17). His nature of holiness enables his resurrection *from* the place of the dead bodily spirits

---

("heart"). Paul's phrase "blameless in holiness" (ἀμέμπτους ἐν ἁγιωσύνῃ) modifying "heart" (καρδίας) combines ideas of blamelessness and holiness. Neither use directly refers to the Holy Spirit but encourages inward anthropological attributes. Paul throughout his writings uses other referent terms for the Holy Spirit.

8. The immediate verse states, "And the glory of the highest will be spoken upon him, and a spirit of understanding and holiness will rest upon him in the water" (T. Levi 18:7 *OTGP*). The phrase "in the water" is thought to be a later interpolation to connect the prophetic tone to Jesus's baptism. Clearly the context is messianic. The term ἁγιασμοῦ differs from ἁγιωσύνης but is the same semantic domain, the former in intent to dedicate oneself in holiness and the later the result of such dedication.

9. L&N, "53.44 ἁγιάζω; ἁγιασμός, οῦ," 1:537. Louw-Nida gloss, "*m*: to dedicate to the service of and to loyalty to deity—'to consecrate, consecration, to dedicate to God, dedication.'"

10. *BNTS*, 371. The other syntactical options when used with resurrection as the object do not make grammatical sense. Wallace writes that in the BDAG this force is considered a "perfectivizing" which aptly applies to the intended meaning in context.

(Heb 7:26; cf. 1 Cor 15:13, 21, 42). In the spatial heavens of Hebrews and the tabernacle outline, Jesus's spirit of holiness begins his rising sequence of the gospel in resurrection (appendix 1, fig. 1, no. 3; appendix 1, fig. 10), his travel from the realm of the dead through the heavens and the reclaimed holy place, by God's previous removal the veil, into the now greater and more complete holy of holies for enthronement at the right hand of God (appendix 1, fig. 1, no. 4). It is highly possible the gospel sequence in Romans has nodal contact with Hebrews conversation about immediate continued living in spiritual form for Jesus's after death and judgment, which would extrapolate to his believers who follow the same path.

1 Timothy 3:16b

The next sequential gospel narrative to compare to Heb 9:14 "spirit of an eternal/perpetual-*place*" (πνεύματος αἰωνίου) and the similar experience of believers in Heb 9:27–28 is the hymn of 1 Tim 3:16b. If one arranges the hymn in the standard couplets, interprets in consistent sequence fashion, and finds points of spatial-temporal contact within the narrative frame of the common first-century CE heavens tabernacle background—it harmoniously depicts a typical sequential gospel account.

Due to space, consideration only looks briefly at the first two lines. The hymn's first line is "who . . . was manifest in the flesh" (ὅς. . .ἐφανερώθη ἐν σαρκί). The inference is probably to Christ's incarnation and life offering (cf. John 1:14, 8:23). Antithetically paired in line two with "flesh" (σαρκί) is "spirit" (πνεύματι). This combination flesh-spirit human contrast permeates the teaching sequences of the gospel theme and Paul's exposition (cf. 1 Cor 5:5; 2 Cor 7:1).

Jesus, as a complete man had both flesh and spirit to qualify in penal substitution for sin in his sacrificial death and intercession (Heb 2:14–18, cf. 1 Tim 2:5). If Heb 9:14 has been correctly understood considering gospel flesh-spirit teaching thus far, then Jesus had an "spirit of an eternal-place" (πνεύματος αἰωνίου Heb 9:14), as a whole human being that can transform to a spirit body compatible with the features of heaven.[11]

---

11. Jesus in both person and nature as fully man also is fully God. His human and divine Spirit are joined in his flesh enabling animated living. As the God-man, Jesus's human spirit would continue living if removed in death to face immediate judgment. In first-century CE understanding, unless the spirit is removed in rising *of* the dead to God for eternal-place judgment (Heb 6:2), Jesus would not be dead in the flesh as a

Matthew reports at the end of Jesus's life, "He gave up the spirit," (ἀφῆκεν τὸ πνεῦμα Matt 27:50) implying for first-century CE readers a transformation in death to Jesus's spirit from his flesh to face the judgment of God. In the hymn of 1 Tim 3:16b *pneumati* (πνεύματι) is joined with an aorist pass. verb *edikaiōthē* (ἐδικαιώθη). The common first-century CE meaning was forensic with ideas of a trial where one is proven right.[12] Therefore, the phrase "was vindicated in spirit" (ἐδικαιώθη ἐν πνεύματι) speaks of the point in the sequential gospel narrative where the spirit of Jesus is legally vindicated at judgment (appendix 1, fig. 1, no. 2). This vindication is similar language to Jesus finding release of redemption in the holy place in Heb 9:12. If both texts explain aspects of the same spatial-temporal point in the sequential gospel narrative (appendix 1, fig. 1, no. 2–3), this enables Jesus's experience to journey during approach of the holy place and to begin his rising sequence *from* the dead as the first to enter the holy of holies of God's presence (appendix 1, fig. 1, no. 3). This understanding separates the gospel teaching from the commonly held ideology often postulated by the early church of *Christus descendit ad inferno*.[13] Jesus's life as blameless, in holiness, and legally just, pre-certifies a different "spirit" destiny than the unrighteous as evidenced of the NT and STL (appendix 1, fig. 3). It is highly possible the gospel sequence in the hymn of 1 Tim 3:16b has nodal contact with Hebrews conversation about Jesus's judgment after death that allowed his continued living in spiritual form, which would extrapolate to his believers who follow the same path. In the basics of the beginning teaching of the Christ in Heb 6:1–2, judgment must take place after rising *of* the dead people before one can rise *from* the dead, if vindicated as blameless (cf. Heb 9:27–28).

1 Peter 3:18–22; 4:5–6

The next sequential gospel to compare to Heb 9:14 "spirit of an eternal-place" (πνεύματος αἰωνίου) and the anticipation of believers in Heb 9:27–28 is in 1 Peter. In context, Peter provides Christ's atonement suffering as

---

necessity for atonement for the Christ. The transition of Jesus's human spirit from flesh does not involve any division of Jesus in the God-man, or any inferior intermediate state of the soul, but only separation of flesh to spirit in transformation to a spiritual body prepared by God (unit F UPt5 Heb 10:5–14; cf. 2 Cor 5:1–11).

12. BDAG, "δικαιόω," 249. See Ziesler, *Meaning of Righteousness*, 18.

13. Gundry, "Form, Meaning and Background," 218–22. Gundry is one of the last modern scholars in the last fifty years to argue this position.

an example for the suffering of believers for doing God's will.[14] Like other sequential gospel narratives, the categories of Jesus's flesh-spirit form an essential element in the description of his atonement and intercessory activity.

While Jesus suffered, Peter states, "But he was entrusting to the one who is judging righteously" (παρεδίδου δὲ τῷ κρίνοντι δικαίως 1 Pet 2:24). This clearly indicates that Jesus expected vindication in judgment before the Father after completion of his atonement of suffering on the cross (cf. John 8:50; Jer 11:20). Peter uses this expectation to teach his readers in this section that God judges both the living and the dead (1 Pet 4:5–6; cf. Heb 9:26–28).

First Peter 3:18 shares another gospel flesh-spirit pairing with a *dikai-* (δίκαι-) word group. Jesus "suffered" (ἔπαθεν) "the just for the unjust" (δίκαιος ὑπὲρ ἀδίκων) signifying common gospel themes of penal substitution. The ἵνα signals for readers an adverbial of result clause where Jesus as "just" (δίκαιος) "could lead to God" (προσαγάγῃ τῷ θεῷ). The path that Jesus led was exercised by his being put to death in the flesh. Following his death, he was quickened in the spirit.

The *men-de* (μὲν-δὲ) construction signals the pairing contrast of the referent datives of σαρκί and πνεύματι with respective descriptive participles. Like the other sequential gospel descriptions, these probably grammatically pair Jesus's nature as both human flesh and spirit. Peter first comments, "on the one hand after being put to death in the flesh" (θανατωθεὶς μὲν σαρκί 1 Pet 3:18). The aorist pass. ptc. *thanatōtheis* (θανατωθεὶς) in the sequential gospel narrative is temporal to designate action antecedent to the main verb "he might bring" (προσαγάγῃ). As verbal nouns, both participles are masc. sg. in agreement with the subject of Christ to describe verbal action that Christ, as subject passively receives, in both flesh and spirit. Jesus was put to death in the flesh in penal substitution for sin before the possibility of bringing others to God.

In contrast, Peter says "but on the other hand after being made alive in the spirit" (ζῳοποιηθεὶς δὲ πνεύματι 1 Pet 3:18). The dat. πνεύματι must be taken with the force meaning of the aorist pass. ptc. *zōopoiētheis* (ζῳοποιηθεὶς) in the context of the verdict Jesus's receives as one "just" before God versus one unjust, and in relation to its paired dat. "flesh" (σαρκί). First, the dat. σαρκί is a dat. of sphere. This then in the μὲν-δὲ contrast would usually make πνεύματι also a dat. of sphere. There are

---

14. Dalton, *Christ's Proclamation to the Spirits*, 100–102.

no grammatical signals otherwise, so contextual evidence must support a change. Therefore, the only problem with πνεύματι as a dat. of sphere would be interpretative theological presuppositions or evidence that negate the option.[15]

Second, if Jesus as an example is in some way judged by God as "just" between fleshly death and fleshly resurrection for qualities to make him alive for resurrection from the dead, then this judgment must be complete before his flesh body resurrection (cf. Heb 9:26–28). Jesus is the object of his own resurrection by the distinction he is blameless before God in a spirit of holiness as one just without sin. This perfection of Jesus is due to his continual filling in power by the Holy Spirt in the Father's will. His flesh resurrection functions as a sign of his spiritual resurrection (cf. John 2:18–22). Such fleshly resurrection is unnecessary for believers (1 Cor 15:50).

Third, the Holy Spirit in a dat. of agency "by the spirit" (πνεύματι) should not directly apply as a subjective to "after being made alive" (ζωοποιηθείς). Jesus is the subjective recipient agent of his own resurrection though the objective capability provided by his own personal submission to the Holy Spirit in the Father's will without sin. The Holy Spirit is present, but not actively providing the way of salvation in death to resurrection. If so, salvation is by the subjective Holy Spirit, rather than primarily Jesus, as the Christ. These persons of God cannot be taken too distinctly since these three persons of God are one, yet in revelation of salvation history there is delegation of salvific duties.

---

15. Patterson, *Pilgrim Priesthood*, 133. Patterson takes rightful theological exception with the *Christus descendit ad inferno* interpretation often placed upon Peter's text. He also agrees the grammar should interpret πνεύματι as a dat. of sphere, but correctly does not think one should be slavishly held to grammar. However, his visible creation logic applied to invisible creation options for Jesus's in spirit making proclamation to the spirits in prison lead him to reject by fallacy of negative inference πνεύματι as a dat. of sphere. The error is rational visible world applications that make invisible realms of all creation of God's house completely oblivious to others (cf. Luke 16:19–31). This project does not intend to answer all the exegetical questions about this spirit activity of Jesus, but strongly suggests it should be evaluated in light of Jesus's spirit intercessory activity after sacrificial death and before fleshy resurrection (appendix 1, fig. 1, nos. 2–4). The option for *pneumati* (πνεύματι) as Jesus's spirit does influence interpretation of these difficult texts. There are two groups of invisible creation here referenced in the text for Jesus's proclamation. First, "to the spirits" (πνεύμασιν 1 Pet 3:19) and second, "to the dead" (νεκροῖς 1 Pet 4:6). These groups are evidence for Peter of God's expected judgment in the unseen realm after death which should ethically motivate believers to suffer in doing what is right in a clear conscience. The viable option of Jesus "in spirit" (πνεύματι) as *Christus ascendens in spiritu* will require much more study.

Jesus's path in death is not as one "unjust" in a continued separation from God in spirit bodily form (fig. 3). As one "just," after being made alive in spirit bodily form a very little while after death on the cross and rising *of* the dead (appendix 1, fig. 1, nos. 1–2), Jesus, as a spirit of an eternal-place, journeys in his priestly ministry to God (appendix 1, fig. 1, nos. 3–4), creating a way in death that others can follow (fig. 2). In harmony with other sequential gospels, this salvation event would take place in the holy of holies, which now has heavenly space reclaimed by cleansing of the sins of the people there, by Jesus's atonement into the greater and more perfect tent. There, Jesus finds eternal-place redemption to proceed through the opened veil of angelic protection into heaven itself.

CONCLUSION

This excursus explores the biblical texts of Hebrews and other sequential gospel narrative accounts for evidential support for a possible *Christus victor* intercessory spirit ministry of Jesus after his penal substitutionary death in atonement before fleshly resurrection *from* the dead. The starting point for the investigation is the modifier πνεύματος αἰωνίου ("a spirit of a holy place") in Heb 9:14 in reference to the priestly intercessory ministry of Christ after completion of atonement and before fleshly resurrection as visible proof of his success in rising to God from the dead.

This example investigation proceeds through the lens of the phrase "spirit of an eternal-place" (πνεύματος αἰωνίου Heb 9:14) in comparison to other sequential gospel narratives in the NT. In summary, the work finds strong nodal links between the use of "spirit" (πνεῦμα) in Heb 9:14 and other NT sequential gospel narratives that directly reference Jesus's human "eternal-place spirit" in his initial priestly intercession after completion of sacrificial atonement. However, this is not mutually exclusive regarding Holy Spirit involvement with Jesus. The evidence of the background, subunit exegesis, and other similar NT sequential gospels, support that the interpretation should naturally integrate both hermeneutical options for a Holy Spirit empowered initial priestly intercessory movement of Jesus's human spirit after sacrificial death (cf. Rom 8:16; 1 John 4:13). Jesus by both the agency of the Holy Spirit and the means of his human "eternal-place spirit" bodily form, begins intercession of his priesthood atonement ministry by the way of his sacrificial death to prepare the way to God's presence before his ascension after resurrection (cf. John 14:1–7). Christopher Rowland and Christopher R. A. Morray-Jones write, "The ascent of Christ into heaven is not the glorious progress of the Son to the Father, as the whole of the understanding of the letter is linked with the cross as the decisive event which made the ascent\entry possible."[16]

The evidence, when taken literally in the first-century CE apocalyptic understanding, supports the intercessory bodily spirit activity of Jesus after completion of atonement on the cross in the invisible creation of God's house before his visible proof of his accomplished entry to God by his fleshly resurrection and later ascension. The affirmative or negative response to the evidence may not have eternal salvific consequences. However, if the evidence is correct, it does impact the present hope of believers concerning the dead. Like Abraham, Isaac, and Jacob, they are still living, just as Jesus corrects the greatly mistaken Sadducees (Mark 12: 25–27). A negative response in objection to the evidence concerning Jesus as consciously active in death in the substance of his "a spirit of an eternal-place" (πνεύματος αἰωνίου) when worked out greatly challenges the common Christian hope of continued living with Jesus after death. If Jesus did not go to the Father in spirit in a human death, then neither do his believers—since they follow his "way" in death, burial, and resurrection. This rationalization leads some in scholarship to assert that no one has yet been saved until Jesus's return.

Hence, a major portion of the academy has no developed theology for Jesus from death to resurrection. The critical historical approach limits acceptance of apocalyptic understanding of the biblically supported elements of the *Christus victor* view of atonement. The academy usually options for the atonement language of Hebrews as either legal, ethical, symbolic, or dramatic. In a casual conversation in the Hebrews research group at the meeting of the Evangelical Theological Society, I asked a Scholar often working in Hebrews, "Why do scholars not have any teaching about what Jesus might have done between the cross and fleshly resurrection?" His response was "I don't know, you will have to research that and find out." This project is part of an attempt to investigate that response.

Dr. David L. Allen, during supervision of my master's thesis, upon reviewing my cosmic mapping of a version of *Christus descendit ad inferno* based on the tabernacle, looked at the visual mapping and said, "Bill,

---

16. Rowland and Morray-Jones, *Mystery of God*, 169.

you have to figure out where your 'Jesus in Hades' fits on your model of the tabernacle in Hebrews." Nothing in Hebrews teaching about Jesus's death and atonement supported such a view with Jesus going into a lower region of Hades. His observation provided a major turning point from my early training in traditional cosmic-*field* oriented understanding (fig. 4) about heaven in relation to Jesus's spatial fulfillment of the gospel (appendix 1, fig. 1) that his believers follow (fig. 2).

The gospel is a process concerning the speech-action of God himself known as the word of God, conversation, the Christ, the seed, the promise, and the gospel that was fulfilled by Jesus, so that he might shepherd believers as his assembling church into the kingdom of God, now in the heaven. This canonical exploration of a handful of NT texts strongly supports the nodal point of continued spirit body living for open heavens in a concrete substance-reality for believers after death and judgment. Areas of future exploration regarding other NT authors in relation to the nodal points of the substance-realty of our living hope with the living God include Matthew's use of plural heavens, with special emphasis on the plural and singular juxtaposition in the model prayer. Another rich source of spatial understanding arises from Paul's discussion of the dead in 1 Thess 4:13–5:10 and his language about their present spatial-temporal status.

Many other first-century CE works provide future opportunities for further investigation into the spatial-temporal background about open heavens in contrast to the now prevalent views toward closed-heaven realities that have dominated scholarship over the last one hundred years. Surveys of noncanonical literature available in the first century CE may further elaborate upon postmortem views and support plural heavens. This would include the spatial statements contained in the Testament of Levi in relation to other pseudepigraphic and apocryphal writings, the works of Philo, the writing of Josephus, and appraisal of the DDS.

Excursus B explores in depth a major example of numerous missteps that shift the first-century CE, spatial-temporal trajectory of death, judgment, intercession, and salvation—earthward. Among those so educated, the language of approach and entrance into heaven now stands in a lowered expectation for an escalated final endpoint of a kingdom on earth (fig. 4).

Excursus B

Avoiding Missteps—An Example of a Detour toward Other Place(s) from Heaven
Martin Luther's Misstep after Five Hundred Years

INTRODUCTION

For successful running, it is important to avoid missteps in accidentally going off the well-marked course by studying the route, wearing proper attire, and adequately preparing oneself. Many a runner has missed a turn, under or over dressed for race conditions, chosen poor equipment, or failed to rest, hydrate, and eat properly before the race, only to lose precious time and waste valuable resources. The Pastor exhorts his audience, "Having laid oneself of every weight and the easily ensnaring sin" (12:1). Believers should prepare well, follow proper signage, and remove any choices that might hinder success. In our heavenly calling while running the race to Jesus, we should evaluate and remove errant misinterpretations that create detours away from a correct conversation concerning the Son's speech recorded in the Letter to the Hebrews.

Do perceived optional themes easily fit coherently the rest of the message, or do they uncomfortably seem to fit another conversation? The question about thematic coherence introduces the trajectory of needed research for greater understanding of the missteps of others. This is not to condemn but to create an awareness of the pitfalls that distort the voice of God's speaking. Any student of God's word can make missteps. Forty years of chart versions support a personal learning curve in listening often to people of God more than the God of the people.

Within a few centuries of the writing of Hebrews, interpreters flip the spatial destiny of hope and thereby relegate the sermon into a collection of proof texts. The cultural theological and political change, from Jesus's promise to build an unseen kingdom now assembling in heaven, to a kingdom expected on the earth, flattens salvific expectation to ancient, often surfacing, alternative traditions (see appendix 1, fig. 4). The growth of this inverse hope accelerates quickly over a second-century CE reaction to heretical missteps concerning access while living into the heavenly spiritual realm.

Early third- to fourth-century CE political anxieties that arise from contemplation about a true spiritual kingdom other than Rome, especially after leaving its long tradition of celestial gods for an organized state Christianity, solidify the change. In Heb 9:28, the early fifth-century CE Latin Bible translation of Jerome still preserves correctly the second position option of the ordinal *secundo* for Jesus present ministry.[1] God's voice can still be heard. However, the popular cosmic-*field* tensions pressure the elders of the speech of God to rationally collapse the present ministry of Jesus into creedal statements regarding his people for an afterlife more compatible with a Greco-Roman underworld (Hades) that rationally anticipates a delay for perceived improvement back to original earthly conditions. Salvation now is from the depths of Sheol and hell, rather than prompt heavenly expectation.[2]

The elders adopt a less threatening method of allegorical interpretation, with no realistic links about heavenly concepts. This approach uncontrollably escalates rational earthly antitypes without regard for the corresponding true types of heavenly reality. Also, a perceived mandate for earthy sovereign rule over the salvation of others through authority by God upon the authorized state-church heavily influences the development of many strange evolving ideas when listening to God's speech regarding what happens in the afterlife after death.[3] Jesus's flesh and blood,

---

1. *DVNT*, "Secondo," 107. Harden glosses "secondly, in second place."

2. Myers, *Apostles' Creed*, 79–84. Cf. MacCulloch, *Harrowing of Hell*; Kay, "He Descended into Hell," 117–29; Zahn, *Apostles' Creed*.

3. Cf. Bass, *Battle for the Keys*. Bass comments that Augustine thought only infidels rejected the view of Christ's decent in hell (1). In his defense of this tradition, Bass documents that it was the fourteenth century until documented rejection is found again.

as bodily proof of resurrection, soon mystically embodies the salvific sacraments and personifies a delayed endpoint after death for a complete salvation with an expectation of resuscitation for return to fleshly bodies.[4] Also, the OT concept for completion in heaven by transfer to a whole body of the spirit and soul rationally downgrades to various speculations about an inferior, postmortem, intermediate-state, while waiting for resurrection in the second coming and a general judgment in establishment of the expected final earthly kingdom.[5] By the Middle Ages entrance into heaven is possible, but only for the pious and faithful or those who have fulfilled penance for their sin in purgatory.

The salvific corrections of the Reformation returned to the importance of God's speech over the now long held traditions. However, those listening to God's speech, still retain the collapsed foundation for earthly kingdom ideals with no settled conception about the present fate of the dead in Christ. Martin Luther in German and other German to English language translators, who follow the lead of other German translators, foresee no problem with translating nearly all Greek texts with the plural heavens as singular against their Latin text used for over one thousand years that allowed the hearing in God's speech about plural heavens in visible and invisible realms.

The philosophical strain of empiricism and rationalism upon faith in the unseen substance-realities mentioned by the Pastor, inspired new philosophical terms of transcendent and supernatural. Much worse, the long neglect of contemplation about heavenly substance-reality results in a lack of descriptive equivalents in modern languages that produces translations with word meanings foreign to the context of Hebrews. For many who study these matters, the confusion supports evidence for the

---

4. Finney, *Resurrection, Hell, and the Afterlife*. Finney argues for OT, STL, and early Christian understanding as a postmortem existence as the soul, with the physical body later becoming a point of theological orthodoxy.

5. Hendriksen, *Bible on the Life Hereafter*, 58. Hendriksen comments, "Never can it be emphasized strongly enough that the redeemed in heaven between the moment of death and that of the bodily resurrection have not yet attained to ultimate glory. They are living in what is generally called 'the intermediate' state, not yet the final state. Though to be sure, they are serenely happy, their happiness is not yet complete." Cf. Gentry and Wellum, *Kingdom through Covenant*. Gentry and Wellum write, "The church—as God's new covenant–new creation people—is constituted now as a believing, regenerate people, although we await the fullness of what Christ inaugurated at his glorious return" (36–37). They envision the promises of salvation only consummate in a land return to an Edenic new heaven and earth (833). Cf. Gooder, *Heaven*, 91–100. Gooder options for the waiting of postmortem life in an undefined inferior state until later bodily flesh resurrection by delayed transformation until the second coming.

language of heaven in Hebrews as nothing but extended metaphor with no coherent view about God's house of all creation seen and unseen.[6] Scholars, in attempting to make sense of the past constructed antithetical straw men to justify traditional positions, now find themselves in opposition to open heavenly hope for people beyond worship and praise.[7]

Nevertheless, from the time of the circulation of Hebrews, nonacademic believers still accept by faith that the heavenly promises of God's speech are truth. The common Christian believes that at death believers will in a very short while be met by Jesus and enter heaven. Also, in the afterlife of continual living there is reconnection with some family ties.[8]

This is true, at least, until corrected by one trained in the now orthodox traditions inherited from those before them. Many people desiring to better educate themselves to serve God, eventually turn from hearing the speech of God to hearing the speech and approved methodology of leaders claiming to possess the true conversation about God's speech. It boils down to the same problem that the Pastor attempts to correct among his listeners. Rather than follow the traditions of the Sinaitic covenant relationships, which were obsolete due to Jesus's fulfillment and changes in the structure of the unseen eternal-places of heaven, the Pastor entreats his listeners to listen to God's speech about the new covenant relationships. They should look to the elders who speak the speech-action of the Word of God by Jesus as the Christ in both his onetime offering and his present ministry to those approaching at death and judgment.

The chapter 5 conclusion lists an orchestra of evidence related to missteps that distort the speech of God about the present anticipation

6. E.g., Allen, *Grounded in Heaven*. Allen follows N. T. Wright in polemic against "Christian hope in terms of 'going to heaven,' of a salvation that is essentially away from this world" (3). Rather, he in line with Reformed theologians offers a distinctly Protestant account of the ascetic calling to both heavenly-mindedness and self-denial (cover).

7. E.g., Moore, *Open Sanctuary*. In an ironic move, Moore, after rejecting open heavens for people in his many previous publications discussed in this project, now uses the term "open heavens" in relation to Jesus and the changes in the "heaven tabernacle," so-called, previously discussed, but still considers entrance by God's people postmortem as delay and detour to only the second coming in flesh resuscitation. At the time of manuscript completion, Moore's complete project is not yet published. Nicholas and I have exchanged thoughts about one of his papers and I sent charts and copies of my earlier work in years past. I appreciate his kindness to review his chapter on Hebrews before publication release. It was exciting to read many common conclusions about Jesus's ministry in his new work, even if our structures differ with his "heavenly temple" against my "tabernacle of/in the heavens" and my prompt ministry of Jesus after death at judgment in transformation to spiritual bodies to bring his people into heaven.

8. Lang, *Meeting in Heaven*.

of believers in seeing Jesus appear promptly at death and judgment. As an example of this line of needed research, excursus B provides a more modern example of another major misstep concerning the translation of the Greek plurals of "heaven" (ουρανος) initially by Martin Luther that is maintained today.

THE BIBLICAL TEXT ABOUT THE HEAVENLY PLACES IN THE OT AND LXX

The structure of the Letter to the Hebrews is built upon exegesis of the OT and in unity with it.[9] OT text about the heavens is centered upon the Hebrew word "the heavens" (השמים), which for unknown reasons is in the dual form of things in pairs. While not denying the possibility of a specific structural existence for creation, from descriptions in the OT many scholars feel there is not enough information given about referents to propose a distinct structure.[10]

---

9. Guthrie, *Structure of Hebrews*, 121–24.

10. E.g., Houtman, *Der Himmel im Alten Testament*, 283–317. Regarding the OT worldview and ideology, Houtman writes, "In our view, it is not possible to draw the conclusion from the information that the OT gives us that ancient Israel had a generally accepted, systematically structured theory about the origin, structure and endowment of the cosmos surrounding man in all it sharing exists" (283). Later he assumes the same conclusion for his arguments, stating, "Although the OT does not give us a uniform picture of how the coming into being and existing and of the structure and equipment of the cosmos" (299). Houtman does not say that there is not a structure to the creation of the cosmos, only which in his opinion there is not enough information in the OT to draw one theory generally accepted by ancient Israel. He rejects purpose of any underlying specific literal cosmic structure for reasons of a greater than scientific purpose for cosmological statements, saying, "The purpose of an investigation of the Old Testament statements about the cosmos is therefore not purely scientific, but goes far beyond that" (317). Houtman goes on to set up a fallacy of false disjunction by assuming if one could understand the order of creation, he would lose his awe of God. Cf. Carson, *Exegetical Fallacies*, 90. Contrary to Houtman, both a heavenly topography and an awe of God are possible in authorial intent. Also, Houtman's common difficulty with making sense of the biblical data does not mean a literal pattern does not exist or that God has not revealed it. Cf. Wright, "Biblical versus Israelite Images," 59–75. Wright argues against a unified view of Israel for the cosmos and follows the theory for late Judean editors of the OT. He concludes, "Based on evidence from both texts and artifacts suggests that the depictions the Hebrew Bible offers of the heavenly realm on the one hand and what ancient Israelites and Judeans actually believed on the other hand may have been very different" (60). Wright follows multiple historical fallacies in his rejection, the worst being uncontrolled historical reconstruction. Cf. Carson, *Exegetical Fallacies*, 131.

It appears that the Pastor's version of the OT was the LXX.[11] As is seen to follow in modern translation for the referent for heaven, the translators of the LXX evidently found no consistent number for the translation of "heaven(s)" (השמים). In the LXX, the Greek οὐρανός (*ouranos*) is used 567 times, translates singular 180 times and plural 453 times, making the plural form 80 percent of the translation occurrences. Therefore, the OT syntax from the referent heaven alone would probably not determine for the Pastor a specific creation cartography for the background spatial work of Jesus as high priest.[12] His LXX understanding about heaven is probably enhanced from multiple other sources, those being the OT typological experiences, direct prophecy from the Holy Spirit, and the recent explosion of first-century CE revelation in the teachings of Christ and the apostles, some of which is contained in the NT record.

THE BIBLICAL TEXT ABOUT HEAVENLY PLACES IN GREEK

In classical and secular Hellenistic Greek, the syntactical form for οὐρανός is always singular in number.[13] In Semitic literature beginning in the fourth century BCE the syntactical form for plural οὐρανός appears to increase in frequency until it is an established option of Semitic views of creation in the day of Jesus.[14] Jesus would use the plural pattern when speaking to or teaching his disciples, but the singular when speaking to forces of opposition.[15] Further, he in his teachings at times used plural-singular juxtaposition (cf. Matt 6:9–10; 24:29–31).

In the NT, a form of οὐρανός appears as text 273 times, with 90 plurals (33 percent) and 183 singulars. The text of οὐρανός is noted 10 times in Hebrews, 7 as plurals and 3 as singulars for 70 percent plurals.

In Hebrews each singular text appears for a particular realm (see table 9): (1) heaven itself of the combined holy place and holy of holies

---

11. Lindars, *Theology of the Letter to the Hebrews*, 124–25.

12. This does not deny that one does not exist. Each decision by OT authors for use of singular and plural under inspiration of the Holy Spirit would have to be evaluated in its context before such determination could be made for an existing unified creation cartography.

13. BDAG, "Οὐρανός," 737–739. Similar findings are noted by other lexical information.

14. Wright, *Early History of Heaven*, 185–86.

15. Pennington, *Heaven and Earth*, 145.

(Heb 9:24) that God created with Jesus's achieved atonement for heavenly entrance, and (2) "the stars of heaven" (11:12) in the "world" (κόσμος) or a temporary heaven that can be shaken (12:26) outside of the substance-reality of the eternal-places of heaven. For the plural use, one text refers to the two temporary realms of the starry heaven and the holy-places (1:10). The other six speak about all heavens, both visible and invisible collectively (4:14; 7:26; 8:1; 9:23; 12:23, 25).

THE PRE-REFORMATION TEXT ABOUT HEAVENLY PLACES

The text for the plural use of οὐρανός maintains significant statistical accuracy for nearly 1,500 years.[16] This stability maintains itself through Greek manuscript copies, over 1,100 years of copies of the translation of the Latin Vulgate, 56 years of seventeen publications of early pre-Luther German translations, and over 100 years of English translations before 1522.

GREEK MANUSCRIPTS COPIES

Of the ninety uses of the plural in the over five thousand known manuscripts, nearly all witnesses have variants involving the plural of "heaven" (οὐρανός). Most of these are a shortened form of οὐρανός that maintain the plural number. Of these variants, only twelve of the ninety texts with the plural οὐρανός change the plural to singular.[17] Seven of these changes were for only one witness and most of these were very late copies. This calculates as 87 percent of the plural references were never changed and 94 percent never more than once. Only about 1 percent of the over five thousand manuscripts with plural texts of οὐρανός were ever questioned in change by those utilizing the copies of the Greek manuscripts concerning referents for heavens (table 12). As is now known, 94 percent of the plural texts of οὐρανός never changed in many years of copying the Greek text. This even includes the Byzantine text-type, which is well

---

16. There are variants where changes were at times made from plural to singular in Greek manuscripts, but these are few. These occasional witnesses show the continued conflict in creation views against a plural topography of the heavens among believers due to theological presuppositions.

17. Matt 3:17 (1); 5:12 (1); 6:9 (9); 13:52 (1); 18:10 (1), 19:21 (12); Mark 1:11 (1); Luke 18:22 (9); Heb 12:25 (18); Eph 3:15 (1); 6:9 (5); 1 Thess 1:10 (1). Parenthetical contents provide the number of text witnesses about the plural to singular change.

known for its trend for distinctive readings away from the original text.[18] There are even some texts that οὐρανός was changed from singular to plural revealing an ongoing heavenly debate since the early autographs.[19]

While beyond the intent of this excursus to evaluate every textual variant of the plural forms of ουρανος, a few examples are discussed to reveal the ongoing heavenly debate. For example, in Matt 6:9 the phrase "in the heavens" (τοῖς οὐρανοῖς) is preferred by all known manuscript copies with the exception that "in heaven" (τω ουρανω) is noted in the Middle Egyptian or Mesokemic and the *Didache*.[20] The NA28 text is preferred as the original text. The singular heaven in the *Didache* may reflect an alternative early heavenly discussion close to the production of the autographs.

Table 12—Early Greek Manuscript and Latin Translator Accuracy of the Greek New Testament Plurals of ουρανος

Source	Percent Accuracy of Ninety NT Plurals
Text Reference Known Greek Manuscript Textual Variations[21]	87 percent
Total Manuscripts Word Accuracy	99 percent
Latin Vulgate circ. 405 CE	98 percent
Latin Vulgate Manuscript Textual Variations[22]	100 percent

Another example is found in Matt 18:10, where the phrase "in heavens" (ἐν οὐρανοῖς) is replaced with sg. "in heaven" (εν τω ουρανω).[23] The change from plural to singular again reflects questions about plural heavens in the theological presuppositions of biblical readers due to difficulty with the conception of angels as omnipresent in multiple heavens as the Father is omnipresent. The plurality of the verse is more a statement of

---

18. Black and Dockery, *New Testament Criticism and Interpretation*, 107.
19. NA28App, "Matthäus 18,18," 58.
20. NA28App, "Matthäus 6,9," 14.
21. In known manuscripts only thirteen have changes from plural to singular. This statistic was determined from evaluation of known textual variants from the following resources. Metzger, *Textual Commentary*; NA28App; HolGNTAp; and *CNTTS*.
22. This statistic is determined from variations listed in VULAp.
23. NA28App, "Matthäus 18,10," 57.

angelic service in the current multiple realms rather than transcendence. For some, the heavens needed to be closed, even to angels.

Also, in Matt 19:21 the word "heavens" (οὐρανοῖς) is replaced with "heaven" (ουρανω).[24] A similar variant is found in Luke 18:22 where the phrase "in the heavens" (ἐν [τοῖς] οὐρανοῖς) is replaced with the sg. "heaven" (ουρανω).[25] However, the "[τοῖς]" bracketed article indicate that the textual critics are not entirely convinced of its authenticity. Another related exchange is in Heb 12:25 where the word "from the heavens" (ἀπ' οὐρανῶν) is replaced with the sg. "from heaven" (οὐρανοῦ).[26] This supports a strong possibility that future eschatological promises are often changed to singular due to theological presuppositions. The dominant amillennial view in the early Reformation conflates the eternal new heaven and earth promises (cf. Rev 21–22) with the ministerial rewards in the temporary millennium. Once conflated, adherents cannot conceive of the continued existence of plural heavens when treasure is given to believers for faithful service. Early German translators felt the same tension.

A final example is Eph 3:15 where the word "heavens" (οὐρανοῖς) is replaced with the sg. "heaven" (οὐρανῷ).[27] The rejection of the idea that at this time the families of God's creation are currently spread across multiple heavens leads many to change the plural text to singular.

LATIN TRANSLATION

The Latin Vulgate used by churches since the fifth century CE also properly translated the Latin *caelum* ("heaven, sky") syntactically correct to maintain a plural and singular contrast (table 12). For example, in Matthew's rendition of the model prayer, it first says, "Pater noster qui in caelis" (Our Father who in heavens; Matt 6:9 VUL) with *caelis* as the dat. pl. for "heavens." It follows with "in caelo et in terra" (in heaven and in earth; Matt 6:10 VUL) with *caelo* as dat. sg. for "heaven." For over one thousand years, there were no known major variants for the plural or singular in the Latin text for this hot spot in Matthew for Jesus's plural-singular juxtaposition (cf. Matt 6:9–10 VUL). Of the ninety uses of the plural, Weber and Gryson mention only one known manuscript from

---

24. NA28App, "Matthäus 19,21," 62.
25. NA28App, "Luke 18,22," 260.
26. NA28App, "Hebrews 12.25," 682.
27. NA28App, "Eph 3:15," 595.

sixth century CE Italy that has a plural to singular variation involving the plural of the Latin *caelum* for heaven.[28]

Table 13—Pre-Luther Greek Collated Textual Accuracy by Erasmus of the Greek New Testament Plurals of ουρανος

Source	Percent Accuracy of Ninety NT Plurals
Erasmus Latin-Greek 1516 CE	98 percent
Erasmus Latin-Greek 1519 CE	98 percent
Erasmus Latin-Greek 1522 CE	98 percent

Erasmus Greek-Latin Text

In the early sixteenth using mostly a half-dozen Byzantine minuscule texts, Desiderius Erasmus published a compiled Greek-Latin text.[29] Pre-Luther publications of the Greek-Latin were published 1516, 1519, and 1522. Erasmus's available manuscripts were incomplete, even requiring corrections, yet these were still significantly accurate for the text of the Greek plurals in the NT (table 13).[30] This accuracy is important, for as subsequently noted, Martin Luther is thought to have used Erasmus second edition for the translation of his 1522 September German NT.[31]

---

28. VULAp, "Rev 8:13." The copyist substituted the Latin genitive singular *caeli*, which usually refers to the heavenly region of the visible sky or stars for the dat. sg. neut. "midheaven" (μεσουρανήματι).

29. Metzger and Ehrman, *Text of the New Testament*, 148.

30. Metzger and Ehrman, *Text of the New Testament*, 145. The few places Erasmus has the grammatical singular substituted for plural are in two texts where manuscript variations (Matt 19:21; Luke 18:22) that today are no longer by textual criticism felt to be the original wording. Erasmus was one hundred percent true to the text that he could determine in available manuscripts to him. He often corrects and consciously chooses the older renderings as the most reliable.

31. Metzger and Ehrman, *Text of the New Testament*, 145. Cf. Tregelles, *Account of the Printed Text*, 22–23.

Table 14—Pre-Luther German and English Translator Accuracy of the Greek New Testament Plurals of ουρανος

Source	Percent Accuracy of Ninety NT Plurals
Wycliffe English 1430 CE	96 percent
German 1466 CE	92 percent
German 1474 CE	89 percent
German 1483 CE	89 percent
German 1490 CE	88 percent
German 1494 CE	87 percent
German 1507 CE	87 percent
German 1518 CE	87 percent

ENGLISH AND GERMAN

The best-known pre-Luther English translation is that of John Wycliffe (table 14). It is debated whether Wycliffe ever really translated a NT text.[32] Those scholars who knew him or his reputation that followed him definitely used the spirit of his name in a tradition of an English NT translation from the Latin Vulgate.[33] The translators were again significantly accurate.

The German translations also significantly maintain the text of the grammatical plural prior to Martin Luther (table 14). In a survey of seven of the seventeen known German translations from the Latin Vulgate that span fifty-six years, a preservation of the plural text for heaven is again noted.[34]

32. Evans, *John Wyclif*, 228–29. Cf. Milligan, *English Bible*, 10–11.

33. Milligan, *English Bible*, 16–17. Cf. González, *Story of Christianity*, 413.

34. Theological presuppositions that effect heavenly views had begun to influence pre-Luther translators to change the plural to the singular. The texts changed were usually those speaking of the "Father in the heavens" and those prophetically referencing some form of future rewards "in the heavens." "God the Father" in German theology of the day could only be conceived as dwelling in a singular heaven. Also, as mainly

These early German translations are divided into fourteen High German and three Low German texts.[35] The 1466, translated by an unknown scholar and printed by Johan Mentel, provides the base text used for the other printings to follow.[36] It is thought that Luther, while claiming to attempt to create a new fresh base text, may have utilized the previous German translations of 1474 and 1483 while at Wittenberg.[37]

REFORMATION TEXT OF BIBLICAL CREATION

For 1,500 years prior to Martin Luther, the Latin, English, German, and Greek texts used by Christians translated the plurals of "heavens" (οὐρανός) as naturally grammatically plural. Several factors appear to have influenced Luther, as a second-generation translator, in this syntactical choice.[38] First, there are the early amillennial theological presuppositions of Luther and other leaders of the Reformation.[39] Second, Luther for vernacular understanding for German popular idiom of the common

---

amillennial in fulfillment of the Parousia, these scholars conflated millennial prophecy with the eternal promises to follow. Since for these scholars, rewards were in the coming kingdom of the new heaven and earth, heaven as depicted in Rev 21–22 must be singular at that time of fulfillment of rewards. This inclination to change the text for theological reasons set the stage for Luther's massive changes regarding the plurals of "heaven" (οὐρανός). Luther did in excess to the text what his predecessors did in moderation.

35. Strand, *German Bibles before Luther*; Strand, *Early Low-German Bibles*; Prime, *Fifteenth Century Bibles*, 89–94.

36. Strand, *German Bibles before Luther*, 29–30.

37. Strand, *Luther's "September Bible" in Facsimile*, 7.

38. Gow, *Contested History of a Book*, 287, 298–300. Gow reveals how little is written in English scholarship since WWII about how Luther drew from a long history of German tradition of vernacular translation that provided the preconditions that help shape the Reformation.

39. The best source for the developing the synchronic theological presuppositions of the early Reformation and Luther that influenced the plural to singular change is found in the Augsburg Confession of Faith in 1530, which was written primarily by Luther. Schaff, *Creeds of Christendom*, 228–32. Also, Tappert, *Book of Concord the Confessions*, 38–39. Particularly important is "XVII. [The Return of Christ to Judgment] It is also taught among us that our Lord Jesus Christ will return on the last day for judgment and will raise up all the dead, to give eternal life and everlasting joy to believers and the elect but to condemn ungodly men and the devil to hell and eternal punishment. Rejected, therefore, are the Anabaptists who teach that the devil and condemned men will not suffer eternal pain and torment. Rejected, too, are certain Jewish opinions which are even now making an appearance, and which teach that, before the resurrection of the dead, saints and godly men will possess a worldly kingdom and annihilate all the godless" (brackets in the original).

person often changes the inspired text frequently exchanging accuracy.[40] Third, Luther was rejecting the Catholic doctrine of purgatory.[41] The result from these and perhaps other unknown factors influenced Luther to remove all but a few plurals (table 15).

POST-REFORMATION TEXT OF BIBLICAL SPATIAL CREATION

English Translations

It is interesting that after 1522 CE almost all subsequent English translations of οὐρανός omit the plural use (table 15). There is compelling evidence that William Tyndale and Miles Cloverdale were significantly influenced by the work of Martin Luther.[42] Also, since both Tyndale's and

---

40. Evans, *Roots of the Reformation*. Evans comments about Martin Luther, "But he was also, like other translators into the European vernaculars at the time, tempted to ensure that the meaning reflected the reforming theology they were embracing.... When he was challenged, he said it was his translation and his business. He wanted his translation to make doctrinal points, to speak to the people of Germany not only in their own language but in language that conveyed a faithful (Lutheran) interpretation." Cf. Bluhm, *Martin Luther, Creative Translator*, 130–31. Bluhm writes, "Luther's procedure as a translator is clear. First, he establishes, to the best of his ability and upon his conscience, the meaning of the text before him. Then he tries hard to find the most suitable, idiomatic German garb for it." Bluhm further explains, "In accordance with his own principle that a translation must in no way tamper with the text, Luther shows that he merely expressed, in the best German at his disposal, the intention of the original author." Cf. Beekman and Callow, *Translating the Word of God*, 24–25. Also, Strand, *Luther's "September Bible" in Facsimile*, 4–6.

41. Luther, *Luther's Works*, 362. Luther writes in January 1522, "On purgatory I have this opinion: I do not think, as the sophists dream, that it is a certain place, nor do I think that all who remain outside heaven or hell are in purgatory. (Who could assert this, since [the departed souls] could sleep suspended between heaven, earth, hell, purgatory, and all else, just as could happen with the living, when they are in a deep sleep?)." Luther was entertaining the doctrine of soul sleep as part of his heavenly view. These soul sleep ideas caused his rejection of purgatory. With one singular heaven for Luther, there was no real place for purgatory. Luther rejected this doctrine of soul sleep later in life.

42. Bluhm, *Martin Luther, Creative Translator*, 170–71, 181. It appears Martin Luther's idiomatic language style that fueled the Reformation greatly influenced early English translators of Tyndale and Coverdale. Bluhm writes concerning Tyndale, "In spite of the fundamental verbal independence of Tyndale's rendering, there are a number of passages where he saw fit to follow, beyond general method of Luther's translation, actual phrases and words found in the German New Testament." Cf. Bruce, *History of the Bible*, 24–36. Bruce notes that the later translation of Tyndale derived from the 1522 Greek text of Erasmus. However, in Bluhm's opinion of Cloverdale,

Cloverdale's native language being English, the highly inflected grammatical form of the German language made it difficult for Englishmen to accurately translate Luther's German text. Luther's desire was to begin a fresh German text rather than use the established German text that was followed from 1466.[43] Regarding the text of the plurals of "heaven" (οὐρανός), Luther made radical innovative grammatical changes that made it difficult for either Tyndale or Cloverdale as Englishman to easily perceive the plural from the German text.[44]

---

he states, "There should never have been any doubt that Cloverdale's translation of the Bible leans heavily on German sources; the translator himself established this fact by indicating on the original title-page that his English Bible was 'faithfully and truly translated out of Douche and Latyn.'" Also, Cheney, "Sources of Tyndale's New Testament," 40. Cheney reviews of a sampling of 915 variations between texts available to Tyndale from Erasmus, Wycliffe, and Luther. He concludes, "First, That Tindale's [sic] Testaments show traces of the influence of the four versions, Wycliffe's, Vulgate, Luther's, Erasmus. Second, that these traces of agreement, quite inconsiderable as regards Wycliffe and the Vulgate, show the influence of Erasmus far more than of Luther. Third. That of the versions by Erasmus, the Latin, as well as the Greek, was followed and the Latin, at times, preferred." In the sampling, Tyndale agrees with Luther alone 19 percent of the time. He also agrees with Luther and either Erasmus or Wycliffe 49 percent of the time. Nevertheless, rather than following the Greek and Latin, both Tyndale and Cloverdale followed Luther's German rendition of the translation of the plural οὐρανοῖς "heavens." The rendering better fit the cosmic-*field* constricted theology of the day.

43. Strand, *Luther's "September Bible" in Facsimile*, 7. This decision may have been by the fact while at the castle in Wartburg; Luther may have not had copies of German translations. It is felt by scholarly evaluation that when later in Wittenberg, where he continued and edited his work, he used the 1474 and 1490 versions to assist in determining the best German vernacular word choices.

44. An examination of the Luther's September Testament reveals several grammatical changes to support existing German theological presuppositions that may be confusing to native English. First, the plurals of "heaven" (οὐρανός) in combination with the kingdom were compounded from *das reich der Himmel* ("the kingdom of the heavens") to *das Himmelreich* ("the kingdom of heaven"). In the former *der Himmel* is gen. pl. but the latter is neut. sg. Second, he follows the early German translator position for a singular heaven in the text of "the Father in heaven." Also, in many of the plural texts, he either drops the article completely or contracts the article with the preposition, which increases the difficulty of determining singular and plural from the German text. Where Luther does have an article, almost all articles are changed to sg. for "heaven" (οὐρανός). This near duplication by Tyndale significantly demonstrates that while Tyndale had accurate information from Greek and Latin, at times he preferentially followed the German text of Luther. Cloverdale's work did not use the Greek or Latin. He was dependent upon the translations in English by Tyndale, in German by Luther and Zwingli, and the existing Latin Vulgate. McKim, *Historical Handbook of Major*, 181.

Table 15—Luther German and Post-Luther English Translator Accuracy of the Greek New Testament Plurals of ουρανος

Source	Percent Accuracy Ninety NT Plurals
Luther German 1522 CE	11 percent
Luther German 1545 CE	9 percent
Tyndale English Cologne 1525 CE[45]	0 percent
Tyndale English 1534 CE	13 percent
Cloverdale English 1535 CE	11 percent
Geneva English 1560 CE	14 percent
AKJV English 1611 CE	19 percent
ASV English 1901 CE	28 percent
NASB English 1995 CE	26 percent

The use by Cloverdale of both Tyndale and Luther providentially influenced the base text for the English Geneva translation in 1560 when Cloverdale was temporarily exiled to Geneva during Mary's reign.[46] The impact upon the 1611 AKJV by Luther, Tyndale, and Cloverdale is also attested by the significant agreement in the grammatical changes of οὐρανός (ouranos) from Luther to Tyndale to Cloverdale then to later English translations. The AKJV became the base text for all subsequent translations to present. This explains the loss of the text for the possibility of plural heavens in the present separated creation.

MODERN LEXICAL AND DICTIONARY FORMS

Scholarly works and commentaries deal very little with the theological reasoning behind this revolutionary change of the plural heavens to the

---

45. This fragment only contains NT text through Matt 22. Gruber, *Truth*. This first edition resembles Luther's 1522 German in every way including Luther's notes except for minor variations. Later editions due to criticism of making England Lutheran probably influenced more originality. With the 1525 as a base text, Tyndale never retracted the copied grammatical change by Luther for heaven from plural to singular but in a few texts.

46. Gruber, *Truth*.

singular heaven.⁴⁷ It remains an unchallenged segment of text within textual criticism and lexicography. About this change, Pennington states, "Most scholars conclude that there is *no difference* in meaning between singular and plural forms, a few studies have argued for the possibility of some pattern."⁴⁸ However, a diachronic survey of modern lexicons and word dictionaries reveals a scholarly drift from a subjunctive possibly, to the indicative reality, to "no difference," with preference now for the diachronic classical Greek singular meaning. For example, concerning οὐρανός, Louw and Nida comment, "Singular or plural; there seems to be *no semantic distinction* in NT literature between the singular and plural forms."⁴⁹ Pennington changes the words of Louw and Nida from "no semantic distinction" to "no difference." Louw and Nida's work published in 1988 is probably not being read correctly here by Pennington. They are not saying, as many read them, that the semantic sense of the word οὐρανός ("heaven"), whether singular or plural, always has only one meaning as singular. Such a position, without proper investigation, would contradict Louw's work in lexical semantics.⁵⁰

47. For a general critique concerning the tradition of lexicography dating back to the sixteenth century, see Lee, *History of New Testament Lexicography*. Lee documents the less satisfactory features of lexicons including a strong reliance on predecessors, the influence of translations and publishers, and shortcomings in traditional methodology. Lee warns, "Lexicons play a pivotal role in all other subjects, yet they are commonly taken for granted and trusted as though they had no faults. Greater awareness of what still needs to be done is desirable" (xi).

48. Pennington, *Heaven and Earth*, 132 (italics mine).

49. Cf. L&N, "οὐρανός," 1:xxiii (italics mine). A search of this Lexicon reveals only two other words are semantically treated in this same manner. Cf. L&N, "ἡμέρα," 1:173; L&N, "ὕψος," 1:3.

50. See Louw, *Semantics of New Testament Greek*. When one looks at Louw's works in semantics, a statement that reads "no difference" contradicts his principles set forth. When Louw's arguments have been read correctly, this statement that the authors of the NT cannot mean literal plural heavens in their writings when using the plural form, does not harmonize with the requirement for such a statement in the principles of semantics he develops. Following Louw's text, to make such a global statement he would have to evaluate all uses of the word semantically to include the author's arguments (88), polysemy (40), context (15), and relation to other words (67) to determine what the author means. Yet, this author is not aware of such a work that does what is semantically required to make such a global canonical statement that discounts an author's grammatical choices in possible intended meaning. Also, in Hebrews, it appears one can argue that the Pastor does have in mind a plural heavenly background that is based on the tabernacle language in symbolic reference to the heavens and Jesus's priestly work. It thus appears without proper study of the entire NT, the "no difference" read into Louw-Nida's statement is an unsupported personal theological bias that is typically uncharacteristic of Louw's work on semantics. Pennington's interpretative position

Other lexical contributions by scholars are gentler on this semantic position with recognition that first-century CE Jewish views include plural heavens. Consider the work Hans Bietenhard in the *NIDNT*. In the OT and late Judaism, he recognizes two possibilities. First, that "it is possible for Yahweh to take chosen people to himself in heaven (Gen 5:24; 2 Kgs 2:11; cf. Ps 73:24)."[51] (2) Second, "In later writings the frequency of plur. increases considerably, indicating that the ancient oriental conception of several heavens had begun to have effect (2 Macc 15:23; 3 Macc 2:2; Wis 9:10; Tob 8:5, etc.)."[52] He further observes that to avoid the name of God, late Judaism used the "substitutes" of "heaven" and even "place" (2 Macc 3:18; 4:10; 12:15), and that God dwelled in heaven with "angels" (4 Macc 4:11; Luke 2:13) and "children of God" (2 Macc 7:34).[53] However, concerning his evaluation of the NT, Bietenhard concludes, "There is clearly no attempt to give definitive instruction about the geography of heaven as in certain Rab. writings (cf. above OT 3). In this context it is striking that there is never any mention of several heavens but only of one. The only passage in the NT which, in agreement with Rab. teaching, speaks of three heavens is 2 Cor. 12:2–4, but we are not given any more precise information."[54]

While technically a correct assessment, Bietenhard ignores the basic evidence of the NT Greek plurals in combination with other spatial-temporal contextual indicators. It may be that he considers the plural heavenly places as late developments, rather than natural differences of emphasis that arise from various genre and contexts in the OT that flow through to the NT. Often forgotten is the observation that no record exists among first-century CE available rhetoric that reacts antithetically to the prominent, plural-heaven, theological views.[55] Where contextually indicated, first-century CE writers universally embrace plural heavenly

---

is not supported by the works of other Lexicons, which do admit the possible sense meaning of Semitic plural heavens.

51. Bietenhard, "οὐρανός," 191.
52. Bietenhard, "οὐρανός," 191.
53. Bietenhard, "οὐρανός," 191.
54. Bietenhard, "οὐρανός," 192.
55. The common use of referents with semantic meaning for multiple heavens must have been familiar to the disciples of the first century CE. Cf. Gooder, *Only the Third Heaven?*; Weeks, "Cosmology in Historical Context," 283–93; Wright, "Biblical versus Israelite Images"; Barker, "Beyond the Veil." Gooder, Weeks, Wright, and Barker give excellent discussion of early heavenly imagery and apocalyptic mysticism apart from canonical Scripture. Cf. Yohann, "Cosmological Aspects in the Sermon."

places as part of their descriptive background language. The only NT record of a first-century CE religious group who probably rejected such views are the Sadducees, who found themselves on the wrong side of Jesus's teachings.

In the *TDNT*, Helmut Traub recognizes the importance of the Greek LXX in contribution to "the *status contructus* form and the plural use" of "heaven" (οὐρανός).[56] Regarding the NT, he stresses the importance for the concept that the messianic work of Jesus serves to bear testimony to "the opening of the heavens" (cf. Matt 3:16; John 1:51).[57] He is probably correct when he writes, "Since there are many reasons for the use of the plur. οὐρανοί in the individual NT writings, one cannot lay down a general rule which applies to the NT as a whole."[58] However, this negation for a general statement about all plural uses does not rule out plural heavenly places supported by proper context that must be evaluated on an individual basis. This is especially true if the only evidence for rejection of the first-century CE option for plural heavenly places is tension with later traditional, cosmic-*field* constrained theology.[59]

In ABD, Mitchell Reddish, without evidence, claims, "In the NT both the singular and plural forms occur with no difference in meaning."[60] As noted, the work has not been done to make such a global semantic statement of the NT. This statement by Reddish in 1992 may be strongly influenced in the popular misread of Louw, who published in 1988.

Cremer's *Biblico-Theological Lexicon* in 1878 reveals hints concerning the modern solidification of Cartesian views among scholars by influences of liberal theology upon lexical glosses and comments.[61] Since

---

56. Traub, "Οὐρανός," 510–11.

57. Traub, "Οὐρανός," 529–30. Jesus's baptism that was commended by the Father in heaven served typologically as an antitype. His immersion in the Jordan depicted his death, burial, and resurrection. This pictorial event symbolized that the expected offering by Jesus would be judged as pleasing to the Father and would result in the opening of the heavens to him. These events correspond to the type fulfilled by Jesus's actual offering after sacrificial death, his judgment as righteous on approach to God, and entrance to the Father that this project explores in chapters 2–4.

58. Traub, "Οὐρανός," 534–35.

59. Traub references without critique other scholarly conversation for the speculation that the NT plural heavens arose under the influence of Hellenistic Gnosticism. Traub, "Οὐρανός," 534n321. This early twentieth century view has been highly critiqued as a scholarly straw man that enabled rejection of Jewish views about plural heavens.

60. Reddish, "Heaven," 390.

61. *BTLNTG*, "Οὐρανός, 'O,'" 467. Cremer writes, "οὐρανός, ὁ, heaven, Hebrew שָׁמַיִם, *probably* a plural of abstraction. . . . Hence also the plural, unused in profane Greek, οἱ

Cremer is not sure, he correctly uses subjective wording that contains "probably," "may," "hardly suppose," and "hardly," since no major studies have been done to support the growing theological assumptions about the heavens. If the plural is proven as *always* an abstraction with no concrete reality, his revealed subjective assumptions would hold true. In the next century, Louw-Nida takes Cremer's statements from subjective to the indicative absolute truth. Cosmic-*field* limited theology has little room in lexical glosses for possible plural heavens referenced in the first-century CE STL and NT.

The lexical and dictionary support just discussed concerning the modification and translation of the plural heavens as singular may be strongly influenced by the fact that most past Greek scholars traditionally learned Greek usage from the classics and may have incurred a modern Classical-Hellenistic Greek syncretism.[62] For example Traub remarks, "Οὐρανός, in class. Gk. almost without exception in the sing., always means 'heaven.' The word always has a double reference. Heaven is the firmament, the arch of heaven over the earth. But it is also that which embraces all things in the absolute."[63]

BDAG, after listing the classical references of heaven, recognizes, "The concept of more than one heaven (the idea is Semitic).... But it is not always possible to decide with certainty just where the idea is really alive and where it simply survives in a formula."[64] The slight disagreement between these camps of lexicographers demonstrates an important point raised by Moises Silva; lexicographers get their word meanings from other dictionaries.[65] While dependent on lexicons, the student of

---

οὐρανοί (perhaps = all that is heaven), which cannot, however, be urged in proof of any opinion concerning heaven. The only expression (we may here remark) which implies a plurality of heavens (2 Cor. xii. 2, ἕως τρίτου οὐρανοῦ) *may* itself have been derived from this use of the plural.... The singular and plural are uses so similarly and interchangeably, that we can *hardly suppose* any difference of meaning between them." Later he writes, "As to the relation of the plural to the singular, there is *hardly* any difference traceable" (italics mine).

62. Young, *Intermediate New Testament Greek*, vii. Young notes, "Many grammars assume that what a particular structure meant before the Koine Greek period dictates what it means when used by New Testament writers. The historical school therefore tends to be prescriptive, a notion shunned by modern linguists. The descriptive school, on the other hand, recognizes that usage in context determines meaning, not prior usage."

63. Traub, "Οὐρανός," 497–98.

64. BDAG, "Οὐρανός," 738.

65. Silva, *Biblical Words and Their Meaning*, 137–38. He asks, "How did Bauer

biblical meaning must realize the dictionaries of these men are heavily dependent upon the descriptive school anchored in glosses of possible meanings determined primarily from Classical to Hellenistic Greek. Silva mentions insight by Edwin Hatch who authored essays on the matter in the late nineteenth century. Hatch was concerned about lack of acknowledgment about differences in biblical and Hellenistic Greek.[66] The work of Louw and Nida offers a major improvement in lexicographic form.[67] Louw and Nida begin by reminding those who use lexicons that the NT Greek is not a distinct form independent of Hellenistic Greek.[68]

It seems the strong diachronic influence of the classical Greek literature yields bias for a singular "heaven" in the face of an obvious natural grammatical plural. It is almost unanimously translated singular from the highly accurate compiled original text into English, even in rejection of the acknowledgment of first-century CE synchronic Semitic ideas of plural heavens in STL and the NT. It is interesting that in modern semantics the usual order is synchronic meaning above diachronic meaning in syntactical choices.[69] However, in the translation of the plural of ουρανος for the last five hundred years, the traditional diachronic influences still

---

then come up with his meanings? We fool ourselves if we do not admit that, by and large, he got them from previous dictionaries. The earliest lexicographers in turn got their meaning from existing 'implicit dictionaries'—information stored in grammar books and literal translations or simply preserved as part of bilingual oral tradition. This somewhat obvious point is emphasized to disabuse any readers of the tacit belief (possibly shared by some lexicographers) that dictionary makers approach their work completely from scratch, that is, without assuming knowledge of the meaning of any words." For numerous examples that support this statement, see Lee, *History of New Testament Lexicography*.

66. Silva, *Biblical Words and Their Meaning*, 57. Silva about Hatch wrote, "He felt these were more than just the passage of time saying, the fact that biblical Greek was spoken in a different country and, more to the point, by a different race. The LXX and the New Testament, he claimed, 'afford clear internal evidence that their writers, in most cases, were men whose thoughts were cast in a Semitic and not in a Hellenic mould.'"

67. Black, *Linguistics for Students*, 139. Black writes, "For Louw, words do not have any meaning, but different *usages*. *Sentences* have meaning. And what is true of the relation of individual words in a sentence is true of the relation of individual sentences in a whole discourse. In the final analysis, the meaning of the smaller unit is always determined by its broader context. This means that the entire text is instrumental, if not decisive, in choosing between the different possible meanings of words and sentences."

68. L&N, "Introduction," 1:xvi. Louw writes, "However, though the Greek New Testament contains some examples of specialized meanings of lexical items, the Greek of the New Testament should not be regarded as a distinct form of Greek, but rather as typical Hellenistic Greek." Also, see discussion *GGBB*, 23–30.

69. *GGBB*, 4. Cf. McKnight, *Introducing New Testament Interpretation*, 103.

prevail. These incorrect ideas are so rooted, it will take many years to correct existing scholarship.

SCHOLARLY POSITIONS

Due to theological presuppositions concerning the structure of the creation in relation to the coming eschatological kingdom and King, many Bible interpreters and translators have attempted to limit the first-century CE synchronic meanings of οὐρανός to only a *singular* application whether grammatically singular or plural.[70] The strong unsupported bias against a grammatical plural is further supported by many influential modern published scholars with sparse support over the last five hundred years.[71]

CONCLUSION

This excursus documents convincing evidence for the possibility of the original canonical text containing the sense option for plural heavens in the first-century CE church. This evidence further supports a high probability that the message of Hebrews syntactically assembles grammatical uses of key referents to support for a contextual sense meaning of a distinct coherent topography of God's creation (table 9). First, there is the plural-singular juxtaposition of "heaven" (οὐρανός). Second, one

---

70. This trend began in the middle of the fifteenth century in German translations of the Latin Vulgate. By 1522, Martin Luther, as a second-generation translator under the influence of contemporary German Reformation theology, changed in his translation nearly all ninety grammatical plurals of the Greek NT to German singular. Tyndale's initial English base text published in 1525, while largely independent English idiom, was often copied from Luther's third edition. Cloverdale, who published in 1534, was more influenced by Luther and largely published Tyndale's work anonymously. While subsequent English versions became more original and corrected, these still maintained the ninety NT plurals as singular. Since these works provided the base English text for the 1560 Geneva and 1611 King James Authorized versions, this modification has been maintained at all language textual levels except Greek compilations and literal translations.

71. Maile, "Heaven, Heavenlies, Paradise," 381. Maile follows traditional opinions, writing, "There appears to be no discernible pattern in Paul's usage of singular and plural." Cf. Scofield, *Scofield Bible Reference Bible*, 1113. Scofield comments, "The Scriptures distinguish three heavens: first, the lower heavens, or the region of the clouds; secondly, the second or planetary heavens; and, thirdly, the heaven of heavens, the abode of God."

finds normal syntactical function for ἅγιος (*hagios*) as an adjective and substantive. Third, the modified and unmodified use of σκηνή (*skēnē*) provides specific locations for priestly work of Jesus as the Christ moving about in the heavens and subsequent changes by God in preparation for his entrance. The Pastor uses these as the *aiōn-field* for his overall contextual message.

Finally, the argument establishes some strong possible implications. First, there is a text that can grammatically support a first-century CE view with plural heavens. Second, the sense meaning option of plural heavens was a real option to both speakers and readers. Third, there has been no adequate research that can globally conclude no difference between singular and plural, despite claims otherwise. Fourth, unity of Scripture in common inspiration and creation descriptions harmonize in the entire canon. Fifth, for nearly 1,500 years those reading Scripture could entertain possible plural sense options for the heavens. Sixth, for nearly five hundred years theological presuppositions have both initiated and helped to maintain the option of plural heavens hidden in the English Bible translation of the text. With modern scholarship's interest in reclaiming the original text, it may be time to allow the text to say what the Holy Spirit intended.

Appendix 1

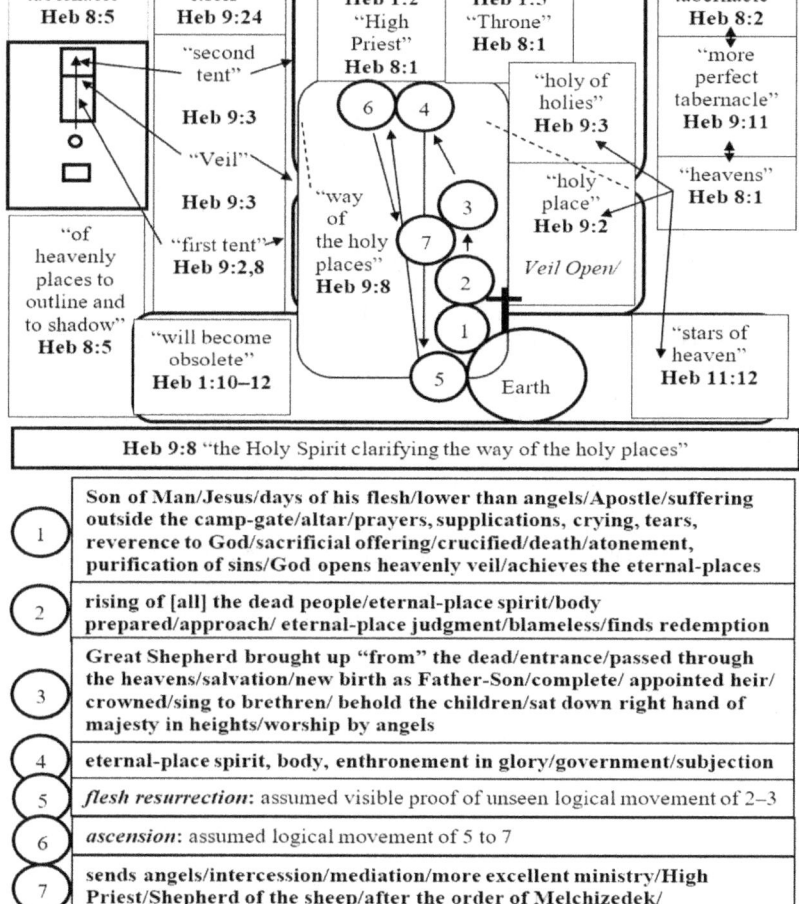

Figure 1—A Minister of the Holy Places: Hebrews 8:2; 9:12, 25

APPENDIX 1

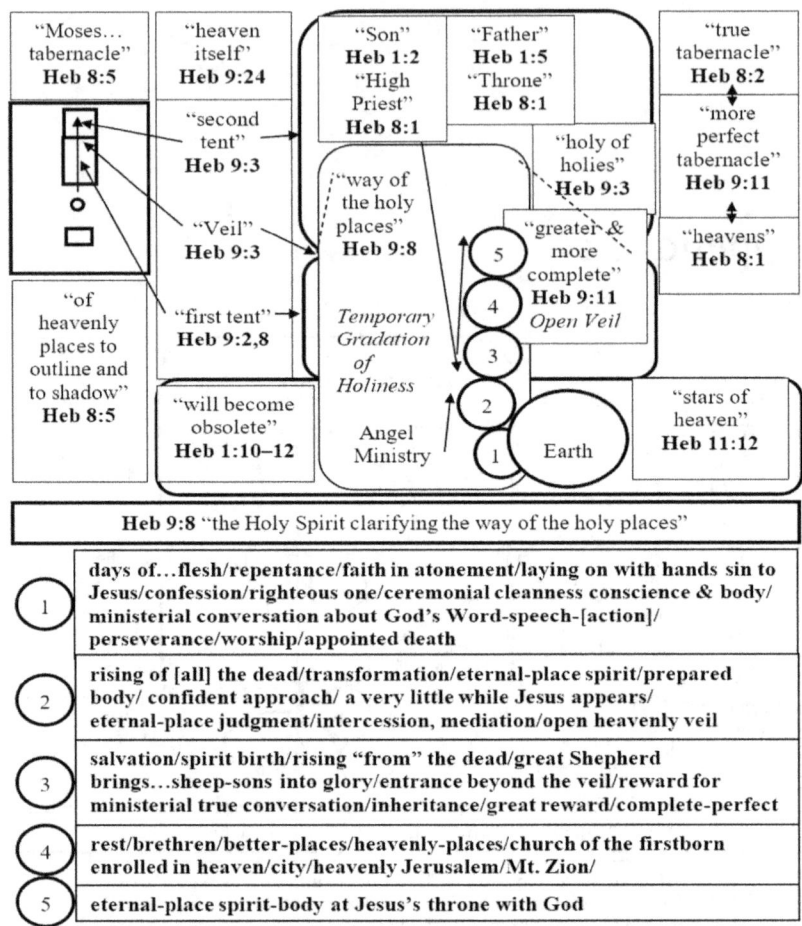

Figure 2—Confident People to Enter the Holy Place

APPENDIX 1

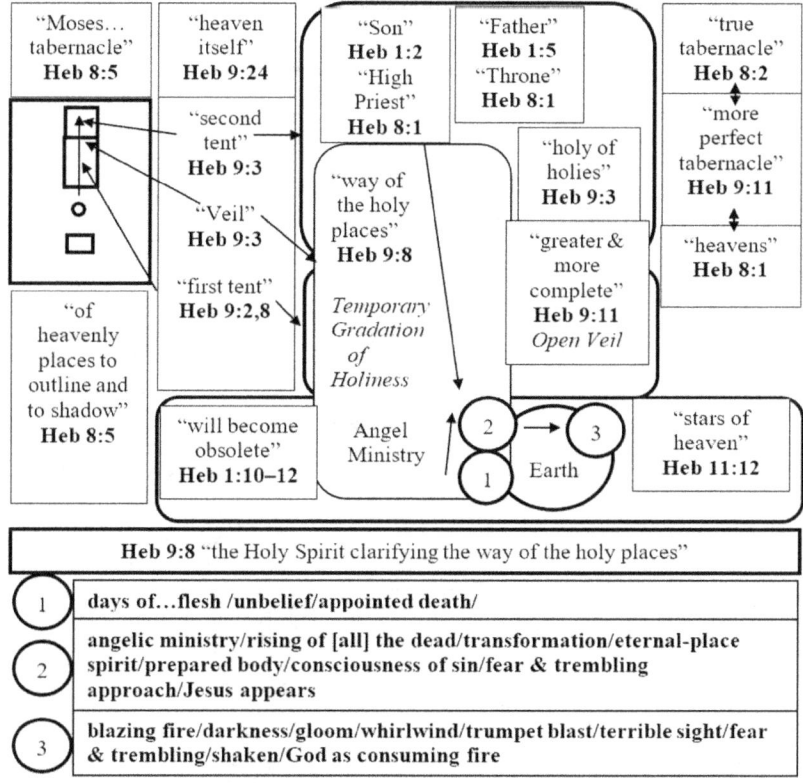

Figure 3—Judgment for Unbelievers at Death

APPENDIX 1

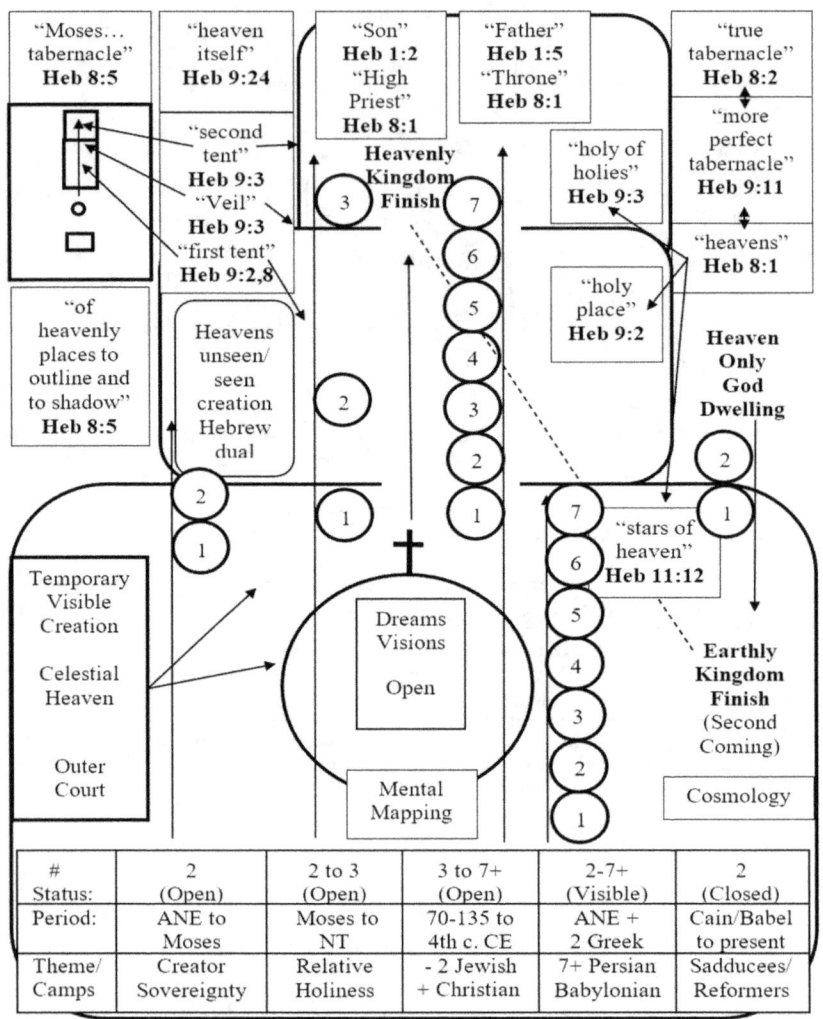

Figure 4—Historical Senses of the Heaven(s)

APPENDIX 1

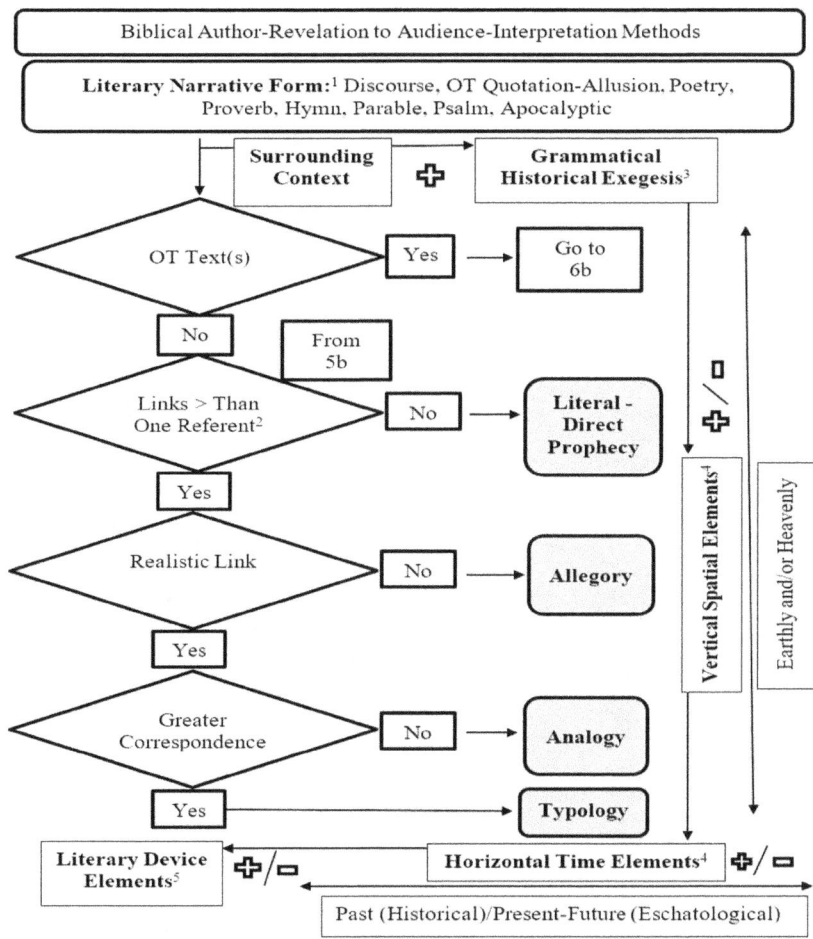

Figure 6a—First-Century Interpretation Methods I

APPENDIX 1

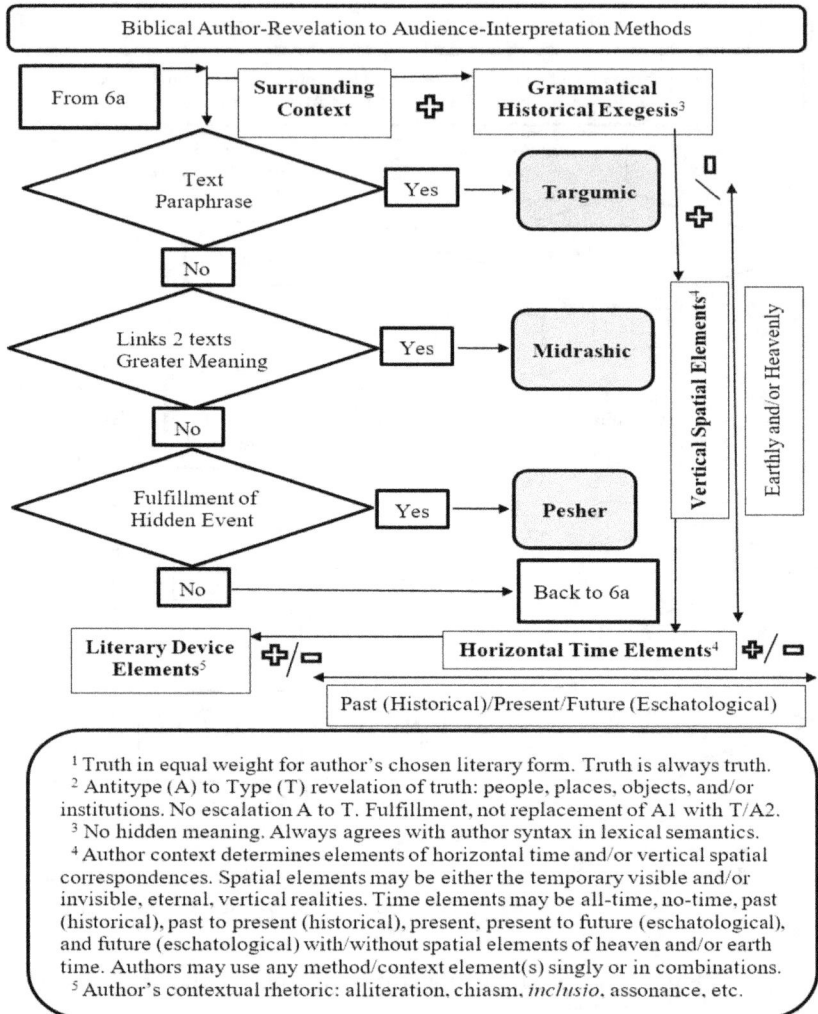

Figure 6b—First-Century Interpretation Methods II

APPENDIX 1

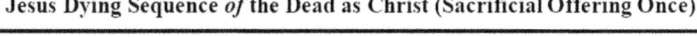

Jesus Dying Sequence *of* the Dead as Christ (Sacrificial Offering Once)

1. Son of Man/Jesus/days of his flesh/lower than angels/Apostle/suffering outside the camp-gate/altar/prayers, supplications, crying, tears, reverence to God/sacrificial offering/crucified/death/atonement, purification of sins/God opens heavenly veil/makes the eternal-places

2. rising "of" [all] the dead people/eternal-place spirit/body prepared/approach/

Jesus Rising Sequence *from* the Dead as Christ (Continual Priestly Ministry)

3. Great Shepherd brought up "from" the dead/entrance/passed through the heavens/salvation/new birth Father-Son/complete/ appointed heir/crowned/sing to brethren/ behold the children/sat down right hand of majesty in heights/worship by angels

4. eternal spirit-body enthronement in glory/government/subjection

5. *flesh resurrection*: assumed visible proof of unseen logical movement of 2-3

6. *ascension*: assumed logical movement of 5 to 7

7. sends angels/intercession/mediation/more excellent ministry/High Priest/Shepherd of the sheep/brings all things by the conversation of his ability

Bold text indicates quotation of Scripture words and phrases. Italic text indicates concepts of corresponding truth from other NT Scripture that must logically occur but are not considered pertinent in the narrative and rhetoric of the narrow focus in Hebrews.

Figure 10—Dying Sequence and Rising Sequence of Salvation

APPENDIX 1

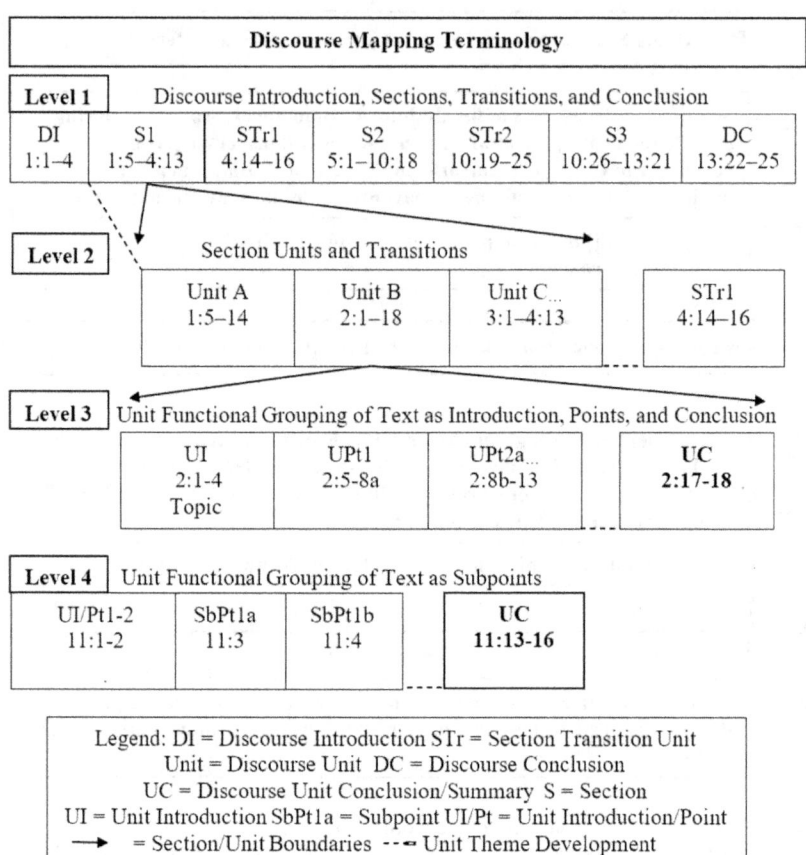

Figure 11—Discourse Mapping Terminology

APPENDIX 1

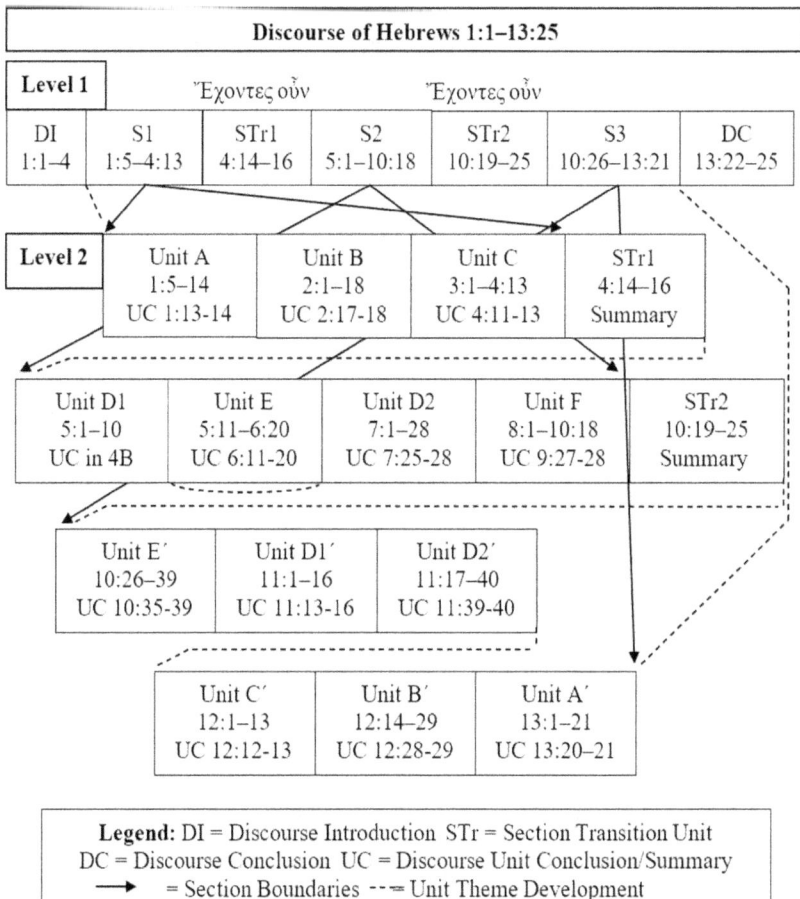

Figure 12—Discourse Structural Mapping of Hebrews

APPENDIX 1

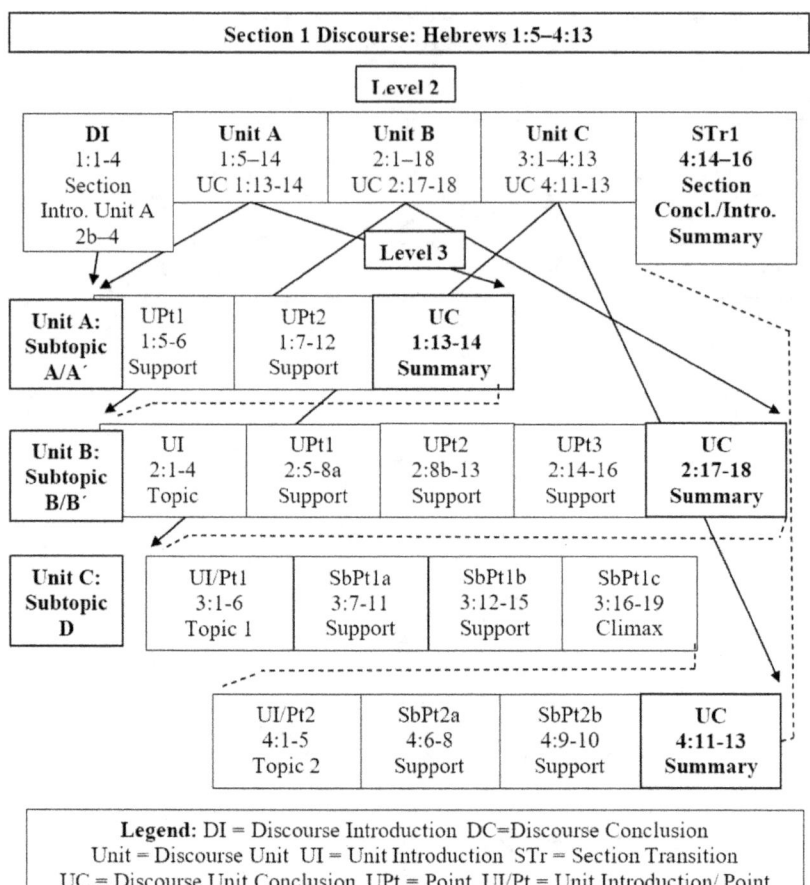

Figure 13—Section 1 Discourse Unit Structural Mapping

APPENDIX 1

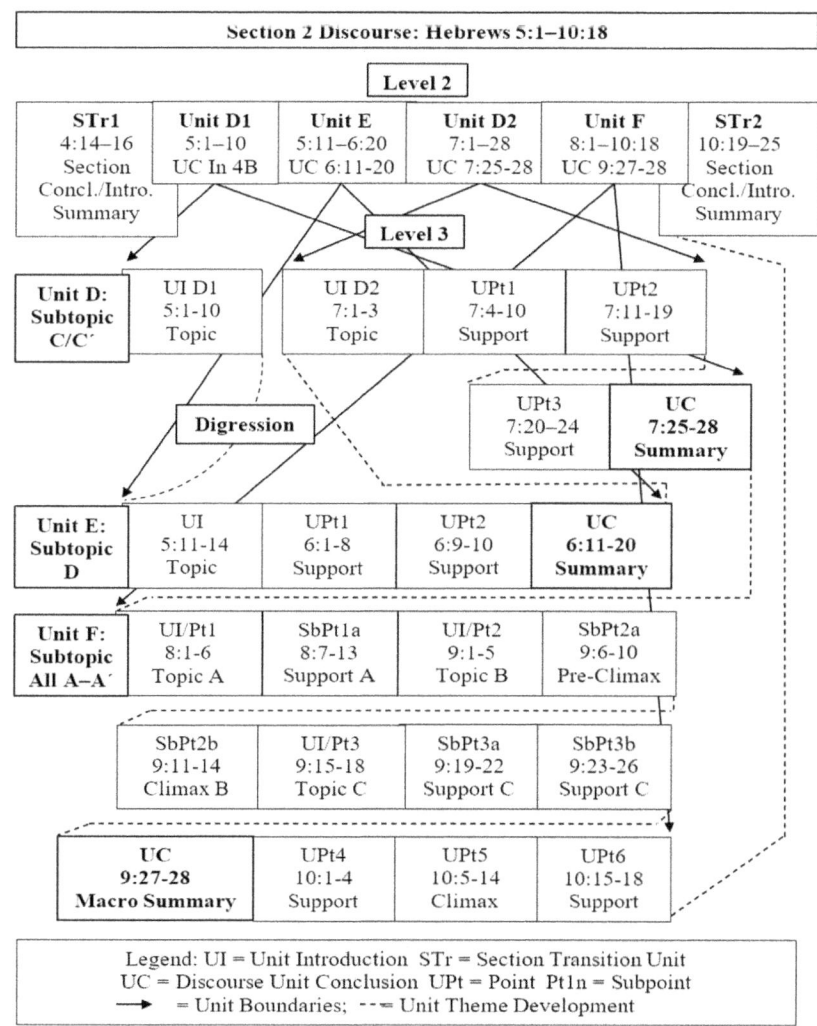

Figure 14—Section 2 Discourse Unit Structural Mapping

APPENDIX 1

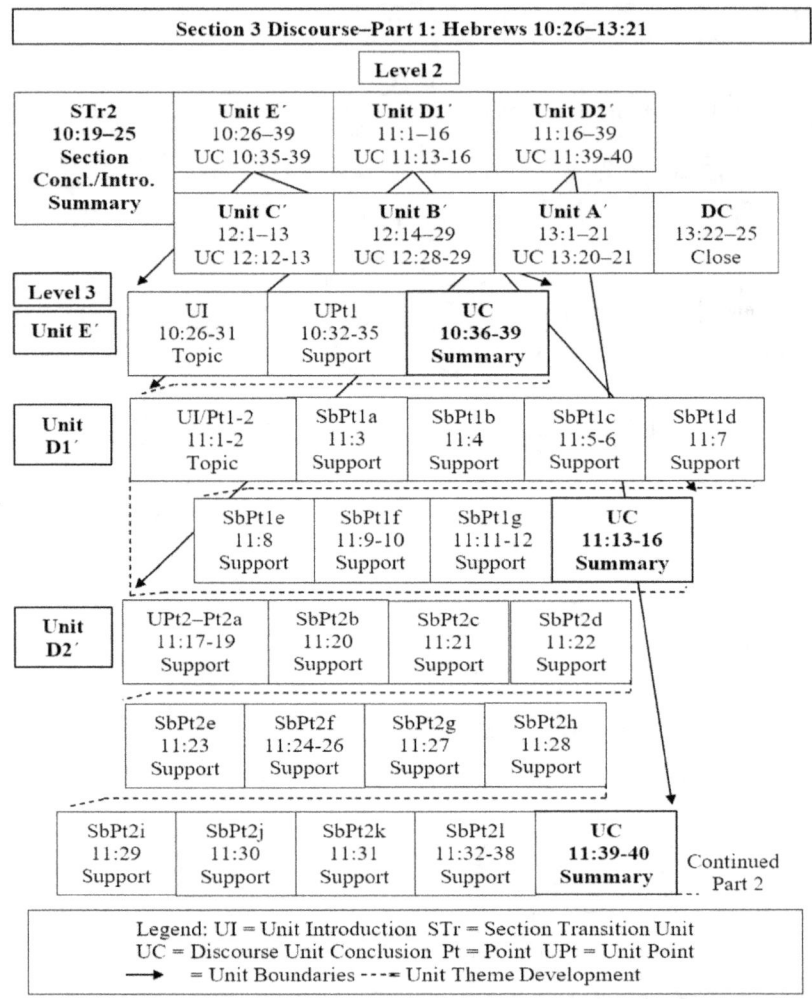

Figure 15—Section 3 Discourse Unit Structural Mapping

APPENDIX 1

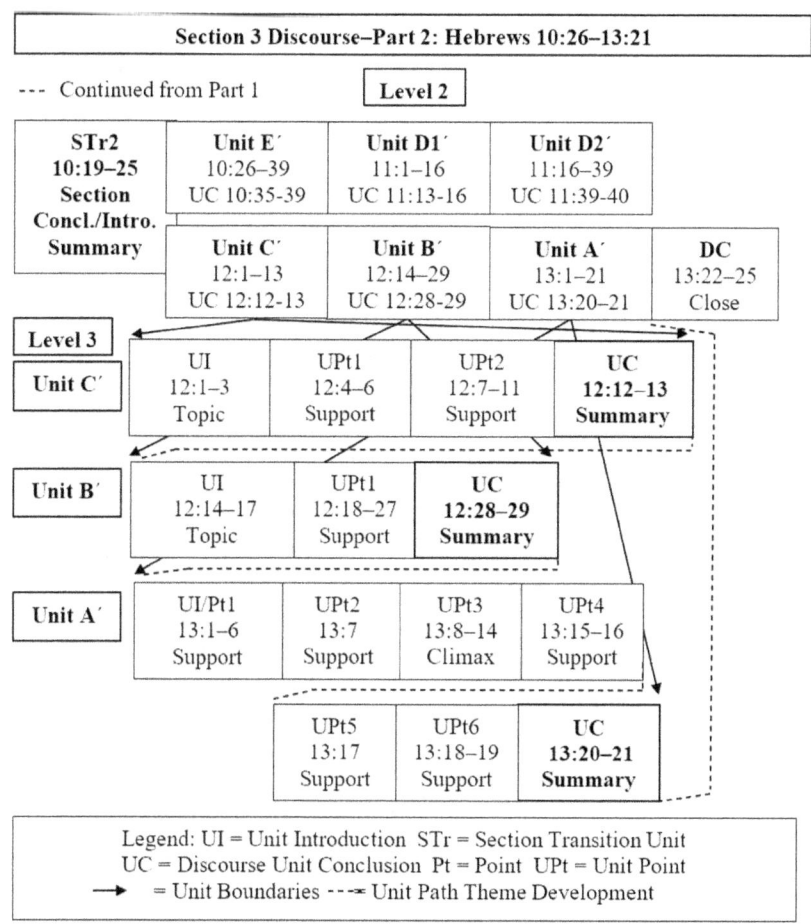

Figure 15—Section 3 Discourse Unit Structural Mapping

APPENDIX 1

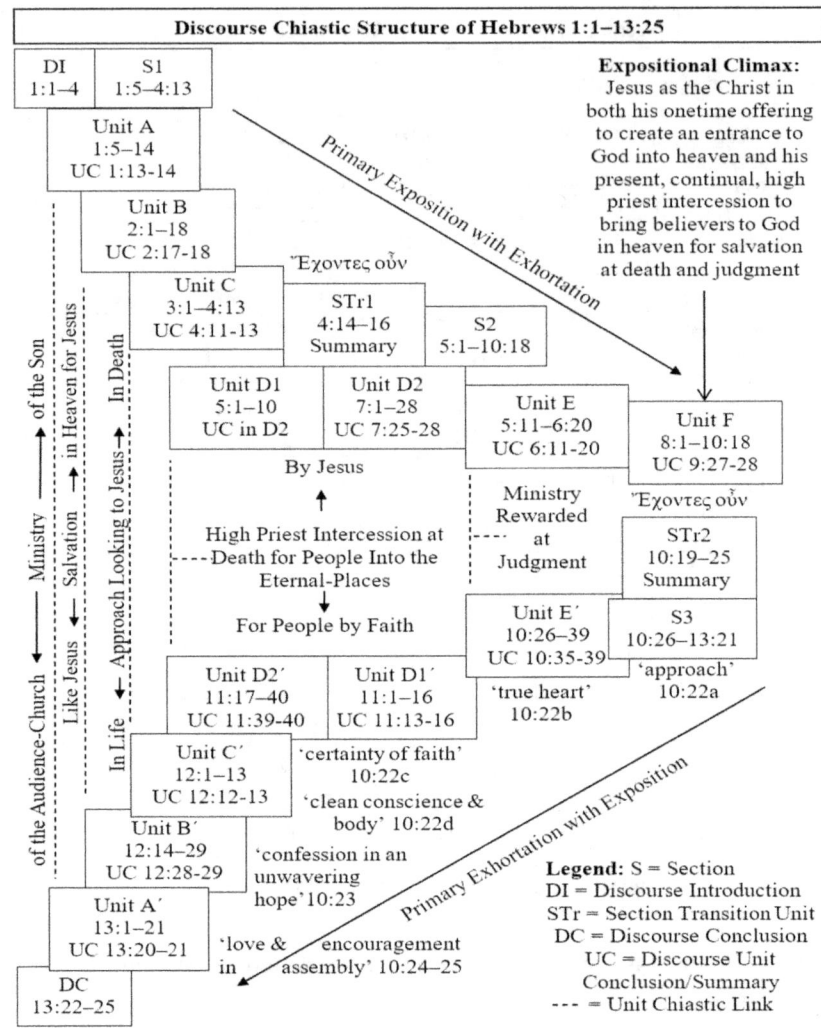

Figure 16—Discourse Chiastic Structure of Hebrews

Appendix 2

NATIVE DISCOURSE LEXEMES OF THE PASTOR'S MAIN CONCLUSION

This section lists tables of the Pastor's word stock used in his narrative and rhetoric. Lexemes subdivide his choices of into categories for comparison. Each table supplies the Greek lexeme, the total number of times used in the message, and a suggested gloss that corresponds with the proposed overarching context.

In chapters 2–4, principles of text linguistics implement to exegete the Pastor's handling of his lexemes for syntactical usage and semantic meaning in the discourse narrative context. Lexemes included that are not in Hebrews signal either possible foreign translator thematic meaning, later Greek-Latin emendations by redactors, or usage of vocabulary with overlapping semantic fields with other documents. Some lexemes appear in multiple tables due to the common usage as either referent identifiers, characteristics, or expressions of the verbal activity of the referents.

Successful exegesis without eisegesis depends on the strength of the exegetical leg work.[1] The Pastor's message blurs when forcing external categories on the text. Knowing the words of the Pastor assists to identify foreign theology and philosophy.

---

1. Cf. Bock, "New Testament Word Analysis," 97–113. Bock shares fundamental rules for the important determination of authorial word meaning and ways to avoid common errors and fallacies that were undeveloped when sixteenth century translators began making the text of Scripture available in the common language of the people. Cf. Erickson, *Beginner's Guide to New Testament*, 21. Erickson reminds in his definition of the task of exegesis, how one must first exegete a qualified text "*to project us back into that ancient world*" (italics Erickson).

APPENDIX 2

TABLES OF REFERENTS, VERBAL NOUNS, AND ACTIVITY

Table 1—Words in Hebrews Linked with God

God Referents					
θεός 63	God	ἀρχιερεύς 17	high priest	ἱερεύς 14	priest
υἱός 21	Son	Ἰησοῦς 14	Jesus	μέγας 10	great
αἷμα 20	blood	κύριος 16	Lord	πατήρ 8	Father
σάρξ 6	flesh	Χριστός 12	Christ[2]	πρωτότοκος 3	firstborn
ὄνομα 4	name	σπέρμα 3	seed	δίκαιος 3	righteous
κληρονόμος 3	heir	πρόδρομος 1	forerunner	ἀρχηγός 2	leader
μεγαλωσύνη 2	Majesty	ποιμήν 1	shepherd	τελειωτής 1	finisher
λειτουργός 2	minister	δίκαιος 3	righteous	κριτικός 1	discerner
τοῦ πνεύματος τοῦ ἁγίου 3		Holy Spirit		ἀπόστολος 1	apostle
ἀμετάθετος 2		unchangeable		κριτής 1	judge

God Verbal Noun Referents			
ἐπαγγελία 13	promise(s)	λόγος 12	Word, word
κρείττων 12	better	ἔργον 10	works
θάνατος 8	death	χάρις 7	grace
κατάπαυσις 7	rest	ὀμνύω 6	oath
δύναμις 6	ability	θέλημα 5	desire, will
δικαιοσύνη 6	righteousness	πιστός 5	faithful
τοσοῦτος 5	so great	φωνή 5	voice, speech
δόξα 5	glory	τιμή 4	honor
		πούς 4	feet
ἀντιλογία 3	argument, opposition, dispute	ῥῆμα 4	conversation, word, statement
μεσίτης 3	mediator	ἐντολή 4	commandment
ἀληθινός 3	true	πάθημα 3	suffering
μισθαποδοσία 3	reward	πρᾶγμα 3	events, matters

2. Bold text signifies lexeme occurs in Heb 9:27–28 MCS. Numbers reflect total number in Hebrews Greek text without distinction of a referent or the subject/object/indirect object of referent verbal activity. The overlap of terms reflects the similar death to life experiences of Christ and believers. Believers both follow him in faith of ministry and in life beginning at death in the eternal creation with entrance to God.

APPENDIX 2

God Verbal Noun Referents			
ἐπιλανθάνομαι 3	forget	ἀνομία 2	lawlessness
ὅρκος 2	oath	μερισμός 2	distribution
εὐλογία 2	blessing, praise	ὁμοιότης 2	likeness
κληρονομία 2	inheritance	εὐλάβεια 2	reverence
κρίσις 2	judgment	ἀθέτησις 2	removal
ὀργή 2	anger	τεχνίτης 1	designer, architect
πέρας 1	end, Limit	δυνατός 1	able
ὅσιος 1	holy	κλῆσις 1	invitation
μισθαποδότης 1	rewarder	ἄμωμος 1	faultless
καθαρισμός 1	purification	πρωτοτόκια 1	firstborn inheritance
τελειότης 1	completeness	ἄδικος 1	not unjust
στοιχεῖον 1	basic principles	δημιουργός 1	builder
δοκιμασία 1	test	βεβαίωσις 1	validation
ἀδύνατον ψεύσασθαι 1	impossible to lie	ἐπεισαγωγή 1	bring in, introduce
ἀπαράβατος 1	unchangeable	ἁγιότης 1	holiness
ἀκατάλυτος 1	indestructible	ἵλεως 1	gracious
ἄκακος 1	innocent	αἴτιος 1	basis, source
ἐλεήμων 1	merciful	ὑπακοή 1	obedience
ἀγαλλίασις 1	gladness	εὐθύτης 1	uprightness
μαρτύριον 1	testimony	ἀμίαντος 1	blameless

God Verbal Activity			
λέγω 43	say, speak	γίνομαι 29	born; become; exist
προσφέρω 18	offer (sacrificial)	λαλέω 17	speak
εἰσέρχομαι 15	enter	τελειόω 9	complete
ζάω 12	live	ὁράω 10	see, pass. appear
δύναμαι 9	able	μαρτυρέω 7	testify, commend
προσέρχομαι 7	approach	ὀμνύω 6	swear by oath
μένω 6	dwell	καλέω 6	call
φέρω 5	lead	εὐλογέω 6	bless
ἔρχομαι 5	come	ὑποτάσσω 5	subjugate
εὑρίσκω 4	find	κατασκευάζω 5	build, construct
κληρονομέω 4	inherit	πειράζω 5	test

APPENDIX 2

God Verbal Activity			
καθαρίζω 4	cleanse	μιμνῄσκομαι 4	remember
θέλω 4	will, desire, decide	καθίζω 4	sit
ἀναφέρω 4	lead up, bring up	ἐπαγγέλλομαι 4	promise
διατίθημι 4	make a last will, execute a covenant	πάσχω 4	suffer
τίθημι 3	put, place	δίδωμι 4	give
γεννάω 3	beget	καθίστημι 3	appoint, give charge
μετέχω 3	share	οἶδα 3	know
χρηματίζω 3	warn	ἥκω 3	have come
πρόκειμαι 3	set before	εὐδοκέω 3	please
ὀφείλω 3	obligate, require	δεῖ 3	it is necessary
καταρτίζω 3	restore	ἐπιλαμβάνομαι 3	take hold, grasp
δηλόω 2	make clear	ἀγαπάω 2	love
σῴζω 2	save	πρέπω 2	fit
τυγχάνω 2	experience	δηλόω 2	clarify
ἀφίημι 2	left, forgive	κρίνω 2	judge
σαλεύω 2	shake	στεφανόω 2	crown
ἐγκαινίζω 2	inaugurate	ἀμελέω 2	ignore
ἐντέλλω 2	command, instruct	ἀπειθέω 2	disobey
συμπαθέω 2	sympathize with	ἀμελέω 2	ignore
ἐλαττόω 2	make lower	ἐμφανίζω 2	show (act.), appear (pass.)
ἐπαισχύνομαι 2	ashamed	παλαιόω 2	make obsolete
ἀπόκειμαι 1	appoint	προσκυνέω 2	worship
ἐντυγχάνω 1	intercede	ἐξάγω 1	lead out
πήγνυμι 1	set up	ἄγω 1	bring
συντελέω 1	complete	εἰσάγω 1	bring into
ἀναδέχομαι 1	receive	ἐγείρω 1	raise
ἱλάσκομαι 1	atone	προάγω 1	lead the way
διέρχομαι 1	travel through	ἀνάγω 1	lead up
διϊκνέομαι 1	penetrate	ποιέω 1	make
ἀπαλλάσσω 1	release	ἀπαγγέλλω 1	proclaim
εἰσακούω 1	be heard	διαλέγομαι 1	address
κάθημαι 1	sit	μισέω 1	hate
χωρίζω 1	separate	ζητέω 1	seek

APPENDIX 2

God Verbal Activity			
πληθύνω 1	abound	ἀνίημι 1	leave
προβλέπω 1	plan ahead	ἐλέγχω 1	reprove
μέμφομαι 1	find fault	μεταμέλομαι 1	change the mind
ὑμνέω 1	sing	ἐπιδείκνυμι 1	show
καταργέω 1	nullify	δείκνυμι 1	explain, detail
ὁμοιόω 1	made like	θεμελιόω 1	lay the foundation
μαστιγόω 1	chastise	κατασκευάζω 1	prepare
δοξάζω 1	glorify	ἐπίκειμαι 1	demand, pressure
ἑτοιμάζω 1	prepare	παραγίνομαι 1	arrive
δέησις 1	pray	συνεπιμαρτυρέω 1	testify together
κραυγή 1	cry	ἱκετηρία 1	petition
βούλομαι 1	desire	φημί 1	declare, explain
προσαγορεύω 1	designate	ἐντρέπω 1	cause shame
ἀπεκδέχομαι 1	eagerly wait	αἱματεκχυσία 1	shed, pour out
ἀναιρέω 1	kill, do away with	μανθάνω 1	learn
ἀνταποδίδωμι 1	repay	παραδέχομαι 1	receive
μεσιτεύω 1	guarantee	σείω 1	tremble
συμφέρω 1	bring together	καταφρονέω 1	despise
ἀναβαίνω 0(NT 81)	raise up, ascend	Χρίω 1	anoint
καταβαίνω 0	descend	ἕλκω 0	draw
ὑψόω 0	raise up	Παρουσία 0	come

Table 2—Words in Hebrews Linked with Creation

Spatial Referents			
ἅγιος 17	holy, holy places	οὐρανός 10	heaven(s)
αἰών 13	eternal/perpetual-places (space-time)	γῆ 10	earth
σκηνή 10	tabernacle, tent	πρῶτος 9	first *place*
οἶκος 9	house	δεξιός 5	right hand
κατάπαυσις 7	rest	δόξης 7	glory
ὅσος 8	so much	πόλις 4	city
ἐπουράνιος 6	heavenly	πούς 4	feet
κόσμος 5	world	τόπος 3	place
δεύτερος 5	second . . . place, time, position	ἁγίων, ἅγια 4	holy place(s)

APPENDIX 2

Spatial Referents			
θρόνος 4	throne	Αἴγυπτος 4	Egypt
καταπέτασμα, ἐσώτερον τοῦ καταπετάσματος 3	veil, inside the veil	ὄρος 4	mountain
ὑπόστασις 3	reality, substance	βασιλεία 3	kingdom
ὑποπόδιον 2	footstool	καταβολή 3	foundation
ἔρημος 2	wilderness	ὁδός 3	way
ὑψηλοῖς 2	heights	ὑπόδειγμα 3	pattern
τέλειος 2	complete	θυσιαστήριον 2	altar
ὕπαρξις 2	possession	οἰκουμένην 2	domain
Σαλήμ 2	Salem	τροχιά 1	path
σκιά 2	shadow	κοσμικός 1	earthly
ὕψιστος 1	highest	ἀντίτυπος 1	copy
ἀόρατος 1	invisible	πρόσωπον 1	presence
σπήλαιον 1	cave	ἀφανής 1	invisible
ὀρθός 1	straight	παντελής 1	completion
Ἅγια 1	holy place	πατρίς 1	homeland
τύπος 1	model, pattern	Ἱεριχώ 1	Jericho
ἐνώπιον αὐτοῦ 1	before him	ὀπή 1	caves
Ἅγια Ἁγίων 1	holy of holies	Σιών 1	Zion
ὑπεράνω 1	high above	εἴσοδος 1	entrance
πόρρωθεν 1	from a distance	ἄκρον 1	top
Ἱερουσαλήμ 1	Jerusalem	ἐρημία 1	desert
ἀκατάλυτος 1	endless place	γέεννα 0	hell
κόλπον Ἀβραάμ 0	Abraham's bosom	ᾅδης 0	Hades
τρίτου οὐρανοῦ 0	third heaven		

Time Referents			
ἡμερῶν 18	day(s)	σήμερον 5	today
αἰών 13	eternal/perpetual-Places (space-time)	πρῶτος 9	first (series)
ἅπαξ 8	once	ὅσος 8	so much
αἰώνιος 6	eternal/perpetual-*places* (adj.)	ἐφάπαξ 3	once for all
νῦν 6	now	ἀρχή 6	beginning

APPENDIX 2

Time Referents

πρότερος 4	first (event)	δεύτερος 5	second . . . place, time, position
διηνεκής 4	continuous	καιρός 4	time
ἔτος 3	years	μέχρι 3	until
πάρειμι 2	for the moment	οὐδέποτε 2	never
πολλάκις	many times	ἐγγύς 2	near
οὐκέτι 1	no longer	ἐχθές 1	yesterday
μηδέπω 1	not yet	ἐνίστημι 1	current
ἡλικία 1	life Age	πρόσφατος 1	recent
ὕστερος 1	later	χρονίζω 1	delay
σαββατισμός 1	Sabbath rest	λοιπός 1	remaining
εὔκαιρος 1	time of need	νυνί 1	now
συντέλεια 1	completion	μίαν	one
πόρρωθεν 1	from a distance	τρίμηνος 1	three months
ἀκατάλυτος 1	endless place	ἀνώτερον 1	previously

Object Referents

θυσία 15	sacrifice	διαθήκη 14	covenant	κρείττων 12	better things
χείρ 5	hand	διάκρισις 5	good	προσφορά 5	offering
δῶρον 5	gift	πῦρ 5	fire	βέβαιος 4	binding, unalterable
τράγος 4	goat	διάφορος 3	superior	ἀγαθός 3	good
Βασιλεία 3	kingdom			ὑποπόδιον 2	footstool
ῥάβδος 3	staff	μάχαιρα 3	sword	σποδός 3	ashes
τροφή 2	food	δικαίωμα 2	regulations	παραβολή 2	parable
καινός 3	new	κιβωτός 2	ark	βρῶμα 2	food
ταῦρος 2	bull	γάλα 2	milk	θεμέλιος 2	foundation
μόσχος 2	oxen	θάλασσα 2	sea	ὕδωρ 2	water
ὁλοκαύτωμα 2	whole burnt offerings	λιθοβολέω 1	throw stones	ἄγκυρα 1	anchor
ἀλήθεια 1	truth	πλοῦτος 1	wealth	ἔξοδος 1	exodus
θησαυρός 1	treasure	χωλός 1	lame	σταυρός 1	cross
γόνυ 1	knee	μάννα 1	manna	βρῶσις 1	meal
στάμνος 1	jar	δάμαλις 1	heifer	πλάξ 1	stone tablets
ἀνάμνησις 1	reminder	ὕσσωπος 1	hyssop	ἄμεμπτος 1	faultless
κόκκινος 1	scarlet	ῥαντισμός 1	sprinkling	ἔριον 1	wool

APPENDIX 2

Object Referents					
μυριάς 1	myriad	βουλή 1	plan	σκεῦος 1	vessel
ῥίζα 1	root	πρόθεσις 1	presentation	χρυσίον 1	gold
τράπεζα 1	table	ἔγγυος 1	guarantee	ἀνωφελής 1	uselessness
μέρος 1	detail	ἄρτος 1	bread	λυχνία 1	lamp stand
πόμα 1	drink	καθαρός 1	pure	κεφαλίδι βιβλίου 1	section of a scroll
θυμιατήριον 1	incense altar	ἱλαστήριον 1	atonement cover (place)	πικρία 1	bitterness
εἰκών 1	image, likeness	ξηρός 1	dried	τεῖχος 1	wall
νήπιος 1	child	βιβλίον 1	scroll	νέφος 1	cloud
ἐρυθρός 1	red	κακός 1	evil	θηρίον 1	animal
χρυσοῦς 1	golden	ἀσθενής 1	weakness	ὄγκος 1	impediment
ἀποκάλυψις 0	revelation	ἔλαιον 1	oil	Φλόξ 1	flame

Creation Verbal Noun Referents					
εἴσοδος 1	entrance	ἐπουράνιος 6	heavenly	ἀφανής 1	invisible
ἀδόκιμος 1	rejection	κατάρα 1	curse	καῦσις 1	burn
ἀκροθίνιον 1	plunder	γνόφος 1	darkness	θύελλα 1	storm
ἦχος 1	blasts, loud noise	ἱλαστήριον 1	atonement place; mercy seat	χειροποίητος 2	handmade
σάλπιγξ 1	trumpet	ζόφος 1	blackness	ἀφανισμός 1	disappear

Creation Verbal Activity					
μέλλω 9	coming, about to, subsequently	ἥκω 3	have come	πίπτω 3	fall
μεταλαμβάνω 2	receive with	καίω 1	light on fire	παλαιόω 2	make obsolete
μετατίθημι 2	change loc.	πίνω 1	drink	παύω 1	cease, stop
περικαλύπτω 1	cover	φαίνω 1	appear, visible	γεωργέω 1	cultivate
ἀπόλλυμι 1	destroy	ἐκφέρω 1	bring out	βλαστάνω 1	sprout
γηράσκω 1	grow old			τίκτω 1	produce
κατασκιάζω 1	overshadow			ἀλλάσσω 1	change form

APPENDIX 2

Table 3—Words in Hebrews Linked with People

People Linked Referents					
λαός 12	people	ἀδελφός 10	brother	μέγας 10	great
οἶκος 9	house	πατήρ 8	fathers	ἄνθρωπος 8	person
μέτοχος 5	companions	ἐκκλησία 2	assembly	παιδίον 3	child
κληρονόμος 3	heir	ὄνομα 4	name	μόνος 3	alone
προφήτης 2	prophets	ἱερωσύνη 3	priesthood	μικρός 2	least
πατριάρχης 1	patriarch	κτίσις 2	creation	φυλή 2	tribe
πνεύματος ἁγίου 2	people-spirit of holy-*place*	πολίτης 1	neighbor	θεράπων 1	servant
ἱερατεία 1	priest office	γενεά 1	generation	συγκληρονόμος 1	coheir
μονογενής 1	only one				

Historical People Referents					
Ἰησοῦς 14	Jesus	Χριστός 12	Christ	Ἀβραάμ 10	Abraham
Μελχισέδεκ 8	Melchizedek	Μωϋσῆς 11	Moses	βασιλεύς 5	king(s)
Ἰσραήλ 3	Israel	Ἀαρών 3	Aaron	Ἰσαάκ 4	Isaac
Κάϊν 1	Cain	Ἰούδας 2	Judah	Ἰακώβ 3	Jacob
Ἄβελ 2	Abel	Σάρρα 1	Sarah	Ἰησοῦς 1	Joshua[3]
Ἰωσήφ 2	Joseph	θυγάτηρ 1	daughter	Ἠσαῦ 1	Esau
Ῥαάβ 1	Rahab	Σαμουήλ 1	Samuel	Φαραώ 1	Pharaoh
Βαράκ 1	Barak	Σαμψών 1	Samson	Γεδεών 1	Gideon
Λευί 1	Levi	προφητῶν 1	prophets	Ἰεφθάε 1	Jephthah
Δαυίδ 1	David	Ἑνώχ 1	Enoch	Νῶε 1	Noah

Person-Linked Subcategory Referents					
αἷμα 20	blood	πνεῦμα 5	spirit of people	καρδία 10	heart
ψυχή 6	soul	σαρκός 6	flesh	σάρξ 6	flesh
συνείδησις 5	conscience	σῶμα 5	body	διάνοια 2	mind
ὀσφῦς 2	loins	πνεύματος ἁγίου 2	people-spirit of holy-*place*	ἐνθύμησις 1	thoughts
ἁρμός 1	joints	ὀστέον 1	bones	μυελός 1	marrow

3. While not important to this discussion, the Jesus versus Joshua debate in Heb 4:8 probably centers on the Pastor's point of view. Joshua led the believers of Israel to the earthly promised land. This event typologically portrayed Jesus leading believers to the heavenly rest in the eternal creation. The analysis of the UC for this dilemma follows in chapter 4.

APPENDIX 2

Person-Linked Subcategory Referents				
νοῦς 0	mind	ἔννοια 1	intentions	

People Verbal Noun Referents					
πίστις 32	faith	ἁμαρτία 24	sin(s)	ἅγιος 17	holy
θάνατος 8	death	νόμος 13	law	ἔργον 10	works
κατάπαυσις 7	rest	σωτηρία 7	salvation	νεκρός 7	dead
δικαιοσύνη 6	righteousness	εὐλογέω 6	blessings	ἀνάγκη 4	necessity
καλός 5	good	τάξις 5	order, succession	ἐλπίς 5	hope
κληρονομέω 4	inherit	παρρησία 4	confidence	χαρά 4	joy
κληρονομέω 4	heirs	ἀσθένεια 4	weakness	εἰρήνη 4	peace
ἀδύνατος 4	powerless	βασιλεύς 4	king	φοβερός 3	terror
ἀντιλογία 3	argument, dispute	μετάθεσις 3	change, taken up	παιδεία 4	train, discipline
μετάνοια 3	repentance	ὁμολογία 3	confession	δίκαιος 3	righteous
ὀνειδισμός 3	insult	χρεία 3	need	ξένος 2	foreigners
νομοθετέω 2	legislate	ἀνομία 2	lawlessness	ἀγάπη 2	love
πόρνος 2	sexually immoral	νωθρός 2	sluggish	κρίσις 2	judgment
ἀκοή 2	hear	ἁμαρτωλός 2	sinner	δέσμιος 2	prisoner
πονηρός 2	evil	δάκρυον 2	tears	πεῖρα 2	attempt
παράβασις 2	transgressions	μάρτυς 2	witness, One commended	τέλειος 2	mature, complete
ἀπιστία 2	unbelief	εἰρηνικός 1	peaceable	νόθος 1	illegitimate
παραπικρασμός 2	rebellion	λατρεία 2	priesthood ministry	ἐκδοχή 1	expectation
βαπτισμός 2	ceremonial washings	ὑπομονή 2	perseverance, Steadfastness	ἄφεσις 2	forgiveness
ἀνάστασις 2	resurrection	ἐπισυναγωγή 2	gathering together	τιμωρία 1	punishment
πληροφορία 2	full conviction	ὑποστρέφω 1	defeat, slaughter	ἁρπαγή 1	confiscation
πληθύνω 1	abounding	λύτρωσις 1	redemption	θλῖψις 1	tribulation
πειρασμός 1	testing	κοινωνός 1	partaker	δέος 1	awe
ἀφίστημι 1	leaving			ἁγιασμός 1	holiness
αἰσθητήριον 1	faculty	ἀπόλαυσις 1	pleasure	ἀστεῖος 1	beautiful
περιποίησις 1	preserve	φόβος 1	fear	ἀδικία 1	iniquities

464

APPENDIX 2

People Verbal Noun Referents					
ὑποστολή 1	hesitate	διάταγμα 1	command	στάσις 1	existence
πρόσχυσις 1	sprinkling	κρίματος αἰωνίου 1	eternal/perpetual-place judgment	ἀγνόημα 1	committed sin in ignorance
κατάσκοπος 1	spy	δωρεά 1	heavenly gift	στεῖρα 1	barren
μακροθυμία 1	patience	κλῆσις 1	calling	θυμός 1	anger
καθαρότης 1	purity	ἀπάτη 1	deception	πόρνη 1	prostitute
ἐκδίκησις 1	vengeance	κοινόω 1	ceremonially unclean	ἄθλησις 1	challenge
ἕξις 1	practice	ἀπολύτρωσις 1	redemption	βέβηλος 1	worldly
παραπικρασμός 1	disobeyed	ἐπίγνωσις 1	spiritual knowledge	ἀκλινής 1	unwavering
ἀγνοέω 1	not understanding	ὑπεναντίος 1	opposition	ἄπειρος 1	inexperience
ἀγών 1	athletic contest, race	πρεσβύτερος 1	elders	μιμητής 1	imitators
αἰσχύνη 1	shamefulness	παρεπίδημος 1	strangers	ἔθος 1	custom
λύπη 1	grief, Sorrowful	εὐπερίστατος 1	entangle	ἐπίθεσις 1	laying on
παιδευτής 1	teacher, trainer	βοήθεια 1	need	σπουδή 1	diligence
ζῆλος 1	zealous	δουλεία 1	slaves	κῶλον 1	corpse
Καθεύδω 0	sleep	Κοιμάω 0	sleep		

People Verbal Activity					
ἔχω 36	have	προσφέρω 18	offer sacrificially	ποιέω 17	do, make, achieve
λαμβάνω 17	receive	εἰσέρχομαι 15	enter into	ζάω 12	live
ὁράω 10	see	τελειόω 9	complete	δύναμαι 9	able
προσέρχομαι 7	approach	μέλλω 9	coming, about to, subsequently	ἀκούω 7	hear
ἀποθνήσκω 7	die	λατρεύω 6	priesthood ministering	ἁγιάζω 6	make holy
ἡγέομαι 6	regard, thought	ἐξέρχομαι 5	come out	μένω 5	dwell
φέρω 5	lead	δοκέω 4	think	ῥαντίζω 4	sprinkle

465

APPENDIX 2

People Verbal Activity					
πείθω 4	trust	καθαρίζω 4	purify, cleanse sin	παρακαλέω 4	encourage
φοβέομαι 4	fear	πειράζω 4	test	γινώσκω 4	know
σκληρύνω 4	harden	ὀφείλω 3	obligate	ὑπομένω 4	endure
κατέχω 3	hold fast	εὐαρεστέω 3	please	παιδεύω 3	instruct
μετέχω 3	share	μνημονεύω 3	remember	γεύομαι 3	taste
κομίζω 3	receive	ὑστερέω 3	be in need	πλανάω 3	stray
παράκλησις 3	encouragement	ἀποδίδωμι 3	return, reward, give up	πίπτω 3	collapse, die
ἁμαρτάνω 2	sin	ὠφελέω 2	benefit	ἀπολείπω 3	remain
παραιτέομαι 3	reject	περίκειμαι 2	surround	ἐγγίζω 2	draw near
καταλείπω 2	remain behind	εὐαγγελίζω 2	proclaim gospel	ὁμοιότης 2	similar, like
διδάσκω 2	teach	ἀμελέω 2	ignore	ἐκλύω 2	losing heart
κατανοέω 2	consider	προσέχω 2	guard	ἵστημι 2	stand
ἐπιτυγχάνω 2	reach	ἀναστρέφω 2	treat	ὁμοιόω 2	made like
ἀξιόω 2	worthy	μερίζω 1	divide	κρατέω 2	hold onto
ἀφίημι 2	leave	ἀσπάζομαι 2	welcome	φωτίζω 2	enlighten
ἐπιζητέω 2	seek earnestly	ἐπιγράφω 2	write upon	συναντάω 2	meeting
σῴζω 2	save	ἐκδέχομαι 2	wait	ὁμολογέω 2	confess
ἀποβάλλω 1	throw away	ἐκζητέω 2	seeking out	γυμνάζω 2	train, exercise
προσδέχομαι 2	welcome	πιστεύω 2	believe	δεκατόω 2	pay a tenth
μετατίθημι 2	change	ὑπακούω 2	answer	παραρρέω 1	drift away
ἐγκαταλείπω 2	forsake	ἐκφεύγω 2	escape	ἐπιτελέω 2	accomplish
ἐνδείκνυμι 2	display	γράφω 1	write	ἰσχύω 1	enable
ἀνασταυρόω 1	crucify again	διαβαίνω 1	pass through	λειτουργέω 1	priesthood ministering
εὐλαβέομαι 1	reverence	συγκακουχέομαι 1	suffer with	διάκρισις 1	discern, critique
καταφεύγω 1	taking refuge	καταβάλλω 1	lay down	τρέχω 1	run, strive
κοινωνέω 1	share	ἀνακαινίζω 1	renew	κρύπτω 1	hide
ἀπαλλάσσω 1	release	κατακρίνω 1	sentence	λούω 1	wash
ὑποστρέφω 1	return	ἐπισκοπέω 1	see to it	ἐμμένω 1	remain

APPENDIX 2

People Verbal Activity					
θεωρέω 1	perceive	ἀποτίθημι 1	set aside	ἐκτρέπω 1	turn away
κωλύω 1	prevent	αἱρέω 1	chose	φύω 1	sprout
καταπίνω 1	drown	κάμνω 1	grow weary	παρίημι 1	weaken
δέχομαι 1	march	λογίζομαι 1	calculate	ἀνορθόω 1	strengthen
ἐνυβρίζω 1	insult	ἐγείρω 1	raise	παραλύω 1	make feeble
μετριοπαθέω 1	deal gently	παραπίπτω 1	fall away	θεατρίζω 1	publicly expose
καρτερέω 1	endure	ὀλιγωρέω 1	despise	ἀρνέομαι 1	deny
μακροθυμέω 1	patience	κατοικέω 1	live in	ἐπικαλέω 1	call upon
συγκεράννυμι 1	combine	εἴσειμι 1	enter	ἀνατέλλω 1	descend
παροξυσμός 1	stir up	ἀνακάμπτω 1	return	ἐκβαίνω 1	leave out
ἀναλογίζομαι 1	consider	ὑπάρχω 1	possess	ἰάομαι 1	heal, restore
γενεαλογέω 1	trace decent	ἀθετέω 1	set aside, reject	ἐλπίζω 1	hope
ἐμπίπτω 1	fall into	ζητέω 1	seek	οἰκτιρμός 1	pity
ἀποδοκιμάζω 1	reject	κυκλόω 1	welcome	ἑκουσίως 1	willful, deliberate
ἀποδεκατόω 1	collect a tenth	φανερόω 1	appear (make visible)	τελευτάω 1	come to the end, die
ἀποστρέφω 1	turning away	καταπατέω 1	trample under foot	ἐπίσταμαι 1	acquaintance
ἀναμιμνήσκω 1	remember	παροικέω 1	live as a stranger	ἀποβλέπω 1	look ahead
ὑποστέλλω 1	hesitate, Timidity	ἐνοχλέω 1	cause trouble	φαντάζω 1	reveal
συναπόλλυμι 1	perish with	ἀφοράω 1	fix eyes, look away	διακονέω 1	serve
παραπικραίνω 1	disobey	ἀπογράφω 1	recorded	περιαιρέω 1	take away
ἀντικαθίστημι 1	resist	ἀφομοιόω 1	to be like	μιαίνω 1	make ceremonially unclean
ἀνταγωνίζομαι 1	struggle against	παραμένω 1	continue	διώκω 1	hasten toward
ἐκλανθάνομαι 1	forget	ψηλαφάω 1	touch	διαστέλλω 1	thing commanded
Παραλαμ-βάνω 1	receive	ἑρμηνεύω 1	interpret	καταβαίνω 0	decent
παραδειγματίζω 1	ridicule	ἀποστρέφω 1	turning away	ἀπεκδέχομαι 1	eagerly await

Table 4—Words in Hebrews Linked with Other Spiritual Beings

APPENDIX 2

Spiritual Being and Verbal Noun Referents					
ἄγγελος 11	angels	ἐχθρός 2	enemies	πνεῦμα 12	spirits
διάβολος 1	devil	Χερούβ 1	cherubim	διακονία 1	ministry
κράτος 1	power	λειτουργικός 1		ministering (adj.)	
λειτουργός 2	minister				

Spiritual Being Verbal Activity		
ἀποστέλλω 1	being sent out	
προσκυνέω 2	worship	
ὀλοθρεύω 1	destroying	

Table 5—Hebrews 9:27–28 Lexemes

καὶ	καί	and	καθ	κατά	in accordance with
ὅσον	ὅσος	just as	ἀπόκειται	ἀπόκειμαι	it is reserved
τοῖς	ὁ	article	ἀνθρώποις	ἄνθρωπος	men
ἅπαξ	ἅπαξ	once	ἀποθανεῖν	ἀποθνῄσκω	die
μετὰ	μετά	after (with)	δὲ	δέ	but
τοῦτο	οὗτος	this	κρίσις	κρίσις	judgment
οὕτως	οὕτω	in the same way	καὶ	καί	likewise
ὁ	ὁ	article	Χριστὸς	Χριστός	Christ
ἅπαξ	ἅπαξ (adv.)	once	προσενεχθεὶς	προσφέρω	having offered himself
εἰς with inf.	εἰς	for the purpose	τὸ	ὁ	article
πολλῶν	πολύς	many	ἀνενεγκεῖν	ἀναφέρω	to bear
ἁμαρτίας acc. pl.	ἁμαρτία	sins	ἐκ	ἐκ	from
δευτέρου gen.	δεύτερος	second series	χωρὶς adv.	χωρίς	without
ἁμαρτίας gen.	ἁμαρτία	sins	ὀφθήσεται	ὁράω	will appear
τοῖς	ὁ	article	αὐτὸν acc.	αὐτός	him
ἀπεκδεχομένοις	ἀπεκδέχομαι	those eagerly awaiting	εἰς acc.	εἰς	for
σωτηρίαν		salvation			

APPENDIX 2

Table 9—Spatial Syntax Cohesion in Hebrews

Text	Adj. Syntax	Subject Noun	Spatial Meaning
1:2c τοὺς αἰῶνας (Son's achievement on cross & judgment)		αἰών "eternal/ perpetual-*places*" masc. pl.	"the eternal/perpetual-*places*" (11:3 invisible creation changes)
1:6 εἰς τὴν οἰκουμένην (Son's enthronement to rule)		οἰκουμένην "dominion-rule" fem. sg.	"into the dominion-rule" (invisible creation)
1:8 εἰς τὸν αἰῶνα τοῦ αἰῶνος (Son's location in heaven at throne)		αἰών "eternal/perpetual-*place*" masc. sg.	"into the eternal/perpetual-*place* of the eternal/perpetual-*place*" (invisible creation)
1:8 τῆς βασιλείας σου (Son's kingdom)		βασιλείας "kingdom" fem. sg.	"your kingdom" (invisible creation)
1:10 οἱ οὐρανοί (Son's ministry)		οὐρανοῖς "heavens" masc. pl.	"the heavens" (all creation)
2:4 πνεύματος ἁγίου μερισμοῖς (believers reception of spirit body)		ἁγίου "holy *place*" neut. sg. + πνεύματος "spirit" neut. sg.	"by a distribution of a spirit of a holy-*place*" (holy pneumatic body in heaven after death)
2:5 τὴν οἰκουμένην τὴν μέλλουσαν (not angelic rule)	pres. act. ptc. acc. fem. sg.	οἰκουμένην "dominion-rule" fem. sg.	"the present subsequently coming dominion-rule" (invisible creation)
4:14 διεληλυθότα τοὺς οὐρανούς (Christ)		οὐρανοῖς "heavens" masc. pl.	"having gone through the heavens" (all creation)
6:4 μετόχους γενηθέντας πνεύματος ἁγίου (believer transformed to spirit)		ἁγίου "holy *place*" neut. sg. + πνεύματος "spirit" neut. sg.	"after becoming partakers of a spirit of a holy-*place*" (pneumatic body into heaven)
6:5 μέλλοντος αἰῶνος (believer in heaven)	pres. act. ptc. gen. masc. sg.	αἰών "eternal/perpetual-*place*" masc. sg.	"the present subsequently coming eternal/perpetual-*place*" (invisible creation)
6:19 εἰς τὸ ἐσώτερον τοῦ καταπετάσματος (Jesus & believers)	acc. neut. sg.	καταπετάσματος "veil" neut. sg.	"into the inner veil" (invisible creation)
7:26 ὑψηλότερος τῶν οὐρανῶν (Jesus)		οὐρανοῖς "heavens" masc. pl.	"exalted above the heavens" (all creation)

APPENDIX 2

5:6; 6:20; 7:17, 21, 24, 28; cf. 13:8, 21 εἰς τὸν αἰῶνα (Jesus)		αἰών "eternal/ perpetual-*place*" masc. sg.	"into the eternal-*place*" (invisible creation)
8:1 ἐν τοῖς οὐρανοῖς (Son ministry)		1:10 οὐρανοῖς "heavens" masc. pl.	"in the heavens" (all creation)
8:2 τῶν ἁγίων (Son ministry)		ἁγίων "holy places" neut. pl.	"of the holy places" (first spatial use)
8:2 τῆς σκηνῆς τῆς ἀληθινῆς (all creation)	gen. fem. sg.	σκηνῆς "tent" fem. sg.	"the true tent or tabernacle" (all creation)
8:5 σκηνήν (earthly)		σκηνῆς "tent" fem.	"tent"
9:1 τό τε ἅγιον κοσμικόν (earthly)	acc. neut. sg.	ἅγιος "holy *place*" neut. sg.	"even the earthly holy place" (first tent)
9:2 Ἅγια (earthly)	nom. fem. sg.[4]	9:2 σκηνή "tent" fem. sg.	"holy place" (first tent)
9:3 δεύτερον καταπέτασμα (earthly)	acc. neut. sg.	καταπέτασμα "veil" neut. sg.	"second veil" (between tents)
9:3 Ἅγια Ἁγίων (earthly)	nom. fem. sg. +gen. neut. pl.	9:2 σκηνή "tent" fem. sg.	"holy of holies," "most holy place"
9:6 τὴν πρώτην σκηνήν (earthly)	9:2 ἅγιος link	9:2 σκηνή "tent" fem. sg.	"the first tent" (holy place)
9:7 δευτέραν (earthly)	acc. fem. sg.	9:2 σκηνή "tent" fem. (subj. by context)	"the second *tent*" (holy of holies)
9:8 τοῦ πνεύματος τοῦ ἁγίου (Holy Spirit)	gen. neut. sg.	πνεῦμα "spirit" neut. sg.	Holy Spirit
9:8 τὴν τῶν ἁγίων ὁδὸν (veil intact & entry closed while first tent standing)	gen. neut. pl. Link 8:2; 9:3, 10:19	ὁδός "way" fem. sg.	"the way of the holy places" (both holy place & holy of holies)
9:8 τῆς πρώτης σκηνῆς (earthly)	9:2 ἅγιος link	9:2 σκηνή "tent" fem. sg.	"the first tent" (holy place)
9:11 διὰ τῆς μείζονος καὶ τελειοτέρας σκηνῆς (through veil & entrance opened in true tent in heaven)	9:2 ἅγιος link	σκηνή "tent" fem. sg.	"through the greater and more complete tent" (holy place & holy of holies now created as one tent)

---

4. The feminine gender is common in the LXX in Exodus and Leviticus in reference to the holy place and holies of holies or most holy place.

9:12 εἰς τὰ ἅγια (Christ)	acc. neut. pl. or acc. fem. sg.	9:11 σκηνή "tent" fem. sg.[5] 9:2 ἅγιος link rep. 9:11	"into the holy *tent*" (holy place & holy of holies now created one tent)
9:14 ὃς διὰ πνεύματος αἰωνίου ἑαυτὸν (Jesus)		πνεύματος "spirit" neut. sg. + αἰωνίου "eternal/ perpetual-*place*" neut. sg.	"who through a spirit of a eternal/perpetual-*place* himself" (Jesus's pneumatic body into heaven)
9:23 ἐν τοῖς οὐρανοῖς (not copy, true tent)	8:1–2 ἅγιος link	1:10; 8:1 οὐρανοῖς "heavens" masc. pl.	"in the heavens" (all creation)
9:24 εἰς...ἅγια (Christ)	acc. neut. pl.or acc. fem. sg.	σκηνή "tent" fem. sg. (subj. "tent" by context)	"into...a holy *tent*" (holy place & holy of holies now created one tent—since veil now gone)
9:24 εἰς αὐτὸν τὸν οὐρανόν (Christ)	acc. masc. sg. 8:2 ἅγιος link	1:10; 8:1 οὐρανοῖς "heaven" masc. sg.	"into heaven itself" (holy place & holy of holies now created one)
9:25 εἰς τὰ ἅγια cf. 9:24 (earthly priests)	acc. fem. sg. or acc. pl. neut. or noun,	9:11 if fem. sg.: σκηνή "tent," if neut. pl. noun: own subject	if adj. with tent: "into the holy *tent*," (probable); if noun: "into the holy *places*"
9:26 ἐπὶ συντελείᾳ τῶν αἰώνων (Christ finished)	7:28—8:2 ἅγιος link	αἰών "eternal/ perpetual-*places*" masc. pl.	"upon the completion of the eternal/ perpetual-*places*" (holy place & holy of holies now created one)
9:28 ἐκ δευτέρου (Christ ministry in heaven at throne)	gen. neut. or masc. sg.	if neut. sg. then ἅγιος "holy *place*"; if masc. then αἰών "eternal/ perpetual-*place*"	"from a second holy-*place*," "from a second eternal/perpetual-*place*," or idiom: "a second time"[6]

5. In the rhetorical context, the audience would probably understand the adjective "holy" (ἅγια) as linked with the feminine noun "tent" (σκηνή). Contra Hughes, *Commentary on the Epistle*, 307. Hughes writes, "At first sight ἅγια looks like a nominative feminine singular describing and agreeing with σκηνή ... ἡ πρώτη, and this would indeed be a legitimate way of construing it; but it is preferable to read it as a nom. neut. pl. corresponding with the LXX term τὰ ἅγια for the 'holy place.' Montefiore, however, is one who prefers to interpret ἅγια as qualifying σκηνή ('this Tent is called holy')" (ellipsis in original). In the FGT, there is no literary indication to signal a transition back to the noun form introduced in Heb 8:2 after changing to the adjective form in Heb 8:3. Either way, the point is moot. At Jesus's entrance there was no longer a distinction between the holy place and the holy of holies.

6. In context for the believer's entrance into heaven after death at judgment and the

APPENDIX 2

10:5 εἰσερχόμενος εἰς τὸν κόσμον (God-Christ body)		κοσμος "world" masc. sg.	"having entered himself into the world"
10:19 εἰς τὴν εἴσοδον τῶν ἁγίων (Christ)		αἰών "eternal/perpetual-*places*" masc. pl. 8:2; 9:3, 8 link	"into the entrance of the holy-*places*"
10:20 ὁδὸν πρόσφατον καὶ ζῶσαν διὰ τοῦ καταπετάσματος (entry opened)		ὁδός "way" fem. sg.; καταπέτασμα "veil" neut. sg.	"a recent and living way through the veil"
11:12 τὰ ἄστρα τοῦ οὐρανοῦ (earthly)		οὐρανός ("heaven") masc. sg.	"the stars of heaven" (visible heaven)
12:23 ἐν οὐρανοῖς (all creation)		οὐρανοῖς "heavens" masc. pl.	"in the heavens"
12:25 ἀπ' οὐρανῶν (all creation)		οὐρανοῖς "heavens" masc. pl.	"from the heavens"
12:26 τὴν γῆν ἀλλὰ καὶ τὸν οὐρανόν (earthly)		οὐρανός "heaven" masc. sg.	"the earth but also the heaven"
12:28 βασιλείαν (believers)		1:10 βασιλείαν "kingdom" fem. sg.	"kingdom" (invisible eternal creation)
13:8 εἰς τοὺς αἰῶνας (invisible creation)		αἰών "eternal/perpetual-*places*" masc. pl.	"into the eternal/perpetual-*places*"
13:21 εἰς τοὺς αἰῶνας (τῶν αἰώνων) (invisible creation)		αἰών "eternal/perpetual-*places*" masc. pl.	"into the eternal/perpetual-places of the eternal/perpetual-*places*"

previous uses of the ordinal δεύτερος ("second") in the unit F FGT about the spatial changes in the invisible creation regarding the holy place, the idiom is weak without context for second coming to earth, with only the repetitive use of "once" as possibly helpful. See chapter 4 unit F UC analysis. Cf. substantive links with either (Heb 9:26 + 1:2c + poss. *inclusio* with 7:28) or οὐρανοῖς ("heavens").

APPENDIX 2

Table 10—Ministry Comparison in Unit F (Heb 8:1–10:18)

Earthly Tabernacle	Text	True Tabernacle	Text
focus mainly first-area (holy place) tabernacle ministry	8:5, 7; 9:2, 6	better second-area/no longer first-area/new covenant ministry	8:6, 7, 8; 9:3, 7, 15
focus mainly holy place entrance	9:1; 10:1	now only holy of holies/heaven entrance	9:24
made with hands by people	8:2; 9:24	made by the Lord at entrance into heaven	8:2; 9:11
earthly creation as the true tabernacle antitype	8:5; 9:1, 24	in the heavens, in the holy places, as the true tabernacle type	8:1–2, 5; 9:8, 11, 23
Moses mediated	8:5; 9:19	Jesus as Christ mediated	10:10
animal blood sacrifice	9:12, 18–22	Jesus's blood sacrifice	9:12, 23, 26
earthly ministry	8:4	heavenly ministry	8:4
first covenant relationship/promises	8:7, 9, 13; 9:1, 15, 18; 10:9	second, new covenant relationship/promises	8:6, 7, 8, 10, 13; 9:15; 10:9; 12:24
fault found when executed at death and judgment	8:8	blameless, faultless when executed at death and judgment	8:7; 9:14, 27–28
cannot cleanse consciousness of sin at judgment in forgiveness	9:9, 23; 10:1–4	can cleanse consciousness of sin at judgment in forgiveness	9:14, 23; 10:18
law is a shadow	8:4; 9:19, 22; 10:1, 8;	Christ is the reality	8:10
sacrifices/offerings	8:3–4; 9:9–10	body of Jesus prepared	10:5–10
repeated offerings many times	8:3–4; 9:25; 10:11	one offering, now once accomplished	9:25, 26; 10:10, 18
many ministers as priests going in and out in mediation daily and annually in Yom Kippur	9:6	one minister as perpetual high priest sitting on throne in mediation	8:1; 9:24; 10:12–14
old, obsolete ministry	8:13; 9:8, 10	now, perpetual ministry	8:6, 8; 9:9; 10:37
near God	10:1	presence of God	8:1; 9:24
out of Egypt	8:9	endpoint heaven	9:15, 26
flesh and blood	9:13; 10:20	bodily transformation	8:10–12; 10:5, 16–17

Appendix 3

HEBREWS 9:27-28 SENTENCE DIAGRAM

[rhetorical argument: 2 sentences in premise support sentence conclusion]
And [connective] [Begin left dislocation literary device *10]
    in accordance with this [macrosummary: connects discourse to this point]
    just as [first statement of premises: protasis]
        it is reserved [PPI3S main vb./sub. it/ antecedent: to die]
        for people [NDMP dat. direct object]
        once ←[ordinal-adv./time-space loc. from discourse context]
        to die ← [subst. inf./sub. it with antecedent: people]
        but [adversative particle contrastive two clauses/premises]
        a judgment ←[NNFS anarthrous/individual before Jesus after death]
        is after this [acc. marker of another point in-space/dem. pron.*1]
Adv. καὶ so also [second statement: apodosis] [End left dislocation *10]
        Christ [NNMS sub. a person subcategory\statement 1 *2]
        who being offered ←[attributive aorist ptc.]
        once ←[ordinal-adv./time-space loc. from discourse context]
        for the purpose to bear sins [εἰς τὰ + inf. adv. inf. purpose]
        of many people [attributive gen. moderates people's sins]
        from a second place ←[ἐκ-δευτέρου-gen.-ordinal of position *3]
        without sins [adv. gen. after word it governs]
        will be appearing [FPI3S main vb. *4]
            to those themselves eagerly [attrib. PMPtcDMP]
            awaiting [presently at time of death/judgment/how long? *5]
            him [AMS per. pron. antecedent Christ]
            for salvation ←[AFS εἰς acc. advantage *6]

*1 μετὰ δὲ τοῦτο "but after this" demon. pron. antecedent death and judgment
*2 messianic force as 1) offering [unit E] 2) anointed priest [unit D]; [both unit F]
*3 ordinal idiom force from context as 1) time/space or 2) position/rank cf. Ps 110
*4 Not ordinarily limited force in STL, LXX, and NT for only a one-time event
*5 Cf. Heb 10:37 μικρὸν ὅσον ὅσον "a very little while"
*6 Subtopics death, judgment, intercession, and salvation linked by cognates, phrases, from OT midrash from DI (Heb 1:1–4) to conclusion about Christ
*7 Two sentence warrants about people assumed true
*8 Conclusion sentence warrant about Christ assumed true
*9 Individual must die and face individual judgment before individual appearing of Christ to individual believers
*10 Return summary of previous themes in protasis to highlight and emphasize statements to follow in apodosis.

Bibliography

Adams, Edward. *Constructing the World: A Study in Paul's Cosmological Language*. Edinburgh: T&T Clark, 2000.

———. "The Cosmology of Hebrews." In *The Epistle to the Hebrews and Christian Theology*, edited by Richard Bauckham et al., 122–39. Grand Rapids: Eerdmans, 2009.

———. "Graeco-Roman and Ancient Jewish Cosmology." In *Cosmology and New Testament Theology*, edited by Jonathan T. Pennington and Sean M. McDonough, 5–27. London: T&T Clark, 2008.

———. *The Stars Will Fall from Heaven: Cosmic Catastrophe in the New Testament and Its World*. New York: T&T Clark, 2007.

Adler, William. "The Pseudepigrapha in the Early Church." In *The Canon Debate*, edited by Lee M. McDonald and James A. Sanders, 211–28. Peabody, MA: Hendrickson, 2002.

Aitken, Ellen Bradshaw. "The Body of Jesus Outside the Eternal City: Mapping Ritual Space in the Epistle to the Hebrews." In *Hebrews in Contexts*, edited by Gabriella Gelardini and Harold Attridge, 194–209. Leiden: Brill, 2016.

Aland, Barbara, et al., eds. *Nestle-Aland Novum Testamentum Graece*. 28th ed. Westphalia: Deutsche Bibelgesellschaft, 2012.

Alexander, Philip S. "3 (Hebrew Apocalypse of) Enoch: A New Translation and Introduction." In OTP 1:223–54.

———. "Geography and the Bible: Early Jewish Geography." In *ABD* 2:977–88.

———. "Jewish Aramaic Translation of Hebrew Scripture." In *Mikra: Text, Reading and Interpretation of the Hebrew Bible in Ancient Judaism and Early Christianity*, edited by Martin J. Mulder and Harry Sysling, 217–53. Grand Rapids: Baker Academic, 2004.

———. *The Mystical Texts*. New York: T&T Clark, 2006.

———. "Mysticism." In *The Oxford Handbook of Jewish Studies*, edited by Martin Goodman, 704–32. Oxford: Oxford University Press, 2004.

———. "Rabbinic Judaism and the New Testament." *ZNW* 74 (1983) 237–46.

Alfeyev, Hilarion. *Christ the Conqueror of Hell: the Descent into Hades from an Orthodox Perpesctive*. Crestwood, NY: St. Vladimirs, 2009.

Allen, David L. *Hebrews*. Nashville: B&H, 2010.

———. *Lukan Authorship of Hebrews*. Nashville: B&H, 2010.

BIBLIOGRAPHY

Allen, David M. *According to the Scriptures: The Death of Christ in the Old Testament and the New*. London: SCM, 2018.

———. "'Forgotten Ages': Times and Space in Hebrews 1:2." *BT* 61 (2010) 144–51.

Allen, Michael. *Grounded in Heaven: Recentering Christian Hope and Life on God*. Grand Rapids: Eerdmans, 2018.

Anderson, Charles P. "Lukan Cosmology and the Ascension." In *Ascent into Heaven in Luke-Acts: New Explorations of Luke's Narrative Hinge*, edited by David K. Bryan and David W. Pao, 175–212. Minneapolis: Fortress, 2016.

Andriessen, Paul. "Das Grossere und vollkommenere Zelt (Hebr 9,11)." *BZ* 15 (1971) 76–92.

———. "De Betekenis van Hebr. 1,6." *StC* 35 (1960) 1–13.

Aquinas, Thomas. *Summa Theologica*. Translated by Fathers of the English Dominican Province. London: Burns, Oates & Washbourne, n.d.

Attridge, Harold W. "God in Hebrews." In *The Epistle to the Hebrews and Christian Theology*, edited by Richard Bauckham et al., 95–110. Grand Rapids: Eerdmans, 2009.

———. "God in Hebrews: Urging Children to Heavenly Glory." In *The Forgotten God: Perspectives in Biblical Theology*, edited by A. Andrew Das and Frank J. Matera, 197–209. Louisville: Westminister John Knox, 2002.

———. "How the Scrolls Impacted Scholarship on Hebrews." In *The Scrolls and Christian Origins*, edited by James H. Charlesworth, 203–30. Vol. 3 of *The Bible and the Dead Sea Scrolls*. Waco, TX: Baylor University Press, 2006.

———. "The Uses of Antithesis in Hebrews 8–10." In *Christians among Jews and Gentiles: Essays in Honor of Krister Stendahl on His Sixty-fifth Birthday*, edited by George W. E. Nickelsburg and George W. MacRae, 1–9. Philadelphia: Fortress, 1986.

Attridge, Harold W., and Helmut Koester. *The Epistle to the Hebrews: A Commentary on the Epistle to the Hebrews*. Philadelphia: Fortress, 1989.

Aune, David E. "Anthropological Duality in the Eschatology of 2 Cor 4:16–5:10." In *Paul Beyond the Judaism and Hellenism Divide*, edited by Troels Engberg-Pendersen, 215–39. Louisville: Westminster John Know, 2001.

———. "Apocalyptic and New Testament Interpretation." In *Method and Meaning: Essays on New Testament Interpretation in Honor of Harold W. Attridge*, edited by Andrew B. McGowan and Kent Harold Richards, 237–58. Atlanta: Society of Biblical Literature, 2011.

Austin, J. L. *How to Do Things with Words*. 2nd ed. Cambridge: Harvard University Press, 1975.

Backhaus, Knut. *Der Hebräerbrief*. Regenburg, Germany: Friedrich Pustet, 2009.

———. "Das Land der Verheißung: Die Heimat der Glaubenden im Hebräerbrief." *NTS* 47 (2001) 171–88.

———. *Der sprechende Gott: Gesammelte Studien zum Hebräerbrief*. Tübingen, Germany: Mohr Siebeck, 2009.

———. "Zwei harte Knoten: Todes—und Gerichtsangst im Hebräerbrief." *NTS* 55 (2009) 198–217.

Bailey, Robert E. "Is 'Sleep' the Proper Biblical Term for the Intermediate State?" *ZNW* 55 (1964) 161–67.

———. "Life after Death: A New Testament Study in the Relation of Body and Soul." PhD diss., University of Edinburgh, 1962.

BIBLIOGRAPHY

Baird, William. *History of New Testament Research.* 3 vols. Minneapolis: Fortress, 1992–2013.

Baker, David L. "Typology and the Christian Use of the Old Testament." In *The Right Doctrine from the Wrong Texts: Essays on the Use of the Old Testament in the New,* edited by G. K. Beale, 313-30. Grand Rapids: Baker, 1994.

Baptist Press Staff. "Billy Graham, 99, Now in 'the Presence of God.'" *Baptist Press,* Feb 21, 2018. https://www.baptistpress.com/resource-library/news/billy-graham-99-now-in-the-presence-of-god/.

Barker, Margaret. "Beyond the Veil of the Temple: The High Priestly Origins of the Apocalypses." *SJT* 51 (1988) 1–21.

Barnard, Jody A. *The Mysticism of Hebrews: Exploring the Role of Jewish Apocalyptic Mysticism in the Epistle to the Hebrews.* Tübingen, Germany: Mohr Siebeck, 2012.

Barrett, C. K. "The Eschatology of the Epistle of Hebrews." In *The Letter to the Hebrews: Critical Readings,* edited by Scott D. Mackie, 146–70. 1956. Reprint, New York: T&T Clark, 2018.

———. "New Testament Eschatology." *SJT* 6 (1955) 137–55.

Barr, James. *Biblical Words for Time.* London: SCM, 1962.

———. *The Concept of Biblical Theology: An Old Testament Perspective.* Minneapolis: Fortress, 1999.

———. *The Garden of Eden and the Hope of Immortality.* Minneapolis: Fortress, 1992.

———. *The Semantics of Biblical Language.* London: Oxford University Press, 1961.

Barth, Christoph. *Die Errettung vom Tode in den individuellen Klage: Und Dankliedern des Alten Testament.* Zollikon: Evangelischer Verlag, 1947.

Barth, Gerhard. *Der Tod Jesu Christi im Verständnis des Neuen Testaments.* Neukirchen-Vluyn, Germany: Neukirchener, 1992.

Bass, Justin W. *The Battle for the Keys: Revelation 1:18 and Christ's Descent into the Underworld.* Eugene, OR: Wipf & Stock, 2014.

Bateman, Herbert W., IV. *Four Views on the Warning Passages in Hebrews.* Grand Rapids: Kregel, 2007.

Bauckham, Richard. *The Fate of the Dead: Studies on the Jewish and Christian Apocalypses.* Atlanta: Society of Biblical Literature, 1998.

———. *Jesus and the God of Israel: God Crucified and Other Studies on the New Testament's Christology of Divine Identity.* Grand Rapids: Eerdmans, 2009.

———. "Life, Death, and the Afterlife in Second Temple Judaism." In *Life in the Face of Death: The Resurrection Message of the New Testament,* edited by Richard N. Longenecker, 80–95. Grand Rapids: Eerdmans, 1998.

Bauckham, Richard, et al. *The Epistle to the Hebrews and Christian Theology.* Grand Rapids: Eerdmans, 2009 .

Bauckham, Richard, et al., eds. *Old Testament Pseudepigrapha: More Noncanonical Scriptures.* Grand Rapids: Eerdmans, 2013.

Bauer, Walter. *Orthodoxy and Heresy in Earliest Christianity.* Mifflintown, PA: Sigler, 1996.

Baugh, Steven M. "The Cloud of Witnesses in Hebrews 11." *WTJ* 68 (2006) 113–32.

———. "Greek Periods in the Book of Hebrews." *NovT* 60 (2018) 24–44.

———. "Whose Spirit? Christ's Spirit or the Holy Spirit in Hebrews 9:14." Paper presented at the Annual Meeting of the Evangelical Theological Society, Denver, CO, Nov 13, 2018.

Bautch, Kelley Coblentz. "Spatiality and Apocalyptic Literature." *HeBAI* 5 (2016) 273–88.

Baxter, Richard. "Whether the Souls Departed Enjoy this Rest before the Resurrection." In *The Saints Everlasting Rest*, edited by John T. Wilkinson, 94–96. Vancouver, BC: Regent College Publishing, 2004.

Baxter, Wayne. *Israel's Only Shepherd: Matthew's Shepherd Motif and His Social Setting*. New York: T&T Clark, 2012.

Beale, G. K. *Handbook on the New Testament Use of the Old Testament: Exegesis and Interpretation*. Grand Rapids: Baker, 2012.

———. *The Temple and the Church's Mission: A Biblical Theology of the Dwelling Place of God*. Downers Grove, IL: InterVarsity, 2004.

Beale, G. K., and D. A. Carson. *Commentary on the New Testament Use of the Old Testament*. Grand Rapids: Baker Academic, 2007.

Beale, G. K., and Mitchell Kim. *God Dwells among Us: Expanding Eden to the Ends of the Earth*. Downers Grove, IL: InterVarsity, 2014.

Beekman, John, and John Callow. *Translating the Word of God: With Scripture and Topical Indexes*. Grand Rapids: Zondervan, 1974.

Beek, William L. Vander. "Hebrews: A 'Doxology' of the Word." *Mid-America Journal of Theology* 16 (2005) 13–28.

Bell, Richard H. *Deliver Us from Evil: Interpreting the Redemption from the Power of Satan in New Testament Theology*. Tübingen, Germany: Mohr Siebeck, 2007.

Ben-Dov, Jonathan. "Apocalyptic Temporality. The Force of the Here and Now." *HeBAI* 5 (2016) 289–303.

Bergh, Ronald H. van der. "A Textual Comparison of Hebrews 10:5b–7 and LXX Psalm 39:7–9." *Neot* 42 (2008) 353–82.

Berquist, Jon L. "Critical Spatiality and the Book of Hebrews." In *Hebrews in Contexts*, edited by Gabriella Gelardini and Harold Attridge, 181–93. Leiden: Brill, 2016.

Berthelot, Katell. "Early Jewish Literature Written in Greek." In *EDEJ* 181–200.

Bertolet, Timothy J. "Hebrews 5:7 as the Cry of the Davidic Sufferer." *Die Skrflig* 51 (2017) 1–10. https://indieskriflig.org.za/index.php/skriflig/article/view/2286.

———. "The Obedience of Sonship: Adamic Obedience as the Grounds for Heavenly Ascension in the Book of Hebrews." PhD diss., University of Pretoria, Pretoria, South Africa, 2017.

Weber, Robertus, and R. Gryson. *Biblia Sacra Iuxta Vulgatam Versionem*. 3rd ed. Stuttgart: Deutsche Bibelgesellschaft, 1969.

Bieberstein, Klaus. "Jenseits der Todesschwelle: Die Entstehung der Auferweckungshoffnungen in der alttestamentlich-frühjüdischen Literatur." In *Tod und Jenseits im alten Israel und in seiner Umwelt*, edited by Herausgegben von Angelika Berlejung and Bernd Janowski, 423–46. Tübingen, Germany: Mohr Siebeck, 2009.

Bietenhard, Hans. *Die himmlische Welt im Urchristentum und Spätjudentum*. Tübingen, Germany: Mohr Siebeck, 1951.

———. "οὐρανός." In *NIDNT* 2:191–92.

Bimson, John J. "Reconsidering a 'Cosmic Fall.'" *Science & Christian Belief* 18 (2006) 63–81.

Black, David Alan. "Hebrews 1:1–4: A Study in Discourse Analysis." *WTJ* 49 (1987) 175–94.

———. *Linguistics for Students of New Testament Greek: A Survey of Basic Concepts and Applications*. 2nd ed. Grand Rapids: Baker, 1995.

———. "The Problem of the Literary Structure of Hebrews: An Evaluation and a Proposal." *GTJ* 7 (1986) 163–77.
Black, David Alan, and Benjamin L. Merkle, eds. *Linguistics and New Testament Greek: Key Issues in the Current Debate*. Grand Rapids: Baker Academic, 2020.
Black, David Alan, and David S. Dockery. *New Testament Criticism and Interpretation*. Grand Rapids: Zondervan, 1991.
Blass, Friedrich, Albert Debrunner, and Robert Walter Funk. *A Greek Grammar of the New Testament and Other Early Christian Literature*. Chicago: University of Chicago Press, 1961.
Bluhm, Heinz Seigfried. *Martin Luther, Creative Translator*. St. Louis: Concordia, 1965.
Bock, Darrell L. *Luke 1:1—9:50*. Vol. 1. Baker Exegetical Commentary on the New Testament. Grand Rapids: Baker Academic, 1994.
———. "New Testament Word Analysis." In *Introducing New Testament Interpretation: Guides to New Testament Exegesis*, edited by Scot McKnight, 97–113. Grand Rapids: Baker, 1989.
Bockmuehl, Markus. "Locating Paradise." In *Paradise in Antiquity: Jewish and Christian Views*, edited by Markus Bockmuehl and Guy G. Stroumsa, 192–209. Cambridge: Cambridge University Press, 2010.
Bolt, Peter G. "Life, Death, and the Afterlife in the Greco-Roman World." In *Life in the Face of Death: The Resurrection Message of the New Testament*, edited by Richard N. Longenecker, 51–79. McNTS. Grand Rapids: Eerdmans, 1998.
Borgen, Peder, Kåre Fuglseth, and Roald Skarsten. *The Works of Philo: Greek Text with Morphology*. Bellingham, WA: Logos, 2005.
Bornkamm, Günther. *Studien Zu Antike Und Urchristentum*. München: Kaiser, 1959.
Bousset, D. Wilhelm. *Die Himmelsreise der Seele*. Darmstadt, Germany: Wissenschaftliche Buchgesellschaft, 1971.
Bowman, John W. "Eschatology in the OT." *IDB* 2:135–40.
Brandon, S. G. F. *The Judgment of the Dead: An Historical and Comparative Study of the Idea of a Post-Mortem Judgment in the Major Religions*. London: Weidenfeld and Nicolson, 1967.
Bremmer, Jan. N. "Descents to Hell and Ascents to Heaven in Apocalyptic Literature." In *The Oxford Handbook of Apocalyptic Literature*, edited by John J. Collins, 340–57. Oxford: Oxford University Press, 2014.
———. *The Early Greek Concept of the Soul*. Princeton: Princeton University Press, 1983.
———. *The Rise and Fall of the Afterlife: The 1995 Read-Tuckwell Lectures at the University of Bristol*. London: Routledge, 2002.
Briggs, Richard S. "Speech-Act Theory." In *DTIB* 763–66.
Bruce, F. F. *History of the Bible in English: From the Earliest Versions*. 3rd ed. New York: Oxford University Press, 1978.
———. *The Epistle to the Hebrews*. Grand Rapids: Eerdmans, 1990.
Bryan, David K. "A Revised Cosmic Hierarchy Revealed." In *Ascent into Heaven in Luke-Acts: New Explorations of Luke's Narrative Hinge*, edited by David K. Bryan and David W. Pao, 61–82. Minneapolis: Fortress, 2016.
Buchanan, George Wesley. *Eschatology: The Doctrine of the Future Life in Israel, in Judaism, and in Christianity, A Critical History*. New York: Schocken, 1963.
Bulley, Alan D. "Death and Rhetoric in the Hebrews 'Hymn to Faith.'" *SR* 25 (1996) 409–23.

Bultmann, Rudolf Karl. *The New Testament and Mythology and Other Basic Writings*. Fortress, 1984.

———. "New Testament and Mythology." In *Kerygma and Myth*, edited by H. W. Bartsch, 1–16. New York: Harper & Row, 1961.

———. *Theology of the New Testament*. 2 vols. Translated by Kendrick Grobel. London: SCM, 1951–55.

Burns, Dylan M. "Apocalypses Among Gnostics and Manichaeans." In *The Oxford Handbook of Apocalyptic Literature*, edited by John J. Collins, 358–72. Oxford: Oxford University Press, 2014.

Burrows, Eric. "Some Cosmological Patterns in Babylonian Religion." In *Cult and Cosmos: Tilting Towards a Temple-Centered Theology*, edited by L. Michael Morales, 27–47. Paris: Peeters, 2014.

Burton, Ernest DeWitt. *Spirit, Soul, and Flesh: πνεῦμα, ψυχή, and σάρξ in Greek Writings and Translated Works from the Earliest Period to 225 AD; And of their Equivalents Rûaḥ, Nepeš and Baśar in the Hebrew Old Testament*. Historical and Linguistic Studies, Second Series 3. Chicago: University of Chicago Press, 1918.

Caird, George B. *The Language and Imagery of the Bible*. London: Duckworth, 1980.

Calaway, Jared C. *The Sabbath and the Sanctuary: Access to God in the Letter to the Hebrews and its Priestly Context*. Tübingen, Germany: Mohr Siebeck, 2013.

Campbell, Constantine R. *Basics of Verbal Aspect in Biblical Greek*. Grand Rapids: Zondervan, 2008.

Caneday, Ardel B. "The Eschatological World Already Subjected to the Son: The Οἰκουμένη of Hebrews 1:6 and the Son's Enthronement." In *A Cloud of Witnesses: The Theology of Hebrews in Its Ancient Contexts*, edited by Richard Bauckham and Nathan MacDonald, 28–39. London: T&T Clark, 2008.

———. "God's Parabolic Design for Israel's Tabernacle: A Cluster of Earthly Shadows of Heavenly Realities." *SBJT* 24 (2020) 103–24.

Carlston, Charles. "The Vocabulary of Perfection in Philo and Hebrews." In *Unity and Diversity in New Testament Theology: Essays in Honor of George E. Ladd*, edited by Robert A. Guelich, 133–60. Grand Rapids: Eerdmans, 1978.

Carmignac, Jean. "Description du phénomène de l'Apocalyptique." In *Apocalypticism in the Mediterranean World and the Near East*, edited by David Hellholm, 163–70. Tübingen, Germany: Mohr Siebeck, 1983.

Carson, D. A. *Exegetical Fallacies*. 2nd ed. Grand Rapids: Baker, 1996.

———. "The Limits of Functional Equivalence in Bible Translation." In *The Challenge of Bible Translation: Communicating God's Word to the World*, edited by Glen G. Scorgie et al., 65–114. Grand Rapids: Zondervan, 2003.

Casey, Edward S. *The Fate of Place: A Philosophical History*. Los Angeles: University of California Press, 1997.

———. *Getting Back to Place: Toward a Renewed Understanding of the Place-World*. 2nd ed. Bloomington: Indiana University Press, 2009.

Casey, Juliana. "Christian Assembly in Hebrews: A Fantasy Island?" *TD* 30 (1982) 323–35.

Cassidy, James J. *God's Time for Us: Barth's Reconciliation of Eternity and Time in Jesus Christ*. Bellingham, WA, Lexham, 2016.

Cavallin, H. C. C. *Life after Death: Paul's Argument for the Resurrection of the Dead in 1 Cor. 15; Part 1: An Enquiry Into the Jewish Background*. Lund, Sweden: CWK Gleerup, 1974.

Cervera i Valls, Jordi. "Jesús, gran sacerdot i víctima, en Hebreus: Una teologia judeocristiana de la mediació i de l'expiació." *RCT* 34 (2009) 477–502.
Charles, Robert Henry. *Eschatology: The Doctrine of the Future Life in Israel, in Judaism, and in Christianity, A Critical History*. New York: Schocken, 1963.
Charlesworth, James H. Editor. *The Old Testament Pseudepigrapha*. 2 vols. New York: Yale University Press, 1983.
Cheney, James Loring. "The Sources of Tyndale's New Testament." PhD diss., University of Leipzig, Leipzig, Germany, 1883.
Clark-Soles, Jaime. *Death and Afterlife in the New Testament*. New York: T&T Clark, 2006.
Cockerill, Gareth Lee. "The Better Resurrection (Heb. 11:35): A Key to the Structure and Rhetorical Purpose of Hebrews 11." *TynBul* 51 (2000) 215–34.
Cody, Aelred. *Heavenly Sanctuary and Liturgy in the Epistle to the Hebrews: The Achievement of Salvation in the Epistle's Perspectives*. St. Meinrad, IN: Grail Publications, 1960.
Coetsee, Albert J. "Die sprekende God in die boek Hebreërs: 'n openbaringshistoriese studie," PhD diss., North-West University, Potchefstroom, South Africa, 2014.
―――. "The Unfolding of God's Revelation in Hebrews 1:1–2a." *HTS Teologiese Studies/Theological Studies* 72 (2016) 1–8.
Cole, Graham A. *Against the Darkness: The Doctrine of Angels, Satan, and Demons*. Foundations of Evangelical Theology. Wheaton, IL: Crossway, 2019.
Collins, John J. "The Afterlife in Apocalyptic Literature." In *Judaism in Late Antiquity, Part 4: Death, Life-After-Death, Resurrection and the World-to-Come in the Judaism of Antiquity*, edited by Alan J. Avery-Peck and Jacob Neusner, 119–39. Leiden: Brill, 2000.
―――. *The Apocalyptic Imagination: An Introduction to Jewish Apocalyptic Literature*. Grand Rapids: Eerdmans, 1998.
―――. "Early Judaism in Modern Scholarship." In *EDEJ* 12.
―――. "The Genre Apocalypse Reconsidered." *ZAC* 20 (2016) 21–40.
―――. "Introduction, Towards the Morphology of a Genre." In *Semeia 14 Apocalypse: The Morphology of a Genre*, edited by John J. Collins, 1–20. Atlanta: Society of Biblical Literature, 1979.
―――. "The Jewish Apocalypses." In *Semeia 14 Apocalypse: The Morphology of a Genre*, edited by John J. Collins, 21–59. Atlanta: Society of Biblical Literature, 1979.
―――, ed. *Semeia 14 Apocalypse: The Morphology of a Genre*. Atlanta: Society of Biblical Literature, 1979.
―――. "The Seven Heavens in Jewish and Christian Apocalypses." In *Death, Ecstasy, and Other Worldly Journeys*, edited by John J. Collins and Michael Fishbane, 59–93. Albany, NY: State University of New York Press, 1995.
―――. "A Throne in the Heavens: Apotheosis." In *Death, Ecstasy, and Other Worldly Journeys*, edited by John J. Collins and Michael Fishbane, 43–58. Albany, NY: State University of New York Press, 1995.
Compton, Jared M. *Psalm 110 and the Logic of Hebrews*. New York: T&T Clark, 2015.
Coogan, Michael D., et al., eds. *The New Oxford Annotated Apocrypha: New Revised Standard Version*. 3rd ed. Oxford: Oxford University Press, 2007.
Cooper, John W. *Body, Soul and Life Everlasting: Biblical Anthropology and the Monism-Dualism Debate*. Grand Rapids: Eerdmans, 1989.

Cortez, Felix. H. "'The Anchor of the Soul that Enters Within the Veil': The Ascension of the 'Son' in the Letter to the Hebrews." PhD diss., Andrews University Seventh-day Adventist Theological Seminary, Berrien Springs, MI, 2008.

———. "From the Holy to the Most Holy Place: The Period of Hebrews 9:6–10 and the Day of Atonement as a Metaphor of Transition." *JBL* 125 (2006) 527–47.

Costley, Angela. *Creation and Christ*. Tübingen, Germany: Mohr Siebeck, 2020.

Cotterell, Peter, and Max Turner. *Linguistics and Biblical Interpretation*. Downers Grove, IL: InterVarsity, 1989.

Cremer, Hermann. "Οὐρανός." In *BTLNTG* 464–67.

Criswell, W. A., ed. *Criswell Study Bible King James Version*. Nashville: Thomas Nelson, 1979.

Crowson, Milton. *The Epistle to the Hebrews*. Nashville: Randall House, 2000.

Crowther, David Carter. "The Rhetorical Function of Jesus's Session: The Exaltation of Christ as the Ground for Moral Exhortation in the Epistle to the Hebrews." PhD diss., Southeastern Baptist Theological Seminary, Wake Forest, NC, 2017.

Croy, N. Clayton. *Endurance in Suffering: Hebrews 12:1–13 in its Rhetorical, Religious, and Philosophical Context*. Cambridge: Cambridge University Press, 2005.

———. "A Note on Hebrews 12:2." *JBL* 114 (1995) 117–19.

Cullmann, Oscar. *Christ and Time: The Primitive Christian Conception of Time and History*. Rev. ed. Philadelphia: Westminster, 1964.

———. *The Christology of the New Testament*. Translated by S. H. Guthrie and C. A. M. Hall. Philadelphia: Westminster, 1959.

———. "Immortality of the Soul or Resurrection of the Dead? The Witness of the New Testament." In *Immortality and Resurrection: Four Essays by Oscar Cullman, Harry A. Wolfson, Werner Jaeger, and Henry J. Cadbury*, edited by Krister Stendahl, 9–53. New York: McMillan, 1965.

———. *Immortality of the Soul or Resurrection of the Dead? The Witness of the New Testament*. New York: Macmillian, 1964.

Culver, Robert Duncan. *Systematic Theology: Biblical and Historical*. Ross-shire, UK: Mentor, 2005.

Cumont, Franz. *After Life in Roman Paganism*. New York: Dover Publications, 1959.

———. *The Oriental Religions in Roman Paganism*. New York: Palatine, 2015.

Dalton, William J. *Christ's Proclamation to the Spirits: A Study of 1 Peter 3:18—4:6*. Rome: Pontifical Biblical Institute, 1965.

D'Angelo, Mary R. *Moses in the Letter to the Hebrews*. Atlanta: Society of Biblical Literature, 1979.

Darnell, John Coleman, and Colleen Manassa Darnell. *The Ancient Egyptian Netherworld Books*. Atlanta: Society of Biblical Literature, 2018.

Das, A. Andrew, and Frank J. Matera. *The Forgotten God: Perspectives in Biblical Theology*. Louisville: Westminster, 2002.

Davidson, Richard M. "Christ's Entry 'Within the Veil' in Hebrews 6:19–20: The Old Testament Background." *AUSS* 39 (2001) 175–90.

———. "The Eschatological Hermeneutic of Biblical Typology." *TheoRhēma* 6 (2011) 5–48.

———. "Inauguration or Day of Atonement? A Response to Norman Young's Old Testament Background to Hebrews 6:19–20 Revisited." *AUSS* 40 (2002) 69–88.

———. *Typology in Scripture*. Berrien Springs, MI: Andrews University Press, 1981.

Davies, J. H. *A Letter to the Hebrews*. Cambridge Bible Commentaries on the New Testament. London: Cambridge University Press, 1967.

Davila, James R. "Heavenly Ascents in the Dead Sea Scrolls." In *The Dead Sea Scrolls After Fifty Years*, vol. 2, edited by James C. VanderKam and Peter W. Flint, 460–85. Boston: Brill, 1999.

———. "The Macrocosmic Temple, Scriptural Exegesis, and the Songs of the Sabbath Sacrifice." *Dead Sea Discoveries* 9 (2002) 1–19.

Delitzsch, Franz. *Commentary on the Epistle to the Hebrews*. Vol. 2. 3rd ed. Clark's Foreign Theological Library, Fourth Series 28. Translated by Thomas L. Kingsbury. Edinburgh: T&T Clark, 1876.

DeSilva, David A. "Exchanging Favor for Wrath: Apostasy in Hebrews and Patron-Client Relationships." *JBL* 115 (1996) 91–116.

———. "Heaven, New Heavens." In *DLNT* 439–43.

———. *Introducing the Apocrypha: Message, Context, and Significance*. Grand Rapids: Baker Academic, 2002.

———. "The Invention and Argumentative Function of Priestly Discourse in the Epistle to the Hebrews." *BBR* 16 (2006) 295–323.

———. *The Letter to the Hebrews in Social-Scientific Perspective*. Eugene, OR: Cascade, 2012.

———. *Perseverance in Gratitude: A Socio-Rhetorical Commentary on the Epistle 'to the Hebrews.'* Grand Rapids: Eerdmans, 2000.

De Vos, J. Cornelis. "Hebrews 3:7—4:11 and the Function of Mental Time-Space Landscapes." In *Constructions of Space III: Biblical Spatiality and the Sacred*, edited by Jorunn Økland et al., 169–83. New York: T&T Clark, 2016.

Dey, Lala Kalyan Kumar. *The Intermediary World and Patterns of Perfection in Philo and Hebrews*. Missoula, MT: Scholars, 1975.

Dickason, C. Fred. *Angels: Elect and Evil*. Rev. and exp. ed. Chicago: Moody, 1995.

Dodd, C. H. *According to the Scriptures: The Substructure of New Testament Theology*. 1952. Reprint, Welwyn, England: Nisbet, 1961.

Dooley, Robert A., and Stephen H. Levinsohn. *Analyzing Discourse: A Manual of Basic Concepts*. Dallas: SIL International, 2001.

Dunn, James D. G. *The Theology of Paul the Apostle*. Grand Rapids: Eerdmans, 1998.

Dyer, Bryan R. *Suffering in the Face of Death: The Epistle to the Hebrews and Its Context of Situation*. New York: T&T Clark, 2017.

Easter, Matthew C. *Faith and the Faithfulness of Jesus in Hebrews*. New York: Cambridge University Press, 2014.

———. "Faith in the God Who Resurrects: Theocentric Faith of Hebrews." *NTS* 63 (2017) 76–91.

Eberhart, Christian A. "Characteristics of Sacrificial Metaphors in Hebrews." In *Hebrews: Contemporary Methods-New Insights*, edited by Gabriella Gelardini, 37–64. Boston: Brill, 2005.

Edersheim, Alfred. *The Temple, Its Ministry and Services as They Were at the Time of Jesus Christ*. 1874. Reprint, London: James Clarke, 1959.

Eisele, Wilfried. "Bürger zweier Welten: Zur Eschatologie des Hebräerbriefs." *ZNT* 29 (2012) 35–44.

———. *Ein unerschütterliches Reich: Die mittelplatonische Umformung des Parusiegedankens im Hebräerbrief*. Berlin: De Gruyter, 2003.

Eisenbaum, Pamela M. *The Jewish Heroes of Christian History: Hebrews 11 in Literary Context*. Atlanta: Scholars, 1997.
Eklund, Rebekah. "'To Us, the Word': The Double-λόγος of Hebrews 4:12–13." *JTI* 9 (2015) 101–15.
Elledge, Casey D. *Life after Death in Early Judaism*. Tübingen: Mohr Siebeck, 2006.
Ellingworth, Paul. *The Epistle to the Hebrews: A Commentary on the Greek Text*. Grand Rapids: Eerdmans, 1993.
———. "Hebrews." In *NDBT* 337–42.
———. "Jesus and the Universe in Hebrews." *EvQ* 58 (1986) 337–50.
Ellis, E. Earle. *Christ and the Future in New Testament History*. Boston: Brill, 2001.
———. *The Making of the New Testament Documents*. Boston: Brill Academic, 2002.
———. *Pauline Theology: Ministry and Society*. Eugene, OR: Wipf & Stock, 1997.
———. *Prophecy and Hermeneutic in Early Christianity: New Testament Essays*. Eugene, OR: Wipf & Stock, 1978.
Emerson, Matthew Y. *"He Descended to the Dead": An Evangelical Theology of Holy Saturday*. Downers Grove, IL: InterVarsity, 2019.
Engberg-Pedersen, Troels. *Cosmology and Self in the Apostle Paul: The Material Spirit*. New York: Oxford University Press, 2010.
Erickson, J. A *Beginner's Guide to New Testament Exegesis: Taking the Fear out of Critical Method*. Downers Grove, IL: InterVarsity, 2005.
Eskola, Timo. *Messiah and the Throne: Jewish Merkabah Mysticism and Early Christian Exaltation Discourse*. Tübingen, Germany: Mohr Siebeck, 2001.
Esler, Philip F. *God's Court and Courtiers in the Book of the Watchers: Re-interpreting Heaven in Enoch 1–36*. Eugene, OR: Cascade, 2017.
Evans, Craig A. *Ancient Texts for New Testament Studies: A Guide to the Background Literature*. Peabody, MA: Hendrickson, 2005.
Evans, G. R. *John Wyclif: Myth and Reality*. Downers Grove, IL: InterVarsity, 2005.
———. *The Roots of the Reformation: Tradition, Emergence and Rupture*. Downers Grove, IL: InterVarsity, 2012.
Ezra, Daniel Stökl Ben. *The Impact of Yom Kippur on Early Christianity: The Day of Atonement from Second Temple Judaism to the Fifth Century*. Tübingen, Germany: Mohr Siebeck, 2003.
Fairbairn, Patrick. *Typology of Scripture*. 2 vols. Grand Rapids: Kregel Publications, 1989.
Fallon, Francis T. "The Gnostic Apocalypses." In *Semeia 14 Apocalypse: The Morphology of a Genre*, edited by John J. Collins, 122–58. Atlanta: Society of Biblical Literature, 1979.
Fanning, Buist M. *Verbal Aspect in New Testament Greek*. Oxford: Clarendon, 1990.
Farris, Joshua R. *An Introduction to Theological Anthropology: Humans, Both Creaturely and Divine*. Grand Rapids: Baker Academic, 2020.
Feinberg, John S. *Four Views on Heaven (Counterpoints)*. Grand Rapids: Zondervan, 2021.
Feldmeier, Reinhard, and Hermann Spieckermann. *God of the Living: A Biblical Theology*. Translated by Mark E. Biddle. Waco, TX: Baylor University Press, 2011.
Ferguson, Everett. *Backgrounds of Early Christianity*. 3rd ed. Grand Rapids: Eerdmans, 2003.
Filson, Floyd V. *"Yesterday": A Study of Hebrews in Light of Chapter 13*. London: SMC, 1970.

Finney, Mark T. *Resurrection, Hell, and the Afterlife: Body and Soul in Antiquity, Judaism and Early Church*. Bible World. New York: Routledge, 2016.
Fischer, Ulrich. *Eschatologie und Jenseitserwartung im hellenistischen Diasporajudentum*. New York: De Gruyter, 1978.
Fishbane, Michael. *Biblical Interpretation in Ancient Israel*. Oxford: Oxford University Press, 1988.
Fisher, Amy Marie. "Celestial Topography: Mapping the Divine Realms of Antiquity." PhD diss., University of Toronto, Toronto, ON, 2015.
Foerster, Werner. "σῴζω and σωτηρία," In *TDNT* 7:989–998.
Foreman, L. D. *The Bible in Eight Ages*. Texarkana, AR-TX: Bogard, 1992.
Fraade, Steven D. "Targum, Targumim." In *EDEJ* 1278–81.
France, R. T. "Relationship between the Testaments." In *DTIB* 666–72.
Fredericks, Daniel C. "A Question of First Importance: ἐν πρώτοις in 1 Corinthians 15:3." *BBR* 32 (2022) 165–81.
Fredriksen, Paula. "Apocalypse and Redemption in Early Christianity: From John of Patmos to Augustine of Hippo." *VC* 45 (1991) 151–84.
———. "Paul, the Perfectly Righteous Pharisee." In *The Pharisees*, edited by Joseph Sievers and Amy-Jill Levine, 112–35. Grand Rapids: Eerdmans, 2021.
Frei, Hans W. *The Eclipse of Biblical Narrative: A Study in Eighteenth and Nineteenth Century Hermeneutics*. New Haven, CT: Yale University Press, 1974.
Friedeman, Richard Elliot, and Shawna Dolansky Overton. "Death and Afterlife: The Biblical Silence." In *Judaism in Late Antiquity, Part 4: Death, Life-After-Death, Resurrection and the World-to-Come in the Judaism of Antiquity*, edited by Alan J. Avery-Peck and Jacob Neusner, 35–57. Leiden: Brill, 2000.
Gäbel, Georg. *Die Kulttheologie des Hebräerbriefes: Eine exegetisch-religionsgeschichtliche Studie*. Tübingen, Germany: Mohr Siebeck, 2006.
Gane, Roy E. *Cult and Character: Purification Offerings, Day of Atonement, and Theodicy*. Winona Lake, IN: Eisenbrauns, 2005.
———. "Re-Opening *Katapetasma* ('Veil') in Hebrews 6:19." *AUSS* 38 (2000) 5–8.
Garland, Robert. *The Greek Way of Death*. Ithaca, NY: Cornell University Press, 1985.
Gärtner, Bertil E. *The Temple and the Community in Qumran and the New Testament: A Comparative Study in the Temple Symbolism of the Qumran Texts and the New Testament*. 1965. Reprint, New York: Cambridge University Press, 2005.
Garuti, Paolo, OP. *Alle Origini Dell'omiletica Cristiana: La lettera agli Ebrei; Note di Analyli Retorica*. Jerusalem: Franciscan Press, 1995.
Geisler, Norman L. *The Battle for the Resurrection*. Rev. 3rd ed. Matthews, NC: Bastion, 2013.
Gelardini, Gabriella. "'As if by Paul?' Some Remarks on the Textual Strategy of Anonymity in Hebrews." In *Deciphering the Worlds of Hebrews: Collected Essays*, edited by Gabriella Gelardini, 13–37. Boston: Brill, 2021.
———. "Charting 'Outside the Camp' with Edward W. Soja: Critical Spatiality and Hebrews 13." In *Deciphering the Worlds of Hebrews: Collected Essays*, edited by Gabriella Gelardini, 210–37. 2016. Reprint, Boston: Brill, 2021.
———. *Deciphering the Worlds of Hebrews: Collected Essays*. Boston: Brill, 2021.
———. "Existence beyond Borders: The Book of Hebrews and Critical Spatiality." In *The Epistle to the Hebrews: Writing at the Borders*, edited by Régis Burnet et al., 187–203. Leuven, Belgium: Peeters, 2016.

———. "Faith in Hebrews and Its Relationship to Soteriology: An Interpretation in the Context of the Concept of *Fides* in Roman Culture." In *Deciphering the Worlds of Hebrews: Collected Essays*, edited by Gabriella Gelardini, 261–72. 2019. Reprint, Boston: Brill, 2021.

———. "Hebrews, An Ancient Synagogue Homily for Tisha Be-Av: Its Function, Its Basis, Its Theological Interpretation." In *Hebrews: Contemporary Methods-New Insights*, edited by Gabriella Gelardini, 107–27. Boston: Brill, 2005.

———. "The Inauguration of Yom Kippur According to the LXX and Its Cessation or Perpetuation According to the Book of Hebrews: A Systematic Comparison." In *The Day of Atonement: Its Interpretations in Early Jewish and Christian Traditions*, edited by Thomas Hieke and Tobias Nicklas, 225–54. Leiden: Brill, 2012.

———. "The Unshakeable Kingdom in Heaven: Notes on Eschatology in Hebrews." In *Deciphering the Worlds of Hebrews: Collected Essays*, edited by Gabriella Gelardini, 308–25. Boston: Brill, 2021.

Gentry, Peter J., and Stephen J. Wellum. *Kingdom through Covenant*. Wheaton, IL: Crossway, 2012.

George, Mark K. *Israel's Tabernacle as Social Space*. Atlanta: Society of Biblical Literature, 2009.

German Bible Society. *Biblia Hebraica Stuttgartensia: SESB Version*. Stuttgart: German Bible Society, 2003. Electronic ed.

Gesenius, Friedrich Wilhelm. *Gesenius' Hebrew Grammar*. Edited by E. Kautzsch and Arthur Ernest Cowley. 2nd English ed. Oxford: Clarendon, 1910.

Gheorghita, Radu. *The Role of the Septuagint in Hebrews: An Investigation of its Influence with Special Consideration to the Use of Hab. 2:2–4 in Heb. 10:37–38*. Tübingen, Germany: Mohr Siebeck, 2003.

Gilders, William K. *Blood Ritual in the Hebrew Bible: Meaning and Power*. Baltimore: John Hopkins University Press, 2004.

Ginzberg, Louis, et al. *Legends of the Jews*. 2nd ed. Philadelphia: Jewish Publication Society, 2003.

Girdwood, James, and Peter Verkruyse. "Hebrews 8:5." In *Hebrews*. The College Press NIV Commentary. Joplin, MO: College Press, 1997.

Gleason, Randall C. "Angels and Eschatology of Hebrews 1–2." *NTS* 49 (2003) 90–107.

———. "The Old Testament Background of Rest in Hebrews 3:7–4:11." *BSac* 157 (2000) 281–303.

Goldingay, John. "Death and the Afterlife in the Psalms." In *Judaism in Late Antiquity, Part 4: Death, Life-After-Death, Resurrection and the World-to-Come in the Judaism of Antiquity*, edited by Alan J. Avery-Peck and Jacob Neusner, 61–84. Leiden: Brill, 2000.

González, Justo L. *The Story of Christianity: The Early Church to the Reformation*. Vol. 1. 2nd rev. and updated ed. New York: Harper One, 2010.

Gooder, Paula. *Heaven*. Eugene, OR: Wipf & Stock, 2011.

———. *Only the Third Heaven? 2 Corinthians 12:1–10 and Heavenly Ascent*. New York: T&T Clark, 2006.

Goodman, Martin. "Paradise, Gardens, and the Afterlife in the First Century CE." In *Paradise in Antiquity: Jewish and Christian Views*, edited by Markus Bockmuehl and Guy G. Stroumsa, 57–63. Cambridge: Cambridge University Press, 2010.

Goppelt, Leonhard. *Typos: The Typological Interpretation of the Old Testament in the New*. Translated by Donald H. Madvig. Grand Rapids: Eerdmans, 1982.

Gordon, Robert. "Better Promises: Two Passages in Hebrews Against the Background of the Old Testament Cultus." In *Templum Amicitiae*, edited by William Horbury, 434–49. Sheffield: Sheffield Academic, 1991.

Gorman, Frank. H., Jr. *The Ideology of Ritual: Space, Time and Status in the Priestly Theology*. Sheffield: Sheffield Academic, 1990.

Gorman, Michael. "Effecting the New Covenant: A (Not So) New, New Testament Model for The Atonement." *Ex Auditu* 26 (2010) 26–59.

"What Was God Doing before He Created the Universe?" Got Questions, Jan 4, 2022. https://www.gotquestions.org/God-doing.html.

Gould, Peter, and Rodney White. *Mental Maps*. Boston: Allen & Unwin, 1986.

Gow, Andrew C. *The Contested History of a Book: The German Bible of the Later Middle Ages and Reformation in Legend, Ideology, and Scholarship*. Piscataway, NJ: Gorgias, 2012.

Graham, Billy. "By the Time You Read This, I Will Be in Heaven." *Gaston Gazette*, Feb 21, 2018. https://www.gastongazette.com/story/lifestyle/faith/2018/02/21/billy-grahams-final-column-by-time-you-read-this-i-will-be-in-heaven/14118799007/.

———. *An Extraordinary Journey: One Ordinary Man. One Ordinary God*. Charlotte, NC: Billy Graham Evangelistic Association, 2018.

Graham, Will. (@TellaGraham). "Even though my grandfather has physically died, he is very much alive in heaven. And you will see him there one day if you have asked Jesus to forgive you of your sins and made him Lord of your life." Twitter, Feb 21, 2018, 10:23 a.m. https://twitter.com/WillGraham_4/status/966347626718400512.

Grässer, Erich. *An die Hebräer*. 3 vols. Zürich: Benziger, 1990–97.

———. *Aufbruch und Verheissung: Gesammelte Aufsätze zum Hebräerbrief*. New York: De Gruyter, 1992.

Gray, Patrick. *Godly Fear: The Epistle to the Hebrews and Greco-Roman Critiques of Superstition*. Leiden: Brill, 2003.

Green, Joel B. *Body, Soul, and Human Life: The Nature of Humanity in the Bible*. Milton Keynes, England: Paternoster, 2008.

Griffiths, Jonathan I. *Hebrews and Divine Speech*. New York: T&T Clark, 2014.

Grimes, Joseph E. *The Thread of Discourse*. Hague: Mouton, 1975.

Gruber, L. Franklin. *The Truth About the So-Called "Luther's Testament in English": Tyndale's New Testament*. St. Paul, MN: Ernst Mussgang, 1917.

Grudem, Wayne A. *Systematic Theology: An Introduction to Biblical Doctrine*. Grand Rapids: Zondervan, 2004.

Gruenwald, Ithamar. *Apocalyptic and Merkavah Mysticism*. Leiden: Brill, 1980.

Gundry, Robert H. "The Form, Meaning and Background of the Hymn Quoted in I Timothy 3:16." In *Apostolic History and the Gospel: Biblical and Historical Essays Presented to F. F. Bruce on His 60th Birthday*, edited by F. F. Bruce, W. Ward Gasque, and Ralph P. Martin, 203–22. Exeter: Paternoster, 1970.

———. *Sōma in Biblical Theology: With Emphasis on Pauline Anthropology*. Cambridge: Cambridge University Press, 1976.

Gurtner, Daniel M. *Introducing the Pseudepigrapha of Second Temple Judaism*. Grand Rapids: Baker, 2020.

———. "Καταπέτασμα: Lexicographical and Etymological Considerations on the Biblical 'Veil.'" *AUSS* 42 (2004) 105–11.

———. "LXX Syntax and the Identity of the NT Veil." *NovT* 47 (2005) 344–53.

BIBLIOGRAPHY

——. *The Torn Veil: Matthew's Exposition of the Death of Jesus*. Cambridge: Cambridge University Press, 2010.

Guthrie, George H. "Conclusion." In *Four Views on the Warning Passages in Hebrews*, edited by Herbert W. Bateman IV, 430–45. Grand Rapids: Kregel, 2007.

——. "Discourse Analysis." In *Interpreting the New Testament: Essays on Methods and Issues*, edited by David Alan Black and David S. Dockery, 253–71. Nashville: B&H, 2001.

——. "Hebrews." In *Commentary on the New Testament Use of the Old Testament*, edited by B. K. Beale and D. A. Carson, 919–93. Grand Rapids: Baker Academic, 2007.

——. "Hebrews in Its First-Century Context." In *The Face of New Testament Studies: A Survey of Recent Research*, edited by Scot McKnight and Grant R. Osborne, 413–33. Grand Rapids: Baker Academic, 2004.

——. *The Structure of Hebrews: A Text-Linguistic Analysis*. Grand Rapids: Baker, 1998.

——. "Time and Atonement in Hebrews." In *So Great Salvation: A Dialogue on the Atonement in Hebrews*, edited by Jon C. Laansma et al., 209–27. New York: T&T Clark, 2019.

Hahn, Scott W. "Covenant, Cult, and the Curse-of-Death: Διαθήκη in Hebrews 9:15–22." In *Hebrews: Contemporary Methods-New Insights*, edited by Gabriella Gelardini, 65–88. Boston: Brill, 2005.

Hallote, Rachel S. *Death, Burial, and Afterlife in the Biblical World: How the Israelites and Their Neighbors Treated the Dead*. Chicago: Ivan R. Dee, 2001.

Haran, Menahem. *Temples and Temple Service in Ancient Israel*. Winona Lake, IN: Eisenbrauns, 2010.

Harlow, Daniel C. "Early Judaism and Early Christianity." In *EDEJ* 257–78.

Harrington, Daniel J. *Invitation to the Apocrypha*. Grand Rapids: Eerdmans, 1999.

——. "The Old Testament Apocrypha in the Early Church and Today." In *The Canon Debate*, edited by Lee M. McDonald and James A. Sanders, 196–210. Peabody, MA: Hendrickson, 2002.

Harris, Dana M. "The Eternal Inheritance in Hebrews: The Appropriation the Old Testament Inheritance Motif by the Author of Hebrews." PhD diss., Trinity Evangelical Divinity School, Deerfield, IL, 2002.

——. "The Use of ERCHOMAI and AGO in Hebrews—Going Where Jesus Has Already Gone." Paper presented at the Annual Meeting of the Evangelical Theological Society, Baltimore, MD, Nov 21, 2013.

Harris, Murray J. *From Grave to Glory: Resurrection in the New Testament*. Grand Rapids: Academie, 1990.

Harrison, R. K. *Introduction to the Old Testament: With a Comprehensive Review of Old Testament Studies and a Special Supplement on the Apocrypha*. Grand Rapids: Eerdmans, 1969.

Hay, David M. *Glory at the Right Hand: Psalm 110 in Early Christianity*. New York: Abingdon, 1973.

Hayward, C. T. R. *The Jewish Temple: A Non-Biblical Sourcebook*. New York: Routledge, 1996.

Heath, David Mark. "Chiastic Structures in Hebrews: A Study in Form and Function in Biblical Discourse." PhD diss., University of Stellenbosch, Stellenbosch, South Africa, 2011.

Heen, Erik M., and Philip D. W. Krey, eds. *Hebrews*. Downers Grove, IL: InterVarsity, 2005.

Hegermann, Harald. "Das Wort Gottes als aufdeckende Macht: zur Theologie des Wortes Gottes im Hebräerbrief." In *Das lebendige Wort: Beiträge zur kirchlichen Verkündigung; Festgabe für G. Voigt*, edited by Hans Seidel and Karl-Heinrich Bieritz, 83–98. Berlin: Evangelische Verlagsanstalt, 1982.

Heike, Thomas, and Nicklas Tobias, eds. *The Day of Atonement: Its Interpretations in Early Jewish and Christian Traditions*. Boston: Brill, 2012.

Heinemann, Joseph. "The Triennial Lectionary Cycle." *Journal of Jewish Studies* 19 (1968) 41–48.

Heiser, Michael S. *Angels: What the Bible Really Says about God's Heavenly Host*. Bellingham, WA: Lexham, 2018.

Helgeland, John. "Time and Space: Christian and Roman." In *ANRW* 2.23.2, edited by Wolfgang Haase, 1285–305. New York: De Gruyter, 1980.

Hendriksen, William. *The Bible on the Life Hereafter*. Grand Rapids: Baker, 1971.

Hengel, Martin. *Judaism and Hellenism: Studies in their Encounter in Palestine during the Early Hellenistic Period*. Translated by John Bowden. Eugene, OR: Wipf & Stock, 1973.

Henry, William W., Jr. "Atonement and the Logic of Resurrection in Hebrews 9:27–28: Jesus's Ministry to Lead Believers for Salvation into Heaven a Very Little While after Individual Death and Judgment." PhD diss., Southwestern Baptist Theological Seminary, Fort Worth, TX, 2023.

———. "The Cosmology of the Heaven(s), Tabernacle, and Sanctuary of the Priestly Work of Christ in Hebrews 8–10." MATh thesis, Southwestern Baptist Theological Seminary, Fort Worth, TX, 2015.

———. *Heaven Past Present Future: The Fulfillment of the Times*. Crossett, AR: William Henry, 2002.

Héring, Jean. *The Epistle to the Hebrews*. Translated by A. W. Heathcote and P. J. Allcock. 1970. Reprint, Eugene, OR: Wipf & Stock, 2010.

Hilber, John W. *Old Testament Cosmology and Divine Accommodation: A Relevance Theory Approach*. Eugene, OR: Cascade, 2020.

Himmelfarb, Martha. *The Apocalypse: A Brief History*. Malden, MA: Wiley-Blackwell, 2010.

———. *Ascent to Heaven in Jewish and Christian Apocalypses*. New York: Oxford University Press, 1993.

———. "The Practice of Ascent in the Ancient Mediterranean World." In *Death, Ecstasy, and Other Worldly Journeys*, edited by John C. Collins and Michael Fishbane, 123–37. Albany: State University of New York Press, 1995.

Hirsch, E. D. *The Aims of Interpretation*. Chicago: University of Chicago Press, 1976.

Hofius, Otfried. "Das 'erste' und das 'zweite' Zelt: Ein Beitrag zur Auslegung von Hebrews 9:1–10." *ZNW* 61 (1970) 271–77.

———. "Inkarnation und Opfertod Jesu nach Hebr 10,19f." In *Der Ruf Jesu und die Antwort der Gemeinde: Exegetische Untersuchungen Joachim Jeremias zum 70; Geburtstag gewidmet von seinen Schülern*, edited by Eduard Lohse, 132–41. Göttingen, Germany: Vandenhoeck & Ruprecht, 1970.

———. *Katapausis: Die Vorstellung vom endzeitlichen Ruheort im Hebräerbrief*. Tübingen, Germany: Mohr Siebeck, 1970.

Horsley, Richard A. *The Pharisees and the Temple-State of Judea.* Eugene, OR: Cascade, 2022.

Horton, Fred L. *The Melchizedek Tradition: A Critical Evaluation of the Sources to the Fifth Century A.D. and in the Epistle to the Hebrews.* Cambridge: Cambridge University Press, 1976.

Hoskins, Paul M. *Jesus as the Fulfillment of the Temple in the Gospel of John.* Milton Keynes: Paternoster, 2006.

———. *That Scripture Might Be Fulfilled: Typology and the Death of Christ.* Longwood, FL: Xulon, 2009.

Houtman, Cornelis. *Der Himmel im Alten Testament: Israels Weltbild und Weltanschauung.* New York: Brill, 1993.

Hughes, Graham. *Hebrews and Hermeneutics: The Epistle to the Hebrews as a New Testament Example of Biblical Interpretation.* Cambridge: Cambridge University Press, 1980.

Hughes, Philip Edgcumbe. *A Commentary on the Epistle to the Hebrews.* The New International Commentary on the Old and New Testament. Grand Rapids: Eerdmans, 1977.

Hurst, L. D. *The Epistle to the Hebrews: Its Background of Thought.* New York: Cambridge University Press, 1990.

Isaacs, Marie E. *Sacred Space: An Approach to the Theology of the Epistle to the Hebrews.* Sheffield: Sheffield Academic, 1992.

Jackson, Paul N. *An Investigation of Koimaomai in the New Testament: The Concept of Eschatological Sleep.* Lewiston, NY: Mellen, 1996.

Jamieson, Robert B. "Hebrews 9.23: Cult Inauguration, Yom Kippur and the Cleansing of the Heavenly Tabernacle." *NTS* 62 (2016) 569–87.

———. *Jesus's Death and Heavenly Offering in Hebrews.* New York: Cambridge University Press, 2019.

———. "When and Where Did Jesus Offer Himself? A Taxonomy of Recent Scholarship on Hebrews." *CurBR* 15 (2017) 338–68.

Jennings, Mark A. "The Veil and the High Priestly Robes of the Incarnation." *PRSt* 37 (2010) 85–97.

Jenson, Phillip Peter. *Graded Holiness: A Key to the Priestly Conception of the World.* Sheffield: Sheffield Academic, 1992.

Jeremias, Joachim. *Der Opfertod Jesu Christi.* Stuttgart: Calwer, 1963.

———. "'Flesh and Blood Cannot Inherit the Kingdom of God' (1 Corinthians 15:50)." *NTS* 2 (1956) 151–59.

———. *New Testament Theology.* Translated by John Bowden. 1971. Reprint, London: Xpress, 1996.

———. "Zwischen Karfreitag und Ostern: Descensus und Ascensus in der Karfreitagstheologie des Neuen Testamentes." *ZNW* 42 (1949) 194–201.

Jipp, Joshua W. "The Son's Entrance into the Heavenly World: The Soteriological Necessity of the Scriptural Catena in Hebrews 1:5–14." *NTS* 56 (2010) 557–75.

Jobes, Karen H. "The Function of Paronomasia in Hebrews 10:5–7." *TJ* 13 (1992) 181–91.

———. "Putting Words in His Mouth: The Son Speaks in Hebrews." In *So Great Salvation: A Dialogue on the Atonement in Hebrews,* edited by Jon C. Laansma et al., 40–50. New York: T&T Clark, 2019.

Jobes, Karen H., and Moisés Silva. *Invitation to the Septuagint*. Grand Rapids: Baker Academic, 2000.

Johnson, Andy. "On Removing a Trump Card: Flesh and Blood and the Reign of God." *BBR* 13 (2003) 175–92.

Johnson, Luke Timothy. *Hebrews: A Commentary*. Louisville: Westminster John Knox, 2012.

Johnson, S. Lewis. "Hebrews 10:5–7: The Place of Typology in Exegesis." In *The Old Testament in the New: An Argument for Biblical Inspiration*, 53–57. Grand Rapids: Zondervan, 1980.

Johnsson, William G. "The Pilgrimage Motif in the Book of Hebrews." *JBL* 97 (1978) 239–51.

Johnston, George. "Oikoumenē and κόσμος in the New Testament." *NTS* 10 (1964), 352–60.

Johnston, Phillip S. *Shades of Sheol: Death and Afterlife in the Old Testament*. Downers Grove, IL: InterVarsity, 2002.

Jones, Alexander, ed. *Time and Cosmos in Greco-Roman Antiquity*. Princeton: Princeton University Press, 2016.

Josephus. *The Jewish War: Books 1–7*. Edited by Jeffrey Henderson et al. Translated by H. St. J. Thackeray. Cambridge, MA: Harvard University Press, 1927–28.

Joslin, Barry C. *Hebrews, Christ, and the Law: The Theology of the Mosaic Law in Hebrews 7:1–10:18*. Eugene, OR: Wipf & Stock, 2008.

Kahn, Charles H. *Anaximander and the Origins of Greek Cosmology*. Indianapolis, IN: Hackett, 1994.

Kaibel, George, ed. *Epigrammata Graeca ex Lapidibus Conlecta*. Berlin: n.p., 1878.

Kärkkäinen, Veli-Matti. *Creation and Humanity*. Grand Rapids: Eerdmans, 2015.

Karrer, Martin. *Der Brief an die Hebräer*. 2 vols. Gütersloh: Gütersloher, 2002–2008.

Käsemann, Ernst. "The Beginning of Christian Theology." In *New Testament Questions of Today*, translated by W. J. Montague, 82–107. Philadelphia: Fortress, 1969.

———. *Das wandernde Gottesvolk: Eine Untersuchung zum Hebräerbrief*. Göttingen: Vandenhoeck & Ruprecht, 1961.

———. "To the Theme of the Early Christian Apocalypse." In *New Testament Questions of Today*, translated by W. J. Montague, 108–37. Philadelphia: Fortress, 1969.

———. *The Wandering People of God: An Investigation of the Letter to the Hebrews*. Translated by Roy A. Harrisville and Irving L. Sandberg. Eugene, OR: Wipf & Stock, 2002.

———. "Zum Thema Der Urchristlichen Apokalyptik." *ZTK* 59 (1962) 257–84.

Katz, Dina. *The Image of the Netherworld in the Sumerian Sources*. Bethesda, MD: CDL, 2018.

Kay, James F. "He Descended into Hell: Descendit ad inferna." In *Exploring and Proclaiming the Apostle's Creed*, edited by Roger E. Van Harn, 117–29. Grand Rapids: Eerdmans, 2004.

Keener, Craig S. "Hebrews 8:1–5: The Heavenly Tabernacle." In *IVPBBCNT*. Downers Grove, IL: InterVarsity, 1993.

———. "Hebrews 8:2." In *IVPBBCNT*. Downers Grove, IL: InterVarsity, 1993.

Keene, Thomas. "Heaven Is a Tent: The Tabernacle as an Eschatological Metaphor in the Epistle of Hebrews." PhD diss., Westminster Theological Seminary, Glenside, PA, 2010.

Kibbe, Michael Harrison. *Godly Fear or Ungodly Failure? Hebrews 12 and the Sinai Theophanies.* Berlin: De Gruyter, 2016.

———. "The God-Man's Indestructible Life—A Theological Reading of Hebrews 7.16." Paper presented at the Annual Meeting of the Evangelical Theological Society, San Antonio, TX, Nov 15, 2016.

———. "Is It Finished? When Did It Start? Hebrews, Priesthood, and Atonement in Biblical, Systematic, and Historical Perspective." *JTS* 65 (2014) 25–61.

Kiene, Paul F. *The Tabernacle of God in the Wilderness of Sinai.* Grand Rapids: Zondervan, 1977.

Kirk, G. S., et al. *The Presocratic Philosophers: A Critical History with Selection of Texts.* 2nd ed. Cambridge: Cambridge Univeristy Press, 2013.

Kistemaker, Simon J., and William Hendriksen. *Exposition of Hebrews.* New Testament Commentary 15. Grand Rapids: Baker, 1984.

Klappert, Bertold. "Begündete Hoffnumg und bekräftgte Verheißung: Exegetisch-systematische Erwägungun zur Eschatologie des Hebräerbriefes." In *Alles in allem: Eschatologische Anstöße*, edited by Ruth Heß and Martin Leiner, 447–74. Neukirchen-Vluyn, Germany: Neukirchener, 2005.

———. *Die Eschatologie des Hebräerbriefs.* Munich: Kaiser, 1969.

Klawans, Jonathan. *Purity, Sacrifice, and the Temple: Symbolism and Supersessionism in the Study of Ancient Judaism.* New York: Oxford University Press, 2006.

Kleinig, John W. *Hebrews.* Concordia Commentary. St. Louis: Concordia, 2017.

Klink, Edward W., III, and Darian R. Lockett. *Understanding Biblical Theology.* Grand Rapids: Zondervan, 2012.

Knöppler, Thomas. *Sühne im Neuen Testament: Studien zum urchristlichen Verständnis der Heilsbedeutung des Todes Jesu.* Neukirchen-Vluyn, Germany: Neukirchener, 2001.

Koch, Klaus. *The Rediscovery of Apocalyptic: A Polemical Work on a Neglected Area of Biblical Studies and Its Damaging Effects on Theology and Philosophy.* Naperville, IL: Allenson, 1972.

Koester, Craig R. *The Dwelling of God: The Tabernacle in the Old Testament, Intertestamental Jewish Literature, and the Old Testament.* Washington, DC: Catholic Biblical Association of America, 1989.

———. *Hebrews: A New Translation with Introduction and Commentary.* London: Yale University Press, 2001.

Koester, Helmut. "'Outside the Camp': Hebrews 13.9–14." *HTR* 55 (1962) 299–315.

Kohler, Kaufmann. "Heaven." In *JE* 6:298.

Köstenberger, Andreas J., and Richard D. Patterson. *Invitation to Biblical Interpretation: Exploring the Hermeneutical Triad of History, Literature, and Theology.* Grand Rapids: Kregel, 2011.

Köster, Helmut. "ὑπόστασις." In *TDNT* 8:572–88.

Kraus, Wolfgang. "Ps 40(39): 7–9 in the Hebrew Bible and in the Septuagint, with Its Reception in the New Testament (Heb 10:5–10)." In *XVI Congress of the International Organization for Septuagint and Cognate Studies: Stellenbosch, 2016*, edited by Gideon R. Kotzé et al., 119–31. Atlanta: SBL, 2019.

Kreitzer, Larry. J. "Intermediate State." In *DPL* 805–12.

Kuhn, Thomas S. *The Structure of Scientific Revolutions.* 3rd ed. Chicago: University of Chicago Press, 1996.

Kurianal, James. *Jesus Our High Priest: Ps 110,4 as the Substructure of Hebrews 5,1–7,28.* New York: Lang, 2000.

Laansma, Jon C. "The Cosmology of Hebrews." In *Cosmology and New Testament Theology*, edited by Jonathan T. Pennington and Sean M. McDonough, 125–43. London: T&T Clark, 2008.

———. "Heaven in the General Epistles." In *Heaven*, edited by Christopher W. Morgan and Robert A. Peterson, 111–37. Wheaton, IL: Crossway, 2014.

———. "Hebrews: Yesterday, Today, and Future: An Illustrative Survey, Diagnosis, Prescription." In *Christology, Hermeneutics and Hebrews: Profiles from the History of Interpretation*, edited by Jon C. Laansma and Daniel J. Treier, 1–32. New York: Bloomsbury, 2012.

———. "Hidden Stories in Hebrews: Cosmology and Theology." In *A Cloud of Witnesses: The Theology of Hebrews in Its Ancient Contexts*, edited by Richard Bauckham and Nathan MacDonald, 9–18. London: T&T Clark, 2008.

———. *"I Will Give You Rest": The Rest Motif in the New Testament with Special Reference to Mt 11 and Heb 3–4.* Tübingen, Germany: Mohr Siebeck, 1997.

Laansma Jon C. et al., eds. *So Great Salvation: A Dialogue on the Atonement in Hebrews.* New York: T&T Clark, 2019.

Ladd, George E. *A Theology of the New Testament.* Grand Rapids: Eerdmans, 1974.

Lampe, G. W. H., and K. J. Woollcombe. *Essays in Typology.* London: SCM, 1957.

Lane, William L. *Hebrews 1–8.* Dallas: Word, 1998.

———. *Hebrews 9–13.* Dallas: Word, 1998.

———. "Life in the Face of Death: The Resurrection Message of the New Testament." In *Life in the Face of Death: The Resurrection Message of the New Testament*, edited by Richard N. Longenecker, 247–69. Grand Rapids: Eerdmans, 1998.

Lang, Bernhard. *Meeting in Heaven: Modernising the Christian Afterlife, 1600–2000.* Frankfurt: Lang, 2011.

Laub, Franz. "'Ein für allemal hineingegangen in das Allerheiligste' (Hebr 9,12)—Zum Verständnis des Kreuzestodes im Hebräerbrief." *BZ* 35 (1991) 65–85.

Le Boulluec, Alain. *The Notion of Heresy in Greek Literature in the Second and Third Centuries.* Edited by David Lincicum and Nicholas Moore. Translated by A. K. M. Adam et al. Oxford, Oxford University Press, 2022.

Lee, Chris W. *Death Warning in the Garden of Eden.* Tübingen, Germany: Mohr Siebeck, 2020.

Lee, Jihye. *A Jewish Apocalyptic Framework of Eschatology in the Epistle to the Hebrews: Protology and Eschatology as Background.* New York: T&T Clark, 2021.

Lee, John A. L. *A History of New Testament Lexicography.* New York: Lang, 2014.

Leithart, Peter J. "Womb of the World: Baptism and the Priesthood of the New Covenant in Hebrews 10.19–22." *JSNT* 22 (2000) 49–65.

Le Moyne, Jean. *Les Sadducéen.* Paris: Librairie Lecoffre, 1972.

Leschert, Dale F. *Hermeneutical Foundations of Hebrews: A Study in the Validity of the Epistle's Interpretation of Some Core Citations from the Psalms.* Lewiston, NY: Edwin Mellen, 1994.

Levenson, Jon D. "Cosmos and Microcosm." In *Cult and Cosmos: Tilting Towards a Temple-Centered Theology*, edited by L. Michael Morales, 227–47. Paris: Peeters, 2014.

———. *Creation and the Persistence of Evil: The Jewish Drama of Divine Omnipotence.* Princeton: Princeton University Press, 1988.

———. *Resurrection and the Restoration of Israel: The Ultimate Victory of the God of Life*. New Haven, CT: Yale University Press, 2006.
———. *Sinai and Zion: An Entry into the Jewish Bible*. New York: Harper One, 1985.
———. "The Temple and the World." *JR* 64 (1984) 275–98.
Levine, Lee I. *The Ancient Synagogue: The First Thousand Years*. New Haven, CT: Yale University Press, 2000.
Levinsohn, Stephen H. *Discourse Features of New Testament Greek: A Coursebook on Informational Structure of New Testament Greek*. 2nd ed. Dallas: SIL International, 2000.
Lewicki, Tomasz. *"Weist nicht ab den Sprechenden!": Wort Gottes und Paraklese im Hebräerbrief*. Paderborn, Germany: Schöningh, 2004.
Lewis, Thomas W. "'. . . And if He Shrinks Back' (Heb. X.38b)." *NTS* 22 (1975) 88–94.
Lincoln, Andrew T. "Hebrews and Biblical Theology." In *Out of Egypt: Biblical Theology and Biblical Interpretation*, edited by Craig Bartholomew et al., 313–38. Grand Rapids: Zondervan, 2004.
———. *Hebrews: A Guide*. London, England: T&T Clark, 2006.
———. *Paradise Now and Not Yet: Studies in the Role of the Heavenly Dimension in Paul's Thought with Special Reference to His Eschatology*. Grand Rapids: Baker, 1991.
———. "Sabbath, Rest, and Eschatology in the New Testament." In *From Sabbath to Lord's Day: A Biblical, Historical, and Theological Investigation*, edited by D. A. Carson, 197–220. Eugene, OR: Wipf & Stock, 1982.
Lindars, Barnabas. "Hebrews and the Second Temple." In *Templum Amicitiae*, edited by William Horbury, 410–33. Sheffield: Shefield Academic, 1991.
———. *The Theology of the Letter to the Hebrews*. New Testament Theology. New York: Cambridge University Press, 1991.
Liss, Hanna. "The Imaginary Sanctuary: The Priestly Code as an Example of Fictional Literature in the Hebrew Bible." In *Judah and the Judeans in the Persian Period*, edited by Oded Lipschits and Mandred Oeming, 663–89. Winona Lake, IN: Eisenbrauns, 2006.
Loader, William R. G. *Sohn und Hoherpriester: Eine traditionsgeschichtliche Untersuchung zur Christologie des Hebräerbriefes*. Neukirchen-Vluyn, Germany: Neukirchener, 1981.
Lohfink, Gerhard. *Die Himmelfahrt Jesu—Erfindung oder Erfahrung?* Stuttgart: Katholisches Bibelwerk, 1972.
Löhr, Hermut. "'Heute, wenn ihr seine Stimme Hört . . .' Zur Kunst der Schriftanwendung im Hebräerbrief und in 1 Kor 10." In *Schriftauslegung: Im Antiken Judentum Und Im Urchristentum*, edited by Martin Hengel and Hermut Löhr, 226–48. Tübingen, Germany: Mohr Siebeck, 1994.
Loiseau, Anne-Françoise. *L'influence de l'araméen sur les traducteurs de la LXX principalement, sur les traducteurs grecs postérieurs, ainsi que sur les scribes de las Vorlage de la LXX*. Atlanta: SBL, 2016.
Longacre, Robert E. *The Grammar of Discourse: Topics in Language and Linguistics*. 2nd ed. New York: Plenum, 1996.
Longacre, Robert E., and Shin Ja J. Hwang. *Holistic Discourse Analysis*. Dallas: SIL International, 2012.
Lookadoo, Jonathon. *The High Priest in the Temple*. Tübingen, Germany: Mohr Siebeck, 2018.

Louw, J. P. "Preface." In Guthrie, *The Structure of Hebrews*, xii. Grand Rapids: Baker, 1998.

———. *Semantics of New Testament Greek*. Atlanta: Scholars, 1982.

Lucas, Earnest C. "Cosmology." In *DOTP* 130–39.

Lund, Nils W. *Chiasmus in the New Testament: A Study in Form and Function of Chiastic Structures*. 1942. Reprint, Peabody, MA: Hendrickson, 1992.

Lundquist, John M. "The Common Temple Ideology of the Ancient Near East." In *The Temple in Antiquity: Ancient Records and Modern Perspectives*, edited by Truman G. Madsen, 53–76. Religious Studies Monograph Series 9. Provo, UT: Brigham Young University, 1984.

Lünemann, Gottlieb. *The Epistle to the Hebrews*. Edinburgh, IN: T&T Clark, 1882.

Luther, Martin. *Luther's Works: Letters I*. Edited by Jaroslav Jan Pelikan et al. Philadelphia: Fortress, 1999.

MacCulloch, J. A. *The Harrowing of Hell: A Comparative Study of an Early Christian Doctrine*. Edinburgh: T&T Clark, 1930.

Mackie, Scott D. "Confession of the Son of God in Hebrews." *NTS* 53 (2007) 114–29.

———. "Confession of the Son of God in the Exordium of Hebrews." *JSNT* 30 (2008) 437–53.

———. *Eschatology and Exhortation in the Epistle to the Hebrews*. Tübingen, Germany: Mohr Siebeck, 2007.

———. "Let Us Draw Near . . . But Not Too Near: A Critique of the Attempted Distinction between 'Drawing Near' and 'Entering' in Hebrews' Entry Exhortations." In *Listen, Understand, Obey: Essays in Honor of Gareth Lee Cockerill*, edited by Caleb T. Friedeman, 17–36. Eugene, OR: Pickwick, 2017.

MacLeod, David J. "The Cleansing of the True Tabernacle." *BSac* 152 (1995) 60–71.

———. "The Present Work of Christ in Hebrews." *BSac* 148 (1991) 184–200.

MacRae, George W. "Heavenly Temple and Eschatology in the Letter to the Hebrews." *Semeia* 12 (1978) 179–99.

Maile, J. F. "Heaven, Heavenlies, Paradise." In *DPL* 381–83.

Malina, Bruce J. and J. J. Pilch. "The Wrath of God: The Meaning of ὀργή θεοῦ in the New Testament World." In *In Other Words: Essays on Social Science Methods and the New Testament in Honor of Jerome H. Neyrey*, edited by A. C. Hagedorn et al., 138–54. Sheffield: Sheffield Academic, 2007.

Marshall, I. Howard. "Soteriology in Hebrews." In *The Epistle to the Hebrews and Christian Theology*, edited by Richard Bauckham et al., 253–80. Grand Rapids: Eerdmans, 2009.

———. "Yes, But . . . Testing the Exegetical Basis for David Moffitt's Proposal." Paper presented at the Annual Meeting of the Evangelical Theological Society, Baltimore, MD, Nov 21, 2013.

Martens, E. A. *God's Design: A Focus on Old Testament Theology*. 3rd ed. Grand Rapids: Baker, 1998.

Martin, Charles T., Jr. "The Household of God: Familial Language and Christology in Hebrews." PhD diss., Southwestern Baptist Theological Seminary, Fort Worth, TX, 2016.

Martin, Dale Basil. *The Corinthian Body*. New Haven, CT: Yale University Press, 1995.

Martin, Michael Wade, and Jason A. Whitlark. *Inventing Hebrews: Design and Purpose in Ancient Rhetoric*. New York: Cambridge University Press, 2018.

Mason, Eric F. "A Call to Renunciation of Judaism or Encouragement to Christian Commitment?" In *The Letter to the Hebrews: Critical Readings*, edited by Scott D. Mackie, 389–403. New York: T&T Clark, 2018.

Mason, Eric F., and Kevin B. McCruden. *Reading the Epistle to the Hebrews: A Resource for Students*. Atlanta: Society of Biblical Literature, 2011.

McCruden, Kevin B. "The Concept of Perfection in the Epistle to the Hebrews." In *Reading the Epistle to the Hebrews: A Resource for Students*, edited by Eric F. Mason and Kevin B. McCruden, 209–29. Atlanta: Society of Biblical Literature, 2011.

McKay, John Michael Jr. "God's Holy Temple Fire as Possible Background to Heb 10:27: 'Fury of Fire.'" Paper presented at the Annual Meeting of the Evangelical Theological Society, Denver, CO, Nov 15, 2022.

———. "Jesus as Faithful in Testing: A Key to the Rhetorical Connection Between Hebrews 3:1–6 and 3:7–4:14." PhD diss., Southwestern Baptist Theological Seminary, Fort Worth, TX, 2016.

McKim, Donald K. *Historical Handbook of Major Biblical Interpreters*. Downers Grove, IL: InterVarsity, 1998.

———. *Westminster Dictionary of Theological Terms*. Louisville: Westminster John Knox, 1996.

McKnight, Scot, ed. *Introducing New Testament Interpretation*. Grand Rapids: Baker, 1989.

———. "The Nature of Bodily Resurrection: A Debatable Issue." *JETS* 33 (1990) 379–82.

McRay, John. "Atonement and Apocalyptic in the Book of Hebrews." *ResQ* 23 (1980) 1–9.

Meier, John. P. "Structure and Theology in Hebrews 1, 1–14." *Biblica* 66 (1985) 168–89.

Mendel, Arthur P. *Vision and Violence*. Ann Arbor: University of Michigan Press, 1999.

Metzger, Bruce Manning. *The Canon of the New Testament: Its Origin, Development, and Significance*. Oxford: Clarendon, 1987.

———. *A Textual Commentary on the Greek New Testament, Second Edition a Companion Volume to the United Bible Societies' Greek New Testament*. 4th rev. ed. London: United Bible Societies, 1994.

Metzger, Bruce Manning, and Bart D. Ehrman. *The Text of the New Testament: Its Transmission, Corruption, and Restoration*. 4th ed. New York: Oxford University Press, 2005.

Michaelis, Wilhelm. "σκηνή." In *TDNT* 7:368–81.

Michel, Otto. *Der Brief and die Hebräer*. 11th ed. Göttingen: Vandenhoeck & Ruprecht, 1960.

Milligan, George. *The English Bible: A Sketch of Its History*. London: A. & C. Black, 1895.

Milligan, J. H. Moulton, and George Milligan. *Vocabulary of the Greek Testament*. London: Hodder and Stoughton, 1930.

Moffatt, James. *A Critical and Exegetical Commentary on the Epistle to the Hebrews*. Edinburgh: T&T Clark, 1952.

Moffitt, David M. *Atonement and the Logic of Resurrection in the Epistle to the Hebrews*. Boston: Brill, 2011.

———. "Blood, Life, and Atonement: Reassessing Hebrews' Christological Appropriation of Yom Kippur." In *The Day of Atonement: Its' Interpretations in Early Jewish and Christian Traditions*, edited by Thomas Hieke and Tobias Nicklas, 211–24. Leiden: Brill, 2012.

———. "Further Reflections on Hebrews, Sacrifice, and Purity." Paper presented at the Annual Meeting of the Evangelical Theological Society, Baltimore, MD, Nov 21, 2013.

———. "Hebrews." In *T&T Clark Companion to Atonement*, edited by Adam J. Johnson, 533–36. New York: Bloomsbury, 2017.

———. "'If Another Priest Arises': Jesus's Resurrection and the High Priestly Christology of Hebrews." In *A Cloud of Witnesses: The Theology of Hebrews in its Ancient Contexts*, edited by Richard Bauckham and Nathan MacDonald, 68–79. London: T&T Clark, 2008.

———. "It Is Not Finished: Jesus's Perpetual Atoning Work as the Heavenly High Priest in Hebrews." In *So Great Salvation: A Dialogue on the Atonement in Hebrews*, edited by Jon C. Laansma et al., 157–75. New York: T&T Clark, 2019.

———. "Jesus as Interceding High Priest and Sacrifice in Hebrews: A Response to Nicholas Moore." *JSNT* 42 (2020) 542–52.

———. "Jesus's Sacrifice and the Mosaic Logic of Hebrews' New-Covenant Theology." In *Understanding the Jewish Roots of Christianity: Biblical, Theological, and Historical Essays on the Relationship between Christianity and Judaism*, edited by Gerald R. McDermott, 51–68. Bellingham, WA: Lexham, 2021.

———. "Perseverance, Purity, and Identity: Exploring Hebrews' Eschatological Worldview, Ethics, and In-Group Bias." In *Sensitivity to Outsiders*, edited by Jacobus Kok et al., 357–81. Tübingen, Germany: Mohr Siebeck, 2013.

———. "Serving in the Tabernacle in Heaven: Sacred Space, Jesus's High-Priestly Sacrifice, and Hebrews' Analogical Theology." In *Hebrews in Contexts*, edited by Gabriella Gelardini and Harold Attridge, 259–79. Leiden: Brill, 2016.

———. "Unveiling Jesus's Flesh: A Fresh Assessment of the Relationship Between the Veil and Jesus's Flesh in Hebrews 10:20." *PRSt* 37 (2010) 71–84.

Moltmann, Jürgen. *Is There Life after Death? (Pére Marquette Lecture in Theology, 1998)*. Milwaukee: Marquette University Press, 1998.

Montefiore, Hugh. *A Commentary on the Epistle to the Hebrews*. Harper's New Testament Commentaries. 1817. Reprint, San Francisco: Harper & Row, 1964.

Moo, Douglas J. *The Old Testament in the Gospel Passion Narratives*. Eugene, OR: Wipf & Stock, 1983.

Moore, Nicholas J. "Heaven's Revolving Door? Cosmology, Entrance, and Approach in Hebrews." *BBR* 29 (2019) 187–207.

———. "'In' or 'Near'? Heavenly Access and Christian Identity in Hebrews." In *Muted Voices of the New Testament: Readings in the Catholic Epistles and Hebrews*, edited by Katherine M. Hockey et al., 186–98. New York: T&T Clark, 2017.

———. "Jesus as 'the One who Entered his Rest': The Christological Reading of Hebrews 4:10." *JSNT* 36 (2014) 383–400.

———. *The Open Sanctuary: Access to God and the Heavenly Temple in the New Testament*. Grand Rapids: Baker Academic, 2004.

———. *Repetition in Hebrews: Plurality and Singularity in the Letter to the Hebrews, Its Ancient Context, and the Early Church*. Tübingen, Germany: Mohr Siebeck, 2015.

———. "Sacrifice, Session, and Intercession: The End of Christ's Offering in Hebrews." *JSNT* 42 (2020) 521–41.

———. "'The True Tabernacle' of Hebrews 8:2: Future Dwelling with People or Heavenly Dwelling Place?" *TynBul* 72 (2021) 49–71.

Morales, L. Michael. "Atonement in Ancient Israel: The Whole Burnt Offering as Central to Israel's Cult." In *So Great Salvation: A Dialogue on the Atonement in Hebrews*, edited by Jon C. Laansma et al., 27–39. New York: T&T Clark, 2019.

———. *Cult and Cosmos: Tilting Towards a Temple-Centered Theology.* Paris: Peeters, 2014.

———. *The Tabernacle Pre-Figured: Cosmic Mountain Ideology in Genesis and Exodus.* Paris: Peeters, 2012.

Morgan, Christopher W., and Robert A. Peterson, eds. *Heaven.* Wheaton, IL,:Crossway, 2014.

Moule, C. F. D. *An Idiom Book of New Testament Greek.* 2nd ed. Cambridge: Cambridge University Press, 2004.

Moulton, James Hope, and Nigel Turner. *A Grammar of New Testament Greek: Syntax.* Vol. 3. Edinburgh: T&T Clark, 1963.

Mounce, William D. *Basics of Biblical Greek: Grammar.* 3rd ed. Grand Rapids: Zondervan, 2009.

Myers, Ben. *The Apostles' Creed: A Guide to the Ancient Catechism.* Bellingham, WA: Lexham, 2018.

Nardoni, Enrique. *Rise Up, O Judge: A Study of Justice in the Biblical World.* Translated by Seán Charles Martin. Grand Rapids: Baker Academic, 2004.

Nauck, Wolfgang. "Zum Aufbau des Hebräerbriefs." In *Judentum, Urchristentum, Kirche: Festschrift für Joachim Jeremias*, edited by Walther Eltester, 199–206. Berlin: Alfred Töpelmann, 1960.

Neeley, Linda L. *A Discourse Analysis of Hebrews.* Dallas: SIL International, 1987.

Nelson, Richard D. "'He Offered Himself': Sacrifice in Hebrews." *Int* 57 (2003) 251–65.

Neyrey, Jerome H. "'Without Beginning of Days or End of Life' (Hebrews 7:3): Topos for a True Deity." *CBQ* 53 (1991) 439–55.

Nichols, Terence. *Death and Afterlife: A Theological Introduction.* Grand Rapids: Brazos, 2010.

Nickelsburg, George W. E. "Enoch, Levi, and Peter: Recipients of Revelation in Upper Galilee." *JBL 100* (1981) 575–600.

———. *Jewish Literature between the Bible and the Mishnah: A Historical and Literary Introduction.* 2nd ed. Minneapolis: Fortress, 2005.

———. "Judgment, Life-after-Death, and Resurrection in the Apocrypha and the non-Apocalyptic Pseudepigrapha." In *Judaism in Late Antiquity, Part 4: Death, Life-After-Death, Resurrection and the World-to-Come in the Judaism of Antiquity*, edited by Alan J. Avery-Peck and Jacob Neusner, 141–62. Leiden: Brill, 2000.

———. *Resurrection, Immortality, and Eternal Life in Intertestamental Judaism and Early Christianity.* Exp. ed. Cambridge: President and Fellows of Harvard College, 2006.

———. "Son of Man." In *ABD* 6:137–50.

Nida, Eugene A., and Charles R. Taber. *The Theory and Practice of Translation.* Leiden: Brill, 1974.

Nida, Eugene A., et al. *Style and Discourse, with Special Reference to the Text of the Greek New Testament.* Cape Town, South Africa: United Bible Societies, 1983.

Niederwimmer, Kurt. "Vom Glauben der Pilger: Erwägungen zu Hebr 11, 8–10 und 13–16." In *Zur Aktualität des Alten Testaments: Festschrift für Georg Sauer zum 65. Geburtstag*, edited by Seigfrie Kreuzer and Kurt Lüthi, 121–31. Frankfurt: Lang, 1992.

Odenberg, Hugo, ed. *Enoch or the Hebrew Book of Enoch*. 1928. Reprint, Memphis: Old South Books, 2020.

Oden, Robert A., Jr. "Cosmogony, Cosmology." In *ABD* 1:1162–71.

Orr, Peter C. *Exalted above the Heavens: The Risen and Ascended Christ*. Edited by D. A. Carson. Downers Grove, IL: InterVarsity, 2018.

Osborne, Grant R. *The Hermeneutical Spiral: A Comprehensive Introduction to Biblical Interpretation*. Rev. and expanded, 2nd ed. Downers Grove, IL: InterVarsity, 2006.

Otto, Rudolf. *The Idea of the Holy: An Inquiry into the Non-rational Factor in the Idea of the Divine and Its Relation to the Rational*. 1923. Reprint, N.p.: Pantianos Classics, n.d.

Ounsworth, Richard. *Joshua Typology in the New Testament*. Tübingen, Germany: Mohr Siebeck, 2012.

Pannenberg, Wolfhart. *Basic Questions in Theology: Collected Essays*. Vol. 1. Philadelphia: Fortress, 1970.

Patai, Raphael. *Man and Temple: In Ancient Jewish Myth and Ritual*. New York: KTAV, 1967.

Pate, C. Marvin, et al. *The Story of Israel: A Biblical Theology*. Downers Grove, IL: InterVarsity, 2004.

Patterson, Paige. *A Pilgrim Priesthood: An Exposition of the Epistle of First Peter*. Eugene, OR: Wipf & Stock, 1982.

Payne, J. Barton. *The Imminent Appearing of Christ*. Grand Rapids: Eerdmans, 1962.

Peeler, Amy L. B. "The Ethos of God in Hebrews." *PRSt* 37 (2010) 37–51.

———. *You Are My Son: The Family of God in the Epistle of Hebrews*. New York: T&T Clark, 2014.

Penner, Ken, and Michael S. Heiser. *Old Testament Greek Pseudepigrapha with Morphology*. Bellingham, WA: Lexham, 2008.

Pennington, Jonathan T. *Heaven and Earth in the Gospel of Matthew*. Grand Rapids: Baker Academic, 2009.

Perrin, Nicholas. *Jesus the Priest*. Grand Rapids: Baker Academic, 2018.

———. *Jesus the Temple*. Grand Rapids, Baker Academic, 2010.

———. "The Origins of Hebrews' High Priest Christology: A Conundrum Revisited." In *So Great Salvation: A Dialogue on the Atonement in Hebrews*, edited by Jon C. Laansma et al., 51–64. New York: T&T Clark, 2019.

Pester, John. "Exhortation to Participate in the Fulfillment of the Eternal Will of God in the Epistle to the Hebrews: The Corporate Perfection of Redeemed Humanity." *Affirmation and Critique* 16 (2011) 33–48.

Peterson, David G. "God and Scripture in Hebrews." In *The Trustworthiness of God: Perspectives on the Nature of Scripture*, edited by Carl R. Trueman and Paul Helm, 118–38. Grand Rapids: Eerdmans, 2002.

———. *Hebrews and Perfection: An Examination of the Concept of Perfection in the Epistle to the Hebrews*. New York: Cambridge University Press, 2005.

Philip, Mayjee. *Leviticus in Hebrews: A Transtextual Analysis of the Tabernacle Theme in the Letter to the Hebrews*. New York: Lang, 2011.

Philo. *Philo*. Vols. 1–10. Translated by F. H. Colson et al. LCL. Cambridge, MA: Harvard University Press, 1929–1962.

Pierce, Madison N. *Divine Discourse in the Epistle to the Hebrews: The Recontextualization of Spoken Quotations of Scripture*. New York: Cambridge University Press, 2020.

BIBLIOGRAPHY

Playoust, Catherine Anne. "Lifted Up from the Earth: The Ascension of Jesus and the Heavenly Ascents of Earthly Christians." ThD diss., Harvard University, Cambridge, MA, 2006.

Plummer, Robert L. *40 Questions About Interpreting the Bible*. Grand Rapids: Kregel, 2010.

Porter, Stanley E. "Defining Discourse Analysis as an Important New Testament Interpretive Framework." In *New Testament Philology: Essays in Honor of David Alan Black*, edited by Melton Bennett Winstead, 194–211. Eugene, OR: Pickwick, 2018.

———. "Discourse Analysis and New Testament Studies: An Introductory Survey." In *Discourse Analysis and Other Topics in Biblical Greek*, edited by Stanely E. Porter and D. A. Carson, 14–35. Sheffield: Sheffield Academic, 1995.

———. *Idioms of the Greek New Testament*. Sheffield: Sheffield Academic, 2005.

———. "Linguistic Schools." In *Linguistics and New Testament Greek: Key Issues in the Current Debate*, edited by David Alan Black and Benjamin L. Merkle, 11–36. Grand Rapids: Baker Academic, 2020.

———. *Verbal Aspect in the Greek New Testament, with Reference to Tense and Mood*. New York: Lang, 2010.

Portier-Young, Anathea. "Jewish Apocalyptic Literature and Resistance Literature." In *The Oxford Handbook of Apocalyptic Literature*, edited by John J. Collins, 145–62. Oxford: Oxford University Press, 2014.

Prime, George Wendell. *Fifteenth Century Bibles: A Study in Bibliography*. 1888. Reprint, Boston: Milford, 1974.

Pulse, Jeffrey. *Figuring Resurrection: Joseph as a Death and Resurrection Figure in the Old Testament and Second Temple Judaism*. Bellingham, WA: Lexham, 2021.

Rahlfs, Alfred. *Septuaginta: With Morphology*. Edited by Alfred Rahlfs. Stuttgart: Deutsche Bibelgesellschaft, 1979. Electronic ed.

Rahlfs, Alfred, and Robert Hanhart, eds. *Septuaginta: SESB Edition*. Stuttgart: Deutsche Bibelgesellschaft, 2006.

Reddish, Mitchell G. "Heaven." In *ABD* 3:390–91.

Reeves, John C., and Annette Yoshiko Reed. *Enoch from Antiquity to the Middle Ages: Sources from Judaism, Christianity, and Islam*. Vol 1. Oxford: Oxford University Press, 2018.

Rhee, Victor. *Faith in Hebrews: Analysis within the Context of Christology, Eschatology, and Ethics*. New York: Lang, 2001.

———. "The Role of Chiasm for Understanding Christology in Hebrews 1:1–14." In *New Testament Philology: Essays in Honor of David Alan Black*, edited by Melton Bennett Winstead, 84–108. Eugene, OR: Pickwick, 2018.

Ribbens, Benjamin J. *Levitical Sacrifice and Heavenly Cult in Hebrews*. Berlin: De Gruyter, 2016.

———. "Typology of Types: Typology in Dialogue." *JTI* 5 (2011) 81–96.

Rice, George. E. "Hebrews 6:19: Analysis of Some Assumptions Concerning *Katapetasma*." *AUSS* 5 (1987) 65–71.

———. "With Which Veil?" *Ministry* (June 1987) 20–21.

Robertson, A. T. *A Grammar of the Greek New Testament in the Light of Historical Research*. 4th ed. Nashville: B&H, 1934.

Robinson, H. Wheeler. "Hebrew Psychology." In *The People and the Book: Essays on the Old Testament*, edited by Authur S. Peake, 353–82. Oxford: Clarendon, 1925.

Robinson, John A. T. *The Body: A Study in Pauline Theology*. London, SCM, 1952.
Rogers, Adrian. *A Place Called Heaven*. Memphis: LoveWorthFinding Ministries with Adrian Rogers, 2012.
Rohde, Erwin. *Psyche: The Cult of Souls and Belief in Immortality among the Greeks*. 2 vols. Translated by W. B. Hillis. 1925. Reprint, Eastford, CT: Martino, 2019.
Roloff, Jürgen. "ἱλαστήριον." In *EDNT* 2:186.
Rowland, Christopher. *The Open Heaven: A Study of Apocalyptic in Judaism and Early Christianity*. 1982. Reprint, Eugene, OR: Wipf & Stock, 2002.
Rowland, Christopher, and Christopher R. A. Morray-Jones. *The Mystery of God: Early Jewish Mysticism and the New Testament*. Boston: Brill, 2009.
Rowlands, Jonathan. "The Faithful Son: Rereading Hebrews 1:3b." *JBL* 142 (2023) 699–716.
Runge, Steven E. *Discourse Grammar of the Greek New Testament: A Practical Introduction for Teaching and Exegesis*. Peabody, MA: Hendrickson, 2010.
Russell, Bertrand. *The History of Western Philosophy*. New York: Simon & Schuster, 1972.
Sandmel, Samuel. "Parallelomania." *JBL* 81 (1962) 1–13.
Sasse, Hermann. "Αἰών, Αἰώνιος." In *TDNT* 1:197–209.
Schaff, Philip. *The Creeds of Christendom, with a History and Critical Notes: The Greek and Latin Creeds, with Translations*. Vol. 2. New York: Harper & Brothers, 1890.
Schenck, Kenneth L. "An Archaeology of Hebrews' Tabernacle Imagery." In *Hebrews in Contexts*, edited by Gabriella Gelardini and Harold Attridge, 238–58. Leiden: Brill, 2016.
———. *A Brief Guide to Philo*. 1st ed. Louisville: Westminster, 2005.
———. "A Celebration of the Enthroned Son: The Catena of Hebrews 1." *JBL* 120 (2001) 469–85.
———. *Cosmology and Eschatology in Hebrews: The Settings of the Sacrifice*. New York: Cambridge University Press, 2010.
———. "God has Spoken: Hebrews' Theology of the Scriptures." In *The Epistle to the Hebrews and Christian Theology*, edited by Richard Bauckham et al., 321–36. Grand Rapids: Eerdmans, 2009.
———. "Keeping His Appointment: Creation and Enthronement in Hebrews." *JSNT* 19 (1997) 91–117.
———. "Philo and the Epistle to the Hebrews: Ronald Williamson's Study after Thirty Years." In *The Letter to the Hebrews: Critical Readings*, edited by Scott D. Mackie, 184–208. Reprint, New York: T&T Clark, 2018.
———. "'Through His Own Blood' (Heb 9:12): Did Jesus Offer His Blood in Heaven?" Paper presented at the Annual Meeting of the Society of Biblical Literature, Atlanta, GA, Nov 22, 2015.
Schierse, Franz Joseph. *Verheißung und Heisvollendung: Zur theologischen Grundfrage des Hebräerbriefes*. Munich: Karl Zink, 1955.
Schnabel, Eckhard. "Jesus's Atoning Sacrifice in Hebrews and Atonement of Sin in the Greco-Roman World." In *So Great Salvation: A Dialogue on the Atonement in Hebrews*, edited by Jon C. Laansma et al., 65–86. New York: T&T Clark, 2019.
———. "The Viability of Premillennialism and the Text of Revelation." *JETS* 64 (2021) 785–95.
Scholem, Gershom G. *Jewish Gnosticism, Merkabah Mysticism, and Talmudic Tradition*. New York: Jewish Theological Seminary, 1965.
———. *Major Trends in Jewish Mysticism*. Jerusalem: Schocken, 1961.

Scholer, David, and Klyne Snodgrass. "Preface to the 1992 Reprint." In *Chiasmus in the New Testament: A Study in Form and Function of Chiastic Structures*, 2nd ed., by Nils W. Lund, xxi. 1942. Reprint, Peabody, MA: Hendrickson, 1992.

Scholer, John M. *Proleptic Priests: Priesthood in the Epistle to the Hebrews*. Sheffield: Sheffield Academic, 1991.

Schoonhoven, Calvin Robert. "The 'Analogy of Faith' and the Intent of Hebrews." In *Scripture, Tradition, and Interpretation: Essay Presented to Everett F. Harrison by His Student and Colleagues in Honor of his Seventy-Fifth Birthday*, edited by W. Ward Gasque and William S. LaSor, 92–110. Grand Rapids: Eerdmans, 1978.

Schreiner, Patrick. *The Ascension of Christ: Recovering a Neglected Doctrine (Snapshots)*. Bellingham, WA: Lexham, 2020.

Schweizer, Eduard. "Σῶμα, Σωματικός, Σύσσωμος." In *TDNT* 7:1024–94.

Scofield, C. I. *The Scofield Bible Reference Bible*. New York: Oxford University Press, 1945.

Scott, James M. "Heavenly Ascents in Jewish and Pagan Traditions." In *DNTB* 447–52.

Searle, J. R. *Speech Acts*. Cambridge: Cambridge University Press, 1969.

Segal, Alan F. "Heavenly Ascent in Hellenistic Judaism, Early Christianity, and Their Environment." In *ANRW* 2.23.2, edited by Wolfgang Haase, 1333–94. Berlin: De Gruyter, 1980.

———. *Life after Death: A History of the Afterlife in Western Religion*. New York: Doubleday, 2004.

Selby, Gary S. "The Meaning and Function of Συνείδησις in Hebrews 9 and 10." *ResQ* 28 (1985–86) 145–54.

Seow, C. L. *A Grammar for Biblical Hebrew*. Rev. ed. Nashville: Abingdon, 1995.

Seow, C. L., et al. *Handbook to A Grammar for Biblical Hebrew*. Rev. ed. Nashville: Abingdon, 2005.

Sigvartsen, Jan A. *Afterlife and Resurrection Beliefs in the Apocrypha and Apocalyptic Literature*. New York: T&T Clark, 2019.

Silva, Moisés. *Biblical Words and Their Meaning: An Introduction to Lexical Semantics*. Grand Rapids: Zondervan, 1994.

Sleeman, Matthew. "The Ascension and Spatial Theory." In *Ascent into Heaven in Luke-Acts: New Explorations of Luke's Narrative Hinge*, edited by David K. Bryan and David W. Pao, 157–73. Minneapolis: Fortress, 2016.

———. *Geography and the Ascension Narrative in Acts*. Cambridge: Cambridge University Press, 2013.

Smillie, Gene R. "Living and Active: The Word of God in Hebrews." PhD diss., Trinity Evangelical Divinity School, Deerfield, IL, 2000.

Smith, Benjamin. "Priest and Sacrifice: The Priestly Background to Isaiah 52:13–53:12." Paper presented at the Annual Meeting of the Evangelical Theological Society, Fort Worth, TX, Nov 17, 2021.

Smith, James D., III. "Faith as Substance or Surety: Perspectives on Hypostasis in Hebrews 11:1." In *Challenges in Bible Interpretation*, edited by Glen G. Scorgie et al., 381–92. Grand Rapids: Zondervan, 2003.

Smith, Morton. "On the History of ΑΠΟΚΑΛΥΠΤΩ and ΑΠΟΚΑΛΥΠΙΣ." In *Apocalypticism in the Mediterranean World and the Near East*, edited by David Hellholm, 9–20. Tübingen, Germany: Mohr Siebeck, 1983.

Sorabji, Richard. *Time, Creation, and the Continuum: Theories in Antiquity and the Early Middle Ages*. Chicago: Chicago University Press, 2006.

Sowers, Sidney G. *The Hermeneutics of Philo and Hebrews: A Comparison of the Interpretation of the Old Testament in Philo Judaeus and the Epistle to the Hebrews.* Richmond, VA: John Knox, 1965.

Spicq, Ceslaus. *L'Épître aux Hébreux: I—Introduction.* Paris: J. Gabalda, 1952.

———. *L'Épître aux Hébreux: II—Commentaire.* Paris: J. Gabalda, 1953.

———. *L'Épître aux Hébreux.* Sources Bibliques. Paris: J. Gabalda, 1977.

Stadelmann, Luis I. J. *The Hebrew Conception of the World: A Philological and Literary Study.* Rome: Pontifical Biblical Institute, 1970.

Stegemann, Ekkehard W., and Wolfgang Stegemann. "Does the Cultic Language in Hebrews Represent Sacrifical Metaphors? Reflections on Some Basic Problems." In *Hebrews: Contemporary Methods—New Insights*, edited by Gabriella Gelardini, 13–24. Boston: Brill, 2005.

Stek, John H. "Biblical Typology Yesterday and Today." *CTJ* 5 (1970) 133–62.

Stemberger, Günter. *Der Leib der Auferstehung.* Rome: Pontifical Biblical Institute, 1972.

Stendahl, Krister. *Immortality and Resurrection: Four Essays by Oscar Cullman, Harry A. Wolfson, Werner Jaeger, and Henry J. Cadbury.* Edited by Krister Stendahl. New York: McMillan, 1965.

———. "Immortality is Too Much and Too Late." In *Meanings: The Bible as Document and as* Guide, 193–202. Philadelphia: Fortress, 1984.

Sterling, Gregory E. "Ontology Versus Eschatology: Tensions between Author and Community in Hebrews." *Studia Philonica Annual* 13 (2001) 190–211.

Stewart, Alexander. "Cosmology, Eschatology, and Soteriology in Hebrews: A Synthetic Analysis." *BBR* 20 (2010) 545–60.

Stewart, Roy A. "Creation and Matter in the Epistle to the Hebrews." *NTS* 12 (1966) 284–93.

Steyn, Gert J. "The Eschatology of Hebrews: As Understood within a Cultic Setting." In *Eschatology of the New Testament and Some Related Documents*, edited by Jan G. Van der Watt, 429–50. Tübingen, Germany: Mohr Siebeck, 2011.

———. *A Quest for the Assumed LXX Vorlage of the Explicit Quotations in Hebrews.* Oakville, CT: Vandenhoeck and Ruprecht, 2011.

Still, Todd. "Christ as Pistos: The Faith(fulness) of Jesus in the Epistle to the Hebrews." *CBQ* 69 (2007) 746–55.

Stock, Augustine. "Chiastic Awareness and Education in Antiquity." *BTB* 14 (1984) 23–27.

Stokes, Ryan E. *The Satan: How God's Executioner Became the Enemy.* Grand Rapids: Eerdmans, 2019.

Stolz, Lukas. *Der Höhepunkt des Hebräerbriefs.* Tübingen, Germany: Mohr Siebeck, 2018.

Strand, Kenneth A. *Early Low-German Bibles: The Story of Four Pre-Lutheran Editions.* Grand Rapids: Eerdmans, 1967.

———. *German Bibles before Luther: The Story of 14 High-German Editions.* Grand Rapids: Eerdmans, 1966.

———. *Luther's "September Bible" in Facsimile: With Brief Historical Introduction.* Ann Arbor: Ann Arbor Publishers, 1972.

Streett, Andrew D. "New Approaches to the Use of the Old Testament in the New Testament." *SwJT* 64 (2021) 14–17.

Strong, James. *The Tabernacle of Israel: Its Structure and Symbolism*. Grand Rapids Kregel, 1987.
Swetnam, James. "On Romans 8,23 and the Expectation of Sonship." *Biblica* 48 (1967) 102–8.
Strum, R. E. "Defining the Word 'Apocalyptic': A Problem in Biblical Criticism." In *Apocalyptic and the New Testament*, edited by Joel Marcus and Marion L. Soards, 17–48. New York: Bloomsbury, 2015.
Stuckenbruck, Loren T. *Angel Veneration and Christology*. Tübingen, Germany: Mohr Siebeck, 1995.
———. "The Interiorization of Dualism within the Human Being in Second Temple Judaism: The Treatise of the Two Spirits (1QS 111:13–IV:26) in Its Tradition-Historical Context." In *Light Against Darkness: Dualism in Ancient Mediterranean Religion and the Contemporary World*, edited by Armin Lange et al., 145–68. Göttingen, Germany: Vandenhoeck & Ruprecht, 2011.
Styers, Randall, ed. *Light Against Darkness: Dualism in Ancient Mediterranean Religion and the Contemporary World*. Oakville, CT: Vandenhoeck & Ruprecht, 2011.
Sullivan, Kevin P. *Wrestling with Angels: A Study of the Relationship between Angels and Humans in Ancient Jewish Literature and the New Testament*. Boston: Brill, 2004.
Suriano, Matthew J. *A History of Death in the Hebrew Bible*. New York: Oxford University Press, 2018.
Tănase, Nichifor. "From 'Veil' (κάλυμμα) Theology to 'Face' (πρόσωπον) Christology: Body as a Veil Concealing Divine Glory—Direct Experience and Immediate Perception (αἴσθησις) of God." *SUBBTO* 62 (2017) 119–82.
Tångberg, K. A. "Linguistics and Theology." *BT* 24 (1973) 301–10.
Tappert, Theodore G. *The Book of Concord: The Confessions of the Evangelical Lutheran Church*. Philadelphia: Mühlenberg, 1959.
Thiessen, Matthew. "Hebrews 12.5–13, the Wilderness Period, and Israel's Discipline." *NTS* 55 (2009) 366–79.
———. "Hebrews and the End of the Exodus." *NovT* 49 (2007) 353–69.
———. "Hebrews and the Jewish Law." In *So Great Salvation: A Dialogue on the Atonement in Hebrews*, edited by Jon C. Laansma et al., 183–94. New York: T&T Clark, 2019.
———. *Jesus and the Forces of Death: The Gospel's Portrayal of Ritual Impurity within First-Century Judaism*. Grand Rapids: Baker Academic, 2020.
Thiselton, Anthony C. *Life after Death: A New Approach to the Last Things*. Grand Rapids: Eerdmans, 2012.
Thompson, James W. *The Beginnings of Christian Philosophy: The Epistle to the Hebrews*. Washington, DC: Catholic Biblical Association of America, 1982.
———. "Outside the Camp: A Study of Hebrews 13:9–14." *CBQ* 40 (1978) 53–63.
———. *Strangers on the Earth: Philosophy and Rhetoric in Hebrews*. Eugene, OR: Cascade, 2020.
Tigchelaar, Eibert. "Dead Sea Scrolls." In *EDEJ* 163–80.
Torrance, Thomas F. *Royal Priesthood: A Theology of Ordained Ministry*. New ed. New York: T&T Clark, 2003.
———. *Space, Time and Resurrection*. Edinburgh, Scotland: T&T Clark, 1976.
Toussaint, Stanley D. "The Eschatology of the Warning Passages in the Book of Hebrews." *Grace Theological Journal* 3 (1982) 67–80.
Traub, Helmut. "Οὐρανός, Οὐράνιος, Ἐπουράνιος, Οὐρανόθεν." In *TDNT* 5:497–543.

Travis, Stephen H. "Judgment." In *DJG* 408–11.
Tregelles, Samuel Prideaux. *An Account of the Printed Text of the Greek New Testament: With Remarks on Its Revision Upon Critical Principles; Together with a Collation of the Critical Texts of Griesbach, Scholz, Lachmann, and Tischendorf, with That in Common Use*. London: S. Bagster and Sons, 1854.
Treier, Daniel J. "'Mediator of a New Covenant': Atonement and Christology in Hebrews." In *So Great Salvation: A Dialogue on the Atonement in Hebrews*, edited by Jon C. Laansma et al., 105–19. New York: T&T Clark, 2019.
———. "Proof Text." In *DTIB* 622–24.
———. "Speech Acts, Hearing Hearts, and Other Senses: The Doctrine of Scripture Practiced in Hebrews." In *The Epistle to the Hebrews and Christian Theology*, edited by Richard Bauckham et al., 337–50. Grand Rapids: Eerdmans, 2009.
Trotter, Jonathan. *The Jerusalem Temple in Diaspora: Jewish Practice and Thought during the Second Temple*. New York: Brill, 2019.
Trueman, Carl R. *Histories and Fallacies: Problems Faced in the Writing of History*. Wheaton: Crossway, 2010.
Turner, Nigel. *Christian Words*. Nashville: Nelson, 1981.
Urga, Abeneazer G. *Intercession of Jesus in Hebrews: The Background and Nature of Jesus' Heavenly Intercession in the Epistle to the Hebrews*. Tübingen, Germany: Mohr Siebeck, 2023.
Vaillancourt, Ian J. *The Multifaceted Saviour of Psalms 110 and 118: A Canonical Exegesis*. Sheffield: Sheffield Phoenix, 2019.
VanderKam, James C. *An Introduction to Early Judaism*. Grand Rapids: Eerdmans, 2001.
VanderKam, James C., and Peter Flint. *The Meaning of the Dead Sea Scrolls: Their Significance for Understanding the Bible, Judaism, Jesus, and Christianity*. San Francisco: HarperOne, 2002.
Van Dijk, Tuen A. "Recalling and Summarizing Complex Discourse." In *Text Processing: Papers in Text Analysis and Text Description*, edited by Wolfgang Burghardt and Klaus Hölker, 49–118. New York: De Gruyter, 1979.
———. *Some Aspects of Text Grammars: A Study of Theoretical Linguistics and Poetics*. Parris: Mouton, 1972.
———. *Text and Context: Explorations in the Semantics and Pragmatics of Discourse*. New York: Longman, 1977.
VanGemeren, Willem A. "Psalms." In *The Expositor's Bible Commentary: Psalms*, vol. 5, rev. ed., edited by Tremper Longman III and David E. Garland, 814. Grand Rapids: Zondervan, 2008.
Vanhoye, Albert. *La structure littéraire de l' Épître aux Hébeux*. Paris: Desclée de Brouwer, 1976.
———. "L'οἰκουμένη dans l'épître Hébreux." *Bib* 45 (1964) 248–53.
———. *A Perfect Priest*. Edited and translated by Nicholas J. Moore and Richard J. Ounsworth. Tübingen, Germany: Mohr Siebeck, 2018.
———. *Situation du Christ: Épître aux Hébeux 1 et 2*. Paris: Cerf, 1969.
———. *Structure and Message of the Epistle to the Hebrews*. Rome: Editrice Pontificio Instuto Biblico, 1989.
Vines, Michael E. "The Apocalyptic Chronotope." In *Bakhtin and Genre Theory in Biblical Studies*, edited by Roland Boer, 109–17. Atlanta: SBL, 2007.
Vlastos, Gregory. *Plato's Universe*. Las Vegas: Parmenides, 2005.

Vos, Geerhardus. *The Teaching of the Epistle to the Hebrews.* Grand Rapids: Eerdmans, 1956.

Walker, Peter. "A Place for Hebrews? Context for a First-Century Sermon." In *The Letter to the Hebrews: Critical Readings,* edited by Scott D. Mackie, 376–88. New York: T&T Clark, 2018.

Wallace, Daniel B. *The Basics of New Testament Syntax: An Intermediate Greek Grammar.* Grand Rapids: Zondervan, 2000.

———. *Greek Grammar Beyond the Basics: Exegetical Syntax of the New Testament.* Grand Rapids: Zondervan, 1999.

Walter, Nikolaus. "'Hellenistiche Eschatologie' im Frühjudentum—Ein Beitrag zur 'Biblischen Theologie.'" *TLZ* 110 (1985) 331–48.

———. "'Hellenistische Eschatologie' im Neuen Testament." In *Glaube und Eschatologie: Festschrift für Werner Georg Kümmel zum 80. Geburtstag,* edited by Erich Gräßer und Otto Mark, 335–56. Tübingen, Germany: Mohr Siebeck, 1985.

Waltke, Bruce K., and Michael Patrick O'Connor. *An Introduction to Biblical Hebrew Syntax.* Winona Lake, IN: Eisenbrauns, 1990.

Weeks, Noel. "Cosmology in Historical Context." *WTJ* 68 (2006) 283–93.

Weiss, Johannes. *Die predigt Jesu vom reiche Gottes.* Göttingen, Germany: Vandenhoeck & Ruprecht, 1964.

Wenell, Karen J. *Jesus and Land: Sacred and Social Space in Second Temple Judaism.* New York: T&T Clark, 2007.

———. "The Kingdom of God as 'Space in Motion': Towards a More Architectural Approach." In *Constructions of Space III: Biblical Spatiality and the Sacred,* edited by Jorunn Økland et al., 135–50. New York: T&T Clark, 2016.

Werner, Martin. *The Formation of Christian Doctrine: An Historical Study of Its Problem.* New York: Harper, 1957.

Wessinger, Catherine. "Apocalypse and Violence." In *The Oxford Handbook of Apocalyptic Literature,* edited by John J. Collins, 422–40. Oxford: Oxford University Press, 2014.

Westcott, Brooke Foss. *The Epistle to the Hebrews: The Greek Text with Notes and Essays.* 3rd ed. London: Macmillan, 1903.

Westfall, Cynthia Long. *A Discourse Analysis of the Letter to the Hebrews: The Relationship between Form and Meaning.* London: T&T Clark, 2005.

———. "Space and Atonement in Hebrews." In *So Great Salvation: A Dialogue on the Atonement in Hebrews,* edited by Jon C. Laansma et al., 228–48. New York: T&T Clark, 2019.

Welch, John W. *Chiasmus in Antiquity: Structures, Analyses, Exegesis.* Hildesheim: Gerstenberg, 1981.

Whitfield, Bryan J. "Pioneer and Perfecter: Joshua Traditions and the Christology of Hebrews." In *A Cloud of Witnesses: The Theology of Hebrews in Its Ancient Contexts,* edited by Richard Bauckham and Nathan MacDonald, 80–87. London: T&T Clark, 2008.

———. "The Three Joshuas of Hebrews 3 and 4." *PRSt* 37 (2010) 21–35.

Whitlark, Jason A. "Cosmology and the Perfection of Humanity in Hebrews." In *Interpretation and the Claims of the Text: Resourcing New Testament Theology, Essays in Honor of Charles H. Talbert,* edited by Jason A. Whitlark et al., 117–28. Waco, TX: Baylor University Press, 2014.

———. *Enabling Fidelity to God: Perseverance in Hebrews in Light of the Reciprocity Systems of the Ancient Mediterranean World*. Eugene, OR: Wipf & Stock, 2008.

Wider, David. *Theozentrik und Bekenntnis: Untersuchungen zur Theologie des Redens Gottes im Hebrerbrief*. Berlin: De Gruyter, 1997.

Wilder, Terry. *Pseudonymity, the New Testament, and Deception: An Inquiry into Intention and Reception*. Lanham, MD: University Press of America, 2004.

Williams, Michael Allen. *Rethinking "Gnosticism:" An Argument for Dismantling a Dubious Category*. Princeton: Princeton University Press, 1996.

Williamson, Paul R. *Death and the Afterlife: Biblical Perspectives on Ultimate Questions*. Downers Grove, IL: InterVarsity, 2018.

Williamson, Ronald. *Jews in the Hellenistic World: Philo*. Cambridge: Cambridge University Press, 1989.

———. *Philo and the Epistle to the Hebrews*. Leiden: Brill, 1970.

Williams, Ronald J., and John C. Beckman. *Williams' Hebrew Syntax*. 3rd ed. Toronto: University of Toronto Press, 2007.

Williams, Sam K. *Jesus's Death as Saving Event: The Background and Origin of a Concept*. Missoula, MT: Scholars, 1975.

———. *Philo and the Epistle to the Hebrews*. Leiden: Brill, 1970.

Wilson, R. McL. *The Gnostic Problem*. London: Mowbray, 1980.

Windisch, Hans. *Der Hebräerbrief*. HNT 14. Tübingen, Germany: Mohr Siebeck, 1931.

Wray, Judith Hoch. *Rest as a Theological Metaphor in the Epistle to the Hebrews and the Gospel of Truth: Early Christian Homilectics of Rest*. Atlanta: Scholars, 1998.

Wright, J. Edward. "Biblical versus Israelite Images of the Heavenly Realm." *JSOT* (2001) 59–75.

———. *The Early History of Heaven*. New York: Oxford University Press, 2000.

Wright, M. R. *Cosmology in Antiquity*. New York: Routledge, 1995.

Wright, N. T. *The New Testament and the People of God: Christian Origins and the Question of God*. Vol. 1. London: Society for Promoting Christian Knowledge. Minneapolis: Fortress, 1992.

———. *Surprised by Hope: Rethinking Heaven, the Resurrection, and the Mission of the Church*. New York: HarperCollins, 2008.

Yamauchi, Edwin M. "Life, Death, and the Afterlife in the Ancient Near East." In *Life in the Face of Death: The Resurrection Message of the New Testament*, edited by Richard N. Longenecker, 21–50. Grand Rapids: Eerdmans, 1997.

Yarbro Collins, Adela. "Ascents to Heaven in Antiquity: Towards a Typology." In *A Teacher for All Generations: Essays in Honor of James C. VanderKam*, edited by Eric F. Mason et al., 553–72. Leiden: Brill, 2012.

———. *Cosmology and Eschatology in Jewish and Christian Apocalypticism*. New York: Brill, 2000.

———. "The Early Christian Apocalypses." In *Semeia 14 Apocalypse: The Morphology of a Genre*, edited by John J. Collins, 60–121. Atlanta: Society of Biblical Literature, 1979.

———. "Introduction." In *Early Christian Apocalypticism: Genre Social Setting; Semeia 36*, edited by Adela Yarbro Collins, 1–11. Decatur, GA: SBL, 1986.

———. "Traveling Up and Away: Journeys to the Upper and Outer Regions of the World." In *Greco-Roman Culture and the New Testament: Studies Commemorating the Centennial of the Pontifical Biblical Institute*, edited by David E. Aune and Frederick Brenk, 135–66. Leiden: Brill, 2012.

Yates, Stephen. *Between Death and Resurrection: A Critical Response to Recent Catholic Debate Concerning the Intermediate State*. New York: Bloomsbury Academic, 2017.

Yohann, Gaveau. "Cosmological Aspects in the Sermon to the Hebrews." PhD seminar, Studies in the Sermon to the Hebrews, Newbold College, Bracknell, England, 2013.

Young, David. *The Concept of Canon in the Reception of the Epistle to the Hebrews*. New York: T&T Clark, 2021.

Young, Francis. "Typology." In *Crossing the Boundaries: Essays in Biblical Interpretation in Honour of Michael D. Goulder*, edited by Stanley E. Porter et al., 29–48. New York: Brill, 1994.

Young, Norman H. "The Gospel According to Hebrews 9." *NTS* 27 (1981) 198–210.

———. "Suffering: A Key to the Epistle to the Hebrews." *ABR* 51 (2003) 47–59.

———. "Where Jesus Has Gone as a Forerunner on Our Behalf." *AUSS* 39 (2001) 165–73.

Young, Richard A. *Intermediate New Testament Greek: A Linguistic and Exegetical Approach*. Nashville: B&H, 1994.

Zahn, Theodor. *The Apostles' Creed: A Sketch of Its History and an Examination of Its Contents*. London: Hodder and Stroughton, 1899.

Zangenberg, Jürgen. "Trochene Knochen, himmlische Seligkeit: Todes- und Jenseitsvorstellungen im Judentum der hellenistisch-frühromischen Zeit." In *Tod und Jenseits im alten Israel und in seiner Umwelt*, edited by Angelika Berlejung and Bernd Janowski, 655–89. Tübingen, Germany: Mohr Siebeck, 2009.

Ziegler, Phillip G. *Militant Grace: The Apocalyptic Turn and the Future of Christian Theology*. Grand Rapids: Baker Academic, 2018.

Ziesler, J. A. *The Meaning of Righteousness in Paul: A Linguistic and Theological Enquiry*. Cambridge: Cambridge University Press, 1972.

Zimmerman, Henrich. *Das Bekenntnis der Hoffnung: Tradition und Redaktion im Hebräerbrief*. Bonner Biblische Beiträge 47. Cologne: Hanstein, 1977.

Author Index

Adams, Edward, 119, 143
Allen, David L., xviii, 170, 275, 417
Attridge, Harold W., 170
Aune, David E., 33

Beckman, John C., 117
Bietenhard, Hans, 435
Black, David Alan, 20, 394

Carson, D. A., 39
Cloverdale, Miles, 431–32, 433
Coetsee, Albert J., 201
Collins, Adela Yarbro, 33, 34
Collins, John J., 14, 32, 33, 146, 147
Cremer, Hermann, 436–37

Deahl, Tim, xvii
Delitzsch, Franz, 170
DeSilva, David A., 124, 263

Ellingworth, Paul, 306
Erasmus, Desiderius, 428

Gelardini, Gabriella, 123, 153
Ginzberg, Louis, 124
Gryson, Roger, 427
Guthrie, George H., 201

Hatch, Edwin, 438
Heath, David Mark, 201
Hellholm, David, 33
Hofius, Otfried, 162

Horsley, Richard A., 145

Jamieson, Robert B., 12
Jeremias, Joachim, 162

Karrer, Martin, 152
Keener, Craig S., 13
Kiene, Paul F., xiv
Koester, Helmut, 170

Laansma, Jon C., 4
Le Boulluec, Alain, 148
Louw, J. P., 434, 436, 437, 438
Luther, Martin, 5, 17, 403, 419, 421,
    423, 428, 429, 430–31, 433

Macabeus, Judas, 55
Mentel, Johan, 430
Moffitt, David M., 12, 140, 141, 151,
    162, 163, 164, 174
Morray-Jones, Christopher R. A., 417
Mounce, William D., 350

Neely, Linda L., 16, 194, 200
Nida, Eugene A., 39, 434, 437, 438

O'Connor, Michael Patrick, 117

Pennington, Jonathan T., 434

Reddish, Mitchell G., 436
Rhee, Victor (Sung Yul), 13

AUTHOR INDEX

Roloff, Jürgen, 307–8
Rowland, Christopher, 34, 417

Silva, Moisés, 437, 438
Smillie, Gene R., 94, 97, 248

Toon, Ronnie, xvii
Traub, Helmut, 436, 437
Tyndale, Wiliam, 431, 432, 433

Van Dijk, Tuen A., 16, 194, 198

Wallace, Daniel B., 330
Waltke, Bruce K., 117
Weber, Robert, 427
Westfall, Cynthia Long, 123, 224
Wilder, Terry, xviii
Williams, Ronald J., 117
Wright, J. Edward, 118
Wycliffe, John, 429

Subject Index

Aaronic ministry, 264
Aaronic priesthood, 206, 263
Abel, 73, 130, 360–61, 362
abilities, of Jesus, 96, 250, 253, 375
Abraham
    as already in heaven, 145, 402
    antitype of to a place as a land of promise, 115
    exampling faith, 363–64
    imagery of bringing up Isaac for sacrifice, 75
    imitation of, 279
    looking for a heavenly city in death, 83
    offered Isaac by faith, 73, 368–69
    paid tithes after his deliverance of Lot, 134
    as the Pastor's main example, 280
Absalom, 77
"according to a spirit of holiness," 411
accountability
    by Israel, 225
    at judgment, 236, 242, 251
Adam, 101, 103, 164, 409
"after themselves occurring," 314
afterlife, 335, 420
aiōn-field
    flattening of, 400
    holiness, 99–100
    language, 5
    motifs related to a present hope, 33
    of the Pastor, 20
    place background, 224
    reality, visible & invisible, 27
    view of the heavens, 122
    word stock introducing the apocalyptic, 89
aiōn-field (apocalyptic) revelation, of the Pastor, 151
aiōn-field background (apocalyptic) language, 14, 27
allegorical hermeneutic, gave rise to major theological changes, 37
allegory, in biblical interpretation, 26
altar of incense, representing prayers ascending to God in heaven, 306
anachronistic hazards, awareness of, 20
ancient afterlife "opinions," debate about, 145
"and in accordance with this," connective-preposition combination, 53
angelic creation, contrasting with the Son who is not created, 219
angelic ministry, of the first heavenly covenant, 220
angels
    as a former way of testifying about the Son, 206
    Jesus also appearing to, 81
    ministering, 220–22, 326
    Moffitt's anthropology in relation to, 174
    omission of created, 180–81

SUBJECT INDEX

angels (continued)
  as omnipresent in multiple heavens, 426
  returning a second time, 77
  serving with prophets and other messengers of the "Word," 225
  as "spirit" and not "human," 174
  worshiping Jesus's enthronement at death, 218
animal sacrifices, 318, 321
"anointed king," Christ as, 69
"anointed priest," 67, 69, 71
anthropological afterlife options, for sinful people, 144–45
Antiochus Epiphanes, torture of Eleazer and his family, 55–56
antitype escalation, into morphed earthly replacements and successionism, 40
antitype sacrificial teaching, foundation of from the beginning, 70
antitypes, 27, 66, 82
antitype-type connection, of "of an eternal/perpetual-place judgment," 62
antitype-type correspondence, in a text, 29–30
apekdechomai, not found in the LXX, 84
apocalypse genre, 31, 32, 33
apocalyptic, distinguishing from eschatology, 34
apocalyptic (*aiōn-field*) thematic frame, 39
apocalyptic *aiōn-field* language, 116, 400–401
apocalyptic language
  criticism against by the late second century CE, 36
  employed by the Pastor, 163
  of heavenly living after death, 49
  in spatial matters for conscious activity of people after fleshly death, 128
  style of revelation, 33
apocalyptic literature, 34
Apostles' Creed, 149
apostolic-led missions, 44

"approach"
  expecting to see Jesus, 381–82
  in faith, 358–59
  to God in judgment, 135
  by Jesus as spirit into heaven, 162
  movement emphasis of, 127
  to the throne of grace, 107
argument from silence, fallacy of, 25
ark of the covenant, highlighted, 306–7
arrival, of Christ, 170
ascent, of Christ into heaven, 417
assembly of the firstborn, as destiny of believers, 384
"at the right hand of the throne of the Majesty," 288
atonement
  achievement of, 9
  Christ's suffering offering of, 334
  complete at sacrificial death on the cross, 318
  finished on the cross, 316
  Jesus's onetime offering for, 266
  of Judas Maccabeus for those who had died, 55
  for the ministry of the new covenant, 168–69
  offering of Jesus, 12, 348
  process of, 8
  requiring Jesus's tasting death for every man, 320
  for sin, 101, 212
  of sins, 71, 231
  in suffering, 330, 413–14
Atonement and the Logic of Resurrection in the Epistle to the Hebrews (Moffitt), 12
audience mental thematic, assembling, 204
author-chosen method, for revelation of truth, 27
authorial intention, interpretational methods, 29
authors, providing summaries, 186

background
  markers, 407
  recent discussion, 12–14
background *aiōn-field*

512

SUBJECT INDEX

determining the narrative, 7
governing the Pastor's word sense, 91
with Philo, 46
places of the Pastor's words, 89
of the reality envisioned by the Pastor, 8
of a reserved judgment linked with one's death, 57
Bar Kokhba Revolt, 35
"becoming," of Christ, 170
beginning teaching, about the Word of Christ, 273–78
"the beginning word of Christ," 271
believers
    after death waiting for the appearance of Christ, 126
    anticipating the ministry of Jesus, 399
    bringing into substance-reality of things not seen, 367
    confession of an unwavering hope for salvation, 382
    at death, 244, 422
    descriptors for the destiny of, 384
    entering heaven a very little while after death, 223
    entering to Jesus in the eternal dwellings of heaven, 136
    entreating others in the message of Christ, 381
    by faith in unseen substance-relities, 404
    finding grace at their time of need before God, 347
    following Jesus "way," 377, 417
    in heaven with Jesus, 230
    heavenly expectation of salvation motivating, 376
    hope by faith to see their Savior at death, 335
    intercession from judgment for sin after death, 7–8
    Jesus's present priestly ministry to after death, 346–47
    made holy after death, 337, 344
    maintaining previous foundation of repentance, 274
    with no conscious living after death, 25
    not hardening their hearts, 245
    not left on their own, 378
    not left outside of heaven, 165
    preparation of, 419
    raising up from the dead, 393
    receiving salvation through Jesus, 133, 260
    striding to God in heaven, 152
    transformation of at death, 324
    transitioning bodily at judgment, 346
    traveling within the veil, 138
    washing the body with pure water, 376
better covenant, 206, 265, 299
better ministry, 219, 222, 233
better resurrection, 373
better teaching, 323
bias, against a grammatical plural, 439
biblical creation, Reformation text of, 430–31
biblical earthly antitypes, orphaned, 37
biblical history, never connecting God's creative acts at "the beginning" to places of holiness, 101
biblical narrative, about Jesus's approach in spirit following flesh resurrection, 24–25
biblical text
    about heavenly places, 423–25
    as nothing more than unreliable history, 94
biblical theology, 15–16, 91, 182
bidirectional movement, between the holy place of God's dwelling and the earth, 112
bitterness, 382–83
blamelessness, of Jesus, 320–21
blessing, pronounced before Isaac's death, 369
blessings of Mount Zion in the City of the Living God, approaching, 383–85
blood of Christ, 318, 319, 323
blood of sprinkling, 384
bodily changes, required for living in God's presence, 302

SUBJECT INDEX

bodily postmortem opportunities, denying in open heavens, 149
bodily transformation, into a perpetual eternal/perpetual-place kingdom, 398
bodily unseen elements of people, dualism of, 160
body of Jesus Christ, self-offering of, 343
boundaries, of the holy place no longer in existence, 315
brethren
    God equipping his for a pleasing relationship, 393
    Jesus participation with other people as, 401
    live loving as God loves, 390
    love of, 387, 391–94
    receiving a spirit bodily transformation, 172
    testifying about the Son, 206
"bring, carry, bear, offer" word, appearing 155 times in the LXX, 74
"bring, carry, lead," broadly encompassing all things, 392
brotherly love, associated with the ministry of Jesus, 389
burnt offering, sacrifice of, 311
"but after this" phrase, not appearing in the LXX, 60
"but you have approached," 384

Cain, 360–61
camp outside the earthly tabernacle ministry, Pastor symbolically using, 390
captive situation, release or deliverance from, 315
Cartesian adversarial problem, of "time" and "eternity," 184
Cartesian philosophy, concerning the unseen/seen creation, 141
Cartesian views, hints concerning the modern solidification of, 436–37
celestial holy place, allowed sinful people and angels temporary residence, 329

ceremonial cleansing law, linking the hearts and conscience of his listeners, 377
ceremonial washings, teaching of, 276
"certainty of faith," 351, 357, 365, 366, 375–76, 394
character of service, emulating God's, 185
cherubim of glory, 307
chiasm, in Greek discourse, 201
chiastic structure, scholars attempted mapping of Hebrews, 203
chosen words of the Pastor, optional meanings for, 406
Christ. *See also* Jesus; Son of God
    after appearing himself as a high priest, 171
    "after finding eternal/perpetual-place redemption," 323
    after himself arriving as a high priest, 170, 171, 255, 314
    after offering himself once to bear the sin of many, 332–36
    anointed one carrying heavy messianic weight, 274
    appearing, 3, 23, 115
    basic requirements of, 160
    as both God and Jesus, 106
    cleansing of things in the heavens, 328–31
    cleansing the conscience, 313–23
    completed priestly work in the flesh, 322
    completing atonement for sin in the holy of holies, 307
    describing the ministry of God as the Son, 211
    endured the same death reserved for all people, 74
    enthronement of as Messiah, 218
    entrance into the holy place in heaven, 172, 323
    errant teaching about, 108
    at eternal/perpetual-place judgment, 70
    "into the eternal/perpetual-place of the eternal/perpetual-place," 219

SUBJECT INDEX

expressing the present ministry of, 333
finding eternal/perpetual-place redemption, 315, 317
"intercedes" for those "waiting completion," 84
intervention at judgment before God, 85
as Jesus, the Son of God, 107
Jesus's high priest ministry as, 266
leading believers into the unseen reality of heaven, 14
ministry "now to appear before God for us," 330
not an earthly replacement for the high priests, 298
offered himself blameless to God, 318
offering himself once, 330, 397
people's rebellious response to and impending judgment, 218
providing transformation from Adam's likeness, 409
sacrificial offering to bear the sin of many people, 332–33
with "salvation" for sinful people, 168
seeing the unseen in, 371
sharing with the same spiritual experience, 160
in spiritual bodily form, 320
as substantive "anointed one," 65
transition completed by, 336
two-fold ministry of after death at judgment, 397
verbal nouns implying spatial camaraderie, 128
"Christ entered," at his dying moment on the cross, 318
Christian churches, second-century CE preserved apocalyptic literature, 34
Christians
in response to the pressure of heresy, 36, 37
turned to the safer hermeneutic of allegory, 35
christological priesthood, link to, 257
Christos, 92, 173

church proposals, neglecting the foundational teaching of Christ, 275
city of the living God, as destiny of believers, 384
classical concept, where all the dead enter Hades, 403
classical Greek literature, bias for a singular "heaven," 438
clean conscience and body, 351, 394
climax, function, 192, 193, 196
closed-heaven
human sin creating spatial-temporal tensions, 230
limitations of, 141
realities, 418
reversals toward exposed concepts, 185
translation decisions building on presuppositions of Cartesian philosophy, 183
where people not allowed in the presence of the living God, 400
Cloverdale, Miles, 431–32, 433
Collins, John, 32
communication rules, essential for successful understanding, 19
communication theory, the structure of discourse and, 190
community finish, of all believers, 376
completeness, leading to, 274
completion, 84–85, 242, 396–404
confession
brethren as "sharers in a heavenly calling," 236
concerning Jesus's ministry, 244
conversation to cohesion, 253
describing a possible errant theological, 273–74
of hope, 386
in Jesus as the Christ, 136
power of in receiving Jesus, 109
that Jesus can bring all things to God, 282
in an unwavering hope, 351, 382, 394
of your heart, 241–42
"confession," and "conversation," about Jesus's ability as the Son, 237

515

SUBJECT INDEX

confessors, receiving an inheritance in heaven, 107
"confidence," at death and judgment, 350
conscience, cleansing of, 301, 321
consuming fire of God, upon errant ministerial conversation, 386
contentment, with God's provision and protection, 387
contextual evidence, supporting a change, 415
"continual, daily" offerings, in the tabernacle, 137
continual priestly mediator, Jesus as, 131
continued living, Jesus experienced in approach to God, 24
continued sacrificial activity by his people, willful ministerial sin of, 346, 354–55
conversation
    about the Son's "ability," 215, 236, 253, 255, 331, 352
    directed "to the certainty of hope until the end," 279
    the Son bringing all things by, 225
conversational witness, about Jesus's personal experience and ability, 211
conversation/biblical theology, exploring the Pastor's, 182
1 Corinthians 15:1–8, as a sequential gospel narrative, 408–9
cosmic limitation, of people after death, 14
cosmic reality, visible, 27
cosmic-field
    antitypes/types, 27
    constrained backgrounds, 139
    constrained fulfillment, 35
    constrained theology, 436
    constrained traditions, 28
    constriction, 7
    fulfillment, 4
    limited background, 31
    limited kingdom traditions eluding, 374
    limited theology, 437
    limited views, 24
    for people, 38
    pointing perpendicular to the *aiōn-field*, 33
    restricted, salvation solutions, 5
    restriction, 14
    tensions, 420
    window of Genesis, 178
cosmos, 222, 294
covenants, 114–15, 136
creation
    God's rest from, 246–47
    originating from much older creation, 181
    proof texting about, 403
    referents are "God" and "Lord," 209–10
    spatial aspect of after death, 84
    structural existence for, 118
    structure of correlated with the temple, 119
    words in Hebrews linked with, 459–62
cries to the Lord, of David, 339
critical historical approach, 417
critical space theory, 123
cross, as the decisive event, 417
crown of righteousness, reserved for Paul, 56
crucifixion and fleshly resurrection, of Jesus, 9
cultic priesthood of Israel, 65
cultural spatial beliefs, available to the Pastor, 119–20
current ministry, of Jesus, 343

daily sacrifices, 136, 309, 312
Daniel, 77, 147
David
    accepting by faith heavenly access "today," 158
    as already with God in heaven, 145, 402
    anticipating a whole, eternal/perpetual-place, spiritual body, 340
    entrance into God's rest, 245–46
    sharing patient trust in God as deliverer, 339

SUBJECT INDEX

Davidic King-Priest language, inferring, 410
Day of Atonement, 71, 306, 311, 323
the dead
  in faith, 165
  now living with Jesus, 133
  rising of, 24, 277
  still without atonement in heaven, 316
dead flesh body, of Jesus remained in a tomb until the third day, 408
dead teachings, work of the earthly covenant as now, 331
dead works, 321, 323
death
  all people experiencing rising of, 403
  of Christ, 58, 320
  enduring, 219
  establishing a peaceful relationship after, 392
  of the flesh, 84
  of flesh and spirit as potential, 320
  hope after for a heavenly inheritance, 23, 323
  Jesus and other sons entering glory after, 229
  Jesus coming at, 91
  Jesus tasted for all people, 228, 232, 411
  Jesus's path in, 416
  judgment and, 302, 351
  link with "the eternal/perpetual-place inheritance," 325
  movement at between the temporary earth and God in heaven, 76
  Paul's thoughts centering on, 56
  people transformed into another form after, 160
  personifying a delayed endpoint after, 421
  requiring assimilation of all Jesus's postmortem heavenly activity, 24
deceased believers, xviii, 321, 399
deceased saints, xix
deductive approach, to avoid presuppositions, 193
Demetrius, second time to send, 77

devil
  as a created being, 177
  ignoring, 400
  Jesus rendering powerless, 230
  sin by "from the beginning," 102–3
  spatially separated from God's presence, 176–77
Diaspora Revolt of 115–117 CE, 35
dictionaries, dependent upon the descriptive school, 438
Didache, singular heaven in, 426
discourse analysis, 190–99, 204
discourse chiastic structure, 287, 382, 454
discourse conclusions, 406
discourse division boundaries, guides mapping, 203
discourse lexemes, successful identification of, 15
discourse mapping terminology, 191–99, 448
discourse structural mapping, of Hebrews, 199, 449
discourse topic/subtopic introduction, analysis of, 204–15
discourse units, 215, 397
disobedient choices of Israel at Sinai, 385
dissertation level investigation, about believers promptly entering heaven, 403
divine king, son of David and serving his people in their needs, 274
divine priest, as both the offering and intercessor for sin, 274
divinity, 237, 322
dominion-rule, present subsequently coming, 227
dualism, 25, 100
dualistic complementary contrast, words having, 161
duality, of place, 110, 126
DUC (Discourse Unit Conclusion) summaries, 51, 285
dwelling places, holiness of God's, 103–4
"dynamic equivalence," "functional equivalence" replacing, 39

517

SUBJECT INDEX

earthly and heavenly, correspondence between, 124
earthly antitypes, elevating or flattening the revelation of, 400
earthly daily and annual ministries, 309, 346
earthly events, representing the truth of heavenly unseen substance-realities, 402
earthly fulfillment, 13, 67
earthly high priest, offering gifts and sacrifices, 298
earthly ministry, 304, 309–13, 336
earthly people, linking in temporal-spatial movement, 75
earthly priests, bringing offerings for sins, 101
earthly sacrifices, promised offering of Christ depicted by, 313
earthly tabernacle
    contrasting with the present heavenly ministry of Christ, 297–98
    ministry as the first covenant relationship, 303–23
    as a model "about" the heavens, 140
    outlines of, 328
    as a useful ministry for God's purpose, 295
earthly veil, torn while Jesus is on the cross promptly at death, 317
earthly view of the gospel, from an eyewitness perspective, 408
earthly worship activity, in assembly with other believers, 350
Egyptian peers, of Moses considering "the reproach of Christ," 370
Egyptians, drowned in the Red Sea, 372
elders
    adopting a method of allegorical interpretation, 420
    approved "by this kind of faith," 359
    choices for a heavenly, rather than an earthly completion, 365
    deriving creedal statements, 403
    emulating the faith of, 367
    Pastor summarizing his list of, 145
Eleazer, torture of, 55

Eli, priestly unfaithfulness of the sons of, 65
Elijah, at Jesus's transfiguration, 155
empiricism, philosophical strain of, 421
endless life, of Jesus, 134, 170
endpoint, 315, 363, 366
enduring, sorrowful training, 380
enemies
    of David, 339
    of Jesus, 220–21
    placed as a footstool, 182–83
English, not utilizing chiasm, 201
English Bible translation, plural heavens hidden in, 431, 440
English paragraph, as more loosely constructed, 201
English words, modern unknown by the Pastor, 20
Enoch, 83, 144, 145, 147, 361–62
entering, to God's presence, 135
enthroned Lord, serving as a priest to his people, 259
enthronement after death, outcome of Jesus's, 228
enthronement and exaltation, of Jesus, 8
entrance, by faith in Christ, 277
entrance to rest, of salvation into God's presence in heaven, 246
Erasmus, Desiderius, 428
errant conversation, about God's speech, 241
Esau, 115, 369, 382–83, 386
eschatological promises, changed to singular, 427
eschatology, 13, 28, 153, 400
eternal beings, God speaking through other, 173–77
eternal creation, judgment in after death, 64
eternal life at death, perpetual heavenly place for, xiii
eternal living, no present place for continuous, 14
eternal "substance-reality," of faith viewed as allegory, 26
eternal/holy place creator, God speaking as, 178–82
eternal/perpetual-place(s)

SUBJECT INDEX

access to, 243
aiōn translating as, 95
Christ as source of salvation, 108, 260
constricting the Son's creativity, 181
designating ontological durative space-time, 322
establishing the Son's throne into, 218
existing with the present, temporary, visible "world," 123
holy place in the heavens functioning till the achievement of, 138
inheritance and, 134, 208, 401
Jesus as high priest, 171, 259
Jesus providing access to, 220
Jesus's achievement of, 173
Jesus's transformation of, 360
judgment and, 62, 161, 277
kingdom and, 219–20, 236
life and, 152, 172
linking with spatial features, 129
living by the agency of the Holy Spirit, 321
living relationship with people in, 111
narrative background on, 127
necessity for "purification of sins" by the Son, 101
"as" the plural "heavens" and earth, 126
of punishment, 146
some separated from his presence, 114
Son's achieving of, 224
Son's recent opening access into, 209
spatial dualism of, 238
understanding by faith, 181
understanding in conversation of God, 360
waiting a very little while for Jesus in, 151–55
eternal/place covenant, 406
"eternal-place spirit," referencing Jesus's human, 416
events, as successive but closely connected, 60
evidence, supporting salvation a very little while after death, 399–402
evil teaching, 272, 273, 278

examples, of approach to God in the face of death, 373–74
excursuses, in this book, 17
exegesis, successful without eisegesis, 455
expectant king, for the antitype of the earthly kingdom, 68
expectation
 linking with belief in both God's existence and reward at God's judgment, 362
 of return to fleshly bodies, 421
expiation, establishment of a new place of, 308

faith
 of Abraham, 363, 368–69
 acceptance of going promptly to Jesus in heaven, 3
 centered on heavenly expectation in death, 82–83
 continuous, governing Moses's decisions, 371
 conversation understanding the eternal/perpetual-places, 359–60
 of David, 340–41
 as an expectation for unseen substance-realities, 366
 in God, 275–76, 375, 404
 for God's calling to invisible heavenly promises, 104
 as hope of the elders at death, 388
 as how to enter God's presence, 375
 living by, 268, 352, 357, 367
 as a mandatory condition for heavenly entrance, 244
 people of anticipating promises in Christ, 358–59
 Rahab as an example of, 372
 seeking the final reward of seeing God, 106
 as "substance-reality of things being presently expected," 105, 359
 testimonials of the Pastor, 73
 testimonies confessing as exiles and strangers, 83
 viewed as allegory, 26
faith-centered speech, 388

SUBJECT INDEX

faithful at death, following through the heavens to God at judgment, 107
faithfulness
   of Christ, Moses becoming an antitype of, 370
   of God through Jesus, 135
   of Jesus as a Judge, 347
   of Jesus's example, 236
   in teaching, 278
falling away, from heaven after entrance, 273, 278
familial relationships, Pastor's language of, 108
family ties, reconnection with, 422
fate, for those waiting for Christ, 144
Father (God), 137, 314, 379
   as a former way of testifying about the Son, 206
   as referent serving to initiate a subtopic, 205
fathers, who died without receiving promises, 365–66
fear, at judgment, 358
festal gathering, as destiny of believers, 384
final termini, history of future earthly antitypes as, 37
findings, summary of, 397–99
first covenant ministry, 308, 343
first man Adam, 409
first ministry, after the pattern of the Son's offering of his blood by death, 328
first steps, in running with perseverance, 18–89
first tent of the holy place, 314
first-century CE
   apocalyptic (*aiōn-field*), word stock of, 31–38
   canonical and noncanonical texts exploring for spatial-temporal markers, 406
   interpretation, observations deduced about, 28–31
   interpretation methods, 445–46
   message of Hebrews, mountain of information about, 401
   original text containing the sense option for plural heavens, 439
   use of "rest" in Greek and Jewish literature, 241
   volatile deliberation between Jewish schools of thought, 147
   word meanings, sifter for the Pastor's, 40–52
   writers embracing plural heavenly places, 435–36
flesh, without durative spirit as a quality of death, 320
flesh and blood resurrection, for believers, 342
flesh resurrection, as a sign of spiritual resurrection, 415
fleshly death of Jesus, verified, 408
fleshly offering, of the life of Jesus for sin, 310
fleshly resurrection
   contrasting with the better resurrection of faith, 374
   doctrine of, 148
   Moffitt's assumption for only, 163
   superfluous debate over, 184
fleshly resuscitation, people who experienced all died again in the flesh, 373
flesh-spirit activity, of Jesus in atonement, 408
flesh-spirit human contrast, permeating teaching sequences of the gospel, 412
"flesh-spirit" language pairing, 410
footstool imagery, 135, 182–83, 220–21
"for people," 57–58
"for salvation," in the LXX, 85 ?page
"for the purpose to bear many sins" form, 74–77
"for you have not approached," 383
foreigners and sojourners upon the earth, elders as, 365
"forerunner," Jesus as, 168, 284, 316, 317
"forever, eternal, everlasting," creating tension with temporal limitation, 182–83
forgiveness, not occurring without the shedding of blood, 328

SUBJECT INDEX

former ways, testifying of God's
  speech about the true covenant
  relationships by the Son, 206
"from a second place without sin,"
  Christ appearing, 8, 22, 77–80,
  115, 178, 182, 210, 222, 285, 406
"from" and "to where" places, of the
  appearing of Jesus, 116
full heavens approach, as exaltation
  instead of fleshly resurrection,
  162
"functional equivalence," with the
  Pastor's contextual meaning, 39
functional groupings of text (FGT),
  above the sentence level, 188
functional units, analysis of, 196
functional-grouping connections, by
  use of a broad cognate word
  cache, 204
future, supernatural world of, 33

gate of Jerusalem, Pastor symbolically
  using, 390
general mission statement, Pastor
  charting, 330
Genesis account, only referring to God's
  recent historical creation, 180
German translations, early, 430
"Get Ready! . . . Get Set!" preparations,
  for heavenly entrance, 1–17
global plan, 194, 197
glory of God, 377
glory of the Son, 349
glosses, 188, 401
Gnosticism, as a straw man, 142–43
God
  abiding in the eternal/perpetual-
    place, 219
  about ministry to others as a
    servant, 216
  as an actual living being
    reproduced as the Son, 97–98
  anger over flawed testimony of
    Israel, 240
  in animated life as the promised
    Son and Christ, 98
  approaching with an expectation,
    353–54
  avenging and repaying when
    judging his people, 355
  bringing all things to, 229
  choice to joyfully anoint his Son, 219
  as a consuming fire, 385–86
  creation as distinct coherent
    topography of, 439
  descriptions of the heavens as his
    temple, 120
  direct prophecy of a future time of
    impermanent return, 106
  dwelled in heaven with "angels" and
    "children of God," 435
  on either dwelling with or "turned
    away" from God, 159
  encouraging desired features, 394
  entrance into his rest is based upon
    the condition of faith, 244
  as an eternally active creator, 103
  extending "atonement" in
    forgiveness of sin, 130
  "having heard" Jesus's appeals by
    faith, 261
  heavenly rest, Jesus judges
    candidates for entrance into, 250
  holiness decoupling of from visible
    temporary dwellings, 101
  house of, 6
  individuals chosen for special
    purposes of, 66
  jealous for obedience, 109
  judging both the living and the
    dead, 414
  judging continued sacrificial
    activity by his people, 354–55
  judging the sacrificial offering of
    the blood of Jesus's animated
    life, 313
  judgment of, 62, 362
  as main subject, 205
  Melchizedekian priesthood
    guaranteeing his intercession
    for sin, 264
  offering a peaceful new covenant
    relationship, 392
  offering of himself as a Father in
    training, 73
  personal intercession for sins, 256–57

God (continued)
    place of rest of, 245–46
    placing at a distance, 400
    placing himself as Son and high priest in the eternal/perpetual-places, 267
    prepared a city for the elders, 366
    promise of, 281
    promising a Son from David's linage, 218
    providing a body, in continuous living after death, 338–44, 393
    raising Jesus up from the dead into his presence, 87
    referents to, 456–57
    remembrance of man, 227
    reserved judgment in Job, 56
    resting from his works on the seventh day, 246
    sharing the glory of his presence in peace, 393–94
    Son as, 209
    as "the source of eternal/perpetual-place salvation," 88
    tabernacle of as substance-reality "about" the plural heavens, 162
    training as a father does, 379, 380
    transferred Enoch, 145, 361
    undertaking plans and projects, 98
    upon Jesus's "approach" promptly at death judges his sacrifice, 129–30
    verbal activity of, 457–59
    will of one coming physically into the cosmos, 72
    words in Hebrews linked with, 456–59
    working in space-time creative relationships, 320, 322
gods, of other religions, 96
God's speech, 93–96
    about holy-places, heavenly places and sinful people, 109–68
    about the Son's ability, 394
    audience of, 268, 270
    complementary contrast between two layers of, 271
    as an eternal/holy place creator, 178–82
    as an eternal/perpetual-place priest, 168–73
    hearing, 404
    heavenly covenants of, 398
    as holy, 99–106
    in intermittent revelations and the law, 225
    listening to about the new covenant relationships, 422
    as living, 97–99
    paying attention to, 225
    by the person of a Son on behalf of sons, 106–9, 171
    in the present and will continue to speak in the future, 93
    as the primary evidence, 15
    shaking the temporary heaven of all substance devoid of God's holiness, 181
    skill of listening to concerning the Jesus's Melchizedekian priesthood, 272
    by a Son as better ministry, 204–15
    speaking even in the present, 249
    through other eternal beings, 173–77
    through the antitype of Israel in the exodus motif, 251
    true teaching about, 269–70
    to us in a Son, 93
    to what constitutes an acceptable ministerial sacrifice, 338–39
going "to Jesus in heaven," expectation of, 3–4
good teaching, 278, 279
gospel accounts, with similar language, 407–16
gospel sequence events, reducing Jesus's to nodal points, 409
gospel teaching, separating from the ideology of *Christus descendit ad inferno*, 413
government, of the Son, 218
grace of God, pursuing, 382
grammatical-historical exegesis, of each UC in analysis of Hebrews, 189

SUBJECT INDEX

grammatical-historical studies, modern sentence to sentence or point-to-point, 196
"grateful reward," for those who "fall asleep" or die with godliness, 55
gratitude, showing, 385–86
Great Shepherd of the sheep, Jesus continuing as, 133–34
Greek basics, going back to, 350
Greek belief, in immortality of the soul, 14
Greek communication, technical language for, 201
Greek discourse and chiasm, communication approach of, 402
Greek Jewish pseudepigrapha, especially with apocalyptic language, 41
Greek language discourse, hearers of, 198
Greek lexemes, expanding broader creation conceptions, 5
Greek manuscripts, copies of, 425–27
Greek Platonism, spatial understanding about, 142
Greek recension(s), of OG/LXX with apocryphal writings, 41
Greek rhetorical discourse, embedded unit conclusions forming a MCS, 16
Greek scholars, may have incurred a modern Classical-Hellenistic Greek syncretism, 437
Greek to English philosophically loaded words, stripped away during analysis, 183
Greek-Roman mythology, no evidence of a line of influence from, 49
Greeks, faith for continued living after death, 146
groupings, of text above the sentence level, 193
guides, for structural mapping, thought analysis, and chiasm, 199–204

hairesis, as a rejection of novel aspects in the development of ancient revelation, 148
hands, laying on of, 276–77
Hannah, 60–61, 65
"has been revealed," suggesting a past event with present effects, 331
Hasmonaean priesthood, escalated the intended antitype of the tabernacle, 47
hearing, of God's speech, 272
heaven
    as a concrete reality, 123
    entering together with brethren, 230
    Jesus's entrance and enthronement into, 398
    as more than just the source of a future earthly salvation, 116
    as one distinct creation divided into distinct places, 117–18
    remaining outside until later time, 63
    singular use in Hebrews appearing for a particular realm, 118
    summary about entrance into, 1–17
    translation of the Greek plurals of by Martin Luther, 423
heavenly access, 133, 211, 246
"heavenly body," 38
heavenly calling of God, for conveyance of God's speech, 236
heavenly changes, exampled by Christ, 303
heavenly city, approaching, 358
heavenly destiny, as guaranteed, 282
heavenly entrance, 3, 158, 305
heavenly focus, xv–xvi
heavenly hope, for people as living "souls" after death, 160
heavenly Jerusalem, 384, 390
heavenly journey, mapping Jesus's, xvii
heavenly kingdom, unseen substance-reality of, 386
heavenly places, 111–26
    biblical text about, 423–25
    continually desiring, 105
    open for sinful people, 126–44
    pre-Reformation text about, 425
heavenly position, placing Jesus between God and people, 264
heavenly promises, available in death at judgment, 400
heavenly realities, "transfer" to, 361

SUBJECT INDEX

heavenly rest, Jesus bringing those who believe into, 253
heavenly reward at judgment, better and lasting possession in, 355
heavenly unseen substance-reality, existence of, 121
heavens
    both visible and invisible collectively, 425
    cartographic studies of, xx
    Greek texts used by Christians translated the plurals, 430
    Hebrew word, 117, 423
    historical senses of, 444
    needing to be closed, even to angels, 427
    teaching about Jesus in, xvii
    three in 2 Cor. 12:2–4, 435
heavens and earth, perishing and growing old, 222
Hebrews (book of)
    analysis of, 189
    comparing with other textual usage and meaning, 405
    discourse chiastic structure of, 454
    discourse structural mapping of, 449
    literary structure for the message of, 395
    not teaching about Jesus going into a lower region of Hades, 418
    observed literary features of, 193
    occupying a unique place of transition from the OT to the NT, 10
    OT recension(s) similar to the MT, 41
    OT text, unknown *Vorlage* of, 43
    OT translated into Greek, 42
    reading of in modern language missing clues, 127
    on rising to God bodily into heaven at the moment of death, 148
    spatial syntax cohesion in, 469–72
    word groupings of, 200
Hebrews 9:27–28
    forming a grid to sample the Pastor's terms in, 41
    introduction to, 1–17
    as MCS, 397, 406
    sentence diagram, 474
    sifting sources with the Pastor's words in, 52–88
Hebrews 9:28, traditional translation of, 38–40
Hellenistic Geek ('grammar'), standard terms for, 191
Hellenistic Greco-Roman and other cultural literature, infuence on the Pastor, 49
heresy, 37
heretical issues, 400
heretical missteps, 420
hermeneutics, common first-century CE, 18
high priest
    created good places in the heavenly eternal/perpetual-places, 318
    into the eternal/perpetual-places according to the order of Melchizedek, 135, 259
    God calling every, 256–61
    Jesus as, 173, 206, 232, 253, 265–67
    making offerings for his people and for himself, 64
    movement into the holy of holies, 58
    not entering without blood on the Day of Atonement, 309
    occurrences of the term, 169
    requiring movements of the anointed, 71
    second place/position in ministry of once a year, 79
high priest ministry
    intercessional function of, 257
    movement of through the tabernacle of all creation, xiv
    properly teaching about as God has spoken, 255
    of the Son in heaven, 288–303, 324
historical activities, of God within a cosmic-field, 5
holiness
    concept of God's personal, 99–106

Jesus's quality of in his human spirit
  nature, 411
necessity of in respect to sin, 376
pursuing, 382
vertical dwelling levels of, 121
"holy brethren," link with those already
  in heaven, 235
holy living, God's cleansing for, 276
holy of holies
  beyond the veil, 162
  having heavenly space reclaimed,
    416
  high priest movement into, 58
  identifying, 79
  Jesus able to instantly enter, 266
  linked with a true and more
    complete tabernacle, 290
  ministry into occurring only once
    a year, 309
  movement of Jesus's entrance into,
    xix
  path to dwelling with God in, 135
  reference to, 219
  shepherding believers into, 327
  two fixtures related to, 306
holy place(s)
  allowing reclamation of the space
    of, 398
  believers' material access to, 349
  changes achieved by Jesus's entry
    into, 403
  confident people entering, 442
  elimination of at the completion of
    Jesus's atonement, 312
  existed before Jesus's atonement for
    sin, 316
  first introduction of the spatial
    concept about, 291
  linked with the tabernacle, 290
  minister of, 441
  ministry entailing continual
    intercessory travel, 94
  no longer existing due to Jesus's
    entrance, 309
  no longer functionally active, 317
  presence or absence of "sins"
    determining the confines of, 101

in relation to the other ministerial
  area of the "holy of holies," 306
remodeling of by merger into the
  holy of holies, 317
restricted the souls of the righteous
  dead from God's dwelling
  presence, 317
symbolizing in the daily sacrifices
  of the Sinai covenant, 137
Holy Spirit
  awkward reference for, 410
  giving understanding, xx
  indwelling agency of, 321
  Jesus's empowerment by, 318–19
  not actively providing the way of
    salvation, 415
  not described as a person of the
    Trinity of God, 322
  revealing things available to all
    believers, 14–15
  speaking, 93
  as the third person of the Trinity, 322
homeland in heaven, desire for, 365
hope
  of access into the substance-reality
    of the unseen, 360
  of believers "reserved" "in the
    heavens," 56
  expectation of contained in good
    teching, 279
  by faith in the reality of unseen
    things, 359–64, 367–74
  inverting from heaven to dominant
    cosmic-field limited tenets, 403
  living by, 352
  of living with Jesus after fleshly
    death, 3
  for those who believe in Jesus, 398
horizontal filter grid line, 50–52
hortatory subjunctive, William Mounce
  on, 350
"house," joining the spatial referents of
  "eternal/perpetual-places," 236
human creation, Pastor not speaking
  directly of, 222
human death, unique situation of
  Jesus's, 322

SUBJECT INDEX

human "eternal/perpetual-place spirit," describing Jesus's, 320
human fleshy resurrection, of Jesus, 164
"human" Jesus, as above the angels, 174
human offering, of Jesus, 163–64
human spirit, of Jesus, 320
humanness, of Jesus, 410
hymn, of 1 Tim 3:16b, 412
hymnic chiasm, 210, 215

illegitimate totality transfer fallacy, utilizing the English "word" for, 10
"image," denoting good things to expect after death, 336
imitation, of others who had faith in the Son, 367
immorality, avoiding, 382–83
immortality of the soul, 146, 167
"in the heavens," 288–89, 292, 426
inductive approach, behind the Pastor's textual meaning for God's speech, 193
indulgences, doctrine of, 149
infant, only tolerating milk, 271
"inferior immortality of the soul," debate over, 184
inheritance
   about the Son's appointed and better name for ministry than the angels, 349
   Abraham going out to a "place" to receive, 363
   describing heavenly access as, 207
   of the "heir" and the verbal activity "to inherit," 325
   by heirs of salvation, 326
   of Jesus as all things, 211
   loss of Esau's rightful, 115
   of the Son, 208, 218, 323
   subtopic concept of, 208
inherited kingdom, of the Son, 251
inner man, worship by, 400
intercession
   of Christ on behalf of sinful people, 171
   of Jesus, 9, 23, 348
   at judgment, 232, 267

interpretation
   by allegorical symbolism, 25
   providing "functional equivalence" with the Pastor's contextual meaning, 39
interpretation methods, the Pastor's intended, 26–31
intersecting operations, involving the current separation of places, 134
introduction topic/subtopic (UI) (UPt), function, 192
invisible creation, 6, 167–68
invitation, from the Pastor, 404
Irenaeus, 148–49
Isaac, 73, 115, 369
Isaiah, suffering servant motif of, 61
Israel
   correspondence to Mt. Zion, 384
   experience in Egyptian deliverance and promise of the land, 134
   failed to enter God's rest, 238–41, 244
   as a former way of testifying about the Son, 206
   impetus for pursuit of requested conduct, 383
   inheriting the land a second time, 77
   not escaping when they refused to listen, 385
   not following the example of, 242
   passed through the Red Sea on dry land, 372
   serving as an example of a chosen people, 379
"It Is Reserved," appearing four times in the LXX, 54

Jacob, 54, 369–70
Jeremiah, 302
Jericho, miracle at, 372
Jerome, Latin Bible translation of, 420
Jesus. *See also* Christ; Son of God
   ability to stand before God as a high priest, 253
   able to enter through the heavens, 266
   already ministering at death, 172–73

SUBJECT INDEX

appearing, 23, 81, 172, 404
approach of in spirit at death for judgment, 163
arose in fleshly resurrection, 262
assisting believers approaching after death, 254
atoned for sins and can now assist in need at testing, 231–33
being brought up into heaven at his ascension, 75
as better than Moses's faithful ministry, 235–43
as blameless, 171, 316, 413, 415
bodily suffering death, 169
bringing believers into the substance-reality of heaven at judgment, 164
bringing people as a free will offering to God at his enthronement, 258
bringing people into the holy-places of the present by becoming the lessor form, 175
bringing "salvation" from consequences of sin, 86
calling and shepherding believers into heaven, 185
coming bodily from the holy of holies to the cosmos, 91
completing hope in heaven for people by faith, 216
confession as a great high priest, 107
delivered by God from the path of death, 87
descending from the tribe of Judah, 264
descending into hell to rescue the dead, 403
dismissing his spirit into the hands of the Father, 314
dwelling in a local heavenly tabernacle, 139
earthly sign of God's acceptance of his atonement, 164
in an endless life, 152
entering once into the holy tent, 314
entering the eternal/perpetual-place at death, 316
escorting believers into the holy of holies, 344
as an eternal/perpetual-place spirit approaching God, 322
experience beyond death in rising to God, xix
fixing eyes upon the author and consummator of faith, 83
following in suffering and possible martyrdom, 75
as "the forerunner," 160
freeing believers from enslavement of the power of the devil, 177
fulfilling the reservation of death and judgment, 70
fulfillment of the Christ of four thousand years of sacrifices, 275
glory in the eternal/perpetual-place of the eternal-perpetual-places, 178
as God-man, 320
as God's chosen king-priest, 69
as the Great Shepherd, 133–34, 397–98
heavenly goal to be with, xiv
as high priest, xv, 80, 91, 169–70, 234–35, 265–67, 268, 285
as a high priest according to the order of Melchizedek, 131
as human, 176
in immediate self-offering after death, 319
interceding a little while after death at judgment, 9, 397
interceding before God, 266
judging the reflections and thoughts of people's hearts, 158
as "just," 414, 415
linking with people as the "apostle" and "high priest," 169
living at the finish in heaven, 404
made lower than the angels and crowned with glory and honor, 228
mediation, only those with rising from the dead, 403
as a Melchizedekian, High Priest successor, 262–64

SUBJECT INDEX

Jesus (continued)
- ministering as God and High Priest after the Order of Melchizedek, 256
- ministry leading people to God at judgment, 164
- neither fell away nor had to start again his atonement at repentance, 170
- not ashamed to call those he makes holy as his "brethren," 230
- not ministering alone, 174
- offering of his life on behalf of sinful people, 130
- offering sinful people a shared holy place, 99
- passed through the heavens to the throne of God, 287
- penal substitution for sin in his sacrificial death and intercession, 412
- pitting in opposing contrast against the angels as lesser inferior beings, 400
- plural-singular juxtaposition in the Lord's Prayer, 427
- position in the *aiōn-field* background governing the message, 22
- positioned by God to be at the right place at the right time, 264–65
- possessing a durative human "spirit," 322
- post-flesh resurrection and ascension, 139–40
- prayers and supplications with loud crying heard by the Father, 108
- present construction as a better enduring house, 237
- put to death in the flesh in penal substitution for sin, 414
- qualification corresponding with the symbolism of Melchizedek, 264
- quickened in the spirit following his death, 414
- receiving life in rising from the dead into salvation of God's presence, 88
- as repetitively crucified again and falling from heaven, 354
- returning to and being present with his people, 151–52
- as the same yesterday and today in the eternal/perpetual-place, 389–90
- as the seed of David "according to the flesh," 410
- seeing at the moment of death, xix
- self-purpose in his relationship to the temple in Jerusalem, 125
- as shepherd, 381
- shepherding believers, 333, 418
- as the Son, 169, 347
- speaking, 93
- stuck on his throne with no active shepherd ministry, 400
- as the subjective recipient agent of his own resurrection, 415
- "suffered" "the just for the unjust," 414
- superior priesthood of in heaven, 268
- sympathizing with the weakness of people, 253
- taking his chosen disciples up on the mountain for his transfiguration, 75
- taking his people with him at death to rest, 244
- teaching of cutting across Sadducean views, 147
- travel from the realm of the dead through the heavens, 412
- travel of the ministry of as the Great Shepherd, 128
- trusting the one who is judging righteously, 414
- use of familial terms "sons" and "brethren," 128–29
- using the plural pattern of heavens, 424
- will come to you and bring you through the entrance, 404
- as the Word and the Christ, 206

SUBJECT INDEX

as yet to begin his ministry to bring sons into glory, 229
Jesus and his people, "in the heavens," 401
Jesus as the Christ
  changelessness of, 389
  finding "eternal/perpetual-place redemption," 129
  offered himself to bear the sins of many, 255
  perpetual priestly movement of, 112
  prompt heavenly shepherd ministry by, 2
  sacrificial offering and present ministry of, 366
"Jesus in Hades," 418
Jewish, messianic hope, pressure of resulting in Jesus's crucifixion, 35
Jewish apocalyptic literature, on creation in heaven of God's dwelling, 179
Jewish belief, in the flesh resurrection, 14
Jewish Essenes, faith for continued living after death, 146
Jewish gnostic elements, Christian incorporation of early, 36
Jewish intertestamental pseudepigraphic writings, as an influential source on the Pastor, 48
Jewish Law, serving as a "shadow" of the eternal/perpetual-places, 62
Jewish talmudic literature, 41
Jewish views, of first century CE include plural heavens, 435
Jewish Wars, 35, 147
Jews in Palestine, some resisted apocalyptic and platonic language, 47
Jews of the diaspora, few knowing Hebrew and Aramaic, 42
Joseph (son of Jacob), 369–70
Josephus, 140, 146
Joshua, 206
Joshua [antitype]/Jesus [type], 246
Judah, 54
judge, Jesus as a capable heavenly, 250
judgment
  of all believers, 375
  between earth and heaven after death, 61
  events of Christ's personal intercession at, 84
  of God, 23, 242–43
  of individuals after death, 33
  in the literal presence of the Son's "eyes," 247
  of the ministry of believers, 386
  place of, 116
  salvation of three groups at, 226
  for unbelievers at death, 443
"a judgment" verbal noun, carrying thematic significance in the LXX, 60
judgment-related senses, processes of, 61
judgment-transformation process, for believers upon entering heaven, 132
"just as...so also" conjunction, signaling Christ's participation, 92
"just as...so" correlative conjunction, 53–54, 70
Justin, 148

kingdom, that cannot be shaken, 385–86
kingdom in heaven, 218, 406
kingdom of the Son, 219
king-priest ministry, of the Son in heaven, 213
kings, serving before God, 66
"knowledge of the truth," 354, 381
Koine Greek, as the common language of the Greco-Roman Empire, 42

Laansma, Jon, 4
last days, background for God's promised inauguration of, 205
last rites, doctrine of, 149
Latin translation, of heaven, 427
Latin transliterations, 141, 183, 401
Latin Vulgate
  translated the Latin *caelum* ("heaven, sky") to maintain a plural and singular contrast, 427
  transliteration of terms to English, 399

SUBJECT INDEX

law
- as only a shadow, 336–38
- perfecting/completing nothing, 264
- of the Sinai covenant, 336

laziness, in hearing God's speech, 274, 280, 285

leaders, 388, 391, 422

less holy place outside, 162

Levi, 262

Levitical priesthood, 262, 266, 267

Levitical priests, 264, 265

lexemes, 21–22, 182, 455, 468

lexical choices, of the Pastor, 15

lexical parts, validity of, 16

lexical repetitions, of the Pastor, 51

lexical semantics, 14, 19–22, 89, 401

lexicographers, getting word meanings from other dictionaries, 437

life after death, belief in, 146

life promptly after fleshly death, as a minority theological position, 23

life rewards, expectation of, 56

"life-achieving, -creating spirit," nodal connection to "spirit of an eternal/perpetual-place," 409

linear topic connections, from unit-to-unit, 204

linguistic analysis, tools of, 18

listener anticipation and expectation, 350

listening ability, desired faith about God's speech in Hebrews, 182

literal ministry, of Jesus, 117

literary elements, governing meaning with, 402

literary structure, for the message of Hebrews, 395

literary works, at Qumran as a possible influence on the Pastor, 47–48

literature, in first-century CE Hellenistic-Jewish milieu, 48

living
- adding to the dead already in heaven, 164, 374–75
- assistance of God as the person of Jesus, 98
- before fleshly death, 115
- by loving others even as Jesus's did, 387

living God, 96, 97, 245

living movement, of both God and his living listeners, 97

living nearness, of God, 185

living soul, of man, 98

logos, 94, 224, 267

LORD
- appearing after Aaron's "approach" to the "altar," 81
- Jesus as, 206
- present place of ministry, 288
- as a priest, 300
- sending out from Zion a scepter, 291

love
- in assemblies, 394
- of the brethren, 387, 390
- and good deeds unto others, 351
- living by, 352
- as more than affection of emotion, 388

lural "heavens, modern lexical semantic meaning of, 121

Luther, Martin, 5, 421, 428, 430, 431, 432

LXX
- with the Apocrypha, 42
- on the christological completion of the forgiveness of sin, 348
- Hebrew words related to, 59
- no consistent number for translation of "heaven(s)," 424
- OT quotations on the speaking of the Father to the Son, 169
- OT text as authoritative speech from God, 94
- Pastor's content utilizing, 43
- Pastor's extensive use of, 11, 51, 424
- sacrificial tradition of, 70
- text concerning Enoch in, 361
- typological interpretation of as God's speech, 401–2

Maccabeus, Judas, 55

macro conclusion/summary (MCS)
- form of the Pastor's discourse, 198
- of God's speech, 7
- key referents underlying, 92
- methodology for evaluation of the Pastor's, 14–17

SUBJECT INDEX

place and time questions about the
  Pastor's, 2–3
place(s) of, 10–14
as the thematic conclusion of the
  Pastor, 203
on the thematic propositions of
  chiasm, 195
words in their function as referents,
  verbal nouns, and verbal
  activity, 51
macrostructure, 188, 193, 194
man
  as an animated fleshly being, 409
  in the image of God, 98
manifest in the flesh, 412
manuscripts, copies of Greek, 425–27
mapping, similar to other approaches
  to Hebrews, 201
marital fidelity, 387
martyrdom, 50, 373
material/nonmaterial duality, of God's
  creation, 139
Matthew, reporting Jesus gave up the
  spirit, 413
mature holiness before God, 410
meat, of Christ's intercessory ministry,
  278
meat/mature metaphoric connection,
  leaving, 271
mediation of Jesus Christ, 326, 382
"mediator," 134, 299, 325
Melchizedek, 53, 131, 134, 135, 259
Melchizedekian, High Priest successor,
  Jesus as, 262–64
Melchizedekian priesthood, 206, 210,
  262, 264–65
Messiah, 67, 86, 258
messianic Christ, salvation activity of
  the promised, 226
messianic work, of Jesus, 436
metaphoric concept, of Enoch, 362
methodology, for discourse analysis of
  Hebrews, 194
Middle Platonic tabernacle, as
  metaphor, 140
Middle Platonism, features of, 46
milk, 273, 274, 278

"milk" and "solid food," pairing with
  "Infant" and "mature," 271
minister, of the holy places, 441
ministerial ability of the Son, 216, 339
ministerial accountability, 268, 278,
  347, 354, 371, 391, 398–99
ministerial confession, 242–43, 358
ministerial conversation
  about Jesus in his ministry as the
    Christ, 251
  in an anticipatory approach to
    Jesus, 375
  audience rectification of, 380–81
  of Cain, 361
  in earthly antitypes of continued
    sacrifices, 331
  by elders, 360
  portraying the promised "true
    heart," 353–54
ministerial message, demonstrating
  the unchangeableness of God's
  purpose, 279
ministerial movements, of Jesus as the
  Son of Man, 125
ministerial objective, "to please" God at
  judgment, 359
ministerial participation, with Christ,
  242
ministerial purity, encouraging, 377
ministerial teaching, accountability
  for, 278
ministerial worship, 399
ministers, 221, 378
ministry
  after the order of a Melchizedekian
    priesthood, 271
  of "another priest" as "to arise," 262
  being certain about, 280
  comparison of, 473
  in death of Jesus, 177
  description of Jesus's adding force,
    172
  of the heavenlies, 100
  holistic bi-vocational of the author,
    xv
  by "minister" and "ministering," 217
  no longer existing due to Jesus's
    entrance, 309

SUBJECT INDEX

ministry (continued)
    Pastor emphasizing Jesus's present, 173
    of the Son, 211, 222–23, 248
ministry of angels, 88, 214, 323
ministry of Christ
    an entry into heaven itself, 329
    as a high priest before God, 325
    involving the ministry of the angels, 222
    recapitulating the two-fold, 378
    in a spatial dualism, 114
ministry of Jesus
    as better than the angelic ministry, 267
    including appearing "now" "in heaven," 330
    listeners experiencing when facing judgment after death, 351
ministry of the law, limited to testimonial matters on earth, 301
misinterpretations, evaluating and removing, 419
missteps, 418, 419–40
modern Greek, additions to assist modern readers, 191
modern straw men, concerning Hellenistic and Jewish philosophy, 168
Montanism, prophecy of, 36
Mosaic history, not documenting everything ever created, 180
Moses
    approached to a fearful situation, 383–85
    created the earthly tabernacle as an antitype, 298
    faith in his choice of Christ above the sin of Egypt, 76
    faith regarding his relationship to Pharaoh, 70
    as faithful to the one who created him, 236
    as a former way of testifying about the Son, 206
    on God's relationships before this creation, 179
    God's warning to before building the tabernacle, 82
    house representing the earthly, covenant relationship, 236
    at Jesus's transfiguration, 155
    kept the Passover, 371–72
    left Egypt, 244, 371
    looking to promised blessings in heaven after death, 83
    ministry over Israel as an example in antitype, 237
    parents hid him alive by faith, 370
    provided an example of Christ to Israel as a servant, 237
    refused to be called a son of Pharaoh, 370–71
    saw the complete source tabernacle "in heaven," 140–41
    use of blood in commandments, 328
mountain typology, symbolizing God's sovereignty, 134
mountains, symbolized the high presence of God, 298
myriad of angels, as destiny of believers, 384

native discourse lexemes, of the Pastor's main conclusion, 455–73
natural language, 29
nature of Jesus, as both human flesh and spirit, 414
"necessity"
    concerning "purification" in the heavens, 328
    that the Son had to die, 324
Neeley, Linda, 200
negated typology, of what listeners should not encounter, 383
negativism, toward apocalyptic concepts, 35
negativized common language, of Platonic influences, 184
new covenant
    accepted by believers, 379
    actions in following, 389
    on approach after death at judgment, 345–46

SUBJECT INDEX

complete, recurring fulfillment of, 302
embodied by the Sinai law appointed an annual sacrifice, 137–38
embracing God's new speech in, 216
features, 351
fulfillment of by Jesus the Christ, 398
Jesus's two-fold ministry, 9
not implying that the believer is free to sin in impurity, 379
not replacing the earthly Sinai covenant, 398
as only effectual for people at death, 324
promise contained in Jeremiah, 345
receiving a new mind and a new heart, 404
requirement of death for, 320
requiring the offering of the blood from an animated life, 327
warrants about, 327
new heavenly covenants, validated in death, 346
new speech, deleting, combining, or concentrating with previous conversation, 198
New Testament
authors deploying "Christ" 529 times, 68
Greek as not a distinct form independent of Hellenistic Greek, 438
writings as a probable influence, 44
Nicene Creed, 149
Nida, Eugene, 39
Noah, 88, 362–63
nobleman's judgment of his servants, Jesus parable about, 56
nomenclature, for identification of different assemblies of text, 191–92
"now and not yet" solutions, regarding the spatial-temporal message in Hebrews, 154

obedience, 260, 261, 363
"of the holy-places," 289
offering, of Christ, 72, 303, 318
offerings, 74–75, 311, 360–61
oikoumene, of the reality envisioned by the Pastor, 8
old covenant, 389, 398
"once" ordinal adverb, 58, 70
one "just," Jesus as before God versus one unjust, 414
"the ones having been called," 327
"the ones having believed," 244
"the ones taking refuge," 281
onetime offering, of Jesus, 323
onetime sacrifice, of Jesus, 343
open heaven
aiōn-field concepts of, 230–31
of six millennia of believers, 126–27
open heavenly access, enabled by Jesus's intercession, 209
open heavens, 127–28, 134
order and rule, of God, 5
order of Melchizedek, 256, 284
"ordered dominion," 111–12, 138
ordinal event, second in order of an, 77
"original" sin, Pastor not speaking directly of, 222
"the originator and consummator of faith," Jesus as, 168
originator/author of salvation, Jesus as, 228
OT (Old Testament)
concepts of heavenly places, 117
contextual self-understanding of Jesus, 125–26
foreshadowing of the anointed priest and king, 68
as foretelling about Jesus, 137
guiding understanding, 28
heavenly afterlife concepts, 184
on judgment by God upon those who reject the way of the Messiah, 258
on the Melchizedekian high priest ministry, 288
messianic textual traditions, 44
quotations common with Philo, 46
sacrifices, 131, 274, 275
support for a current transformation, 302

SUBJECT INDEX

OT (continued)
    supporting the Son's priestly ministry, 300–303
    theology of the creation, 179
"Our Father who in heavens," 427
outside the camp, symbolizing regions of God's creation, 390
"outspokenness," not throwing away, 355
outward cleansing, overt cultic demonstration of, 321

pace and split times, improvement in, 186
Palestinian influence, upon the Pastor's Jewish educational background in rabbinic schools, 48
"parable," testing of Abraham as, 368
"paradigm shift," entailing a change in the background field, 14
"parallelomania," muddling salvation, 4
parenesis of the Pastor, described, 57–58
Parousia, early church debate over delay of, 154
partners
    directional movement of people in a heavenly calling of Jesus's house, 158
    in the heavenly calling with Jesus for believers "to enter" rest by faith at judgment, 248
    ministering underneath the better ministry of the Son in heaven, 238
"passing through the heavens," by Jesus to the holy of holies, 317
Passover, events of revealing unseen realities, 371–72
past eternal activity, of the Son as God, 210
Pastor
    affirming that the Son "achieved the eternal/perpetual-places," 208
    on afterlife activity of believers, 14
    as apocalyptic in analogy, 140
    asserting homogeneity in death by Jesus with all people, 53
    atonement for sin as a sacrifice once and perpetually as an active priest, 113
    on a "better" two-fold heavenly "ministry" to people by atonement, 175
    on Christ appearing "from a second place without sin," 178
    complementary *aiōn-field* background views with Philo, 142
    conceptions of Jesus's continual second ministry, 23
    concern for his brethren embracing incongruent ministry, 108
    considering those who have already been judged, 374
    cuing his listeners to hear God speaking, 93
    direct prophecy of Jesus's priestly enthronement, 126
    discourse unit summary/conclusions, 187
    earth and cosmos having no lasting appeal, 164
    emphasizing Jesus's present ministry, 173
    envisioning salvation, 151
    envisioning the wait for Jesus, 398
    exegetical method as close to midrash, 49
    exhorting believers to follow Jesus's faith, 177
    exhorting his audience to "approach" places of the unseen living God, 104
    on first-century CE dualism, 163
    following an apocalyptic trajectory with an *aiōn-field* background, 181
    framing this theme of God speaking with an introductory formula, 94
    frequent terms of "blood," "body," and "flesh," 161
    on God's holiness as an attribute of the creation, 99

on hearing and imitating what God "spoke," 11
hearing the OT LXX speaking directly from the ministry of Christ, 94
on the heaven(s), 126
including detailed spatial-temporal background information, 13
inferring places for the movements of the ministry of Christ, 115
introducing the OT text with "say, speak," 94
inviting all to accept the Christ of faith, 404
Jesus appearing for intercession, 331
learning the language and culture of, 20
main motifs typologically, 134
maintaining a Jewish theological and philosophical view, 49
modern English words unknown by, 20
on Moses, 83, 105
moving along his propositional path in the chiastic structure, 202
not anticipating a long delay after death and judgment, 356
not following Greek or later Jewish Christian cultural options, 166–67
not mentioning eschatological waiting after death for fleshly resurrection, 105
orderly arrangement of the heavens as substance-reality, 119
original spatial intentions in vertical movement of the Christ, 28
on people entering to a "heavenly place…city" with other brethren, 162
predicting that Jesus will appear for salvation to those awaiting "for him," 161
providing temporal when options for movement to open heavens for access now to God, 152
on putting to death without mercy those who invalidate the law, 354–55
as quite a Greek wordsmith, 40
quotation of OT texts, 26
quoting Hag 2:6 in the phrase "still once," 58
repeated subtopics in relation to the "veil," 135
spoke as moved by God's Holy Spirit, 199
summarizing four synchronized tracks of exposition, 23
tables of his word stock, 455
typology of heavenly access "today," 158
using common Jewish methods and normative language, 168
using Greco-Roman Hellenized philosophical terms, 49
utilizing different words to describe features of people, 160
word meanings derived from thematic and verbal correspondences, 43
Pastor's macro conclusion/summary, tensions, 3–7
path
of falling away, 278
Moses followed others before him in, 105
patristic emphasis, acknowledgment of an orthodoxy toward the future resurrection, 38
patron system, of Jesus's/God's house of the heavens, 134
pattern, about "all" the plural heavens, 140
Paul, on a crown of righteousness reserved for him, 56
peace, with all relationships, 382
peaceful relationships, God providing, 392, 393
"pejorative" arguments, pushing back against, 143

SUBJECT INDEX

penal substitutionary atonement, of Jesus's death requiring fleshly death, 322
penitence for sin, before fleshly resurrection, 149
people
  of faith, 136
  invisible features of, 160
  of Israel, 242
  that pleased God, 57
  waiting for an unknown eschaton, 400
  words in Hebrews linked with, 463–67
"perfection," understood as "consecration," 263
perfection/completion, concept of, 263
persecution, mentioned by the Pastor, 49
persecutory harm, man's limitations when enduring, 57
perseverance
  as an example of faith, 356–57
  in the knowledge of the truth, 366
  needed to receive "the promise," 356
  in "a race," 377–78
  during suffering and training on earth, 380
personal judgment, after fleshly death, 115
persons of God, cannot be taken too distinctly, 415
1 Peter 3:18–22, 4:5–6, as a sequential gospel narrative to compare to "spirit of an eternal-place" and the anticipation of believers in, 413–16
Pharisaical schools, Josephus describing, 146
Philo
  discussion of the unchangeableness of God, 62
  Greek works of, 41
  introducing the OT text with "say, speak," 94
  as metaphor, 140
  possible influence of, 44–45, 142

philosophical intermediate-state, developed alongside heavenly kingdom teaching, 335
philosophies, all cosmic-field constrained having no lasting value in the eternal/perpetual-places for believers, 371
physical death, 58–59, 60
place(s)
  achieved changes accomplished by Jesus, 114
  of atonement ("mercy seat"), 311
  balancing the concept of, 183
  of God's ordered dominion, 112
  Pastor deploying on three occasions, 114
  of the Pastor's macro conclusion/summary, 7–14
  and time questions, 2–3
place/position sense, adding to the idiomatic force of ordinal idiom, 22
Platonic Hellenistic spatial thought, versus wholistic Jewish temporal afterlife, 184
"please imitate the faith!" 388
"Please look!" 241
please pursue, 382
"please remember!" 388
"please submit!" to the Word of God, 391
plural heavens
  charting activities across, xvi
  Matthew's use of, 418
  as metaphor for simply heavenly grandeur, 292
  tabernacle outline of, xviii
plural heavens and holy-places, and holy places, 400
plural holy-places, in a seen-unseen heavenly dualism, 119
plural references, to heaven in Greek manuscripts, 425
plural sense options, entertained for nearly 1,500 years for the heavens, 440
plural text, preservation of for heaven, 429

plural-singular juxtaposition, by Jesus in his teachings for heaven, 118
pneuma
  referring to "angels," a transformed "human spirit" at death, and the "Holy Spirit," 319
  separation of in death for Jesus, 322
pneumato saioniou, 323
points, 192, 193
post-Reformation text, of biblical spatial creation, 431–33
praying, for other ministers, 391
preexistence, of the Son, 210
pre-Luther German and English translator accuracy of "heaven(s)," 429
pre-Luther Greek collated textual accuracy, 428
pre-Reformation text, about heavenly places, 425
present heavenly dwelling, turning topsy-turvy, 400
present imperfective aspect, 350–51
present ministry of Jesus, to people at judgment, 229
present spirit bodily access, by people rising to God, 156
present subjunctive, 350, 351
"presently being sent for service," angels as, 221–22
"presently/subsequently coming," providing force for a spirit body of substance-reality, 161
presuppositions, unlikely, 139–40
priest(s)
  called by God like Aaron, 257
  continued offering daily burnt offerings, 310–11
  interceding on behalf of another's sin, 171
  of the law, 300
  registering the present sacrificial offerings of earthly, 76
  spatial-temporal (*aiōn-field*) movements and actions of, 82
  standing between the people and God as a mediator, 262
priesthood

appointed by law from the tribe of Levi, 169
atonement ministry of Jesus, 416–17
change from Zadok to Hasmonaean, 145
of Jesus, 53
ministries, 300
as only "until" the "enemies" are subjugated, 135
significance in matters before God, 257
in which Melchizedek served, 259
priestly language, concerning ceremonial cleanness, 376
priestly ministry, 310, 334
priestly sacrifices, 336–38, 360
prisoners, remembrance of, 387
promise(s), 281, 364, 365
promised land, 115, 243, 364
promised Lord, locating his priestly ministry, 264
prompt access after death, clear teaching about, 399
prompt eternal life in heaven after death, view of, xix
proof texting, coherence in, 198
prophets, as referents, 205
propositions, in a cohesive path, 204
psalm of David, on hearing the voice of God, 239
purgatory, doctrine of, 149, 431
purification, 212, 328, 329, 349
purified eternal/perpetual-place, 178
purpose, indicating in intent, 171

Qumran documents, 48, 121

Rabbinic Judaism, surviving as mainly Sadducean, 35
race, running, xiv, 377–79
Rahab, 372
rational earthly antitypes, escalating, 420
rationalism, philosophical strain of, 421
Red Sea, events of added by the Pastor, 372
redemption, 317, 413

SUBJECT INDEX

referent antitype examples, expressed in the LXX, 43
referents, 7, 19, 456–57
Reformation, salvific corrections of, 421
Reformation text, of biblical creation, 430–31
relationship, of God and creation, 98
relationships, pursuing peace and holiness, 382–83
Religionsgeschichtliche Schule, 37, 94
renewed repentance option, 277
repentance of dead works, 108, 275, 276
repetitive sacrifices, emphasizing judgment, 354
rest
    centering on the concept of, 243
    enjoying God's, 406
    entrance by faith into at judgment, 247–51
    in heaven as better life, 374
    of Jesus and his people, 246–47
    in the presence of the living God, 240, 245
resurrection
    Adam-Christ contrast of body composition, 409
    contra claims against prompt, 162–68
    of the dead, 73, 147
    from the dead demanding holiness of Jesus, 411
    expectation of for (all) the dead by the Christ, 129
    Pastor not using, 392
    steering clear of thinking about at all, 163
revelation, mediated by an otherworldly being, 32
Revelation (book of), as a pure apocalypse, 34
Rhee, Victor (Sung Yul), 13
rhema, referring to external conversation, 94
rhetorical cohesion, within the topicintroduction, 204
right hand of God, Son in access to, 209
the righteous, awaited the Christ, 392
righteous in innocence, 63

righteousness of faith, 366
rising from the dead, 130, 262, 413
rising to God, 3, 14, 341–42
rising/resurrection, from the dead into heaven, 165
Roman persecution and possible death, Pastor anticipating, 49–50
Romans (book of), clauses modifying "gospel of God," 410

Sabbath rest, for the people of God, 246
sacred space, movement through, 253
sacrifice(s)
    as acceptable to God, 275
    criteria for the acceptance of, 129
    Enoch offering proper, 362
    specified in the law, 336
sacrificial blood requirement, for forgiveness and holiness before God, 324
sacrificial burnt offering, Isaac as, 368
sacrificial living, 390
sacrificial offerings, 74
sacrificial suffering, of Jesus, 130
Sadducean ruling class, 147
Sadducean school, 146
Sadducees, 67, 146, 417, 436
salvation
    available to those taking a step of repentance, 404
    Christ appearing for "from a second place/position without sins," 22
    dying sequence and rising sequence of, 447
    eagerly awaiting a very little while after death, 80, 85
    with eternal/perpetual-place inheritance, 404
    as future for the audience, 223
    from God's judgment of wrath upon sin, 86
    having Christ and his believers falling away, 242
    having no future delay after death, 155
    at judgment, 88, 211

SUBJECT INDEX

lengthy postponements and alternative endpoints for, 1
limiting to a merited incorruptibility by sin and death, 38
not neglecting, 225–26
into a present, new, covenant relationship for believers, 23
present experience of at death and judgment, 357
as a process of living events, 262
as promises internally realized, 13–14
in the realm about to come, 227
in the realm of the presently coming rule of God, 227
rest in God's dwelling presence, 116
taking place over plural heavens, 56
for those waiting for Jesus's appearing, 406
"Sanctuary," Latin transliterated gloss, 292
Sarah, 364
Saul of Tarsus, 82
scholarly constructed speculations, toward adversarial straw men, 184
scholarly works and commentaries, behind change of the plural heavens, 433–34
scholars
　failure to unlock the message of Hebrews, 197
　incorrect traditional themes or new novel ideas for publication, 395
　in opposition to open heavenly hope for people, 422
　promoting an earth-centric ideology, xviii
　on what Jesus might have done between the cross and fleshly resurrection, 417
scientific Cartesian timeless solution, 155
second coming
　of Christ not mentioned, 334
　the living in the flesh are gathered to Jesus, xix
　as an outlier subtopic about the NT alternative truth of, 397
　promises of as not the major focus of the Pastor's concern, 50
　waiting for resurrection in, 421
second covenant, 80, 324, 333, 407
"second place without sin," where Jesus lives, 115
"second tent," as the tent called holy of holies, 23
second time, 39, 77
second-Adam, Christ as, 409
sections, 192, 196, 397
seed of Abraham, as who God helps into heaven, 231
self-offering, of Jesus, 338–44
self-offering events, of Jesus's death and rising, 68
semantic deep structure, guiding the selection of lexemes, 193
semantic meaning, in context, 291
semantic spatial correspondence, of Psalm 109:2–3 with Hebrews 8:1–2, 291
Semitic views, of creation in the day of Jesus, 424
"sense," intended for word choices, 19
sense meaning option, of plural heavens, 440
sentence diagram, for Hebrews 9:27–28, 474
sequential gospel accounts, 407–16
sermon genre, of Hebrews, 11
servant, words of reserving judgment he receives, 56
service, offering acceptable, 385–86
"shadow"
　law as, 62, 336
　tabernacle service as, 288–303
shepherd
　intercession of Jesus, 8
　Jesus as, 108, 206
　Son in ministry as, 393
sifting, sources with the Pastor's words in Hebrews 9:27–28, 52–88
sifting function, of both vertical and horizontal lines, 51
sin(s)
　atoned by Jesus, 80
　cleansing of, 226

sin(s) (continued)
    Jesus sacrificed himself for once, 72, 266
    laying aside during approach to Jesus, 376–77
    needing atonement, 392
    outcome of God's judgment upon, 88, 384
    of the people in making atonement, 316
    presence of necessitated God's wrath, 101–2
    purification of, 212
    symbolic transfer of for atonement, 74
    transference of to Jesus, 404
Sinai covenant, 136, 379, 398, 422
"since presently receiving," 386
sinful beings, separation due to, 135
sinful people
    anthropological afterlife options for, 144–45
    creation accommodating, 329
    problem of in the holy place of heaven, 317
    Son's sacrificial offering transmitted to, 215
    transformation to enable dwelling with God in heaven, 115
singular text, in Hebrews for "heaven," 424–25
smoke, burning from offering(s) judged by aroma, 129
"so also," comparing corresponding statements, 64–65
Sodom and Gomorrah, God's judgment upon the sin of, 86
Solomon, made king a second time, 77
Son of God. *See also* Christ; Jesus
    abilities of, 96, 250, 253, 375
    able to appear for salvation, 205
    achieving a purification of sins, 209
    achieving the eternal/perpetual-places, 349
    appointed according to a spirit of holiness, 410
    assisting as a merciful and faithful high priest in heaven before God, 233
    atoning for the sins of the people, 251
    bringing all things by the conversation of his ability, 229, 350, 388
    bringing all things to God in heavenly access, 211
    bringing many brethren to God in heaven, 228–30
    bringing salvation to people before God at testing, 223–25
    bringing to God all things into heaven and God's presence, 255
    as Christ, had to die, 327
    cleansing of sins, 226
    continually crucifying again, 273
    created access to the eternal/perpetual-places, 169
    creating the necessary piercing, 250
    current role as the Christ doing the will of the Father, 389–40
    describing the salvation of, 224
    first person into heaven to God's presence, 213
    freed people from the realm of the devil, 230–31
    fulfilling the new covenant as the Christ, 398
    functioning in his role of Judge, 251
    as God himself from the glory of heaven, 211
    as heir, 208, 214
    as high priest in an active ministry, 107
    interceding in heaven on behalf of believers, 286–87
    intercession of in heaven as high priest, 240, 256
    listening to the tabernacle ministry, 309
    made atonement for sins, 347
    as mediator of a new covenant, 324–28
    as a "minister," 288
    ministering as God and worshiped by angels, 217–18

SUBJECT INDEX

ministering in the heavens, 294
ministry, subtopics concerning, 207
ministry to people suffering death and judgment, 211
narrative about abilities of, 96
new inherited ministry at death, 347
occupying the seat at the throne of God, 107
as the owner-agent of an "inheritance," 96
Pastor speaking about, 97
priestly ministry in the heavens, 297
rendering powerless the devil's power of death, 310
saved by the Father after his death, 108
speaking by ministry, 217
subtopics related to the activity of, 206
as the Word of God, 158, 248
Son of Man
 contrast with "man," 57
 doing now and in heaven today, 169
 greatness and faithfulness of Jesus as, 176
 reception of Jesus as, 131
 salvation accomplished by, 228
sons of God, confession by, 109
soteria, combining with *kyrios* in the LXX, 85 ?
souls, of people entering heaven after death remain in heaven, 283
sovereign rule, 420
space and time, indicating a second ordinal event in, 78–79
space-time, 7, 96, 135
spatial access to God, language of, 135
spatial and temporal elements, depending on contextual background, 34
spatial benefits, of the second ministry, 301
spatial changes, 312, 324, 398, 401
spatial concepts, balancing the Pastor's spatiality, 123
spatial descriptions, Pastor intending accurate, 117

spatial destiny of hope, interpreters relegating the sermon into a collection of proof texts, 420
spatial domain, covered by the ministry of the Son, 294
spatial force consideration, referent meanings in context requiring, 401
spatial heavenly destiny, 213–14
spatial listing, in Heb 8:1–2 condensing the place described in the LXX, 291
spatial location, for the event(s) where Jesus initially shepherds his sheep, 161–62
spatial movement, of terms the Pastor applies to the Son's, exemplary, atoning ability, 107
spatial place, as "heaven" in a "city," 105
spatial possibilities, of heavenly places, 122
spatial reality, moving errantly toward a closed, 37
spatial rising smoke, of offerings, 129
spatial statements, in pseudepigraphic and apocryphal writings, 418
spatial syntax cohesion, in Hebrews, 469–72
spatial understanding, of freeing people from enslavement by the devil, 128
spatial-temporal background, 405, 406, 418
spatial-temporal conceptions, often codified into prescribed traditions, 4
spatial-temporal contact, points of, 412
spatial-temporal language, gospel fulfillment containing, 407
spatial-temporal place, envisioned by the Pastor, 406
speech-action, about the anticipated Son of God, 405–6
spies, Rahab assisting, 372
"spirit, Spirit," options of human spirit, Holy Spirit, or a human spirit filled with the Holy Spirit, 319

541

spirit bodies, transformation to at death, 155–62
spirit body living, for open heavens, 418
spirit in death, of Jesus, 411
"spirit" life intercession, hints of possible invisible not part of the visible earthly witness, 409
"a spirit of a holy place"
    experience of, 161
    modifying *pneuma* as "an eternal/perpetual-place spirit," 319
    in reference to the priestly intercessory ministry of Christ, 416
    salvation event of Jesus at death and judgment, 157
"spirit of an eternal-place"
    in comparison to other sequential gospel narratives, 416
    Jesus having, 412
    Jesus journeying in his priestly ministry to God, 416
    Jesus's continual living in transformation as, 407–8
"spirit of grace," 319
spirit of holiness, of Jesus, 411, 412
spiritual beings, words in Hebrews linked with other, 468
"spiritual body," no revealed eternal creation transitions to, 38
spiritual creation, in contrast to the material, 143
spiritually born offspring, of Abraham and Sarah, 364
standing before Jesus, as high priest, 254
starry heaven and the holy-places, as two temporary realms, 425
state-church, authority upon the authorized, 420
Stephen, Jesus came for at death, 163
strangers, showing hospitality to, 387
strangers and sojourners, upon the earth, 107
straw men
    examples of, 184
    including Gnosticism, 142–43

inventing first-century CE, 400
modern, 168
structural guides, distanced from Hellenistic Greek culture, 199
structural outlines, of Neeley, 200
substance-reality
    adhering steadfast the beginning of, 158
    angels and Jesus possessing the form of, 175
    everything created consisting of, 6
    as "evidence of things not presently being seen," 359
    participating with Jesus in, 156
    of the Son, 97
substitutionary atonement, by the Christ, 127
substitutionary death, Jesus enduring, 177
substitutionary sacrifice, 76, 129, 277
subtopics, 194, 206
suffering, 355–56, 378, 380
suffering servant motif, 76
summaries/conclusions, 186, 194
summary language, of the Pastor's structured discourse analyzed, 198
supernatural, as a new philosophical term, 421
symbolic antitypes, as the salvific final endpoint of God's purposes, 37–38

tabernacle
    distinctive divisions and furnishings of, 306
    divisions of holiness in a cosmic-field constrained eschatology, 140
    functioned as a "parable," 310
    link with plural heavens, 294
    as a model about the plural heavens, 144
    separate parts of having a symbolical significance, 124
    service, outline and shadow of, 288–303
    symbolizing all of God's creation, 134

SUBJECT INDEX

typology language, 140
"within" or "in" heaven, 290
tabernacle ministry, 50, 82, 124
tabernacle/tent, 289–90, 298, 314
talmudic commentary literature, knowledge of, 48
teaching
    building upon the foundation of the word of Christ, 272
    concerning an impossible Logos teaching about God's speech, 270–73
    concerning Christ, 216
    God having reward for good productive at judgment, 278–79
    illustrating impossible, 273–78
    imitating Abraham and those who follow the promise inside the veil, 279–84
    not following strange, 389–90
teaching alternative, to "those having fallen away," 108
teaching "conversation," concerning confession of eternal/perpetual-place hope, 10
temple spatial typological language, limiting, 401
temptation, 273, 323, 354
testimonial narrative, historical evidence of familiar, 51
testimonial witness, about salvation, 226
testimony, about the Son's "ability," 215
testing, at God's judgment, 232, 285
text
    compilations of, 194
    original designs, 402
text linguistics, 190–91, 455
textual interpreters, ignored methods of interpretation, 26
thematic investigation, information overwhelming, 40
thematic subtopics, in analysis of Hebrews, 189
theology
    accepted by the Pastor, 402
    developed for Jesus from death to resurrection, 417
    of God, background places within, 94
    modern on the Genesis creation cosmogony, 181
    of the Pastor, 169
"therefore," as an inferential conjunction, 238
thought structure, greatly indebted to the work of Albert J. Coetsee, 200–201
threshold criteria, for division, 200
threshold indicators, in analysis of Hebrews, 189
throne
    direct prophecy of the Pastor about the place of, 135
    in the eternal/perpetual-place of the holy of holiness, 178
    of God, 128
    of grace approaching with confidence, 254
    of the Son located in heaven, 220
time, after death to judgment as but a moment, 356
timing, of Jesus's ministry, 334
"to after have said," on God's speech, 345
"to complete," Pastor's verbal concept of, 131
"to die" verb, appearing often in the Pastor's environment, 58
"to enter his rest," positively linking with "salvation," 251
to God, the Judge of all people, as destiny of believers, 384
to Jesus, mediator of the new covenant, as destiny of believers, 384
"to the ones eagerly awaiting him" phrase, not found in the LXX, 84–85
to the spirits of the righteous, as destiny of believers, 384
topic introduction, FGTs positioned, 193
topics/subtopics, missing due to ill-fitting word glosses, 196
topological and typological images, stimulating mental mapping questions, 111

SUBJECT INDEX

topos, "nonliteral" interpretation as "occasion," 114
tradition argument, countering or affirming a spatial translation, 25
training, receiving from the Father, 73, 376–77, 379, 380–81
transcendent, as a new philosophical term, 421
transcendent eschatology, 33
transcendent immaterial timelessness, philosophical Cartesian ideas of, 96
transformation, in death to Jesus's spirit, 413
transition summary (STr), for audience orientation, 192
transition units, connecting three major sections, 204
"true," referent reflecting congruency with unseen heavenly realities, 357
true church, catalyst for later conflicts over, 335
"true heart"
  as a desired feature, 394
  embracing the quality of, 375
  Pastor considering, 366
  reflecting substance-realities of the unseen heavens, 381
  subtopic expanded, 351
  unit topic as, 357
true tabernacle, 292, 329
truth, that it is impossible for God to lie, 281
Tyndale, William, influenced by the work of Martin Luther, 431–32
types, of *aiōn-field* heavenly reality fulfillment in places, 27
typological events, of Israel's deliverance, judgment, and inheritance, 158
typological interpretation, under the pretext of all things hidden as allegory, 46
typological links, between an antitype and type, 30
typology, in Hebrews, 27

unbelievers, judgment for at death, 443
uncleanness, at Jesus's judgment, 316
unholiness, potential of, 410
unit, functional summaries of text groupings, 196
unit shift, speaker/author providing a threshold of indicators for, 224
unit-to-unit shifts, signaled by threshold changes, 204
"universe," Latin transliterated term, 292, 294
unproductive teaching, receiving loss of reward at judgment, 278
unseen changes, achieved by Jesus, 371
unseen creation, recent spatial changes, 295
unseen descriptors, believers not enduring, 383–84
unseen realities, modern bias against, 121
unseen substance-realities, kind of faith anticipating, 367
"unshakable kingdom," 385–86
using "your last things," 153

"valid covenant," 327
vegetation, analogy about two classes of, 277–78
veil
  believers traveling within, 138
  earthly torn while Jesus is on the cross promptly at death, 317
  holy of holies as beyond, 162
  Jesus's entrance through, 360
  obstacle of, in the "house of God," 349
  Pastor repeating subtopics in relation to, 135
  removal of the inner enabling approach for people, 296
  separating everything unholy and unclean from the presence of the living God, 136
  teaching on Abraham and others inside, 279–84
  tearing of opening at Jesus's entrance for others to follow, 282
verbal activity, of God, 457–59

SUBJECT INDEX

verbal noun referents, 456
vertical and horizontal *aiōn-field* categories, 52
vertical filter grid line, involving vertical stratification of the Pastor's words, 41–50
vertical reality, of the Pastor, 184
vindication, of Jesus, 413, 414
visible and invisible substance-reality, 6
visible cosmic reality, 27
visible creation, xvi, 182
visible heavens, distinguishing from the heaven/the heavens, 143
visible proof, of Jesus's rising to God, 408
visible realm of creation and its duration, the Son providing evidence about, 219

walls of Jericho, 372
warrants, about the new covenant, 327
"way of the holy-places," 312
weak hands and feeble knees, strengthening, 380
"weakness," when standing before God, 255
weaknesses, strengthening by God's training, 380–81
"Where are we going when we die?" 2
"who being offered" word, 70–74
"who having passed," suggesting completed passage to God, 253
the wicked, descending outside of heaven, 166
wilderness generation, unbelief of, 239
"will appear" future passive verb, 81–83
"without sin" adverbial modifier, 79, 80
witnesses, 226, 377, 381
the "Word," accountability of, 225, 234
word choices, meaning of the Pastor's, 18–89
word meanings, 19, 22–25, 42
"word of exhortation," Hebrews as, 11
Word of God [Jesus]
 as a capable judge, 247–51
 as God speaking, 93
 gospel known as, 418
 judging all, 268
 "presently giving" at judgment, 302
 word of the Lord, came a second time, 77
word pool, 15, 51
word study, filtering, 91
"word/message of righteous," describing missing, 270
words
 establishing familiarity with the Pastor's chosen, 18
 flattening translation of several Greek, 399–400
 linked with creation, 459–62
 linked with God, 456–59
 linked with other spiritual beings, 468
 linked with people, 463–67
 not retaining original meanings throughout their history, 20
 of the Pastor, 455
 sampling method sifting the available information, 40
"the Word/word of God" phrase, interpreted in several ways, 249
work of Christ, teaching error concerning, 216
"world," modern translations of multiple Greek terms to the English word, 183
worldly resurrection of the flesh, 374
writer of Hebrews, not seeing the heavenly reality, 13
writers, on believers seeing Jesus coming in intercession for those at death, 17
Wycliffe, John, 429

Yahweh, 65–66, 217–18, 220, 435
Yom Kipper, 309
Yom Kippur, 287, 330

Zechariah, 77

Scripture Index

OLD TESTAMENT

Genesis

	xvin7, 96n19, 103, 103n39, 104n40, 111, 179, 180, 257n139
1	100n31
1:1	xvin7, 95n18, 103n39, 178n221, 209
1:1–2	xvin7
1:1—2:4	178n221
1:1—2:4a	119
1:2	103n39
1–2	111
1:2 LXX	63n125
1–3	103n37, 139n125
1:14	112n59
1:31	100n31, 103n39
2–3	178n221
2:7	98
2:7 LXX	98
2:7 MT	98
2:7c BHS	98n28
2:8	209
2:17 BHS	59n112
2:17 LXX	59n112
2:24	57n108
3	102n36
3:14–19	103
3:15	101, 180, 211, 259n145, 261n150, 271n162, 361
3:22	257n139
3:22 BHS	259n145
3:22 LXX	259n145
3:24	257n139
3:24 LXX	259n145
4	289n191, 362
4:1–10	362
4:1–16	360
4:3–7	241n109, 272n165
4:6	130
4:7	70n142, 73
4:7 LXX	70n142
4:11	84n184
5:15	120n77
5:17	120n77
5:22–24	83n183, 144
5:24	133n112, 435
5:24 BHS	362
5:24 LXX	361, 362
6:3	95n18
6:4	179n223
8:20–21	74n153
8:20–22	88
12:7	81n176, 115
13:15	183n230
14:18	259
18:1	161n185
19:1	161n185
19:17	86

Genesis (continued)

19:20	86
19:22	86
21:33 LXX	95n18, 178
22	73n151
22:1–19	368
22:6	74
22:7	280n179
22:7 LXX	280
22:8–4	73n151
22:14 LXX	81, 81n177
22:14 LXX/OT	81n177
22:15 LXX/MT	77n163
22:17 BHS	280n178
22:17–18	369
22:18	73
24:10	161n185
27:27–29	369
27:39–40	369
28:12	120n77
32:20	307n227
37:35	59n113
42:38	59n113
43:9	84n184
44:29	59n113
44:31	59n113
47:22	71n142
48:1–20	369
48:4	369
48:4 LXX	369
49:10	54
49:10 LXX	54, 54n101
49:18 LXX	86n188
49:18 LXX/MT	85
50:17	84n184

Exodus

	304n219, 470n4
2:2	370
2:10–14	370
2:14	371
2:15	371
3:5	99
3:5 BHS	99n30
3:6 LXX	24n7
10:28–29	371
12:21–50	372
12:50	371
14:22–31	372
24:8	328
25:8–9	337n268
25:9	124
25:9 LXX	82n180
25:17	307n227
25–31	119
25–40	305n221
25:40	124
25:40 LXX	82
26:1	222n83
26:2	99n29
26:31	222n83
28:3	304n219
28:29	304n219
28:30	304n219
28:35	304n219
29:18	129
29:25	74, 129
30:10	304n219
30:13	304n219
30:24	304n219
30:35	304n219
33:17–23	105
33:20	141n132
36:8	222n83
36:35	222n83
38:25	304n219
40:34–35	377

Leviticus

	81, 81n177, 304n219, 470n4
1:4	74
1:10	74
1:13	129
4:1—6:7	326n255
4:3 LXX	65
4:4	65n129
4:4–5	74
4:5 LXX	65
4:6	65n129, 137n119
4:7	65n129
4:13–21	65n129
4:15	74
4:16 LXX	65

4:20	137n119	16:20	290n196
4:22–35	65n129	16:21	74
4:24	74	16:23	290n196
4:26	130	16:24	304n219
4:31	130	16:27	290n196
4:33	74	16:30	137n119
6:7	130	17:11	130, 307n226, 307n227, 309n230
6:9	304n219		
6:11	65n129	19:2	99
6:12–16	137	20:26	99
6:13 LXX	71n143	21:8	99
6:15	65n129	21:10 LXX	65
6:15 LXX	65	21:12 LXX	65
6:19	304n219	22:25	84n184
6:20	304n219	23:26–27	307n227
6:20 MT	71n143	24:9	304n219
6:22 MT	65	25:8–9	100n31
6:26	65n129	25:40	100n31
6:29	65n129	26:15	325n254
6:30	130	26:31	129
7:6	304n219	26:44	325n254
7:7	130		
8	311n233	## Numbers	
8:3	304n219	4:16	137
8–9	305n221	7:89	307n227
8:14	74	9:15–23	377
8:18	74	18:17	74n153
9:4 LXX	81	20:11	30n28, 241n109
9:6 LXX	81	23:19	264
9:7	130	24:17	54n102
9:22	74	35:6–28	281n180
10:1–2	241n109		
10:1–3	102, 130, 316	## Deuteronomy	
10:9–11	104	1:17	75
10:13	304n219	5:23	95n18
10:14	304n219	5:28	383n332
10:17	130, 304n219	10:14	253n134
10:18	304n219	17:2–6	354
11:44–45	99	30:16 LXX	60n117
14:13	304n219	31:16	325n254
16	304n219, 311n232, 311n233, 326n255, 329n258	31:20	325n254
		32:35–36	62
16 LXX	303n218	32:35–36 LXX	355
16:2	304n219	32:39	366
16:2 LXX	282n183	32:40	95n18
16:16	290n196		
16:17	290n196		

Joshua

2:1–24	372
6	372
10:24	221n81
11:21–23 LXX	158
11:23	157n179
24:19	99

Judges

20:38	74n153

1 Samuel

2:2	99
2:6	366
2:10 MT	65
2:35	66n131
2:35 MT	65
6:15 MT	74n153
6:20	99
12:5–6	66n131
12:5–6 MT	66
15:29	264
24:7	66
24:11	66
26:11	66
26:16	66
26:23	66
27:8	179n223

1 Samuel (1 Kingdoms)

2:10 LXX	61n118, 65
2:35 LXX	65
6:15 LXX	74n153
12:5–6 LXX	66
17:10	50n90
17:25f	50n90
17:36	50n90
17:45	50n90
24:7 LXX	66
24:11 LXX	66
26:11 LXX	66
26:16 LXX	66
26:23 LXX	66

2 Samuel

1:14	66
1:16	66
2:5 [omitted MT]	66
7:12–16	98
7:13 LXX	218
7:14	217, 218, 271n162
19:21	66
23:1	66

2 Samuel (2 Kingdoms)

1:14 LXX	66
1:16 LXX	66
2:5 LXX	66
14:29 LXX	77
19:21 LXX	66
21:21	50n90
23:1 LXX	66

1 Kings

4:18–37 MT	373
5:3	221n81
6:29	222n83
8:10–11	377
8:27	119, 120n77, 253n134
9:2 MT	81, 81n176, 81n177
17:17–24 MT	373
18:15	253n134

1 Kings (3 Kingdoms)

9:2 LXX	81, 81n176, 81n177
19:7 LXX	77

2 Kings

2:1	133n112
2:11	133n112, 366, 435

1 Chronicles

16:22 LXX/MT	66
20:7	50n90
28:2	221n81
29:22 LXX	77

2 Chronicles

2:5–6	253n134
2:6	119, 120n77
3:7	222n83
6 LXX	86n188
6:18	86n188, 253n134
6:21	86n188
6:23	86n188
6:41–42	86n188
22:7	66
22:7 MT	66
30:8 LXX	179n222

Ezra

	159n183
6:18	157n179
9:8 MT	86n188

Nehemiah

9:6	253n134

Job

	220n80
1:7	176
14:13	59n113
38:4–7	181n224
38:23 LXX	54, 56

Psalms

	201n48, 220n80
2	68n137, 171n206, 221n81, 257n139, 299n213
2:2 LXX	66
2:2 LXX/MT	218
2:4	218
2:7	217, 257n140
2:7 LXX	260n148
2:7 LXX/MT	217, 258
2:7 LXX/OT	69
2:12 BHS	258
2:12 LXX	218, 258
3:8 MT	86n188
3:9 LXX	86n188
6	264
8	13n38
8:4 MT	57
8:4–6 MT	227
8:5 LXX	57
8:5–7 LXX	227
9	264
9:13	106n45
9:17	106n45
11:6 LXX	86n188
12:5 MT	86n188
15:9–10 LXX	59n112
16:8–11	59n113
16:9–10 MT	59n112
16:10	106n45, 166n191, 317n245
16:10–11	341
17:8 LXX	138n123
17:51 LXX	66
18	264
18:7 MT	138n123
18:50 MT	66
19:7 LXX	66
20:6 MT	66
21:4 LXX	99
21–23 LXX	138n123
21:23 LXX	230
22:3 MT	99
22:22 MT	230
22–24 MT	138n123
23	264, 341
23:3 LXX	138n123
23:5 LXX	138n123
24:3 MT	138n123
24:5 MT	138n123
25:6	179n223
27:8 LXX	66
28:8 MT	66
30:3	166n191
31:17	106n45, 166n191
37:23 LXX	86n188
38:22 MT	86n188
39 LXX	339
39:3 LXX	339
39:4–5 LXX	339
39:5–7	339
39:6 LXX	72n148
39:6–7 LXX	72
39:7 LXX	71, 340, 340n271

Psalms (continued)

39:7–9 LXX	338
40 MT	339
40:2 MT	339
40:5–6 MT	339
40:5–7	340n271
40:6 BHS	72n148
40:6 MT	340
40:6–7 MT	72
40:6–8 MT	338
40:7 BHS	340n271
40:7 MT	71
41:3 LXX	136, 136n116
42:2 MT	136
44:6 LXX	219
44:6–7 LXX	219
44:7–8 LXX	69
44:8 LXX	69n138
45:6–7 MT	69, 219
49:15	166n191
50:21 LXX	74n153
51:21 MT	74n153
53:3 LXX	86
54:1 MT	86
56	264
56:13	106n45
65:10–12 LXX	323n97
66:10–12	323n97
68:20	106n45
71:4 LXX	86
72:4 MT	86
73:24	435
74	231n94
74:22	231n94
75:10 LXX	86
76:9 MT	86
76:19 LXX	138n123
77:18 MT	138n123
78:69	119
83:10 LXX	66
84:9 MT	66
86:13	106n45, 166n191
87:2 LXX	86n188
88	166n190
88:1 MT	86n188
88:3	59n113
88:12 LXX	138n123
88:39 LXX	66
88:52 LXX	66
89 MT	221n81
89:1 LXX	99n30
89:1–5 LXX	173n210
89:2 LXX	112n59, 138n123, 179
89:3	179n222
89:11 MT	138n123
89:18	99
89:38 MT	66
89:48	106n45
89:51 MT	66
90:1 MT	99n30
90:1–2	104n39
90:1–4	xvin7, 97
90:1–5	173n210
90:2 MT	112n59, 138n123, 179
93:2	179n223
94:7 LXX	242, 246
94:7–11 LXX	238
94:11 LXX	244, 245
95 MT	239
95:7	341
95:7 MT	242, 246
95:7–11 MT	238
95:11 MT	244, 245
96:7 LXX	218
97:6 MT	218
97:7	217
99:5	221n81
101:13 LXX	219
101:19 LXX	219
101:25–27 LXX	219
102 MT	219
102:12 MT	219
102:19 MT	219
102:22 LXX	209
102:25–27 MT	219
103:4 LXX	219, 261, 261n150
103:17	179n223
104	119, 259
104:4 MT	219, 261
109 LXX	213n70, 291, 303n218
109:1 LXX	3, 72, 135, 213n70, 264, 288, 288n190
109:1–4 LXX	288
109:2 LXX	291

SCRIPTURE INDEX

109:2–3 LXX	291, 303n218	8:22–31	119, 178n221
109:3 LXX	258, 288, 291	8:23	178n221
109:4 LXX	3, 69, 131, 135, 169, 213n70, 219n78, 258, 258n144, 259, 260n148, 266, 267, 268, 288, 318	12:28	366
		28:3	179n223
110	91, 171n206, 183, 213, 213n71, 257n139	**Ecclesiastes**	
			220n80, 313n235
110 MT	213n70, 221n81, 352n290	12:5–7	59n113
		12:5–7 LXX	313n235
110:1	13n38, 220, 221n81	**Isaiah**	
110:1 BHS	264		
110:1 MT	3, 72, 135, 213n70	6:1–6	142n132
110:1–4 MT	288	6:1–11	120n77
110:3 BHS	258n144	6:3	99
110:4	97, 257n140, 264, 271n162	6:17 LXX	77
		8:17–18	230
110:4 BHS	259	11:1	54n102
110:4 MT	3, 69, 131, 135, 169, 213n70, 219n78, 258, 266, 267, 268, 318	12:2 LXX/MT	86n188
		14:9–10	59n113
		19:20 LXX	86
116:8	106n45	19:20 MT	86
117:6 LXX	57	26:11	62
117:14–15 LXX		26:19	366
	86n188	34:5 LXX	248n123
118:6 MT	57	37:3	50n90
118:14 MT	86n188	38:10	59n113
119:89	179n222	38:20 LXX/MT	86n188
119:123	63	40:28	95n18, 320n248
131:17 LXX	66	40:28 LXX	178
131:10 LXX	66	45:1 LXX	66
132:7	221n81	45:17 LXX/MT	86n188
132:10 MT	66	49:8 LXX/MT	86n188
132:17 MT	66	51:3	5n9
136:5	179n222	51:23	221n81
139:8	106n45, 166n191	53	176
139:8 LXX	86n188	53:8 LXX	61n119
139:23–24	166n191	53:10 LXX	169n198
140:7 MT	86n188	53:11–12	76
148:4	253n134	53:12	338n269
149:4 LXX	86n188	53:12 LXX	260n147
149:4 MT	86n188	55:9	126n97
		55:10	169n198
Proverbs		57:15	320n248
	220n80	59 LXX/MT	86n189
3:11–12 LXX	379	59:11 LXX/MT	85
8:22	178n221	60:19–20	112n59

553

Isaiah (continued)

63:16	179n223
65:20	356n298
66:1	221n81

Jeremiah

1:13 LXX	77
3:23 LXX/MT	86n188
6:29	323n97
10:12	138n123
11:20	414
25:31 MT	248n123
28:15 LXX	138n123
31:31–34	302, 326n255
31:33	345, 346
32:31 LXX	248n123
38:22 LXX/MT	86n188
51:15 MT	138n123

Lamentations

2:1	221n81
4:20 LXX	66

Ezekiel

1	142n132
28:13	5n9
32:21	59n113
36:35	5n9
40:2	75n157
40–48	120n77
41:15–26	222n83
43:24 LXX	74n153

Daniel

	120n77, 147, 227n90, 342n275
2:7 LXX	77
7	125n96, 227n90
7:13	68n137
7:13 LXX	125n96
7:13–14	68n137, 125, 130n109, 131, 168n197, 227n90, 299n213
7:14	125n96
7:18	227n90
7:22	227n90
7:26	168n196
7:27	227n90
9:26	66n133, 67n133
9:26 LXX	66
12:1–3	130n109, 174n211, 373
12:2	55n103
12:2–3 LXX	131n109
12:3	364
12:3 LXX	131n109
12:7	179n222

Hosea

8:7	84n184

Amos

4:13	65n128
4:13 LXX	66
4:13 MT	66

Jonah

3:1 LXX	77

Micah

2:12	84n184
5:2	54n102

Habakkuk 357n300

2:3–4 LXX	356n296
3:13	65n128
13:3 LXX	66

Haggai

2:6	58, 138n123
2:6 LXX	385
2:20 LXX	77
12a	253n134

Zechariah

4:12 LXX	77
13:9	323n97

SCRIPTURE INDEX

DEUTEROCANONICAL BOOKS

1 Enoch

83n183, 102n36, 120n77, 159n183, 293n201, 368n313

1:4	122n83
1:7	168n196
3:6	280n179
3:8	137n119, 281n179
3:10	281n179
3:19	281n179
5:6	168n196
9:2	137n119
10:4–7	102n36
12:3	102n36
12:5	102n36
13:2	137n119, 281n179
14:5	102n36
14:8—15:2	124
14:10	281n179
15:3 GP	179n222
17–19	159n183
18:14	102n36
18:15	102n36
22:3	281n179
22:3–14	137n119, 281n179
25:3	75n157
37–71	227n90
50:1–5	168n196
50:53–56	168n196
71:5–11	122n83
77:4–5?	75n157
77:87?	75n157
92:3	55n103
100:5	55n103

Book of the Watchers

179n222

Enoch

144, 144n139, 147, 342n275

2 Esdras

9:8 LXX	86n188

4 Ezra 120n77

11–13	227n90

Jubilees

120n77

23:31	55n103, 349n283

1 Maccabees

4:46	170
9:1 LXX	77

2 Maccabees

1:10	65n130
3:18	435
4:10	435
7	342n275
7:34	435
7:35 LXX	66n131
7:36 LXX	342n275
11:6 LXX	86n188
12:15	435
12:42	55n104
12:44–45	55n104
12:45	55
12:45 LXX	54
15:23	435

3 Maccabees

2:2	435

4 Maccabees

228n91

4:11	435
7:18–19	55n103
7:19	136n115
8:11	55
8:11 LXX	54
16:25	55n103, 136n115

555

Sirach (Wisdom of Ben Sira)

	43n65, 120n77
7:36 LXX	153
38:3	43n65
38:23	241n108
39:28–31	102n36
47:4	50n90

Tobit

1:22	78
1:22 LXX	77
3:6	137n119, 281n179
8:5	435

Wisdom of Solomon

	46n79, 120n77, 281n179
1–6	227n90
1:14	281n179
2:1	281n179
3:1	137n119
3:1–13	281n179
3:6	323n97
4:10	137n119, 281n179
4:14	137n119, 281n179
7:26	43n65
9:10	435
17:14	281n179

PSEUDEPIGRAPHA (OLD TESTAMENT)

Apocalypse of Abraham

120n77

Apocalypse of Zephaniah

33, 120n77

Ascension of Isaiah

120n77

2 Baruch

	227n90
76:3	75n157

3 Baruch

33, 120n77

2 Enoch

	120n77
20:5	122n83

Testament of Abraham

	120n77
12:14	323n97
13:13	323n97
20:10–12	174n211

Testament of Levi

	120n77, 293n201, 418
18:7	411, 411n8

DEAD SEA SCROLLS

1 QS IV

18–26	341n272

4Q400

120n77

Songs of the Sabbath Sacrifice

293n201

ANCIENT JEWISH WRITERS

Ezekiel the Tragedian

120n77

Josephus

46n79, 120n77, 142, 142n133, 144n138, 146, 147, 147n149, 147n150, 148, 151, 166n192, 293n201, 342n276, 418

SCRIPTURE INDEX

Antiquities of the Jews

3:123	293n201
3:180–181	293n201
3.123	46n79
3.180–187	46n79

Philo

13, 26n15, 41, 42, 44, 44n73, 45n73, 45n76, 46, 46n76, 46n78, 46n79, 46n80, 47n80, 62n122, 94, 110n54, 117n67, 120n77, 124n93, 139n125, 141n131, 142, 142n133, 142n134, 143n134, 144n138, 148, 151, 184n234, 185n234, 250n126, 293n201, 298n212, 299n212, 418

Allegorical Interpretation

1.61	47n80
2.58 PAGM	85n186
3.135	290n194
3.96	45n73

On the Creation of the World

8	44n73
109	62n122

On Dreams

	46n80
1.164 PAE	47n80
1.215	46n79
1.28	62n122
2.24	62n122

On Drunkenness

36	47n80

On Flight and Finding

93	290n194
118	62n122
196	62n122

On the Life of Abraham

268	44n73

On the Life of Joseph

28	46n80

On the Life of Moses

2.17	45n73
2.76	47n80
2.88	46n79

Questions and Answers on Exodus

2.91	46n79

On Rewards and Punishments

30	44n73
117	44n73
152	45n73, 142n133
169–172	45n73

Special Laws

1:66–67	110n54, 124n93
1.239–244	137n119
1.66	46n79
2:45	142n133
8:2	124n93
9:11	124n93

That Every Good Person is Free

83	46n80

That God Is Unchangeable

74–76	62

Who Is the Heir

162	62n122
181	47n80
311	62n122

RABBINIC WORKS

Midrash

	48n86

NEW TESTAMENT

Matthew

1:18	158n179
2:1–2	67
2:2	35, 67
2:6	54n102
3:1	170
3:16	63n125, 436
3:17	425n17
3:29	61n121
5:8	38n52, 106, 141n132
5:12	425n17
5:17	30n27, 354n294
6:9	425n17, 426
6:9 VUL	427
6:9–10	112n58, 118, 122n83, 424
6:9–10 VUL	427
6:10	138, 228
6:10 VUL	427
7:21–23	xxn20, 67n135, 87n193, 131n109, 160, 176n214, 237n101, 276n174
10:15	272n166
11:2–6	67n135
11:5	133n112
11:23	63n125
11:25	3n4, xviin11, 184
12:36	80n174
12:40	63n125
13:11	113
13:52	425n17
14:30	86
16:12–28	67n135
16:18	37n49, 63n125, 237
16:20	67n135
16:21	63n125, 263n151
16:23	135n114
16:27	172
17:1	75
17:1–8	155
17:2	364n308
17:3	82n179, 317n245
17:23	263n151
18:10	425n17, 426
18:12	338n269
19:21	425n17, 427, 428n30
19:29	88
20:19	263n151
22	433n45
22:23	148
22:29–30	368n313
22:41–45	xxn20
22:42	67
23:13	68n136
23:33	61n121
24	173n210
24:4–14	354n292
24:5	xx, 68n136, 274n169
24:9–12	149
24:29–31	3n3, 118, 424
25:31	127n99
25:31–46	168n196
25:34	101
26:28	327
26:31–36	127
26:59–68	67n135
26:63	68n137
26:64	67n135, 135
27:11	35
27:11–14	67n135
27:29	35
27:37	35
27:46	339
27:49	86
27:50	413
27:51	315
27:51–53	108n49, 155n174, 366
27:52	133n112
27:52–53	xiii, 63n125, 155, 209, 226, 236
28:2	63n125

Mark

	64n126
1:1	68n137
1:10	63n125
1:11	425n17
1:44	71n145
6:49	161n185
8:31	227n90
8:33	3n4
9:2	75

SCRIPTURE INDEX

9:2–8	155
9:4	82n179, 317n245, 364n308
9:9	263n151
9:9–12	227n90
9:10	263n151
9:31	227n90
10:33–34	227n90
10:45	175, 227n90
12:18	148
12:18–27	23n7, 67
12:24–27	131, 133n112, 147
12:25	263n151
12:25–27	417
12:26	133n112
14:24	327
14:26	161n185
14:61–62	67n135
15:18	315
15:20	86
15:32	67n135
16:19	24

Luke

1:5	158n179
1:11	82n179
1:31	86n190
1:41	158n179
1:67	158n179
1:76–79	87
2:10–11	86n190
2:13	435
2:21	86n190
2:25–32	67
2:29–32	317n245
2:49	125
3:15	67
3:22	63n125
4:1	158n179
4:6	112n58
4:16	11, 201n48
4:41	67n135, 68n137
7:22	133n112
8:31	363n307
9:22	263n151
9:28–36	155
9:30–31	364n308

10:1	276n172
10:18	102n36
12:51	170
13:22–35	160
14:30	112n58
15:1–6	127
15:4	338n269
16:11	112n58
16:19–31	54n102, 133n112, 137n119, 147, 159n183, 281n179, 340, 415n15
16:22	59, 59n115, 60n115, 74n152, 87, 176, 183n230, 280n179
16:23	132, 281n179
16:23–31	317n245
16:31	63n125, 263n151
16:41–42	183n230
17:20	67
18:4	11
18:13	308n227
18:14	63n125
18:22	425n17, 427, 428n30
18:33	263n151
19:11	3n4, 35, 67
19:20	56
19:38	35
20:27	148
20:34–39	133n112
20:34–40	351, 357
20:35	133n112
22:20	327
22:43	82n179
22:46	263n151
23:2	67n135
23:35	68
23:39	86
23:43	63n125, 159n183, 209, 236, 263n151, 366
23:45	315
23:46	130, 157, 275, 313, 314, 319, 368n313

Luke (continued)

24:7	263n151
24:21	3n4
24:26	68

559

SCRIPTURE INDEX

24:34	81, 81n178	5:25–32	24n7
24:36	161n185	5:29	61n121
24:39	133n112, 161n185, 339	5:30	61n121
24:44	354n294	6:33	63n125
24:46	68, 263n151	6:38	63n125
24:51	24, 75	6:41–42	63n125
26:22	174n211	6:46	141n132
26:25–30	175	6:50–51	63n125
		6:58	63n125

John

		6:62	63n125, 125
		7:24	61n121
1:1–18	43n65, 127	7:26–27	68
1:5	5n9	7:31	68
1:12	107n47	8:16	61n121
1:14	105n41, 211, 412	8:23	218, 334n266, 412
1:18	133n112, 141n132, 283n183	8:44	102, 102n36
		8:50	414
1:25	68	8:56–58	81n176
1:32–33	63n125	9:39	68n136
1:41	67, 86n190	11:27	68n137
1:51	63n125, 125, 436	12:25	64
2:18–22	8, 9, 131n109, 147, 163, 164, 229n92, 260n146, 262, 263n151, 393n343, 408, 409, 415	12:27	86
		12:31	61n121, 112n58
		12:33	64
		12:34	3n4, xviin11, 68, 68n137, 184
3:1–21	168, 351n289	12:35	5n9
3:2	366	12:46	5n9
3:3	168	12:48	80n174
3:5–7	157, 168	13:31–32	163
3:6	157	14:1	105n41
3:10	3n4, xviin11, 184	14:1–6	xiii, 3n3, 173n210, 209, 331
3:12	298n210		
3:13	63n125, 125, 133n112, 168n197	14:1–7	67n135, 176, 417
		14:1–12	xviin11, 184
3:14	168n197	14:2	281n179
3:15–16	172	14:3	85
3:17	38n52	14:6	258, 259n145
3:18	80n174	16:2	149
3:19	61n121	16:8	80n174
3:28	67, 86n190	16:11	64
4:25	67, 86n190	16:16	68n137
4:29	67, 86n190	16:22	81
5:22–30	80n174	17:5	211, 228
5:24	24n7, 61n121, 80	17:22	228
5:24–32	54n102	17:23	132n110
5:25	134, 136	17:24	103n38, 211, 228
5:25–29	131n109		
5:25–30	130n109		

SCRIPTURE INDEX

18:36	67n135, 218, 334n265, 334n266
19:20	316
19:30	130, 313
20:8	263n151
20:9	35
20:17	63n125, 125, 133n112
20:26–28	133n112
21:19	275n171
21:23	xviin11, 184

Acts

	44, 237n102
1:2	24, 158n179
1:6	35, 37n50
1:9	24
1:11	3n3, 24, 173n210
1:22	24
2:4	158n179
2:24	133n112
2:34	63n125, 125
2:47	87n193
3:15	138
3:18	68
3:21	37n50
3:35	73n152
4:8	158n179
4:25	158n179
5:27	145
5:31	138
6:5	158n179
6:7	201n48
7	47, 334n265
7:2	81n177
7:30	82n179
7:55	158n179
7:55–56	163, 163n188
7:55–60	115
7:56	107
9:17	82, 158n179
10:40	263n151
10:41	263n151
10:42	172
11:19	201n48
11:24	158n179
13:9	158n179
13:14–31	11, 201n48
13:15	11
13:31	81
13:34	263n151
13:34–35	411
13:42	11, 201n48
13:44	11, 201n48
13:52	158n179
15:5	145
17:2–4	201n48
17:3	68, 263n151
17:31	62n123, 80n174, 131n109, 229n92, 260n146, 262, 263n151, 393n343, 409
18:4	201n48
21:26	71, 71n145
23:6–10	147
23:7–8	67
23:8	68n136, 148
24:5	145
24:14	145
24:17	71
24:25	80n174
26:5	145
26:16	82
26:18	5n9, 112n58, 176
26:23	68
27:20	86
27:31	86
27:34	86

Romans

	228n91, 408n3, 410, 412
1:1	410
1:1–6	407, 409–12
1:3	410
1:3–5	408
1:4	130, 410
1:16	10n20
1:18–32	120n76
1:28	120n76
2:3	80n174
2:4	102n35

SCRIPTURE INDEX

Romans (continued)

2:5	80n174, 102n35
2:16	80n174, 172
3:4	63n125
3:22	237n101
3:25	307n226, 308n227
4:1–8	337n269
5:5	158n179
5:8	68
5:9	87
5:9–10	87n193
5:12	101, 103
5:20	338
6:4–11	345n281
6:8	67n135
7:7	338
8	110n53
8:1	84
8:1–17	340
8:1–39	84
8:2–4	337
8:9	84
8:11	38n52
8:13	84
8:14–16	84
8:16	87n193, 157n178, 158n179, 321, 416
8:18–22	139n125
8:18–25	122n82, 329n258
8:18–30	112n58
8:19	84
8:23	84
8:24–25	84
8:25	84
8:27	84
8:29	63n125
8:34	84, 213n71
8:38–39	281
9:4	327n256
9:5	411
9:8	31n28
9:10–13	115
9:30–33	337n269
9:31	336
9:31–33	337
10:4	337
10:4–7	67n135
10:6	125
10:6–7	63n125
10:7	228n92
10:17	10n20, 269
12:2	64
13:11	87
14:9	67n135
14:10	80n174
14:10–12	172
15:13	158n179
15:16	71
15:19–20	68
16:22	179n223
16:25	113

1 Corinthians

	408n3
1:7–8	85
1:8	272n166
1:17	68
1:23	68
2:6–16	47n80
2:7	113
2:9	263n151
2:9–10	xxn19, 142n132, 360
2:9–16	15
2:14	371
3:8–15	88
3:9–15	251
3:10–15	272n166
3:11	272n165
3:13–15	323n97
3:15	86n189
3:18–19	371
3:19	68n136
4:5	3n3, 80n174, 173n210, 272n166
5:4	132n110
5:5	412
10:6	30n28
10:11	30n28
11:25	327
11:29	80n174
11:31–32	80n174
15	131n109, 153, 166n190, 340n272
15:1–8	407, 408–9

15:1–58	409	2:14–16	129
15:3	408	3:6	327, 327n256
15:3–5	408	3:14	67n135
15:4	263n151, 408	4:4	112n58
15:5	408	4–5	xiii, 155
15:5–6	82	4:16–18	168, 370
15:5–8	39, 81	4:18	6, 327n256
15:12–49	340n272	5	366
15:12–58	xiii, 155, 375	5:1–8	172
15:13	412	5:1–11	413n11
15:15	131n109, 133n112	5:6–8	57n107, 213n71
15:16	133n112	5:6–10	250
15:18	131n109	5:7	135n114, 142n132
15:20	263n151	5:7–8	327n256
15:20–21	88n196	5:8	68
15:20–28	183n230	5:9–10	172
15:21	411, 412	5:10	3n3, 80n174, 172, 173n210
15:21–22	87n194		
15:22–23	68	5:11–21	169
15:22–26	135	5:16–17	160
15:23	131n109	5:17	156, 172
15:24–26	115n64	7:1	410n7, 412
15:29	131n109, 133n112, 351n289	7:10	87
		9:4	97
15:32	131n109, 133n112	11:17	97
15:35	133n112	12:1–4	122n83, 141n132, 142n132
15:35–38	131n109, 342n275		
15:35–50	36n47, 38n52	12:2	294n203, 437n61
15:35–57	164	12:2–4	435
15:35–58	155n174, 368n313		
15:40	38, 133, 341n273	**Galatians**	
15:42	412	1:6–7	274n169
15:42–49	250	1:6–10	272n165
15:44	342n275	3:16	73n152
15:44–45	319	3:19	73n152
15:44–58	157	3:19–20	299
15:45	130, 340, 368n313, 409	3:24	338
15:47–49	38, 133	3:29	73n152
15:50	36n47, 132n111, 340, 340n272, 373n317, 415	4:21–26	25n13
		5:5	85
15:50–58	160		
15:52	133n112	**Ephesians**	
15:58	131n109		34, 177n216
		1:3	298n210
2 Corinthians		1:4–5	103n38
	150n161	1:10	37n50, 310n231
1:9–10	133n112		

Ephesians (continued)

1:13	10n20
1:13–14	87n193, 321
1:14	157n179
1:18	208
1:20	135
2:2	112n58
2:6	298n210
2:8	87n193
3:10	298n210
3:11	210n65
3:15	425n17, 427
4:8	63n125
4:8–10	63n125, 125
4:9	63n125
4:30	87n193, 321
5:2	71
5:14	263n151
6:9	425n17
6:12	122n83, 181n226, 298n210

Philippians

	150n161
1:20–23	134, 366
1:21–23	68
1:21–24	xiii, 155, 340n272
1:22–24	2n2
1:23	57, 57n107, 213n71
1:28	87
2:3–11	175
2:6–11	260n147
2:10	298n210
3	45n73
3:6	337n269
3:10–11	130
3:14	208
3:17–21	xiii, 155, 368n313
3:19–20	135n114
3:20	85, 172, 172n208
3:20–21	38, 340n272, 366

Colossians

	34, 177n216
1:1–4	135n114
1:5	56
1:13	5n9
1:13–23	250
1:15	141n132
1:15–20	43n65
1:16	112n58, 122n83, 296n207
1:18	63n125
1:20	37n50
1:22	411
2:8	2n1, 110n52
2:12	345n281
3:1	135
3:1–4	3n3, 156n177, 173n210

1 Thessalonians

1:5	87n193
1:6	158n179
1:7–10	272n166
1:10	213n71, 263n151, 425n17
3:13	410n7
4:13—5:10	418
4:13–17	159n181
4:13–18	3n3, 87n193, 150n161, 152, 165n189, 169, 173n210, 331, 356n298
4:14	150n161, 153n167
4:15	133
4:16	68, 150n161, 153n167, 263n151
4:17	164, 213n71
5:1–11	24n7, 366
5:6–11	3n3, 173n210
5:9	87

2 Thessalonians

1:5	80n174
2:1	3n3, 173n210, 338n269
2:3	273n167
2:10	87
2:12	80n174, 168n196

1 Timothy

	408n3, 410
1:7	122n83
2:5	134, 208, 299, 412

SCRIPTURE INDEX

3:16	82, 113
3:16b	63n125, 82n179, 314, 407, 408, 412–13
4:4	100n31
5:24	80n174
6:15	122n83
6:16	112n58, 141n132

2 Timothy

1:6	57n107
1:9	103n38, 179n223
1:10	133n112
1:12	272n166
1:18	272n166
2:14	158n179
3:16–17	405
4:1	80n174
4:6	56, 57
4:7	56
4:8	56, 80n174, 272n166

Titus

1:2	179n223
3:5	158n179, 351n289

Hebrews

xiii, xiv, xviii, xixn16, xxn17, 2n1, 8, 10, 10n22, 11, 11n24, 12, 12n28, 13, 13n38, 14, 17, 21, 26n15, 34, 37n48, 38n51, 40, 43n65, 45n76, 46n76, 46n78, 47, 48, 48n82, 49, 49n87, 56, 58, 58n110, 64n126, 71n145, 75, 79, 81, 95n18, 97n22, 103n39, 104n40, 104n41, 105n41, 111, 113n60, 118, 120, 122, 123n86, 123n87, 123n88, 127, 127n100, 128n104, 144n138, 145, 146, 150n161, 154, 155, 157n178, 157n179, 164, 175n213, 182, 185n234, 192, 192n22, 193, 195, 196, 197, 200, 201, 201n48, 202n51, 203, 203n52, 204n54, 205n57, 228n92, 237n101, 237n102, 239n104, 249, 254n135, 258n141, 263n151, 277n176, 283n184, 289n191, 289n192, 289n193, 292n199, 293n201, 296n206, 297n208, 301n215, 304n219, 306n223, 311n232, 313n235, 315n237, 323n96, 332n262, 336n268, 337n268, 339n270, 352n290, 357n300, 359n303, 363n307, 370n316, 375, 379n325, 382n329, 392, 395, 397, 401, 403, 407, 412, 419, 420, 422, 423, 424

1	169
1:1	93, 94, 132n111, 205, 236, 259, 308, 405
1:1–2	11, 12, 106, 241n109
1:1–4	10n20, 12, 24n8, 76, 93, 94, 106, 107n47, 192, 204–15, 206n58, 212n67, 216, 250n126, 252, 253, 255, 275, 325, 347, 348, 349, 352, 365n309, 448, 449, 450, 454, 474
1:1—10:18	23
1:1—13:25	449, 454
1:1–14	387n339
1:2	6, 81n176, 93, 95, 101, 111, 111n56, 112n57, 125n94, 127n100, 153, 157n178, 157n179, 169, 173, 207n62, 236, 250n126, 441, 442, 443, 444
1:2a	205
1:2b	205, 207, 215, 217, 299, 325, 349
1:2b–4	206n58, 212n67, 216, 217, 224, 234, 251, 287, 323n97, 450
1:2bc	223
1:2c	138, 171, 205, 208, 208n63, 209, 210, 210n66, 215, 222, 224, 236, 250n126, 349, 469, 472n6
1:3	11n27, 23, 43n65, 76, 94, 97, 123, 135, 142n132, 159, 162, 163, 164, 176

565

SCRIPTURE INDEX

Hebrews (continued)

1:3–4	76n160
1:3–9	9
1:3–14	69n138
1:3a	176n214, 205, 215, 255, 256, 269, 349
1:3b	10, 10n20, 11, 91, 182, 205, 211, 215, 216, 225, 229, 235n99, 237, 250, 252n131, 253, 254, 254n135, 255, 266n157, 269, 299, 331, 333, 339, 352, 384, 388, 390, 392
1:3bd	223
1:3c	3n3, 101, 132n111, 173n210, 205, 208n63, 212n67, 215, 222, 223, 223n85, 232, 233, 234, 255, 256, 269, 274, 316, 349, 358n301
1:3c–14	24
1:3d	205, 209, 210, 215, 224, 250n126, 312n234, 349, 384n333
1:4	88n196, 157n179, 170, 175, 205, 206n59, 207, 215, 217, 223, 299, 325, 349
1:5	62n123, 97n22, 106n46, 112n59, 125n94, 168, 218, 229, 236, 257, 257n140, 441, 442, 443, 444
1:5—4:13	215–16, 235, 253, 254n135, 347, 448, 449, 450, 454
1:5–6	211, 217–18, 258n142, 450
1:5–7	223
1:5–9	175
1:5–12	62n124, 69n138, 82n179, 209, 314
1:5–14	131, 192n21, 206, 206n58, 214, 215, 216–17, 217n76, 218n76, 240, 387, 388, 448, 449, 450, 454
1:5–18	225
1:6	63n125, 111, 111n56, 134, 138n123, 164, 174n212, 176, 217n76, 218, 223, 236, 252n131, 469
1:7	181, 217, 219, 227n90, 319
1:7–12	219–20, 236, 450
1:8	97, 170, 178, 178n220, 211, 218, 219n78, 237, 259n145, 261n150, 334n266, 469
1:8–9	209, 219
1:8–10	295n205
1:8–12	223, 313
1:9	69n138, 209, 219, 236, 276
1:9b	223
1:10	81n176, 118, 219, 220n79, 271n162, 425, 469, 470, 471, 472
1:10–12	6, xvin7, 101, 103n39, 114, 122n82, 164, 181, 209, 209n64, 210n66, 222, 227n90, 441, 442, 443
1:11	299n213
1:12	222
1–12	387n339
1:13	23, 123, 257
1:13–14	88, 125n96, 154n170, 176, 216–17, 220–22, 223, 251, 307n226, 326, 347, 449, 450, 454
1:14	157n179, 159n183, 174n212, 175, 181n224, 207, 221, 221n82, 222n84, 223, 223n85, 239n104, 319, 326
1:14–16	363n307
1:39–40	449
2	169, 172n208
2:1	223n85, 225, 243n111, 247n120
2:1–3	88
2:1–3a	235

SCRIPTURE INDEX

2:1–4	12, 93, 97, 224, 224n87, 225–26, 234, 241, 272, 319n247, 321n251, 448, 450		228, 252n131, 258n141, 262, 316
		2:10–13	9, 235, 258
		2:11	82n179, 134n113, 136n116, 137n120, 157n178, 215, 227n90, 229, 230, 236, 317, 327
2:1–18	62n124, 215, 223–25, 240, 309, 381n328, 382, 383, 448, 449, 450, 454		
2:2	223n85, 225, 354, 358n301	2:11–13	63n125, 93n9, 107, 136, 159n181, 209, 211
2:2–3a	223n85	2:12	230
2:2a	223n85, 358n301	2:12–14	137
2:3	11n26, 88, 174n212, 225, 226, 233, 242, 271n162, 276	2:13	108n49, 230, 235n99, 261
		2:14	63n124, 63n125, 82n179, 112n58, 128n102, 135, 140n129, 181n226, 230
2:3–4	157		
2:3–4 LXX	356		
2:4	99n29, 132n111, 156, 158n179, 160, 163, 164, 172, 226, 319, 469	2:14–15	63n124, 102, 176, 231n95, 310
		2:14–16	230–31, 450
2:5	111, 134, 138, 138n123, 157n178, 175, 227, 236, 469	2:14–18	87n194, 135, 412
		2:15	98, 98n27, 177, 231
2:5–8a	227, 448, 450	2:16	73, 363n307
2:5–8b	228	2:17	8, 66n131, 76, 101, 169, 171, 171n205, 177n216, 231, 232, 234, 234n99, 235n99, 256n138, 261, 308n227, 410, 411
2:5–16	63n124		
2:5–18	175, 218n76, 227n90		
2:6	57, 93n10, 98		
2:6–8a	227		
2:7	175, 211, 228	2:17–18	4, 62n124, 134n113, 176, 176n214, 223–25, 228, 231–33, 251, 308, 325, 347, 448, 449, 450, 454
2:8	112n58, 218		
2:8b	228		
2:8b–13	206, 228–30, 317n245, 448, 450		
		2:18	62, 173, 232, 233, 252n131, 254, 323n97
2:8b–18	317		
2:9	63n124, 63n125, 81n176, 87n194, 169, 175, 228, 235n99, 411	3:1	12, 63n125, 99n29, 107, 136, 158, 169, 171n205, 208, 216, 234n99, 235n99, 236, 245n116, 248, 253, 327
2:9–10	211, 227n90		
2:9–11	63n125, 172		
2:9–13	226	3:1—4:13	107n47, 158, 215, 234, 235, 240n107, 251, 281, 302, 321n251, 370, 376, 385n335, 448, 449, 450, 454
2:9–15	325		
2:9–18	25, 97n22, 99, 108, 113, 115, 131, 134, 137, 172, 172n208, 393		
		3:1–6	86n188, 112n57, 125n95, 235–41, 245n116, 370, 370n316, 450
2:10	106n46, 107n47, 133n112, 134, 134n113, 137, 137n120, 138, 145, 164, 165, 165n189, 168,		

567

Hebrews (continued)

3:1–7	66n131
3:1–19	206
3:2	236
3:3	53n98
3:3–4	101, 237
3:4	6
3–4	38n52
3:4	209, 237
3:4b	112n57
3:5	175, 235n99, 237
3:6	69n139, 81n176, 107n47, 176n214, 234n99, 237, 279n177, 280
3:7	62n123, 93n9, 97n22, 99n29, 112n59, 125n94, 238, 242, 319
3:7—4:11	238n103
3:7—4:13	245n116
3:7–11	238–41, 450
3:8	160, 242
3:9	232n98, 242
3:10	160, 240, 242, 258
3:11	102, 128n101, 159n181, 240, 240n105, 243, 248n122
3:11 VUL	240n105
3:12	97, 97n22, 98, 102n35, 159, 160, 241, 242, 243n111, 247n120, 261
3:12—4:13	63n124
3:12–15	241–42, 450
3:13	62n123, 112n59, 125n94, 376
3:14	66n131, 69n139, 97, 98n25, 158, 158n180, 241, 242, 262, 271n162, 278, 279n177, 280
3:15	62n123, 93n9, 97n22, 112n59, 125n94, 160, 242
3:16–19	242–43, 450
3:18	128n101, 243, 248n122
3:19	102n35, 128n101, 159n181, 242, 248n122, 261
4:1	128n101, 159, 159n181, 243, 243n111, 247n120, 248n122, 279n177, 280, 364n308
4:1–5	243–45, 450
4:1–13	206
4:2	10n20, 176n214, 244, 260, 358n301
4:3	54n102, 102, 123n86, 128n101, 159n181, 209n64, 210n66, 220n79, 243, 243n111, 244, 248n122, 260, 348
4:3–4	209
4:3c–4	209
4:4	93n10, 243, 243n111, 245
4:5	128n101, 159n181, 243, 245, 248n122
4:6	10n20, 128n101, 248n122, 261
4:6–8	245–46, 450
4:6–9	173n210
4:6–10	158
4:7	62n123, 93n10, 112n59, 125n94, 160, 245, 341
4:8	246, 463n3
4:8b–13	136n116
4:9	246
4:9–10	246–47, 450
4:10	128n101, 159n181, 246
4:11	30n28, 128n101, 159n181, 243, 247n120, 248, 248n122, 251, 261
4:11–12	248, 251
4:11–13	63n125, 93, 115, 131n109, 234–51, 252n130, 302n217, 327, 347, 449, 450, 454
4:11–16	116
4:12	62, 80n174, 97, 97n22, 98, 131n109, 157, 158, 160, 163, 247n120, 249, 249n126, 250n126, 252n130, 319, 349n283, 358n301
4:12–13	10, 62, 249n126, 251, 274

SCRIPTURE INDEX

4:13	247, 247n120, 249	5:8	260
4:13–16	115, 268, 282n181	5:9	88, 97, 165, 165n189, 174, 260, 262
4:14	12, 66n131, 107, 107n47, 118, 132n110, 136, 169, 171, 171n205, 245n116, 252n131, 253, 273, 281, 282, 313n235, 317, 348n282, 425, 469	5:10	171n205, 347
		5:10—6:20	252n131, 255, 346, 348n282
		5:11	269n160, 270, 279n177, 280, 358n301
4:14—5:10	212n67	5:11—6:8	88, 108
4:14—10:18	206	5:11—6:18	211, 251, 256n137, 273n167, 287, 289n191, 344
4:14–15	252n131, 256n138		
4:14–16	63n124, 85, 107n47, 117, 216, 252–54, 254n135, 282, 347, 448, 449, 450, 451, 454	5:11—6:20	210, 215, 249n125, 269, 271, 313, 326, 326n255, 349n283, 353, 353n291, 354, 359, 371, 449, 451, 454
4:15	76, 79, 80, 232, 233n98, 252n131, 253, 254, 266, 323n97, 335n266		
		5:11–14	270–73, 451
		5:12	11, 271, 271n162, 273, 325n254
4:15–16	132n110	5:13	270
4:16	9, 85n186, 107, 128n101, 252n131, 254, 265n157, 329n258	5:13–14	271
		5:14	262, 272
5:1	72, 76, 101, 171	5:22–24	241n109
5:1—7:28	206, 256n137	6:1	11, 66n131, 70n142, 108, 176n214, 262, 271, 271n162, 271n163, 273, 274, 275, 276n174, 277n176, 279n177, 305n220, 325n254, 358n301
5:1–10	211, 215, 255, 256–61, 271, 287, 288, 299n213, 305n220, 314, 325n254, 326, 337n269, 339, 358, 367, 449, 451, 454		
5:1—10:18	72, 107n47, 254n135, 255, 285, 286, 347, 348, 448, 449, 451, 454	6:1–2	66n132, 69n139, 70n142, 71n146, 73n152, 74, 113n61, 127, 129, 131, 140n126, 169, 273n168, 287, 348, 361, 413
5:3	64, 76		
5:4	295		
5:4–6	235n99		
5:5	62n123, 64, 66n131, 69, 112n59, 125n94, 257	6:1–5	105, 129
5:5–6	218n76	6:1–6	37n48, 170
5:5–7	157	6:1–8	273–78, 451
5:5–10	134, 138n123, 275	6:2	8, 55n103, 62, 62n121, 64, 73, 73n152, 80n174, 87n193, 108, 115, 129, 159, 160, 161, 228n92, 283, 313, 345n281, 392, 412n11
5:6	97, 173, 219n78, 259n145, 261n150, 470		
5:7	9, 82n179, 87, 88n196, 108, 140n129, 259, 266n157, 314, 325, 339		
5:7–8	248		
5:7–9	260n148	6:3	275, 275n171
5:7–10	260n147		

569

SCRIPTURE INDEX

Hebrews (continued)

6:4	51, 99n29, 157, 158n179, 159, 160, 226, 276, 277n175, 319, 469
6:4–5	161, 163
6:4–6	273, 276, 276n174
6:5	11, 108, 129, 159, 164, 243n111, 247n120, 249n126, 273, 366, 469
6:6	108, 129, 242, 273, 274, 276n174, 277, 277n176, 283
6:7–8	274, 278
6:8	262, 278, 279n177, 280
6:9	88, 233n98, 278
6:9–10	251, 278–79, 451
6:10	99n29, 157n178, 279
6:11	262, 279, 279n177, 280
6:11–18	321n251
6:11–20	160, 269–84, 347, 385n335, 449, 451, 454
6:12	88, 176n214, 207, 279n177, 280, 326
6:13–15	108
6:13–20	163
6:15	73n152, 145, 280, 364, 375
6:17	207, 279, 281, 326, 364n308
6:17–18	305n221
6:17–20	117
6:18	30n27, 279n177, 281, 282
6:18–20	3, 56, 63n124, 79n170, 168, 175n213, 317
6:19	125n94, 128n101, 160, 248n122, 279n177, 281n180, 282, 282n183, 283, 469
6:19–20	9, 88, 115, 127, 131, 159n181, 211, 258n141, 263, 283n183, 284n185, 295n205, 314, 326
6:20	97, 123n86, 128n101, 133n112, 160, 170, 171, 171n205, 219n78, 259n145, 261n150, 283n183, 284, 316, 470
7:1–2	66n132
7:1–3	256–61, 451
7:1–18	212n67
7:1–28	71n142, 134, 211, 215, 218n76, 255, 256, 271, 287, 288, 299n213, 305n220, 314, 325n254, 326, 337n269, 339, 358, 367, 449, 451, 454
7:3	261, 261n150, 262
7:4–10	262, 451
7:6	364
7:8	55n103, 98, 98n27
7:11	262, 263, 392
7:11–19	262–64, 451
7:12	337, 337n269, 338n269
7:13–14	169
7:14	54n102
7:15	262, 392
7:15–17	170
7:16	11n27, 24, 24n8, 63n125, 107, 263n151, 264
7:17	219n78, 259n145, 470
7:19	165, 165n189, 263, 264
7:20	53, 53n98, 264
7:20–24	264–65, 451
7:21	219n78, 259n145, 264, 470
7:21–22	132n110
7:22	265, 287, 299n213, 301n215, 326
7:23–24	94
7:23–25	67n135
7:24	219n78, 259n145, 265, 470
7:24–25	132n110
7:25	3n3, 9, 62n121, 63, 78n168, 79n170, 84, 87, 87n193, 87n194, 97n22, 98, 98n27, 99n30, 116, 128n101, 132n110, 140n126, 173, 239n104, 265n157, 266n157, 267, 272n166, 348
7:25—8:13	115

570

SCRIPTURE INDEX

7:25–26	4, 9, 117, 135, 171		100, 124, 134, 141n131,
7:25–28	58, 76n160, 256, 265–		141n132, 298, 314n235,
	67, 325, 347, 449, 451,		336, 441, 442, 443, 444,
	454		470, 473
7:26	73n152, 115, 118, 170,	8:5–6	265n155, 300
	171n205, 265n157, 316,	8:6	134, 172, 208, 281,
	412, 425, 469		298n210, 299, 301n215,
7:26–28	132n110		324n252, 325, 364, 473
7:27	51, 75n159, 76,	8:7	79n171, 114, 114n63,
	265n157, 267, 276		299n213, 300, 473
7:28	165, 165n189, 219n78,	8:7–13	265n155, 300–303,
	259n145, 264, 265n157,		301n215, 304n218, 351,
	266n157, 267, 358n301,		451
	470, 472n6	8:8	299n213, 302, 473
7:28—8:2	471	8:8–12	327
8:1	6, 23, 118, 123, 135,	8:9	164, 473
	171, 171n205, 217,	8:10	160, 302, 473
	286n186, 288, 288n190,	8:10–12	302, 473
	291, 292n200, 296n207,	8:12	76, 312
	303n218, 314n235, 425,	8:13	30n27, 67n135, 137,
	441, 442, 443, 444, 470,		138n121, 299n213, 302,
	471, 473		306, 473
8:1–2	3n3, 67, 100n31, 106,	9	303n218
	162, 171, 258n141, 288,	9:1	290n194, 299n213,
	291, 292, 298n210, 471,		303n218, 305, 306n222,
	473		470, 473
8:1–5	86n188, 159n182, 237	9:1–2	82, 99n29
8:1–6	xvii, 66n131, 288–303,	9:1–5	303–9, 303n218, 451
	301n215, 303n218, 451	9:1–8	136
8:1—9:26	343	9:1–10	295, 306n222
8:1—9:28	207n60, 286n187	9:1–14	63n125, 95n19, 287n1,
8:1—10:18	215, 252n131, 286, 287,		291n198, 299n213, 303,
	289, 324, 332, 337n269,		337
	339, 345, 449, 451, 454,	9:2	22n5, 290n194,
	473		299n213, 303n218, 305,
8:1—10:25	349n283		306n222, 441, 442, 443,
8:1–13	286n187		444, 470, 471, 473
8:2	23n5, 99n29, 144n137,	9:2–5a	306
	175, 289n192, 290n194,	9:3	23, 23n5, 79, 79n172,
	291, 292n199, 295,		290n194, 299n213,
	301n215, 441, 442, 443,		306n222, 441, 442, 443,
	444, 470, 471, 471n5,		444, 470, 472, 473
	472, 473	9:5	134n113, 307, 307n226,
8:3	471n5		308, 308n227
8:3–4	71, 298, 473	9:6	299, 299n213, 306n222,
8:4	113n61, 473		309, 470, 473
8:5	xiv, 8, 26n15, 30n28,	9:6–10	309–13, 311n233,
	46n79, 69n139, 82,		312n233, 314, 325, 451

571

Hebrews (continued)

9:7	23, 51, 58, 71, 80n173, 299n213, 306n222, 309, 311n233, 470, 473
9:8	9, 15, 23n5, 24, 63n125, 66n131, 76, 99n29, 113n61, 135, 137, 157n179, 209, 215, 258, 259n145, 290n194, 297n207, 299n213, 303n218, 305n221, 306n222, 310, 312, 314n235, 317, 319, 319n246, 336, 341, 441, 442, 443, 444, 470, 472, 473
9:8–9	26n15, 93, 94, 138n121
9:8–14	113
9:9	85n186, 160, 165n189, 301, 310, 312, 312n234, 324, 325, 473
9:9–10	473
9:9—10:25	136
9:10	312, 345n281, 473
9:11	xiv, 6, 66n131, 67, 69n139, 86n188, 113n61, 122n83, 159n182, 170, 171, 171n205, 179n222, 182n228, 296n207, 313, 314, 318, 330, 441, 442, 443, 444, 470, 471, 473
9:11—10:18	306n222
9:11–12	170, 258n141
9:11–14	313–23, 328, 363n307, 451
9:11–23	311n233
9:12	23n5, 51, 99n29, 100n31, 113n61, 128n101, 129, 130, 170, 290n194, 303n218, 304n218, 313, 314, 315, 315n239, 317, 323, 413, 441, 471, 473
9:12–15	127
9:13	157n178, 160, 316, 317, 473
9:13–14	318, 408
9:14	24, 63n125, 66n131, 69n139, 85n186, 97, 98, 113n61, 116, 130, 133n112, 157, 157n179, 160, 163, 164, 171, 171n205, 172, 226, 274, 275n172, 278, 283, 301, 304n218, 305n220, 310n230, 312n234, 313, 316, 318, 319, 320n248, 321n251, 323, 340, 368n313, 373, 408, 409, 410, 412, 413, 416, 471, 473
9:14–22	208n62
9:15	134, 207, 208, 299n213, 324n252, 325, 325n252, 326, 364, 473
9:15–18	320, 324, 327, 451
9:15–22	301n215, 325n254
9:15–23	311n233
9:15–26	299n213, 324
9:15–28	308n227
9:16	324, 327
9:16–17	208, 325n254
9:17	55n103, 98, 327, 333
9:18	299n213, 329n258, 473
9:18–22	473
9:19	328, 473
9:19–22	324, 328, 451
9:22	328, 354n294, 473
9:23	xiv, 30n28, 106, 118, 178, 222, 298n210, 314n235, 328, 329n258, 336, 337n268, 425, 471, 473
9:23–24	122n83, 127, 131, 258n141
9:23–26	317, 317n245, 324, 328–31, 392, 451
9:24	23n5, 26n15, 30n28, 67, 69n139, 78n168, 99n29, 100n31, 123, 125n94, 128n101, 131, 133n112, 172, 290n194, 296n207, 303n218, 304n218, 315n239, 329, 330, 333,

	336, 425, 441, 442, 443, 444, 471, 473	9:28 3, 8, 18, 22, 23, 25, 25n12, 39n55, 50, 62n121, 65,
9:24–25	159n181	67n135, 76, 78n168,
9:24–28	117	79, 80, 82, 84, 89, 93,
9:25	23n5, 71, 99n29, 128n101, 131, 248n122, 290n194, 303n218, 304n218, 330, 441, 471, 473	106, 115, 127, 139n124, 151, 154n170, 157, 164, 172n208, 173, 176, 213n71, 214, 216n75, 239n104, 251, 276, 285,
9:26	58, 76, 78n168, 79n172, 125n94, 220n79, 330, 331, 471, 472n6, 473	299n213, 304n218, 331, 332n261, 333, 333n263, 338n269, 344n278, 373,
9:26–28	51, 334, 414, 415	406, 409, 420, 471
9:27	53, 53n98, 54n100, 55n103, 56, 62, 63n124, 64n126, 82n179, 83, 84, 113n61, 115, 129, 172, 208n62, 248n121, 251, 310n230, 313, 326n254, 332n261, 333, 350, 367, 374, 386	10 314n235
		10:1 62, 71, 72n147, 128n101, 165n189, 336, 348, 473
		10:1–2 278
		10:1–3 325n254
		10:1–4 336–38, 360, 451, 473
		10:1–10 286n187
9:27–28	xiii, xix, xxn18, 1, 2, 3, 4, 7, 9, 14, 15, 16, 17, 18, 19, 23, 38, 40, 41, 52, 53, 54, 58, 63n125, 64, 64n126, 71, 76n160, 79n170, 82, 84, 85n186, 86n188, 87n194, 88, 89, 91, 92, 106, 108, 115, 116, 129, 131, 131n109, 144, 152, 158, 161, 163, 182, 185, 187, 188, 189, 193, 196n34, 198, 208, 209, 210, 211, 212, 212n67, 222–23, 233–34, 233n98, 251–52, 252n130, 255, 260n147, 263n151, 267, 274, 276, 284–85, 286–331, 332–36, 338n269, 340, 343, 344, 346–47, 346n281, 348, 357–58, 365n309, 366, 375–76, 381, 383n331, 386, 394, 396–404, 406, 407, 412, 413, 449, 451, 454, 468, 473, 474	10:1–18 71, 76
		10:2 51, 85n186, 160, 312, 312n234, 338
		10:3 338
		10:4 338
		10:4–10 310n230
		10:5 3, 63n125, 72, 72n148, 91, 93n9, 111n56, 128n101, 159n181, 160, 164, 220n79, 248n122, 250, 334n266, 339, 341, 344n278, 351n289, 368n313, 373, 472, 473
		10:5–9 72
		10:5–10 327, 343, 473
		10:5–14 72n148, 260n148, 298, 302n217, 338–44, 368n313, 413n11, 451
		10:7 314
		10:7–9 340n271
		10:8 72, 473
		10:8–9 93n9
		10:9 80, 299n213, 316, 343, 473
9:27–28 MCS	330n260, 456n2	10:10 51, 69n139, 72, 157n178, 317, 343, 354n294, 473

Hebrews (continued)

10:11	71, 473
10:11–12	343
10:11–18	286n187
10:12	23, 123, 135, 212n68
10:12–13	343
10:12–14	473
10:13	239n104
10:14	72, 157n178, 165, 165n189, 317, 343, 343n277, 343n278
10:15	93n9, 97n22, 99n29, 319, 345
10:15–18	76n160, 345–46, 451
10:16	160, 346
10:16–17	473
10:17	346
10:18	72, 164, 274, 346, 473
10:19	23n5, 99n29, 128n101, 290n194, 295n205, 348n282, 349, 350, 470, 472
10:19–20	79n170, 87n192, 284n185, 295n205, 314, 315
10:19–21	389n340
10:19–22	86n188, 351n289
10:19–23	117, 135
10:19–25	107n47, 255, 272n166, 286, 348–52, 353, 357, 358, 366, 375, 385n334, 448, 449, 451, 452, 453, 454
10:20	98, 130, 135, 136, 258, 348, 348n282, 349, 349n283, 350n283, 472, 473
10:21	6, 66n131, 134, 348n282, 349, 350n283
10:22	9, 85n186, 128n101, 160, 278, 301, 312n234, 329n258, 348n282, 350
10:22–23	176n214
10:22–25	376, 376n320, 381, 381n328, 382, 386, 387, 387n338, 394
10:22a	454
10:22b	354, 357, 366, 454
10:22c	357, 358, 365, 366, 367, 376, 454
10:22d	376, 454
10:23	12, 66n131, 107, 107n47, 135, 136, 348n282, 351, 357, 381, 382, 386, 454
10:24–25	454
10:25	50, 79n170, 125n94, 239n104, 346n281, 350, 351, 357
10:26	353n291, 356n296
10:26—13:21	72, 255, 348, 351, 352, 448, 449, 452, 453, 454
10:26—13:30	254n135
10:26—13:31	203n53
10:26–29	64
10:26–31	63n125, 64, 80n174, 319, 354–55, 452
10:26–39	54n102, 109, 233n98, 269, 274, 351, 353, 357, 359, 371, 375, 449, 452, 453, 454
10:26a	354
10:26b	354
10:26c	354
10:27	62, 353n291
10:27–28	353n291
10:27a	354
10:27b	354
10:28	55n103, 354
10:29	157n178, 160, 317, 319, 353n291, 355
10:29–30	93
10:29–39	248n121
10:30	62, 353n291, 355
10:31	97, 97n22, 98, 353n291, 355
10:31–35	379
10:32	233n98, 355
10:32–33	353n291
10:32–35	11, 355–56, 452
10:33a	355
10:33b	355
10:34	355
10:35	355

SCRIPTURE INDEX

10:35–39	3n3, 173n210, 353–58, 449, 452, 453, 454	11:3–12	358
10:36	355n295, 356, 364n308, 376n320	11:4	55n103, 66n132, 70n142, 99n30, 272n165, 359n304, 360–61, 374, 448, 452
10:36–37	239n104, 353n291		
10:36–39	356–57, 366, 452	11:4–5	83n182
10:37	79n170, 80, 94, 115, 223, 356, 373n317, 383n331, 398, 473, 474	11:4–6	85n186, 87n192, 116, 130
		11:5	83, 133n112, 145, 361, 362, 368n313
10:37–38	93, 172, 356n296, 357n300	11:5–6	241n109, 359n304, 361–62, 368n313, 452
10:38	98, 98n25, 353n291, 359	11:6	9, 54n102, 85n186, 99n30, 106, 113, 128n101, 135, 140n126, 176n214, 233n98, 237n101, 239n104, 243n111, 251, 276, 305n221, 307n225, 314n235, 362, 371, 375
10:38–39	135, 160, 176n214		
10:39	86n189, 160, 233n98, 250, 277, 278, 283, 353n291, 355n295, 356n296, 357, 357n300, 358n301		
11	26n15, 72, 83n182, 98n25, 104, 373n317	11:7	88, 207, 220n79, 276, 362–63, 452
11:1	6, 26, 97, 98n25, 105, 113, 117, 135n114, 139n125, 159, 242, 358n301, 359, 363, 365, 377n321	11:8	114, 115, 207, 208, 363, 452
		11:8–12	368
		11:8–16	115
		11:9	115, 239n104
11:1–2	83n182, 105n42, 359, 367, 367n312, 371, 448, 452	11:9–10	83n182, 364, 452
		11:10	83, 159n182
		11:11	66n131
11:1–3	116, 139n125, 142n134	11:11–12	364, 452
11:1–6	360	11:12	83n182, 118, 179n222, 377n321, 425, 441, 442, 443, 444, 472
11:1–16	256, 358, 359, 365, 366, 367, 367n312, 449, 452, 453, 454		
		11:13	55n103, 83, 107, 208n63, 365n309
11:1–38	206		
11:1–40	351, 366, 375, 376, 388, 389	11:13–15	98n25
		11:13–16	xiii, xv, 5, 13, 57, 83n182, 157, 165n189, 173n210, 176n214, 276, 358–66, 367n312, 448, 449, 452, 453, 454
11:1a	359		
11:1b	359		
11:2	358n301, 359, 367, 371		
11:3	6, xvin7, 57, 96n19, 97, 101, 103n39, 114, 127n100, 181, 182n228, 210n66, 249n126, 250n126, 295n205, 315n238, 358n301, 359–60, 365n309, 448, 452, 469	11:16	105, 123n86, 145, 162, 172
		11:16–39	452, 453
		11:16–40	358, 367
		11:17	232n98, 369

575

Hebrews (continued)

11:17–19	73, 73n151, 368, 373n317, 452
11:17–40	192n21, 256, 359, 367, 373n317, 449, 454
11:19	55n103, 73n151, 83n182, 132, 228n92, 276, 368
11:20	369, 452
11:21	55n103, 452
11:21–22	83n182
11:22	369–70, 452
11:23	370, 452
11:23–28	30n28
11:24–26	370–71, 452
11:24–27	142n132, 237
11:25–26	76
11:26	70, 83, 105, 142n132, 370–71
11:26–27	83n182
11:27	83, 105, 142n132, 371, 452
11:28	371–72, 452
11:28–31	83n182
11:29	372, 452
11:30	372, 452
11:31	372, 452
11:32	341
11:32–38	373, 452
11:33–35	83n182
11:34	132n111
11:35	8, 55n103, 132, 228n92, 276, 276n173, 373, 373n317, 392
11:35–37	83n182
11:35a	373
11:35b	373
11:37	55n103, 102
11:38	220n79
11:39	374, 374n319, 375
11:39–40	9, 79n170, 87n193, 115, 131, 133, 154n170, 164, 165, 169, 173n210, 223, 229n92, 273n166, 325n253, 331, 338n269, 367, 373n317, 374–75, 374n319, 452, 453, 454
11:40	164, 165, 165n189, 374n319, 375
12	72
12:1	xiv, 18, 90, 104n41, 152, 186, 376, 376n320, 377, 377n321, 378, 405, 419
12:1–2	104, 136n115, 140n129
12:1–3	218n76, 377–79, 378n323, 453
12:1–11	258n141
12:1–13	xx, 235, 351, 376, 449, 452, 453, 454
12:1–17	73n150
12:2	9, 23, 26, 83, 83n182, 123, 133n112, 135, 138, 168, 212n68, 228, 233n98, 316, 378
12:2–3	376n320
12:3	160, 233n98, 378
12:3–4	11
12:4	379, 380
12:4–6	379, 453
12:5–6	107n47
12:5–8	106n46
12:7	73n150, 233n98
12:7–11	380, 453
12:8	380
12:9	83n182, 97n22, 98, 160, 319, 380
12:12	380n326
12:12–13	177n215, 376–81, 380n326, 449, 452, 453, 454
12:13	380
12:14	82n181, 157n178, 381n328, 382
12:14–17	382–83, 384, 453
12:14–29	224, 351, 381, 382, 449, 452, 453, 454
12:15	243n111, 247n120
12:17	88, 114, 115, 207
12:18	5n9, 128n101, 383
12:18–19	6
12:18–21	63n125
12:18–22	75n157
12:18–24	134, 254n135
12:18–27	230, 383–85, 453
12:18–29	346n281

SCRIPTURE INDEX

12:22	97, 97n22, 98, 128n101, 136n115, 174n212, 175, 384	13:9	160
		13:10	217, 360, 361
12:22 KJV	221n82	13:11	76, 99n29, 290n194
12:22–24	5, 9, 31n28, 99, 136, 145, 160, 163, 165n189, 173n210, 283, 317, 351n289	13:11–12	260n148
		13:11–13	140n129
		13:12	157n178, 317
		13:13	208n63
		13:14	6, 159n182, 239n104, 390
12:22–25	105		
12:22–29	354n292	13:15	390
12:23	37n49, 62, 63n125, 80n174, 99n30, 116, 118, 123n89, 160, 162, 165, 165n189, 168, 220n79, 319, 425, 472	13:15–16	390, 453
		13:16	241n109, 390
		13:17	160, 391, 453
		13:18	85n186, 160, 278, 391
		13:18–19	391, 453
12:23 KJV	221n82	13:20	3n3, 8, 24n9, 55n103, 108n49, 112n58, 130, 132n111, 133, 137n120, 162, 163, 164, 173n210, 211, 223, 229, 236, 276, 327, 331, 338n269, 388, 392, 392n342
12:24	71n142, 130, 134, 208, 250n126, 299, 473		
12:24–27	130		
12:25	118, 385, 385n336, 425, 425n17, 427, 472		
12:25–27	6		
12:25–29	64, 114, 115n64, 154n170, 164, 181, 295n205, 315n238, 329n258, 356n298	13:20–21	69, 93n8, 333, 387, 391–94, 449, 452, 453, 454
		13:21	69n139, 134n113, 170, 178, 219n78, 307n225, 470, 472
12:26	58, 134, 385, 385n336, 425, 472		
12:26–27	51	13:22	11
12:27	6, 58, 182n228	13:22–25	11, 352, 448, 449, 452, 453, 454
12:28	183n230, 334n266, 385n337, 386, 386n337, 472		
		13:24	99n29, 157n178
12:28–29	381–82, 385–86, 449, 452, 453, 454	**James**	
		1:2–4	232
12:29	386n337	2:5	3n4
13	387n339	2:21	75
13:1–6	387, 453	2:26	320
13:1–21	333n264, 351, 387, 449, 452, 453, 454	**1 Peter**	
13:4	64, 80n174		34, 408n3, 410, 413
13:6	57	1:7	323n97
13:7	249n126, 388, 389, 391, 453	1:12	363n307
		2:4	363n307
13:8	62n123, 69n139, 112n59, 125n94, 219n78, 389, 470, 472	2:4–5	237
		2:5	75
13:8–14	389–90, 453		

577

1 Peter (continued)

2:23	63n125, 82n179, 314
2:24	75, 414
2:25	133
3:9	88
3:18	75, 134, 319, 363n307, 368n313, 414
3:18–22	85, 363, 363n307, 407, 408, 413–16
3:19	415n15
3:21	30n28, 363n307
3:21–22	88
4:5	80n174
4:5–6	407, 408, 413–16
4:6	415n15
4:11	112n58
4:12	323n97
5:5	175
5:11	112n58

2 Peter

	34
1:20	405
1:21	158n179
2:4	102n36, 181n226
2:9	61n121
3:5	181n226
3:8	112n59, 173n210, 180n223

1 John

1:1	81
1:3	81
1:8–10	276n172
2:2	38n52
2:28	3n3, 173n210
3:1–3	3n3, 173n210
3:2	36n47, 38, 132n111, 133, 157n177, 160, 340
3:2–3	377
3:8	102, 102n36
3:12	272n165, 361n305
4:1–6	xx
4:12	141n132
4:13	87n193, 158n179, 321, 416

5:19	112n58

Jude

1:5	58, 78n169
1:6	102n36, 181n226
1:9	61n121, 174n211
1:11	272n165, 361n305
1:13	102n36
1:15	61n121

Revelation

	34, 120n77, 202n51
1:5	63n125, 68
2:2–3	37
2:7	259n145
3:2	59
3:8	208
3:21	99
4–5	142n132
5:5	54n102
5:11–14	181n224
7:9–17	164
9:6	59n114
11:15	68
11:18	64
12:1	102n36
12:4	102n36
12:10	68
13:2	112n58
14:13	43n65
14:14	356n298
16:6	149
17:5–6	149
18:10	61n121
20:4	68
20:5–6	63n124
20:6	68
20:12	168n196
20:13–14	346n281
21:1	356n298
21:1–3	310n231
21:3	38n52, 103n39
21:10	75n157
21–22	38, 115n64, 134, 427, 430n34
21:23	112n59, 142n132

22:2	259n145	**Didache**	426
22:5	103n39, 112n59, 142n132		
22:14	259n145	**Ephrem the Syrian**	25n12

APOCRYPHA (NEW TESTAMENT)

Eusebius

Ecclesiastical History

Testament of Job

47:10–11	174n211	6.14	49n87
52:1–12	174n211	7.14.1–3	35

Irenaeus

148, 149

EARLY CHRISTIAN WRITINGS

Apostles' Creed

149

Against Heresies

4. Pref. 4	149n156
5:31.1	36n47
5.13.3	36n47
5.2.2	36n47
5.31	36n47
5.31.9	36n47

Aquinas, Thomas

Summa Theologica

I, Q. 31, Art. 3	103n38
II–II, Q. 11. Art. 3	149n159

Jerome

91n6, 420

Augustine

420n3

Justin

148, 149

City of God

22.21	38n52

Nicene Creed

149

Confessions

11.12.14–11.31.41	143n135

Origen

Against Celsus

4.87	35

Clement of Alexandria

49n87

On First Principles

2.11.2–3	35

Clement of Rome

First Epistle of Clement

60:1	111n57

SCRIPTURE INDEX

GREEK AND ROMAN LITERATURE

Aristotle
  96n20, 143n135

Letter of Aristeas
  41n61

Parmenides
  96n20

Plato
  13, 46n78, 96n20, 111n55, 117n67, 141n131, 142n133, 143n135, 293n201

Republic
10.614b–621d   168n196

Timaeus
37D–38A   96n20, 143n135

Plutarch

Moralia. On the Face Which Appears in the Orb of the Moon
942d–945d   168n196

www.ingramcontent.com/pod-product-compliance
Lightning Source LLC
Chambersburg PA
CBHW052041290426
44111CB00011B/1580